Faculty in the AI Era

Rethinking Teaching, Supervision, and Academic Integrity

Steve Munkeby, DM

Barbara Turner, DM

Title: Faculty in the AI Era – Rethinking Teaching, Supervision, and Academic Integrity

Authors: Drs. Steve Munkeby and Barbara Turner

NextGen Publications, LLC

Website: https://SteveMunkeby.com, Email: drstevemunkeby@gmail.com, Phone: 470-302-4626

AI Use Disclosure Statement

This book was authored by Drs. Steve Munkeby and Barbara Turner with minimal support from generative AI tools, specifically OpenAI's GPT-5 (ChatGPT). AI assistance was used in the following ways:

- **Idea development and drafting**: AI was engaged as a thought partner to generate outlines, expand initial arguments, and draft sample paragraphs for refinement.
- **Revision and refinement**: Drafted passages provided by AI were critically evaluated, fact-checked against peer-reviewed literature, and revised for clarity, coherence, and alignment with scholarly standards by the authors.
- **Citation and reference support**: AI suggested draft writing from the author's pre-established and curated reference list were verified against the authoritative publications within the references list by the authors to ensure accuracy and integrity.
- **Stylistic and organizational assistance**: AI was used to restructure and expand key author selected paragraphs and suggest transitions between selected paragraphs while preserving authorial voice.

All final decisions regarding content, framing, interpretation, and argumentation were made by the authors. AI contributions were treated as drafting assistance, not as authoritative sources or substitutes for scholarly judgment. This disclosure reflects the book's broader commitment to transparency in AI use, demonstrating how generative tools can be integrated responsibly into academic work without compromising human authorship, ethical accountability, or disciplinary rigor.

ISBNs:

Paperback: 979-1968702526

ebook: 978-1968702533

First Edition: August 2025 Printed in the United States of America

Cover Design: NextGen Publications, LLC

Interior Formatting: NextGen Publications, LLC

For more books and free resources, visit https://SteveMunkeby.com

Table of Contents

Foreword

Standing at the Threshold of an AI-Transformed Academy

We are living through the most profound transformation in education since the invention of the printing press. At the center of this seismic shift stands artificial intelligence - an invisible yet omnipresent force already reshaping how students learn, how knowledge is produced, and how intellectual work is evaluated.

And yet, amid this accelerating revolution, many educators - especially those entrusted with supervising the highest levels of academic work - find themselves underprepared. Doctoral faculty, long regarded as guardians of scholarly integrity and rigorous inquiry, are now navigating a landscape that feels unfamiliar, even disorienting. While students increasingly explore or embrace generative AI tools, many faculty continue to operate within pedagogical, research, and evaluative frameworks grounded in 19th- and 20th-century traditions. The result is a growing disconnect between how students engage in learning and how that learning is mentored, supervised, and assessed.

Across educational levels, a common refrain echoes: *"Is this cheating?"* But in the context of AI, that question has become more difficult - if not impossible - to define, detect, or deter. The harder truth is this: academic dishonesty did not begin with artificial intelligence, and our capacity to reliably identify it has always been imperfect. If we struggled to detect plagiarism or misconduct before this new era, what makes us believe we can outpace it now - especially without evolving our own methods, mindsets, and expectations?

These challenges are not limited to doctoral programs. From elementary classrooms to undergraduate lecture halls, educators are asking new versions of familiar questions:

- *"Did the student actually write this?"*
- *"Is this their voice?"*
- *"Can I trust what I am reading?"*

These concerns are legitimate - but they represent only one side of the story. The more urgent and generative question is this: **"How do we teach, mentor, and evaluate in a world where AI is not optional, but ambient - an ever-present co-author, co-pilot, and co-thinker?"**

This book does not treat AI as a threat to be resisted, nor as a novelty to be indulged. Instead, it offers a pragmatic and principled guide for educators - from K–12 teachers to doctoral advisors - who are ready to work *with* AI, not against it. It asks:

- *"What new supervisory, cognitive, and evaluative skills must educators develop?"*
- *"How must assignment design and assessment evolve to preserve integrity while enabling innovation?"*
- *"What does 'originality' mean when machine-generated fluency becomes indistinguishable from human prose?"*
- *"How do we uphold academic rigor and ethical standards in a world where AI will shape every discipline and professional domain?"*

The age of AI is not on the horizon - it is here. It permeates our homes, classrooms, laboratories, and offices. And just as we once adapted to the rise of the internet or the expansion of digital scholarship, educators must now reimagine their roles in this next epoch. This is not a time for fear. It is a time for clarity, courage, and leadership.

This book is written for faculty who are prepared to meet that moment. Whether you supervise dissertations or capstone projects, design syllabi, evaluate student writing, or mentor original research, your work now stands at the forefront of educational reinvention. What you do next will determine not whether faculty remain relevant - but whether we become more essential than ever before.

Welcome to the new frontier of education!

A Historical Evolution of Doctoral Guidance: From Protégé to Mentor in the AI Era

As artificial intelligence reshapes nearly every dimension of knowledge production and human inquiry, the academic world finds itself caught between tradition and transformation. Nowhere is this tension more visible than in the relationship between faculty and doctoral students - a relationship historically regarded as the cornerstone of scholarly development. For centuries, the process of guiding a doctoral student has reflected not only the academic priorities of its time but also the structure of the broader society in which research occurs.

Today, that structure is under profound stress.

Faculty trained under 20th-century paradigms now supervise students who are increasingly using 21st-century tools. Dissertation or capstone chairs, committee members, and mentors often operate within institutional frameworks that were never designed to account for algorithmic co-authorship, real-time data generation, or AI-augmented problem solving. In this evolving reality, the once-clear boundaries of authorship, originality, and mentorship are becoming blurred.

To understand where we must go, we must first understand how we got here.

This section traces the evolution of doctoral guidance from its earliest master-apprentice origins to the rise of formal dissertation or capstone committees, and finally to the more recent mentor based models that emphasize flexibility and personalization. Each stage of this evolution emerged in response to the cultural, intellectual, and technological needs of its time - and each has struggled, in turn, to adapt to the demands of the next.

By examining this history, we gain more than just perspective - we gain clarity about what must change in how faculty engage with students in the AI era. It is not only our research tools that must evolve, but also our thinking about what it means to guide others through the research process itself.

The Expert-Apprentice Model: Academic Lineage in the Pre-Modern World

The origins of doctoral mentorship can be traced to early models of **expert-apprentice relationships**, seen in Socratic dialogues, Confucian academies, Islamic madrasas, and medieval European guilds. In these structures, the protégé learned through immersion, imitation, and oral instruction, aiming not to generate novel insights but to master existing traditions (Schon, 2017; Vaughan, 2017).

The **objective** of this system was the preservation of knowledge and replication of established frameworks. The **method** was deeply personalized and reliant on long-term intellectual relationships. This model thrived in eras where knowledge progressed slowly, and education focused on cultural continuity.

The Dissertation or Capstone Committee: Emergence from the German University Tradition

In the 19th century, with the rise of the **Humboldtian model of higher education** in Germany, a new form of doctoral training emerged - one centered on the production of original research (Clark, 2008). The University of Berlin, founded in 1810, became the template for modern research universities worldwide. Doctoral education now demanded not only mastery of content, but also **the creation of new knowledge**.

To maintain rigor and reduce the influence of any one individual, universities institutionalized the **dissertation or capstone committee**, a group of faculty charged with supervising and evaluating the dissertation or capstone. This structure introduced key benefits:

- **Distributed expertise** across committee members.
- **Increased academic accountability**.
- **Standardization** of doctoral rigor across institutions (Gardner, 2009).

The committee model was suited to a period of **disciplinary consolidation** when academic knowledge was neatly organized into fields and specialization was rewarded.

The Mentor Model: Personalized Guidance for Diverse Doctoral Paths

In the late 20th century, doctoral education underwent further transformation. Students diversified in age, background, and professional goals, and the number of **practice-oriented doctoral programs** (e.g., EdD, DBA, DNP) grew dramatically (Walker et al., 2009). Traditional committee structures began to feel rigid, bureaucratic, and impersonal.

As a result, many institutions embraced the **mentor model** - a model emphasizing one-on-one relationships between faculty and doctoral candidates. The mentor became more than a subject expert; they were expected to serve as guide, coach, and sometimes even career advisor (Lee, 2008).

This model worked well in **non-traditional or online programs**, where flexibility and continuity were more important than formal committee deliberations. It provided:

- **Customized academic support**.
- **Responsive research direction**.
- **Psychosocial guidance** (Zellers et al., 2008).

Yet even as the mentor model grew in prominence, cracks began to appear - especially with the rise of artificial intelligence and data-centric research.

Why the Mentor Model Is Now Under Strain

While the mentor model once offered a refreshing alternative to rigid committee structures - providing individualized guidance, responsiveness, and relational depth - it is now showing signs of systemic stress. The very flexibility that made mentorship appealing in an era of growing student diversity and nontraditional doctoral pathways has become insufficient in the face of today's research complexity.

We have entered an academic era defined by **velocity, variability,** and **volume** - fueled in large part by artificial intelligence. Doctoral students are engaging with rapidly evolving technologies, transdisciplinary problems, and hybrid methodologies that far exceed the training of many faculty mentors. The result is a widening mismatch between what students need and what mentors are prepared to offer.

This section explores the root causes of this strain - not to undermine the value of mentorship, but to critically examine the structural, technological, and cognitive gaps that have emerged. By surfacing these tensions, we can begin to identify what must be reimagined for mentorship to remain relevant, ethical, and effective in a world where AI is no longer peripheral to research, but central to it.

The Pace and Nature of Knowledge Has Changed

The information landscape has become **nonlinear, interdisciplinary, and exponential**. AI systems now support rapid literature synthesis, data analysis, and even ideation - changing not only how research is done but how fast it evolves (Luckin et al., 2016). Mentors trained in traditional methods often lack:

- Experience with AI-augmented research tools.
- Familiarity with computational or interdisciplinary methods.
- Capacity to evaluate outputs generated by AI (Floridi et al., 2018).

Methodological Expansion Exceeds Mentor Capacity

Today's doctoral students engage with **blended research approaches**, including mixed methods, design-based research, and data-informed ethnography (Creswell & Clark, 2017). Faculty accustomed to qualitative interviews or statistical regression may struggle to support:

- Machine learning models used in qualitative coding.
- AI-assisted meta-analysis.
- Experimental simulations or synthetic data (X. Wang et al., 2024).

The traditional assumption - that one mentor or committee can sufficiently guide a dissertation or capstone within a single methodological paradigm - no longer holds in many domains.

Lack of Institutional Support and Faculty Development

Despite the growing complexity of doctoral supervision, **many faculty mentors receive no formal training** in supervising research in the AI era (Caillaud & Skec, 2024). Time constraints, unclear role expectations, and limited exposure to evolving research technologies further exacerbate the problem (Lovitts, 2001).

This has led to a troubling paradox: doctoral students are increasingly capable of leveraging AI tools to generate advanced outputs, yet their mentors may lack the framework to evaluate, guide, or even understand the tools being used. This **asymmetry in capability** can undermine both the mentoring relationship and the integrity of the research process.

The Way Forward: Faculty as Research Architects in the AI Era

To address the growing mismatch between traditional academic preparation and rapidly evolving technological realities, doctoral education must once again adapt. This shift calls for a **reimagining of the faculty role** - from mentor-as-guide focused on linear scholarly progression to faculty-as-architect responsible for designing adaptive, AI-aware learning and research environments. Such a transformation equips emerging scholars to thrive in complex, data-driven contexts while preserving the critical and ethical foundations of advanced inquiry (Damsa et al., 2024). This shift requires:

- **Reimagining assignments** to engage AI tools critically, rather than prohibitively.
- **Redefining academic integrity** to distinguish between augmentation and misrepresentation.
- **Rebuilding faculty development models** that prioritize interdisciplinary literacy and technological fluency.

The AI era demands **flexibility, foresight, and fluency** - not only from students, but also from the faculty who guide them through increasingly complex learning environments. Faculty must lead not from a place of fear or rigid adherence to tradition, but from a position of informed innovation that embraces change while safeguarding academic values. Ultimately, the future of research will not be shaped solely by algorithms, but by those who possess the ethical judgment and intellectual wisdom to harness AI responsibly and creatively (Zawacki-Richter et al., 2019).

And that future begins with us.

Chapter 1: Rethinking Rigor - Redefining Academic Integrity in the Age of AI

Academic integrity has traditionally been anchored in authorship, originality, and verifiability. But in a world where AI can co-author text, generate citations, and summarize research at scale, these definitions must evolve. This chapter explores how integrity can be preserved - and redefined - through transparency, attribution, and intentional design, rather than outdated prohibition. Faculty must learn to separate human dishonesty from machine assistance and guide students in ethical collaboration with AI tools (Balalle & Pannilage, 2025; Lancaster & Cotarlan, 2021).

Section 1: The Historical Foundations of Academic Integrity

To understand how academic integrity must evolve, we must first examine how it began. This section explores the origins of academic integrity in the Western university model, where individual authorship, originality, and truth-seeking became the hallmarks of scholarship. Drawing on traditions from Socratic teaching to Humboldtian research ideals, this section traces how integrity was historically tied to a clear authorship trail, limited access to knowledge, and trust in the solitary scholar. It also surfaces implicit assumptions - such as the student always working alone - that no longer apply in today's AI-rich environments (Fishman, 2009).

The Birth of Integrity: Truth and Trust in Early Universities

Academic integrity, as a formalized concept, traces its roots to the early structures of Western higher education, particularly the universities of medieval Europe such as Bologna, Paris, and Oxford. These institutions emerged not merely as places for learning but as centers for knowledge production, preservation, and verification (Cobban, 1975). At the heart of their mission was a fundamental commitment to truth-seeking. In an era when manuscripts were copied by hand and the transmission of knowledge was painstaking and limited, the trust placed in scholars to be accurate, honest, and original was not just a virtue - it was a necessity.

Originality was valued not for creativity alone but for the assurance that each contribution to scholarship could be traced, verified, and built upon (Sutherland-Smith, 2016). Academic dishonesty, whether in copying texts or falsifying arguments, was a threat to the fragile ecosystem of knowledge production. As universities grew in complexity and influence, formal codes of conduct began to emerge, reinforcing norms of attribution, individual labor, and the moral responsibility of scholars (Bok, 2003).

Philosophical Foundations: Socratic Dialogue and Ethical Inquiry

Long before the establishment of these institutions, philosophical traditions in ancient Greece laid the groundwork for the ethical dimension of learning. The Socratic method, characterized by questioning, dialogue, and critical reasoning, emphasized not only the acquisition of knowledge but the moral responsibility of the learner (Brickhouse & Smith, 2000). Socrates modeled intellectual humility, insisting that admitting ignorance was a starting point for wisdom. Integrity, in this context, meant aligning one's pursuit of knowledge with ethical conduct.

This legacy passed through Plato and Aristotle and shaped future intellectual traditions. The teacher-student relationship was not merely instructional but transformational. It implied trust, mutual respect, and a shared commitment to truth (Nussbaum, 1997). These foundations became embedded in Western academic systems, evolving into expectations of honesty, independence, and ethical behavior in scholarship.

The Humboldtian Shift: Originality and the Independent Scholar

In the 19th century, Wilhelm von Humboldt introduced a transformative model of higher education in Germany that profoundly influenced the modern research university. His vision emphasized **Bildung** (self-cultivation) and the integration of teaching and research (M. G. Ash, 2006). Under Humboldt's model, the ideal scholar was an autonomous individual engaged in the independent pursuit of universal truths. This model institutionalized the expectation that knowledge creation was the product of solitary, rigorous effort.

The Humboldtian framework not only redefined the role of faculty as both researchers and educators but also entrenched originality and independence as central pillars of academic integrity. Students, too, were expected to mirror this model by demonstrating their intellectual growth through original work, unaided by others (Taebi et al., 2019).

Cultural Norms: How "Working Alone" Became Virtue

As the research university model spread across Europe and North America, it shaped not just institutional structures but cultural expectations. The rise of the peer-reviewed journal and the monograph positioned individual authorship as the gold standard of scholarly merit (Biagioli, 2002). The scholar was increasingly seen as a lone figure, producing work through personal insight and sustained, solitary labor.

Honor codes, particularly in American universities, codified these ideals. Students pledged not to cheat, plagiarize, or seek undue assistance. The underlying assumption was clear: academic integrity was synonymous with working alone, proving one's worth through unassisted effort, and demonstrating mastery without shortcuts (Gallant, 2008). These norms were enforced through institutional policies, cultural narratives, and peer expectations.

Challenging Assumptions: A Legacy at Odds with the Present

Embedded within this historical legacy are several implicit assumptions that no longer align with today's educational and technological reality. First, the assumption that students work alone does not reflect the collaborative nature of modern knowledge work. Second, the belief that knowledge is scarce and must be discovered individually ignores the reality of digital abundance and open access. Third, the idealization of unaided learning disregards the transformative potential of tools and technologies that enhance understanding, including generative AI (Selwyn, 2019).

These foundational assumptions were not inherently flawed for their time; they were built to safeguard the integrity of learning and truth-seeking in specific historical contexts. However, as new tools and environments reshape how knowledge is accessed, processed, and produced, it becomes necessary to reassess these assumptions. To uphold academic integrity today, educators must shift from enforcing outdated norms to guiding students in ethical, transparent, and responsible engagement with modern technologies (Fahad & Donni, 2024).

This requires not abandoning integrity but redefining it. In the age of AI, integrity should no longer be viewed solely as the preservation of academic tradition, but as an evolving commitment to honesty, trust, and accountability. Such a reframing allows institutions and faculty to intentionally adapt ethical standards to new technological realities without compromising their foundational values (Bailey et al., 2023).

Section Reflection: Redefining Integrity for a New Era of Learning

This section reveals that academic integrity, historically rooted in solitary authorship, originality, and truth-seeking, emerged from traditions such as Socratic ethics and the Humboldtian model of independent scholarship. These foundations, developed in eras of limited access to knowledge and analog tools, emphasized working alone as a virtue and codified integrity through honor codes and institutional norms. However, the assumptions behind these models - such as the lone learner or the scarcity of knowledge - no longer align with today's AI-enhanced, collaborative learning environments.

Upholding academic integrity now requires redefining it as a dynamic commitment to honesty, trust, and accountability in the context of digital abundance and intelligent tools. This evolution calls for institutional courage to reward thoughtful risk-taking and pedagogical innovation, ensuring that integrity remains a living, relevant principle in an era of rapid educational transformation.

Section 2: The Fragile Line Between Assistance and Cheating

Generative AI has challenged the traditional boundaries between support and misconduct in academic work. In doing so, it has exposed a fragile and often subjective line between acceptable assistance and cheating (Vincent-Lancrin & Van der Vlies, 2020). Unlike calculators or spelling tools, which were slowly integrated into education with clear guidelines, AI tools arrived quickly and with much broader capabilities (Yu et al., 2025). Today, faculty and students face a chaotic, inconsistent, and ethically gray terrain where the rules are unclear, and trust is under strain (Dabis & Csaki, 2024).

At what point does using AI become *"too much help?"* This question is not merely academic. Consider the following scenarios:

- A student asks an AI to improve grammar and sentence clarity. *"Is this cheating, or just modern proofreading?"* (Gulya, 2023).
- Another asks the AI to summarize a dense research article to better understand the material. *"Is this unethical, or a new form of scaffolding?"* (Smutny & Schreiberova, 2020).
- A computer science major uses AI to suggest lines of code but later adapts them for an assignment. *"Is this academic dishonesty, or a real-world coding norm?"* (Luckin et al., 2016).

The answers vary - not only by institution but often from one instructor to another within the same department (Kallunki et al., 2024). The absence of shared definitions leaves students confused, and faculty divided (Gundu, 2024). Underlying this uncertainty is a more fundamental question: "**What constitutes authorship and intellectual contribution in the age of intelligent machines**?"

"If AI assists in shaping a student's idea but the student makes the final judgment call, who owns the thought?" "If AI generates content that is edited and personalized by the learner, is the work co-authored, ghostwritten, or merely assisted?" (Bailey et al., 2023). These are not just technical questions - they are philosophical ones, tied deeply to evolving definitions of originality and fairness (Floridi & Chiriatti, 2020).

From a traditional lens, originality implies unmediated production of thought. But in the AI era, originality may increasingly mean making informed decisions with the aid of powerful tools. **It is the act of judgment, not the absence of assistance, which may become the new measure of academic integrity** (Buckingham-Shum et al., 2019).

This reframing demands that we move away from static rules and toward dynamic norms. Institutions must work collaboratively to:

- Clearly define categories of acceptable, assisted, and prohibited use.
- Involve students in creating shared norms, so they understand not just what is allowed but why (Eden et al., 2024).
- Develop assignment types that differentiate between AI-generated scaffolding and student-driven synthesis.
- Encourage transparency: students should disclose when and how they used AI, just as they would cite a human source (Mienye & Swart, 2025).

Fairness is not just about banning tools to ensure equality. It is about ensuring that all students know how to use those tools wisely, ethically, and transparently. Those who lack access to AI support may be disadvantaged, just as those who misuse AI may compromise their learning (Zawacki-Richter et al., 2019).

In this context, academic integrity is no longer defined by the simple act of abstaining from external help. Instead, **it involves taking ownership of one's intellectual process**, transparently declaring sources, and engaging thoughtfully with the tools at one's disposal. As artificial intelligence becomes a collaborative partner in cognitive tasks, students must understand their evolving role as thinkers in partnership with technology (Uanachain & Aouad, 2025).

The next section will propose structured frameworks and design principles that can help faculty and institutions construct a clearer, fairer, and more adaptable model of academic integrity in the AI age.

Section Reflection: Navigating the Ethics of Help in the AI Age

This section underscores the growing tension between assistance and academic misconduct in an educational landscape increasingly shaped by generative AI. It highlights how AI blurs long-standing distinctions between support and cheating, leaving both students and faculty in ethically ambiguous territory with inconsistent guidance and definitions. As traditional notions of originality - once rooted in solitary, unassisted work - give way to more nuanced understandings of judgment, synthesis, and transparency, the challenge lies in redefining academic integrity to reflect this shift.

Integrity today must be measured not by the absence of help, but by the quality of engagement, the ownership of ideas, and the openness about how tools are used. To maintain fairness and uphold educational values, institutions must move beyond rule enforcement to co-create dynamic norms with students, establishing clear, contextual boundaries that reflect both ethical principles and the realities of modern learning.

Section 3: The Myth of Detection - Why Policing AI Use Is Futile

---

As institutions confront the rapid adoption of generative AI, many have defaulted to a familiar strategy: detection and punishment. Policies banning unauthorized AI use are being enforced with tools designed to identify machine-generated text - AI-output detectors, plagiarism software, and behavior-monitoring platforms. These efforts may offer a sense of control, but they are largely ineffective and, worse, often harmful to the trust-based educational environment that academic integrity depends on (Eden et al., 2024; Floridi & Chiriatti, 2020).

The promise of AI-detection tools is seductive. In theory, they can distinguish between human and AI-generated writing and offer a tidy solution to misconduct. In practice, they are deeply flawed. Most detection models rely on probabilistic estimations rather than definitive proof (Solaiman et al., 2019). Their outputs - such as "70% AI-generated" - do not withstand academic or legal scrutiny. False positives are common, especially among non-native English speakers or students using legitimate writing aids such as translation tools or grammar checkers (Tan & Maravilla, 2024; Weber-Wulff et al., 2023).

These tools are also easily circumvented. With minor edits or paraphrasing, students can "fool" detection algorithms, creating an arms race between those trying to catch misconduct and those trying to avoid being caught (Rafiq & Qurat-ul-Ain, 2025). Instead of fostering ethical thinking, this approach incentivizes secrecy, workarounds, and technical manipulation. What results is not a culture of integrity, but a culture of avoidance (Yadav, 2024).

The harms extend beyond technical failure. Detection-based enforcement fosters an atmosphere of surveillance. Students begin to perceive their faculty not as mentors but as adversaries (Bailey et al., 2023). Honest students feel pressure to defend legitimate work. Some may avoid using AI tools altogether - even when permitted - for fear of triggering suspicion. Others may be punished unjustly, damaging their academic record and trust in the institution (Yu et al., 2025).

More broadly, **the very act of framing AI use as something to police sends the wrong message**. It treats technology as inherently suspect, and students as inherently deceptive. This mindset reflects a punitive model of education rather than a developmental one (Buckingham-Shum et al., 2019). It fails to recognize that students need support in navigating a rapidly changing information landscape - not interrogation.

Rather than obsess over whether AI was used, educators should ask deeper questions: *"Did the student engage meaningfully with the material?" "Did they make intellectual decisions, demonstrate understanding, and apply critical thought?"* These are the hallmarks of authentic learning, regardless of whether an AI tool was involved (Eden et al., 2024).

The future of academic integrity does not lie in detection. It lies in design - intentional course structures, assignment formats, and evaluation strategies that assume AI use will happen and that help students use it wisely. This might include:

- Designing assignments that require process documentation, such as draft comparisons or tool-use reflection logs.
- Creating multi-stage assessments where feedback, iteration, and in-person synthesis play central roles.
- Encouraging transparency by normalizing AI usage declarations, just as we expect citations (Mienye & Swart, 2025).
- Emphasizing skill development over content regurgitation, shifting the goal from "getting it right" to "understanding it deeply."

By shifting from detection to design, institutions can empower students to use AI ethically, creatively, and responsibly. Academic integrity, then, becomes not a matter of catching misconduct but of cultivating character - supporting students as they learn not just what to think, but how to think well in a machine-augmented world.

Section Reflection: From Surveillance to Stewardship in the AI Classroom

This section dismantles the illusion that policing AI use through detection technologies can meaningfully preserve academic integrity. It reveals how reliance on flawed AI-detection tools not only fails to provide reliable proof of misconduct but also actively undermines trust, equity, and the learning environment itself. By turning faculty into enforcers and students into suspects, institutions risk fostering a culture of avoidance rather than one of integrity.

The true path forward lies not in surveillance, but in thoughtful instructional design - one that assumes AI use, channels it constructively, and emphasizes process, reflection, and transparency. When academic work is structured to reward critical engagement over mere compliance, integrity becomes less about catching wrongdoers and more about cultivating responsible, empowered learners in a technologically complex world.

Section 4: Transparency and Attribution as the New Pillars of Integrity

---

In the AI era, the foundations of academic integrity must shift from invisibility and assumption to openness and accountability (Bailey et al., 2023). Traditional models often assumed that students worked independently unless proven otherwise. In contrast, today's educational environments must expect and embrace the use of advanced tools - and require students to be transparent about how those tools are used (Kallunki et al., 2024).

Transparency and attribution are not about encouraging AI use blindly. Rather, they are about creating a culture of academic honesty where tool use is openly acknowledged and ethically integrated into the learning process (Eden et al., 2024). Just as citations give credit to human sources, declarations of AI assistance can give credit to non-human collaborators - acknowledging their role without diminishing the student's intellectual agency (Cotton et al., 2024; Khreisat et al., 2024).

A new academic norm must emerge: students should declare when and how they use AI in the research and writing process. Likewise, faculty should model this openness in their own use of AI tools for research, communication, or content generation (Gundu, 2024). The conversation must evolve from *"Did you use AI?"* to *"How did AI help you think more deeply, and how did you control its influence?"* (Buckingham-Shum et al., 2019). This cultural shift can be reinforced through practical strategies:

- **Declaration Statements**. Faculty can require a brief AI usage statement at the end of each assignment. Example: *"I used ChatGPT to help outline my argument structure and rephrase one paragraph. All ideas and final wording were reviewed and edited by me"* (Mienye & Swart, 2025).
- **Assignment Prompts**. Include directions that encourage students to reflect on their learning process. Example: *"If you used any AI tools in your work, describe how they helped and what decisions you made as the final author"* (Gulya, 2023).
- **Syllabus Policies**. Add a clearly defined section outlining expectations for AI tool usage, including what types of use are permitted, encouraged, or prohibited - and how transparency should be demonstrated (Zawacki-Richter et al., 2019).

- **Faculty Modeling**. Professors can disclose when AI tools help develop syllabi, generate quiz questions, or explore lecture ideas. This demystifies tool use and sets a tone of integrity from the top (Bailey et al., 2023).
- **Conversation Starters**. Build dialogue between faculty and students about ethical technology use. Questions such as *"What is the difference between using AI to understand versus to replace?"* can guide students to think critically about their choices (Yadav, 2024).

Transparency empowers students to own their process. Attribution respects the collaborative nature of modern learning. **Together, they help establish a future-ready model of integrity that does not resist technological change but channels it ethically** (Floridi & Chiriatti, 2020). In the next section, we will explore how these redefined pillars of integrity can be operationalized in course design and institutional policy - ensuring that integrity remains meaningful, measurable, and resilient in the age of AI.

Section Reflection: Owning the Process in a Transparent Age

This section reframes academic integrity as an open practice of accountability rather than an invisible presumption of independence. In an educational landscape increasingly shaped by generative AI, the focus must shift from whether a tool was used to how it was used and disclosed. Transparency and attribution become essential - empowering students to articulate their engagement with AI while preserving their role as the final authorial voice.

By normalizing declarations of AI assistance and encouraging reflective ownership of the learning process, institutions can foster a culture where integrity is not compromised by technological advancement but strengthened by ethical clarity. When both students and faculty model openness and intentionality, academic honesty evolves from suspicion to stewardship, building trust and resilience in a digitally integrated future.

Section 5: Designing Assignments that Make Integrity Visible

The most effective safeguard against academic dishonesty is not surveillance - it is smart design. Rather than rely on flawed detection tools or restrictive bans, educators can protect academic integrity by creating assignments that emphasize originality, personal insight, and developmental process (Gundu, 2024). These are the very attributes that generative AI still struggles to reproduce meaningfully (Floridi & Chiriatti, 2020).

AI excels at synthesizing surface-level responses, retrieving information quickly, and mimicking style. But it lacks the human capacity for reflection, nuanced reasoning, emotional interpretation, personal experience, and iterative learning (Buckingham-Shum et al., 2019; Geethanjali & Umashankar, 2025). These gaps offer educators powerful opportunities to design assessments that elevate integrity through authentic intellectual engagement.

To accomplish this, faculty must shift from product-focused assignments to **process-visible assignments** - those that make the student's thinking traceable, explainable, and accountable (Bailey et al., 2023; Cotton et al., 2024). Below are several strategies for creating such assignments:

---

1. Use Scaffolding to Track the Learning Journey

Break large assignments into smaller, sequential components that must be submitted at regular intervals throughout the term. This scaffolding encourages sustained engagement, provides opportunities for feedback and revision, and makes academic dishonesty - such as AI overuse or last-minute outsourcing - easier to detect. By structuring assignments in this way, faculty promote process-based learning and uphold academic integrity through transparent student progress (Gundu, 2024). Examples include:

- *Initial topic proposal and rationale.*
- *Annotated bibliography with reflections on source relevance.*
- *Draft submission with margin notes or revision history.*
- *Final submission accompanied by a reflective process statement.*

This layering reveals more than just the final product - it showcases the student's evolution of thought over time. **It also demonstrates their meaningful engagement with feedback**, illustrating how ideas are refined through revision and dialogue. As a result, it becomes significantly more difficult for students to conceal unauthorized shortcuts or overreliance on AI tools, reinforcing academic integrity through transparency (Nikolopoulou, 2025).

---

2. Design Prompts That Require Personalization

Assignments should be designed to invite personal opinion, lived experience, or references to local context - dimensions of thought that AI cannot easily or convincingly fabricate. These authentic prompts challenge students to draw from their own identities and communities, making their responses more original and less susceptible to generic or AI-generated content. By incorporating such elements, educators strengthen academic integrity while fostering deeper, more meaningful engagement with the material (Gulya, 2023). Examples:

- *"Describe how this theory applies to a decision you made in your workplace."*
- *"Compare two texts, including your personal reaction to each."*
- *"Reflect on how your cultural background influences your interpretation of this data."*

When questions are grounded in personal insight, **they prompt responses that reflect the unique experiences and perspectives of the individual learner**. This personalization reduces the likelihood that answers will be vague, formulaic, or easily generated by artificial intelligence. By fostering this level of authenticity, educators help students produce work that is more meaningful, original, and resistant to AI replication (Gulya, 2023).

---

3. Embed Process Documentation Requirements

Require students to explicitly explain their method and decision-making process as part of their assignments. This not only deepens their understanding of the material but also makes their intellectual journey more transparent to faculty. **By incorporating reflective components, educators can better assess authenticity and critical thinking**, reinforcing academic integrity in an AI-assisted learning environment (Mienye & Swart, 2025). Examples include:

- *A short paragraph explaining why certain sources were chosen.*
- *A screenshot of an outline or mind map.*
- *A "thought trail" log. A brief narrative of how the student moved from topic selection to final conclusion.*
- *AI-use declaration. A brief note on where and how AI was used (if at all).*

These metacognitive elements bring to light the often-overlooked "invisible labor" that contributes to the creation of a final academic product. By encouraging students to reflect on their thinking processes, challenges, and decisions, **such elements foster a deeper understanding of how learning unfolds**. This reflection not only supports academic integrity but also cultivates greater self-awareness and ownership of one's educational journey (Mienye & Swart, 2025).

---

4. Incorporate In-Class Synthesis Activities

Even in hybrid or online learning environments, educators can incorporate brief, spontaneous writing or speaking activities during class sessions. These tasks - such as responding to readings, explaining a concept, or debating a position without external aid - act as real-time integrity checkpoints. **They also provide faculty with a reliable baseline** for each student's authentic voice and comprehension level, making deviations in later work easier to detect (Geethanjali & Umashankar, 2025).

---

5. Use Iterative Feedback Loops

Build opportunities for feedback and revision into the structure of major assignments to promote deeper engagement with learning. When students are required not just to submit work but to revisit, refine, and reflect on it, they become more invested in the development of their ideas. **This process-oriented approach discourages one-time, AI-generated submissions** and fosters a culture of continuous improvement and academic integrity (Eden et al., 2024; Gundu, 2024).

---

6. Shift the Purpose from Performance to Exploration

When assignments are framed as opportunities to learn rather than as mere demonstrations of competence, students are more inclined to engage with sincerity and purpose. Prompts that encourage curiosity, experimentation, and even failure - such as *"What surprised you most during your research?"* - foster a mindset oriented toward intellectual growth. **This shift away from performance-based assessment supports a more ethical and resilient learning**

environment, where integrity and exploration are valued over perfection (Zawacki-Richter et al., 2019).

Bridge Topic

Integrating These Strategies into the Curriculum

Faculty should be supported in the process of redesigning their syllabi, rubrics, and assessments to align with evolving approaches to AI-integrated learning. This includes not only technical guidance but also pedagogical training that equips faculty to promote transparency, critical engagement, and integrity in student work. When institutions invest in such support, they empower educators to create learning environments that are both innovative and ethically grounded (Ray & Ray, 2024). Institutions can:

- Offer workshops on AI-informed assignment design.
- Provide exemplar prompts and rubrics.
- Encourage departments to co-develop shared standards for process-oriented evaluation.

When educators intentionally design assignments and learning environments with integrity in mind, they significantly reduce both the opportunity and the temptation for academic misconduct. **This proactive approach shifts the focus from policing behavior to creating conditions where ethical engagement is the norm**. Most importantly, it cultivates a culture in which originality becomes visible, student effort is traceable, and trust is built through transparent and accountable learning journeys (Bailey et al., 2023; Nikolopoulou, 2025).

Section Reflection: Designing for Integrity, Not Just Assessment

This section emphasizes that academic integrity is best preserved not through policing or punishment, but through intentional assignment design that makes student thinking visible. By structuring coursework around processes rather than products - through scaffolding, reflection, personalization, and iterative feedback - educators can reduce the appeal and effectiveness of AI misuse while promoting deeper, more authentic engagement.

Thoughtfully crafted assignments that ask students to document their learning journey, incorporate their lived experiences, and reflect on their decision-making foster a transparent academic environment where integrity is naturally reinforced. This design-centered approach not only protects against dishonesty but also cultivates critical thinking, ownership, and ethical academic habits - values essential for learning in an AI-augmented world.

Section 6: Teaching Students to Collaborate Ethically with AI

In the age of generative AI, academic integrity must expand beyond the avoidance of misconduct to include the development of responsible practices. Ethical engagement with AI means not just refraining from unauthorized use but actively learning how to work with these tools in thoughtful, transparent, and critical ways (Geethanjali & Umashankar, 2025). Integrity, therefore, becomes not only a matter of restraint - but of intelligent, ethical collaboration (Bailey et al., 2023).

This section presents practical strategies for faculty to teach students how to engage with AI tools in a way that strengthens their own thinking, promotes honest attribution, and fosters a deeper understanding of both human and machine roles in the learning process (Mienye & Swart, 2025).

Teaching Responsible Prompting

Students often treat AI tools as oracles, entering vague prompts and accepting the responses without question or critique. This passive approach can limit learning and reinforce surface-level thinking, as students miss opportunities to guide or refine the technology's output. Faculty should help students shift from passive querying to intentional prompting, encouraging them to see AI as a tool that responds best to thoughtful, precise, and context-aware engagement (Yu et al., 2025). This means teaching them to:

- Frame precise, multi-layered prompts to extract depth.
- Avoid suggestive or biased language.
- Experiment and iterate on prompts to see how phrasing changes outcomes.
- Reflect on whether the prompt encourages thinking or bypasses it.

Responsible prompting plays a vital role in cultivating critical thinking skills, especially in AI-assisted learning environments. **By carefully considering how a question is framed**, students begin to recognize the influence that prompt structure has on the nature and tone of the AI's response. This awareness empowers learners to approach generative tools more critically and thoughtfully, reinforcing both digital literacy and academic integrity (Khreisat et al., 2024).

Guiding Students to Edit and Evaluate AI Output

One of the biggest misconceptions among students is that AI responses are final or authoritative. Faculty should emphasize that AI output is a draft - not a destination (Floridi & Chiriatti, 2020). Students must be taught to:

- Fact-check claims and verify sources independently.
- Edit AI-generated language for clarity, tone, and personal voice.
- Compare multiple outputs to detect inconsistencies or logical flaws.
- Challenge the reasoning of AI outputs and substitute their own.

This approach positions students as the final decision-makers in the learning process, emphasizing their active role in shaping outcomes. **By doing so, it underscores the importance of cultivating sound judgment**, especially when interacting with AI-generated content. Ultimately, this reinforces a sense of accountability and ethical responsibility, which are essential components of academic integrity in the digital age (Buckingham-Shum et al., 2019).

Introducing Bias Detection and Ethical Scrutiny

AI tools inherit the biases present in the data on which they are trained, often reflecting historical, cultural, or societal prejudices embedded in those sources. These biases can manifest in subtle ways, influencing the tone, framing, or accuracy of generated responses. Recognizing this limitation is essential for faculty and students alike, as it promotes a more critical and informed use of AI in academic contexts (Binns, 2018). This makes them prone to:

- Repeating cultural stereotypes.
- Omitting marginalized voices.
- Misrepresenting scientific uncertainty.

Faculty can incorporate short assignments or in-class activities that challenge students to:

- Identify bias in AI-generated content.
- Compare AI summaries to peer-reviewed literature.
- Reflect on who benefits or is excluded by a given response.

Doing so transforms students into more than passive users of AI - they become active participants in evaluating its outputs and ethical implications. **By critically examining the limitations, biases, and consequences of AI-generated content, students learn to question rather than blindly accept technological assistance**. This shift empowers them to act as ethical evaluators, fostering responsible academic practices in a digitally mediated learning environment (Bender et al., 2021; Kallunki et al., 2024).

Modeling and Requiring Attribution of AI Use

If a student cites a book, they are expected to name the author as a matter of academic honesty and proper attribution. The same principle should apply when students use AI tools to summarize, generate, or enhance text - transparency about the source remains essential. Acknowledging AI assistance not only upholds academic integrity but also models responsible and ethical use of emerging technologies in scholarship (Ray & Ray, 2024). Faculty can:

- Provide models for how to cite AI tools in bibliographies or footnotes (e.g., APA, MLA, or institutional standards).
- Require AI use declarations, as discussed in earlier sections.
- Explain that attribution does not discredit a student's work - it enhances transparency.

By making attribution a normative part of academic work rather than a response to misconduct, educators can shift students' perceptions of acknowledgment. **Instead of viewing citation as a defensive act or admission of wrongdoing, students come to understand it as a marker of intellectual integrity and scholarly maturity**. This perspective reinforces that proper attribution is a strength - an ethical practice that honors both transparency and the collaborative nature of knowledge creation (Eden et al., 2024; Mienye & Swart, 2025).

Promoting Human-AI Collaboration as a Learning Partnership

Finally, faculty must guide students in reframing AI not as a shortcut to bypass effort, but as a valuable thought partner in the learning process. When used critically and ethically, AI can support idea development, enhance clarity, and spark deeper inquiry. This mindset shift encourages students to collaborate with technology in meaningful ways while still taking full ownership of their intellectual work (Holmes et al., 2022). This means designing exercises that explicitly ask students to:

- Compare their own ideas to those generated by AI.
- Use AI to identify counterarguments or alternative viewpoints.
- Reflect on how their thinking changed through interaction with the tool.

Such tasks deepen learning by transforming the interaction between humans and AI into an active site of cognitive development. **Rather than simply using AI as a tool for output, students engage in reflective dialogue with the technology**, analyzing its responses and adjusting their thinking accordingly. This dynamic exchange not only enhances subject mastery but also cultivates higher-order reasoning and digital discernment (Luckin et al., 2016; Nikolopoulou, 2025).

Building a Culture of Ethical AI Engagement

To embed these practices across the institution, faculty development programs must move beyond optional workshops and instead become integral components of institutional strategy. These programs should be designed to equip educators with the pedagogical, ethical, and technical skills needed to engage with AI in meaningful and responsible ways. By offering sustained, collaborative opportunities for professional learning, institutions can ensure that faculty are prepared to lead with integrity in an evolving educational landscape using:

- Workshops on AI tool literacy.
- Collaborative syllabus design sessions.
- Shared repositories of sample prompts, assignments, and usage statements.

The goal is not merely to tolerate AI in education as an inevitable tool, but to proactively shape a generation of students who are ethical, thoughtful, and fluent in collaborating with intelligent systems. This requires more than technical instruction - it involves cultivating critical thinking, self-awareness, and a strong foundation in digital ethics. By teaching students how to engage with AI critically and transparently, we empower them to navigate the future with both technological confidence and moral clarity.

Section Reflection: Cultivating Ethical Thinkers in an AI-Augmented World

This section advances the conversation from AI avoidance to ethical AI engagement, positioning students not merely as users of technology but as critical collaborators in the learning process. By teaching students to prompt intentionally, evaluate AI outputs critically, detect embedded biases, and attribute assistance transparently, educators help transform AI from a passive shortcut into an active cognitive partner. This shift reframes academic integrity as a practice of judgment, reflection, and accountability rather than restraint alone.

When students are guided to view AI as a thought partner - not a crutch - they develop essential digital ethics and intellectual maturity. Building a culture where ethical AI use is normalized and openly discussed empowers learners to take ownership of their thinking and prepares them to thrive in a world where human-machine collaboration is the norm, not the exception.

Section 7: Faculty as Role Models of Integrity in the AI Era

Faculty cannot expect students to uphold principles they do not see practiced. In the context of AI, academic integrity becomes a shared enterprise - not just a student obligation, but a professional standard that educators must embody (Bailey et al., 2023). The credibility of any integrity policy or classroom guideline depends largely on whether faculty visibly model the values they promote (Mienye & Swart, 2025).

In this new era, faculty themselves must wrestle with questions of appropriate AI use. *"Have they used ChatGPT to draft a lecture outline, brainstorm discussion questions, or generate rubric language?" "Have they disclosed this use to students?" "Do they distinguish between AI-assisted drafting and original scholarship in their own publications or academic materials?"* These questions are not trivial - they shape the cultural norms that guide student behavior (Geethanjali & Umashankar, 2025; Gundu, 2024).

Modeling Transparent AI Use in Teaching

Faculty can normalize transparency by openly discussing how AI supports their own teaching practices, whether in course design, grading, or content development. When educators model this openness, they create a culture where responsible AI use is seen as thoughtful and intentional rather than secretive or taboo. This approach fosters trust and encourages students to engage in similar ethical and reflective use of AI tools in their academic work (Ray & Ray, 2024). For example:

- *"I used ChatGPT to brainstorm topics for this week's lecture, but I reviewed and revised everything myself."*
- *"The rubric you are using was adapted with the help of an AI writing assistant, and I checked it against our department's standards."*

These disclosures demonstrate what responsible AI collaboration looks like in practice, showing that ethical integration involves intentionality rather than avoidance. They reinforce the essential role of human judgment, emphasizing that technology should support - rather than replace - critical decision-making. In doing so, they also demystify AI's role in the learning process, helping students recognize that ethical use involves active engagement, not passive reliance (Khreisat et al., 2024).

Ethical AI Use in Grading and Feedback

Some faculty now use AI tools to help draft grading comments or generate initial feedback on written assignments, leveraging these technologies to streamline their workload. While this approach can save considerable time, its effectiveness and appropriateness depend on how thoughtfully and transparently the tools are applied. To maintain trust and uphold academic integrity, it is essential that such use is disclosed to students and supplemented with individualized, human judgment (Holmes et al., 2022). Faculty should:

- Review and personalize all AI-generated feedback to reflect authentic evaluation.
- Acknowledge if AI assisted in summarizing or organizing student feedback.
- Avoid over-delegating pedagogical judgment to automated tools.

When feedback is overly generic or clearly algorithmic, students can quickly sense a lack of personal engagement from their faculty. This perception may undermine trust and reduce the impact of the feedback, leading students to disengage from the learning process. However, when **faculty use AI to enhance - rather than replace - thoughtful, personalized feedback, they reaffirm their commitment to meaningful teaching** and uphold the relational core of education (Nikolopoulou, 2025; Yadav, 2024).

Leading by Example in Research and Professional Writing

Faculty who write scholarly articles, grant proposals, or public commentaries are increasingly turning to AI tools to support their writing processes. These tools can assist with drafting abstracts, refining grammar, or improving structural coherence, thereby streamlining the often time-intensive task of professional communication. When used ethically and transparently, AI becomes a valuable aid in academic productivity without compromising intellectual authorship or scholarly rigor (Kacena et al., 2024). While there is no universal standard yet, faculty should:

- Credit AI contributions in footnotes, author's notes, or acknowledgments where appropriate.
- Distinguish between AI-generated text and original argumentation.
- Disclose AI use in contexts that emphasize transparency (e.g., presentations, preprints, institutional reports).

By setting clear standards for AI use in their own professional work, faculty model the behaviors they hope to see in their students. **This practice cultivates a professional culture that values proper attribution, communicative clarity, and ethical engagement with emerging technologies**. Through these actions, educators demonstrate that innovation and integrity are not opposing forces but can - and should - coexist in the evolving academic landscape (Bender et al., 2021; Floridi & Chiriatti, 2020).

Engaging Students in Integrity Conversations

Faculty who are open about their own learning curve with AI demonstrate humility and authenticity in their professional practice. By acknowledging that they, too, are navigating new technologies, educators model the mindset of lifelong learning for their students. This openness fosters a learning environment where curiosity, adaptation, and continuous growth are valued as much as expertise (Rahm, 2023). Rather than positioning themselves as authorities untouched by these tools, they invite students into a collaborative conversation:

- *"Here is what I have been exploring with AI - what about you?"*
- *"How do you decide when to use AI in your writing, and how do you know when it is too much?"*

These kinds of questions - posed by faculty to students and vice versa - create opportunities for open dialogue about the ethical dimensions of technology use. By inviting honest reflection and mutual inquiry, they help to foster trust and build stronger relational dynamics within the learning community. Such exchanges flatten traditional hierarchies and promote a shared responsibility for ethical decision-making in the use of AI and other emerging technologies (Bailey et al., 2023; Eden et al., 2024).

Departmental Leadership and Policy Alignment

Departmental leadership and institutional policy play a crucial role in shaping how AI is integrated across academic programs. Beyond the efforts of individual faculty, faculty can work collectively to establish shared guidelines, coordinate professional development, and advocate for ethical norms in AI use. This alignment not only strengthens consistency across courses but also reinforces a unified institutional culture that supports transparency, integrity, and innovation in the AI era so faculty can:

- Participate in drafting or revising departmental AI policies.
- Share assignment models and teaching strategies in faculty workshops.
- Mentor colleagues who are hesitant or unsure about AI integration.

Integrity becomes a systemic value when faculty at every level - from adjunct faculty to senior scholars - engage in collaborative efforts to define and uphold shared norms. This collective approach fosters a sense of unity and mutual accountability, ensuring that ethical standards evolve alongside technological advancements. By supporting one another in adapting to new educational realities, faculty create a resilient academic culture rooted in trust, transparency, and continuous growth (Cotton et al., 2024; Geethanjali & Umashankar, 2025).

Bridge Topic

The Ethical Role Model in Practice

Being a role model for integrity in the AI era does not mean being perfect. It **means being transparent, thoughtful, and consistent in one's own engagement with technology**. Students watch not only what faculty say - but what they do. And when educators model the principles of transparency, attribution, discernment, and responsible innovation, they transform integrity from a policy into a lived culture (Gundu, 2024).

Section Reflection: Leading with Integrity in a Transparent AI Era

This section affirms that faculty are not just enforcers of academic integrity - they are its most influential role models. In an era shaped by generative AI, students look to their faculty for cues on how to use emerging technologies ethically, thoughtfully, and transparently. When faculty openly disclose their own AI use in teaching, grading, or scholarship, they demystify the tools and model responsible engagement.

Through visible practices such as attribution, reflective dialogue, and feedback transparency, educators show that integrity is not about avoiding technology but using it with care and clarity. By fostering open conversations, aligning departmental norms, and embracing their own learning curves, faculty help build a culture of shared responsibility. Integrity, then, becomes a lived standard - something students absorb not through policy alone, but through the everyday actions and examples of those who lead them.

Section 8: Toward a Culture of Integrity by Design, Not Discipline

Academic integrity cannot be sustained through surveillance, prohibition, or punishment alone. These reactive strategies may enforce compliance in the short term, but they do little to cultivate genuine ethical engagement in the long term. In the age of AI, the more effective and enduring path forward is to design academic environments where integrity is built in - visible, supported, and expected - not just enforced (Eden et al., 2024; Ray & Ray, 2024).

This closing section challenges institutions to move from discipline to design, from policing misconduct to empowering ethical scholarship. It calls for a whole-campus approach that integrates course design, faculty support, policy alignment, and student voice into a shared culture of academic responsibility (Geethanjali & Umashankar, 2025; Gundu, 2024).

Redesign Curricula to Reflect AI-Integrated Learning

Institutions must take an active role in supporting faculty as they design courses that acknowledge the presence of AI as an integral part of the learning landscape. Rather than treating AI as an external threat or anomaly, educators should be empowered to teach students how to engage with these tools critically, ethically, and effectively. By embedding AI literacy and responsibility into the curriculum, institutions prepare students for real-world contexts where thoughtful human-AI collaboration is increasingly essential (Holmes et al., 2022). This includes:

- Revising learning outcomes to include AI literacy, critical thinking, and ethical decision-making (Zawacki-Richter et al., 2019).
- Offering interdisciplinary courses that explore the societal, ethical, and technical dimensions of AI (Floridi, 2019).

- Embedding transparency expectations into course materials (e.g., AI-use declarations in assignment guidelines) (Mienye & Swart, 2025).

Integrity is more likely to flourish when it is integrated into the realities of modern learning environments, rather than positioned in opposition to them. **As education evolves to include digital tools, AI, and flexible learning modalities, ethical practices must evolve alongside these changes** to remain relevant and effective. When integrity is framed as compatible with innovation and not a constraint on it, students and faculty alike are more likely to embrace it as a guiding principle (Nikolopoulou, 2025).

Update Syllabi and Honor Code Language

Institutional policies must move beyond vague or overly broad bans on AI use, which often create confusion and inhibit meaningful engagement. Instead, policies should offer clarity, articulate nuanced guidelines, and provide resources that help both faculty and students navigate ethical use. When institutions adopt supportive and well-defined approaches, they foster a culture of trust, accountability, and innovation rather than fear or avoidance (Ray & Ray, 2024). Suggested updates include:

- Differentiating between unauthorized use, transparent use, and encouraged exploration of AI tools.
- Including examples of acceptable and unacceptable AI uses in syllabi.
- Encouraging faculty to include personal statements about their AI expectations and practices.

By aligning policy language with actual pedagogical practices, institutions create consistency between what is expected and what is enacted in classrooms. **This coherence helps eliminate ambiguity**, ensuring that both students and faculty clearly understand how to engage with AI tools responsibly. As a result, educational communities are better equipped to act with integrity, guided by shared expectations and supported through practical implementation (Bailey et al., 2023; Cotton et al., 2024).

Create Shared Institutional Norms and Resources

Siloed efforts by individual departments or faculty will not be sufficient to address the complex challenges and opportunities introduced by AI in education. Institutions must foster intentional collaboration across departments, academic disciplines, and administrative offices to ensure cohesive and inclusive strategies. By uniting diverse perspectives and areas of expertise, schools can build comprehensive approaches that support ethical, innovative, and institution-wide integration of AI (Luckin, 2017). This can include:

- Establishing working groups or task forces to regularly update academic integrity guidelines.
- Hosting faculty development sessions on AI-informed pedagogy.
- Creating a centralized repository of sample assignments, policies, and citation models that emphasize ethical AI use.

Shared resources play a crucial role in reducing individual uncertainty among faculty who may feel overwhelmed by the rapid pace of technological change. **When institutions provide clear guidelines, exemplar practices, and centralized tools, educators are better equipped to respond confidently and consistently to the challenges and opportunities presented by AI**. This collective approach promotes a unified, coherent institutional response, ensuring that the integration of emerging technologies aligns with shared values and pedagogical goals (Geethanjali & Umashankar, 2025; Khreisat et al., 2024).

Engage Students as Partners in Integrity Culture

Integrity cannot simply be imposed from the top down - it must be co-created through inclusive and ongoing dialogue between faculty and students. When students are treated not merely as recipients of institutional policies but as collaborators in shaping academic norms, they are more likely to take ownership of ethical behavior. This shared responsibility fosters a deeper commitment to integrity and strengthens the academic culture as a whole (Iloka, 2025). Institutions can:

- Include student representatives in policy and curriculum revision committees.
- Invite students to write reflection pieces or case studies on their experiences with AI and academic honesty.
- Create peer mentoring programs focused on academic integrity and responsible technology use.

When students are actively involved in shaping academic policies and expectations, they are more likely to develop a genuine understanding of the rules and their underlying purpose. This participatory approach fosters a sense of ownership and respect, making students more inclined to follow guidelines they helped create. By including student voices in the development of integrity frameworks, institutions promote ethical engagement grounded in mutual trust and shared accountability (Bretag et al., 2011; Gundu, 2024).

Shift from Rigor as Restriction to Rigor as Engagement

Traditional notions of academic rigor have often emphasized difficulty, solitary effort, and strict restraint as markers of excellence. However, in the AI era, rigor must be redefined to reflect intellectual depth, reflective engagement, transparent processes, and ethical responsibility. This shift acknowledges that true academic challenge lies not in exclusion or restriction, but in cultivating the skills and integrity required to navigate complex, AI-enhanced learning environments (Williamson & Eynon, 2020). This shift requires:

- Redefining assessment to emphasize synthesis, analysis, and originality.
- Emphasizing effort and ethical reasoning as much as final outcomes.
- Designing intellectually demanding work that uses AI while still requiring student insight.

Rigor by design engages students in authentic, meaningful learning experiences that emphasize growth, reflection, and application. In contrast, rigor imposed through excessive restriction often leads to anxiety, surface-level compliance, and performances that prioritize appearance over understanding. **By shifting toward rigor that is intentionally designed and student-centered, educators can cultivate deeper learning and promote academic integrity** in an age shaped by AI (Eden et al., 2024; Nikolopoulou, 2025).

Leadership and Long-Term Vision

Institutional leaders must reframe integrity not as a constraint on progress, but as the very foundation upon which meaningful and ethical innovation is built. When integrity is positioned as a catalyst rather than a barrier, it encourages creativity that is guided by purpose and principle. This perspective empowers faculty and students alike to embrace emerging technologies while staying grounded in shared academic values (Floridi & Chiriatti, 2020). They must:

- Advocate for investment in faculty training and support.
- Communicate openly about the challenges and opportunities AI brings to education.
- Evaluate integrity initiatives not by how many infractions are punished, but by how many ethical habits are cultivated.

Sustaining integrity in the AI era requires more than enforcement - it demands vision, humility, and collaboration across all levels of the academic community. **Faculty and institutional leaders must be willing to let go of outdated assumptions about control and compliance and instead design learning environments that actively support ethical behavior**. When structures and systems are built to make integrity easier to practice than to avoid, academic honesty becomes a natural and sustainable part of the educational experience (Bailey et al., 2023; Floridi & Chiriatti, 2020).

Section Reflection: Integrity as a Designed Experience, Not a Disciplinary Threat

This final section reframes academic integrity as a proactive, systemic design challenge rather than a reactive disciplinary concern. It calls on institutions to build integrity into the educational fabric - through curriculum design, policy clarity, faculty development, and student partnership - so that ethical behavior becomes a natural outcome of the learning environment, not just a rule to follow. By embedding transparency, AI literacy, and critical engagement into assignments and expectations, schools can align rigor with relevance and prepare students to act ethically in real-world, AI-rich contexts.

When faculty model integrity and students help shape its norms, a shared culture of trust and responsibility emerges. Rather than policing misconduct, educators and leaders are urged to foster conditions where ethical thinking is visible, valued, and practiced. In doing so, integrity becomes not just preserved - but redefined - as a foundation for innovation, reflection, and intellectual courage in the AI era (Davis et al., 2011).

Chapter 1 Conclusion: Reclaiming Purpose and Pedagogical Integrity in the Age of AI

As artificial intelligence continues to reshape the contours of higher education, Chapter 1 has argued that faculty must respond not with fear or passive compliance, but with intentional design, ethical imagination, and renewed professional agency. Across its eight sections, this chapter has charted a clear trajectory: from naming the existential and structural challenges of generative AI to reimagining teaching, assessment, mentorship, and academic culture in ways that center human judgment, reflective learning, and shared responsibility.

In **Section 1**, we redefined **empowerment** for both students and educators - not as mere access to tools, but as the capacity to question, contextualize, and retain authorship in a world of automated fluency. This theme was deepened in **Section 2**, where faculty were encouraged to teach AI as a **reflective mirror**, inviting students to critique, compare, and revise machine outputs as a path to deeper self-awareness and intellectual integrity.

Section 3 introduced **ethical reasoning** as a core competency, urging the use of case-based, situated learning that develops moral agency and anticipatory judgment. **Section 4** expanded this lens by spotlighting **creativity and divergence**, positioning faculty as curators of assignments that reward imaginative risk and subversion of algorithmic norms.

In **Section 5**, the chapter turned toward **discernment** - teaching students to assess the credibility and bias of AI outputs, cultivating habits of evaluation that resist surface-level fluency. **Section 6** built on this by arguing that **faculty modeling** is not a supplemental practice but a foundational form of leadership, shaping students' understanding of ethical technology use through transparency, dialogue, and visible boundary-setting.

Section 7 offered practical and philosophical tools for **designing learning goals** that reflect the complexity of human–AI collaboration. These goals emphasize not only technical fluency, but process awareness, ethical disclosure, and creative co-authorship. Finally, **Section 8** elevated the role of faculty as **legacy-builders** - ethical leaders who shape institutional values through mentorship, policy participation, and public engagement.

Together, these eight sections converge around a central theme: that AI's arrival in higher education is not merely a technological disruption - it is a pedagogical reckoning. It forces us to ask: *"What do we value as educators?" "What must remain human?" "And how do we prepare students not simply to* ***use*** *intelligent systems, but to* ***critique, question, and shape*** *them?"*

The **path forward** is neither a rejection of AI nor an embrace of its efficiencies alone. It is a deliberate act of reclaiming purpose - ensuring that, even amid automation, education remains a relational, reflective, and justice-oriented endeavor. Faculty, when empowered to lead with clarity and care, can guide the AI transition not as a crisis to be managed, but as a moment to be defined - by values, by vision, and by the shared mission to cultivate thoughtful, ethical, and empowered learners.

Chapter 2: Designing Assignments for a Post-Textbook World

The internet - and now generative AI - has rendered traditional, fact-based assignments obsolete. The question is no longer **what** students know, but **how** they think. This chapter introduces flexible frameworks for designing AI-resilient assignments that focus on reasoning, synthesis, problem-solving, and reflection. Faculty will learn how to craft prompts that reveal student thinking, not just student output.

Section 1: Beyond Recall - Moving Past Fact-Based Testing

In the age of generative AI and instant access to information, assignments that focus on factual recall are quickly becoming obsolete. Students no longer need to memorize what can be retrieved in seconds. Instead, faculty must shift from **"What do you know?"** to **"What can you do with what you know?"** This section explores how to move beyond traditional multiple-choice tests, short-answer quizzes, and copy-pasteable essay prompts. Faculty will learn to design assessments that prioritize analysis, application, and synthesis - skills that require active cognitive engagement and cannot be outsourced to AI tools. Strategies include scenario-based questioning, real-world problem framing, and timed critical response tasks that demonstrate comprehension rather than repetition. By shifting away from rote recall, educators can build intellectual resilience in students and foster more meaningful engagement with content that endures far beyond the classroom.

In the age of generative AI and instant access to vast databases of information, the utility of assignments based solely on factual recall has drastically declined. Students no longer need to memorize what they can retrieve in seconds from a search engine or a chatbot such as ChatGPT (Selwyn, 2021). The emphasis in pedagogy should shift from measuring **"What knowledge do students hold?"** to examining **"How can they apply that knowledge in meaningful, authentic contexts?"**

Why Factual Recall Falls Short

- Consider a common multiple-choice question:
  - *"What year did the Berlin Wall fall?"*

Within seconds, a student can retrieve the correct answer - which is 1989 - using any AI tool or search engine. There is no need for deep thought, interpretation, or contextual understanding. This type of question rewards quick lookup skills rather than critical engagement with the material. As Lang (2013) argued, students often resort to strategic short-term memorization for these tasks, **leading to superficial learning and quick forgetting**.

Reframing Assessment for Higher-Order Thinking

To foster deeper learning, faculty must design assessments that require cognitive effort and decision-making. According to L. W. Anderson and Krathwohl's (2001) revision of Bloom's Taxonomy, the higher-order thinking skills - analyzing, evaluating, and creating - form the bedrock of meaningful education. Assignments that activate these skills are far less susceptible to AI automation.

Example 1: Comparative Reasoning Prompt

- **Instead of Asking:**

  "List the causes of the French Revolution."

- **Ask:**

  "Compare the political and economic grievances that led to the French Revolution with those that fueled the American Revolution. Which factors played a more significant role in triggering change, and why?"

This type of question demands more than surface-level information retrieval - it requires **synthesis, historical interpretation, and evidence-based justification**. These are cognitive tasks that depend on deep understanding, critical thinking, and the ability to contextualize information within a broader intellectual framework. Such complexity cannot be reliably outsourced to AI without substantial human engagement and refinement, reinforcing the value of authentic student work (Wineburg, 2018).

Example 2: Contextual Application

- **Replace a Standard Science Prompt Such As:**

  "What is the function of mitochondria?"

- **With:**

  "Your friend has been diagnosed with a mitochondrial disorder. Explain how this might affect their overall health and energy levels, using what you have learned in class."

This approach compels students to apply their knowledge in real-world scenarios, bridging academic learning with practical relevance. **While AI can assist in this process by offering suggestions or simulations, it lacks the ability to fully personalize or contextualize those applications without meaningful human insight**. Ultimately, it is the student's judgment, experience, and situational awareness that bring depth and authenticity to applied learning tasks (Yadav, 2024).

Scenario-Based and Problem-Framed Assignments

Assignments that ask students to respond to simulated or real-world dilemmas are particularly effective in fostering critical engagement. These tasks go beyond content recall by requiring students to exercise judgment, prioritize competing considerations, and apply ethical reasoning - skills that remain distinctly human and context-dependent. Such assessments not only deepen learning but also help students prepare for complex decision-making in professional and civic life (Glaser et al., 2001; Wiggins & McTighe, 2005).

Example 3: Ethical Scenario in Technology

- *"A city plans to implement facial recognition technology to reduce crime. As a policy advisor, write a briefing note outlining the social, ethical, and technological implications of this decision."*

This prompt effectively merges critical thinking with applied learning and real-time engagement with current events. By doing so, it **challenges students to move beyond memorization or surface-level responses and toward nuanced analysis and informed interpretation**. This kind of task promotes critical synthesis, encouraging students to integrate diverse perspectives and demonstrate higher-order thinking (Brookhart, 2010).

Timed Critical Reflection and In-Class Responses

Incorporating timed reflections or short, spontaneous writing tasks encourages students to engage in active processing and immediate articulation of their thoughts. These low-stakes, real-time exercises prompt authentic responses that reflect individual understanding rather than polished or AI-assisted outputs. As a result, they serve as effective tools for discouraging overreliance on generative technologies while promoting deeper cognitive engagement (Deneen & Boud, 2014).

Example 4: Timed In-Class Writing

- *"After watching a short documentary on climate adaptation, write a 5-minute reflection on how individual behavior intersects with structural climate policy. No outside materials allowed."*

This style of assessment is designed to evaluate student comprehension in a timely and targeted manner, helping learners internalize key concepts more quickly. When paired with follow-up discussions, peer reviews, or reflective activities, it deepens understanding by prompting students to articulate and defend their thinking. At the same time, **it fosters accountability**, as students become more engaged in their own learning process and in the collaborative academic community (Lang, 2013).

Designing for AI-Resiliency

Rather than banning AI, **design assignments that make AI insufficient**. In other words, even if students were to use generative AI, they would still have to provide **personal insights, real-world connections, or reasoning under constraint**.

Example 5: Reflection with AI Transparency

- *Use an AI tool to generate a summary of this week's article.*
- *Then, in your own words, critique the AI summary:*
    - *"What did it get right?"*

- *"What did it miss?"*
- *"How would you improve it based on your understanding?"*

This dual-layer prompt is designed to cultivate both critical AI literacy and reflective thinking by requiring students to engage with content at multiple levels. It places the student at the center of interpretation, **prompting them to assess, critique, and contextualize AI-generated responses through a human lens**. These essential skills - reflection, judgment, and meaning-making - cannot be fully automated, highlighting the irreplaceable role of human insight in academic work (Lang, 2013).

Section Reflection: Redefining Rigor Through Critical Engagement

This section urges a necessary departure from fact-based testing and challenges faculty to redesign assessments for deeper learning in the AI era. As instant information access renders rote memorization obsolete, the focus must shift toward evaluating what students can **do** with knowledge rather than simply what they **know**. By integrating scenario-based prompts, real-world applications, ethical dilemmas, and timed reflections, educators can cultivate critical thinking, judgment, and synthesis - skills that remain uniquely human and resistant to AI automation.

These assignment designs not only strengthen academic integrity but also build intellectual resilience, encouraging students to engage with material in ways that are personal, contextualized, and meaningful. Integrity in this context is no longer preserved by restricting access to tools, but by elevating the kinds of thinking those tools cannot replicate.

Section 2: Designing Prompts that Prioritize Process Over Product

---

One of the greatest weaknesses of traditional assignments in the AI era is their overemphasis on the final deliverable. Whether it is a polished essay, a finished lab report, or a neatly formatted presentation, such assignments focus heavily on appearance and not enough on **how** students got there. This approach creates two problems: (a) it obscures authentic student learning and (b) it invites students to use generative AI to bypass the thinking process entirely (Lang, 2013).

By contrast, process-oriented prompts elevate the **journey** over the **destination**. These prompts make visible the evolving stages of thinking, reasoning, and revision - facets that generative AI cannot authentically simulate. According to Brookhart (2010), assessing students' metacognitive development and decision-making processes fosters deeper understanding, supports long-term retention, and cultivates academic honesty.

Why the Process Matters in the Age of AI

While tools such as ChatGPT can produce fluent, grammatically correct responses in seconds, they cannot reveal **why** a student chose a particular approach, **what** they struggled with, or **how** their thinking changed over time. This makes the final product a poor proxy for intellectual growth. Instead of focusing solely on polished submissions, educators must design prompts that track and reward process milestones.

Example 1: Thinking Journals

- *Rather than assigning only a final paper, faculty can ask students to submit weekly "thinking journals" that capture how their thesis or argument is evolving.*
- ***Prompt**: "Each week, write a short entry (150–250 words) detailing what you have learned, what has challenged your thinking, and how your ideas are shifting. Include quotes, questions, or research you are considering."*

This **strategy highlights intellectual progress** by making the learning journey itself visible, rather than focusing solely on final outcomes. When students are required to document their evolving ideas, revisions, and reflections over time, it encourages deeper engagement and self-awareness. Additionally, it serves as a deterrent to AI-generated submissions, as the requirement for continuity and developmental transparency reveals whether the work is authentically student-produced (Lang, 2013).

Tools to Make Process Visible

There are multiple ways to design assessments that illuminate the student's thinking process and promote deeper engagement with the material. Strategies such as think-aloud protocols, annotated drafts, or process journals help faculty trace how ideas are developed, revised, and justified over time. These approaches not only support authentic learning but also **make it more difficult for students to conceal reliance on AI-generated content** (Nicol & Macfarlane-Dick, 2006).

Iterative Submissions

Encouraging students to produce drafts, outlines, and participate in incremental feedback cycles creates a more rigorous and reflective academic workflow. Instead of relying on one-time submissions or superficial edits, this process gives students the opportunity to revisit their ideas, respond meaningfully to critique, and strengthen their arguments over time. As Wiggins and McTighe (2005) emphasized, structured opportunities for revision make learning deeper and more purposeful, since students actively engage in refining both their thinking and their writing.

Example 2: Multi-Stage Research Paper

- **Stage 1: Topic Proposal + Annotated Bibliography**. Students select a research question, articulate its significance, and compile an annotated bibliography that demonstrates early engagement with credible sources.
- **Stage 2: Outline Submission with Preliminary Thesis**. Students submit a structured outline and draft thesis, clarifying their argument's direction and organization before moving to full drafting.

- **Stage 3: Rough Draft + Peer Feedback Exchange**. A complete rough draft is shared with peers, who provide structured feedback on clarity, argumentation, and evidence use.
- **Stage 4: Final Submission with Reflection Letter**. In the final stage, students submit a polished paper accompanied by a reflection letter. In this letter, they explain how feedback shaped their revisions, what choices they made in response, and how their argument evolved.

In the reflection letter, students articulate how they integrated feedback into their work and what specific revisions they made in response. **This practice makes the writing process transparent**, allowing faculty to see the student's progression, decision-making, and engagement with critique. It also individualizes the learning experience, helping to verify authorship and reinforce metacognitive awareness (Taczak et al., 2016).

Annotated Bibliographies

These assignments move beyond the basic task of listing sources by requiring students to engage in critical evaluation and purposeful selection. When students annotate why they chose each source, explain what it contributes to their argument, and describe how they intend to use it, they reveal their analytical reasoning and research strategy. This approach gives faculty valuable insight into students' evaluative thinking and supports the development of information literacy and source integration skills (Head & Eisenberg, 2010).

Example 3: Annotated Bibliography Entry

- *Illustrative Example:*
- *Source: Jones, J. (2022). "Urban Resilience and Climate Policy."*
- *Annotation: I chose this article because it focuses on climate adaptation strategies in cities - directly relevant to my case study on New York. I plan to use its policy framework in my section on zoning reform.*

AI tools can suggest sources based on keywords or patterns, offering a useful starting point for research. However, **they cannot independently justify the relevance or credibility of those sources within the context of a student's evolving argument**. Doing so requires deep prompting, critical evaluation, and human reflection - skills grounded in higher-order thinking that AI alone cannot replicate (L. W. Anderson & Krathwohl, 2001).

Reflection Checkpoints

Built-in reflection moments during a project encourage students to pause and critically assess their own learning trajectory. These checkpoints foster metacognitive awareness by prompting learners to evaluate their progress, challenges, and evolving understanding. At the same time, they provide faculty with natural opportunities for formative assessment, enabling timely feedback and instructional adjustment (Boud, 2001).

Example 4: Midway Reflection Prompt

- *"Now that you have completed your first draft, answer the following: What do you feel confident about? What still feels uncertain? What feedback would help you most at this stage?"*

This kind of introspective writing **prompts students to take ownership of their learning by examining their thought processes, decisions, and areas for growth**. Through regular reflection, learners strengthen self-regulation and build academic resilience - skills essential for sustained, independent inquiry. These habits not only deepen engagement but also reduce the temptation to outsource cognitive effort to AI, reinforcing integrity and personal accountability (Brookhart, 2010).

Process-Based Rubrics

Assessment tools should reflect process-based values that emphasize how students develop and apply knowledge over time - not just what they produce at the end. Rather than focusing solely on correctness or final presentation, rubrics can be designed to assess critical thinking, reflection, and engagement with feedback. By incorporating such criteria, educators reinforce learning as an iterative, thoughtful process rather than a one-time performance (Brookhart, 2010). Rubrics can include criteria such as:

- Demonstrates idea development across stages.
- Engages meaningfully with feedback.
- Reflects on learning challenges and growth.
- Justifies research and writing choices.

Example 5: Rubric Language for Process Evaluation

- *"Student shows evidence of growth from draft to final version, including at least two major conceptual changes based on peer or instructor feedback."*

This approach **shifts the focus of grading away from superficial polish and toward deeper indicators of learning such as engagement, effort, and adaptability**. By valuing how students think, revise, and respond to challenges, faculty create space for authentic growth and meaningful progress. As Wiggins and McTighe (2005) argued, this kind of assessment fosters a more accurate and supportive picture of student learning in complex, real-world context.

Reducing AI Dependency through Metacognition

By focusing on how students think rather than solely on the final product they submit, faculty promote deeper metacognitive engagement throughout the learning process. When students are encouraged to reflect on their decisions, strategies, and intellectual growth, they develop a stronger sense of agency and awareness. As a result, they are not only less likely to misuse AI but are also more likely to achieve learning that is lasting and transferable across contexts (Brookhart, 2010).

Example 6: End-of-Term Meta-Reflection

- *"Describe how your thinking evolved throughout this course. What assignment challenged you most? What strategies helped you grow as a writer, researcher, or problem solver?"*

These reflections can take a variety of forms, including written submissions, short videos, or live one-on-one conversations. **Each format invites students to articulate their thinking in personal and authentic ways that are less easily outsourced to AI**. By selecting modes that prioritize voice, presence, and individualized expression, faculty create meaningful opportunities for genuine engagement and academic integrity (Ryan & Ryan, 2013).

Section Reflection: Elevating Learning Through Visible Thinking

This section champions a vital pedagogical shift: from emphasizing polished products to illuminating the thinking that produces them. In an AI-saturated academic landscape, where tools can fabricate fluent outputs in seconds, the most authentic learning emerges when students are asked to document, reflect on, and refine their intellectual journey. By designing prompts that prioritize process - through iterative drafts, annotated bibliographies, reflection checkpoints, and metacognitive assessments - faculty empower students to engage deeply, think critically, and take ownership of their growth.

These process-oriented strategies not only make learning visible but also reduce reliance on generative AI by making it difficult to bypass genuine cognitive effort. Ultimately, this approach redefines academic rigor as the development of thinking over time, fostering integrity through engagement and cultivating learners who value their own evolving understanding.

Section 3: Creating Multistage Assignments that Build Intellectual Scaffolding

---

Multistage assignments - those broken into defined components across time - are one of the most effective ways to promote deep learning while reducing opportunities for academic dishonesty and AI overreliance. Unlike single high-stakes submissions that can be entirely generated by an AI tool in minutes, multistage assignments emphasize development, feedback, and iteration - elements that AI cannot authentically simulate (Lang, 2013).

This process-driven approach aligns with principles of scaffolding in cognitive theory, which suggest that learners acquire complex skills more effectively when supported through structured, sequential tasks (L. W. Anderson & Krathwohl, 2001). As students are progressing through stages such as idea generation, research planning, drafting, and reflection, they are building both confidence and capacity for independent thought.

Benefits of the Multistage Model

Scaffolded assignments discourage one-time AI use by requiring students to submit work in incremental phases, making it difficult to produce a complete, credible submission all at once. This structure encourages ongoing reflection and revision, as students are asked to explain their thinking, adjust their ideas, and build upon previous efforts - practices that develop metacognitive awareness. In turn, faculty gain valuable insight into the student's learning process and intellectual growth, visibility that is often absent in final products alone (Brookhart, 2010). Therefore, these benefits:

- **Discourage One-Time AI Use**. Students cannot produce a complete, credible submission at once because each phase is evaluated incrementally.
- **Encourage Reflection and Revision**. By requiring students to explain, adjust, and build on prior work, these assignments develop meta-cognitive awareness (Brookhart, 2010).
- **Reveal the Learning Process**. Faculty gain insight into how a student's ideas evolve - insight not visible in final products alone.

Framework for Multistage Assignment Design

A robust multistage assignment typically includes several key checkpoints; each strategically aligned with different cognitive levels of Bloom's Taxonomy. This structure ensures that students are not only recalling information but also applying, analyzing, evaluating, and creating as they progress through the assignment. By scaffolding tasks in this way, educators can support deeper learning while maintaining clarity, rigor, and transparency at every stage (L. W. Anderson & Krathwohl, 2001). Here is a sample framework with examples:

Stage 1: Exploration and Ideation (Cognitive Domain: Understanding + Applying)

Example Prompt:

"Submit a 300-word proposal identifying your topic of interest. Include three guiding questions and at least two initial sources explaining your rationale."

At this initial stage, students are encouraged to articulate what genuinely sparks their curiosity and begin shaping a focused, researchable question. This process fosters personal investment, helping students connect academic work with their own interests and values. By narrowing their focus early, learners set the foundation for purposeful inquiry and sustained engagement throughout the research process (Kuhlthau, 2025).

Stage 2: Research Organization and Evaluation (Cognitive Domain: Analyzing)

Example Prompt:

"Submit an annotated bibliography with at least six credible sources. For each entry, explain its relevance, credibility, and how you plan to use it."

This checkpoint requires students to make informed, intentional decisions about which sources to include and how they support their emerging arguments. By engaging in this selection process before they begin drafting, students practice critical evaluation and source justification - key components of information literacy. It also allows faculty to assess students' research skills early, providing guidance before misconceptions or weak sources shape the final product (Head & Eisenberg, 2010).

Stage 3: Draft Submission and Peer Feedback (Cognitive Domain: Creating + Evaluating)

Example Prompt:

"Turn in a rough draft of your argument. Then, provide peer feedback to two classmates using a guided rubric that includes commentary on clarity, evidence, and organization."

Peer interaction at this stage promotes audience awareness by encouraging students to consider how others interpret and respond to their work. It also reinforces academic standards through collaborative critique, allowing students to learn from one another's approaches and feedback. The draft serves as a mid-process snapshot of student thinking, revealing the development of ideas and offering a valuable opportunity for formative assessment (Wiggins & McTighe, 2005).

Stage 4: Revision with Reflective Commentary (Cognitive Domain: Creating + Reflecting)

Example Prompt:

"Submit your final draft along with a one-page reflection: What feedback did you receive? What changes did you make? What still challenges you about this topic?"

This final stage embeds metacognition by requiring students to reflect on how their thinking and ideas have evolved throughout the assignment. It prompts them to articulate the choices they made, the feedback they incorporated, and the reasoning behind their revisions. In doing so, students demonstrate intellectual ownership of their work, reinforcing deeper learning and personal accountability (Brookhart, 2010).

Bridge Topic

Assessment Strategies for Each Stage

Each stage of a multistep assignment should be assessed using criteria that directly reinforce the purpose and learning goals of that specific phase. Rather than applying a uniform rubric across the entire process, faculty can tailor feedback to emphasize developmental progress, critical thinking, and process-based learning. The following examples illustrate how grading criteria can be aligned with each stage to support meaningful student growth and academic integrity:

- **Proposal**. Originality, clarity of intent, and scope.
- **Annotated Bibliography**. Source diversity, relevance, and evaluation quality.
- **Draft**. Coherence, structure, and preliminary support of claims.

- **Final + Reflection**. Incorporation of feedback, depth of revision, synthesis, and insight.

By distributing points across multiple stages of an assignment, faculty send a clear message that the thinking process is just as important as the final product. This approach values effort, reflection, and intellectual development, rather than rewarding only polished outcomes. It aligns with the broader goals of academic integrity and transparency by encouraging students to engage authentically throughout each phase of their work (Lang, 2013).

Bridge Topic

AI-Resilience in Multistage Assignments

AI can assist in isolated tasks (e.g., grammar editing or idea generation), but it cannot convincingly simulate the continuity and evolution of thought over a 3–5 week cycle of submissions, feedback, and revision. Moreover, by requiring personal reflections and feedback connections, faculty create artifacts that AI cannot fabricate (Lang, 2013).

Even if a student used AI to generate an initial draft, a well-crafted reflection essay can reveal the extent to which they internalized the material, responded to instructor feedback, and developed more nuanced perspectives. This reflective component adds a crucial layer of transparency, allowing faculty to assess not just the product but the depth of student engagement with the learning process. These reflections act as intellectual fingerprints - distinct indicators of authenticity, effort, and cognitive ownership (Brookhart, 2010).

Section Reflection: Building Integrity Through Structured Progression

This section highlights the powerful role of multistage assignments in fostering authentic learning and safeguarding academic integrity in an age of generative AI. By breaking complex tasks into sequential, scaffolded stages - such as ideation, research organization, drafting, peer review, and reflection - educators create an environment where intellectual growth is visible, iterative, and personalized. This structured approach deters one-time AI misuse by requiring continuous engagement, self-reflection, and developmental transparency, all of which are difficult for AI to convincingly replicate.

As students revise their thinking in response to feedback and document their evolving insights, they build essential metacognitive skills and demonstrate ownership of their work. Multistage design not only deepens understanding but also redefines rigor as a process of cognitive investment and ethical engagement, making integrity not an afterthought, but a natural outcome of thoughtful academic design.

Section 4: Embedding Real-World Relevance and Contextual Complexity

---

As AI becomes increasingly adept at mimicking surface-level responses, the most effective way to ensure authentic student work is to design assignments that demand lived insight, critical interpretation, and local relevance. AI struggles not because it lacks language skills, but because it lacks context. It cannot draw on personal experience, engage with evolving human dynamics, or adapt flexibly to real-time, real-world complexity (Selwyn, 2021).

Assignments grounded in real-world relevance challenge students to think like problem-solvers rather than merely repeat information. These tasks often involve navigating uncertainty, weighing competing values, and exercising informed judgment - cognitive domains where human reasoning continues to surpass even the most advanced generative AI tools. By emphasizing these dimensions, educators promote deeper learning and cultivate critical thinking skills that are transferable beyond the classroom (Brookhart, 2010).

Why Real-World Relevance Increases AI Resistance

Real-world and contextualized assignments are inherently less vulnerable to AI misuse because they require students to draw on personal insight, situational awareness, and adaptive reasoning. These types of tasks often demand localized knowledge, lived experience, or dynamic problem-solving - elements that AI tools cannot convincingly replicate without human input. The following points outline several key reasons why such assignments promote authenticity and discourage overreliance on generative technologies:

- They require ***local knowledge*** **and** ***lived experience***.
- They incorporate ***disciplinary judgment*** **and** ***applied reasoning***.
- They often require ***timely responses*** to evolving events.
- They embed ***personal accountability*** that AI-generated responses cannot mimic.

As Wiggins and McTighe (2005) explained, the transfer of learning is most effective when students are able to apply their knowledge and skills in unpredictable and meaningful contexts. These situations require learners to adapt, problem-solve, and connect prior understanding to new challenges - abilities that extend beyond rote memorization or static application. By designing learning experiences that mirror real-world complexity, educators help students internalize concepts in ways that are both durable and transferable.

Strategies for Embedding Relevance and Complexity

---

1. Leverage Local or Community Contexts

AI cannot meaningfully speak to the nuanced dynamics of communities it has never experienced or inhabited. In contrast, when students are asked to analyze, interpret, or engage with their own environments - whether cultural, social, or geographic - they draw on lived knowledge that AI simply cannot replicate. These assignments become inherently human, grounded in personal context, authenticity, and reflective insight that strengthens both learning and integrity (Zawacki-Richter et al., 2019).

Example 1: Local Impact Study

"Conduct a mini environmental impact report on a development project in your city or region. Include perspectives from local stakeholders, and recommend changes based on community values."

This task demands authentic engagement through real research, interviews, or interaction with policies and institutions - experiences that AI cannot convincingly fabricate. Such assignments require students to gather and interpret firsthand information, navigate complex human interactions, and synthesize diverse perspectives. These elements not only promote deeper understanding but also safeguard academic integrity by anchoring the work in verifiable, real-world experiences (Kolb, 2014).

---

2. Use Discipline-Specific Scenarios

Real-world application in professional fields such as business, nursing, law, and education requires practitioners to exercise sound judgment under complex, context-specific constraints. These constraints often involve ethical considerations, rapidly changing conditions, and human-centered variables that AI cannot reliably anticipate or respond to with appropriate nuance. As a result, students must develop situational awareness and adaptive reasoning - skills that are essential for professional competence and resistant to automation (Schon, 2017).

Example 2: Clinical Decision-Making (Nursing)

"You are a nurse in a rural clinic with limited equipment. A patient presents with ambiguous symptoms. Based on current best practices and rural healthcare policy, describe your assessment plan and justify your triage decision."

This task requires students to engage in ethical reasoning while navigating resource constraints and applying evolving medical standards. Such challenges are deeply embedded in real-world professional practice, where decisions must balance evidence, policy, and patient-centered care. By confronting these complex variables, students develop critical competencies that AI cannot replicate - reinforcing the importance of human judgment and contextual sensitivity in professional fields (Lang, 2013).

---

3. Integrate Current Events and Emerging Issues

Assignments grounded in recent events require students to interpret fast-changing dynamics and consider multiple, often conflicting, perspectives. Because AI tools are typically trained on static or outdated datasets, they frequently lack the timeliness, nuance, and contextual awareness necessary for accurate real-time analysis. Engaging students with contemporary issues not only sharpens critical thinking but also ensures that their work reflects current understanding and lived realities (Peters, 2008).

Example 3: Civic Debate (Political Science)

"Choose a current local or national issue (e.g., housing policy, gun reform, education funding). Research arguments on both sides. Then write a position paper that outlines your stance and defends it with contextualized evidence from your state or region."

This type of assignment promotes critical judgment, civic literacy, and personal investment by requiring students to engage meaningfully with complex, real-world issues. These attributes foster responsible citizenship and reflective thinking - qualities that AI tools cannot replicate with depth, accountability, or ethical discernment. By centering human values in the learning process, educators empower students to take ownership of their learning and participate more thoughtfully in public discourse (Brookhart, 2010).

---

4. Encourage Lived Experience and Personal Connection

Assignments that prompt students to reflect on their lived identity, cultural background, or emotional experiences foster deeper, more meaningful learning. These reflections allow students to connect academic content with their personal narratives, cultivating both self-awareness and intellectual authenticity. Because they require introspection and emotional nuance, such tasks create a uniquely human imprint that is difficult - if not impossible - to outsource to AI tools (Gay, 2018).

Example 4: Identity and Representation Essay

"How has your cultural background shaped your views on environmental sustainability? Connect personal experience with scholarly sources to explore the relationship between identity and policy preference."

Even if AI is used to assist with organizing ideas or structuring content, the deeper work of reflection and personal connection remains firmly in the domain of human cognition. Genuine introspection involves interpreting experiences, identifying meaning, and expressing emotion - tasks that require self-awareness and cannot be authentically replicated by machines. This distinction reinforces the value of human insight in academic work, even when supported by technological tools (Hoggan & Kloubert, 2020).

---

5. Include Actionable Proposals or Change-Making Projects

Assignments that lead to real-world consequences - such as proposals, interventions, or public campaigns - require students to demonstrate original thinking, initiative, and accountability. These tasks go beyond theoretical exercises by challenging learners to apply their knowledge in ways that may impact actual communities or systems. Because of their tangible outcomes and contextual demands, such assignments resist automation and highlight the value of human agency in learning (S. L. Ash & Clayton, 2009).

Example 5: Social Impact Proposal (Business or Social Work)

"Design a realistic, low-cost initiative that could reduce food insecurity among students on your campus. Include stakeholder analysis, a basic budget, and potential implementation steps."

Because the solution must be tailored to a real context, students are required to engage deeply with their community, gaining insight into its specific needs, values, and challenges. This level of engagement promotes empathy, civic responsibility, and critical problem-solving, as students must adapt academic knowledge to local realities. Through this process, learning becomes both applied and transformative, reinforcing authenticity and ethical accountability (Jacoby, 2014).

Bridge Topic

Assessment Criteria for Contextual Assignments

Rubrics for real-world assignments should prioritize the depth of analysis, contextual accuracy, originality of insight, and feasibility of proposed solutions. While grammar and structural clarity remain important, they should not overshadow the assessment of critical thinking and authentic engagement. By aligning evaluation criteria with these higher-order skills, faculty can more accurately measure meaningful learning and promote academic integrity (Brookhart, 2010).

Example Rubric Criteria:

- Demonstrates understanding of local/regional dynamics.
- Connects personal perspective to broader issues.
- Proposes feasible, context-specific solutions.
- Engages with timely and credible sources.
- Reflects thoughtful judgment under ambiguity.

This approach encourages students to take ownership of their reasoning by requiring them to articulate ideas that are specific, original, and grounded in context. By moving beyond vague or universal arguments, students are challenged to think critically and defend their positions with evidence and clarity. In doing so, they are less likely to rely on generic AI-generated content and more likely to engage in authentic, higher-order thinking (L. W. Anderson & Krathwohl, 2001).

Section Reflection: Authentic Learning Through Context and Complexity

This section emphasizes the power of real-world relevance in cultivating academic integrity and deeper learning. By grounding assignments in lived experience, local dynamics, and timely societal challenges, educators create conditions that demand human insight, personal judgment, and adaptive reasoning - capacities that AI cannot replicate.

Whether through community-based research, discipline-specific case studies, or reflective identity work, these context-rich tasks engage students as thinkers, not just producers. They make learning more meaningful, discourage generic outputs, and reinforce intellectual ownership by requiring students to synthesize knowledge within complex, human-centered frameworks. Ultimately, embedding relevance and complexity into assignments does not just build AI resilience - it fosters critical citizenship, empathy, and ethical responsibility, reshaping assessment as a transformative act rooted in real-world engagement.

Section 5: Integrating Reflection to Promote Ethical Awareness

In an academic landscape increasingly shaped by generative AI, reflection emerges as one of the most humanizing - and underused - tools in assignment design. While AI can replicate facts, synthesize summaries, and mimic academic tone, it cannot replicate introspection, ethical tension, or emotional nuance. Reflective writing allows students to narrate their *learning journey*, giving faculty access to the cognitive and emotional dimensions of student development - something a final product alone cannot provide (Brookhart, 2010).

Reflection not only deepens learning but also strengthens academic integrity. When students are asked to think about *how* they learned, *what* challenged them, and *why* they made certain choices, they are more likely to engage with the material authentically and less likely to outsource their work to an AI tool (Lang, 2013).

Why Reflection Resists AI Automation

Reflection is a deeply personal and cognitive act that resists AI automation due to the uniquely human qualities it demands. Unlike content generation, which AI can assist with, reflection requires the learner to engage in introspection, assess their own thought processes, and make meaning from experience. The following elements illustrate why true reflection cannot be convincingly outsourced to machines and must originate from the learner's authentic perspective. Reflection requires the learner to:

- Make personal meaning from experience.
- Express uncertainty and growth.
- Examine ethical and emotional responses.
- Connect learning to values or identity.

Because reflective tasks are inherently individualized and subjective, they require a depth of personal insight and emotional nuance that AI tools struggle to replicate. As a result, AI-generated responses often come across as generic, superficial, or emotionally flat, lacking the authenticity that characterizes true reflection. This makes reflection an ideal integrity checkpoint within any assignment, providing faculty with a reliable way to assess genuine engagement and original thinking (Hoggan & Kloubert, 2020).

Reflection as a Layered Pedagogical Strategy

Reflection can be meaningfully implemented at multiple stages of the learning process, from pre-assignment framing to post-assessment analysis. When integrated thoughtfully, it supports deeper cognitive engagement, metacognition, and personal connection to the material. The following formats and examples illustrate how reflective practices can be embedded throughout a course to enhance learning and reinforce academic integrity:

1. Learning Journals (Ongoing Reflection)

These reflective practices encourage students to consistently record their thoughts, observations, and questions throughout the duration of a course or project. By doing so, they are able to track their intellectual and emotional development over time, gaining greater self-awareness and insight into their learning process. This sustained engagement fosters metacognitive growth and provides faculty with a rich view of student progress that extends beyond any single assignment (Moon, 2006).

Example 1: Weekly Learning Log Prompt

"What was the most important idea you encountered this week? What confused or challenged you, and how did you respond? How do you see this connecting to your personal goals or values?"

This kind of journal makes both cognitive and affective engagement visible, allowing students to document not just what they learn, but how they feel and think about their learning. It invites them to personalize their educational journey by connecting course content to their experiences, values, and evolving perspectives. Such reflective practice strengthens motivation and deepens understanding, while also offering faculty meaningful insight into each student's learning process (Boud et al., 2013).

---

2. Ethical Reflection Prompts (Decision-Making + Integrity)

By posing questions that invite students to consider concepts such as right and wrong, fairness, and purpose, faculty encourage the development of moral reasoning. These prompts help students grapple with ethical dilemmas, evaluate competing values, and reflect on the implications of their choices. In doing so, educators not only deepen critical thinking but also foster ethical awareness and civic responsibility (Rest et al., 1999).

Example 2: Ethics in Action Prompt (Business or Technology)

"During your group project, what ethical dilemmas did you encounter? How did you navigate group dynamics, workload sharing, and decision-making? Were there moments where the easy option conflicted with the right one?"

Such prompts help normalize ethical dialogue by creating space for open discussions about values, responsibility, and academic integrity. When students are regularly invited to reflect on topics such as plagiarism, citation, and the fair use of AI tools, these conversations become part of the learning culture rather than reactive interventions. This proactive approach reinforces ethical awareness and equips students to make responsible decisions in their academic and professional lives (Brookhart, 2010).

---

3. AI Transparency Reflections

Instead of banning AI tools outright, faculty can embed structured reflections that encourage students to be honest and thoughtful about their use of such technologies. These reflections provide an opportunity for students to evaluate how, why, and to what extent they relied on AI, fostering transparency and ethical awareness. By normalizing responsible AI engagement, educators shift the conversation from restriction to accountability and learning (Selwyn, 2021).

Example 3: AI Use Reflection Prompt

"Did you use any AI tools while working on this assignment? If so, which ones? How did they help or hinder your thinking? Would you make different choices next time?"

This type of prompt helps reduce students' fear of punishment by creating a safe space for honest disclosure about their use of AI tools. In doing so, it fosters a culture of openness where ethical conversations can flourish, rather than be avoided. Such an environment is essential for helping students develop responsible digital habits and long-term integrity in an AI-mediated world (Selwyn, 2021).

---

4. Post-Assignment Meta-Reflections

Used after a major submission, these reflective prompts encourage students to look back on their learning process, identify challenges they encountered, and articulate the gains they have made. This backward-looking analysis helps learners make sense of their experiences, recognize growth, and refine strategies for future tasks. By integrating this form of reflection, faculty promote deeper learning and support the development of self-regulated, independent thinkers (Zimmerman, 2002).

Example 4: Meta-Reflection Prompt (Humanities or STEM)

"What part of this project was most difficult, and how did you handle it? What feedback influenced your final submission the most? What do you wish you had done differently?"

This type of reflection can be submitted as a cover letter alongside the final product, providing faculty with valuable context for evaluating the student's work. It allows learners to explain their choices, describe how they responded to feedback, and articulate the evolution of their thinking. In doing so, it fosters metacognitive skill development by encouraging students to become more intentional and reflective about their learning process (L. W. Anderson & Krathwohl, 2001).

---

5. Designing Reflection for Depth and Authenticity

Designing reflection for depth and authenticity requires careful attention to the structure and intention behind each prompt. To move beyond superficial or performative responses, reflection must invite students to engage in honest self-assessment, critical thinking, and personal meaning-making. The following principles outline key characteristics of effective reflection prompts that foster genuine insight and intellectual growth:

- Open-ended (not yes/no).
- Rooted in personal or process-based language.
- Specific enough to generate substance, but flexible enough to allow diverse answers.

Example 5: Comparison Prompt

"Compare your initial understanding of the assignment topic with your perspective now. What changed, and what caused that change?"

These kinds of comparisons - such as analyzing early drafts against final submissions or pre-course beliefs against post-course insights - help students recognize and articulate their own growth. They provide concrete evidence of how learning has developed over time, reinforcing the idea that education is a dynamic and evolving process. This practice not only promotes self-awareness but also demonstrates authentic learning progression that goes beyond rote achievement (Moon, 2006).

Bridge Topic

Assessment of Reflection

Assessment of reflection should prioritize the quality of thought, not the surface-level presentation. Instead of focusing on grammar, spelling, or stylistic polish, faculty should evaluate the reflection based on its thoughtfulness, honesty, and depth of engagement. The following rubric criteria offer examples of how reflective work can be meaningfully assessed to support authentic learning and metacognitive development:

- Clarity of thought.
- Evidence of self-assessment.
- Ethical reasoning or emotional insight.
- Connection to course content.

Grading reflection on a pass/fail or low-stakes basis encourages students to take intellectual risks and be honest in their self-assessments. This approach removes the pressure to perform for a grade and instead emphasizes authentic engagement with the learning process. These conditions are essential for fostering genuine ethical awareness and supporting deeper, more meaningful reflection (Wiggins & McTighe, 2005).

Section Reflection: Reflection as a Catalyst for Ethical Learning

This section underscores the transformative power of reflection as both a pedagogical tool and a mechanism for cultivating academic integrity in the AI era. Unlike outputs that can be fabricated or polished by machines, reflective work demands personal insight, ethical reasoning, and emotional authenticity - dimensions that generative AI cannot convincingly imitate. By integrating reflective practices throughout the learning journey - from ongoing journals to post-assignment meta-analyses - educators invite students to think deeply about their choices, challenges, and growth.

These insights not only promote metacognition and critical thinking but also serve as a reliable integrity checkpoint that reveals the learner behind the work. When students are asked to narrate their own intellectual development, engage with ethical dilemmas, and transparently disclose their use of AI tools, reflection becomes a space for honesty, ownership, and identity formation. In doing so, it elevates learning from a task to be completed to a journey to be understood - and transforms academic integrity into a personal and enduring commitment.

Section 6: Reimagining Group Projects with AI Collaboration Guidelines

Group projects have long been a staple of active learning. They foster communication, negotiation, problem-solving, and leadership skills. However, in the age of generative AI, they require a significant rethink. The rise of tools such as ChatGPT, Grammarly, or Claude introduces new layers of complexity - especially when AI is used inconsistently or without disclosure (Luckin, 2017). One team member might use AI extensively while another avoids it entirely. This creates uneven learning, ethical ambiguity, and potential grading disparities.

To meet this moment, faculty must **reimagine group projects** not just as collaborative exercises but as **learning laboratories for responsible AI use**. By providing guidelines for equitable AI integration and shared accountability, educators can teach students how to collaborate with each other - and with intelligent tools.

Why Group Projects Need Redesign

The rise of AI presents both new opportunities and distinct risks within group project settings, challenging traditional models of collaboration and accountability. While AI tools can streamline communication, support research, and enhance productivity, they also complicate authorship, effort distribution, and ethical boundaries. The following considerations highlight why group projects must be thoughtfully redesigned to ensure meaningful learning and maintain academic integrity in the AI era:

- It can help teams brainstorm faster, summarize research, or generate prototypes.
- But without structure, it can lead to **plagiarism**, **free-riding**, or **misrepresentation** of individual effort (Lang, 2013).

By integrating AI collaboration norms into group projects, faculty can transform traditional group work into a realistic simulation of modern team dynamics. In today's professional environments, human and machine contributions increasingly coexist, making it essential for students to learn how to navigate these hybrid workflows ethically and effectively. This approach prepares learners for future work contexts while reinforcing transparency, accountability, and critical engagement with AI tools (Luckin, 2017).

Design Strategies for AI-Integrated Group Work

1. Set Clear Expectations for AI Use

Setting clear expectations for AI use is essential to maintaining transparency and integrity in group projects. Faculty must communicate at the outset whether AI tools are permitted, restricted, or conditionally allowed, and under what circumstances. The following categories offer a framework for defining acceptable AI use, helping students navigate these tools responsibly and ethically within collaborative settings:

- Prohibited.
- Permitted for specific tasks (e.g., grammar, brainstorming).
- Required with disclosure and explanation.

Example 1: AI Use Policy on Syllabus or Assignment Sheet

"AI tools such as ChatGPT may be used for brainstorming or outlining. All usage must be disclosed in the final report and attributed to the tool used. Students are responsible for fact-checking and final interpretation."

Establishing clear AI usage guidelines in group work fosters transparency and shared responsibility among students. It encourages them to make intentional decisions about when and how to incorporate AI, rather than relying on it passively or inappropriately. In doing so, faculty model real-world expectations for ethical collaboration in digitally enhanced environments (Luckin, 2017).

---

2. Require AI Use Logs or Collaboration Journals

Requiring AI use logs or collaboration journals adds a layer of transparency to the group work process. Just as students are often asked to document peer contributions, they can also record when, how, and why AI tools were used during the project. This practice reinforces accountability, promotes ethical reflection, and helps faculty assess the authenticity and balance of both human and machine inputs (Selwyn, 2021).

Example 2: Group AI Collaboration Log

Date | Team Member | Task | AI Tool Used | Summary of Prompt | How Output Was Used/Modified

This documentation provides a visible audit trail of both group member and AI contributions throughout the project lifecycle. By making inputs traceable, the documentation promotes accountability and ensures that credit is appropriately distributed among team members and tools. Additionally, it discourages hidden or inappropriate AI use, reinforcing a culture of transparency and ethical collaboration (Ray & Ray, 2024).

---

3. Use Role-Based Structures to Distribute Responsibility

Using role-based structures in group projects helps distribute responsibility equitably and ensures that all students actively contribute. Assigning rotating roles - such as researcher, editor, presenter, or AI integrator - not only fosters accountability but also exposes students to a range of collaborative skills. This approach balances participation, deepens engagement, and prepares students for real-world teamwork dynamics where diverse roles and tools intersect (D. W. Johnson & Johnson, 2009).

Example 3: Sample Group Roles with AI Literacy Embedded

- **Research Lead.** Uses AI to find articles and generate initial summaries.
- **Skeptic.** Validates AI outputs and identifies bias or error.
- **Writer.** Integrates AI-generated and human content with proper attribution.
- **Editor.** Finalizes language and checks ethical compliance.

By distributing AI engagement responsibilities across different group members, students are encouraged to approach machine-generated input with a critical lens. This shared responsibility fosters dialogue around the accuracy, appropriateness, and limitations of AI contributions, turning passive use into active evaluation. As a result, students are more likely to question, refine, and thoughtfully integrate AI tools rather than accept their output uncritically (Brookhart, 2010).

---

4. Build Individual Accountability into the Grading Model

Building individual accountability into the grading model helps ensure that each student's contribution is fairly assessed within a collaborative project. While group grades can foster teamwork and shared responsibility, incorporating individual reflections or deliverables allows faculty to evaluate personal engagement, learning, and growth. This dual approach discourages freeloading and reinforces the value of both collaboration and individual effort in group work (Oakley et al., 2004).

Example 4: AI + Peer Evaluation Prompt

"Describe your contributions to the group project. If you used AI tools, explain how you used them, what you learned, and how your team responded to AI-generated content."

Evaluating both the collaborative process and individual self-awareness helps reinforce ethical engagement and reflective learning. When students are assessed not just on what they produce, but also on how they think about their contributions and decision-making, metacognition is strengthened. This dual focus encourages learners to be more intentional, transparent, and responsible in their academic work (L. W. Anderson & Krathwohl, 2001).

---

5. Design Projects with Contextual Complexity

Designing projects with contextual complexity makes it more difficult for students to rely on AI as a shortcut. When prompts are rooted in real-world scenarios, require localized knowledge, or involve layered decision-making, they demand human insight and adaptive reasoning. The following prompt characteristics illustrate how faculty can embed complexity that promotes authentic learning and reduces the effectiveness of generic AI responses:

- Tied to local or evolving issues.
- Require negotiation or team-based judgment
- Include live presentations, Q&A, or decision simulations.

Example 5: Complex Team Scenario

"Your team is consulting for a city council considering a smart traffic system. You must evaluate the risks and benefits of using AI-driven surveillance in public spaces. Draft a policy recommendation and present it to a mock board."

Tasks designed with contextual complexity demand more than information recall - they require ethical reasoning, live engagement, and a nuanced understanding of localized context. These elements call upon students to interpret real-world dynamics, respond to unpredictable variables, and make value-based decisions. In such scenarios, AI can serve as a tool, but it cannot lead the conversation, as human judgment remains central to authentic learning and responsible action (Rest et al., 1999).

Bridge Topic

Grading AI-Enhanced Group Projects

Grading AI-enhanced group projects requires a balanced approach that evaluates both collective collaboration and individual contribution. Faculty should assess how effectively the group worked together - including communication, coordination, and ethical AI use - while also recognizing each student's unique role and engagement. The following suggested rubric elements offer guidance for capturing the multidimensional nature of group work in the AI era:

- Ethical and transparent use of AI tools.
- Integration and modification of AI-generated outputs.
- Accuracy, originality, and judgment.
- Reflective accountability from each member.

Scoring should reflect more than just the quality of the final product - it should also reward the process by which the group arrived at that outcome. Emphasizing shared responsibility encourages collaboration, ethical engagement, and mutual accountability among group members. As Wiggins and McTighe (2005) emphasized, valuing the process alongside the outcome promotes deeper learning and more authentic teamwork.

Bridge Topic

Benefits Beyond the Classroom

The benefits of thoughtfully designed group projects that incorporate AI extend well beyond the classroom. When students learn to collaborate effectively with both peers and AI tools, they develop critical workplace competencies such as digital literacy, communication, ethical reasoning, and adaptive problem-solving. The following points highlight how these collaborative experiences prepare students for success in real-world, AI-augmented environments:

- They **mirror modern workplace environments**.
- They develop **AI literacy**, which is now essential for digital citizenship.

- They learn **ethical reasoning in digital collaboration**, a skill critical for leadership and trust in any profession.

Group projects evolve beyond traditional exercises in teamwork when they incorporate the realities of emerging technology. In these redesigned experiences, students learn to navigate the complexities of collaborating not only with peers but also with machine intelligence. As a result, group work becomes a simulation of the modern world - one where AI functions not merely as a tool, but as a digital colleague requiring critical oversight and ethical partnership (Luckin et al., 2016).

Section Reflection: Designing Group Work for Human-AI Collaboration

This section reconceptualizes group projects as dynamic ecosystems where students learn to collaborate not only with each other but also with intelligent tools. In an age where AI can contribute to everything from brainstorming to drafting, educators must provide clear structures, role-based responsibilities, and reflection mechanisms that ensure transparency, equity, and ethical engagement. By embedding AI collaboration guidelines, requiring usage logs, and building individual accountability into grading, group projects evolve from static teamwork exercises into simulations of real-world professional environments.

These designs help students navigate complex decisions, negotiate values, and critically assess both human and machine contributions - skills essential for the AI-integrated future. In doing so, group work becomes not just about managing tasks but about cultivating shared responsibility, ethical fluency, and digital discernment - hallmarks of academic integrity in collaborative, AI-enhanced learning spaces.

Section 7: Using Oral and Visual Assignments to Strengthen Authenticity

---

As generative AI becomes more capable of producing polished written work, faculty must increasingly turn to alternative formats that showcase spontaneity, presence, and personal voice. Oral and visual assignments - such as podcasts, video reflections, live presentations, and slide-based storytelling - are powerful tools for assessing authentic understanding. Unlike text, which can be easily outsourced or fabricated, oral and visual artifacts capture performance, tone, interpretation, and synthesis in real time, making them highly AI-resilient (Brookhart, 2010; Lang, 2013).

These formats also align with **Universal Design for Learning (UDL)** principles by honoring diverse modes of communication. Students who struggle with traditional writing assignments may excel in verbal explanation, visual argumentation, or audio storytelling - thus promoting equity, inclusion, and engagement (CAST, 2018).

Why Oral and Visual Work Strengthens Academic Integrity

Oral and visual assignments offer unique advantages for strengthening academic integrity in an age of widespread AI access. These formats allow students to demonstrate understanding through voice, expression, and spontaneous reasoning - elements that are difficult to replicate with generative tools alone. The following examples suggest how incorporating such modalities fosters authenticity, promotes accountability, and deepens learning by engaging multiple dimensions of student understanding (Boud & Falchikov, 2006):

- **Real-time delivery** reduces the likelihood of AI-generated content.
- **Spontaneity and body language** are difficult to fake.
- **Voice and expression** reflect cognitive and emotional investment.
- **Creative formats** promote engagement, which in turn reduces temptation to cheat (Wiggins & McTighe, 2005).

Moreover, many oral and visual assessment formats closely mirror the demands of professional communication, making them both pedagogically valuable and career-relevant. From client briefings and project pitches to TED-style presentations and stakeholder updates, students are asked to demonstrate clarity, persuasion, and adaptability - skills essential in today's workforce. By practicing these forms of communication in academic settings, students build confidence while reinforcing integrity through real-time, performative expression (Knight & Yorke, 2003).

Examples of Authentic Oral and Visual Assignment Formats

---

1. Video Reflections (Personal Voice + Process Thinking)

When students record a short video reflecting on their learning, choices, or challenges, they provide insight into their cognitive and emotional engagement with the assignment. This format captures not just what they produced, but how they approached the task - revealing their decision-making process, growth, and areas of struggle. Video reflections promote authenticity and serve as powerful tools for evaluating metacognition, especially in contexts where written work may be supplemented or generated by AI (Ryan & Ryan, 2013).

Example 1: End-of-Unit Video Journal Prompt

"In under 3 minutes, describe your biggest 'aha' moment with this unit. What confused you at first, and how did you resolve it? What will you take with you into future courses or projects?"

These reflections help humanize students' thinking by capturing their voice, personality, and unique learning journey in ways that written text alone often cannot. They make the process of learning visible - highlighting not just outcomes, but how students wrestle with ideas, adapt to challenges, and grow over time. Because of their immediacy and personal authenticity, these reflections reveal dimensions of student work that AI tools cannot convincingly emulate (Lang, 2013).

---

2. Podcast Segments or Audio Essays (Synthesis + Communication)

Audio assignments offer an alternative to traditional essays by requiring students to organize their thoughts, interpret content meaningfully, and convey ideas through storytelling. These tasks still demand critical thinking and structure but allow for more flexible and expressive formats that reflect students' authentic voices. As such, they promote engagement and academic integrity while supporting multimodal literacy skills increasingly valued in professional contexts (Kapucu & Avci, 2020).

Example 2: Audio Commentary Assignment

"Record a 5-minute podcast episode where you explain a controversial issue in your field, present opposing perspectives, and offer your own take, supported by research."

To complete audio or oral assignments successfully, students must think critically about their message, script their content with purpose and precision, and deliver it with clarity and confidence. This process integrates analytical and communication skills, requiring learners to move beyond content knowledge into thoughtful expression. By combining cognitive depth with performance, such tasks reinforce academic integrity and mirror real-world demands for persuasive and responsible communication (Knight & Yorke, 2003).

---

3. Live or Recorded Slide Presentations (Structure + Insight)

Slide decks paired with live or recorded narration require students to convey their understanding in a format that emphasizes clarity, organization, and brevity. This multimodal task compels them to explain content coherently and concisely, reinforcing both conceptual mastery and communication skills. Because it blends visual design with verbal reasoning, this format strengthens academic integrity by showcasing students' ability to articulate their thinking in real time (Mayer, 2014).

Example 3: Slide & Speak Assignment

"Create a 6-slide deck that explains your capstone project to a non-expert audience. Narrate each slide in your own words, demonstrating clarity, relevance, and passion."

Grading for oral and visual assignments should prioritize the quality of content, clarity of explanation, and effectiveness of delivery rather than focusing solely on production value or polish. This approach ensures that assessment remains accessible to all students, regardless of their technical resources or design expertise. By emphasizing substance over style, faculty reinforce the core goals of learning and academic integrity (Brookhart, 2010).

---

4. Digital Storytelling Projects (Creativity + Contextual Complexity)

In digital storytelling assignments, students combine images, voiceover, music, and narrative to explore a topic both deeply and creatively. This format allows learners to synthesize content in a multimodal way, drawing on emotional resonance and personal expression to enhance understanding. It encourages originality, critical thinking, and engagement - skills that are difficult to replicate through AI-generated work (Robin, 2008).

Example 4: Visual Argument Project (Humanities or Social Sciences)

"Using Canva, Adobe Spark, or another visual tool, create a 2–3-minute digital story that explores the lived experience of a policy issue, historical figure, or ethical dilemma."

These assignments activate emotional intelligence, ethical judgment, and empathy - human capacities that are difficult for AI to mimic with authenticity. By engaging students on both intellectual and emotional levels, such tasks foster deeper connections to the material and more meaningful learning outcomes. As Wiggins and McTighe (2005) suggested, learning is most powerful when it integrates head and heart, encouraging students to think critically and feel responsibly.

---

5. Debates or Oral Defense Panels (Critical Thinking Under Pressure)

Live discourse challenges students to think on their feet by requiring them to articulate ideas, respond to counterarguments, and adapt to questions in real time. Unlike scripted assignments, this format emphasizes spontaneous reasoning, active listening, and the ability to defend or refine one's position under pressure. These skills mirror real-world communication demands and are difficult for AI to simulate authentically, making live dialogue a valuable tool for assessing understanding and promoting academic integrity (Mercer & Howe, 2012).

Example 5: Structured Oral Defense

"Prepare a 2-minute statement of your position on a case study. Then, field two follow-up questions from peers or the instructor to defend your stance."

This format mirrors real-world discussions, interviews, and professional interactions where individuals must communicate ideas clearly and respond thoughtfully without external aids. In these settings, AI assistance is far less practical, as success depends on human qualities such as adaptability, empathy, and real-time judgment. Incorporating such experiences into academic assessment prepares students for authentic communication challenges beyond the classroom (Mercer & Howe, 2012).

Bridge Topic

Assessment Strategies for Oral and Visual Work

Assessment strategies for oral and visual work should be designed to ensure fairness, clarity, and consistency across diverse student performances. Faculty can use rubrics that prioritize intellectual substance, clarity of communication, and the learner's ability to connect ideas effectively. The following criteria illustrate how thoughtful assessment can reinforce academic integrity while valuing both content and delivery over technical polish:

- Content mastery.
- Clarity of message.
- Engagement with the audience.
- Organization and logical flow.

- Originality and ethical AI use (e.g., whether visuals or scripts were AI-generated and disclosed).

Example Rubric Criteria:

- *Demonstrates depth of understanding.*
- *Communicates ideas clearly and coherently.*
- *Integrates evidence appropriately.*
- *Reflects creativity and authenticity.*
- *Discloses and reflects on any AI tool usage.*

Assessing oral and visual projects holistically allows faculty to focus on the overall quality and authenticity of student work rather than isolated technical elements. This approach supports academic integrity by encouraging students to take ownership of their ideas and communicate them with confidence and clarity. When students feel their expression is valued as a whole, they are more likely to engage sincerely and less likely to rely on shortcuts or AI-generated content (Brookhart, 2010).

Bridge Topic

Supporting Diverse Learners and Ethical Practice

Oral and visual formats support Universal Design for Learning (UDL) by offering multiple means of expression, allowing students to demonstrate knowledge in ways that align with their strengths and needs. These formats are especially empowering for neurodivergent, multilingual, or creatively inclined students, who often thrive when given alternatives to traditional written assessments (CAST, 2018). At the same time, embedding AI-use disclosure within these assignments helps establish an ethical standard, encouraging transparency and responsible technology integration; for example:

> *"If you used any AI tools to help plan, script, or visualize your presentation, please explain where and how in a 1-paragraph addendum."*

Requiring students to disclose their use of AI in oral or visual assignments promotes AI literacy by prompting them to think critically about how and why they engaged with these tools. It also reinforces a sense of responsibility and encourages transparency - cornerstones of ethical academic and professional conduct. These are essential skills in modern digital citizenship, where thoughtful, informed use of emerging technologies is increasingly expected (CAST, 2018).

Section Reflection: Amplifying Authenticity Through Oral and Visual Expression

This section highlights the growing importance of oral and visual assignments as powerful tools for reinforcing authenticity, equity, and integrity in the age of generative AI. Unlike text-based submissions that can be polished - or even fully generated - by AI, oral and visual formats showcase spontaneity, voice, emotion, and real-time reasoning, making them far more resistant to automation. These assignments allow students to communicate in diverse ways that reflect their identities, experiences, and learning processes, while simultaneously developing essential skills in storytelling, synthesis, and public speaking.

Whether through video reflections, debates, digital storytelling, or live presentations, students are invited to demonstrate their thinking with clarity and ownership. By incorporating AI-use disclosures into these formats, faculty foster a culture of ethical transparency while modeling responsible digital literacy. In doing so, oral and visual assignments not only support authentic assessment - but they also prepare students for the communication demands of an AI-augmented world where integrity and human insight matter more than ever.

Section 8: Shifting the Grading Focus to Insight, Not Polish

Generative AI tools such as ChatGPT are capable of producing grammatically correct, structurally sound, and stylistically "academic" writing. What these tools struggle to replicate, however, is the **cognitive substance** beneath the surface: original insight, nuanced interpretation, ethical reflection, or conceptual breakthrough (Wiggins & McTighe, 2005). As such, grading practices that overemphasize grammar, formatting, and form may unintentionally reward students for AI-assisted polish and penalize those who engage more messily - but more authentically - with their thinking.

To meet the challenge posed by AI-assisted work, faculty must fundamentally rethink how they evaluate student performance. This shift does not mean abandoning standards of quality, but rather acknowledging that surface-level polish - often achievable through AI - is no longer a reliable measure of genuine learning. Instead, assessment must prioritize what matters most: the student's thinking, reasoning, and ability to engage deeply with content (Wiggins & McTighe, 2005).

Why Insight Should Be the Center of Assessment

In an educational landscape increasingly influenced by AI, insight must become the central focus of assessment. Unlike surface-level correctness or mechanical completion, insight reveals a student's depth of understanding, originality of thought, and ability to make meaningful connections. Centering assessment on insight allows educators to evaluate learning that is authentic, personal, and far less likely to be outsourced or fabricated (Brookhart, 2010). For example:

- **AI can generate well-structured text, but cannot demonstrate personal struggle, curiosity, or growth**.
- **Human writing - especially at early stages - often includes hesitations, inconsistencies, and questions.** These are not flaws; they are **evidence** of learning in motion (Brookhart, 2010).
- **Insightful work is marked by risk-taking, reflection, and connection-making - not just clean prose**.

As Lang (2013) noted, **students who fear being penalized for imperfect writing are more likely to take shortcuts or seek unauthorized assistance to protect their grades**. When perfection becomes the primary expectation, learners may prioritize appearance over genuine understanding. In contrast, a grading system that values process, thought, and revision fosters a culture of engagement rather than avoidance - encouraging students to take intellectual risks and develop authentic skills.

Recalibrating Rubrics to Assess Thinking, Not Just Writing

To promote depth over decoration, assessment rubrics should shift the emphasis away from superficial polish and toward the cognitive dimensions of student work. This includes prioritizing elements such as analysis, synthesis, reasoning, and reflection - skills that signal genuine engagement and critical thinking. **The following rubric criteria illustrate how educators can foreground these dimensions to evaluate insight and intellectual growth more effectively**.

- Argument clarity.
- Original interpretation.
- Thoughtful use of evidence.
- Reflective or ethical reasoning.
- Personal or contextual engagement.

Effective assessment rubrics can foreground insight by evaluating key cognitive and reflective elements. These include the clarity of the student's argument, the originality of their interpretation, and the thoughtful integration of evidence to support their claims. Additionally, rubrics should recognize reflective or ethical reasoning and the student's ability to engage personally or contextually with the material - criteria that collectively reward deep thinking over surface-level presentation (Brookhart, 2010).

Example: Essay Rubric Comparison

Traditional Rubric Focus:

- 10 pts Grammar and Mechanics.
- 10 pts Structure and Organization.
- 10 pts Use of Sources.
- 10 pts Content Accuracy.

Insight-Focused Rubric:

- 10 pts Clarity and Depth of Argument.
- 10 pts Interpretation of Evidence.
- 10 pts Personal or Contextual Relevance.
- 10 pts Reflection and Self-Awareness.

Notice that grammar, formatting, and citation style are de-emphasized in this rubric - or included only with minimal weight. This intentional shift allows faculty to focus on

what truly matters: the student's thinking, analysis, and ability to engage meaningfully with the material. By rewarding intellectual engagement over technical perfection, educators create space for deeper learning, reduce fear of failure, and discourage reliance on AI-generated polish (Brookhart, 2010).

Examples of Insight-Focused Assignments and Evaluation

---

1. Conceptual Clarity Over Syntax

Example Prompts:

- *"Explain a concept from this unit in your own words, then apply it to an experience or observation outside of class."*
- *"Be honest about any part of the concept you still find confusing."*

Insightful Response Criteria:

- Demonstrates effort to understand and connect ideas.
- Acknowledges ambiguity or partial understanding.
- Applies concept in an original, authentic way.

Even if a student's explanation is not grammatically perfect, it can still offer a far more valuable window into their understanding than a flawlessly worded definition copied from a textbook or generated by a chatbot. Original, imperfect expression often reveals how students are grappling with ideas, making connections, and developing their own interpretations. In contrast, polished responses that lack personal reasoning or context may mask gaps in comprehension and undermine authentic learning (Brookhart, 2010).

---

2. Risk-Taking and Intellectual Ambition

Example Prompt:

- *"Challenge something we have discussed in class. Use evidence, counterexamples, or theoretical alternatives to defend your position."*

Insightful Response Criteria:

- Proposes a unique perspective.
- Supports ideas with thoughtful justification.
- Engages critically with course material, not just repeats it.

This approach encourages students to take ownership of their ideas rather than simply echo what they believe the instructor wants to hear. **By prioritizing original thought and authentic engagement over formulaic correctness, learners are empowered to express uncertainty, explore nuance, and develop their own voice**. As Wiggins and McTighe (2005) argued, such environments foster true understanding by rewarding meaning-making over mimicry.

3. Reflective and Ethical Engagement

Example Prompt:

- *"Describe a moment in this course when you changed your mind about something. What influenced you? What did that reveal about your values or assumptions?"*

Insightful Response Criteria:

- Shows emotional or ethical self-awareness.
- Engages with course content at a values-based level.
- Emphasizes transformation or learning over correctness.

Reflection prompts such as these encourage students to integrate intellectual content with their personal development, fostering deeper, more authentic learning experiences. **By making space for introspection and self-connection, these prompts help learners articulate not just what they know, but why it matters to them**. This kind of engagement is not only more meaningful but also significantly harder to fake or outsource, strengthening the integrity of the learning process (Brookhart, 2010).

Building Insight-Focused Feedback Mechanisms

Just as rubrics should prioritize insight over surface polish, feedback should also focus on the depth of student thinking. When faculty respond with curiosity - inviting students to elaborate, question assumptions, or consider alternative perspectives - they foster a culture of reflection and growth. The following examples illustrate how feedback framed as inquiry can promote deeper learning and reinforce intellectual ownership:

- *"Can you say more about why you believe this?"*
- *"This is a strong idea - what is the evidence that made you confident in it?"*
- *"What other perspectives could challenge this position?"*
- *"Where did you struggle or rethink your approach here?"*

Feedback that emphasizes student thinking over surface-level polish promotes metacognition by encouraging learners to reflect on their cognitive processes and decision-making. It communicates that their ideas, reasoning, and growth matter more than producing a flawless presentation. As Lang (2013) noted, this type of feedback fosters a learning environment where authenticity is valued and intellectual risk-taking is supported.

Bridge Topic

Balancing Form and Function

Of course, mechanics and clarity still have an important place in academic work, as they help students communicate their ideas effectively. However, these elements should serve the expression of thought - not replace it - as the primary focus of assessment. The following strategies show how to integrate both intellectual depth and clear communication in a balanced, pedagogically sound way:

- Use **minimal penalties** for grammar or APA errors - especially if the ideas are rich.
- Allow revision opportunities where students can polish their expression after receiving feedback on their ideas.
- **Separate Rubrics**. One for *thinking quality*, one for *communication mechanics*.

Consider using separate rubrics to assess different dimensions of student work - one focused on the quality of ideas and another on communication mechanics. **This separation ensures that students are evaluated fairly, with clear recognition of both their intellectual contributions and their efforts to express those ideas effectively**. As Brookhart (2010) suggested, this approach reinforces the message that strong thinking is the primary goal, while still supporting the development of clear and accurate communication skills.

Section Reflection: Valuing Thought Over Finish in the Age of AI

This section advocates for a critical shift in grading philosophy - one that places intellectual insight, reflection, and cognitive depth at the center of assessment, rather than surface-level polish. As AI tools become increasingly capable of producing grammatically flawless but intellectually hollow work, traditional grading metrics risk rewarding the appearance of quality over the substance of learning. By prioritizing students' original thinking, conceptual clarity, and ethical engagement, faculty not only discourage AI misuse but also create space for authentic exploration and intellectual risk-taking.

Insight-focused rubrics, reflective prompts, and inquiry-based feedback honor the human elements of learning - uncertainty, struggle, growth - that cannot be convincingly replicated by machines. This approach redefines rigor not as perfection, but as the willingness to wrestle with ideas and express them honestly, even imperfectly. In doing so, educators foster a culture where learning is measured by meaning-making, and integrity is preserved through deep, personal engagement with knowledge.

Chapter 2 Conclusion: Cultivating Epistemic Agency in the Age of Generative Systems

Chapter 2 has explored the fundamental shift from teaching **about** artificial intelligence to teaching **with** and **through** it - framing AI not as a passing tool or a threat to educational integrity, but as a generative mirror that reveals how knowledge is produced, mediated, and challenged in contemporary learning environments. Across its eight sections, the chapter has argued that the true challenge of AI in education is not technical, but epistemological: *"What do we count as knowing, thinking, or creating in an age when machines can simulate all three?"*

In **Section 1**, we introduced AI as a **mirror for thought**, capable of exposing students' assumptions, habits, and blind spots. This set the stage for **Section 2**, which focused on **epistemic humility** - teaching students that AI-generated fluency does not equal truth, and that every machine output is a product of human-designed training data, cultural bias, and probabilistic logic.

Section 3 expanded the lens to **epistemic diversity**, emphasizing that knowledge systems vary across disciplines, identities, and cultures. Teaching AI in this context requires surfacing whose ways of knowing are amplified, and whose are excluded. **Section 4** built on this by exploring **epistemic injustice**, where certain student voices, languages, or knowledge forms are systematically erased or devalued by dominant algorithms.

In **Section 5**, the focus shifted toward **critical literacy** - developing students' capacity to interrogate the credibility, traceability, and logic of AI outputs. This was followed by **Section 6**, which offered strategies for faculty to create **epistemically just classrooms** - spaces where transparency, consent, and positionality are core to any AI use.

Section 7 provided a framework for **disciplinary AI fluency**, inviting faculty to teach AI through the lens of their own fields: what constitutes evidence, argument, originality, or rigor in biology, history, art, or engineering. Finally, **Section 8** reminded us that **student voice** must remain central - AI use should amplify reflection, not erase authorship; encourage curiosity, not collapse it into statistical prediction.

Together, these eight sections point to a central conclusion: The pedagogical challenge of AI is a challenge of **epistemic agency**. Faculty must teach students not just how to use AI, but how to **see themselves as knowledge creators** in a world where machines increasingly produce plausible versions of everything. This requires new literacies, new safeguards, and a recommitment to critical inquiry as the foundation of education.

The future of teaching with AI is not about mastering the interface - it is about reclaiming the authorship of thought. When students learn to see AI outputs as starting points, not endpoints - and when faculty design learning environments that support questioning, dissent, and ethical discernment - higher education becomes not a site of technological assimilation, but a catalyst for epistemic liberation.

Chapter 3: From Evaluator to Architect - Building AI-Aware Learning Environments

In the AI era, educators must evolve from traditional gatekeepers of knowledge to intentional designers of learning environments that foster discovery, creativity, and ethical engagement. This chapter supports faculty in reframing their roles as learning architects - building structures that position AI as a powerful resource rather than a disruptive threat. From collaborative research labs to AI-assisted simulations and mentoring strategies, readers will explore practical, innovative models that redefine teaching and supervision for a rapidly changing academic landscape.

Section 1: Reframing the Faculty Role - From Knowledge Gatekeeper to Learning Designer

---

For centuries, faculty were positioned as the gatekeepers of knowledge. They determined what counted as legitimate content, when it would be shared, and how it would be assessed. In this traditional model, teaching was largely about **content transmission** - the delivery of lectures, assignments, and exams aimed at assessing how well students could absorb what had been taught (Brookhart, 2010). However, in the **AI era**, this model is increasingly untenable.

Students now have instant access to encyclopedic knowledge through search engines, digital libraries, and AI tools such as ChatGPT or Perplexity. These technologies are not just repositories of static facts; they are interactive engines that can explain, rewrite, summarize, and even co-generate new content. As a result, the faculty role must evolve - not by competing with machines, but by designing learning ecosystems that foster **critical thinking, ethical reasoning, and creative application** (Selwyn, 2021).

---

1. From Deliverer to Curator: Designing Learning Pathways

Rather than delivering all content directly, faculty now take on the role of curators - designing rich, purposeful learning pathways that empower student exploration. This involves identifying high-quality resources, including vetted AI tools, and thoughtfully integrating them into the learning experience. By framing critical questions and scaffolding inquiry-based projects, faculty guide students toward deeper understanding while encouraging independence, reflection, and ethical engagement.

Example 1: Scaffolded Research Sprint

- *Instead of assigning a traditional research paper with pre-defined sources, a faculty member acting as a learning designer might structure the task to emphasize inquiry, autonomy, and critical thinking. This approach invites students to navigate the research process more actively, making decisions about sources, framing questions, and evaluating credibility. The following illustrates how such a design can support deeper engagement and foster intellectual ownership:*

- *A curated list of open-access databases.*
- *Optional AI tools for literature discovery (with usage guidelines).*
- *Reflection prompts at each stage (e.g., "What did the AI tool miss?" or "What sources were most persuasive to you, and why?").*

In this model, **the instructor shifts from the role of lecturer to that of a navigator of complexity, helping students make sense of an ever-expanding landscape of information**. Rather than simply transmitting knowledge, the educator guides learners through the critical evaluation of both human- and machine-generated content. As Wiggins and McTighe (2005) emphasized, this approach cultivates thoughtful engagement and deep understanding by encouraging students to analyze, question, and synthesize knowledge from multiple sources.

---

2. Modeling Thinking, Not Just Providing Answers

Becoming a learning architect also involves making your thinking visible to students in intentional and transparent ways. Faculty must model key intellectual practices - such as judgment, ethical reasoning, and evaluative decision-making - in real time, whether during discussions, feedback, or demonstrations. By externalizing their thought processes, faculty provide students with a framework for how to navigate complex academic and technological challenges with integrity and purpose.

Example 2: Think-Aloud Analysis Session

- *During a class, the instructor takes a student-generated AI summary and publicly evaluates it. "Let us look at this response."*
  - *"What is accurate?"*
  - *"What is misleading?"*
  - *"Why might this source be biased?"*
  - *"What lens is it missing?"*

This approach supports the development of discernment rather than just digital fluency - an essential distinction when students are interacting with AI-generated content. Discernment involves the ability to evaluate, question, and contextualize information, empowering learners to navigate complexity with confidence and integrity. As Brookhart (2010) noted, cultivating this kind of critical awareness prepares students to be thoughtful consumers and creators of knowledge in an AI-driven world.

---

3. Embedding Values Through Structure

In a world where content is virtually infinite and instantly accessible, values - not just information - must become the central pillar of education. Faculty who act as learning designers embed core principles such as academic integrity, curiosity, collaboration, and resilience directly into the architecture of their courses. By structuring learning experiences around these values, educators equip students not only to navigate AI-enhanced environments, but rather to do so with purpose, accountability, and ethical clarity.

Example 3: Integrity by Design

- *Require AI-use disclosure statements.*
- *Integrate process-based grading.*
- *Include peer-review checkpoints and self-reflection essays.*

These practices intentionally decenter instructor control and shift the focus toward student agency, trust, and responsibility. Rather than relying on surveillance to enforce compliance, educators cultivate ethical learning environments that emphasize self-awareness, reflection, and internalized accountability. As Lang (2013) suggested, this approach fosters more authentic engagement by encouraging students to own their learning and act with integrity from within, rather than in response to external policing.

---

4. Leveraging AI as a Cognitive Partner

The evolving faculty role includes helping students view AI not as an unquestioned authority, but as a cognitive partner that must be used critically and ethically. This shift requires educators to teach AI literacy alongside subject literacy, guiding students to understand how AI tools work, where their limitations lie, and how to use them responsibly. By doing so, faculty empower learners to collaborate with technology while maintaining ownership of their thinking and academic integrity.

Example 4: AI Collaboration Module

- *Add a unit on "How to Prompt Responsibly" in a research methods course.*
  - *Students learn prompt design.*
  - *Compare outputs from different tools.*
  - *Evaluate limitations and biases.*
  - *Write a reflection on ethical boundaries.*

This approach teaches students not just how to use AI, but how to think critically with and around it - an essential skill in both digital scholarship and modern professional practice. It fosters awareness of AI's capabilities and constraints, encouraging learners to engage with these tools as collaborators rather than infallible sources. By developing this kind of nuanced understanding, students are better prepared to navigate real-world environments where responsible and reflective AI use is increasingly expected (Lang, 2013).

---

5. Designing for Emergence: Building Adaptive Systems

Finally, faculty must design learning systems that are flexible and responsive to the evolving landscape of educational technology, including AI. This does not require constant syllabus overhauls, but rather a shift in mindset - one that builds in room for student-driven inquiry, real-time reflection, and adaptable learning pathways. By embedding structural flexibility, educators can stay current with emerging tools while empowering students to take ownership of their learning in a rapidly changing world (Kallunki et al., 2024).

Example 5: Modular Learning Framework

- *Each unit includes a "student-led exploration" day.*

- *Students vote on a topic, co-design the class session, and prepare short briefings or provocations.*
- *AI tools can be used for preparation but must be cited and critiqued in discussion.*

This approach **empowers students to become co-constructors of knowledge rather than passive recipients of content**. By inviting learners to ask questions, make decisions, and contribute meaningfully to the learning process, faculty create environments where inquiry and collaboration drive engagement. As Brookhart (2010) emphasized, this shift is a hallmark of an architected learning environment - one that fosters autonomy, critical thinking, and shared responsibility for learning.

Section Reflection: Redefining Faculty as Architects of Learning in the AI Era

This section repositions the faculty role from that of content gatekeeper to learning designer - an essential transformation in a world where knowledge is instantly accessible and AI tools can simulate expertise. Rather than delivering prepackaged information, faculty are called to curate learning pathways, model intellectual discernment, and embed values such as integrity, curiosity, and ethical responsibility into the structure of their courses. Through scaffolded inquiry, reflective dialogue, and transparent AI integration, educators create dynamic environments where students are not just passive consumers of content, but active participants in knowledge construction.

By designing flexible, emergent systems that invite co-creation, faculty foster critical thinking, metacognition, and adaptive learning - skills that AI cannot replicate and that modern learners urgently need. In embracing this new role, faculty preserve their most vital function: cultivating thoughtful, responsible, and engaged learners who can navigate complexity with purpose and integrity.

Section 2: Principles of AI-Aware Pedagogy

Designing effective AI-aware learning environments requires more than tweaking old lesson plans - it demands a **new pedagogical orientation**. Traditional instruction emphasized content mastery, factual recall, and controlled progression. In contrast, **AI-aware pedagogy** is grounded in principles that support agility, inquiry, transparency, and ethical engagement. As digital tools evolve, these principles offer educators a roadmap for aligning educational design with both human growth and technological transformation (Selwyn, 2021).

This section introduces four foundational principles that support effective and ethical AI-aware pedagogy. These principles are designed to guide faculty in rethinking instructional design, classroom culture, and student assessment in ways that integrate AI responsibly. Together, they provide a framework for cultivating academic integrity, intellectual engagement, and adaptive learning in an AI-enhanced educational environment:

- Human–AI complementarity.
- Cognitive transparency.

- Learner agency.
- Ethical integration of tools.

These principles are not merely reactive adjustments to AI - they serve as a blueprint for shaping a future-ready classroom culture grounded in integrity, adaptability, and critical thinking. Rather than treating AI as a disruption, they position it as a catalyst for reimagining how learning is structured and supported. In doing so, educators foster environments where students are equipped to thrive intellectually and ethically in a rapidly evolving digital world (Selwyn, 2019).

---

1. Human–AI Complementarity: Teaching Beyond the Machine

The first principle is to focus on what humans do best, especially in an AI-enhanced learning environment. While AI can efficiently summarize, sort, and generate ideas, it lacks key human capacities such as empathy, ethical reasoning, lived experience, and contextual understanding. Faculty should design learning activities that strategically leverage AI's speed and scope while foregrounding human judgment, nuance, and moral discernment as central to the educational experience (Brookhart, 2010).

Example: Partnered Writing Assignment

- *Students use an AI tool to generate an outline or initial draft. Their task is to critique the AI's ideas, identify weaknesses, and revise them into a more nuanced, contextually grounded argument.*

This kind of activity reframes AI not as a substitute for human effort but as a foil - a productive counterpoint that provokes deeper thinking. **By comparing their reasoning with AI-generated output, students are challenged to analyze, critique, and improve upon machine responses**. In doing so, they learn not just how to use AI, but **how to outthink it** - an essential skill in developing critical literacy and responsible digital citizenship (Brookhart, 2010).

---

2. Cognitive Transparency: Making Thought Processes Visible

AI-aware pedagogy encourages students to externalize their thinking, shifting the focus from final answers to the reasoning that produced them. This means prompting learners to reflect not only on what they learned, but how they approached the task and why they made specific choices. Faculty can support this process by asking students to describe their reasoning, document iterations, and explain decision-making practices that foster metacognition and strengthen academic integrity (Zimmerman, 2002).

Example: Thinking Trace Assignment

- *In a project-based class, students submit a "thinking log" alongside their final product:*
    - *"What questions guided their research?"*
    - *"What mistakes or revisions shaped the outcome?"*
    - *"How did tools (including AI) influence their process?"*

This approach shifts grading away from product perfection and toward the richness of the student's learning process. **By valuing reflection, revision, and self-awareness, faculty help students develop metacognitive skills** that extend far beyond a single assignment. As Brookhart (2010) and Lang (2013) emphasized, this process-based focus also reinforces academic integrity by rewarding authentic engagement over polished shortcuts.

---

3. Learner Agency: Empowering Decision-Making and Adaptation

AI-aware pedagogy empowers students by offering meaningful choice and ownership in how they learn, think, and create. Instead of prescribing every step of the learning process, faculty act as facilitators - designing conditions that support guided autonomy while maintaining academic rigor. This balance fosters motivation, creativity, and ethical decision-making, helping students become active participants in their learning journey (Brookhart, 2010).

Example: Inquiry Track Assignment Model

- *For a unit on sustainability, students choose one of three project paths:*
    - *Policy analysis.*
    - *Community-based design.*
    - *Philosophical reflection.*

Each learning path leads to shared outcomes, but students are encouraged to reach those outcomes through diverse methods that align with their interests and strengths. **AI can be used strategically to assist with tasks such as data gathering or idea framing, but its role should be intentional and reflective - not automatic**. Students must articulate why they chose their specific path and how they adapted content to their goals, reinforcing ownership, critical thinking, and ethical AI use (Zimmerman, 2002).

This approach aligns with the principles of Universal Design for Learning (UDL) by offering students multiple means of engagement, representation, and expression. By allowing flexibility in how students interact with content and demonstrate understanding, it accommodates diverse learning preferences and needs. As CAST (2018) noted, such inclusive design not only increases student motivation and responsibility but also fosters deeper, more personalized learning experiences.

---

4. Ethical Integration: Teaching Responsible Use of Tools

Finally, AI-aware pedagogy requires that the ethical use of technology is not simply assumed, but explicitly taught and regularly reinforced. Students need clear guidance to understand what constitutes appropriate, transparent, and value-aligned use of AI tools in academic contexts. By embedding discussions of ethics, responsibility, and digital citizenship into course design, faculty help students build habits of integrity that extend beyond the classroom (Floridi & Chiriatti, 2020).

Example: AI Use Policy + Self-Audit

- *Faculty include a course statement:*

    - *"AI tools are permitted for ideation and grammar checks. They may not be used to draft entire assignments. You must disclose any use of AI in your submission."*
- *Students also complete a short AI self-audit:*
    - *"What tools were used?"*
    - *"For what purpose?"*
    - *"What decisions did the student make independently?"*

This strategy normalizes transparency by making it a regular and expected part of academic practice, rather than an exception triggered by suspicion. It simultaneously **builds students' digital literacy by requiring them to think critically about how AI tools are used, and it strengthens ethical reasoning by encouraging reflection on their choices**. As Brookhart (2010) emphasized, such habits are essential for cultivating responsible learners in an AI-integrated world.

Balancing Innovation and Rigor

Some fear that embracing AI will dilute academic rigor. But rigor in the AI era means teaching students to **question, critique, and collaborate with technology**, not just memorize facts. Rigor becomes a matter of **depth, flexibility, and reflection**, not formality or control (Wiggins & McTighe, 2005).

In addition, some fear that embracing AI in education will dilute academic rigor by making learning too dependent on automated tools. However, when thoughtfully integrated, AI can actually raise expectations by shifting the focus from rote output to deeper reasoning, reflection, and application. **The challenge for educators is not to lower standards, but to redesign them in ways that prioritize insight, integrity, and human judgment** in an AI-augmented environment (Wiggins & McTighe, 2005).

Creating Cultures of Conversation, Not Control

AI-aware pedagogy thrives in classroom cultures that promote open dialogue, critical thinking, and shared responsibility rather than denial or avoidance. Instead of banning AI outright or pretending it does not exist, faculty should engage students in conversations that explore its appropriate use, ethical implications, and impact on learning. The following prompts illustrate how educators can guide these discussions to foster transparency, discernment, and collaborative inquiry (Selwyn, 2021):

- *"What does it mean to 'own' your ideas in a machine-assisted world?"*
- *"Where should we draw ethical boundaries around tool use?"*
- *"How can AI help us learn - and how might it hinder us?"*

These discussions model the principles of critical digital citizenship by teaching students how to engage with emerging technologies thoughtfully, responsibly, and ethically. By **exploring the nuances of AI use - its benefits, limitations, and ethical implications - students build the skills needed to navigate a digitally complex world**. As Lang (2013) and

Selwyn (2021) emphasized, such conversations prepare learners not only for academic success but also for the ethical challenges they will encounter beyond the classroom.

Section Reflection: Establishing a Pedagogical Blueprint for the AI Era

This section lays the foundation for a future-ready approach to teaching by introducing four core principles - Human–AI Complementarity, Cognitive Transparency, Learner Agency, and Ethical Integration - that redefine the pedagogical relationship between students, faculty, and technology. Rather than viewing AI as a threat to learning, these principles frame it as an opportunity to deepen engagement, empower decision-making, and elevate the role of human judgment. By designing learning environments that foreground thinking over output, process over perfection, and responsibility over automation, educators foster classrooms grounded in trust, intellectual rigor, and ethical awareness.

These AI-aware strategies emphasize open dialogue, critical inquiry, and reflective use of tools - helping students develop the discernment and digital citizenship necessary for success in a rapidly changing world. In doing so, faculty shift from enforcing control to cultivating insight, creating learning cultures where technology supports - not supplants - human development and academic integrity.

Section 3: Constructing Learning Spaces that Welcome AI Literacy

---

As generative AI continues to reshape how we search, write, design, and communicate, AI literacy has become a foundational skill - not only for students in technology-related fields, but for every learner across disciplines. Despite this, many classrooms remain anchored in a pre-AI paradigm, where the use of external tools is often equated with cheating and conversations about emerging technologies are infrequent or reactionary. As Selwyn (2021) noted, such outdated models limit both ethical awareness and digital preparedness, underscoring the urgent need for curricular and cultural transformation in education.

To prepare students for a future in which AI is embedded across nearly every profession and discipline, educators must intentionally design learning environments that welcome, explore, and critically question AI. Fostering AI literacy involves more than just technical skill - it requires building a classroom culture grounded in experimentation, transparency, and ethical reflection. In this setting, students learn to think with AI as an active cognitive partner, rather than relying on it passively or using it in secrecy (Brookhart, 2010).

What is AI Literacy?

AI literacy goes far beyond simply learning how to operate tools such as ChatGPT or DALL·E. It encompasses the ability to understand how these tools work, evaluate their limitations, and use them ethically, transparently, and purposefully within academic and professional contexts. The following elements illustrate the key dimensions of AI literacy that educators should cultivate to prepare students for responsible engagement in an AI-infused world (Southworth et al., 2023):

- Understanding how AI models work (at a basic level).
- Recognizing the limitations and biases of AI systems.
- Knowing when and how to use AI responsibly.
- Interpreting and critiquing AI-generated content.
- Reflecting on ethical, social, and professional implications.

As Brookhart (2010) suggested, building any form of literacy - including reading, writing, or critical thinking - requires intentional scaffolding, repeated practice, and engagement with meaningful, context-rich tasks. **The same holds true for AI literacy, which must be developed through guided exploration, reflective use, and real-world application**. Without this structured approach, students risk using AI superficially or uncritically, missing the opportunity to cultivate the discernment and responsibility that true literacy demands.

Strategies for Building AI-Literate Classrooms

---

1. Create "Sandbox" Spaces for AI Experimentation

A sandbox is a low-stakes learning environment where students can explore an AI tool's capabilities without fear of making mistakes or facing penalties. Within this space, faculty can guide learners through experimentation with prompts, outputs, and ethical use cases - encouraging curiosity while demystifying how the AI works. This approach turns the AI from a mysterious "black box" into a subject of study, fostering transparency, critical thinking, and deeper digital literacy (Southworth et al., 2023).

Example 1: AI Sandbox Assignment (First-Year Seminar or Writing Course)

- *Students test three AI tools (e.g., ChatGPT, Grammarly, Bing Copilot) by inputting the same writing prompt. They compare the outputs and reflect on:*
  - *"What is accurate?"*
  - *"What is generic or missing?"*
  - *"How did each tool shape your understanding of the topic?"*

This activity positions AI as a visible thinking partner rather than an invisible assistant quietly completing tasks in the background. **By interacting openly with AI-generated content, students begin to observe the distinctions between machine logic and human nuance** - recognizing where AI may oversimplify, generalize, or miss context. This awareness lays the foundation for critical AI literacy, enabling students to use these tools thoughtfully and with greater discernment (Southworth et al., 2023).

---

2. Compare AI-Generated vs. Human-Generated Work

Direct comparisons between human and AI-generated responses help build students' critical literacy by encouraging them to analyze, question, and refine what they read. This process highlights the strengths and limitations of machine outputs, prompting students to engage more actively with the material. As a result, learners are less likely to blindly accept AI responses and more likely to exercise informed judgment and academic integrity (Floridi & Chiriatti, 2020).

Example 2: Side-by-Side Evaluation Activity

- *Provide students with one paragraph written by a peer and one generated by AI (without saying which is which).*
- *Students evaluate both using a rubric focused on clarity, originality, tone, and nuance.*
- *Then, they guess which is which and justify their reasoning.*

This activity reveals both the strengths and weaknesses of AI-generated prose, helping students evaluate writing beyond surface-level fluency. It **encourages learners to distinguish between coherence - which AI often achieves - and true insight, which requires human interpretation, context, and originality**. As Lang (2013) noted, fostering this kind of discernment strengthens students' ability to think critically about not just what is written, but how and why it was constructed.

---

3. Embed Critical Discussions Across Disciplines

AI should not be confined to computer science classrooms - it is a cross-disciplinary force that touches nearly every academic and professional field. Faculty across all disciplines have a vital role to play in leading conversations about how AI is reshaping their domains, from diagnostic tools in medicine and personalization in marketing to ethical dilemmas in philosophy and automation in engineering. By embedding these discussions into diverse curricula, educators help students contextualize AI's influence and develop the field-specific literacy needed to navigate it responsibly (Selwyn, 2021).

Example 3: AI Roundtable Series

- *Host a "monthly AI moment" in your class:*
    - *Week 1: Explore how AI is reshaping publishing in English studies.*
    - *Week 2: Debate facial recognition in criminal justice.*
    - *Week 3: Analyze copyright implications in digital art.*

These interdisciplinary prompts frame AI not merely as a technical tool, but as a complex social and professional issue with ethical, cultural, and economic implications. **By exploring AI through the lenses of various disciplines, students gain a more holistic understanding of its impact on real-world systems, professions, and communities**. As Selwyn (2021) emphasized, this broader framing equips learners to engage with AI critically and responsibly, beyond the confines of computer science or engineering.

---

4. Require AI Use Disclosures

Normalize transparency by requiring students to reflect on whether, how, and why they used AI tools during their work. This reflective practice removes shame or secrecy around AI use and instead fosters open dialogue about responsible engagement. It also gives educators insight into students' AI literacy and ethical reasoning, allowing them to assess not just the outcome, but the integrity and intentionality of the learning process (Brookhart, 2010).

Example 4: AI Use Statement Requirement

- *At the end of each major assignment, students include a 3–5 sentence note, such as:*
  - *"I used Grammarly to polish my grammar and ChatGPT to brainstorm my outline. ChatGPT suggested three possible structures, but I revised them and selected the one that best fit my thesis. I also added my own analysis, integrated peer-reviewed sources, and rewrote several AI-generated sentences for clarity. Overall, the AI tools helped me start the process, but the final arguments and evidence are my own."*

This practice helps students build essential habits of disclosure, accountability, and tool fluency in their academic work. **By regularly reflecting on their use of AI, students become more intentional and transparent in how they engage with technology**. Over time, this cultivates a mindset of ethical responsibility and digital competence that extends beyond the classroom into professional and civic life (Brookhart, 2010).

---

5. Encourage Student-Led AI Dialogues

AI is evolving at a rapid pace - often faster than faculty development or institutional policies can keep up. Creating space for students to share how they are using AI tools fosters a culture of peer learning, where strategies, questions, and challenges are explored collectively. This not only promotes shared responsibility but also encourages student ownership of the learning process, helping the classroom adapt in real time to a shifting technological landscape (Ray & Ray, 2024).

Example 5: "Tool Talk" Peer Presentation

- *Students research and demo an emerging AI tool relevant to the course. They present:*
  - *What the tool does.*
  - *How it could be used ethically in coursework.*
  - *Risks, limitations, or abuse potential.*

This approach promotes student agency by positioning learners as active contributors to the evolving use of AI in the classroom. As students engage with emerging tools and share their experiences, they not only strengthen their own understanding but also support the collective development of digital fluency. As Brookhart (2010) noted, fostering this kind of participatory learning empowers students to navigate complex technologies with confidence and critical awareness.

Aligning AI Literacy with Educational Values

Faculty may understandably worry that the presence of AI in the classroom will dilute academic rigor or compromise authenticity. However, when AI literacy is intentionally integrated into teaching, it can actually enhance both - by requiring students to be more reflective, intentional, and discerning in how they engage with information and express their ideas. Rather than lowering standards, this approach deepens learning by fostering metacognition, ethical reasoning, and thoughtful communication (Brookhart, 2010; Selwyn, 2021). The key is to **embed AI in values-based learning**, not just as a utility but as a lens for ethical and intellectual growth.

Sample Syllabus Language

- *"AI tools may be used for ideation and support in this course. However, you are expected to critically assess any AI-generated content and reflect on your use in a required disclosure. This course treats AI as a subject of learning, not a shortcut to avoid it."*

Section Reflection: Cultivating AI Literacy as a Core Educational Competency

This section reframes AI literacy not as a niche skill, but as an essential component of modern education across all disciplines. In classrooms still shaped by pre-AI assumptions, the integration of generative tools demands a pedagogical shift toward experimentation, transparency, and ethical reflection. Rather than avoiding or banning AI, this section argues for building structured, intentional learning spaces where students are invited to explore AI's potential and limitations.

Through sandboxes, side-by-side comparisons, cross-disciplinary debates, and student-led dialogues, educators can demystify AI and foster critical engagement with it. Importantly, regular AI-use disclosures and reflective practices transform tool use from a secretive shortcut into an opportunity for integrity and metacognition. When framed within the values of intellectual rigor, personal agency, and ethical responsibility, AI literacy becomes more than technical fluency - it becomes a foundation for thoughtful participation in an evolving digital world.

Section 4: Scaffolding Student Autonomy in AI-Augmented Learning

---

AI's power to personalize and accelerate learning presents educators with an exciting - but challenging - opportunity. On one hand, students can now explore new ideas instantly, get feedback on writing drafts, or use intelligent systems to simulate real-world problems. On the other hand, without **intentional scaffolding**, student autonomy can quickly veer into **over-reliance**, **misuse**, or **intellectual disengagement** (Brookhart, 2010).

AI-augmented learning environments must be intentionally designed to nurture responsible independence, not passive dependence on technology. Faculty play a crucial role in striking this balance by offering students enough freedom to make meaningful academic choices, while also embedding clear guardrails that guide ethical tool use. As Brookhart (2010) and Wiggins and McTighe (2005) emphasized, this structure promotes reflective, self-regulated learning - empowering students to act with both autonomy and integrity in complex digital contexts.

What is Scaffolding Autonomy?

Scaffolding autonomy involves gradually increasing student responsibility by offering choice, flexibility, and freedom - while maintaining a structured environment that supports growth and accountability. This balance is especially critical in the context of AI tools, which can easily complete tasks for students but often bypass the deeper learning those tasks are meant to promote. By carefully blending freedom with thoughtful guidance, educators help students develop the judgment and discipline needed to use AI as a support, not a substitute (Brookhart, 2010; Zimmerman, 2002).

Key Strategies for Scaffolding Autonomy in AI-Augmented Classrooms

---

1. Offer Guided Choice in Assignments

Student agency increases significantly when learners are given the opportunity to choose how they approach a task, as this fosters motivation, engagement, and a sense of ownership. However, these choices must be carefully curated and supported to ensure they align with learning objectives and ethical use of tools such as AI. Well-designed frameworks that guide - but do not dictate - student decisions help build confidence, responsibility, and deeper learning (Brookhart, 2010; CAST, 2018).

Example 1: Tiered Project Menu

- *In a sociology class, students can select from the following paths:*
    - *Write a policy brief (use AI for structural suggestions).*
    - *Create a community interview report (no AI assistance permitted).*
    - *Develop a media analysis using AI to identify patterns in news headlines.*

Each learning path should include clearly defined expectations for AI use, along with graded reflections that prompt students to explain why they chose a particular approach. This structure ensures that students experience meaningful autonomy while remaining accountable for their decisions. As CAST (2018) emphasized, such design fosters structured freedom - teaching students to align technological tools with learning goals, rather than using them indiscriminately.

---

2. Teach Critical Evaluation of AI Outputs

Many students enter the classroom with the assumption that AI-generated responses are inherently accurate or superior, often mistaking fluency for authority. Teaching them to critically evaluate AI output is essential for developing autonomous, reflective thinkers who can distinguish between surface coherence and substantive insight. This skill not only strengthens academic integrity but also equips students to navigate a world increasingly shaped by algorithmic influence (Floridi & Chiriatti, 2020).

Example 2: AI Output Deconstruction Exercise

- *Provide students with an AI-generated summary of an academic article. Ask them to:*
  - *Identify factual errors or omissions.*
  - *Compare the summary to their own reading.*
  - *Rate the depth and bias of the AI's interpretation.*

This approach encourages students to exercise judgment rather than simply consume information - whether from AI tools or traditional sources. By challenging them to analyze, compare, and question content, educators help students build confidence in their own reasoning abilities. As Brookhart (2010) noted, fostering this kind of analytical self-trust is essential to developing independent thinkers who value their own intellectual contribution.

---

3. Use Metacognitive Checkpoints

Encourage students to pause and reflect on their process, especially when engaging with AI tools. Taking time to consider how they used AI, what it contributed, and why they made certain choices fosters deeper awareness of their learning strategies. This kind of reflection supports metacognitive growth and helps students become more intentional, ethical, and self-directed in their academic work (Zimmerman, 2002).

Example 3: Weekly AI Use Reflection

- *"What AI tools did you use this week?"*
- *"What decisions did you make independently?"*
- *"What did you learn that the tool could not teach you?"*

These reflective checkpoints help transform basic autonomy into conscious autonomy - where students not only make choices, but understand and justify them. By pausing to evaluate their own decisions, especially when using AI, students cultivate ethical habits and sharpen their self-awareness. As Lang (2013) emphasized, this kind of intentional learning reinforces academic integrity and builds the foundation for long-term intellectual growth.

---

4. Recognize Over-Reliance and Intervene Early

It is common for students to drift into passive use of AI - letting it summarize readings, outline essays, or smooth out grammar without much critical engagement. While these tools can enhance productivity, over-reliance can erode deeper learning and obscure original thought. Faculty must become attuned to the subtle signs of this dependence - uniform writing tone, lack of contextual nuance, or missing voice - and step in early to redirect students toward more active, reflective use.

Red Flags May Include:

- Flat, overly polished writing with no trace of revision.
- Disconnected reflections that echo AI tone.
- Lack of growth across drafts or stages.

Example 4: Instructor Response Strategy:

- *Meet privately to explore the student's process.*
- *Offer a revision opportunity using peer collaboration instead of AI.*
- *Emphasize the value of struggle and uncertainty in authentic learning* (Brookhart, 2010).

This approach safeguards academic integrity not through surveillance or punitive measures, but by fostering trust, transparency, and meaningful engagement. It redirects the focus from catching misconduct to cultivating habits of honesty and responsibility. In doing so, it sustains a culture where integrity is practiced, not policed.

---

5. Scaffold Toward Independent AI Decision-Making

The point is not to block AI from the classroom - it is to teach students how to engage with it thoughtfully. When used well, AI can support learning without replacing the learner. The real goal is to empower students to make ethical, informed decisions about when and how to use these tools, so their independence grows alongside their digital fluency.

Example 5: "AI Use Planning Worksheet" (Before Major Projects)

- *"What part of your process might AI support?"*
- *"What are the ethical limits of using AI for this task?"*
- *"How will you verify or revise what the tool provides?"*

After submitting the worksheet, students return to it - not just to see how they performed, but to think critically about what they would do differently next time. **This act of revisiting encourages self-awareness and fosters habits of thoughtful digital engagement.** As Brookhart (2010) emphasized, such reflection lays the groundwork for lifelong digital self-regulation, helping learners grow beyond the assignment and into responsible, adaptive tool users.

When Autonomy is the Learning Outcome

Autonomy is not just a method - it is a goal. As educators, we are preparing students for a world where they must make choices about technology use, ethics, and learning pathways on their own. Faculty who scaffold AI-literate autonomy equip students not just with knowledge, but with **judgment, confidence, and responsibility**.

This means shifting our focus from compliance to capacity-building. Instead of asking, ***"Did the student follow the rules?"*** we begin to ask, ***"Can the student explain their choices?"*** Autonomy as a learning outcome requires us to create environments where students not only practice ethical decision-making with AI, but also reflect on the impact of those decisions. In doing so, we prepare them to act with discernment in complex, unsupervised digital spaces - where the most meaningful academic and professional growth often takes place.

Section Reflection: Nurturing Responsible Autonomy in AI-Enhanced Learning

This section reframes autonomy as both a process and a purpose in AI-augmented education. Rather than fearing students' access to powerful tools, it calls on educators to scaffold autonomy intentionally - guiding learners to use AI with discernment, integrity, and reflective judgment. Through strategies such as offering guided choice, fostering metacognitive checkpoints, and designing AI planning tools, faculty help students transition from passive users to ethical decision-makers.

The emphasis is not on preventing AI use, but on teaching students to make informed, transparent, and self-regulated choices about when and how to engage with these tools. Early intervention when over-reliance emerges reinforces the idea that learning is about growth, not perfection. Ultimately, this section reminds us that autonomy is not just a means to academic integrity - it is the integrity. By equipping students with the tools and mindset to navigate AI critically, educators empower them for lifelong, ethical engagement in an increasingly digital world.

Section 5: Integrating AI Tools into the Learning Environment - When, Why, and How

---

For many faculty, the idea of bringing AI tools into the classroom raises concerns: *"Will students rely on them too much?" "Will it replace authentic thought?" "Will it erode integrity or academic rigor?"* While these concerns are valid, they stem from a defensive posture that sees AI as a threat to learning. But when **purposefully integrated**, AI tools can become **powerful pedagogical allies** - enhancing, not replacing, the thinking process (Brookhart, 2010).

This section explores the intentional integration of AI tools in higher education, with a focus on when, why, and how their use can meaningfully support - rather than supplant - student learning. As generative AI becomes more accessible and powerful, faculty face growing pressure to either embrace or exclude it from the classroom. But the most productive path lies between these extremes. By incorporating AI into pedagogical design, educators can enhance instruction, expand student access to formative support, and foster creativity without undermining intellectual rigor or agency.

The goal is to demystify generative AI and reframe it not as a threat to learning, but as a tool - one that, when used with discernment, can enrich the learning experience. **Faculty do not need to become AI experts overnight, but they do need a clear framework for making pedagogically sound decisions about AI's role in their teaching**. This section provides strategies, examples, and reflection points to help faculty critically evaluate the purpose of AI in their courses, align its use with learning outcomes, and empower students to engage with these technologies ethically and transparently. In doing so, AI becomes not a shortcut, but a catalyst for deeper learning.

When is AI Use Pedagogically Appropriate?

Determining when to integrate AI into instruction is not just a matter of technological access - it is a matter of pedagogical intent. AI tools should be used in ways that enhance learning rather than bypass it, deepening students' understanding, expanding creative possibilities, or scaffolding difficult tasks without undermining core cognitive skills. The key is to align AI use with educational goals: not because the tool is novel, but because it meaningfully contributes to student growth, engagement, or reflection. AI tools are pedagogically appropriate when:

- They **scaffold early-stage thinking** (e.g., brainstorming, outlining).
- They support **language fluency and access** for multilingual or neurodiverse learners.
- They **reinforce feedback**, revision, or skill development.
- Their limitations are **openly discussed and critiqued** in class.

AI should be introduced strategically - at moments in the learning process where it complements, rather than overrides, human thought. When used to amplify cognitive processes such as brainstorming, organization, or revision, AI can extend what students are capable of doing without diminishing their role as thinkers. As Lang (2013) emphasized, it is essential that faculty avoid inserting AI into stages of learning that demand critical judgment, ethical reasoning, or original synthesis - areas where human discernment must remain central.

Why Does Integration Support Learning Goals?

Integrating AI into the learning process - when done thoughtfully and transparently - can support a range of instructional goals. Rather than replacing core academic skills, responsible AI use can scaffold complex tasks, personalize feedback, and promote deeper engagement with material. By aligning AI tools with well-defined learning outcomes, educators can help students build not only knowledge but also transferable skills such as critical thinking, digital discernment, and ethical reasoning. The aim is not to outsource student work, but to enrich the process through timely support, modeling, and exploration. When used responsibly, AI tools:

- **Accelerate feedback loops**, allowing students to revise more frequently.
- **Support differentiation**, helping students learn at their own pace.
- **Model cognitive apprenticeship**, where students learn by watching machines reason - and by reflecting on those patterns.
- **Encourage metacognitive growth** when tool use is paired with guided reflection.

Integrating AI into the classroom does not eliminate rigor - it redefines where rigor lives. Instead of emphasizing surface-level polish or formulaic performance, educators can redirect students toward more substantive forms of intellectual engagement. **True rigor lies in interpretation, critique, insight, and synthesis** - all of which remain firmly in the domain of human cognition, even in AI-supported environments (Wiggins & McTighe, 2005).

How to Introduce AI Tools Intentionally

1. AI for Brainstorming and Idea Generation

Think of AI not as a shortcut to answers, but as a collaborator in the early stages of thought. When positioned as a creativity partner rather than a content provider, AI can help students overcome writer's block, explore multiple perspectives, or generate initial directions for research or design. The key is to ensure that students remain the drivers of the process - using AI to spark ideas, not to substitute for originality or critical thinking. This keeps ownership with the learner and preserves the integrity of the creative process (Brookhart, 2010).

Example 1: Idea Prompting Activity (Writing or Business Class)

- *Students use ChatGPT to generate five topic ideas for a position paper.*
- *Then, students critique their list and revise it to include only ideas that feel relevant and original.*

Engaging AI in the brainstorming phase teaches students far more than how to generate ideas - it cultivates the ability to initiate inquiry, evaluate the relevance of suggestions, and ultimately take ownership of their intellectual direction. **Rather than passively accepting what the tool produces, students must make choices, justify their reasoning, and refine their focus**. This kind of guided autonomy is foundational to developing reflective, independent learners who understand how to shape their own thinking in complex environments (Brookhart, 2010).

2. AI for Language Support and Revision

AI tools can offer meaningful assistance to students who struggle with grammar, syntax, or written fluency - particularly multilingual learners or students with language-based learning differences. Used thoughtfully, these tools act as scaffolds rather than shortcuts, helping students express their ideas more clearly without altering their meaning or voice. The goal is not to erase imperfection but to empower students to communicate more effectively while still taking ownership of their thinking and structure. When supported by feedback and reflection, this approach can enhance both confidence and competence in academic writing (Brookhart, 2010; CAST, 2018).

Example 2: Revision Station Activity

- *After writing a draft, students use Grammarly or ChatGPT to revise for clarity.*
- *Students then annotate their draft to explain what changes they accepted, what they rejected, and why.*

By pairing AI-assisted language support with opportunities for critical reflection, faculty ensure that students remain actively engaged in the learning process. **Rather than relying on passive automation, learners are prompted to consider how and why revisions were made, what they learned in the process, and how they can apply those insights independently**.

This reflective integration not only supports accessibility but also fosters deeper, more transferable skill development (CAST, 2018).

---

3. AI for Peer Review and Feedback Practice

AI tools can serve as simulated peer reviewers - offering early-stage feedback that helps students practice giving and receiving critique. By analyzing clarity, structure, or tone in a low-stakes context, AI can model what constructive feedback might look like, giving students a foundation to build their own evaluative skills. Rather than replacing peer interaction, this approach prepares students to engage more meaningfully in real peer review by strengthening their feedback literacy and increasing confidence in the revision process (Brookhart, 2010; Nicol & Macfarlane-Dick, 2006).

Example 3: Simulated Feedback Activity

- *Students paste a sample essay into an AI tool and prompt it to "offer constructive feedback."*
- *Then, they critique the AI's comments, identifying what is useful, vague, or missing.*

This approach gives students a safe space to practice both giving and receiving feedback before engaging in high-stakes peer evaluation. **By working with AI-generated drafts or critique models, learners can build confidence, clarify expectations, and develop the language of constructive feedback.** Such practice is essential for cultivating meaningful peer review skills and promoting a reflective, improvement-oriented mindset (Brookhart, 2010).

---

4. AI for Coding and Technical Reinforcement

In science, technology, engineering, and mathematics (STEM) and computer science classrooms, tools such as GitHub Copilot and Amazon CodeWhisperer can serve as real-time coding companions - reinforcing correct syntax, suggesting relevant functions, and even explaining segments of code as students work. These tools do not just speed up coding tasks; they can support comprehension by modeling problem-solving patterns and providing immediate, contextual feedback. When integrated thoughtfully, they help students move beyond trial-and-error coding toward a more reflective, iterative approach to software development (Becker et al., 2023).

Example 4: Explain-the-Code Challenge

- *Students write a small program, then use an AI tool to comment on each line.*
- *Their task is to compare the AI explanation to their own, identifying gaps or misinterpretations.*

This approach strengthens students' technical confidence by providing just-in-time support while they code, but it does more than that - it also cultivates critical code literacy. As students engage with AI-generated suggestions, they must evaluate accuracy, relevance, and efficiency, rather than blindly accepting every line. This kind of active decision-making deepens their understanding of coding principles and prepares them to write, critique, and debug with greater independence and skill.

---

5. AI for Concept Reinforcement

AI tools can certainly help clarify complex or abstract concepts by offering accessible explanations, analogies, or visual representations. However, the educational value lies not in copying these outputs, but in learning to question, validate, and apply them thoughtfully. Encouraging students to cross-reference AI-generated explanations with trusted sources and course materials fosters discernment and reinforces that understanding - not replication - is the goal.

Example 5: Concept Clarification Prompt (Philosophy or Economics)

- *Students ask ChatGPT to explain a key theory (e.g., Utilitarianism or Keynesian Economics).*
- *Then, they compare the response to two scholarly sources and identify differences in depth, tone, and nuance.*

This practice supports triangulation and evaluative reading - two foundational skills in digital-era scholarship. By comparing AI-generated explanations with academic texts, lecture notes, and empirical evidence, students learn to weigh sources, detect inconsistencies, and build informed interpretations. These habits are critical in a landscape where information is abundant but not always trustworthy, and where discernment is as valuable as knowledge itself (Selwyn, 2021).

Building a Culture of Transparent AI Use

Integrating AI into the classroom is not just about access to tools - it is about shaping the norms and habits that govern how those tools are used. Every AI strategy must be paired with clearly communicated guidelines and structured opportunities for reflection. Transparency does not emerge by chance; it must be modeled, scaffolded, and embedded into the course culture from day one. This not only protects academic integrity but also prepares students to use AI ethically and responsibly beyond the classroom. Effective practices for cultivating transparency include:

- Disclose when and how tools are permitted.
- Teach students how to cite or acknowledge AI.
- Require reflections that assess the tool influence on thinking.
- Model thoughtful use by using AI in class demonstrations.

Sample Syllabus Language:

- *"In this course, AI tools may be used for brainstorming, language support, or ideation. All use must be disclosed in writing. Final products should reflect student thinking, not machine output."*

This shift transforms AI from a secretive shortcut into a visible, acknowledged part of a healthy learning ecosystem. When students are encouraged to be open about their use of AI - and when faculty respond with structured guidance rather than suspicion - it normalizes transparency and accountability. Cultivating this openness helps students develop ethical digital habits and positions AI as a support for learning, not a replacement for it (Selwyn, 2021).

Section Reflection: Moving from Avoidance to Purposeful Integration of AI

This section presents a critical shift in pedagogical mindset - from viewing AI as a threat to academic integrity to embracing it as a tool for deepening learning when used intentionally. Rather than banning or ignoring generative AI, faculty are encouraged to integrate it strategically - at moments that align with learning goals and foster student agency, reflection, and growth. Through guided brainstorming, revision support, simulated peer feedback, and conceptual clarification, AI can scaffold rather than replace cognition, particularly when paired with metacognitive reflection and ethical boundaries.

Importantly, integration is not about using AI because it is available, but because it can help students build confidence, independence, and critical literacy across disciplines. When faculty create transparent, structured environments that model and require thoughtful AI use, they demystify the technology and transform it into a pedagogical ally. This reorientation equips students to engage with AI tools reflectively and ethically - skills they will need far beyond the classroom.

Section 6: Designing Transparent Policies for AI Use and Academic Integrity

---

As AI tools become more powerful and accessible, confusion about their role in education grows. *"Should students be allowed to use ChatGPT to outline a paper?" "Is grammar correction acceptable?" "What if a student generates a full draft but edits it extensively?"* Without **clear and transparent policies**, students and faculty are left to navigate these questions based on inconsistent assumptions, often resulting in **mistrust, academic misconduct, or unnecessary anxiety** (Lang, 2013).

Transparent AI policies are not about locking down innovation or restricting creativity - they are about establishing thoughtful boundaries that support ethical, purposeful, and informed use. Rather than policing technology, these policies create a shared understanding of how AI can be integrated to enhance learning while preserving academic integrity. When crafted collaboratively and communicated clearly, such policies empower both students and faculty to navigate AI with confidence and accountability (Lang, 2013).

This section explores how to design, communicate, and adapt AI use policies at both the course and institutional levels. From syllabus language to institutional guidelines, you will find strategies for making policies flexible, inclusive, and responsive to the evolving technological landscape.

Why Transparent AI Policies Matter

In an age where AI tools are rapidly entering classrooms - often faster than institutional norms can adapt - transparent policies are no longer optional; they are essential. Clear AI guidelines create a shared framework for what is permitted, expected, and encouraged, helping students navigate grey areas with confidence rather than confusion. Without such policies, students may rely on peer assumptions, hidden use, or accidental misuse, undermining both learning outcomes and academic integrity (Selwyn, 2021).

Transparent AI policies do more than set rules - they signal values. They show that faculty and institutions are not ignoring technological change but are engaging with it intentionally and reflectively. When students see that AI can be used openly, ethically, and with purpose, they are more likely to develop responsible habits that carry into future academic, civic, and professional contexts. As Brookhart (2010) noted, transparency builds the trust needed for deeper engagement, turning policy into a foundation for learning rather than a barrier to innovation. Transparencies require the need to:

- **Clarify Expectations.** Students need to know what is permitted and what is not.
- **Promote Ethical Reflection.** Disclosure requirements foster honesty and integrity.
- **Support Pedagogical Goals.** Policies align AI use with course outcomes.
- **Reduce Inequity.** Clear guidelines prevent advantaging students who interpret silence as permission.
- **Adapt to Change.** Dynamic policies can evolve with the tools and their capabilities (Selwyn, 2021).

Key Elements of an Effective AI Use Policy

1. Define Acceptable and Unacceptable Use

When expectations around AI use are unclear, students often default to extremes - either avoiding helpful tools entirely or overusing them without understanding boundaries. To support ethical engagement, faculty must clearly define which AI tools are permitted, what functions they may serve, and the conditions under which they can be used. For example, allowing AI to assist with brainstorming or grammar revision may be acceptable, while using it to generate final drafts or bypass peer review would not. These distinctions help students differentiate between support and substitution - an increasingly vital skill in digital learning environments (Zawacki-Richter et al., 2019).

Establishing acceptable and unacceptable use also contributes to a culture of transparency and shared responsibility. Research shows that students are more likely to follow guidelines when those guidelines are framed in terms of values and supported by examples (Flick & Lederman, 2004). Including explicit AI-use scenarios in syllabi, assignment instructions, or learning contracts invites conversation and reduces ambiguity. Policies that are too vague leave room for misinterpretation, while well-defined boundaries foster clarity, trust, and deeper learning (Floridi & Chiriatti, 2020).

Example 1: Policy Language for a Syllabus

- *"AI tools such as Grammarly and ChatGPT may be used for brainstorming, outlining, and grammar correction in this course. However, generating full drafts or responses to prompts using AI is not permitted unless explicitly stated. Any use of AI must be disclosed in a brief statement at the end of the assignment."*

Establishing **clear parameters for AI use fosters autonomy by helping students make informed decisions within defined ethical boundaries**. Rather than relying on guesswork or hidden norms, learners are empowered to act responsibly and with confidence. Research in instructional design emphasizes that transparent expectations promote academic integrity and self-regulation, particularly in tech-enhanced environments (Floridi & Chiriatti, 2020; Nicol & Macfarlane-Dick, 2006).

---

2 Require Disclosure and Reflection

Students should be encouraged - and expected - to reflect on how and why they used AI tools in their work. This is not about catching wrongdoing; it is about building self-awareness, transparency, and ethical reasoning. When students articulate their decision-making process, they begin to recognize the role of AI as a support, not a shortcut. This also gives faculty valuable insight into students' thought patterns and developmental needs, supporting more personalized and constructive feedback (Ryan & Ryan, 2013; Zimmerman, 2002).

Disclosure normalizes responsible AI use and helps foster a classroom culture where students are not afraid to acknowledge digital assistance. Paired with reflective prompts - such as ***"How did AI help you clarify your thinking?"*** or ***"What decisions did you make that the AI could not?"*** - these practices promote integrity while reinforcing cognitive ownership. Metacognitive reflection deepens learning by making it visible, intentional, and connected to ethical action (Ryan & Ryan, 2013).

Example 2: Disclosure Prompt

- *"In 3–5 sentences, describe how you used AI tools for this assignment."*
    - *"What tool did you use?"*
    - *"What was helpful?"*
    - *"What decisions did you make as a result?"*

This practice helps cultivate a learning environment grounded in trust and openness. **When students know they can acknowledge AI use without penalty** - as long as it is done ethically and reflectively - **they are more likely to engage honestly and critically**. Normalizing transparency reduces fear, fosters accountability, and reinforces the development of digital ethics as a core academic habit, not just a policy requirement (Ryan & Ryan, 2013).

---

3. Align Policies with Course Goals

AI use should serve learning, not sidestep it. The purpose of integrating AI into education is to enhance students' cognitive development, not to bypass it. If an assignment is designed to build argumentation skills, for example, AI might be appropriately used to assist in researching sources, organizing ideas, or generating counterpoints. However, the core analytical work - developing a thesis, weighing evidence, and crafting the argument - must remain the student's responsibility. Aligning tool use with intended learning outcomes ensures that AI acts as a scaffold, not a surrogate (Becker et al., 2023; Zawacki-Richter et al., 2019).

Example 3: Assignment-Specific AI Guideline

- *"For this position paper, AI may be used to help identify opposing viewpoints. However, all reasoning, writing, and citations must be your own. Include a disclosure at the end."*

When AI use is aligned with the intended learning outcomes of an assignment, it reinforces - not undermines - learning integrity. Students come to understand that tools are meant to support their development, not replace the thinking process that the assignment is designed to cultivate. Meaningful learning happens when tasks, tools, and assessments are purposefully connected to deepen understanding rather than distract from it (Wiggins & McTighe, 2005).

---

4. Make Policies Dynamic and Context-Aware

AI tools are evolving at an extraordinary pace - what seems harmless or narrowly scoped today may introduce unanticipated challenges tomorrow. A tool that currently offers basic writing assistance might soon generate multimedia projects or simulate scholarly reasoning. For this reason, institutional and course-level AI policies should be treated as living documents: revisitable, revisable, and responsive to both technological developments and pedagogical insight. Building in periodic review cycles, faculty feedback mechanisms, and student input ensures that policies remain relevant, equitable, and ethically grounded in a changing landscape (Flick & Lederman, 2004; Floridi & Chiriatti, 2020).

Example 4: Dynamic Policy Model

- *Include an AI policy version number in your syllabus (e.g., "AI Use Policy v1.2").*
- *Invite students to propose policy revisions mid-semester.*
- *Reassess AI guidelines annually or when new tools emerge.*

Maintaining flexible, evolving AI policies models the very kind of adaptive digital leadership we hope students will carry into their academic, professional, and civic lives. It shows that responsible technology use is not about having all the answers upfront - but about staying engaged, reflective, and responsive as tools and contexts shift. Effective educators lead not by controlling every variable, but by modeling how to navigate complexity with clarity and integrity (Brookhart, 2010).

---

5. Incorporate Policy into Classroom Culture

An effective AI policy should not exist only as fine print on a syllabus - it should live within the everyday rhythms of the classroom. When policies are treated as active, evolving agreements rather than static rules, they become part of the culture of learning. Faculty can reinforce this integration through regular check-ins, reflective discussions, and assignment-specific reminders that revisit ethical tool use and expectations. Embedding policy into classroom dialogue not only increases understanding but also invites students to participate in shaping norms around AI, making them more invested in following those norms (Niemi & Multisilta, 2016).

Moreover, open conversations about what AI can and should do help students think critically about their role in digital environments. These discussions normalize transparency, reinforce trust, and cultivate ethical judgment - outcomes that no static document alone can achieve. As Niemi and Multisilta (2016) emphasized, when students are treated as co-constructors of digital learning cultures, they are more likely to internalize shared values and act with integrity in ambiguous or evolving situations.

Example 5: Class Activity – "Build the Policy"

- *Early in the semester, lead a discussion or small group activity where students draft proposed AI use boundaries.*
- *Compare their drafts to your policy.*
- *Finalize a hybrid version together.*

When policies are embedded into classroom dialogue and co-owned by students, the result is more than compliance - it is a genuine investment. **Students are more likely to engage thoughtfully with expectations when they have had a voice in interpreting or applying them**. This cultivates a climate of shared accountability, where academic integrity becomes a collective responsibility rather than an imposed rule (Lang, 2013).

Sample Policy Statements (for Adoption or Adaptation)

---

1. Full Integration Model (Upper-Level Course or Seminar)

- *"AI tools are integral to this course. You are encouraged to experiment with generative AI for ideation, argument mapping, and editing. All AI use must be disclosed in your submission. Your final grade will reflect not just your content, but your ethical and reflective engagement with the tools."*

---

2. Limited Integration Model (Skills-Based Course)

- *"AI may be used for grammar or spelling support. No part of your content or structure should be generated by an AI tool. Assignments may be audited for originality. Failure to disclose use may result in academic penalties."*

---

3. No Integration Model (Foundational or Integrity-Building Courses)

- *"To support the development of foundational thinking and writing skills, AI use is not permitted in this course. Students must complete all assignments independently. Violations of this policy will be treated as academic misconduct."*

Section Reflection: Establishing Clarity and Trust Through Transparent AI Policies

This section addresses the critical need for clear, adaptive, and transparent policies to guide AI use in educational environments. As generative AI tools grow more powerful and accessible, ambiguity around their ethical application can erode trust, increase misuse, and compromise learning integrity. By proactively defining acceptable and unacceptable uses, embedding disclosure and reflection requirements, and aligning tool use with course outcomes, educators create a framework that not only safeguards academic integrity but also fosters a culture of ethical autonomy.

These policies are not static rulebooks - they are living, co-created agreements that evolve alongside technology and pedagogy. When thoughtfully crafted and integrated into classroom dialogue, they promote student investment, reduce inequity, and transform AI from a source of confusion into a catalyst for transparency, accountability, and intellectual growth. Ultimately, transparent AI policies signal to students that responsible innovation is not only allowed but expected, and that learning with integrity is a shared and evolving responsibility.

Section 7: Fostering a Culture of Inquiry and Ethical Curiosity

---

Creating an AI-aware classroom is not simply about integrating tools - it is about cultivating **a mindset of critical inquiry and ethical reflection**. As generative AI becomes a regular feature of both academic and professional life, students must be equipped to ask not only ***"How do I use it?"*** but also ***"Should I use it?"***, ***"What are its limits?"***, and ***"Who does it affect?"***

Fostering a culture of inquiry and ethical curiosity transforms the classroom from a space of rule enforcement into one of value exploration. Instead of treating AI use as a checklist of permissions and prohibitions, educators can create opportunities for students to engage with the deeper questions surrounding intelligent tools: *"What are the limits of machine reasoning?" "How do we define authorship and originality in a hybrid human-AI world?" "What does it mean to use technology responsibly in contexts that are still evolving?"*

By inviting students into these moral, social, and epistemological conversations, faculty model that ethics is not a barrier to innovation - it is its foundation. As Brookhart (2010) and Selwyn (2021) argued, classrooms that encourage this kind of critical discourse do not just teach content; they prepare students to navigate uncertainty, challenge assumptions, and become ethically informed contributors in a digitally mediated society.

Why Ethical Curiosity Matters in an AI Era

In a time when generative AI can produce essays, solve equations, generate images, and simulate conversations in seconds, ethical curiosity becomes not just a virtue - but a necessity. The question is no longer whether students **can** use AI, but whether they understand the implications of **how**, **when**, and **why** they use it. Ethical curiosity invites learners to interrogate the boundaries of tool use, explore unintended consequences, and reflect on their own roles as decision-makers in a world where artificial intelligence increasingly shapes knowledge, communication, and power.

This form of curiosity pushes beyond compliance with academic policies. It encourages students to think critically about authorship, originality, consent, labor, and even the biases embedded within algorithmic systems. As digital tools become more sophisticated and embedded into everyday life, fostering ethical curiosity ensures that students do not simply learn to **use** AI - they learn to question it, challenge it, and coexist with it responsibly. A classroom grounded in ethical inquiry prepares learners not just for academic success, but for lifelong digital citizenship in an age of intelligent systems. This mindset equips them to engage with technology thoughtfully and responsibly, fostering habits that support academic integrity, social awareness, and lifelong ethical reasoning. Specifically, ethical curiosity:

- Prepares students to lead in uncertain environments.
- Builds resilience against misinformation and manipulation.
- Reduces reliance on surveillance by reinforcing internal ethical standards.
- Connects academic learning to real-world responsibilities (Lang, 2013).

When students learn to think ethically, they move beyond the mechanics of tool use and step into the role of responsible digital citizens. They begin to see themselves not just as consumers of technology, but as active participants in shaping its impact on knowledge, society, and human connection. This kind of ethical fluency does not just prepare them to use AI wisely - it prepares them to lead thoughtfully in a world where technological choices carry real-world consequences.

Strategies for Fostering Ethical Inquiry in the Classroom

1. Begin with Wonder: How AI Works and Why It Matters

Before students can think critically about AI, they must first be invited to *wonder* about it. Demystifying how AI works - what it can do, what it cannot, and how it "learns" - is a powerful starting point for ethical inquiry. When students understand that AI is not magic but pattern recognition, probability, and data-driven prediction, they are better equipped to question its capabilities and its limitations. Ethical reflection often begins not with answers, but with curiosity - about the tool, its origins, its consequences, and its place in human systems. By encouraging students to ask, *"How does this work?"* and *"Why was it built this way?"*, educators plant the seeds of responsible and informed engagement.

Example 1: AI Origins Discussion Prompt

- *"What is generative AI?"*
- *"How does it work?"*
- *"Who builds it?"*
- *"Whose data trains it?"*
- *"Who benefits - and who might be harmed?"*

Use brief, accessible explainers (e.g., short readings, podcasts, or visualizations) to anchor these conversations. This helps students view AI as something **built by people, not magic** - making it subject to critique and improvement (Lang, 2013).

---

2. Integrate Case Studies on Bias, Ethics, and Impact

Bring real-world examples of AI into the classroom to spark curiosity and provoke meaningful discussion. Whether it is a news article about AI bias in hiring algorithms, a viral example of AI-generated misinformation, or a case study on ChatGPT's role in academic writing, concrete scenarios help students connect abstract ethical concepts to lived realities. These examples ground conversation in context, allowing students to grapple with nuance, ask better questions, and reflect on their own assumptions and responsibilities in an AI-shaped world (Zawacki-Richter et al., 2019).

Example 2: Case Study – AI and Facial Recognition in Law Enforcement

- *Students read about misidentifications caused by facial recognition software. In small groups, they discuss:*
    - *"What went wrong?"*
    - *"How could these tools be redesigned or regulated?"*
    - *"Who should be held accountable?"*

Such discussions take ethical questions out of the abstract and place them into socially grounded, personally relevant contexts. When students analyze real-world examples, they begin to see **how AI intersects with issues of justice, equity, authorship, and accountability in tangible ways**. As Brookhart (2010) noted, anchoring reflection in lived experience deepens understanding and helps learners internalize values - not just memorize rules.

---

3. Use Debate and Ethical Dilemmas to Encourage Moral Reasoning

Structured debates give students the opportunity to take a position, articulate their reasoning, and engage with opposing viewpoints in a respectful, evidence-based environment. This format cultivates essential skills such as critical analysis, ethical reasoning, and active listening - particularly valuable when discussing the societal implications of AI. By defending a stance while considering alternative perspectives, students learn to navigate complexity, build empathy, and sharpen their ability to reason through real-world dilemmas.

Example 3: Classroom Debate Prompt

- *"Should students be required to disclose all AI tool use in their coursework? Why or why not?"*

Assigning roles - such as student, employer, faculty member, or AI developer - invites students to step into diverse perspectives and grapple with the competing priorities each role might hold. This exercise encourages empathy, highlights the complexity of ethical decision-making, and reveals the real-world trade-offs involved in deploying AI across different contexts. By inhabiting these viewpoints, students learn that ethical dilemmas are rarely clear-cut, and that responsible leadership requires understanding not just individual outcomes, but systemic impacts.

---

4. Design Reflective Writing That Builds Integrity

Invite students to reflect not only on the actions they took during an assignment or discussion, but on the values, assumptions, and priorities that informed those choices. This shift from *"What did I do?"* to *"Why did I do it that way?"* encourages deeper ethical awareness and helps students identify the principles guiding their decisions - whether fairness, efficiency, transparency, or accountability. Over time, this kind of reflection fosters a stronger sense of moral agency, empowering learners to act with purpose and integrity in AI-mediated environments.

Example 4: Ethical Reflection Journal Prompt

- *"Describe a moment in this course where you considered using an AI tool."*
    - *"What factors influenced your decision?"*
    - *"What do you think the responsible choice was, and why?"*

This type of **reflective writing cultivates moral imagination - the ability to envision the consequences of one's actions on others** - and supports the development of an ethical identity. As students articulate the values behind their decisions, they begin to see themselves not just as learners completing tasks, but as emerging professionals with responsibilities to communities, institutions, and systems. These habits of ethical reflection are foundational to lifelong integrity and essential for navigating the evolving moral landscape of an AI-driven world (Brookhart, 2010; Lang, 2013).

---

5. Make Ethical Inquiry a Norm, Not an Add-On

Ethical questioning should be woven into the fabric of everyday classroom practice - not reserved only for special assignments or end-of-term reflections. By embedding moments of moral inquiry into routine discussions, peer feedback, project planning, and tool selection, faculty normalize ethical reflection as a core part of the learning process. This steady, low-stakes integration helps students develop the habit of thinking critically about their choices, fostering ethical agility that grows stronger through repetition and relevance (Niemi & Multisilta, 2016).

Example 5: "Ethics Moment" Weekly Discussion

- *Start each class with a short prompt or news story related to AI ethics.*
- *Students can respond on discussion boards, in pairs, or as an exit ticket.*

Over time, **consistently engaging students in ethical questioning builds a habit of ethical vigilance** - an attentiveness to the broader implications of their decisions, both in and beyond the classroom. This habit not only deepens critical thinking but also connects academic material to real-world contexts, making learning more relevant and socially grounded. In an era shaped by rapid technological change, developing this kind of ethical awareness is as essential as mastering content (Selwyn, 2021).

Shifting Culture: From Surveillance to Stewardship

Rather than watching students for signs of dishonesty, AI-aware educators **coach students to reflect on power, ownership, and responsibility**. This transition fosters trust, not fear, and builds a community where curiosity and conscience thrive. When students understand that ethics is not about rules to avoid punishment - but **questions to shape a better world** - they are more likely to internalize values and less likely to offload thinking to machines.

Section Reflection: Cultivating Ethical Curiosity as a Cornerstone of AI-Aware Education

This section reframes ethical engagement not as a compliance mechanism, but rather as a powerful catalyst for learning, leadership, and digital responsibility. In an age where AI can generate content effortlessly, students must be equipped not only with technical fluency but with the ethical imagination to question the purpose, consequences, and values embedded in their technological choices. Fostering a culture of inquiry and ethical curiosity transforms the classroom into a space of moral exploration - where students interrogate the boundaries of machine reasoning, grapple with real-world dilemmas, and reflect on the impact of their decisions.

Through strategies such as case study analysis, role-based debates, reflective journaling, and weekly ethics prompts, educators help students see themselves as active participants in shaping the digital future - not just users of tools. This mindset shift - from surveillance to stewardship - builds trust, deepens critical thinking, and lays the foundation for academic integrity grounded in conscience, not compliance. In doing so, students develop the ethical fluency needed not only to navigate AI, but to lead with integrity in a rapidly evolving world.

Section 8: Building Feedback Loops That Reinforce Human Insight

---

Despite the rise of AI in education, **human insight remains the anchor** of authentic learning. As generative tools become better at producing grammatically correct, even persuasive content, the educator's role must be re-centered on **providing feedback that**

recognizes and reinforces human judgment, reflection, and complexity (Brookhart, 2010; Lang, 2013).

Feedback is no longer just about fixing what is wrong - it is about probing the student's thought process, surfacing assumptions, and inviting deeper intellectual engagement. Especially in an AI-aware classroom, where polished output can sometimes mask superficial thinking, feedback must reach beyond the surface. It becomes a conversation - an interactive, reflective exchange that prompts students to consider **how** they arrived at their answers, **why** they made certain choices, and **what** they might explore next. In this environment, **feedback shifts from being a red pen of correction to a mirror of cognition** - one that reflects the learners' reasoning back to them and challenges them to refine it. This shift fosters not only academic growth but also ethical awareness, intellectual independence, and metacognitive confidence.

Why Feedback Must Change in AI-Augmented Classrooms

As generative AI tools become more integrated into student workflows, the traditional model of feedback - focused largely on correctness, formatting, and grammar - no longer meets the moment. In an environment where AI can produce highly polished writing or code with minimal student input, feedback must evolve to target the underlying cognitive and ethical dimensions of student learning. It must shift from evaluating surface-level outputs to exploring the quality of thought, the use of tools, and the learner's decision-making process. Traditional feedback often focuses on:

- Correcting grammar, syntax, or formatting errors.
- Identifying factual inaccuracies.
- Checking whether students followed instructions.
- Assigning points or grades with minimal context.

In AI-augmented classrooms, feedback must also address:

- How students used AI tools and why.
- The reasoning behind their claims or choices.
- Their ability to reflect on and revise their thinking.
- Their ethical judgment and alignment with learning goals.

These aspects of learning - reasoning, reflection, ethical decision-making - cannot be fully replicated or meaningfully assessed by machines (Nicol & Macfarlane-Dick, 2006). While AI can generate fluent responses, it cannot grasp the nuances of a student's intention, growth, or internal conflict. For this reason, faculty must intentionally rebuild feedback loops that prioritize thinking over output. In an AI-aware classroom, feedback is not just a tool for refinement - it becomes a space for intellectual dialogue, where learners are invited to explain, justify, and deepen their understanding in partnership with their instructor.

Strategies for Reinforcing Human Insight Through Feedback

---

1. Shift Feedback from Evaluation to Conversation

Feedback should do more than justify a grade - it should invite students into deeper thinking about their choices, strategies, and interpretations. Rather than focusing solely on corrections or surface-level fixes, effective feedback poses questions that prompt reflection: ***"Why did you choose this approach?" "What alternative might you consider?" "How does this align with your intended message?"*** When framed this way, feedback becomes a tool for growth rather than evaluation, guiding students to refine their judgment and develop a more intentional relationship with their work (Nicol & Macfarlane-Dick, 2006).

Example 1: Question-Based Feedback on a Paper Draft

Instead of Writing:

- *"Unclear thesis."*

Try:

- *"What is the central tension in your argument?"*
- *"Could you explain it in one sentence as if you were convincing a skeptical reader?"*

This kind of question nudges students to articulate their own reasoning rather than reverse-engineering what they think the instructor wants to hear. **By shifting the focus from performance to thought process, it fosters authenticity and encourages students to take intellectual ownership of their work**. This approach empowers learners to trust their judgment and engage in learning as active participants - not passive responders (Brookhart, 2010).

---

2. Use Midpoint Check-Ins to Support Iteration

Midpoint check-ins provide students with a valuable opportunity to receive formative feedback while learning is still in progress - not after it is concluded. When students receive feedback too late in the process, they may view it as a postmortem critique rather than a tool for growth. But when feedback comes midstream, it enables them to reflect, adjust, and redirect their efforts in real time. This approach supports a mindset of learning as **iterative**, not fixed, and helps students understand that excellence is built through refinement.

In AI-aware classrooms, midpoint check-ins can also reveal how students are using digital tools - offering faculty a chance to affirm appropriate use, raise questions, or prompt reflection. Whether through low-stakes conferences, annotated drafts, or structured self-assessments, these check-ins reinforce process over product and promote self-regulation, ethical reasoning, and deeper cognitive engagement (Nicol & Macfarlane-Dick, 2006).

Example 2: Midpoint Reflection and Conference (Writing or STEM Project)

- *Students submit a process memo answering:*
  - *"What is working?"*
  - *"What is unclear?"*
  - *"What feedback would be most helpful now?"*

This approach allows faculty to coach thinking **in motion - guiding students as their ideas are still forming** - rather than offering commentary only after the fact, when the opportunity for meaningful revision has passed. Midpoint feedback turns the learning process into a conversation rather than a verdict, enabling faculty to support not just what students produce, but *how* they are thinking, deciding, and evolving along the way. It is a shift from evaluation to mentorship - one that affirms growth over perfection.

---

3. Design Peer Review for Human Insight - not Copy Editing

Peer review too often drifts into the realm of surface-level commentary - praising grammar, formatting, or word choice while overlooking the deeper layers of argumentation or insight. In AI-aware environments, this becomes even more critical, as students may submit work that is grammatically flawless but intellectually thin. To counter this, peer feedback should be intentionally structured to focus on idea development, the quality of reasoning, and the student's engagement with the assignment's core purpose. By shifting the focus from polish to substance, peer review can become a meaningful tool for collaborative thinking, not just commentary.

Example 3: Peer Feedback Questions (Social Sciences or Humanities)

- *"What surprised you in your peer's argument?"*
- *"Where does their thinking feel incomplete or ambiguous?"*
- *"What questions does this draft raise for you?"*

This shift humanizes the review process by emphasizing shared exploration over judgment, fostering an environment where students learn **with** and **from** each other. When feedback focuses on ideas rather than errors, students are more likely to feel respected, engaged, and intellectually invested. Such peer interactions support mutual cognitive development by encouraging students to articulate their thinking, challenge assumptions, and refine their understanding through dialogue (Brookhart, 2010).

---

4. Use AI to Support - but Not Replace - Feedback Workflows

AI tools can be thoughtfully integrated into the feedback process to assist - not override - the human elements that make feedback meaningful. For example, AI can help faculty identify common patterns or recurring misunderstandings across a group of student submissions, making it easier to target instructional interventions where they are most needed. These insights can help scale feedback in large classes without sacrificing depth or nuance.

However, the heart of effective feedback lies in relational judgment - responding to the **way** a student is thinking, not just **what** they have written. AI can flag issues or suggest phrasing, but it cannot interpret student intent, acknowledge personal growth, or pose the kinds of questions that prompt deeper reflection. When used as a support tool rather than a substitute, AI can streamline logistical burdens while preserving the instructor's most vital role: coaching thoughtful, ethical, and independent learners (Ryan & Ryan, 2013; Zawacki-Richter et al., 2019).

Example 4: AI-Aided Feedback Summary

- *Use AI to analyze and summarize student journal entries, especially in large classes where tracking individual trends manually is difficult. Ask the AI to identify:*
  - *Common misconceptions.*
  - *Frequently asked questions.*
  - *Recurring themes of confusion.*

Then address these trends in a **personalized class-wide video or email**. This saves time while **retaining faculty voice** (Zawacki-Richter et al., 2019). Using this kind of summary helps faculty prioritize where to focus in upcoming lessons, tailor clarifications, or adjust pacing - without having to comb through each entry individually. It also reinforces a responsive teaching model, where student thinking shapes instructional direction. Importantly, this process should complement - not replace - direct reading and human interpretation to ensure nuance and tone are not lost in automation (Zawacki-Richter et al., 2019).

---

5. Build Feedback Literacy in Students

For feedback to be effective - especially in AI-aware classrooms - students must be taught not only how to receive it, but how to interpret, question, and apply it meaningfully. This is especially important as students increasingly engage with both human and machine-generated feedback, which differ in tone, depth, and reliability. Without guidance, learners may misinterpret AI suggestions as authoritative or disregard instructor feedback that feels less polished by comparison.

To build feedback literacy, faculty can model how to read comments for intent, ask reflective follow-up questions, and differentiate between revision for clarity versus revision for content. Structured activities - such as annotating feedback, setting personal goals based on comments, or comparing peer and AI responses - help students move beyond passive reception and toward active use of feedback as a tool for growth (Carless & Boud, 2018). In doing so, students learn that feedback is not a final judgment, but a conversation designed to support their evolving thinking.

Example 5: Feedback Response Memo Assignment

- *After receiving comments, students submit a short response:*
  - *"What feedback surprised you?"*
  - *"What will you change and why?"*
  - *"What feedback did you decide not to implement?"*

Developing feedback literacy fosters more than revision skills - it **strengthens metacognition, nurtures learner autonomy, and sharpens discernment**. These capacities are especially critical when students must decide whether to accept, reject, or modify AI-generated suggestions. As CAST (2018) emphasized in its Universal Design for Learning framework, empowering students to make informed choices about tools and strategies supports deeper learning and ensures that technology serves, rather than supplants, their thinking.

Designing Feedback to Promote Reflection and Resilience

In AI-augmented classrooms, feedback should do more than correct - it should cultivate intellectual resilience, curiosity, and a growth-oriented mindset. **Rather than reinforcing the illusion that good work is flawless work, faculty can design feedback systems that reward persistence, reflection, and thoughtful revision**. This shift supports students in becoming adaptable learners who are open to challenge and willing to revisit their thinking. Instead of rewarding perfection, faculty can create a culture where:

- **First Drafts are Invitations, not Endpoints.** Students are encouraged to see early work as a launch point for deeper exploration, not a finished product to defend.
- **Mistakes are Learning Signals, not Penalties.** Errors become diagnostic tools for growth, guiding both students and faculty toward what needs deeper attention.
- **Feedback is a Dialogue, not a Verdict.** Comments spark reflection, invite response, and foster mutual understanding between learner and teacher.

When feedback is framed this way, students are more likely to take intellectual risks, own their learning process, and develop the confidence to refine their thinking over time - skills essential for navigating both AI-enhanced and real-world challenges (Carless & Boud, 2018; Dweck, 2006)

Sample Feedback Mantra:

- *"I am not here to correct you. I am here to help you see your thinking more clearly."*

This mindset helps students remain engaged - even in the face of struggle, uncertainty, or failure - because they come to see difficulty not as a signal to withdraw, but as an invitation to grow. When feedback is framed as guidance rather than judgment, students are more likely to persist through challenges, reflect on their progress, and adjust their strategies. Over time, this builds not only academic resilience but also a sense of agency and confidence in their ability to learn from setbacks.

Section Reflection: Reimagining Feedback as a Catalyst for Thoughtful Learning

This section powerfully reframes feedback as a developmental process rather than a corrective one - especially in classrooms shaped by generative AI. As polished outputs become easier to produce, the educator's role shifts toward recognizing and cultivating what machines cannot replicate: human insight, reasoning, and ethical decision-making. In AI-aware learning environments, feedback must go beyond fixing grammar or formatting and instead function as an ongoing conversation that probes the learner's thinking, values, and choices.

Through strategies such as midpoint check-ins, peer dialogue focused on substance over surface, reflective response memos, and intentional use of AI for instructional support - not evaluation - educators can design feedback systems that nurture metacognition, integrity, and resilience. This human-centered feedback loop does not just support academic growth - it builds intellectual confidence and ethical agency, equipping students to think critically with and beyond AI. Ultimately, the shift from correction to coaching transforms feedback into one of the most vital tools for sustaining authentic learning and trust in a world of accelerating automation.

Chapter 3 Conclusion: From Rules to Reasoning - Reclaiming Ethical Agency in AI-Integrated Education

Chapter 3 has reframed ethical engagement in higher education as a dynamic, lived practice - not a static list of rules or prohibitions, but a cultivated form of reasoning that evolves alongside emerging technologies. Across the chapter's eight sections, a clear trajectory emerges: ethical competence in the AI era must move from compliance to discernment, from avoidance to intentional integration, and from reactive policy enforcement to proactive moral imagination.

Section 1 opened by challenging the tendency to equate ethics with rule-following, especially in the context of AI-generated outputs. It called for a shift from punitive language to frameworks that encourage **judgment, context, and transparency**. This laid the foundation for **Section 2**, which explored **human–AI ethical case studies** as a means of teaching situated reasoning. By confronting real-world dilemmas, students begin to see that ethical decisions are rarely black-and-white - they are shaped by stakeholder values, disciplinary norms, and systemic complexity.

Section 3 positioned **ethical reasoning as a professional skill**, noting that in fields such as healthcare, journalism, business, or engineering, the ability to interpret and respond to ambiguous AI involvement is fast becoming essential. In **Section 4**, faculty mentorship emerged as a powerful site for cultivating ethical literacy - where reflective conversations about tool use, attribution, and authorship create a relational framework for value clarification.

The chapter continued in **Section 5** by demonstrating how **ethical questions can be embedded across disciplines**, even in traditional technical or quantitative fields. Through collaborative dialogue, assignments, and assessment strategies, educators can make moral inquiry visible and participatory. **Section 6** urged institutions to go beyond academic integrity policies by **building campus cultures where ethical reflection is not feared or outsourced - but expected, modeled, and supported**.

In **Section 7**, we returned to the student perspective - emphasizing that learners must be taught to recognize power dynamics, algorithmic bias, and the limitations of automation. Ethics, here, is not about learning what **not** to do - it is about developing the courage and clarity to act when systems fail. Finally, **Section 8** envisioned ethical reasoning as a form of **civic preparation**, positioning students not merely as consumers or users of AI, but as **shapers** of technological futures grounded in justice, care, and democratic responsibility.

Together, these sections make a decisive argument: **ethical reasoning in the AI era must be reclaimed as a faculty-led, student-empowering, and institutionally embedded practice**. The goal is not to keep pace with technology through regulation alone, but to slow down, think critically, and design learning environments where **discernment becomes the norm**.

In an educational culture often pressured by acceleration and optimization, the concluding theme of Chapter 3 is this: **ethical agency is not about predicting every risk - it is about preparing students and faculty to respond with judgment, humility, and integrity when those risks inevitably arise**. And that preparation begins not with policies, but with pedagogies of moral imagination.

Chapter 4: Understanding Generative AI - What Every Faculty Member Needs to Know

You do not need to be a computer scientist to supervise research in the AI era - but you do need AI literacy. As generative tools such as ChatGPT, Claude, and Gemini become part of students' academic workflows, faculty must understand enough to ask the right questions, guide responsible use, and evaluate AI-assisted outputs with discernment. This chapter demystifies the core principles behind generative AI, explaining how these tools function, where their boundaries lie, and what ethical considerations they raise. Faculty will gain a working knowledge of prompt engineering, model limitations, bias risks, and the practical fluency needed to confidently supervise and assess student work that intersects with AI.

Section 1: What Is Generative AI? Foundations for Non-Technical Faculty

---

For faculty without a background in computer science, the rise of generative AI can feel like stepping into a new and unfamiliar territory - one filled with complex terminology, invisible algorithms, and tools that appear to "think" on their own. But engaging with generative AI does not require fluency in coding or expertise in machine learning. What it does require is clarity, curiosity, and approachable metaphors that make the invisible visible.

This section offers non-technical educators a clear, accessible introduction to how generative AI works, what it can and cannot do, and how to interact with it confidently - as both a teaching tool and a supervisory aid. Whether you are guiding students through research, evaluating assignments, or simply trying to understand what AI means for academic integrity, this section equips you with the foundational knowledge to lead with confidence, not hesitation.

What Is Generative AI? A Plain-Language Definition

Generative AI refers to systems - like ChatGPT, Claude, or Gemini - that are designed to produce new content in response to human input. **Unlike traditional tools that retrieve existing information from databases, generative models can compose original outputs based on patterns learned from massive datasets**. These tools can generate content such as:

- Written text (e.g., essays, summaries, emails, poems).
- Code (e.g., Python scripts, HTML templates).
- Images (e.g., digital art, photo-realistic scenes through tools such as DALL·E or Midjourney).
- Audio and music (e.g., synthetic voices, compositions).
- Data visualizations or interactive responses.

These systems are powered by large language models (LLMs), which are trained on vast datasets of text, code, and media to learn patterns and relationships between words, concepts, and formats. At their core, LLMs function by predicting what is most likely to come next in a sequence - whether it is the next word in a sentence, the next line of code, or the next step in a reasoning chain. While these models can produce impressively coherent content, they do so without true understanding - **relying on probability, not comprehension** (Selwyn, 2021).

How Does It Work? The "Next Word Predictor" Analogy

At its core, generative AI is not truly intelligent - at least not in the way humans are. It does not **understand** meaning, context, or intention in the way people do. Instead, it functions like an extremely advanced autocomplete engine, generating the most statistically likely next word, sentence, or image based on patterns it has learned from training data. What feels like fluent conversation or coherent reasoning is actually a probabilistic sequence, not a product of conscious thought or comprehension. This distinction is critical for educators and students alike: while generative AI can mimic understanding, it does not possess it.

Analogy: Writing a Sentence

- *Imagine typing, "The professor walked into the..." and your phone suggests "classroom."*
- *LLMs do this at scale - predicting word-by-word based on probabilities from their training data. If a certain word tends to follow another word in similar contexts, the model is more likely to choos*e it.

So when ChatGPT writes an essay, it is not **thinking** in any human sense of the word - it is calculating which word is most statistically likely to come next based on the prompt and its training data. There is no awareness of argument, no grasp of truth or nuance - just a high-speed prediction engine assembling plausible-sounding sentences. Understanding this difference helps educators evaluate AI-assisted work more critically and guide students toward responsible, reflective use.

Key Terms, Simplified

Term	What It Means in Simple Terms
Token	A piece of text - often a word or part of a word - the AI reads or writes at each step.
Neural Network	A digital structure inspired by the brain, made of layers that "learn" patterns from data.
Training	Feeding the AI model billions of examples (books, websites, articles) so it can find patterns.
Prompt	The question or input you give to the model to get a response.

Term	What It Means in Simple Terms
Inference	The model using what it learned to generate a prediction (i.e., the answer or response).

These concepts empower faculty to move beyond uncertainty and into informed engagement - not by mastering the underlying code, but by understanding the logic behind the machine. When faculty grasp **how** generative AI works, they are better equipped to ask the right questions, guide student use, and integrate these tools with clarity and confidence - instead of apprehension or avoidance. In short, understanding the mechanism replaces fear with confidence.

Why Does It Seem "Smart"?

Generative AI **appears** intelligent because its outputs often mimic the tone, structure, and coherence of human communication. It has been trained on enormous amounts of data - books, articles, websites, and code - allowing it to replicate patterns that **sound** thoughtful, well-reasoned, or even creative. When it produces an articulate response or insightful summary, it is easy to assume it understands what it is saying. But in reality, it is predicting the most likely next word or idea based on statistical patterns - not processing meaning or intent. Its "smartness" is a well-polished illusion, powered by pattern recognition rather than comprehension. Therefore, AI seems smart because:

- It has been trained on **so much data** that it can mimic human speech convincingly.
- It uses **reinforcement learning with human feedback (RLHF)** to fine-tune outputs (Ouyang et al., 2022).
- It can carry on coherent conversations, apply stylistic tone, and simulate reasoning.

But it does **not** understand:

- Context or meaning, the way humans do.
- Right or wrong.
- Personal experience or emotion.

It is undeniably powerful - able to generate fluent essays, debug code, or mimic human tone with remarkable speed - but it remains fundamentally mechanical. Behind the polished language and seamless delivery is a system of probabilities, not perception. Generative AI can replicate the **form** of intelligence, but not the **substance** of understanding.

What Are Its Strengths and Weaknesses?

Strengths	Weaknesses
Fast text generation	Can produce false or misleading content ("hallucinations")
Helps to brainstorm ideas or organize arguments	Can mimic bias, stereotypes, or unethical reasoning
Supports multilingual or neurodiverse learners	Struggles with nuanced ethical or emotional judgment
Provides alternate explanations of concepts	Lacks personal insight, lived experience, or original creativity

Understanding what generative AI is capable of - such as summarizing, rephrasing, or generating stylistically coherent content - and where its limitations lie - such as lacking source verification, critical reasoning, or contextual awareness - enables faculty to evaluate student work with greater nuance. This insight helps educators distinguish between productive AI-assisted engagement and overreliance or misuse. Faculty AI literacy is foundational to maintaining academic integrity and supporting meaningful, outcome-aligned assessment in an AI-enhanced learning environment (Gundu, 2024; Reiss, 2021).

Practical Example: Faculty Use in a Research Supervision Context

Scenario:

- *A student uses ChatGPT to summarize three journal articles before submitting a research proposal.*

Faculty Role:

- *Ask to see the original articles.*
- *Compare the submitted summaries to the original articles for accuracy and nuance.*
- ***Discuss**: "What did the AI miss? Did it oversimplify any arguments? How might you revise the summaries for clarity or accuracy?"*

This approach reframes supervision as a dialogue - one focused on tool use, intellectual synthesis, and academic responsibility - rather than a reactive process rooted in suspicion, punishment, or confusion. When faculty engage students in open conversations about **how** and **why** they have used AI, the emphasis shifts from rule enforcement to ethical reasoning. It becomes an opportunity to mentor students in the thoughtful integration of technology into scholarship, fostering trust, transparency, and deeper learning along the way.

Practical Example: Teaching AI in a Humanities Course

Activity: Prompt Comparison Exercise

- *Students give ChatGPT the same literary prompt: "Analyze the theme of alienation in The Metamorphosis."*

Then Students:

- *Compare responses.*
- *Evaluate what is generic vs. insightful.*
- *Write their own improved version using both human reasoning and contextual evidence.*

This approach encourages students to engage in critical reading of AI-generated content rather than accepting it at face value. By prompting them to question accuracy, detect bias, and evaluate coherence, faculty help students move from passive consumption to active interpretation. Over time, **this cultivates discernment** - an essential skill for navigating an information-rich, AI-mediated world where credibility and context matter as much as fluency (Lang, 2013).

Section Reflection: Empowering Non-Technical Faculty Through Foundational AI Understanding

This section demystifies generative AI for non-technical faculty, offering a clear and accessible introduction to its mechanisms, capabilities, and limitations. By breaking down complex concepts into approachable metaphors and plain-language explanations, it equips educators to engage with AI not as an intimidating black box, but as a powerful - yet fundamentally mechanical - tool. Understanding that generative AI predicts rather than understands helps faculty evaluate AI-assisted student work more critically and ethically.

The section also models how faculty can confidently integrate AI into supervision and teaching without becoming technologists themselves, emphasizing dialogue, discernment, and reflective practice. Ultimately, this foundation empowers faculty to lead AI-aware classrooms with clarity and curiosity - replacing fear with confidence and positioning themselves as ethical guides in a rapidly evolving academic landscape.

Section 2: Prompt Engineering - The Art of Asking AI the Right Questions

---

At the heart of every AI interaction lies a deceptively simple but powerful question: ***"What exactly are you asking it to do?"*** Generative AI models - such as ChatGPT, Claude, or Gemini - do not possess consciousness or understanding. They respond based on the patterns and probabilities embedded in their training data. Thus, **the clarity and structure of the prompt** dramatically affect the **quality, depth, and relevance** of the output (Selwyn, 2021).

This process of shaping effective input is called **prompt engineering**. Though it may sound technical, prompt engineering is essentially the art of crafting instructions. For educators, mastering this skill can lead to better use of AI in creating rubrics, generating lesson plans, designing assignments, and guiding student inquiry. For students, prompt literacy supports ethical AI use, encourages critical thinking, and empowers autonomy in an AI-augmented learning environment.

Why Prompt Engineering Matters for Faculty

Generative AI is not "smart" in a human sense. It does not **know** anything in the way we do. Rather, it predicts the next word (**or token**) based on statistical relationships it has learned from enormous volumes of training data. In other words, it is not solving problems or reasoning - it is **pattern-matching at scale** (Brookhart, 2010; Selwyn, 2021).

This means that poor prompts can lead to vague, shallow, or misleading responses, while well-designed prompts can produce surprisingly clear, insightful, and structured results. A faculty member who understands prompt design is no longer at the mercy of the machine - they become an active participant in shaping how AI supports the learning process.

Types of Prompts and How They Work

---

1. Open-Ended vs. Closed Prompts

A **closed prompt** requests a fixed, specific response. These are ideal for fact-based retrieval or list generation.

Closed Example:

- *"List three causes of the American Civil War."*

An **open-ended prompt**, by contrast, encourages elaboration, comparison, synthesis, or judgment.

Open Example:

- *"Which political, economic, and cultural factors most contributed to the start of the American Civil War?"*
- *"Defend your answer with historical examples."*

In **educational settings**, **closed prompts** - those with specific, limited responses - are especially useful for checking basic understanding, identifying misconceptions, or collecting initial ideas. They work well for formative assessments, knowledge checks, or quick AI-generated responses where precision and clarity are needed. However, for fostering higher-order thinking, **open-ended prompts** are far more effective. These invite students (or AI) to engage in interpretation, analysis, argumentation, and self-reflection, making them ideal for critical writing, discussion preparation, or ethical inquiry. The quality of student thinking is shaped not just by the tool they use - but by the **questions** they are asked to engage with (Gundu, 2024; Reiss, 2021).

---

2. Sequential Prompting: Building Learning Step-by-Step

Sequential prompting involves asking AI a series of logically connected questions that build on one another to deepen understanding over time. Rather than relying on a single prompt for a complete answer, this approach mirrors how a skilled teacher scaffolds instruction - starting with foundational concepts and gradually introducing more complexity. For example, a student might first ask for a summary of a theory, then request examples, followed by a comparison with another framework, and finally, an application to a real-world scenario. This layered interaction encourages learners to think critically, refine their questions, and actively shape the learning process - rather than passively consuming AI-generated output (Reiss, 2021).

Example Sequence (STEM Application):

- **Prompt 1**: *"Summarize Newton's three laws of motion in plain language."*
- **Prompt 2**: *"Provide one real-world example for each law."*
- **Prompt 3**: *"Design a short classroom demonstration to teach each law."*

This approach empowers faculty or students **to guide the AI iteratively**, transforming it from a one-time responder into a responsive partner in learning. Each prompt builds on the last, creating a layered sequence that deepens understanding, sharpens focus, and encourages synthesis over summary. As the dialogue progresses, the AI's output becomes more relevant and tailored - reflecting the student's growing clarity and the instructor's intentional scaffolding of the learning journey.

---

3. Recursive Prompting: Revising and Refining AI Output

Recursive prompting - sometimes referred to as "prompt-refine-prompt" - is the practice of engaging the AI in a cycle of revision, expansion, or rethinking based on its previous responses. Rather than accepting the first answer as final, the user critically evaluates the output and then prompts the AI to improve it: to elaborate on a point, offer an alternative perspective, clarify reasoning, or align more closely with academic standards. This iterative exchange mirrors the process of critical revision that underpins scholarly thinking, helping students see learning as a recursive journey rather than a linear task. In modeling habits of refinement and reflection, recursive prompting not only improves the quality of AI-generated content - but it also strengthens the learner's own evaluative skills (Gundu, 2024).

Example (Writing Assignment):

- **Prompt**: *"Draft a 100-word thesis on climate change policy in the U.S."*
- **Follow-Up**: *"Revise this thesis to include a counterargument and a call to action."*
- **Follow-Up**: *"Improve the tone to be more persuasive and accessible to a general audience."*

By working in cycles, students come to understand that writing - and thinking - is not a one-and-done activity, but a process of refinement, rethinking, and growth. Recursive prompting helps shift their mindset from product to process, where early drafts are starting points, not final answers. In this context, AI becomes a tool for **iterative ideation** - a partner in exploration and revision - not a shortcut to bypass cognitive effort. This fosters habits of persistence, curiosity, and self-editing that are essential for academic and professional success.

---

4. Prompt Engineering for Faculty Tasks

Faculty can use prompt engineering across multiple dimensions of teaching - not only to generate content, but to shape learning experiences, scaffold complex tasks, and guide student inquiry. Well-crafted prompts can support tiered assignments, enable adaptive learning pathways, and model analytical reasoning by gradually increasing complexity. **Prompt engineering is becoming an essential pedagogical skill**, allowing faculty to engage AI tools not as static resources, but as dynamic partners in personalized, reflective, and inquiry-driven learning design (Abdullah & Zaid, 2023).

---

5. Designing Rubrics

AI can assist faculty by generating an initial draft of a grading rubric aligned with specific learning outcomes, saving valuable time during course planning or assessment design. This not only accelerates workflow, but also helps faculty clarify their own expectations by translating broad goals into concrete, evaluable criteria. AI can serve as a co-designer in instructional planning, enabling educators to focus on refining language, emphasizing transparency, and aligning rubrics more closely with what they truly value in student work (Ruiz-Rojas et al., 2023).

Prompt Example:

- *"Generate a rubric for a 1,500-word persuasive essay in a college-level English course. Include categories for thesis, evidence, organization, counterargument, and writing clarity."*

This AI-generated output serves as a starting point - one that faculty can then revise and tailor to align with institutional standards, accreditation requirements, or course-specific expectations. Rather than replacing the educator's expertise, the draft acts as a scaffold for customization, allowing faculty to refine language, adjust criteria for equity, and ensure the rubric reflects disciplinary norms and academic integrity. This collaborative approach preserves professional judgment while streamlining the design process.

---

6. Crafting Assignments and Scenarios

Prompt engineering empowers faculty to quickly generate and iterate on ideas for engaging, interdisciplinary assignments that connect course content to real-world issues. By experimenting with different prompts, faculty can explore novel ways to frame questions, simulate scenarios, or merge concepts across fields - whether combining ethics and computer science, literature and data analysis, or environmental studies and policy. This process not only jumpstarts creativity but also enables faculty to design assignments that are more relevant, inclusive, and adaptable to diverse learning styles (Abdullah & Zaid, 2023).

Prompt Example:

- *"Create a case-based assignment for a criminal justice course focused on the ethical use of facial recognition AI in public surveillance. Include three discussion questions."*

Used this way, generative AI becomes more than a productivity tool - **it acts as a creative collaborator, offering fresh perspectives and helping faculty explore connections they might not have considered on their own**. This is especially valuable during course redesign, when faculty are rethinking structure, learning goals, or thematic coherence, and during interdisciplinary planning, where blending concepts across fields can be both challenging and generative. As generative AI surfaces variations, analogies, and framing options, it supports innovation while still leaving the educator in full control of curation and refinement (Ruiz-Rojas et al., 2023).

---

7. Teaching Prompt Literacy to Students

One of the most powerful applications of prompt engineering in education is teaching students how to ask better questions. In an age where answers are increasingly generated on demand, the real intellectual skill lies in formulating prompts that are precise, layered, and curious. Guiding students to refine vague queries into purposeful, open-ended prompts not only improves the quality of AI interactions - it also sharpens their critical thinking, deepens their inquiry, and fosters habits of intellectual exploration that extend far beyond the screen (Reiss, 2021).

Student Assignment Example:

- *"Design three prompts to ask ChatGPT to explain the concept of 'sustainability.' Then compare the outputs. Which prompt gave the clearest answer? Why do you think that is?"*

This approach cultivates AI fluency by teaching students not just how to use generative tools, but how to question, evaluate, and interpret their outputs critically. **When students are encouraged to probe AI responses** - especially in light of known issues such as hallucinations, misinformation, or embedded bias - **they begin to develop the discernment necessary for responsible tool use**. Paired with classroom discussions about the limitations and ethical risks of AI, this practice fosters critical evaluation and digital ethics, both of which are essential in an age of machine-generated information (Reiss, 2021).

Prompting Tips for Faculty and Students

Prompt Design Tip	What It Does
Add context or role	Improves relevance and tone (e.g., "Act as a professor of ethics…")

Prompt Design Tip	What It Does
Specify format	Guides output style (e.g., "Write a bulleted summary")
Ask for examples or analogies	Improves clarity and conceptual depth
Set word limits or structure	Helps tailor scope and conciseness
Request multiple options	Encourages comparison and flexibility

These techniques elevate prompting from a mechanical input-output exchange into a flexible, inquiry-driven pedagogy. When used intentionally, **prompting becomes a way to scaffold learning, differentiate instruction, and cultivate curiosity** - empowering students to shape not just what they learn, but how they engage with knowledge. It shifts AI use from a technical trick to a thoughtful teaching strategy that supports exploration, iteration, and critical reflection (Abdullah & Zaid, 2023).

Section Reflection: Elevating Thinking Through the Craft of Prompting

This section highlights prompt engineering as a transformative skill that empowers both faculty and students to engage with generative AI as a thinking partner - not just a tool for convenience. By unpacking how prompt clarity shapes AI outputs, the section demystifies AI interactions and reframes them as purposeful, pedagogical acts. For educators, prompt design becomes a dynamic strategy to support lesson planning, rubric creation, assignment design, and creative exploration across disciplines. For students, learning to craft, revise, and evaluate prompts cultivates critical thinking, intellectual ownership, and ethical engagement.

Through open-ended, sequential, and recursive prompting strategies, this approach encourages deeper inquiry, metacognition, and iterative learning. Faculty are shown not only how to model effective prompting but how to teach it as a core literacy - developing students' ability to question, discern, and reflect in an AI-mediated world. Ultimately, this section reframes prompt engineering as a foundational practice for AI-integrated education - one that enhances both the process and the product of learning.

Section 3: What AI Can Do (and What It Cannot)

It is easy to be impressed - or intimidated - by generative AI. Tools such as ChatGPT, Claude, and Gemini can produce grammatically fluent essays, summarize dense academic texts, write computer code, generate lesson plans, translate language, and even simulate conversation in real time. But despite these remarkable abilities, **generative AI is not a "thinking machine."** It is a tool - powerful, yes, but **limited by its design, data, and purpose** (Selwyn, 2021).

For educators, developing a **clear, realistic understanding of what generative AI can and cannot do** is critical. Overestimating AI's intelligence can lead to overuse or misplaced trust. Underestimating it can result in missed opportunities for enhancing learning and instruction. This section offers a grounded overview of the strengths, weaknesses, and pedagogical implications of generative AI in higher education.

What Generative AI Can Do Well

---

1. Summarization and Simplification

AI can summarize complex readings, distill main ideas, or explain difficult terms in accessible language. This can support students struggling with comprehension or allow faculty to scaffold instruction across varied skill levels.

Example (Humanities):

- *A student uses ChatGPT to summarize a 30-page philosophy article on moral relativism. The model produces a 250-word summary, highlighting core arguments and terminology.*

Use Case: Faculty can permit - or even encourage - the use of generative AI during the pre-reading or review stages of an assignment. For instance, students might use AI to generate a summary of a scholarly article or chapter as a way to preview key ideas or refresh their understanding before class discussion. However, this should be paired with a clear **expectation**: *students must cross-check the AI-generated summary against the original source material for accuracy, nuance, and completeness*. This not only prevents overreliance but also reinforces critical reading skills, helping students identify where AI succeeds, where it falls short, and why fidelity to the original text matters.

---

2. Grammar and Syntax Correction

AI tools such as Grammarly and ChatGPT can help students refine sentence structure, correct spelling and grammar errors, and improve overall clarity. These supports are particularly useful for multilingual learners and students with language-based learning differences, as they provide real-time feedback that can reduce cognitive load and increase writing fluency. When paired with explicit instruction and ethical guidance, these tools promote accessibility and learner agency - empowering students to express their ideas more effectively while gaining confidence in their academic voice. Integrating AI into writing instruction can enhance equity when its use is transparent, reflective, and tied to clear learning outcomes (Holmes et al., 2022).

Example (Composition):

- *A student drafts an essay in a second language and uses an AI tool to polish grammar. The student then submits both versions along with a reflection on what changed.*

Use Case: Incorporating AI-assisted revision - such as using tools such as Grammarly or ChatGPT to address grammar, punctuation, and phrasing - allows faculty to shift their feedback toward higher-order concerns. When students use AI to improve surface-level mechanics before submission, faculty can devote their time and attention to more meaningful dimensions of writing: the clarity of ideas, the strength of argumentation, and the logic of structure. This approach supports Universal Design for Learning (UDL) principles by giving all students access to linguistic scaffolds, while ensuring that human feedback remains focused on cognitive and conceptual development (CAST, 2018).

---

3. Brainstorming and Idea Generation

Generative AI excels at producing lists, brainstorming options, and offering starting points for writing, projects, or creative exploration. Its speed and breadth make it particularly useful for overcoming creative blocks, identifying alternative approaches, or surfacing perspectives students may not have initially considered. While it cannot replace the depth, originality, or critical reasoning required for advanced academic or creative work, it can act as a catalyst - nudging students toward new directions and helping them iterate more confidently. Used this way, AI becomes a spark for exploration, not a substitute for inquiry.

Example (Creative Writing):

- *A student asks ChatGPT: "Give me five different story ideas that explore the theme of isolation in a futuristic society."*

Use Case: Faculty can frame AI interaction as a structured prewriting exercise, where students begin by generating a list of ideas, arguments, or examples using a tool such as ChatGPT. Rather than adopting these suggestions wholesale, **students are tasked with evaluating the AI-generated content** - identifying gaps, questioning assumptions, and refining ideas to better suit their goals. This positions AI as a brainstorming partner rather than an author, and encourages students to take ownership of the direction, tone, and depth of their final work. By building their writing from this critical foundation, students engage in a reflective process that promotes both creativity and discernment.

---

4. Pattern Recognition and Structuring

In certain disciplines - such as law, programming, and data analysis - AI can be especially effective at identifying logical structures, recurring patterns, or standardized forms. For example, it can help law students analyze the components of a legal brief, assist programmers in recognizing common function structures, or support data analysts in generating hypotheses from trends. When used as a pattern-recognition tool, AI can deepen students' understanding of disciplinary conventions and improve their ability to replicate or critique those forms with greater confidence and precision. However, its effectiveness depends on thoughtful integration and guided reflection, ensuring students develop insight - not just automation.

Example (STEM):

- *A student uses ChatGPT to debug a short piece of Python code or ask for common structures in research abstracts.*

Use Case: Faculty can permit the use of AI as a scaffold for technical tasks - such as generating code snippets, outlining legal arguments, or formatting data queries - provided that students are required to demonstrate a clear understanding of **why** the AI-generated structure works. This might involve annotating the AI output, explaining the logic behind a function or clause, or identifying potential flaws or limitations. By pairing AI-assisted scaffolding with explanatory reflection, faculty can ensure that students are not just replicating patterns - they are internalizing the underlying logic and applying it with purpose. This approach reinforces both technical fluency and critical reasoning, making AI a learning aid rather than a shortcut.

What Generative AI Cannot Do Reliably (or Ethically)

---

1. Evaluate Evidence or Interpret Nuance

AI does not truly "understand" the content it generates - it lacks consciousness, contextual awareness, and the ability to engage in meaning-making. While it can replicate the **form** of human reasoning, it cannot weigh conflicting interpretations, evaluate the credibility of sources, or exercise ethical or disciplinary judgment in ambiguous scenarios. These are fundamentally human capabilities, rooted in lived experience, critical thinking, and academic training. Recognizing these limitations is essential for both students and faculty, ensuring that AI is used to **support** thinking - not to replace it.

Example (Social Sciences):

- *A student asks AI to compare two theories of globalization. The response is generic and fails to engage with the historical or political complexities.*

Where It Falls Short: Despite its fluency and speed, generative AI lacks the contextual sensitivity required for complex academic reasoning. It cannot account for nuance, cultural perspective, evolving disciplinary standards, or the intent behind a particular interpretation. While it may approximate the structure of a well-formed response, it cannot replicate the deliberative process that scholars and students engage in when weighing competing arguments or applying theoretical frameworks. This limitation becomes especially visible in tasks that demand human judgment, disciplinary rigor, or moral reasoning - areas where insight, not just pattern prediction, is essential (Selwyn, 2021).

---

2. Think Ethically or Morally

Generative AI models are fundamentally amoral - they do not possess an internal moral compass, ethical awareness, or the ability to reflect on the consequences of their outputs. While they can generate language that mimics ethical reasoning, they cannot distinguish between responsible and harmful advice, nor can they assess the values that inform human decisions. Their outputs are based on patterns in training data, not ethical principles or social accountability. This makes it crucial for educators to guide students in recognizing that ethical judgment must come from the user - not the tool - and that meaningful decision-making cannot be outsourced to an algorithm.

Example (Business):

- *A student asks AI to recommend strategies for cutting costs in a nonprofit. The tool suggests downsizing staff with no consideration of community impact.*

Where It Falls Short: Faculty can actively engage students in critiquing AI-generated responses - highlighting not just factual limitations, but also the absence of ethical reasoning and value-based judgment. For example, faculty might present an AI-generated policy recommendation, medical case analysis, or legal argument and ask students to identify where ethical considerations are missing or oversimplified. Assignments can then require students to apply ethical frameworks, reflect on competing values, or justify decisions based on disciplinary standards. Cultivating this kind of ethical evaluation supports critical reflection and helps students develop the moral imagination needed to navigate complexity - something AI cannot do on their behalf (Brookhart, 2010).

---

3. Produce Genuinely Original Insights

While AI is remarkably adept at remixing existing content - reassembling ideas, styles, or formats in novel combinations - it cannot offer **authentic, lived,** or **creatively disruptive** thinking. True creativity often stems from contradiction, personal experience, cultural context, or emotional insight - all dimensions that lie beyond the reach of statistical prediction. AI generates what is most likely to follow based on past patterns; it does not surprise, dissent, or innovate in the way human minds can. This distinction is essential for students and educators alike: creativity is not about producing what is probable, but what is possible.

Example (Literary Analysis):

- *A ChatGPT-generated essay on Toni Morrison's Beloved might rehash clichés or repeat common interpretations found in public data.*

Where It Falls Short: Students should be encouraged to take intellectual risks - asking bold questions, challenging assumptions, and exploring unfamiliar territory. These are the very qualities that generative AI cannot replicate. While AI excels at producing plausible, well-structured responses, it does not innovate, dissent, or imagine beyond the boundaries of its training data. The value of human insight lies precisely in its unpredictability, its capacity to make leaps, forge connections, and introduce ideas that have not been modeled before. The deepest learning happens not through repetition, but through exploration - and that is something only students, not algorithms, can authentically do (Lang, 2013).

---

4. Attribute Sources or Track Knowledge

Most generative AI tools cannot reliably cite their sources significantly in academic contexts where attribution, accuracy, and transparency are essential. Even when prompted to provide references, these models may fabricate citations entirely or blend information from multiple sources without acknowledging their origin. This "hallucination" effect arises because generative models do not access a real-time database of verifiable references; instead, they predict what a plausible citation might look like based on patterns in their training data. For educators and students alike, this underscores the importance of verifying all AI-generated claims and treating its outputs as starting points, not authoritative sources.

Example (Research Essay):

- *A student includes an AI-generated quote attributed to a journal article that does not exist.*

Where It Falls Short: Faculty should explicitly train students to verify and cross-reference all AI-generated content, particularly when it is used in support of academic claims. This includes fact-checking statistics, confirming quotations, and independently locating original sources referenced in AI output. For formal research assignments - especially those requiring peer-reviewed or discipline-specific evidence - faculty should discourage unsupervised reliance on AI tools, which may fabricate citations or blend unverifiable content. Promoting these habits not only protects academic integrity but also develops students' digital literacy and evaluative judgment in an era where misinformation can be algorithmically convincing (Lang, 2013).

---

5. Reflect, Feel, or Understand Emotion

AI cannot authentically express or interpret human emotion - it lacks consciousness, self-awareness, and the lived experience that gives emotion its depth and meaning. While generative models can **mimic** empathy through tone, phrasing, or emotionally resonant language, these outputs are performative, not felt. The AI does not understand suffering, joy, frustration, or compassion; it simply reproduces the patterns of language associated with those states. This distinction matters in fields such as counseling, education, and writing - where emotional insight is not just a communicative device, but a relational and ethical practice rooted in human connection.

Example (Reflective Assignment):

- *A student asks AI to write a reflection on their growth during a service-learning project. The response feels sterile and generic.*

Where It Falls Short: Emotional intelligence, self-awareness, and personal growth are not just desirable traits - they are core dimensions of authentic learning that generative AI cannot replicate. These qualities emerge through reflection, vulnerability, and the ability to connect knowledge to lived experience - all of which require a human learner at the center. True learning is not just about information transfer - it is about transformation. In classrooms that value emotional insight alongside intellectual rigor, students develop as whole thinkers, capable of empathy, ethical reasoning, and lifelong self-directed growth. These are the traits that distinguish education from automation - and students from algorithms (Brookhart, 2010; CAST, 2018).

Section Reflection: Clarifying the Boundaries of AI to Preserve Human-Centered Learning

This section offers an essential balance to the growing fascination - and apprehension - around generative AI by clearly delineating what these tools **can** do effectively and what they **cannot** replicate or replace. It empowers faculty with a realistic, nuanced understanding, reminding educators that AI's strengths - summarization, grammar correction, pattern recognition, and brainstorming - can enhance teaching and learning when used with structure, intention, and reflection.

However, the section also underscores the limits of AI: its inability to reason ethically, cite accurately, feel or reflect authentically, or generate truly original insight. These are distinctly human faculties - rooted in experience, emotion, critical judgment, and moral awareness - that no algorithm can automate. By exploring both capabilities and constraints, this section calls on faculty to integrate AI in ways that **support** student learning while reaffirming the irreplaceable value of human cognition, creativity, and connection. Ultimately, it reframes AI not as a substitute for thinking, but as a tool that - when paired with critical guidance - can sharpen the very skills that distinguish human learning in an AI-augmented world.

Section 4: Key Tools Every Faculty Member Should Explore

The generative AI landscape is evolving rapidly - sometimes overwhelmingly so. With new tools released or updated every week, it is easy for faculty to feel uncertain or even avoidant. But **AI literacy does not require mastering every platform**. Instead, fluency begins with curiosity: engaging with a few carefully chosen tools, testing them in low-stakes settings, and asking, ***"How could this enhance teaching, learning, or research in my discipline?"***

This section introduces a **curated toolkit** of widely used generative AI tools, organized by function. For each, we provide a short description, example use case, educational benefits, and important cautions. Faculty from all backgrounds can use this guide to make informed decisions about what tools to explore and how to align them with their pedagogical goals (Selwyn, 2021).

Large Language Models (LLMs)

---

1. ChatGPT (OpenAI)

Function: Text generation, summarization, brainstorming, and basic coding.

Use Case: A faculty member teaching a first-year seminar uses ChatGPT to generate three alternative discussion questions for an article on climate justice, then refines them based on course themes.

Benefits:

- **Easy to Use and Widely Available**. Most generative AI platforms are accessible via web or app, requiring no technical background to operate. Their interfaces are simple, making them approachable for both educators and students.
- **Capable of Generating Coherent, Grammatically Sound Content**. These tools excel at producing fluent language across a variety of formats, from summaries to explanations, often with impressive speed and surface-level polish.
- **Useful for Ideation, Drafts, Email Templates, or Lesson Brainstorming**. AI can serve as a creative partner in the early stages of planning, helping faculty generate assignment ideas, refine phrasing, or explore alternative ways to structure content or communication.

Cautions:

- **May "Hallucinate" Facts or Generate False Information**. AI tools can produce confident-sounding statements that are factually incorrect or misleading, especially when asked about niche topics, data, or recent events beyond their training window.
- **Struggles with Nuanced Argumentation or Citation Accuracy**. While AI can replicate the form of an argument, it lacks the depth of reasoning and critical engagement required for higher-level academic work. It may gloss over counterarguments, oversimplify complexity, or fail to maintain logical coherence across a longer piece.
- **Does not Cite Sources Unless Specifically Prompted - and Even Then, Citations may be Fabricated**. Even when asked to include references, generative AI often creates convincing but entirely fictional citations or merges content from multiple sources without proper attribution. This makes it unreliable for evidence-based academic writing unless carefully verified by the user.

---

2. Claude (Anthropic)

Function: Similar to ChatGPT but known for a more "conversational" and aligned tone.

Use Case: A professor uses Claude to compare AI-generated summaries of student reflections to identify common themes across a class.

Benefits:

- **Emphasizes User-Aligned Responses and Safety**. Many newer AI systems are fine-tuned to align with user intent while avoiding harmful, biased, or inappropriate outputs. This focus on safety can make them more suitable for classroom or instructional settings.
- **Often Produces More Cautious and Balanced Writing**. Compared to earlier versions, today's models tend to hedge claims, acknowledge uncertainty, and avoid overly strong or controversial statements - helpful for promoting reflective, academically appropriate output.
- **Accepts Larger Documents in Uploads (with Pro Versions)**. Some AI tools (e.g., Claude or GPT-5 with Pro) allow users to upload long documents such as syllabi,

student writing, or academic articles for analysis. This opens up new use cases for summarization, feedback, and lesson planning at scale.

Cautions:

- **Less Consistent Access than ChatGPT**. Some AI platforms may have limited availability depending on region, user tier (e.g., free vs. pro), or institutional access. This can make adoption uneven across classrooms or campuses.
- **Still Prone to Factual Errors or Overly General Responses**. Despite improvements, generative AI can default to vague or oversimplified answers, especially on complex topics. It may confidently present incorrect information, requiring users to critically evaluate and cross-reference output.
- **May Avoid Answering Direct Prompts Involving Controversy or Moral Complexity**. Many AI models are trained to avoid sensitive or polarizing topics, which can result in overly neutral or evasive responses. While this improves safety, it can limit usefulness in disciplines that rely on ethical reasoning, critical debate, or deep interpretive analysis.

AI Research Assistants

---

1. Scite.ai

Function: AI-powered research database with citation context.

Use Case: A student asks Scite to show peer-reviewed articles that support (or contrast with) a claim about online learning effectiveness.

Benefits:

- **Helps Students Find Evidence with Citation Context**. These tools can retrieve research articles and indicate whether a source *supports*, *disputes*, or *mentions* a specific claim, giving students a more nuanced understanding of scholarly conversations.
- **Encourages Deeper Source Analysis**. By surfacing how studies relate to one another, AI-powered research tools prompt students to go beyond "finding any article" and instead evaluate relevance, strength of evidence, and methodological quality.
- **Integrates with Reference Managers (e.g., Zotero)**. Many platforms allow students to export citations directly into reference managers, streamlining the research process and reinforcing good academic habits around attribution and organization.

Cautions:

- **Not All Disciplines are Equally Represented**. Many AI-based research tools draw heavily from open-access scientific databases or well-indexed journals, meaning that fields such as STEM, medicine, or psychology are better covered than others, such as the arts, humanities, or region-specific studies.

- **Faculty Should Guide Students on How to Validate Article Relevance and Impact**. Students may assume that any AI-suggested article is credible or appropriate. Faculty play a key role in helping students evaluate the relevance, methodology, and scholarly weight of sources - especially in disciplines where nuance and context are critical.

---

2. Elicit.org (by Ought)

Function: AI-supported literature review assistant.

Use Case: An instructor working with a research student uses Elicit to generate a table comparing methods used in 10 recent studies on climate migration.

Benefits:

- **Extracts Key Methods, Samples, and Findings from Papers**. Some AI tools (e.g., Elicit or Scite Assistant) can automatically pull out study designs, participant details, and main results, helping students quickly grasp a paper's structure and contribution.
- **Speeds up Early-Stage Research Design**. By summarizing relevant studies and organizing them by themes or methods, AI can accelerate the literature review process and help students form stronger research questions or hypotheses.
- **Great for Teaching How to Ask Literature-Driven Questions**. These tools expose students to the types of questions scholars investigate, allowing faculty to scaffold how to frame inquiries that are grounded in existing evidence rather than guesswork or opinion.

Cautions:

- **Best for Structured Abstracts; Struggles with Less Standardized Formats**. AI tools perform best when analyzing papers with clearly labeled sections (e.g., "Methods," "Results," "Conclusion"). Articles with narrative formats - common in humanities or qualitative research - often yield less accurate or more generic summaries.
- **Still in Beta (at time of this writing) - Faculty Should Review All AI Summaries before Using Them in Instruction**. Many of these tools are still under development and may misinterpret findings, miss nuance, or oversimplify complex arguments. Faculty should critically evaluate any AI-generated summary before sharing it with students or integrating it into class materials.

Visual Generation Tools

---

1. DALL·E (OpenAI)

Function: Text-to-image generation.

Use Case: In an art history course, students generate AI images inspired by Romanticism and compare them to original works - identifying aesthetic inconsistencies.

Benefits:

- **Sparks Creativity and Visual Literacy**. Tools such as DALL·E, integrated into ChatGPT for Pro users, can inspire students to think visually and critically about how meaning is conveyed through images, not just words. This supports creative disciplines and enhances visual communication across subjects.
- **Helps Visualize Abstract Concepts**. AI-generated images can be used to depict scientific processes, historical reconstructions, symbolic themes in literature, or imagined environments - making complex or intangible ideas more concrete and accessible.
- **Integrated into ChatGPT for Pro Users**. For faculty and students with access to ChatGPT's Pro tier, image generation is built into the interface, enabling seamless experimentation with text-to-image prompts during lectures, assignments, or creative brainstorming.

Cautions:

- **May Embed Biases from Training Data**. AI image tools are trained on massive, often uncurated datasets, which can reproduce harmful stereotypes, gender/racial imbalances, or skewed cultural representations - sometimes in subtle ways.
- **Cannot Replicate Culturally Specific Nuance or Symbolism**. While AI can mimic styles or generate literal representations, it often fails to capture the deeper meanings, traditions, or cultural contexts embedded in visual storytelling. This makes it unreliable for assignments involving historical accuracy, Indigenous art forms, or symbolism tied to specific communities.
- **Raises Ethical Concerns About Artistic Originality**. As Selwyn (2021) pointed out, generative tools blur the line between inspiration and imitation, challenging our definitions of authorship, creativity, and intellectual property - especially when AI-generated images draw on existing artistic styles without attribution.

---

2. Midjourney

Function: More photorealistic and stylized visual generation.

Use Case: A digital design professor tasks students with comparing Midjourney-generated branding materials to those created by human designers.

Benefits:

- **High-Resolution, Stylized Visuals**. Tools such as DALL·E, Midjourney, and Stable Diffusion can generate detailed, polished images in a variety of artistic styles, making them useful for digital storytelling, design exploration, or visual supplements in presentations and assignments.
- **Encourages Discussion of Aesthetics, Authorship, and Creative Process**. AI-generated art opens the door to rich classroom conversations about what constitutes originality, how style is defined and imitated, and how artistic intent is (or is not) present in machine-created works. These discussions foster critical engagement with both visual media and evolving definitions of creativity in the age of AI.

Cautions:

- **Requires a Discord-based Interface, which may be Less Intuitive for Some Users**. Midjourney operates through a Discord server, which can present a learning curve for students or faculty unfamiliar with the platform. This may limit accessibility or slow down adoption compared to browser-based tools such as DALL·E.
- **Usage Rights are Unclear in Some Versions - Good for Critique, not Commercial Use**. Depending on the subscription tier and platform terms of service, users may not retain full ownership of generated images. This makes AI-generated visuals best suited for classroom critique, exploration, or discussion - not for commercial or public-facing projects without a careful review of licensing terms.

Educational and Instructional AI Tools

---

1. Khanmigo (by Khan Academy)

Function: Educational AI assistant trained on pedagogical principles.

Use Case: Faculty in a flipped classroom have students use Khanmigo to practice math problems with Socratic questioning before class.

Benefits:

- **Built with Learning Science in Mind**. These tools are developed with research-backed principles such as spaced practice, retrieval-based learning, and cognitive load theory, making them more than just content generators - they are designed to support how students actually learn.
- **Offers Feedback Loops Tailored for Formative Learning**. Instead of simply delivering answers, many of these platforms offer hints, scaffolded support, and iterative feedback that encourage reflection, persistence, and skill development over time.
- **Integrates with Standards-Aligned Content**. Many AI-driven platforms are embedded within curriculum-aligned ecosystems, allowing educators to connect AI-driven feedback and instruction directly to course goals, standards, or personalized learning plans.

Cautions:

- **Limited Subject Range Compared to Broader AI Tools**. While tools such as Khanmigo or Scribe excel in core academic areas (e.g., math, grammar, basic science), they often lack depth in specialized or interdisciplinary subjects. This makes them highly effective in structured learning environments, but less flexible for open-ended exploration or niche topics.
- **Students may Attempt to use it as a Shortcut Rather Than a Tutor Without Clear Guidance**. Without instructor framing, students might treat the AI as a source of quick answers rather than a partner in learning. Faculty should clarify expectations and

encourage metacognitive reflection to ensure students engage with these tools as scaffolds for thinking - not substitutes for effort.

---

2. Perplexity.ai

Function: AI search engine with real-time citation integration

Use Case: A faculty member models how to use Perplexity to answer a student research question: *"What are current theories on social media burnout?"* - then compares results to Google and JSTOR.

Benefits:

- **Cites Sources In-Line with Answers**. These tools provide real-time responses with clickable source references, allowing students to trace claims back to original articles, databases, or websites - an essential feature for teaching information literacy.
- **Great for Introductory Research or Fact-Checking**. Their concise, citation-backed summaries make them useful starting points for students who are learning how to explore unfamiliar topics or verify information before diving into deeper research.
- **Encourages Search Evaluation and Comparison**. By surfacing multiple perspectives and source types, these tools help students practice critical search habits - like comparing claims, checking publication credibility, and assessing how different sources frame the same issue.

Cautions:

- **Answers can Still be Shallow or Oversimplified**. While these tools are helpful for quick overviews, they often lack the nuance, depth, and critical framing required for academic research. Students should be encouraged to treat AI responses as entry points - not final sources.
- **Citations Should be Verified - Perplexity Sometimes Links to Less Rigorous Sources**. Although it cites sources, Perplexity may pull from forums, outdated blogs, or unreviewed content alongside scholarly material. Faculty should guide students in evaluating the credibility, relevance, and authority of each source before relying on it in assignments.

Encouraging Exploration Without Overload

Integrating AI into teaching does not require an overhaul - it starts with intentional, low-pressure steps. Faculty can ease into AI-enhanced pedagogy by:

- **Choosing one or two tools** that align with their discipline, teaching style, or student learning goals. For example, a writing instructor might explore ChatGPT for idea generation, while a science faculty member might try Elicit for sourcing relevant literature.

- **Using those tools in low-stakes settings**, such as brainstorming, prewriting, question generation, or summarizing readings. These activities help students engage with AI as a support - not a shortcut - while giving faculty space to experiment.
- **Reflecting regularly** on what is working, what is not, and what could be improved. Faculty can jot down quick notes, gather student feedback, or compare outcomes to previous semesters to iterate thoughtfully.

Example: Faculty Learning Community (FLC) Prompt

- *"Try using an AI tool to support one instructional task this week - like generating quiz questions or writing a syllabus blurb. Reflect with colleagues: What surprised you? What will you try next?"*

This approach promotes **collaborative experimentation**, where faculty feel supported in trying new tools without the pressure to become immediate experts. By normalizing small, shared steps into AI integration, institutions lower the barrier to entry and create a culture where curiosity and reflection are more important than perfection. As Brookhart (2010) emphasized, environments that support risk-taking and dialogue are essential for authentic professional growth - especially when navigating emerging technologies.

Section Reflection: Empowering Faculty Through Targeted AI Tool Exploration

This section serves as a practical bridge between AI awareness and AI action, providing faculty with a curated, approachable introduction to generative AI tools organized by function and educational value. Rather than overwhelming educators with a flood of unfamiliar platforms, it emphasizes intentional exploration - encouraging faculty to experiment with one or two tools that align with their specific instructional goals. By framing tools such as ChatGPT, Claude, Scite, Elicit, and DALL·E not just as tech novelties but as pedagogical partners, the section reinforces that AI can support creative thinking, streamline planning, enhance accessibility, and facilitate inquiry when used thoughtfully.

Importantly, each tool's strengths are balanced with candid cautions - reminding faculty to critically evaluate outputs, guide student use ethically, and maintain the centrality of human judgment. This grounded, use-case-driven approach helps demystify AI, lower barriers to entry, and cultivate a reflective mindset where small, collaborative experimentation becomes the foundation for responsible AI integration. Ultimately, this section empowers faculty to move from hesitation to confidence - reframing AI not as a disruptive threat, but as a strategic ally in supporting teaching, learning, and innovation.

Section 5: Generative AI and Academic Misconduct - Understanding the Risk Factors

---

Generative AI has reframed the conversation around academic integrity in profound ways. It does not just change how students write, research, or problem-solve - it also alters **why and when** they might cross ethical boundaries. While AI tools such as ChatGPT, Claude, and

Perplexity can support learning, they also present **new avenues for academic dishonesty** that existing plagiarism frameworks often fail to capture (Lang, 2013).

This section examines common forms of AI-related misconduct, explores the underlying motivations, and highlights the structural and pedagogical responses that can **prevent misuse while promoting ethical engagement**. Rather than approaching AI with fear, faculty are encouraged to cultivate **trust, transparency, and thoughtful course design**.

Redefining Misconduct in the AI Era

Traditional definitions of academic misconduct have largely focused on clear-cut violations - such as copying another person's work without attribution, commonly referred to as plagiarism. But the rise of generative AI has introduced a new layer of complexity, with student behaviors that blur the boundaries between assistance and authorship, intention and oversight. These actions often fall into ethical gray zones that do not align neatly with conventional policies, yet still raise serious questions about transparency, accountability, and learning. For example:

- A student asks ChatGPT to rewrite their original essay to sound "more sophisticated," masking their voice behind a polished, AI-generated veneer.
- A learner pastes an entire assignment prompt into Claude and turns in the AI-generated response, avoiding the task of constructing their own understanding.
- Another uses AI to generate citations - only to discover that several are fabricated, incorrectly formatted, or inaccurately quoted, jeopardizing both credibility and academic standards.

These cases do not always stem from deliberate dishonesty; they often reflect confusion about what is allowed, what counts as "original," and how much help is too much. Faculty and institutions must therefore evolve both policy and pedagogy - not only to prevent misconduct, but to teach students how to engage with AI tools ethically, reflectively, and with clear academic purpose.

"Are these cases examples of misconduct, poor judgment, or something in between?" The truth is that many students are not sure - and many faculty do not agree. What once felt like a clear boundary between acceptable and unacceptable behavior has been blurred by tools that are easy to access, socially normalized, and rarely discussed in depth during academic onboarding. The challenge is not just about defining rules - it is about navigating shifting cultural and technological norms that outpace institutional responses. This ambiguity creates uncertainty on all sides, underscoring the urgent need for dialogue, clarity, and shared definitions of integrity in the age of AI (Selwyn, 2021).

Common Forms of AI-Related Misconduct

---

1. Ghostwriting by AI

Definition: Submitting AI-generated content - whether a paragraph or an entire essay - as one's own work without disclosure.

Example: A student struggling with a tight deadline asks ChatGPT to write a complete 1,500-word paper on feminist theory and submits it unchanged.

Risk Factors for Unethical or Unreflective AI Use

Several conditions can increase the likelihood that students will misuse AI tools - not necessarily out of intent to deceive, but out of confusion, desperation, or misunderstanding. Key risk factors include:

- **Time Pressure**. When students are overwhelmed by deadlines or juggling multiple commitments, the appeal of a quick, polished AI response becomes stronger - especially in low-stakes or high-stress situations.
- **Lack of Confidence in Writing**. Students who struggle with academic language, structure, or fluency - particularly multilingual learners or those with language-based learning differences - may turn to AI for rewriting or rephrasing without fully understanding the boundary between support and substitution.
- **Belief that AI is a Neutral "Tool," not a Co-Author**. Some students see AI like a calculator: something that helps "get the job done" without requiring acknowledgment. This belief leads them to skip disclosure, reflection, or citation.
- **Absence of Policy Clarity**. Without explicit course-level or institutional guidance, students are left to interpret faculty expectations on their own, often defaulting to what peers are doing or what "feels allowed."

Prevention Strategies, Encouraging Integrity in the Age of AI

Rather than relying solely on enforcement, faculty can adopt practical, student-centered strategies that promote ethical use of AI and reduce the temptation to misuse it. These approaches foster transparency, reflection, and a culture of learning over perfection:

- **Require AI use Disclosures**. As outlined in *Chapter 3, Section 6*, prompt students to explicitly state whether and how they used AI tools in their assignments. This normalizes responsible use, builds trust, and provides faculty with insight into student thinking and habits.
- **Design Assignments with Process Checkpoints**. Break larger tasks into components such as outlines, drafts, annotated bibliographies, or reflections. These checkpoints encourage metacognition, provide opportunities for feedback, and make one-time AI-generated submissions easier to detect.
- **Foster Classroom Norms where Struggle and Imperfection are Normal**. When students know that messy drafts, evolving ideas, and iterative thinking are part of the process, they are less likely to feel pressure to present polished - but artificially generated - work. Celebrate learning over "looking right."

---

2. Fabricated or Inaccurate Citations

Definition: AI tools often "hallucinate" citations - creating plausible but non-existent sources or misattributing quotes.

Example: A student uses ChatGPT to create a reference list for a research paper. Several of the journal articles listed cannot be found in any database.

Risk Factors for Unethical or Unreflective AI Use

Even when students have good intentions, certain conditions make it more likely they will rely on AI in ways that compromise academic integrity or critical thinking. Understanding these risk factors helps educators proactively design instruction and support systems that reduce confusion and misuse:

- **AI is Trained to Produce Text that *Sounds Plausible*, not Verify Real-World Accuracy**. Tools such as ChatGPT are optimized for linguistic fluency, not factual correctness. As Ouyang et al. (2022) explained, the model's objective is to predict the most likely next word - not to retrieve reliable data - making it prone to "hallucinations" and confident-sounding misinformation.
- **Students may Assume the Tool is Trustworthy, Especially if they are Inexperienced Researchers**. Without proper instruction, students may view AI as a research shortcut or knowledge authority, failing to recognize the need for source validation, critical comparison, or triangulation. This is especially common among first-year students or those unfamiliar with scholarly research practices.

Prevention Strategies, Encouraging Integrity in the Age of AI

As AI tools become more integrated into student research habits, preventing citation-related misconduct requires proactive, skill-based instruction. These strategies focus on helping students critically engage with sources, rather than blindly accepting AI-generated references:

- **Teach Students to Cross-Check Citations**. Instruct students to verify that every source cited by AI tools exists, is accurately formatted, and truly supports the point being made. This not only prevents fabricated citations but builds foundational research habits.
- **Prohibit AI use for Final Citation Generation Unless Combined with Human Validation**. Allow students to use AI for initial searches or formatting support, but make clear that final citation lists must be manually checked using databases, academic search engines, or original source materials.
- **Include Source Verification Activities in Research Instruction**. As Brookhart (2010) emphasized, helping students develop higher-order thinking includes teaching them to assess the credibility, relevance, and accuracy of sources. Activities such as "Citation Fact-Check Challenges" or "Source Reliability Audits" can turn verification into an engaging, collaborative process.

---

3. Undetected AI Paraphrasing

Definition: AI can rewrite existing content in ways that avoid plagiarism detection but still lack originality or insight.

Example: A student pastes a classmate's summary into an AI tool and asks it to "paraphrase this to make it unique."

Risk Factors for Unethical or Unreflective AI Use

AI-generated text often does not trigger plagiarism detection systems because the language is technically "original." However, originality does not equal integrity. When students submit AI-produced work without engaging in the thinking process themselves, they bypass essential elements of learning - like analysis, reflection, and synthesis. Key risk factors include:

- **Misunderstanding What Constitutes Misconduct**. Students may believe that using AI is acceptable as long as they are not copying another human's work.
- **Assuming AI-Generated Work is Academically Valid**. If it passes through a plagiarism checker, they may assume it is acceptable to submit.
- **Lack of Emphasis on Learning Process**. Courses that only assess final products, without checkpoints, make it easier to substitute AI output for student thinking.
- **No Clear Policy or Classroom Norms**. When expectations about AI use are vague, students are more likely to make decisions based on convenience or peer behavior.

Prevention Strategies, Encouraging Integrity in the Age of AI

Rather than relying solely on detection or restriction, faculty can build integrity into the structure of assignments and classroom expectations. By designing tasks that center students' own thinking and voice, faculty help reduce the appeal - and effectiveness - of unreflective AI use. Consider the following strategies:

- **Encourage Personal Voice and Require Process Explanations**. Ask students to reflect on how they developed their ideas, what challenges they faced, and where they made key decisions. These metacognitive checkpoints make it harder to submit AI-generated work without meaningful engagement.
- **Use Assignments that Demand Localized Context or Student Reflection**. When tasks require personal experience, campus-specific examples, or community-based issues, AI tools become less relevant or convincing - pushing students to think critically and authentically.
- **Educate Students on the Distinction Between Using Language Tools and Outsourcing Thinking**. The goal is not to restrict all forms of support, but to help students recognize when they have crossed the line from receiving assistance to avoiding intellectual effort.

---

4. Unauthorized AI Assistance

Definition: When a course policy prohibits or limits AI use, any unpermitted reliance on AI may be considered misconduct.

Example: In a no-AI course, a student uses Claude to rewrite their conclusion for clarity.

Risk Factors for Unethical or Unreflective AI Use

Even when policies are in place, students may not fully understand what is permitted - or may interpret AI use as harmless, especially if the output feels like minor "editing help" rather than full authorship. Contributing factors include:

- **Perceived Similarity to Tools such as Grammarly or Spellcheck**. Students may view AI-generated rewrites as equivalent to grammar correction, especially when the tool improves phrasing without changing core ideas.
- **Lack of Clear Examples in Course Policy**. If AI use is not contextualized with examples (e.g., what is allowed for brainstorming vs. what is prohibited in final submissions), students may make assumptions that do not align with faculty expectations.
- **Social Normalization of AI Support**. With AI tools increasingly marketed as "writing assistants," students may feel justified in using them for any stage of the assignment unless told otherwise.

Prevention Strategies, Encouraging Integrity in the Age of AI

Fostering academic integrity in AI-enhanced learning environments is not about blanket bans - it is about clarity, conversation, and guided boundaries. The following strategies help students make informed, ethical choices while reinforcing institutional values.

- **Policies Must be Clear, Contextual, and Reiterated Regularly**. As outlined in *Chapter 3, Section 6*, policies should include concrete examples of acceptable and unacceptable AI use, tailored to your discipline or assignment type. Reinforcing these policies verbally during key stages of a course (e.g., before major assignments) ensures they stay top of mind.
- **Create Spaces for Ethical Gray-Area Conversations**. Students need space to ask, *"Is this okay?"* without fear of being penalized. Hosting low-stakes discussions or reflection activities around AI use encourages transparency, surfaces confusion, and helps build ethical reasoning skills.
- **Allow Certain AI Uses with Disclosure Requirements**. Rather than outlawing AI completely, consider allowing specific uses (e.g., brainstorming, grammar support) as long as students clearly disclose how and where the tool was used. This encourages metacognition and helps students learn where the line between support and substitution lies.

Understanding Student Motivation

To design meaningful interventions, faculty must first seek to understand - not just penalize - why students may misuse AI tools. Academic dishonesty is rarely driven by malice alone; more often, it is the result of stress, confusion, or misaligned expectations. By recognizing the pressures students face, faculty can respond with both structure and compassion. Common motivational drivers include:

- **Fear of Failure**. When students feel academically overwhelmed or underprepared, AI can seem like a safety net. In high-stakes contexts, the pressure to "get it right" may outweigh concern for how it is done.
- **Perceived Ubiquity**. If students believe "everyone is doing it," they may rationalize unreflective or dishonest AI use as normal, or even necessary, to compete.
- **Ambiguity**. A lack of explicit guidance about what counts as acceptable AI use can lead to accidental misuse or conflicting interpretations of policy.
- **Overconfidence in AI**. Students may assume that AI-generated answers are more accurate, sophisticated, or authoritative than their own thinking, especially in unfamiliar subjects.
- **Desire for Efficiency**. In a time-starved world, students balancing coursework, jobs, and personal responsibilities may see AI as a tool to help them "just get through" assignments.

Understanding these motivations allows faculty to shift from a reactive stance to a preventative one - creating learning environments that support clarity, confidence, and ethical decision-making.

Ethical Gray Zones: Real Student Questions

Not all AI use is clearly wrong or clearly right. Much of what students wrestle with falls into ethical gray areas - contexts where the intention may be honest, but the boundaries are blurry. Faculty should not only **expect** these questions - but they should also **welcome** them as learning opportunities. When students feel safe asking, they are more likely to engage reflectively rather than make risky assumptions in silence. Common and important student questions include:

- **"Can I Use AI to Summarize a Reading if I do not Quote it Directly?"** This raises questions about comprehension versus substitution. "*Is the student using AI to support their understanding - or to bypass it?*"
- **"What if I Use ChatGPT to Help me Brainstorm, but not Write the Actual Paper?"** A valuable conversation starter about process support versus authorship. "*What does it mean to retain intellectual ownership?*"
- **"Is it Cheating to Ask an AI to Explain a Concept I do not Understand?"** This reflects a desire to learn - but also a need to distinguish between tutoring, outsourcing, and responsible use.

Rather than responding punitively to uncertain or inappropriate AI use, faculty can take a teaching-centered approach that promotes transparency, reflection, and ethical growth. The goal is to shift the focus from catching misconduct to **building digital judgment**. Instead, faculty can:

- **Facilitate Discussions about Appropriate and Inappropriate Use**. Invite students to explore scenarios, debate edge cases, and reflect on their own assumptions. These conversations help clarify expectations while reinforcing that academic integrity is about more than just avoiding "cheating."
- **Build Reflection Prompts into Assignments**, such as:

- *"Did you use any AI tools while completing this assignment? If so, how?"*
- *"What part of the task did you complete on your own, and what did you use as support?"*
- *"How did you verify the accuracy of any AI-generated content?"*

These strategies help students internalize responsibility, normalize questions, and reduce the likelihood of unintentional misuse. Over time, they also reinforce a classroom culture where integrity is practiced, not just policed.

A powerful way to encourage ethical AI use is by prompting students to reflect on their decision-making process. For example, faculty can include prompts such as:

- *"How did you use technology while completing this work?"*
- *"What choices did you make?"*

This invites students to think critically about their workflow, clarify their intentions, and distinguish between helpful support and dependency. To reinforce the value of transparency, **faculty can model their own engagement with AI tools**. For instance, faculty might say:

- *"I used ChatGPT to help brainstorm ideas for this week's discussion, but I revised the language to reflect my own tone and priorities."*
- *"This slide graphic was generated using DALL·E, and I will explain how I guided the tool to match our course context."*

When faculty share how they use AI responsibly, they show students that ethical technology use is not about hiding - it is about **owning and articulating one's process**. This helps normalize disclosure and fosters a culture of openness and mutual trust.

Section Reflection: Reframing Academic Integrity for the AI Era

This section thoughtfully addresses the evolving landscape of academic misconduct in a world where generative AI is both widely available and poorly understood. It moves beyond punitive frameworks to examine the motivations, misunderstandings, and structural conditions that often lead students to misuse AI - not out of malice, but out of confusion, pressure, or misplaced trust. By exploring real-world scenarios, risk factors, and common gray areas, the section reveals how easily traditional definitions of cheating break down when confronted with AI tools that blur the line between assistance and authorship.

Importantly, the section does not advocate for surveillance or blanket bans, but instead calls for proactive, trust-building strategies - clear policies, transparent conversations, reflective prompts, and assignment designs that emphasize process, voice, and ethical reasoning. Faculty are encouraged to model responsible AI use, foster metacognitive awareness, and create spaces where questions about integrity are welcomed, not punished. In doing so, educators reframe misconduct prevention as a form of pedagogy - one rooted in clarity, compassion, and the shared goal of cultivating digital judgment. This shift transforms integrity from a set of rules into a set of habits, empowering students to navigate AI with confidence, responsibility, and care.

Section 6: The Human-AI Partnership - Redefining Originality and Contribution

---

Generative AI is reshaping foundational concepts in education - including one of its most cherished values: originality. As tools such as ChatGPT, Claude, and Gemini increasingly assist students with brainstorming, outlining, translating, and even drafting, educators are faced with a complex question: *"**What does it mean to be original when students are working in partnership with intelligent systems?**"* Traditional definitions of authorship - centered on solitary effort, unassisted output, and a single voice - may no longer reflect the realities of how thinking, writing, and problem-solving happen in digital environments.

Rather than resisting this shift, faculty have the opportunity to **reframe originality** not as the absence of assistance, but as a **practice of transparency, transformation, and intellectual ownership**. In this new model, originality is not compromised by the use of tools - it is redefined by the quality of decisions students make, the reflections they offer, and the evidence of their thinking behind the final product.

This section explores how to evaluate student work when digital assistance is common - but human reasoning, curiosity, and judgment must remain central. It offers strategies for designing assignments, building rubrics, and framing feedback in ways that uphold academic integrity without clinging to outdated notions of authorship. Because in the AI era, the question is not simply ***"Did the student use a tool?"*** but rather: ***"How did they use it, and what did they learn along the way?"***

The Myth of Pure Originality

Originality in academia has long been equated with **solitary effort** - the idea that to be truly original, a student must work independently, free from outside influence. But this view is increasingly outdated - and, in practice, unrealistic. Students collaborate with peers, learn from exemplars, draw on mentor feedback, and make use of a growing array of digital tools. The introduction of AI does not mark a sudden rupture; rather, it **amplifies a long-standing truth**: all academic work is scaffolded by prior knowledge, social interaction, and shared resources (Brookhart, 2010).

This mirrors what happens in the professional world. Writers work with editors, designers use templates and stock assets, and researchers rely on statistical software, citation managers, and collaborative platforms. In each of these domains, the **use of tools is not seen as a weakness**, but as part of a thoughtful, layered process. What matters is not the absence of assistance, but the quality of the human decisions - what is kept, what is changed, what is questioned. As Selwyn (2021) argued, the integrity of the work lies not in whether a tool was used, but in how responsibly and transparently it was used in the service of the task.

What Is "Original" in AI-Augmented Work?

In an AI-augmented learning environment, we must move beyond narrow definitions of originality that focus solely on **who typed the words**. Instead, originality should be redefined to reflect the intellectual presence of the student - how they engage with content, tools, and ideas. Generative AI may assist with phrasing, structure, or initial drafts, but it cannot substitute for the cognitive and ethical work that defines true academic contribution. In this context, originality should center on:

- **The Intentional Choices a Student Makes**. *"What prompts were used? What content was accepted, revised, or rejected?"* Originality emerges in the reasoning behind these decisions.
- **The Transformative Thinking Applied to Ideas**. Whether refining AI-generated content or building from a peer conversation, students should demonstrate how they have interpreted, challenged, or expanded on existing input.
- **The Ethical Transparency About How and Why Tools were Used**. Disclosing AI involvement is not a confession - it is a marker of academic maturity and reflective judgment.
- **The Evidence of Intellectual Ownership and Reflection**. Through process notes, reflections, or revisions, students show not just what they produced, but how they thought through it.

This reframed definition of originality does not lower the bar - it raises it. It asks students to engage more deeply with their process, to think critically about their tools, and to claim their role as the architects of meaning in an AI-rich world. **Authentic learning in the AI era must focus less on isolated output and more on transparency, the learner's ability to take ownership and responsibility, and the intentional navigation of digital tools** - where originality is demonstrated through ethical and reflective engagement, not just authorship alone (Han, 2025).

A Continuum of Human–AI Collaboration

To navigate the evolving role of generative AI in education, it is helpful for both faculty and students to visualize AI use as a **continuum of support** - a progression from minimal assistance to near-total dependence. This continuum clarifies **how much AI is assisting the student**, and how that support **impacts the student's ownership, effort, and judgment**.

The goal is not to ban all assistance, but to ensure that AI supports learning **without replacing it**. Framing AI use this way helps make decisions transparent, guide reflection, and shape policies that promote integrity and cognitive engagement.

A Continuum of Human-AI Collaboration: From Minimal AI Support to Full Substitution

Here is one way to visualize the continuum:

- **Minimal AI Support (AI as Tool)**

    - **Who is Supporting Whom**? The student is doing the thinking; AI assists with surface-level mechanics.
    - **Examples**. Grammar correction, spellcheck, and rewording individual sentences.
    - **Educational Impact**. No major influence on the student's thought process.
    - **Faculty Stance**. Generally permitted without disclosure.
- **Moderate AI Support (AI as Learning Scaffold)**
    - **Who is Supporting Whom**? The student drives the thinking; AI scaffolds ideas or structure.
    - **Examples:** Brainstorming with AI, asking for an outline, requesting clarification of a concept.
    - **Educational Impact**. Can support metacognition, but still preserves student authorship.
    - **Faculty Stance**. Allowed with disclosure; useful for early-stage thinking.
- **Substantive AI Support (AI as Writing Assistant)**
    - **Who is Supporting Whom**? AI begins shaping the student's expression; the student is still involved.
    - **Examples**. Using AI to rewrite a draft for tone or organization, smoothing transitions, and rephrasing large blocks of text.
    - **Educational Impact**. Risks diluting the student voice or masking gaps in understanding.
    - **Faculty Stance**. Requires careful boundaries and reflection.
- **Heavy AI Support (AI as Content Generator)**
    - **Who is Supporting Whom**? AI does most of the composition; the student edits or lightly modifies.
    - **Examples**. Asking AI to write an essay draft based on a prompt, then editing and submitting.
    - **Educational Impact**. Student judgment and originality are significantly reduced.
    - **Faculty Stance**. Likely discouraged or prohibited unless explicitly built into the assignment design.
- **AI Substitution (AI as Surrogate)**
    - **Who is Supporting Whom**? Student relies almost entirely on AI; little to no active intellectual contribution.
    - **Examples**. Submitting an AI-generated response with minimal revision or oversight.
    - **Educational Impact**. Undermines learning outcomes and violates academic integrity.
    - **Faculty Stance**. Typically prohibited under academic honesty policies.

Why This Matters

When students - and faculty - can identify **how AI is supporting the learner**, they can make more informed, ethical, and pedagogically sound decisions. This continuum also helps distinguish between **supporting learning** and **short-circuiting it**. Assignments and policies can then be built not just around what tools are used, but **how and why** they are used.

Professional Analogies: Learning from Industry

Understanding how professionals use AI across fields can help faculty and students reframe its educational role - not as a shortcut, but as a **collaborative tool**. These analogies ground AI use in real-world expectations, where tools assist - but never replace - human insight, creativity, and accountability.

The following analogies show that **ethical AI use is already embedded in professional practice**. The classroom challenge is not preventing tool use - it is **teaching students to use tools reflectively, responsibly, and with intellectual clarity**.

---

1. Journalism

Journalists increasingly use AI to draft headlines, summarize press releases, or generate bullet points for background research. However, **editorial judgment** - fact-checking, narrative framing, tone selection, and source validation - remains firmly in human hands.

Classroom Insights that Should be Realized from Journalism. Students may use AI to generate early drafts or summarize complex texts, but **conceptual analysis, argument structure, and evidence selection must reflect the student's voice and reasoning**.

---

2. Graphic Design

Professionals in design fields often rely on tools such as Canva, Adobe Firefly, or Midjourney for inspiration, templates, or asset generation. Yet true originality lies in how elements are arranged, **how visual choices reflect intent**, and how the message is crafted for the intended audience.

Classroom Insights that Should be Realized from Graphic Design. When students submit multimedia or visual work aided by AI, evaluation should focus on **storytelling, audience alignment, interpretive choices, and originality of execution** - not just production quality.

---

3. Research and Programming

Researchers regularly use AI tools and statistical software to generate graphs, model outputs, or visualize data trends. Programmers use GitHub Copilot or ChatGPT to generate boilerplate code or suggest function names. However, in both cases, the **interpretation of output, logical structure, debugging, and innovation** remain human responsibilities.

Classroom Insights that Should be Realized from Research and Programming. In data, STEM, or computing courses, AI use should be permitted for repetitive or scaffolding tasks - **but students must explain the rationale behind methods, validate outputs, and annotate decisions** to demonstrate ownership.

These analogies demonstrate that **ethical AI use is not futuristic** - it is **already a standard in many professional domains**. From journalism to programming, success depends not on avoiding tools, but on **how thoughtfully humans work alongside them**. The classroom challenge, then, is not about preventing AI use altogether - it is about equipping students to engage with these tools **reflectively, responsibly, and with intellectual clarity**. By doing so, educators help students build habits of transparency, critical evaluation, and creative decision-making that will serve them far beyond the walls of any single course.

How to Teach Originality in an AI-Aware Classroom

In AI-augmented classrooms, teaching originality is no longer about preventing tool use - it is about **guiding students to make thoughtful, ethical, and creative decisions with tools**. To foster meaningful originality in this new landscape, faculty must explicitly teach the **skills, habits, and awareness** that help students retain ownership of their thinking - even when digital assistance is involved. Here is what students need to learn to demonstrate true originality in an AI-aware environment:

---

1. Metacognitive Awareness of Process

Students must be taught to **reflect on how they approach a task** - including when and why they choose to use AI tools. Faculty should:

- Assign brief process reflections or tool-use logs.
- Prompt students to explain how their ideas evolved through drafts and iterations.
- Emphasize that originality involves **how** they think, not just **what** they write.

---

2. Intellectual Decision-Making

Originality stems from the ability to make purposeful, content-driven decisions. Students need support in:

- Distinguishing between AI-generated suggestions and their own analytical contributions.
- Evaluating AI outputs critically rather than accepting them at face value.
- Choosing what to keep, revise, reject, or expand - and articulating why.

---

3. Ethical Transparency

Students should learn that originality includes being honest about their process. Faculty should:

- Require AI-use disclosures in writing assignments or presentations.
- Normalize conversations around appropriate and inappropriate tool use.
- Reinforce that transparency is not a confession - it is a skill.

4. Transformative Thinking

Rather than simply summarizing or remixing ideas, students must be challenged to transform them. That means:

- Making personal, creative, or disciplinary connections.
- Applying course concepts to unfamiliar contexts.
- Asking new questions that go beyond what AI can predict or reproduce.

5. Tool Fluency with Boundaries

Students must know how to use AI tools **as collaborators**, not substitutes. Educators should:

- Teach prompt design, result evaluation, and verification techniques.
- Clarify which AI uses are permitted in each assignment - and why.
- Encourage tool use during ideation or revision stages, not for full substitution.

When students are taught to combine **transparency, discernment, and creativity**, originality becomes visible not just in the final product - but in the process itself. As Han (2025) emphasized, **in the age of generative AI, originality is no longer about isolation - it is about responsibility, reflection, and intentional human contribution**.

Section Reflection: Reclaiming Originality Through Ethical Human-AI Collaboration

This section offers a timely and profound reframing of originality for the AI era, encouraging educators to move beyond outdated definitions that equate unassisted output with intellectual merit. As students increasingly engage with AI tools for brainstorming, drafting, and revising, the challenge is no longer to prevent tool use, but to cultivate discernment, reflection, and transparent authorship. Originality, this section argues, is not compromised by digital assistance - it is demonstrated through the **quality** of a student's engagement with those tools, the intentional decisions they make, and the clarity with which they articulate their process.

By presenting a continuum of AI support and drawing on professional analogies from journalism, design, and programming, the section situates AI use as a norm in both academic and real-world contexts. Educators are encouraged to teach students how to think **with** AI - critically, ethically, and creatively - rather than delegating thought to it. Strategies such as process reflections, AI-use disclosures, and assignments requiring transformative thinking ensure that human contribution remains central.

Ultimately, this section reframes originality not as the absence of assistance, but as **ownership of thinking**. It empowers faculty to foster classrooms where students are not penalized for using tools, but are recognized for using them responsibly - and where originality is defined by intention, insight, and ethical presence in the learning process.

Section 7: Teaching Students to Think Critically About AI

As AI tools become more integrated into education, workplaces, and everyday decision-making, it is not enough to teach students **how** to use AI. We must also teach them to think critically **about** AI. That means helping students move beyond efficiency, novelty, or convenience and toward **analysis, skepticism, and inquiry**.

Generative AI systems are not neutral. They are built on human data, shaped by commercial incentives, and embedded with limitations, assumptions, and biases. For students to engage responsibly in an AI-enhanced world, they need to become **AI-literate thinkers** - capable of asking hard questions about how these tools operate, what they omit, and how they shape understanding (Hagerty & Rubinov, 2019).

This section explores how faculty can intentionally embed **critical AI literacy** into courses across disciplines - not as an add-on, but as a vital part of helping students navigate an AI-enhanced world. The goal is to develop students' **discernment** (knowing when and how to use AI), **ethical awareness** (understanding the implications of AI use), and **agency** (making informed, responsible choices). Whether in the humanities, STEM, social sciences, or the arts, educators can equip learners to think **with** AI - without outsourcing their curiosity, creativity, or judgment.

Why Critical Thinking About AI Matters

As generative AI tools become deeply integrated into students' writing, research, and decision-making processes, the need to **teach critical engagement with AI-generated content** has never been more urgent. These systems can produce language that appears fluent and authoritative - yet their outputs often **lack accuracy, context, or ethical reflection**. Key concerns include:

- **AI Outputs Often Sound Confident - Even When They are Wrong.** Because language models are optimized for fluency, not truth, they can generate factually incorrect or misleading information with a persuasive tone (Hagerty & Rubinov, 2019).
- **Models May Reflect or Amplify Social, Cultural, or Racial Bias.** AI systems inherit the biases of their training data, sometimes subtly reinforcing stereotypes or privileging dominant perspectives (Birhane et al., 2022).
- **Responses are Shaped by Training Data, Prompt Design, and System Limitations.** The apparent neutrality of AI output masks the influence of **who** built the model, **what** data it was trained on, and **how** the user frames a prompt (Weidinger et al., 2022).
- **Students May Mistake Fluency for Truth.** A well-structured paragraph or confident tone can lead users - especially novices - to assume credibility without verification.

To safeguard academic integrity, civic reasoning, and ethical decision-making, students must be taught to engage with AI analytically. That means questioning outputs, verifying claims, recognizing limitations, and reflecting on ethical implications. Critical AI literacy is not just a technical skill - it is a form of ethical and epistemological empowerment in an increasingly automated world (Birhane et al., 2022).

Teaching Strategies for Critical AI Thinking

---

1. Compare Human vs. AI-Generated Work

Ask students to evaluate two pieces of writing - one produced by a human and one by an AI - and reflect on which is stronger and why.

Example Assignment: Side-by-Side Analysis (Writing or Communication)

- *Provide students with two brief position papers on climate policy. One is written by a former policy advisor; the other is generated by ChatGPT.*

Prompt Students To:

- *Identify strengths and weaknesses in each response.*
- *Evaluate clarity, originality, logic, and emotional resonance.*
- *Reflect on which they find more convincing and why.*

Learning Outcome: Students develop skills to distinguish between **polished language and substantive insight**, a vital distinction in academic writing and public discourse (Lang, 2013).

---

2. Fact-Check AI Responses

Have students test AI-generated outputs for **accuracy, citation validity, and logical consistency**.

Example Assignment: AI Fact-Checking Lab (Research or STEM Course)

- *Students ask an AI tool a complex question (e.g., "Explain how CRISPR works in gene editing").*

Then They:

- *Verify claims against scholarly sources.*
- *Identify inaccuracies, missing nuance, or logical flaws.*
- *Write a paragraph summarizing their findings.*

Learning Outcome: Students learn that **credibility must be earned**, not assumed, and they begin to see AI as **a draft - not a destination** (Brookhart, 2010).

---

3. Analyze Prompt Influence on Output

Show how small changes in phrasing can **shape AI responses dramatically** - and why this matters.

Example Assignment: Prompt Tuning Workshop (Any Discipline)

- *Students create three different prompts to explore the concept of "justice."*

For Example:

- *"Define justice in one sentence."*
- *"Explain how justice varies across cultures."*
- *"Debate whether justice is possible without equality." After generating responses, they compare tone, depth, and focus.*

Reflection Questions:

- *"How did your prompt influence the response?"*
- *"Which version produced the most nuanced answer, and why?"*
- *"What might be the dangers of poorly phrased prompts?"*

Learning Outcome: Students learn **metacognition** and a deeper understanding of AI's limitations in **interpretive reasoning** (Brookhart, 2010).

---

4. Explore Bias and Ethical Implications

Use case studies or simulations to expose students to **bias in AI outputs** and provoke ethical reflection.

Example Case Study: Hiring Discrimination and AI

- *Students analyze reports on biased hiring decisions made by AI resume screening tools.*

Discussion Questions Include:

- *"How did the bias arise?"*
- *"Who is accountable for correcting it?"*
- *"What regulatory or ethical frameworks are needed?"*

Extension Activity:

- *Have students test bias in generative tools by prompting for images or stories with stereotyped inputs (e.g., "Draw a CEO," "Describe a nurse").*

Learning Outcome: Students see AI as **a reflection of societal bias**, not a neutral actor, and practice **ethical critique** (Selwyn, 2021).

---

5. Create Ethical Reflection Assignments

Encourage students to articulate **how they use AI, what they learned, and what they questioned**.

Example Assignment: AI Use and Ethics Reflection

- *"Describe a recent task for which you used an AI tool. What did the tool do well? What did it miss or misunderstand? Would you use it again - and if so, how differently?"*

Discussion Questions Include:

- *Transparency of tool use.*
- *Evaluation of reliability.*
- *Thoughtfulness about ethical boundaries.*

Learning Outcome: Students practice **intellectual honesty**, build **AI fluency**, and become **ethical stewards** of technology - not just consumers (Brookhart, 2010).

Building a Culture of AI Inquiry Across Disciplines

Critical AI literacy is not the sole domain of computer science. As generative AI increasingly influences how we write, design, analyze, and make decisions, every academic field has a stake in preparing students to engage thoughtfully and ethically with intelligent systems. Each discipline brings a unique lens to the conversation:

- **Humanities**. *"What does authorship mean in the age of machine-generated text?"* As Fenwick and Jurcys (2023) argued, AI challenges longstanding assumptions about originality, interpretation, and the human voice in writing and storytelling.
- **STEM**. *"Can we trust AI-generated scientific abstracts or code?"* Research by Stokel-Walker (2023) highlighted how AI-generated science content may appear valid but lacks the methodological depth or reproducibility required for rigor.
- **Social Sciences**. *"How do algorithms reinforce systemic inequality?"* Noble's (2018) work revealed how search engines and recommender systems can reproduce racial and gender bias - inviting social science students to interrogate the hidden values behind algorithms.
- **Arts and Design**. *"How do we define creativity when machines can imitate style?"* McCormack et al. (2019) explored how AI-generated art blurs the line between creative output and imitation, pushing students to reconsider what counts as authorship, inspiration, or aesthetic innovation

Rather than viewing AI integration as a **disruption**, faculty should approach it as a **realignment** - an opportunity to anchor disciplinary knowledge in the ethical, creative, and epistemological questions shaping the 21st century. By collaborating across departments, educators can help students develop not just technical fluency, but the **critical agency** needed to navigate a world increasingly co-authored by machines.

Section Reflection: Cultivating Critical AI Literacy as a Core Educational Priority

This section repositions AI not simply as a tool to be used, but as a subject to be interrogated - calling on educators to develop students' ability to question, critique, and ethically engage with generative systems. As AI becomes a ubiquitous influence in academic and professional life, critical thinking about **how** AI works, **what** it produces, and **why** it matters becomes a foundational skill across disciplines. Rather than treating AI literacy as a technical add-on, this section argues for its integration into the heart of curriculum - where students compare human and AI work, fact-check outputs, explore bias, reflect on ethical boundaries, and evaluate how prompts shape meaning.

Importantly, the section provides concrete, adaptable strategies that emphasize discernment over automation and reflection over convenience. By embedding these practices across humanities, STEM, social sciences, and the arts, educators help students build intellectual independence, resist passive consumption, and approach AI as a co-constructed system - not a neutral authority. In doing so, they empower students to become thoughtful digital citizens who understand that fluency without scrutiny is not literacy at all. This shift - from teaching how to use AI to teaching how to **think** about AI - fosters ethical reasoning, creative agency, and long-term integrity in an AI-shaped world.

Section 8: Staying Current - Strategies for Lifelong AI Learning

---

The pace of generative AI development is unprecedented. In just a few years, tools such as ChatGPT, Gemini, Claude, Midjourney, and Perplexity have gone from experimental novelties to widely used platforms in classrooms, workplaces, and research labs. New capabilities are added monthly. Interfaces change. New ethical dilemmas emerge. In such a rapidly evolving environment, faculty face a core challenge: **how to stay informed without being overwhelmed**.

The answer lies not in mastering every tool or reading every paper but in cultivating a **sustainable mindset of lifelong AI learning**. This final section offers **practical strategies to help educators stay current, agile, and confident** - not by chasing the latest tech trends, but by embedding AI learning into their personal and professional rhythms.

The Goal: Agility, Not Exhaustion

Let us be clear: you **do not** need to become an AI expert to guide students effectively in this new era of education. You do not need to code, fine-tune models, or understand every algorithmic detail. What you **do** need is:

- **Conceptual Clarity**. A basic understanding of how generative AI tools function and where their limits lie.
- **Pedagogical Judgment**. The ability to align AI use (or restriction) with learning goals, disciplinary norms, and academic integrity.

- **Ethical Grounding**. A commitment to modeling transparency, fairness, and responsible technology use.
- **Curiosity and Adaptability**. A willingness to learn alongside your students and adjust as the tools evolve (Brookhart, 2010; Selwyn, 2021)

Individual Strategies for Ongoing AI Literacy

---

1. Subscribe to a Few Curated Newsletters

Well-designed newsletters offer bite-sized, easily digestible updates that keep readers informed without overwhelming their inbox. When curated thoughtfully, they distill key insights, resources, or announcements into a quick, accessible format - perfect for busy educators who want to stay current without sorting through information overload. The best newsletters balance brevity with value, making each message feel timely, relevant, and worth the click.

Recommended Sources:

- ***The Algorithm – MIT Technology Review***

Focus: AI trends, ethics, breakthroughs, and policy.

Why it is useful: Written for a general but informed audience, *The Algorithm* offers weekly insights into how AI is shaping the world - from scientific advances to societal implications. It is well-curated, succinct, and often includes expert commentary and links to deeper readings.

- ***Import AI – By Jack Clark***

Focus: Research, industry developments, and implications of advanced AI.

Why it is useful: Especially valuable for educators and researchers, this newsletter breaks down recent papers, policy shifts, and model developments in a way that is both accessible and analytically sharp. Clark often includes reflections on long-term risks, governance, and equity.

- ***The Rundown AI***

Focus: Daily summaries of major AI announcements, tools, and use cases.

Why it is useful: Ideal for staying up-to-date with fast-moving developments in generative AI (like ChatGPT, Claude, or Gemini), this newsletter delivers short, actionable updates with a practical edge - great for faculty integrating AI into teaching.

Faculty Habit Tip: Schedule time each **Friday morning or Monday afternoon** to scan headlines or read one deep dive.

---

2. Join a Teaching and Technology Community

Faculty do not need to explore AI in isolation. In fact, some of the most meaningful insights emerge from interdisciplinary conversations, where diverse perspectives challenge assumptions and enrich practice. A literature professor might learn from a computer scientist how AI handles language, while a sociologist might raise questions about bias and equity that reshape how a business course integrates generative tools. These cross-disciplinary dialogues help translate AI from a technical tool into a pedagogical resource - grounded in values, relevance, and shared learning goals.

Example: Interdisciplinary Faculty Learning Communities (FLCs)

- *A writing professor partners with a computer science colleague to co-host monthly "AI teaching huddles." They compare notes on student tool use, prompt design, and ethical conversations across disciplines.*

Benefit: You learn not just from AI updates - but from **how others are implementing them in real time**.

---

3. Set a Monthly "Experimentation Hour"

Schedule personal experimentation for one hour a month for AI play and discovery.

Example:

- *First Monday of the month, 12–1 pm, try a new tool (e.g., Claude, Scite.ai, DALL·E).*
- *Ask it a teaching-related question.*
- ***Reflect:** "Could this be helpful to my students or for course design?"*

You do not need to use every feature or master every AI tool you encounter. The goal is not comprehensive expertise - it is **comfort with exploration**. Staying familiar enough to ask good questions, model responsible use, and lead with curiosity is what matters most. When faculty approach AI with openness rather than pressure, they create space for students to do the same. Curiosity - not perfection - is the foundation of meaningful digital teaching and learning.

---

4. Follow Key Thought Leaders or Education Communities on Social Media or YouTube

Examples:

- ***Ethan Mollick**. Known for approachable AI in education content.*
- ***Dr. Ruha Benjamin**. She emphasizes the intersection of ethnicity, justice, and technology.*
- ***Edutopia and EDUCAUSE**. Provides faculty-focused, practical guidance.*

These thought leaders or education communities offer **low-friction, high-value updates** on how AI is shaping teaching and learning. Designed to fit into busy faculty schedules, they deliver insights in digestible formats that spark reflection without demanding large time investments. Over time, they build awareness, confidence, and a shared vocabulary around AI-enhanced pedagogy.

Institutional Strategies for Faculty AI Development

1. Create Peer-Led Learning Cohorts

Faculty often learn best from one another - through shared stories, trial-and-error, and practical wisdom that cannot always be found in formal training. Peer-led communities foster trust, normalize experimentation, and create a safe space to ask questions, share missteps, and celebrate breakthroughs. When educators see their colleagues engaging with AI tools thoughtfully and imperfectly, it reduces fear and builds collective confidence. These communities transform uncertainty into collaboration and position faculty not just as adopters of technology, but as co-creators of its responsible use in education.

Example: AI Explorers Group

- *A campus teaching center launches a semester-long group of 6–8 faculty. Each week, a different member demos how they have used AI in their course - successes, failures, and takeaways.*

Outcomes: When institutions support faculty collaboration around AI - through time, conversation, and experimentation - the result is more than technical skill. It fosters **trust** among colleagues, builds **accountability** around ethical use, and encourages **locally relevant practice-sharing** that feels grounded in real teaching contexts. These outcomes create a foundation for sustained community-driven innovation in an AI-enhanced educational landscape.

2. Launch AI Teaching Fellowships or Microgrants

Institutions should provide faculty with **dedicated time, recognition, or funding** to explore and experiment with AI tools in their teaching and research. Without space to reflect, test, and iterate, meaningful innovation is difficult to sustain. Whether through course release, mini-grants, teaching fellowships, or public recognition of AI-informed pedagogical work, supporting faculty experimentation signals that exploration is not only permitted - but valued. This investment cultivates a culture of learning, curiosity, and shared advancement that benefits both educators and students.

Example:

- *Faculty apply for a $1,000 microgrant to redesign an assignment or module that embeds AI literacy. Results are shared in a faculty showcase or published online.*

Outcomes: This kind of support encourages **practical innovation** in the classroom, especially when connected to the **Scholarship of Teaching and Learning (SoTL)**. When faculty are given the time and resources to explore AI meaningfully - and to document and reflect on their findings - they contribute not just to improved practice, but to the broader academic conversation on how teaching evolves alongside emerging technologies. It transforms experimentation into inquiry, and inquiry into impact.

3. Embed AI Inquiry into Existing Personal Development Structures

Rather than launching entirely new initiatives, institutions can **integrate AI-related topics into existing faculty development days, orientations, or teaching and learning workshops**. Embedding these conversations within established structures lowers the barrier to participation, normalizes AI as part of the broader pedagogical landscape, and reaches a wider range of faculty. This approach encourages sustainable engagement by building on what already works - while gently introducing faculty to the evolving opportunities and challenges of teaching in the AI era.

Examples:

- *"How to Read an AI Essay: Teaching Beyond the Output"*
- *"Prompting for Pedagogy: Using AI to Design Assignments"*
- *"AI and Academic Integrity: A New Conversation"*

Outcomes: This approach helps **mainstream AI learning**, embedding it into the daily rhythms of academic life rather than isolating it as a niche interest or a tech-only concern. By positioning AI as a shared pedagogical and ethical topic - not just a technological one - institutions signal that all faculty, regardless of discipline or digital expertise, have a role to play in shaping its responsible use. This fosters campus-wide dialogue, reduces intimidation, and promotes a more inclusive culture of innovation.

---

4. Support Dynamic Syllabus Language and Policy Templates

Faculty often avoid creating or enforcing AI policies simply because they are unsure how to write them - or what should even be included. Uncertainty around tone, scope, or institutional alignment can lead to inaction. Institutions can support faculty by providing clear, adaptable templates; sample syllabus language; and discipline-specific examples that reflect both academic integrity and evolving AI use cases. Offering workshops, drop-in consultations, or collaborative policy-writing sessions also empowers faculty to draft policies with confidence, consistency, and pedagogical purpose - without having to start from scratch. Support should include:

- **Policy templates with examples** of disclosure language.
- **Syllabus addenda** with guidance on acceptable AI use.
- **Student-facing FAQs** that clarify norms, expectations, and rights.

When AI policies are both **adaptive and accessible**, more faculty feel confident engaging with them - not just as compliance tools, but as meaningful extensions of their teaching values. Clear, flexible language helps faculty tailor policies to their course context, while avoiding overly rigid rules that may quickly become outdated. This balance encourages participation, reduces anxiety, and fosters a shared sense of ownership over how AI is integrated into the academic experience (Lang, 2013).

Model the Mindset You Want Students to Adopt

Perhaps the most powerful thing faculty can do in the AI era is to **model responsible adaptability** - not having all the answers, but showing a willingness to learn, reflect, and adjust in real time. That means saying things like:

- *"This tool is new to me too - let us figure it out together."*
- *"I am still learning how to use AI responsibly, and I would love to hear how you are thinking about it."*
- *"Here is what I allow in this class - and here is why."*
- *"If something feels unclear or uncomfortable, let us talk about it."*

Students do not need their faculty to have perfect answers - **they need to witness what it looks like when thoughtful people navigate complexity** with both curiosity and caution. In a world where tools, norms, and expectations are shifting rapidly, the most powerful lesson faculty can offer is how to ask good questions, make principled choices, and revise one's thinking when needed. Modeling this kind of intellectual humility and adaptive leadership teaches students not just about AI, but about how to live and learn responsibly.

Section Reflection: Embracing Lifelong AI Learning with Agility and Purpose

This final section offers a reassuring and actionable roadmap for faculty navigating the ever-evolving landscape of generative AI. Rather than demanding expertise or exhaustive tool mastery, it emphasizes **mindset over mastery** - encouraging curiosity, agility, and ethical intentionality as the hallmarks of responsible AI engagement. The core message is empowering: faculty do not need to keep up with every new development to stay relevant - they need sustainable habits, trusted networks, and reflective routines that support **lifelong learning** in an AI-rich world.

By offering both individual strategies (like subscribing to curated newsletters, setting up experimentation hours, and joining interdisciplinary conversations) and institutional supports (such as AI-focused learning communities, microgrants, and adaptable policy templates), the section models a culture of shared responsibility. It highlights how AI fluency grows best through collaborative exploration and thoughtful reflection - not technical perfection.

Crucially, this section also underscores the importance of **modeling the mindset** we hope to instill in students: a willingness to ask hard questions, adjust when necessary, and lead with values over novelty. By doing so, educators transform uncertainty into opportunity, fostering not just digital competence but principled confidence - for themselves and the learners they guide. In a time of accelerating change, this approach makes staying current not only feasible - but deeply meaningful.

Chapter 4 Conclusion: Creativity, Voice, and Human Presence in the Age of Generative AI

Chapter 4 has explored one of the most urgent pedagogical challenges of the AI era: how to preserve and expand student creativity, authorship, and originality when machines can now produce fluent text, visual media, and structured argumentation on demand. Rather than framing AI as a threat to human expression, the chapter repositions it as an invitation to deeper pedagogical design - where creative divergence, critical remix, and intellectual agency are intentionally cultivated across disciplines.

Section 1 introduced the foundational idea that **creative work must not be replaced by AI, but redefined through it**. Faculty are not competing with generative tools; they are tasked with creating learning environments that reward process over polish, risk over repetition, and insight over imitation. This theme was developed further in **Section 2**, which examined how **AI-enhanced creative work** can be used to surface reflection and divergence. By encouraging students to critique, revise, or annotate machine-generated outputs, educators help them develop **creative judgment** - the capacity to identify gaps, insert voice, and reclaim authorship.

In **Section 3**, **designing for failure and iteration** was presented as a core strategy for AI-era creativity. Assignments that build in ambiguity, remix, and play help students become more resilient and imaginative, even as AI tools flatten originality into prediction. **Section 4** explored **multimodal creativity**, where AI outputs are used as raw material to prompt audio, visual, spatial, or performative responses - ensuring that learning is not confined to linguistic mimicry but extends across expressive domains.

The importance of faculty modeling was reinforced in **Section 5**, where faculty were shown to influence not just assignment structure but classroom culture. Faculty who share their own iterative processes - what they generate with AI, what they discard, and why - teach students that creativity is not fast or perfect; it is **reflective, relational, and courageous**. **Section 6** built on this idea by showing how **creative mentorship** fosters trust, ownership, and experimentation. When mentors invite students to take aesthetic or intellectual risks - even when those risks lead to failure - they open space for genuine exploration.

Section 7 extended creativity into **assessment design**, offering rubrics that reward critical remixing, ethical boundary-setting, and process-based documentation. Here, creativity becomes more than expression - it becomes a **form of ethical authorship**. And in **Section 8**, this work was scaled to the institutional level. It argued that campuses must recognize and resource creativity in the AI era - not just through tech tools or policy statements, but by validating reflection, supporting cross-disciplinary partnerships, and protecting space for ambiguity, play, and non-instrumental learning.

Taken together, the eight sections converge on a core conclusion: **in the age of generative AI, human creativity must be taught as a practice of intentional difference**. Faculty must equip students not merely to produce novel content, but to **recognize when AI defaults are too safe, too narrow, or too hollow - and to push past them**. This is not only a creative act - it is a civic one.

The central theme that emerges from Chapter 4 is this: **originality in the AI era is no longer defined by starting from scratch, but by knowing when - and how - to break from the machine.** Faculty who center creative divergence are not just preserving human presence in education; they are preparing students to author a future in which meaning, not mimicry, is the measure of success.

Chapter 5: Guiding Research in the Age of Augmented Thinking

AI now supports nearly every stage of the research process - from refining a research question and summarizing literature, to generating code, visualizing data, and even drafting portions of manuscripts. As these tools become embedded in student workflows, faculty must adapt their supervisory role to account for a new kind of researcher: one who works **with** AI, not simply around it.

This does not mean lowering standards - it means **reframing mentorship** to help students remain intellectually responsible, methodologically rigorous, and ethically grounded. Faculty must learn how to guide students who are not merely consumers of AI output, but **co-researchers in dialogue with intelligent systems**.

This chapter outlines practical strategies for mentoring:

- **Literature reviews** where AI tools summarize or recommend sources.
- **Methodologies** that involve AI-assisted design, data collection, or coding.
- **Analysis and writing** where AI contributes structure or synthesis.

The goal is to embrace AI's potential **without surrendering scholarly rigor or human insight**. In this new landscape, the role of the faculty advisor becomes even more vital - not to gatekeep technology, but to **cultivate judgment, originality, and reflective research practice** in the presence of technology.

Section 1: Reframing Research - From Solo Discovery to Human–AI Collaboration

---

For generations, academic research has been rooted in the model of **independent inquiry**. Students were taught to identify questions, collect sources, evaluate data, and synthesize findings through a solitary, labor-intensive process - one that reinforced intellectual ownership through individual effort. In many ways, this model was designed to ensure academic rigor, traceable methodology, and original contribution.

But in the **age of AI**, this paradigm is rapidly evolving. Tools such as ChatGPT, Elicit, Scite, and Claude are now capable of **summarizing literature, generating hypotheses, organizing outlines, refining language, and suggesting citation structures** - all within minutes. The image of the lone scholar working quietly in a library is giving way to a new reality: **research as a human–machine partnership** (Selwyn, 2021).

To respond to this shift, faculty must reframe research not as something that AI threatens - but as a **process that is augmented by AI**, provided students maintain control over their thinking and methodological rigor. This new model requires **guidance, reflection, and supervision**, not prohibition.

From Isolation to Augmentation: Defining "Augmented Thinking"

Augmented thinking refers to the use of AI tools to **enhance - but not replace** - critical reasoning, judgment, and interpretation. The goal is not to outsource intellectual work, but to amplify human cognition through computational assistance. As Reiss (2021) explained, AI can serve as a cognitive partner in tasks such as idea generation, summarization, or code scaffolding, while leaving analysis, ethical reasoning, and synthesis in the hands of the human researcher.

Key Traits of Augmented Thinking

- **AI assists with routine or repetitive tasks**, such as reformatting references, suggesting synonyms, or summarizing long texts.
- **The human researcher makes interpretive, ethical, and methodological decisions** - from choosing what tools to use, to validating outputs, to contextualizing findings.
- **There is transparency about tool use and clear ownership of intellectual contributions**, ensuring that AI is acknowledged but does not obscure human insight (Han, 2025).

By teaching students to use AI in ways that **expand - not eclipse - their thinking**, educators help cultivate not only **technological fluency**, but also **academic integrity and reflective agency**. Students must be equipped to engage with AI tools critically, transparently, and ethically - treating them not as shortcuts, but as opportunities to develop thoughtful and responsible scholarly practice.

Reframing Research Stages with Human–AI Collaboration

1. Topic Selection and Idea Refinement

AI can support early-stage research by helping students **explore topic ideas**, identify trends, and brainstorm directions.

Example: Exploratory Prompt in ChatGPT

- *"List five emerging research topics related to renewable energy policy in the Global South."*

When students use AI to generate ideas, outlines, or prompts, faculty play a vital role in helping them maintain intellectual ownership. Rather than passively accepting the first suggestion, students should be encouraged to **interact with AI critically and reflectively** - treating it as a conversational partner, not an answer engine.

Faculty Role: Encourage Students To

- **Critically Evaluate Which Suggestions are Most Viable or Relevant**. Prompt students to explain why a certain idea aligns (or does not) with their purpose, audience, or assignment goals.

- **Modify Questions for Deeper Exploration**. Guide students to reframe or extend their prompts to get more nuanced responses, supporting a recursive process of inquiry.
- **Reflect on Why They Chose a Direction - Not Just What Sounded Interesting**. Embed reflection prompts that ask students to justify their choices and demonstrate alignment with learning goals or disciplinary thinking (Gundu, 2024).

Learning Outcome: Students practice **intellectual discernment**, not idea outsourcing. They develop habits of **metacognition, intentionality, and ethical creativity** - skills that are essential for academic work and transferable to AI-enhanced professional environments.

---

2. Literature Review Acceleration

AI tools such as **Elicit.org** and **Scite.ai** can save hours by surfacing relevant academic sources and mapping research questions to existing findings.

Example: Elicit in Action

- *A student researching burnout among healthcare workers uses Elicit to pull 10 studies, organized by methodology and sample size.*

Faculty Role:

- Require students to cross-check AI-sourced articles for relevance and peer-review status.
- Encourage annotation or synthesis notes that describe how each article contributes to the research question.

Caution: AI may **miss seminal works** or misrepresent findings - thus, faculty must reinforce **source validation as a core scholarly habit** (Gundu, 2024).

---

3. Methodology and Design Support

While AI cannot design studies independently, it can help students explore research models, frameworks, or even simulate arguments for and against different methods.

Example: Prompting AI to Compare Designs

- *"What are the strengths and weaknesses of a mixed-methods approach for studying social media addiction?"*

Faculty Role: As AI tools become capable of generating summaries, explanations, and even methodological suggestions, faculty must help students move from **acceptance to evaluation**. Rather than treating AI output as inherently trustworthy, students should be guided to examine its accuracy, completeness, and alignment with disciplinary standards. Faculty can embed this critical literacy by assigning tasks that prompt students to:

- **Compare AI-Generated Summaries with Textbook or Peer-Reviewed Sources**. This exercise teaches students how to cross-check content, note discrepancies, and determine which explanations are more credible or contextually appropriate.

- **Identify What the AI Missed - or Oversimplified**. Encourage students to look for gaps in reasoning, misrepresentations of nuance, or the absence of key theoretical perspectives.
- **Write a Justification Statement Detailing their Final Methodological Choice**. When using AI to explore research design or problem-solving strategies, require students to explain **why** they chose a particular approach and **how** they validated the tool's suggestions.

These strategies reinforce **analytical judgment, transparency, and methodological awareness** - skills that align with what Holmes et al. (2022) described as essential for navigating AI in knowledge-rich environments.

---

4. Data Analysis and Coding Support

In quantitative research, generative AI tools can assist students with a range of technical tasks, such as **writing basic statistical code**, **interpreting output**, or **generating data visualizations**. Tools such as ChatGPT, GitHub Copilot, and AI-enabled plugins for platforms such as RStudio or Python environments can offer students just-in-time support - especially in scripting syntax, formatting graphs, or explaining common statistical procedures. These capabilities can lower the barrier to entry for students new to data analysis, helping them focus more on research design and interpretation.

Example: Stats in Psychology Course

- *A student asks ChatGPT: "Explain what a p-value of 0.03 means in simple language."*

Faculty Role:

- Encourage this as a **starting point**, but reinforce that interpretation must be based on **data context**, not just statistical thresholds.
- Consider AI as a **TA-level assistant**, not a peer reviewer.

In **qualitative research**, generative AI tools can offer support by **summarizing interview transcripts**, identifying frequently used phrases, or suggesting **preliminary coding categories** based on linguistic patterns in the data. These features can be especially helpful in the early stages of analysis, where students often feel overwhelmed by the sheer volume of unstructured information. For instance, a student conducting interviews about first-generation college students' experiences might use AI to extract common expressions such as *"imposter syndrome," "family pressure,"* or *"navigating resources"* - which could point toward emerging themes.

Example: AI-Assisted Coding in a Thematic Analysis of Student Belonging

- *A graduate student is conducting a qualitative study on first-year university students' sense of belonging. They have collected eight semi-structured interview transcripts, each 30–45 minutes long.*
- *To begin analysis, the student uses a generative AI tool (e.g., ChatGPT or Claude) to summarize each transcript and extract* ***frequent phrases or candidate codes****, such as*

"finding my people," "office hours felt intimidating," and *"did not see anyone like me in class."*

Faculty Role: The supervising instructor guides the student to:

- **Compare AI-suggested codes with hand-coded excerpts** from two transcripts to assess alignment and gaps.
- **Annotate decisions** in a coding memo - explaining which AI-generated suggestions were retained, modified, or discarded, and why.
- **Reflect on their positionality**, discussing how their own background may influence code interpretation or the themes they prioritize.
- **Use a theoretical lens** (e.g., Tinto's Model of Student Integration or Critical Race Theory) to frame their interpretation beyond surface-level categorization.

As AI tools become increasingly integrated into research workflows, they offer valuable support during the **data analysis and coding phases** of both quantitative and qualitative studies. These tools can enhance efficiency and reduce cognitive load - **but they cannot replace the researcher's role in interpretation, decision-making, and ethical oversight** (Gundu, 2024; Han, 2025).

In **quantitative research**, AI can assist with organizing datasets, generating visualizations, running descriptive statistics, and recommending models. Tools such as ChatGPT or code-based copilots (e.g., GitHub Copilot) can scaffold students through repetitive or technical tasks. However, faculty must ensure that students **justify their analytical choices**, explain how models align with research questions, and verify results independently.

In **qualitative research**, AI can summarize interview transcripts, highlight frequently used terms, or suggest initial coding categories. These functions can help students manage large data sets and identify entry points for thematic analysis. Yet, students must still **engage deeply with the data**, evaluating the contextual meaning of codes, aligning interpretations with theoretical frameworks, and reflecting on their own positionality.

Across both domains, **faculty play a critical role** in guiding students to:

- Use AI outputs as **starting points**, not conclusions.
- Pair AI-generated insights with human reasoning and methodological rigor.
- Disclose how tools were used, and reflect on the boundaries between support and substitution (Van Dis et al., 2023).

By teaching students to collaborate with AI without deferring to it, educators foster intellectual agency, methodological transparency, and disciplinary integrity in the research process.

---

5. Drafting and Revising the Manuscript

Many students now use generative AI tools to assist with grammar correction, rephrasing, and structural revision - particularly when writing in a second language or under deadline pressure. These tools, when used responsibly, can enhance clarity and reduce mechanical errors. However, the risk lies in students outsourcing too much of the writing process, unintentionally obscuring their voice and intellectual contribution.

To maintain integrity and encourage ownership, faculty should position AI use in revision as a reflective and accountable process - not passive improvement.

Example: Improving a Paragraph with AI Support

- *A student submits two versions of their methods section:*
  - *The **original draft**, written independently.*
  - *The **revised version** improved using ChatGPT for clarity and organization.*
- *Alongside the two drafts, the student provides **annotations** highlighting what was changed and why. In a brief reflection, they answer:*
  - *"What did you agree with in the AI's changes?"*
  - *"What did you reject, and why?"*
  - *"How did the AI revision affect your thinking or understanding of your own work?"*

This assignment models **augmented authorship**, where AI assists the writing process, but the student remains in control.

Faculty Role:

- **Require annotated drafts** when AI is used during revision stages.
- **Embed structured reflection prompts** to support metacognition, such as:
  - *"What decisions did you make in response to AI suggestions?"*
  - *"How did AI support your thinking, and where did you disagree?"*
- **Assess for reasoning, not just fluency** - rewarding students for thoughtful engagement, not just polished output.

As Reiss (2021) suggested, AI can help students improve clarity and fluency, but maintaining authorship requires transparency, reflection, and instructional scaffolding. Faculty play a key role in ensuring that AI becomes a tool for learning, not ghostwriting.

Balancing Use and Overuse: Faculty Red Flags

Generative AI can be a powerful tool for **augmenting student thinking**, but it also carries the risk of overuse - particularly when it begins to obscure the student's voice, judgment, or disciplinary understanding. Faculty must be equipped to recognize when students have **crossed the line from support to substitution**, and to respond in ways that promote reflection, not just punishment. **Red flags that may signal overreliance or inappropriate use**:

- **Work Lacks Personal Voice or Disciplinary Nuance**. The writing feels generic, detached from the course content, or inconsistent with the student's past work.
- **Citations are Inaccurate, Fabricated, or Overly Generic**. AI-generated references may include plausible-sounding but nonexistent sources, or fail to meet academic standards for evidence and attribution.
- **Student Cannot Explain Key Arguments or Methodological Choices**. In conversation or supervision, the student struggles to articulate the logic behind their submission, signaling possible detachment from the content (Han, 2025).

Faculty Response: Supporting Integrity Without Punishment. When red flags arise, the goal should be to re-engage the student in the learning process - not simply to police outcomes. Faculty are encouraged to:

- **Hold a Non-Punitive, Curiosity-Driven Conversation**. Ask open-ended questions such as *"How did you approach this task?"* or *"What tools did you use and why?"* to create space for honesty.
- **Request Earlier Drafts, Planning Notes, or AI Reflection Logs**. These artifacts can help clarify the student's process and level of engagement.
- **Clarify Expectations Moving Forward**. Reiterate the course's AI use policy and discuss what kinds of support are allowed, encouraged, or prohibited.

As Han (2025) emphasized, maintaining academic integrity in the age of AI requires rethinking surveillance-based approaches and focusing instead on restoring transparency, trust, and student agency.

Guiding Questions for Faculty: Centering Human Judgment in AI-Augmented Research

As research workflows increasingly incorporate AI tools, faculty must shift from asking whether a tool was used to asking how it was used - and what the student learned through that process. The goal is not to detect technical errors or inconsistencies, but to evaluate the depth of student thinking, ownership, and reflection. These guiding questions help faculty assess the authenticity of intellectual contribution in AI-supported academic work. Key questions to consider:

- **What is the Intellectual Contribution of the Student, Versus the Tool?** *"Does the work reflect the student's decision-making, synthesis, and disciplinary insight - or merely the structure and polish typical of AI generated output?"*
- **How did the Student Engage with the Content - Interpret, Evaluate, or Challenge it?** *"Is there evidence that the student critically assessed the material, posed questions, or applied a theoretical lens?"*
- **Has the Student Reflected on How and Why They Used AI Support?** *"Do they disclose tool use transparently and explain the reasoning behind incorporating - or rejecting - AI suggestions?"*
- **Can They Explain Their Choices if Asked?** *"In supervision, presentations, or defense-style conversations, does the student demonstrate command of their methods, claims, and conclusions?"*

These questions **recenter human intention, critical reasoning, and ethical transparency** as the hallmarks of quality research - not just technical polish or linguistic fluency. As Reiss (2021) noted, in the AI era, what matters most is not whether a student used a tool, but how responsibly they partnered with it to produce meaningful, original work.

Section Reflection: Redefining Research as Reflective Human–AI Partnership

This section offers a thoughtful and forward-looking redefinition of academic research in the age of generative AI. It moves away from the traditional model of isolated, labor-intensive scholarship and toward a more modern, collaborative vision - where AI supports, but never supplants, human judgment, ethical reasoning, and intellectual ownership. Rather than viewing AI tools as shortcuts or threats, the section positions them as **cognitive partners** capable of enhancing efficiency and supporting early-stage tasks such as brainstorming, summarizing, and organizing - provided that students remain actively engaged in interpretation, validation, and decision-making.

By introducing the concept of **augmented thinking**, the section reframes research as a recursive, reflective process where AI assistance is not only permitted but expected - so long as it is accompanied by critical engagement, transparency, and methodological rigor. The breakdown of each research stage - from topic selection to data analysis to drafting - shows how faculty can intentionally scaffold AI use to deepen learning, not dilute it. Moreover, the inclusion of reflective annotations, process memos, and guided faculty-student dialogues provides actionable strategies for maintaining student voice and disciplinary authenticity.

Importantly, this section also helps educators distinguish between **support** and **substitution**, providing a continuum of AI collaboration and clear red flags for overreliance. The shift in emphasis - from detecting misconduct to understanding and guiding AI use - fosters a classroom culture rooted in trust, reflection, and responsible innovation. In doing so, the section empowers both students and faculty to navigate AI-integrated research with ethical clarity and intellectual agency, helping reshape academic integrity for a new era of collaborative scholarship.

Section 2: Supporting Research Question Development in an AI-Supported Landscape

The rise of generative AI tools such as ChatGPT, Claude, Perplexity, and Elicit has dramatically altered how students approach the earliest stages of research. With a few keystrokes, learners can generate long lists of potential research topics, suggested thesis statements, and even pre-written outlines. But this convenience introduces a new pedagogical challenge: AI-generated content often lacks context, depth, originality, and relevance to the student's own disciplinary lens (Selwyn, 2021).

The **illusion of productivity** - a full page of neatly generated ideas or suggested topics - can obscure a deeper learning gap: students who have not yet wrestled with the why, how, or so what of their inquiry. Generative AI can rapidly produce lists of plausible-sounding research questions, but these often lack disciplinary depth, original framing, or conceptual grounding.

In response, faculty must take on an even more intentional role: guiding students to move beyond AI-generated prompts toward refined, researchable questions rooted in critical thinking, theoretical relevance, and scholarly curiosity. This requires not just filtering AI output, but helping students interrogate its logic, identify gaps, and personalize the inquiry process.

This section offers strategies to:

- Teach students to evaluate and improve AI-suggested questions.
- Embed scaffolds and reflection prompts into early-stage research assignments.
- Reinforce that technology can amplify inquiry, but cannot replace the human work of wondering well.

As Gundu (2024) noted, AI is changing the shape of academic work - but faculty remain essential in helping students **formulate questions that are not only answerable, but meaningful**.

From Prompt to Question: Teaching the Difference

One of the most important conceptual shifts students must make is understanding the distinction between:

- A **prompt** written for an AI to generate content, and
- A **research question** designed to explore, interrogate, or extend knowledge.

Example:

- ***AI Prompt***. *"List ten interesting topics in environmental science."*
- ***Research Question***. *"How do community-led conservation efforts influence environmental policy adoption in sub-Saharan Africa?"*

The first invites surface-level listing; the second demands focused inquiry, scope consideration, and contextual awareness. Faculty can teach this distinction by modeling the process of transforming an AI-generated suggestion into an academic question.

Strategies for Faculty to Guide Student Question Development

---

1. Use AI for Idea Generation - Then Interrogate the List

AI tools are useful for helping students brainstorm possible areas of interest, especially when they are unsure where to begin. But students must be taught to treat this as a starting point, not a destination.

Assignment Example: Guided Topic Triage

- *Use ChatGPT or Perplexity to generate 10 potential research topics.*

Then:

- *Circle the three that interest you most.*
- *For each, identify: "Who might care?" "What is missing from the current discourse?" "What scope is realistic for this assignment?"*
- *Refine one into a draft research question.*

Faculty Role: Lead a workshop where students critique each other's AI-generated lists and ask clarifying questions about feasibility, specificity, and scholarly value.

---

2. Model How Scholars Narrow Questions Over Time

Inexperienced researchers often believe that a "good" question must appear fully formed. Faculty can dispel this myth by demonstrating iterative refinement.

Example: From General to Researchable (Psychology)

- **General Topic**. *Adolescent social media use*
- **AI Suggestion**. *"What are the effects of social media on teenagers?"*
- **Faculty Refinement**. *"In what ways does daily exposure to TikTok's algorithmic content influence body image perception among high school girls in urban U.S. schools?"*

Key Dimensions to Teach:

- **Scope**. "*Can this question be answered within the project timeline?*"
- **Specificity**. "*What demographic, region, or theoretical framework is in focus?*"
- **Feasibility**. "*Is there sufficient, reliable data or scholarship available?*"

By walking students through this process, faculty **make research feel achievable - and grounded in inquiry, not automation** (Brookhart, 2010).

---

3. Encourage Iterative Question Journaling

The best research questions rarely emerge in a single sitting. Encourage students to maintain a **research journal or "question notebook"** throughout the ideation stage.

Example: Research Question Log

- *Each week, write down your current version of your research question.*
- *Include a few sentences on why you are keeping or changing it.*
- *Reflect on how conversations, AI tools, or reading have shaped your thinking.*

Assessment Tip: Grade this **formatively**, emphasizing **growth and reflection**, not perfection.

---

4. Use Comparison Exercises to Build Discernment

Faculty must help students understand what differentiates a weak research question from a strong one through comparative analysis.

Example: In-Class Activity - Rank the Questions

- *Provide a list of 5 research questions (some too broad, some narrow, some well-structured).*
  Students rank them based on:
  - *Clarity.*
  - *Researchability.*
  - *Alignment with a scholarly problem.*
  - *Ethical and practical feasibility.*

Follow-Up Discussion Prompt:

- *"Which question would you most want to explore and why? How could AI help you think further - but not think for you?"*

This process builds critical agency - the ability to question, interpret, and take ownership of intellectual work - a skill that AI cannot supply or simulate. Fostering critical agency means empowering students to use AI tools reflectively and ethically, ensuring that technology enhances rather than displaces human judgment and scholarly identity (Han, 2025).

---

5. Encourage Student Ownership Through Justification

After finalizing a question, students should be required to **justify their selection** - explaining how the question evolved and why it matters.

Example Prompt: Question Rationale Essay

- *Describe the process you used to select your research question.*
  - *"What questions or tools helped you get there?"*
  - *"Why do you believe this question is significant, answerable, and relevant to your field?"*

This exercise reinforces **intellectual ownership** by requiring students to make - and explain - their own decisions, rather than simply submitting polished results. It also provides faculty with valuable insight into the student's reasoning process, enabling them to assess how the student arrived at their conclusions, not just what they produced. As Reiss (2021) suggested, embedding reflective checkpoints in AI-augmented tasks ensures that faculty can still evaluate thinking, not just output - a critical safeguard for preserving academic integrity in an AI-rich classroom.

Balancing Support and Rigor: Guiding Research Question Development in the AI Era

As generative AI becomes a common brainstorming companion, faculty must strike a careful balance: welcoming AI-assisted ideation while ensuring that final research questions remain student-driven, critically reasoned, and academically relevant. AI tools can suggest plausible-sounding topics, but without intentional guidance, students may default to surface-level phrasing or disengage from the deeper work of question formation.

Signs of Overreliance on AI in Research Questioning:

- **Vague or overly polished phrasing** that lacks a clear connection to course content, frameworks, or disciplinary language.
- **Overly broad or generic scope**, such as "The effects of climate change" or "Social media and mental health," without refinement or narrowing.
- **Inability to explain the rationale**, scholarly motivation, or research gap the question addresses during one-on-one discussions or reflections.

Instructor Response Strategies: To re-engage students in the intellectual work of inquiry, faculty can:

- **Ask for revisions** following targeted feedback focused on specificity, relevance, or theoretical alignment.
- **Require a reflection statement or oral check-in** where students articulate how they used AI (if at all), what changes they made, and why they chose the final version.
- **Offer structured scaffolds** such as templates, question frameworks (e.g., PICO, "how/why" models), or graphic organizers that guide students toward sharper, researchable questions.

Ensuring academic integrity in the age of AI requires not just policy, but pedagogical design that reinforces agency, ownership, and iterative thinking. Faculty remain essential in helping students translate machine-generated possibilities into meaningful academic inquiry (Ruiz-Rojas et al., 2023).

Section Reflection: Guiding Inquiry in the Age of AI-Generated Possibilities

This section offers a critical and timely reframing of faculty roles in supporting early-stage research development amid the rise of generative AI. It highlights a key pedagogical paradox: while AI tools can rapidly generate lists of plausible research topics, they often bypass the intellectual struggle and contextual understanding that make research **meaningful**. The section emphasizes that the core challenge in this AI-supported landscape is not access to ideas, but depth of thought - and that the faculty's role is now more vital than ever in cultivating discernment, curiosity, and intellectual ownership.

Rather than resisting AI use, this section provides practical strategies to transform it into a catalyst for deeper learning. Through techniques such as topic triage, comparison exercises, justification essays, and reflective question journals, students are taught to interrogate AI-generated suggestions, refine them through critical and disciplinary lenses, and ultimately claim authorship over their inquiries. These scaffolds empower students to engage with AI as a tool for exploration - not substitution - anchoring their questions in relevance, specificity, and scholarly purpose.

Importantly, the section underscores the necessity of **process visibility** in maintaining academic integrity. When students reflect on how they arrived at their research questions, they demonstrate not just what they know, but how they think. In doing so, faculty shift the focus of assessment from product to process - ensuring that even in an AI-rich environment, research remains a human-driven act of wonder, responsibility, and rigorous inquiry.

Section 3: Teaching AI-Augmented Literature Reviews - Efficiency Without Sacrificing Depth

Literature reviews remain one of the most intellectually demanding and time-intensive components of the research process. They require far more than summarization - they demand critical synthesis, including drawing connections between studies, identifying gaps in knowledge, and positioning one's own work within an evolving scholarly conversation.

With the emergence of AI tools such as Elicit, Scite, Perplexity, and ChatGPT, students can now generate article summaries, compile citation lists, and identify recurring themes in a matter of minutes. These tools offer significant efficiencies - but they also introduce new risks. Chief among them is the illusion of depth: the appearance of scholarly engagement without the underlying cognitive work. A machine can summarize, but it cannot synthesize in a meaningful way. It cannot weigh competing arguments, identify methodological limitations, or connect trends to emerging debates (Brookhart, 2010). As such, faculty must play an active role in guiding students to use AI tools strategically and transparently, without allowing them to replace the essential practices of critical reading, annotation, and interpretive synthesis.

This section will outline practical strategies to help students move beyond AI-generated summaries and develop authentic scholarly synthesis in their literature reviews. It will provide guidance for faculty on how to:

- Distinguish between summary and synthesis in student writing and instruction.
- Use AI tools as scaffolds, not substitutes - clarifying when and how AI can support (but not do) the work.
- Embed annotation, comparison, and critique as part of the review process.
- Design reflection prompts that help students surface their reasoning, positionality, and engagement with sources.

By focusing on integration over imitation, this section will demonstrate how faculty can preserve the rigor and depth of the literature review process - while responsibly incorporating the efficiencies AI can offer. Faculty will leave with tools to assess synthesis authentically, ensuring that students engage with their sources as active thinkers, not passive compilers.

The Core Principle: AI Supports the Process, Not the Thinking

Generative AI is not a shortcut to scholarship - it is an accelerator of certain tasks. The goal is to free cognitive space for students to reflect more deeply, compare more rigorously, and write more persuasively. But achieving this requires faculty to model and scaffold AI-aware research practices that balance efficiency with depth (Brookhart, 2010).

How AI Tools Can Assist in Literature Reviews

---

1. Locating Sources with Smart Queries

AI research assistants such as **Elicit** and **Scite.ai** can help students surface peer-reviewed articles, generate comparative tables, and rank sources based on alignment with a research question.

Example:

- *A student exploring "burnout in K–12 teachers" uses Elicit to find 10 articles and auto-generates a table comparing sample sizes, methodologies, and outcomes.*

Faculty Guidance:

- Require source validation: Have students confirm the publication status and relevance of each article.
- Use this as a first draft bibliography - not a final one.

---

2. Summarizing Articles (With Verification)

AI tools such as ChatGPT can summarize individual articles quickly, but summaries must be verified against the original source.

Example: AI Summary Audit

- *Students use ChatGPT to summarize two journal articles.*

Then They:

- *Read the original.*
- *Annotate the AI's summary for omissions, inaccuracies, or oversimplifications.*
- *Write a short analysis on whether they would trust the tool again and under what conditions.*

Learning Outcome: Students learn that AI-generated content must be approached critically, not blindly trusted. They develop the ability to assess credibility, identify gaps or errors in AI output, and cross-check claims against scholarly sources. As Van Dis et al. (2023) emphasized, promoting skepticism toward machine-generated content is essential for building digital resilience and academic integrity in AI-enhanced learning environments.

---

3. Thematic Clustering and Synthesis Support

Tools such as Perplexity.ai and Claude can help group articles by theme or methodology - but students must make meaning of those patterns.

Example:

- *Perplexity identifies three dominant themes in literature on remote learning: access inequality, engagement strategies, and assessment models.*

Students Then:

- *Trace how each theme develops across 3–5 articles.*
- *Compare these machine-suggested themes with themes they developed independently.*
- *Choose which interpretation to foreground and justify why.*

Learning Outcome: This process builds **synthesis skills** - the highest-order thinking required in a literature review. Students learn to integrate ideas across sources, evaluate differing perspectives, and construct original insights. As Gundu (2024) and Reiss (2021) emphasized, fostering this level of engagement ensures that AI supports **higher-order reasoning**, not rote aggregation, and that students remain the central agents of meaning-making in the research process.

Faculty-Supported Workflow: Blending Traditional and AI-Supported Review

---

Workflow Model: "Human-Centered Literature Mapping"

To support students in using AI tools responsibly during the literature review process, faculty can introduce a **human-centered workflow** - one that strategically integrates AI at appropriate stages without compromising scholarly ownership. The following model outlines how students can collaborate with AI tools across key phases of literature mapping while maintaining critical agency, evaluative judgment, and original synthesis.

This table offers a practical breakdown of **who does what**: where AI can enhance efficiency and where human interpretation remains essential. By clearly defining both tool use and cognitive responsibility, this model helps ensure that students engage with research as thinkers - not just assemblers of content.

Stage	Activity	AI Tool	Human Task
Topic Exploration	Brainstorm related concepts, refine keywords	ChatGPT, Claude	Identify what is missing from AI-generated ideas
Source Location	Search for peer-reviewed sources	Elicit, Scite	Evaluate journal quality, date, and methodology
Summary Drafting	Generate first-pass article summaries	ChatGPT	Verify for accuracy, highlight nuances
Theme Identification	Ask AI to group articles by focus or theory	Claude, Perplexity	Reorganize themes based on student understanding
Synthesis Writing	Draft outline of the literature review	None (manual)	Integrate voice, contrast perspectives, cite sources

Faculty Role:

- Provide **note-taking templates** (e.g., literature matrix with columns for findings, critiques, connections)
- Emphasize **reflection checkpoints**, asking students to assess their own interpretations alongside AI outputs

---

Assignment Example: "AI-Augmented Lit Review Portfolio"

This assignment is designed to teach students how to **collaborate with AI tools thoughtfully and transparently** throughout the literature review process - while maintaining full ownership of analysis, structure, and voice. By emphasizing **process over product**, it helps students develop critical synthesis skills and ethical research habits in an AI-enhanced academic environment.

Assignment Components: Students submit a literature review portfolio containing:

- **AI-Generated Summaries with Human Verification Annotations**. Students highlight where summaries were accurate, misleading, or incomplete.
- **A Reflection Explaining How AI Tools were Used, Avoided, or Adapted**. Prompts may include: *"What decisions did you make when reviewing AI output?"* or *"What did AI miss that you needed to supply?"*
- **A Synthesis Map Showing How Sources were Organized Thematically or Conceptually**. It can be a concept map, chart, or written overview demonstrating how studies relate to one another.
- **A Final Draft of a Literature Review Section**. Reflects integrated understanding, correct citation, and student-authored synthesis.

Rubric Elements:

- **Accuracy of Source Use**. *"Are key arguments, findings, and citations correctly represented?"*
- **Depth of Synthesis and Comparison**. *"Does the student connect studies meaningfully, not just list them?"*
- **Transparency in Tool Use**. *"Is AI use clearly disclosed, with thoughtful commentary on its role and limits?"*
- **Evidence of Critical Thinking and Authorial Voice**. *"Does the student interpret, evaluate, and shape the conversation?"*

This format reinforces that the **literature review is a thinking task**, not a mechanical one. When students are asked to document how they evaluate and interact with AI output, they learn that **true scholarly synthesis requires more than summarizing - it requires discernment, structure, and insight** (Reiss, 2021).

Cautions and Ethical Boundaries

Even when students intend to use AI responsibly, the ease and speed of these tools can lead to **unintentional misuse** - particularly in the context of literature reviews, where accuracy, synthesis, and critical reading are essential. Faculty must help students recognize that AI efficiency should never come at the cost of scholarly integrity.

Common Pitfalls to Watch For:

- **Submitting AI-Written Summaries Without Reading the Original Sources**. This undermines deep engagement and risks misrepresenting arguments or context.
- **Relying on Non-Peer-Reviewed or Fabricated Sources "Sourced" by AI**. Tools such as ChatGPT or Perplexity may suggest articles that sound plausible but are either unreliable or nonexistent.
- **Copying AI-Generated Thematic Interpretations Without Attribution**. Without transparency, students may present machine-structured insight as their own, compromising authorship.

Faculty Strategies to Prevent Misuse: To reinforce ethical use and reflective engagement, faculty can:

- **Require Brief Reading Logs, Citation Pull Quotes, or Annotation Highlights**. These demonstrate that students have read and verified key sections of their sources.
- **Dedicate Class Time to "AI Audit" Practice**. Have students analyze the strengths and weaknesses of AI-generated summaries and correct inaccuracies collaboratively.
- **Define the Boundary Between Assistance and Authorship**. Offer concrete examples of what is permitted (e.g., keyword generation, scaffolding outlines) versus what constitutes intellectual outsourcing.

By **building ethical awareness into assignment design**, faculty help students develop both academic integrity and digital discernment. Clear boundaries and transparent expectations are essential for fostering trust and learning in AI-enhanced environments (Gundu, 2024).

Section Reflection: Preserving Depth in the Age of AI-Accelerated Literature Reviews

This section offers a crucial blueprint for navigating the dual reality of AI-augmented research: while tools such as ChatGPT, Elicit, and Scite can drastically reduce the logistical burden of conducting literature reviews, they also introduce the risk of superficial engagement disguised as scholarly synthesis. By clearly distinguishing **summary** from **synthesis**, the section calls on faculty to move beyond automation and reassert the human work of discerning patterns, weighing competing perspectives, and constructing scholarly narratives.

Rather than rejecting AI's efficiency, this section encourages a nuanced integration - positioning AI as a scaffold for organizing information, not as a substitute for thinking. Through workflows such as "Human-Centered Literature Mapping" and reflective assignments such as the "AI-Augmented Lit Review Portfolio," faculty are equipped to teach students how to critically interact with machine outputs, verify claims, and articulate their interpretive reasoning. Emphasis is placed not only on producing a final synthesis but on making visible the intellectual process behind it - ensuring that authorial voice, ethical awareness, and disciplinary understanding remain central.

Ultimately, this section reframes the literature review as a metacognitive task - one that AI can support but never complete. It empowers educators to reinforce process over polish, judgment over generation, and reflection over replication, preserving the integrity and rigor of scholarly work in an era where fluency can be machine-made, but insight must remain human.

Section 4: Supervising Research Methodology in a Data-Rich, AI-Enhanced World

---

The rise of generative AI and machine learning has transformed how students approach research design. Today's learners have access to tools that can analyze large datasets, extract patterns from qualitative sources, simulate real-world processes, and even predict future outcomes. For faculty supervising undergraduate or graduate research, this new reality requires a shift in how we understand - and teach - methodology.

The modern research landscape is no longer divided between "manual" and "automated." Instead, it is defined by augmented methodologies, where AI functions as a powerful partner in data processing, pattern recognition, visualization, and exploratory analysis (Selwyn, 2021). While this opens new doors for insight and innovation, it also raises questions about methodological rigor, bias, transparency, and intellectual ownership.

This section offers faculty practical strategies for supervising research that integrates AI tools, whether in quantitative, qualitative, or mixed-methods designs. The goal is not to discourage AI use, but to ensure that it enhances rather than compromises the research process.

Understanding Where AI Fits in Methodological Design

Faculty must first understand that AI tools do not "design" research - people do. AI can assist with **execution**, but it cannot:

- Choose valid operational definitions.
- Align methods with theoretical frameworks.
- Interpret significance in context.

With this basis established, AI can augment research at **several methodological stages**:

Research Stage	AI Enhancement Possibility
Instrument Development	Suggesting survey questions based on themes
Data Collection	Chatbots for structured interviews or survey deployment
Text/Data Analysis	Natural language processing, machine learning, statistical modeling

Research Stage	AI Enhancement Possibility
Visualization	Generating charts or heat maps from large data sets
Simulation/Prediction	Running hypothetical scenarios or regression-based forecasts

---

Supervising Methodology in the Age of AI

---

1. Begin with Alignment: AI Must Serve the Research Question

AI tools should never be chosen just because they are available. They must be justified by the research purpose, aligned with the study's epistemology, and suitable for the dataset or context.

Example (Quantitative Study):

- *A student wants to study factors predicting student burnout using a survey dataset. They propose using an AI regression tool to identify correlations.*

Faculty Supervision Strategies:

- Ensure the student can **define variables clearly.**
- Review **assumptions of regression analysis.**
- **Ask**: *"What does the model tell you - and what does it leave out?"*

Key Tip: Require students to **explain in writing** why they chose an AI-assisted method and how it connects to their hypothesis.

---

2. Support Ethical Use of NLP and Machine Learning

AI can accelerate coding in qualitative studies, such as identifying themes in interview transcripts or sentiment in social media posts. However, these tools often:

- Miss nuance.
- Mislabel emotional tone.
- Reinforce bias from training data.

Example (Qualitative Study):

- *A student uploads open-ended survey responses into a natural language processing (NLP) tool to categorize feedback.*

Faculty Supervision Strategies:

- Compare automated coding to **manual human coding.**
- Require a **bias analysis**: *"What assumptions might the model hold?"*

- Encourage the student to **triangulate findings** with another method (Brookhart, 2010).

This practice supports **ethical research design, interdisciplinary integrity, and informed tool use** when students incorporate natural language processing (NLP) or machine learning (ML) into their academic work. By requiring students to explain how models are trained, validated, or applied - and to disclose both tool limitations and interpretive boundaries - faculty help prevent overreliance on opaque algorithms or uncritical data use.

These expectations promote **transparency**, **replicability**, and **methodological alignment** between the student's research goals and the capabilities of the tools they use. Meaningful AI use in research depends not just on technical output, but on students' ability to understand and communicate the risks, assumptions, and ethical stakes embedded in their computational methods (Weidinger et al., 2022).

---

3. Reinforce Transparency and Reproducibility

Many AI tools are proprietary or constantly updated, making methodological transparency and reproducibility challenging. Faculty should help students document:

- What tool or platform did they use (e.g., version, date)?
- How did they configure settings (e.g., training parameters, filters)?
- The exact input (e.g., prompts, datasets).

Assignment Example:

- *"Include an appendix with a screenshot or transcript of your AI tool's output and your reflection on how you used it in analysis."*

This practice supports research transparency, enhances replicability, and ensures accountability in AI-integrated studies. By documenting how AI tools were used in the research process - whether for summarization, coding, or drafting - students and scholars **make their methods more traceable and their findings more trustworthy**. Clear disclosure of AI involvement is essential for upholding scholarly standards in an era of rapidly evolving automation (Van Dis et al., 2023).

---

4. Monitor for Overreliance on Predictive Power

Predictive models are tempting - but they can obscure causal reasoning and domain knowledge. Faculty should challenge students to interpret, not just report, AI-generated forecasts.

Example (Simulation Study):

- *A student builds an AI simulation to model traffic flow after policy changes. The tool predicts congestion reduction but does not explain why.*

Faculty Supervision Strategies:

- **Ask**: *"How do you know the simulation is valid?"*

- Require a **limitations section** acknowledging assumptions and errors.
- Encourage ethical reflection on **real-world applicability**.

This practice supports **critical reasoning, methodological integrity, and academic transparency** when students use AI tools for predictive modeling or trend analysis. By encouraging students to question the scope, assumptions, and limitations of AI-generated predictions - such as correlations in social data or sentiment in text mining - faculty help students avoid treating statistical outputs as unquestionable truths.

Monitoring for overreliance ensures that students are not just reporting predictions, but evaluating **why a model produces certain outputs**, whether those outputs are valid in context, and what alternative interpretations exist. Students must learn that **predictive success does not equate to conceptual accuracy**, and that critical inquiry must guide - not be guided by - the algorithm (Hagerty & Rubinov, 2019).

---

5. Integrate AI-Awareness into Methodology Rubrics

As students increasingly use AI tools in data collection, analysis, and interpretation, faculty should update grading rubrics to explicitly evaluate how responsibly and reflectively these tools are integrated into the research process. Methodology rubrics should not only assess what tools were used, but also how students justified, interpreted, and contextualized their use.

Suggested Evaluation Criteria:

- **Clarity of AI Tool Selection Rationale**. *"Has the student explained why a specific tool was chosen, and how it aligns with the research question or methodology?"*
- **Critical Reflection on the Tool's Limitations**. *"Does the student demonstrate awareness of bias, error, or design constraints within the AI system?"*
- **Transparency in Methodological Reporting**. *"Are the steps taken with AI tools clearly documented, including prompt design, output selection, and any post-processing?"*
- **Evidence of Student Insight Beyond the Tool's Output**. *"Does the student engage with the results critically, adding interpretation rather than simply accepting automated outcomes?"*

Sample Rubric Language:

- *"Demonstrates thoughtful justification for AI use in data analysis."*
- *"Acknowledges and mitigates model limitations or bias."*
- *"Reflects on how AI-supported insights were interpreted, challenged, or validated."*

By integrating AI-awareness into assessment, faculty reinforce that **student agency, not automation, remains central to methodological rigor**. Clear documentation and critical oversight of AI use are essential for ensuring responsible, reproducible, and ethically grounded research (Van Dis et al., 2023).

Mixed-Methods Example: AI in an Undergraduate Capstone

Project Overview: An undergraduate business student conducts a **mixed-methods capstone project** exploring consumer behavior in online shopping environments.

- **Quantitative Component**. The student uses ChatGPT to assist with survey design, automate basic data cleaning, and generate initial statistical summaries from a Google Sheets export.
- **Qualitative Component**. The student also uses ChatGPT to assist in identifying preliminary themes from interview transcripts, using the tool to group responses and surface patterns.

Faculty Role: Ensuring Academic Integrity and Critical Oversight. To maintain scholarly rigor and support ethical AI use, the supervising faculty member:

- **Approves survey design and AI deployment strategy** before data collection begins, ensuring alignment with research goals and responsible tool use.
- **Reviews raw interview transcripts alongside AI-generated codes** to evaluate which themes were accurate, which were superficial, and where human insight was needed.
- **Poses reflective prompts** such as:
    - *"Did the AI miss any emotional tone, nuance, or contradictions that stood out to you?"*
    - *"How did you verify whether the AI's grouping aligned with your own interpretation?"*
- **Requires an appendix** in the final report that documents:
    - Which tools were used?
    - When and why were they employed?
    - What limitations or biases were encountered?
    - What decisions did the student make independently?

This example models how AI can serve as a supportive tool across research modalities - without replacing the analytical responsibility of the student. Responsible AI integration in student research must be grounded in critical engagement, transparency, and ongoing faculty guidance (Han, 2025).

Section Reflection: Supervising Methodology in an Era of Human–AI Co-Inquiry

This section powerfully repositions faculty as **methodological stewards** in an era where students increasingly rely on AI tools to support data analysis, instrument design, pattern recognition, and even predictive modeling. Rather than discouraging AI use, it urges faculty to embrace their evolving role: ensuring that AI enhances research design rather than replacing critical reasoning. The emphasis is not on eliminating automation, but on preserving **academic intentionality** - ensuring that every tool serves the research question, aligns with disciplinary standards, and is transparently reported.

By breaking down the research process into stages and identifying appropriate (and inappropriate) uses of AI across each phase - from NLP-supported qualitative coding to automated survey suggestions - the section provides a practical roadmap for guiding students in real time. It offers faculty concrete tools for identifying red flags of overreliance, embedding reflection and bias analysis into methodology, and updating rubrics to reward AI-awareness, critical oversight, and intellectual ownership.

Ultimately, this section reinforces a central message: in a data-rich, AI-enhanced world, methodological rigor is not achieved by resisting technology, but by ensuring students remain **thinkers first, tool-users second**. It reframes the faculty role from detector of misconduct to mentor of discernment - helping students build ethical, reflective, and transparent research habits that endure long after the latest AI tool fades from view.

Section 5: Fostering Ethical Use of AI Throughout the Research Lifecycle

---

In traditional research ethics, most attention is paid to **data collection** and **human subject protections** - often framed within the scope of Institutional Review Board (IRB) protocols. However, the widespread adoption of generative AI tools has expanded the ethical landscape considerably. Today, responsible research extends not only to how data are collected and managed, but also to **how AI is used across the entire lifecycle of a study** - from question generation to analysis to final presentation.

Faculty now play a critical role in helping students understand that ethics is not a formality or a compliance step; it is a continuous thread woven through every stage of scholarly work. That includes promoting thoughtful disclosure, data transparency, ownership clarity, and sustained reflection on the social and disciplinary implications of AI-assisted research.

This section addresses how faculty can **embed ethical thinking into AI-integrated research supervision**, offering strategies to guide students in evaluating tool limitations, disclosing AI involvement, and reflecting on the broader impact of automation on knowledge creation. Ethical scholarship in the AI age is not just about **what** you study - it is about **how** you think about the tools that help you study it (Brookhart, 2010; Selwyn, 2021).

Ethics Is a Process, Not a Policy

While policies and IRB oversight are important, ethical research behavior must be cultivated through conversation, modeling, and mentorship. Faculty should initiate and sustain ethical dialogue throughout the research process, guiding students as they navigate unfamiliar territory with tools that are powerful but not always transparent or well understood (Brookhart, 2010).

Ethical Considerations Across the Research Lifecycle

---

1. Ideation and Question Development

Ethical Risk: Overreliance on AI-generated questions may dilute originality and introduce bias from the model's training data.

Faculty Practice:

- **Ask Students**: *"Why is this research question meaningful to you?"*
- Require a short rationale for **how they selected and refined** their research question.
- If AI tools are used to generate ideas, prompt reflection:
    - *"What assumptions are embedded in the AI's suggestions?"*

Example:

- *A student uses ChatGPT to brainstorm potential topics in disability studies. Faculty challenge the student to consider whether the tool's suggestions reflect inclusive or deficit-based language, and to revise accordingly.*

---

2. Literature Review

Ethical Risk: Using AI to summarize articles can lead to misrepresentation or shallow engagement. Hallucinated citations are also a known problem.

Faculty Practice:

- Require students to verify AI-generated citations and submit **annotation logs** for selected sources.
- Encourage students to reflect on the reliability of AI outputs:
    - *"How accurate was the AI's interpretation of this article? What did it miss?"*

Example:

- *In a senior thesis, a student submits a literature review that includes two AI-summarized articles. The summaries omit methodological limitations, which the student only discovers during faculty-guided verification.*

---

3. Methodology and Data Collection

Ethical Risk: AI-assisted tools (e.g., survey bots, transcription software, NLP coding) may collect or process sensitive data, sometimes through third-party platforms.

Faculty Practice:

- Review **data privacy policies** of any tools used.
- Discourage uploading identifiable human subject data into public or unsecured platforms.
- Include explicit questions in the methodology proposal:
    - *"Are any third-party tools being used?"*
    - *"How will participant confidentiality be protected?"*

Example:

- *A student wants to use Otter.ai to transcribe interviews. Faculty guides the student to anonymize files before upload and includes this step in the IRB protocol.*

---

4. Analysis and Interpretation

Ethical Risk: AI-generated insights may reflect algorithmic bias or obscure methodological transparency.

Faculty Practice:

- Require students to disclose **what tools were used for analysis**, including prompts, parameters, and settings.
- Encourage students to reflect on **how AI outputs shaped their interpretation.**

Discussion Prompt:

- *"If the AI had produced a different pattern or theme, would your conclusions have changed? Why or why not?"*

Example:

- *A student analyzing social media posts uses sentiment analysis. When the AI categorizes critical political discourse as "negative," the student investigates potential bias in the training data and reframes the analysis to account for tone and rhetorical strategy.*

---

5. Writing and Presentation

Ethical Risk: Students may use AI for drafting large portions of their paper without understanding the implications for originality or intellectual ownership.

Faculty Practice:

- Require an **AI disclosure section** in all written submissions.
- Teach students to cite AI tools when they contribute substantively to content development.
- Use rubrics that reward **transparent and critical reflection on AI use.**

Example Disclosure Statement:

- *"I used ChatGPT to suggest subheadings during my outline phase. I revised the suggestions for alignment with my argument and incorporated only headings that supported my framework."*

Teaching Ethical Reflection in Real Time

Integrating ethical reflection into AI-augmented research does not require standalone lectures or isolated modules - it requires ongoing, embedded conversations that treat ethics as an essential part of the learning process. When ethics is practiced in real time, students learn to engage with AI tools transparently, critically, and responsibly as their work unfolds - not just after it is completed.

Faculty Strategies for Ongoing Integration:

- **Begin Each Research Milestone with a 10-Minute Ethics Check-In**. Ask students what new tools they have tried, where they encountered uncertainty, or what assumptions they made about automation.
- **Assign "AI Use Diaries."** Have students maintain short weekly logs that document which tools they used, how those tools shaped their decisions, and what ethical questions or limitations they encountered.
- **Incorporate Case-Based Learning**. Analyze real-world examples of AI misuse in academia, journalism, or policymaking to spark discussion about accountability, bias, and decision-making under uncertainty.

These practices help students build **ethical reflexes** in parallel with technical fluency - an essential pairing in a research landscape where AI may assist with reasoning, but cannot replace it. As Han (2025) noted, effective AI ethics education is not about identifying a single right answer - it is about **building student agency through reflective, value-driven decision-making** at every step of the research process.

Rethinking Attribution and Ownership

One of the most **complex and evolving challenges** in AI-augmented research is determining what counts as **authorship** - and when AI use requires **attribution**. As generative tools become more capable of producing fluent text, summaries, or analytical suggestions, students and faculty must learn to navigate the blurred boundaries between support and co-creation. Authorship is no longer defined solely by who typed the words, but by who shaped the ideas, structure, and intellectual direction.

Guiding Questions for Students and Faculty:

- *"Did the AI generate new content or simply help organize pre-existing thoughts?"*
- *"Did the student revise, reinterpret, or transform the output meaningfully?"*
- *"Would the final product still reflect the student's intellectual contribution if the AI's role were removed?"*

These questions help surface whether AI was used as a tool or as an authorial agent, and whether the student can demonstrate ownership, reasoning, and originality.

Institutional Implications: Building a Culture of Integrity

While individual faculty play a vital role in guiding ethical AI use, lasting change depends on **institutional commitment**. To foster a culture where students and educators engage with AI tools transparently, thoughtfully, and responsibly, institutions must create clear structures, shared language, and consistent expectations across departments. Ethical AI integration requires coordinated action, including:

- **Updating academic integrity policies** to explicitly address generative AI use across research, writing, and collaboration.
- **Establishing clear standards** for when and how students should cite or disclose AI assistance, including assignment-level expectations and examples.
- **Providing ongoing faculty development** on AI tools, research ethics, and the pedagogical implications of automation.
- **Creating interdisciplinary ethics panels** to advise on emerging technologies, address gray zones, and provide guidance for complex cases involving authorship, data use, or bias.

When institutions lead with clarity and support, they empower faculty and students alike to **navigate AI with confidence and integrity**. As Gundu (2024) emphasized, institutional culture must evolve alongside technology - ensuring that ethical use of AI is not only encouraged, but **sustainably embedded** into the academic fabric.

Section Reflection: Embedding Ethics Across the AI-Enhanced Research Lifecycle

This section reframes research ethics as a dynamic, ongoing process - one that must now extend far beyond data collection and IRB compliance to account for the expanding influence of generative AI. As students increasingly turn to tools such as ChatGPT, Elicit, and NLP platforms across all phases of research - from idea generation to analysis and writing - faculty must guide them in making **informed, transparent, and ethically grounded choices**. Rather than policing AI use, this section emphasizes **mentorship over monitoring**, advocating for real-time conversations that build ethical reflexes alongside technical fluency.

By offering stage-by-stage ethical checkpoints, reflective prompts, and disclosure strategies, the section equips educators to ensure that AI supports inquiry without undermining originality, authorship, or critical thinking. Whether addressing the risks of AI-generated bias in qualitative analysis, concerns about authorship during writing, or data privacy in transcription tools, the emphasis remains on cultivating student agency and responsibility. Key takeaways - like the use of "AI use diaries," process disclosures, and guided attribution questions - demonstrate how ethical reasoning can be woven seamlessly into research supervision.

Ultimately, the section moves beyond compliance to **culture change** - calling on institutions to update policies, create interdisciplinary advisory structures, and invest in faculty development. In doing so, it empowers both students and educators to treat AI not as a shortcut or threat, but as a context for ethical growth. In a world where automation can accelerate research, it is human integrity - modeled and taught by faculty - that must shape how that research is done.

Section 6: Developing Rubrics and Evaluation Criteria for AI-Enhanced Work

---

As generative AI becomes increasingly integrated into student research, **traditional grading rubrics are beginning to show their age**. Most were designed under the assumption that all writing, synthesis, and design decisions were made solely by the student - without algorithmic assistance. Today, however, research projects may include AI-generated outlines, machine-curated literature searches, or AI-drafted summaries. Faculty are now asking:

- *"How do I assess work shaped by tools such as ChatGPT or Elicit?"*
- *"What does originality look like when students collaborate with AI?"*
- *"How can evaluation encourage ethical, thoughtful tool use instead of penalizing or ignoring it?"*

To address these questions, educators need to update assessment strategies that reflect the realities of AI-augmented research - while still maintaining clear standards for rigor, reflection, and ethical practice (Brookhart, 2010).

This section will address how faculty can revise rubrics and assessment practices to evaluate student thinking - not just output - in AI-enhanced academic work. It will provide examples of rubric criteria, sample language, and strategies for encouraging responsible tool use without compromising academic integrity. Rubrics in the AI era must do more than reward polish or formatting. They must prioritize:

- Evidence of critical engagement with sources and tools.
- Transparency about AI use and decision-making processes.
- Demonstrated ownership of insight, argument structure, and methodology.
- An emphasis on learning and process, not just product.

Core Goals of AI-Aware Rubrics

As AI becomes a common part of research and writing workflows, **assessment must evolve** to reflect the tools students are using - without lowering academic expectations. An effective rubric for AI-enhanced work should do more than assess the final product; it should **illuminate the thinking, choices, and ethical reasoning** that shaped it. The core goals of an AI-aware rubric include:

- **Reinforcing the Value of Human Thinking**. Centering analysis, interpretation, and originality as non-negotiable components of academic work.
- **Encouraging Ethical and Transparent Tool Use**. Requiring students to disclose how AI supported their process and to reflect on its role in shaping outcomes.
- **Rewarding Iteration and Critical Analysis**. Giving credit for revisions, reasoning, and evidence of intellectual development - not just polish.
- **Distinguishing Between Acceptable Support and Intellectual Outsourcing**. Helping faculty evaluate whether students used AI to scaffold their thinking or substitute for it.

These goals ensure that rubrics **incentivize ethical engagement, metacognition, and academic ownership** - even in a world where generative tools are only a click away.

Updating Rubric Categories for Modern Research Practices

---

1. AI Use and Disclosure (Transparency)

Why It Matters: Undisclosed AI use undermines academic transparency and **obscures authorship**, making it difficult for faculty to accurately assess student thinking, voice, and effort. When students openly disclose how they used AI - and reflect on their choices - it becomes part of their scholarly narrative, demonstrating ethical engagement, metacognition, and ownership of the learning process.

Rubric Language Example:

- *"The student clearly identifies any AI tools used during the research process."*
- *"Disclosure includes rationale for use, impact on decisions, and critical reflection on benefits and limitations."*

These criteria encourage students to treat AI not as something to hide, but as something to **account for thoughtfully**.

---

2. Assignment Integration Strategy

To embed this expectation consistently across courses and assignments, **faculty can require an AI Reflection Statement** to accompany every major submission. This short, structured component invites students to articulate their use of generative tools and demonstrate intentionality in their decision-making process. The reflection should address:

- **When** the AI tool was used in the research or writing process.
- **Why** the student chose to use it, including the task it was meant to support.
- **How** it influenced the final product, including what was accepted, adapted, or rejected.

This practice not only promotes **ethical transparency** but also encourages **metacognitive awareness** - helping students understand the boundaries between support and substitution. Embedding structured reflection into assessment is key to ensuring that AI tools are used in ways that **reinforce academic integrity and student growth**, rather than replace cognitive effort (Gundu, 2024).

---

3. Critical Evaluation of AI-Generated Content

Why It Matters: AI outputs are not always accurate, relevant, or meaningful. Students must show discernment in deciding what to accept or reject.

Example (Literature Review):

- *A student uses Elicit to summarize six studies but cross-checks each summary with the original article and highlights inconsistencies.*

Rubric Language Example:

- *Student evaluates the accuracy and relevance of AI-generated summaries or outputs.*
- *Student demonstrates independent judgment when incorporating AI insights.*

Faculty Tip: Ask students to annotate or highlight **AI-supported sections** and explain **why** those outputs were accepted or revised.

---

4. Intellectual Ownership and Contribution

Why It Matters: Students must demonstrate that they are not just assembling content - but shaping it with original interpretation, synthesis, or analysis.

Rubric Language Example:

- *Student demonstrates conceptual clarity and contributes a unique academic perspective.*
- *AI-assisted sections are transformed through interpretation, commentary, or theoretical framing.*

Example (Capstone Project):

- *Two students use ChatGPT to generate research subtopics. One pastes them into the final paper untouched. The other writes a rationale for rejecting three, choosing two, and merging one into their custom framework. The latter shows ownership; the former does not.*

---

5. Process and Iteration

Why It Matters: AI can produce a clean draft in seconds, but deep research happens through **drafting, revising, and refining**. Faculty should reward visible thinking, not just the final product.

Rubric Language Example:

- *Student documents stages of project development, including AI integration, revisions, and feedback responses.*
- *Final product reflects thoughtful evolution of the research question, method, or analysis.*

Assignment Example:

- *Include a "Process Portfolio" submission option:*
  - *Outline - Annotated AI output - Revised draft - Reflection.*

This practice makes intellectual effort and the evolution of thought both visible and assessable - shifting the focus from polished output to the process of learning and decision-making. When students reflect on how they interacted with AI tools, it provides faculty with insight into their reasoning, adaptability, and ethical awareness. **Evaluating how students think with AI - not just what they produce - ensures that grading captures authentic learning in an AI-enhanced academic environment** (Reiss, 2021).

---

6. Ethics and Attribution

Why It Matters: AI tools raise questions about authorship, citation, and fairness. Rubrics should encourage students to **articulate their ethical reasoning**.

Rubric Language Example:

- *Student reflects on ethical implications of AI use and addresses fairness, authorship, and responsibility.*
- *All tools and data sources are cited appropriately, including AI platforms when used for content generation.*

Faculty Practice:

- *Provide examples of when AI should be acknowledged like a tool (e.g., Grammarly), and when it becomes part of the intellectual process (e.g., ChatGPT summaries or code suggestions).*

Formative vs. Summative Evaluation in AI Contexts

In an academic environment increasingly shaped by generative AI, assessment strategies must differentiate between formative and summative purposes - supporting student growth early on, while upholding academic standards in final submissions. This distinction helps educators encourage ethical experimentation without compromising rigorous evaluation.

Formative Assessment *(Low-Stakes, Developmental)*: Designed to support learning in progress, formative tasks should:

- **Encourage experimentation** with AI tools and allow space to learn from error or misjudgment.
- **Focus on growth** in areas such as critical thinking, ethical awareness, and research independence.
- **Provide actionable feedback** on skills such as prompt design, AI output evaluation, and tool literacy - not just content accuracy.

Summative Assessment *(Final Product Evaluation).* Summative assessments evaluate the end result of learning, and should:

- **Emphasize originality**, authorship clarity, and thoughtful integration of AI use.
- **Assess the depth of insight**, quality of argumentation, and scholarly contribution - rather than surface-level fluency or formatting.
- **Use rubrics aligned with modern research practices**, reflecting responsible AI integration, transparency, and intellectual ownership.

By clearly separating formative space for risk-taking from summative expectations of scholarly rigor, faculty empower students to develop ethical AI fluency over time. Thoughtful assessment redesign is essential to ensure that AI supports inquiry, rather than substituting for it (Gundu, 2024).

Sample Rubric Snapshot for AI-Augmented Research Paper

As generative AI tools become more integrated into student research and writing, faculty need rubrics that assess how students use these tools, not just whether the final product appears polished. This sample rubric snapshot illustrates how faculty can evaluate transparency, critical thinking, ethical engagement, and authorship clarity in AI-enhanced academic work.

The categories below emphasize process, judgment, and originality, helping faculty recognize the student's intellectual contributions - even when AI is part of the workflow. Each dimension prioritizes accountability, reflection, and academic rigor, aligning assessment with the realities of contemporary research practices. This rubric can be adapted to fit a range of disciplines and assignment types.

Category	Exceeds Expectations
AI Use and Disclosure	Clear, honest disclosure with thoughtful rationale and impact reflection
Critical Analysis	Demonstrates independent thinking; critiques AI outputs; integrates human insight
Research Process Visibility	Provides evidence of iteration, drafting, and decision-making over time
Original Contribution	Offers unique interpretations or connections beyond AI-generated content
Ethical Reflection	Engages with ethical questions related to tool use and authorship
Citation and Attribution	Properly cites AI use where appropriate; distinguishes tool support from co-authorship

---

Section Reflection: Redesigning Assessment for the Age of AI-Augmented Scholarship

This section addresses one of the most pressing challenges of the AI-integrated classroom: how to fairly and rigorously evaluate student work shaped by generative tools. It calls for a decisive shift in assessment culture - from grading polished outputs to **evaluating process, discernment, and intellectual ownership**. As tools such as ChatGPT and Elicit reshape research workflows, traditional rubrics - rooted in assumptions of solitary authorship - no longer suffice. Instead, faculty must develop **AI-aware rubrics** that reward transparency, critical reflection, and ethical reasoning alongside scholarly rigor.

Through practical guidance and concrete rubric categories, the section empowers educators to assess how students think **with** AI, not just what AI helps them produce. Core dimensions such as disclosure of tool use, evaluation of AI-generated content, iterative development, and authorship clarity redefine originality in ways that preserve academic integrity without denying the realities of modern research. It also distinguishes formative from summative evaluation, advocating for low-stakes experimentation early in the learning process and rigorous expectations at the point of submission.

Ultimately, this section reframes assessment as a mirror of **intellectual agency** - where students are asked to demonstrate not only what they did, but **why, how,** and **with what awareness**. In doing so, it ensures that AI becomes a partner in learning, not a proxy for it - and that students are held accountable not just for product quality, but for ethical, reflective, and authentic engagement with the research process.

Section 7: Supporting Writing and Synthesis with AI as a Cognitive Partner

---

Writing remains one of the most **intellectually integrative** acts students perform. It requires them to **synthesize sources**, **construct arguments**, **consider the audience**, and **express ideas clearly and ethically**. Traditionally, the greatest challenge was internal - facing the blank page alone. But today, students have powerful new allies - and new risks - thanks to the rise of generative AI.

Tools such as ChatGPT, Claude, and Grammarly can assist with outlining, suggesting transitions, rephrasing awkward sentences, or adjusting tone. When used reflectively and sparingly, they can help students write with greater clarity and confidence. However, uncritical or over-reliant use can easily overpower a student's voice, obscure the origin of ideas, or shortcut the cognitive effort required to develop a thoughtful argument.

The challenge for faculty is no longer whether students will use AI - but how to guide them in using it responsibly, transparently, and productively. As Van Dis et al. (2023) emphasized, the key is to treat AI as a cognitive partner - one that supports ideation and revision, but never replaces the student's own reasoning, synthesis, or authorship.

This section offers strategies for integrating AI into the writing process in ways that reinforce metacognitive awareness, preserve student voice, and strengthen - not supplant - intellectual engagement.

From Crutch to Catalyst: Redefining the Role of AI in Student Writing

Used thoughtfully, AI becomes not a crutch for struggling writers, but a **mirror** - one that reflects a student's clarity, coherence, or confusion back to them. When students use AI to **refine ideas**, **improve flow**, or **generate structural alternatives**, they gain insight into the logic and rhythm of their own thinking. These moments of interaction can enhance metacognition and confidence.

However, when students rely on AI to generate arguments, compose full paragraphs, or "complete" an assignment, the result shifts from augmentation to intellectual outsourcing. In such cases, the student's cognitive engagement is displaced, and the tool becomes the author - not the assistant.

The key is for faculty to help students **distinguish between mechanical assistance and cognitive contribution** - teaching them when AI supports the writing process and when it begins to substitute for the very thinking writing is meant to develop. Reiss (2021) noted that true learning occurs when students use AI as a reflective partner - not as a shortcut around reasoning and authorship.

Faculty Strategies for Supporting AI-Assisted Writing

---

1. Differentiate Levels of AI Support

One of the most important skills students must develop in an AI-enhanced writing environment is the ability to **recognize the role AI plays in their own process**. Not all AI support is equal - and not all types of assistance carry the same academic or ethical implications. By helping students **differentiate between mechanical, structural, and cognitive support**, faculty can empower them to make informed choices, disclose appropriately, and retain ownership of their thinking.

The following table offers a framework to classify AI use in writing. It can be used to shape rubric expectations, guide reflection assignments, or scaffold classroom conversations around authorship, responsibility, and transparency.

Type of Support	Examples	Disclosure Required?
Mechanical Assistance	Grammar correction, spelling, formatting suggestions (e.g., Grammarly)	Optional (especially in low-stakes work)
Structural Support	Outline generation, paragraph reordering, thesis refinement	Yes (brief acknowledgment or comment)
Cognitive Contribution	Drafting arguments, proposing conclusions, rewording claims or interpretations	Yes, with reflective explanation

Classroom Activity: Classifying AI Use

Provide students with a range of **sample AI outputs** (e.g., a grammar fix, an outline, a rewritten paragraph). In small groups or as a class, ask them to:

- ***"Label each example** as mechanical, structural, or cognitive support."*

- ***"Discuss what level of disclosure or reflection would be appropriate** for each type."*
- *"Reflect on which forms of support are **most appropriate during brainstorming, drafting, or final revision."***

This activity reinforces the idea that responsible AI use is not about prohibition - it is about awareness and authorship. Han (2025) noted that ethical engagement with AI begins when students are taught to understand and articulate their own role in shaping the tools they use.

---

2. Embed Version Comparisons in the Writing Process

To help students build authorship awareness and evaluate the role of AI in their writing, faculty can embed version comparison activities into the drafting process. These assignments ask students not just to produce polished work, but to reflect on how their ideas evolved - and how AI may have shaped that evolution. By comparing an original draft, an AI-assisted version, and their final submission, students learn to:

- Analyze which suggestions were helpful - and which they chose to reject.
- Justify their writing decisions in light of tool-generated input.
- Recognize their own voice, logic, and reasoning within the revision process.

This encourages a shift from passive use to active authorship, helping students become more intentional about what they accept from AI and what they revise or push back against. As Reiss (2021) emphasized, supporting students in interrogating the role of AI in their learning fosters metacognitive growth and responsible digital literacy.

Assignment Example: "Before and After" Exercise

- *To foster **authorship awareness and critical reflection**, ask students to **track and reflect on how AI influenced their writing decisions**.*
  - *This low-stakes assignment highlights the difference between using AI as a support tool versus a surrogate, and helps students internalize when and how their thinking evolved.*

Student Submission Includes:

- **Original paragraph** (written independently).
- **AI-suggested revision** (generated using a tool such as ChatGPT, Grammarly, or Claude).
- **Final student revision** (after critically evaluating and editing the AI output).
- **Short reflection** answering prompts such as:
  - *"What did the AI change?"*
  - *"What did you keep, revise, or reject - and why?"*
  - *"How did AI help or hinder your ability to clarify your thinking?"*

Learning Goal:

- This assignment builds metacognition, ownership, and discernment - teaching students to question how tools influence their choices rather than passively accepting suggestions. Encouraging students to reflect on their interaction with AI fosters ethical awareness and deeper engagement with the writing process (Reiss, 2021).

---

3. Use Writing Checkpoints with Reflection Prompts

Rather than assessing only the final product, faculty can promote ethical and intentional writing by breaking the process into structured milestones, each paired with a reflection opportunity. These checkpoints allow faculty to monitor AI use in real time, reinforce authorship, and help students make thoughtful decisions about how - and when - AI supports their process.

Example Writing Timeline (for a Research Paper):

- **Week 1: Topic Selection + AI-Assisted Brainstorming**. Students generate 3–5 potential topics with optional AI support. They submit a short note disclosing if and how AI was used in ideation.
- **Week 2: Annotated Outline with AI-Generated Suggestions**. Students use AI to draft section headers or structure ideas. They highlight AI contributions and comment on their usefulness or limitations.
- **Week 3: First Draft + Reflection on AI Use and Manual Revisions**. Alongside the draft, students submit a paragraph explaining how they used AI, what they kept, and what they changed through independent revision.
- **Week 4: Final Paper + AI Disclosure + Metacognitive Memo**. The final submission includes an AI use statement and a short reflective memo addressing questions like: *"How did your voice evolve in the process?"* and *"What decisions reflect your authorship?"*

Why It Works:

- Each checkpoint creates an opportunity for **instructor feedback and ethical coaching** before tool reliance becomes problematic. It also encourages students to **see writing as an iterative, reflective process** rather than a task to be completed in one sitting.
- As Gundu (2024) emphasized, embedding formative moments for reflection and feedback is essential to **maintaining academic integrity and supporting ethical AI integration** in writing-intensive courses.

---

4. Design Assignments That Require Human Voice and Judgment

To preserve student voice and intellectual ownership in an AI-enhanced environment, faculty should design prompts that require personal engagement, disciplinary framing, or reflective synthesis - tasks that AI cannot meaningfully replicate. These assignments make space for AI-supported comprehension while ensuring the core interpretive and analytical work remains human-led.

Example Prompt:

- *"After reading three peer-reviewed articles on climate migration, describe how your personal context - such as your geographic location, cultural background, or prior knowledge - shapes your interpretation of the findings. Use AI tools only for summarizing articles, not for writing this reflection."*

Rationale:

- This prompt allows students to **leverage AI for efficiency** in reading, while making clear that **meaning-making, reflection, and interpretation are theirs alone**. It builds critical agency, reinforces ethical boundaries, and helps students practice judgment, not just synthesis.
- Fostering ethical AI use is not about avoidance - **it is about teaching students where machine-generated output ends and human insight begins** (Han, 2025).

---

5. Require AI Reflection Statements

For **summative writing assignments**, requiring students to submit a short **AI Reflection Statement** encourages transparency, ethical reasoning, and metacognitive awareness. Rather than penalizing AI use, this practice creates space for students to **account for their decision-making**, articulate boundaries, and reflect on how AI influenced their process - positively or negatively.

Example Prompt:

- *"In 3–5 sentences, explain how you used AI tools while writing this paper. What decisions did the tool help you make? What did you revise or reject? How did you ensure your voice and ideas remained central to the work?"*

Rubric Criteria:

- **Thoughtfulness of Reflection**. *"Is the student engaging critically, or simply offering surface-level acknowledgment?"*
- **Evidence of Revision and Decision-Making**. *"Does the student show how they shaped or reworked AI input based on their own goals and insights?"*
- **Transparency and Ethical Reasoning**. *"Has the student clearly explained how, when, and why they used AI - demonstrating awareness of tool limitations and authorship responsibility?"*

By embedding reflection into the writing assessment process, faculty reinforce that **authorship is more than writing - it is about choice, judgment, and voice**. Documenting how AI is used in academic work is essential for maintaining scholarly accountability and ensuring students learn to engage with intelligent tools **ethically and transparently** (Van Dis et al., 2023).

What to Watch for: Signs of Overreliance on AI

As AI tools become more accessible and integrated into student writing, it is essential for faculty to recognize when students may be **leaning too heavily on automation** - not out of dishonesty, but often due to uncertainty, time pressure, or lack of confidence.

Common Indicators of Overreliance:

- **Language uniformity** across sections with little variation in tone or rhetorical voice.
- **Lack of conceptual depth** or minimal engagement with disciplinary frameworks.
- **Inability to explain key terms, transitions, or rhetorical choices** when asked in supervision or discussion.
- **Grammatically flawless writing** that reads as cognitively flat or disconnected from course content.

Faculty Response Strategies:

- Rather than assume misconduct, faculty should treat these moments as opportunities for **re-engagement and support**:
    - **Invite the student to an informal conversation** about their writing process, asking open-ended questions such as, *"What was most challenging in this section?"* or *"How did you arrive at this argument?"*
    - **Request draft versions, annotations, or brainstorming notes** to understand how the student's ideas developed over time.
    - **Offer support in building writing confidence** by helping students shift from tool dependency to intentional authorship through peer review, workshops, or one-on-one scaffolding.

Reiss (2021) suggested that the goal is not to ban the use of AI tools, but to teach students how to use them ethically, reflectively, and in ways that enhance rather than replace their cognitive contribution.

Section Reflection: Reclaiming Student Voice in AI-Augmented Writing

This section delivers a thoughtful, pedagogically grounded framework for supporting writing instruction in an AI-enhanced environment - where tools such as ChatGPT, Claude, and Grammarly are as accessible as a keyboard. Rather than framing AI as an ethical threat or writing crutch, the section encourages faculty to position it as a **cognitive partner** - one that, when used transparently and reflectively, can strengthen student clarity, confidence, and metacognition. At the same time, it clearly warns against overreliance, highlighting how unchecked automation can erode voice, obscure authorship, and displace critical thought.

The section equips educators with tangible strategies to preserve human agency in student writing: from assigning version comparison exercises and embedding writing checkpoints, to distinguishing between mechanical, structural, and cognitive forms of AI assistance. These practices reinforce that writing is not just output - it is **intellectual authorship** grounded in intentional decisions. Reflection prompts and rubric language emphasize voice, ethical boundaries, and process visibility, ensuring that students remain active, self-aware participants in their writing journey.

Ultimately, this section reframes writing instruction for the AI age. It affirms that students still need to struggle productively, revise purposefully, and write with integrity - and that faculty are essential in teaching how to **think with tools** without outsourcing the thinking itself. In doing so, it helps preserve what matters most in writing: the emergence of a student's unique voice and the thoughtful ownership of their ideas.

Section 8: Preparing Students to Present and Defend AI-Influenced Research

---

No research journey is complete until a student is able to **present, justify, and defend their work** in a scholarly setting. This is especially true in an era where AI tools - like ChatGPT, Claude, Elicit, or Copilot - may have played an active role in shaping the design, execution, or writing of that research. As a result, faculty must now prepare students not only to discuss their findings but also to explain the role that AI played in the process: what was assisted, what was original, and how ethical standards were maintained.

Whether the student is facing an **oral defense**, preparing a **conference presentation**, or submitting a **manuscript for publication**, questions about AI use are no longer hypothetical - they are expected. Faculty guidance at this stage can mean the difference between a student who stumbles over questions of integrity and one who confidently explains the human thinking behind their choices.

This section provides strategies for preparing students to articulate, defend, and ethically justify their AI use during high-stakes presentations or submissions. It includes sample prompts, reflective checkpoints, and discussion techniques that help students take ownership of their research process - ensuring that the work they present is not just completed, but fully understood.

Why This Matters: From Researcher to Scholar

In an academic culture increasingly shaped by automation, **credibility is earned through articulation**. It is no longer enough to produce a polished paper or present clean data - students must be able to explain the thinking behind their work, especially when AI tools have supported the process. The ability to communicate how tools were used - clearly, ethically, and reflectively - is now essential to maintaining scholarly trust and demonstrating academic maturity. A well-prepared student does not just report findings. They can:

- **Defend their methods**, including decisions made during AI-assisted analysis or drafting.
- **Clarify the origin of their ideas**, distinguishing between human-generated insight and machine-generated suggestions.
- **Explain how technology was used responsibly**, with attention to tool limits and ethical boundaries.

- **Demonstrate that human judgment** guided each stage of the project - from design to revision.

This is the **final test of intellectual ownership**, not just delivering a product, but being able to **account for the process** that produced it. As Van Dis et al. (2023) and Han (2025) indicated in the age of generative AI, trust is not built on the absence of automation - but on the presence of reflective, responsible human oversight.

Strategies for Coaching Students Through AI-Era Presentations

---

1. Start with a Disclosure Framework

As part of research presentations, publications, or defenses, students should be encouraged to **proactively include an AI Use Statement** - a brief, transparent disclosure of how AI tools were used throughout their project. Rather than treating AI use as something to hide, this approach promotes accountability, clarity, and scholarly integrity. A strong AI Use Statement should:

- **Identify which AI tools were used** (e.g., ChatGPT, Elicit, Scite, Copilot).
- **Clarify at what stages of the research process** they were used (e.g., brainstorming, outlining, literature synthesis).
- **Explain how the student ensured ethical and methodological rigor**, including verification, revision, and independent judgment.

Example Disclosure Slide (for a defense or presentation):

- *"AI tools such as Elicit and ChatGPT were used to assist in the early stages of literature review and brainstorming. All AI-generated summaries were manually verified, and all arguments, synthesis, and conclusions were developed and revised independently to ensure academic integrity."*

Why It Works:

- This practice **disarms skepticism** and **preemptively answers questions** about authorship, accuracy, and ethical use. By showing that AI use was transparent, verified, and limited to appropriate stages, students reinforce their credibility and demonstrate reflective, intentional research practice.

Van Dis et al. (2023) emphasized that **clear disclosure is essential to building trust** in AI-integrated scholarship - not because AI use is inherently problematic, but because scholarly integrity now requires accounting for digital assistance with honesty and care.

---

2. Use Practice Questions to Prepare for AI-Related Skepticism

As AI becomes more integrated into academic workflows, students should expect to face **questions about their tool use** during thesis defenses, conference presentations, and manuscript reviews. These questions are **not punitive;** they reflect a growing expectation that researchers can articulate the boundaries between human authorship and machine assistance. By practicing thoughtful responses in advance, students become more confident in defending their methodological choices, demonstrating both ethical awareness and intellectual ownership.

Sample Practice Questions:

- *"What role did AI play in shaping your research design?"*
- *"How did you verify the accuracy of AI-generated content?"*
- *"How did you ensure your voice remained distinct from automated suggestions?"*
- *"Did any ethical concerns arise during your use of AI tools?"*
- *"Would your conclusions have been different without AI assistance?"*

Faculty Tip:

- Incorporate **mock Q&A sessions** into thesis seminars, research methods courses, or lab group meetings. Encourage students to present an AI Use Statement, followed by 2–3 of the sample questions above. This low-stakes practice builds rhetorical fluency and prepares students to answer with clarity, transparency, and confidence when the stakes are higher.
- Preparing students to explain how they engaged with AI is no longer optional - it is part of **maintaining trust and authorship in a rapidly evolving scholarly landscape**.

---

3. Embed Reflection Prompts Throughout the Writing Process

Students who engage in ongoing reflection throughout the research and writing process are better prepared to discuss, defend, and explain their choices - particularly when AI tools are involved. Reflection transforms tool use into a transparent, intentional narrative rather than an invisible assist. It also fosters intellectual accountability, helping students articulate where their own thinking begins and how technology played a role.

Example Prompt: AI Reflection Entry (Journal or Appendix)

- *"Describe a moment in your project where AI helped you move forward. What was your next step, and how did you ensure that the output aligned with your academic goals?"*

This kind of prompt can be used in a **process journal**, project appendix, or regular writing log. It encourages students to **track decisions in real time**, rather than trying to reconstruct them after the fact.

Why It Works:

- When reflection is embedded across the research lifecycle - not reserved for the final submission - students build a coherent **narrative of authorship and agency**. This narrative can then be used during oral defenses, peer review, or publication submissions to show that AI use was guided by human intention, not convenience.

---

4. Emphasize Process Over Product in Presentations

In an era of AI-augmented research, students should be encouraged to **present not just what they produced, but how they produced it**. Emphasizing the research journey - including the use of AI tools, revision decisions, and ethical choices - helps students claim intellectual ownership and reinforces that credibility stems from transparency, not perfection.

Rather than focusing solely on outcomes, faculty can guide students to structure their presentations around the **decision-making process**, showing where human thinking shaped the research at every stage.

Slide Outline Model (for Conference or Oral Defense):

- **Research Question**. *"What was the focus, and how was it framed?"*
- **Methods**. Include any AI tools used during design, analysis, or writing.
- **AI Use Reflections**. *"What support was helpful?" "What limitations were encountered?"*
- **Literature Synthesis Strategy**. *"How were sources identified, categorized, and critiqued?"*
- **Analysis Process**. Highlight data interpretation decisions and tool influence.
- **Limitations and Ethical Considerations**. Address tool reliability, bias, and verification.
- **Conclusion and Future Directions**. Summarize insights and suggest next steps.

Why It Works:

- This presentation structure reinforces that **insight comes from process, not polish**. It teaches students to value transparency over performance and provides faculty and peers with **a clear view of the student's intellectual contributions**, including how AI was used responsibly along the way.

Gundu (2024) emphasized that making the research process visible is one of the most effective ways to preserve **authorship integrity and academic trust** in the AI age.

Teach Attribution and Ethical Framing

Just as we teach students to **cite sources and acknowledge collaborators**, they must also learn to **frame AI as a visible contributor** - not a ghostwriter or silent assistant. Responsible AI integration includes not only **disclosing tool use** but rather **reflecting on how it shaped the final product**. Attribution in the AI age is not about technical transparency alone - it is about teaching students to take **ethical ownership** of their process.

Guiding Questions for AI Attribution

Encourage students to reflect on and answer the following:

- ***"Did the AI contribute structure, language, content, or all three?"***
- ***"Was the AI-generated output revised, reworded, or reinterpreted by the student?"***

- ***"What would the work look like without the AI's influence - and what remained distinctly student-driven?"***

Students should be able to respond to these questions both **in writing and in conversation**. If they struggle to articulate their answers, it may indicate overreliance, insufficient reflection, or unacknowledged substitution of thought.

Why It Matters:

- Teaching attribution in the context of AI ensures that students not only **follow citation norms** but also **practice intellectual accountability** in an evolving academic landscape.
- Preparing students to ethically explain and justify AI use is central to preserving **authorship integrity and scholarly trust** (Selwyn, 2021).

Faculty Roles in Final-Stage Mentorship

In the final stages of the research journey - whether preparing for a defense, publication, or public presentation - **faculty shift from editors to coaches**. At this point, the goal is not to refine the student's work for them, but to empower them to **own, defend, and articulate** their decisions with confidence and clarity.

Your Role as Faculty Mentor:

- **Ask Difficult But Supportive Questions**.
  - *"Can you explain why you chose this method?"*
  - *"How would you respond if asked about AI's role in this section?"*
- **Challenge Students to Clarify Murky Rationale**.
  - Encourage precision in how they describe their decision-making, especially where AI was used.
- **Help Them Rehearse Their Framing of AI Involvement**.
  - Use mock Q&A sessions to help students practice honest, reflective responses to questions about authorship and tool use.
- **Reaffirm that Integrity comes From Transparency - Not Avoidance**.
  - Normalize open discussion about AI as part of the scholarly process, reinforcing that disclosure builds credibility.

By modeling curiosity, clarity, and ethical accountability, faculty can help students become not just researchers - but **researchers who are ready to explain, defend, and ethically own their work** in a world increasingly shaped by intelligent tools.

Section Reflection: Empowering Students to Ethically Defend AI-Enhanced Research

This section delivers a crucial and future-facing contribution to the evolving role of research mentorship: preparing students not just to complete a project, but to **defend it credibly and ethically** in an AI-integrated academic world. As tools such as ChatGPT, Claude, and Elicit become common research companions, the burden of authorship no longer ends at submission - it extends into oral defenses, presentations, and publication inquiries. Faculty must now coach students to articulate how AI shaped their process, what remained distinctly theirs, and how they made ethical, transparent choices along the way.

By emphasizing **process over polish**, the section models a powerful pedagogical shift - from output-based evaluation to process-centered authorship. Strategies such as AI use disclosures, version tracking, reflection prompts, and mock Q&A sessions reinforce metacognition and scholarly accountability. These techniques not only help students trace their thinking - but they also prepare them to communicate it clearly, confidently, and ethically to diverse academic audiences.

Ultimately, this section affirms that the final stage of research is not about hiding AI involvement, but **owning it with integrity**. It calls on faculty to reframe their role as final-stage mentors - from editors to coaches - who help students construct defensible narratives of intellectual contribution in an age of intelligent tools. In doing so, students emerge not just as users of AI, but as authors, scholars, and ethical agents equipped for the realities of modern research.

Chapter 5 Conclusion: From Detection to Discernment - Reclaiming Judgment in the AI Era

Chapter 5 has addressed one of the most pressing and overlooked imperatives of AI-integrated education: the need to teach students how to assess the **integrity** of algorithmic outputs. In a landscape increasingly populated by machine-generated essays, summaries, analyses, and arguments, the educational focus must shift from detecting AI use to **discerning its accuracy, reliability, and epistemic value**. This chapter positions that shift as central to preserving academic rigor, civic responsibility, and informed agency.

In **Section 1**, the foundation was laid by highlighting that generative AI tools, while rhetorically fluent, are not sources of **knowledge** in any human sense - they are statistical engines producing content based on likelihood, not understanding. This demands a fundamental pedagogical pivot: students must be trained to **read AI outputs with skepticism**, much like they would assess a biased news article or a flawed Wikipedia entry.

Section 2 introduced the practice of **lateral reading and source triangulation**, empowering students to cross-check AI claims with primary sources and peer-reviewed literature. This practice cultivates a habit of verification, reinforcing that fluent prose is different from **truthful or valid** content.

Section 3 deepened this critical lens by foregrounding **algorithmic bias**, helping students identify how AI systems reflect cultural norms, stereotypes, and systemic exclusions embedded in their training data. Through reflective exercises, students learn to spot whose voices are missing, what perspectives are flattened, and how language choices shape meaning.

In **Section 4**, disciplinary norms were brought into the frame. What counts as trustworthy, rigorous, or accurate varies across fields. Whether in STEM, law, or the humanities, students must learn to evaluate AI through the **epistemological standards of their discipline**, not simply through general rules of correctness.

Section 5 argued for **faculty modeling** as a cornerstone of critical AI literacy. Faculty who think aloud, critique AI outputs in real time, or share their own experiences with tool limitations demonstrate the **habits of academic judgment** that students are expected to develop.

This modeling was expanded in **Section 6**, which offered assessment strategies to evaluate not just student outputs, but their **process** - including documentation of AI use, decision rationales, and revisions. These assessments affirm that intellectual integrity is not about tool avoidance, but about **transparent, thoughtful engagement**.

Section 7 introduced the concept of **evaluation rubrics tailored for AI collaboration**, measuring student learning by how they modified, contextualized, or interrogated AI-generated material. These frameworks reinforce the idea that the AI itself is not being assessed - the **student's discernment** is.

Finally, **Section 8** tied these efforts to broader institutional goals: embedding AI output assessment into curriculum design, writing center practices, and academic integrity policies. AI literacy must not be left to chance or contained in isolated assignments - it must be treated as a **core component of 21st-century education**.

Together, these eight sections point to a concluding theme: **in the AI era, intellectual rigor is not about policing the line between human and machine authorship - it is about teaching students to stand at that line with discernment, responsibility, and voice**. Students must learn to challenge fluency with fact, coherence with context, and automation with intention.

The central pedagogical task, then, is to cultivate a generation of **critical interpreters of algorithmic content** - students who can engage AI as a partner in inquiry, but never confuse its outputs with authority. Chapter 5 affirms that the heart of academic integrity is not in detection, but in **discernment** - and that this discernment must be actively taught, modeled, and assessed in every classroom that embraces or encounters AI.

Chapter 6: Reimagining the Dissertation or Capstone - New Formats for New Questions

The traditional dissertation or capstone - structured around a five-chapter model and a linear argument - may no longer fully serve the complex, interdisciplinary, and AI-enhanced questions that today's graduate students are exploring. This chapter examines alternative dissertation or capstone formats, including portfolio-based, design-based, and interactive models that allow for greater adaptability, creativity, and real-world alignment. Faculty will gain strategies to support innovation in dissertation or capstone design while upholding scholarly rigor and institutional standards.

Section 1: The Traditional Dissertation or Capstone Model - Origins, Strengths, and Limitations

---

The five-chapter dissertation or capstone has become a fixture of doctoral education in the United States and many other academic systems around the world. Its formulaic structure - Chapter 1: Introduction, Chapter 2: Literature Review, Chapter 3: Methodology, Chapter 4: Results, Chapter 5: Discussion and Conclusion - has offered clarity, predictability, and a scaffolded pathway for students undertaking one of the most complex intellectual challenges of their academic lives. But as the **research landscape evolves**, so too must our frameworks for doctoral inquiry.

This section provides faculty with a **comprehensive overview of the traditional dissertation or capstone model**, tracing its historical roots and explaining its continued relevance in structuring complex doctoral work. It highlights the strengths of this model - such as its clarity, logical flow, and alignment with conventional scholarly expectations - while also acknowledging its growing limitations. In an era marked by AI integration, digital research methods, and interdisciplinary inquiry, faculty must understand where the five-chapter structure supports student learning and where it may inhibit innovation and responsiveness to contemporary research challenges.

Historical Origins of the Traditional Dissertation or Capstone

The five-chapter dissertation or capstone format became a standard feature of U.S. graduate education in the mid-20th century, particularly as higher education expanded in the post–World War II era to meet increasing demands for trained researchers and scholarly professionals (Walker et al., 2009). This model gained traction because it offered **institutional consistency**, **clear academic benchmarks**, and a **scaffolded process** for novice scholars navigating the complexities of original research. It also aligned well with a **positivist epistemology**, making supervision more efficient, assessment more uniform, and expectations more transparent - especially in fields such as education, psychology, and the health sciences (Golde & Walker, 2006).

This standardization emerged from a widespread desire to promote **consistency across institutions and disciplines**, enabling comparability in how doctoral research was structured and evaluated. It aimed to establish **clear metrics for academic rigor**, ensuring that expectations for scholarly quality were transparent and defensible. At the same time, the format offered a **practical roadmap for novice researchers**, while also supporting **efficient assessment and replication** processes for faculty, committees, and external reviewers alike.

This standardization made **dissertation or capstone supervision more manageable**, giving faculty a shared template for guiding students through each stage of research. It also created **uniform expectations for dissertation or capstone committees**, reducing ambiguity in evaluation and aligning faculty across departments. Underlying the structure was a commitment to a **positivist epistemology** - a worldview emphasizing objectivity, measurement, and generalizability - which was especially dominant in fields such as education, psychology, and the health sciences (Golde & Walker, 2006).

Strengths of the Traditional Model

Despite growing critique, the traditional dissertation or capstone structure still offers valuable pedagogical and professional benefits for many doctoral students. Its familiar format provides a clear framework for organizing complex research, guiding students through a sequential and disciplined inquiry process. Additionally, it helps faculty mentor more effectively by offering predictable checkpoints for supervision, feedback, and assessment.

---

1. Structural Clarity

The five-chapter dissertation or capstone model guides students through a **logical and disciplined progression of inquiry**, offering a clear structure for organizing their research. This progression typically moves from identifying a compelling problem, to situating that problem within existing literature, to designing an appropriate methodology. It then leads students through data collection and culminates in the **interpretation of findings**, helping them build both scholarly confidence and academic coherence.

Example:

- *A student in educational leadership studying teacher attrition follows the model precisely - framing the issue (Chapter 1), reviewing retention literature (Chapter 2), using a mixed-methods survey (Chapter 3), presenting quantitative results (Chapter 4), and exploring implications for school districts (Chapter 5).*

This format provides a structured approach that helps students scaffold their work in manageable stages, reducing cognitive overload and uncertainty. It also allows faculty to monitor progress effectively by anchoring feedback and guidance to clear chapter milestones. As a result, the process becomes more transparent and navigable for both students and advisors throughout the dissertation or capstone journey.

---

2. Replicability and Comparability

The model is intentionally built to support **methodological consistency**, ensuring that research follows a predictable and rigorous sequence. This structure is especially effective in disciplines that emphasize empirical replication, where standardized procedures enhance the reliability of findings. Fields such as psychology, education, and the health sciences often favor this model because it aligns with expectations for statistical validation and generalizability, reinforcing the norms of evidence-based inquiry.

Example:

- *In clinical psychology, students often use experimental designs or validated instruments. The structured format ensures that another researcher could reproduce the study design and test results under similar conditions.*

---

3. Academic and Institutional Legitimacy

The traditional dissertation or capstone model has long been regarded as a **symbol of scholarly credibility**, signaling that a student has mastered the conventions of academic research. Its structured design produces a final product that is **coherent, comprehensive, and accessible** to both reviewers and future scholars. Because of its familiarity and format, the dissertation or capstone can be **easily reviewed, archived, and defended**, fulfilling institutional and disciplinary expectations for rigor and professionalism.

For many dissertation or capstone committees and external evaluators, the traditional five-chapter structure provides a **familiar and efficient framework** for assessment. Its standardized format allows reviewers to navigate content easily, compare submissions across students, and identify strengths or weaknesses without needing to interpret unconventional formats. This consistency offers a practical advantage in institutions managing dozens of doctoral projects simultaneously, streamlining evaluation while upholding academic expectations.

Growing Limitations in a Changing Research Landscape

This model, while structurally clear, also imposes **significant constraints**, especially for students whose research does not follow a linear or conventional pathway. It can limit flexibility in how knowledge is constructed and communicated, making it difficult to fully capture the nuances of **emerging, interdisciplinary, or practice-based problems**. As research questions become more complex and context-driven, the rigidity of the five-chapter format may **inhibit innovation or misrepresent the researcher's true process and findings**.

---

1. It Assumes Linear Thinking in a Nonlinear World

Today's research questions increasingly call for **agile, iterative, or cyclical modes of inquiry**, rather than rigid, linear progressions. This is particularly true in methodologies such as **design-based research, participatory action research, and data science**, where findings evolve through repeated refinement or real-time collaboration. These approaches challenge the assumptions of the five-chapter model by requiring **flexibility in framing, analyzing, and presenting research**.

Example:

- *A doctoral student in human-computer interaction (HCI) develops a prototype, collects user feedback, redesigns, and repeats - yet the traditional five-chapter format does not accommodate this iterative loop.*

The result is that students often feel pressured to **compress a complex, non-linear process** into the rigid confines of the methods or results chapters. In doing so, they may omit important contextual decisions, iterations, or theoretical shifts that shaped their inquiry. This can lead to a **loss of transparency and nuance**, as students prioritize conformity to the model over accurately representing their research journey.

---

2. It Marginalizes Interdisciplinary and Creative Inquiry

Research conducted at the intersections of **technology, the arts, business, and design** often resists being broken down into neatly segmented chapters. These fields tend to rely on **fluid, exploratory, and integrative approaches**, where knowledge is generated through iteration, reflection, and creative synthesis. As a result, the five-chapter format can feel overly restrictive, **failing to capture the dynamic and interconnected nature** of these research processes.

Example:

- *A student in a digital humanities program develops an interactive archive on Black feminist literature using AI-assisted text analysis. Their work is part curation, part tool development, and part literary analysis.*

Traditional dissertation or capstone formats leave **little space for multimodal expression**, limiting students to text-heavy submissions even when their work involves diverse forms of knowledge production. This becomes especially problematic when the research process itself is grounded in **creative practice, visual analysis, or applied project work**. As a result, students may struggle to **represent key dimensions of their inquiry**, such as design iterations, media artifacts, or performative components, within a structure that privileges written analysis alone.

---

3. It Minimizes the Role of AI-Augmented Thinking

Generative AI now plays an increasingly prominent role in supporting various stages of the research process. Students use these tools for **brainstorming ideas, organizing literature, generating thematic summaries, drafting preliminary analyses**, and even creating **data visualizations** to clarify trends and patterns. This level of integration challenges traditional assumptions about the boundaries between student-generated work and tool-assisted output, reshaping how dissertations or capstones are conceived and executed.

Yet despite the increasing use of generative AI in doctoral research, the **current 5-chapter dissertation or capstone structure** offers little guidance on how to incorporate these evolving practices transparently and ethically. As a result, students are often left to navigate critical dimensions of AI use without institutional scaffolding. Specifically, the traditional model does not clearly support students in:

- **Disclosing AI use** in a systematic way, leaving questions about tool involvement, authorship, and academic integrity open to interpretation or omission.
- **Reflecting on how AI shaped their thinking**, such as recognizing how suggestions from language models may have influenced research framing, synthesis, or argument structure.
- **Integrating iterative, AI-assisted refinements** into chapters such as methodology or discussion, where real-time tool use and recursive insight challenge the linearity and fixity expected by the traditional format.

Faculty Challenge: Without meaningful structural flexibility in dissertation or capstone design, educators face a critical dilemma in how to engage with AI-integrated research. On one hand, ignoring AI use risks fostering a culture of secrecy or non-disclosure; on the other, rigidly adhering to outdated models may misrepresent the evolving relationship between student agency and machine assistance. As Selwyn (2021) argued, **failing to adapt our frameworks could obscure the realities of human-machine collaboration**, ultimately undermining both academic integrity and innovation.

---

4. It Can Feel Misaligned With Professional Practice

Many students in applied doctoral programs - such as those pursuing an EdD, DNP, or DBA - enter their studies with the goal of creating **practical solutions to complex, real-world challenges**. Their research often emphasizes implementation, systems thinking, and stakeholder engagement rather than narrowly defined, theory-driven hypotheses. As such, traditional dissertation or capstone structures may fail to accommodate the **iterative, adaptive, and context-sensitive nature** of the problems these students are trying to solve.

Example:

- *A doctoral candidate working in community health co-leads a youth mental health intervention. Their results are embedded in workshops, implementation reports, and co-authored narratives. But the five-chapter dissertation or capstone requires converting this dynamic process into a static write-up, distorting both findings and meaning.*

Looking Forward: Why This Matters for Faculty

Faculty must recognize that the growing interest in alternative dissertation or capstone formats does not signal a **rejection of academic rigor or scholarly standards**. Instead, it reflects a desire for greater **relevance, authenticity, and alignment between research design and real-world complexity**. By embracing new structures, faculty support students in representing their intellectual work more accurately - ensuring that rigor is measured not by format conformity, but by the **depth, coherence, and impact of their inquiry**.

Supervising doctoral students effectively in today's AI-augmented and interdisciplinary landscape requires a **shift in faculty mindset and mentoring practice**. As research formats diversify and technological tools reshape inquiry, faculty must adapt how they guide, assess, and support emerging scholars. To do so, effective supervision now demands:

- **Understanding both the strengths and limitations of the five-chapter model**, including when it provides helpful scaffolding and when it may constrain innovation, complexity, or authentic knowledge representation.
- **Being open to alternative formats**, such as project-based, portfolio-based, or design-based dissertations or capstones - that better align with iterative research, creative practice, or applied problem-solving in real-world contexts.
- **Learning to assess scholarly rigor through process, reflexivity, and contribution** rather than relying solely on structural conventions, ensuring that evaluation is based on depth of thought, ethical transparency, and impact.

As faculty shift into roles as **research architects**, their responsibilities extend beyond guiding content - they must also help students **select a dissertation or capstone format that aligns with the nature of their inquiry**. This involves engaging students in thoughtful conversations about structure, purpose, and the representational needs of their research questions and methods. Throughout this process, faculty must ensure that whatever format is chosen, it upholds the standards of **clarity, accountability, and scholarly integrity** (Brookhart, 2010).

Section Reflection: Reexamining the Dissertation or Capstone as a Structure for Scholarly Growth in a Changing Era

This section offers a critical and timely exploration of the traditional five-chapter dissertation or capstone model, recognizing both its enduring strengths and its growing limitations in an era shaped by interdisciplinary inquiry, real-world complexity, and AI-augmented thinking. While the model has long served as a scaffolding tool - providing clarity, consistency, and institutional legitimacy - it increasingly risks constraining authentic research expression when applied rigidly across evolving methodological and epistemological contexts.

By tracing the model's historical roots in positivist traditions, the section helps faculty appreciate its foundational value, especially for novice researchers or fields requiring replicability. Yet, it also illuminates how the model falters in capturing nonlinear processes, collaborative or creative methods, and the iterative logic of practice-based or AI-integrated inquiry. The discussion of how generative tools now play a formative role in shaping literature reviews, analysis, and synthesis is especially salient, highlighting a structural disconnect between modern research workflows and legacy formats.

Importantly, the section reframes interest in alternative dissertation or capstone designs not as a dilution of academic rigor, but as a call for greater relevance, reflexivity, and alignment with real-world scholarly practices. Faculty are invited to evolve from format enforcers to research architects - mentors who help students select or adapt structures that best support the depth, complexity, and integrity of their inquiry. In doing so, the dissertation or capstone becomes not just a credentialing mechanism, but a truer reflection of how knowledge is now constructed: collaboratively, iteratively, and with critical awareness of the tools that shape our thinking.

Section 2: Portfolio Dissertations or Capstones - Integrating Diverse Forms of Scholarship

In an era of multimodal communication, interdisciplinary inquiry, and increasingly public-facing scholarship, the conventional monograph dissertation or capstone no longer meets the needs - or reflects the contributions - of all doctoral students. As students engage in research that spans **multiple domains, audiences, and platforms**, they require a more flexible structure to demonstrate their impact. The **portfolio dissertation or capstone model** answers this need by allowing candidates to compile a set of **thematically unified scholarly works** - such as journal articles, policy briefs, digital tools, videos, blogs, or applied research reports - rather than a single, book-length document.

This model reflects the way scholarship often unfolds in the real world: **incrementally, collaboratively, and in diverse formats**. It also offers doctoral students a chance to **connect academic research to professional practice**, preparing them for careers that demand communication across contexts - not just within the ivory tower (Golde & Walker, 2006; Walker et al., 2009).

What Is a Portfolio Dissertation or Capstone?

A portfolio dissertation or capstone allows for a **diverse range of scholarly outputs**, each tailored to different audiences, purposes, and mediums of knowledge dissemination. These components reflect the **realities of modern research**, where impact is no longer confined to traditional print formats and scholarly contribution often extends beyond academia into professional, digital, and public spheres. As Boud et al. (2023) emphasized, such models support **practice-based, applied, and multimodal forms of inquiry**, enabling students to demonstrate intellectual rigor, creativity, and relevance across multiple forms of knowledge production.

These individual products are not stand-alone artifacts; they are accompanied by a **cohesive set of framing and reflective documents** that unify the portfolio and demonstrate the candidate's intellectual development over time. These components typically include:

- **A unifying introduction** that clearly articulates the overarching research question or theme, explains the rationale for using a portfolio format, and describes how each product contributes to the broader inquiry.

- **A synthesis or concluding chapter** that integrates the collective findings across the portfolio, discusses their significance, and identifies implications for practice, policy, or further research - bringing cohesion to the work as a whole.
- **Reflective components** that offer insight into the student's methodological evolution, key learning moments, and emerging scholarly identity, positioning the candidate as a thoughtful practitioner and contributor to their field.

Typical Components Included

A portfolio dissertation or capstone allows for a **diverse range of scholarly outputs**, each tailored to different audiences, purposes, and mediums of knowledge dissemination. These components reflect the **realities of modern research**, where academic impact is not limited to traditional print formats and meaningful scholarly contribution increasingly extends into **professional, digital, and public domains**. As Carless and Boud (2018) noted, portfolio and capstone models enable doctoral students to **demonstrate intellectual rigor, creativity, and applied relevance** across multiple platforms - expanding the definition of what counts as scholarly work while maintaining high standards of academic integrity.

The following examples represent common elements within a portfolio dissertation or capstone or capstone, illustrating how students can demonstrate intellectual rigor, creativity, and applied relevance through multiple modes of knowledge production:

- **A Peer-Reviewed Journal Article or Manuscript Prepared for Submission**. This academic product showcases the student's ability to contribute to disciplinary conversations, present evidence-based findings, and engage with scholarly literature in a format widely recognized for its credibility and rigor.
- **An Applied Policy Report Tailored for a Practitioner Audience**. Designed for use by educators, healthcare professionals, business leaders, or policymakers, this report demonstrates the student's capacity to translate research into **actionable insights** - bridging the gap between theory and practice.
- **A Digital Product, Such as an AI-Enabled Dataset, Web-Based Tool, or Interactive Visualization**. These outputs highlight technical fluency and innovation, offering scalable or replicable tools for future researchers or practitioners. They exemplify the growing role of **data-driven inquiry and digital scholarship** in contemporary doctoral work.
- **A Multimedia Documentary or Instructional Video**. Incorporating narrative, audiovisual elements, and/or interviews, this product may serve to communicate findings to **non-academic audiences** or to document community-based or participatory research processes in accessible, engaging formats.
- **A Teaching Guide or Curriculum Framework**. This component demonstrates the application of research to **pedagogical design**, often used in education, health professions, or leadership programs. It allows the student to contribute directly to the learning environments they aim to influence.
- **A Traditional Chapter or Conceptual Paper**. Grounded in theory-building or critical analysis, this element allows the student to explore foundational or emerging frameworks in their field, establishing their position within **ongoing academic debates**.

Together, these components reflect a **multimodal approach to doctoral scholarship**, emphasizing adaptability, relevance, and impact. The portfolio model recognizes that scholarly contribution today must often reach across sectors, platforms, and formats - while still meeting the highest standards of integrity and academic excellence.

Why Use a Portfolio Model?

---

1. Supports Interdisciplinary and Applied Work

Some students produce scholarly work that cannot be confined to a single discipline, methodology, or medium - particularly when their research engages with **complex, real-world challenges** that demand interdisciplinary thinking and multimodal communication. Traditional dissertation or capstone formats often constrain their ability to integrate **creative practices, applied problem-solving, or cross-sector collaboration**, especially in fields where innovation and social impact are central. Portfolio models address this need by offering **academic breadth and methodological diversity**, enabling students to synthesize multiple forms of inquiry while preserving **intellectual coherence and scholarly rigor** (Blair & Monske, 2009).

Example:

- *A student in environmental justice research publishes one article in a climate policy journal, develops a GIS-based digital map for affected communities, and creates a reflective essay on integrating Indigenous knowledge systems.*

This type of work may **resist the linear progression** of the traditional five-chapter dissertation or capstone, particularly when it evolves through iterative, interdisciplinary, or community-engaged methods. However, it still represents a **substantive and coherent intellectual contribution**, even if its format departs from convention. Through reflective framing, synthesis, and intentional design, these projects can be **woven into a compelling narrative** that demonstrates both scholarly rigor and practical impact in real-world contexts.

---

2. Reflects Real-World Scholarly Practice

In today's scholarly and professional environments, work is increasingly disseminated through **multiple, iterative platforms**, including journal articles, digital tools, policy briefs, podcasts, and multimedia outputs - not solely through monographs. This shift reflects a broader evolution in how knowledge is **produced, circulated, and consumed** across academic, public, and professional sectors. The portfolio dissertation or capstone format prepares students for this reality by equipping them with the **flexibility and communication skills** needed to engage diverse audiences and participate in scholarly dialogue across multiple formats and platforms (Bengtsen, 2023).

Example:

- *A doctoral candidate in public health contributes to a CDC white paper, co-authors a publication on community health metrics, and builds a public data dashboard with explanatory texts.*

Their dissertation or capstone portfolio serves as more than just an academic requirement - it becomes a **professional calling card** that showcases the breadth and relevance of their scholarly contributions. By including multiple formats and products, the portfolio offers tangible evidence of the student's ability to **disseminate research across varied contexts and audiences**. It reflects a readiness to operate within today's dynamic knowledge ecosystems, where impact is measured not only by publication but by **reach, utility, and adaptability**.

---

3. Aligns with Equity and Inclusion Goals

By recognizing **non-traditional scholarly forms**, portfolio dissertations or capstones offer a more inclusive and adaptable framework for doctoral work. This format is particularly well-suited for students engaged in **community-based research, multilingual scholarship, or practice-oriented inquiry**, where the value of the work may lie in its applied impact rather than its adherence to conventional academic structures. As a result, portfolio models can **better accommodate diverse ways of knowing and communicating**, ensuring that scholarship remains both rigorous and relevant across cultural, linguistic, and professional boundaries.

Example:

- *A student working with refugee populations co-produces an oral history video with participant collaborators, writes a theoretical paper on trauma-informed research methods, and builds a bilingual web archive.*

These artifacts enable students to **honor the voices, experiences, and knowledge** of the communities with whom they collaborate - something that is often difficult to capture fully in traditional dissertation or capstone formats. At the same time, they allow for the **development and extension of theoretical frameworks**, bridging the gap between practice and scholarship. This dual commitment to **community relevance and academic contribution** is often constrained by

the rigid structure of the five-chapter model, but is more easily realized through the flexibility of a portfolio approach.

Faculty Guidance: How to Support Portfolio Dissertation or Capstone Development

---

1. Start With a Unifying Framework

Help students **identify and clearly articulate a central research question or thematic thread** that unifies the portfolio as a cohesive body of work. This thematic through-line serves as the intellectual anchor, ensuring that each product - regardless of its audience, genre, or methodology - **contributes meaningfully to the overarching inquiry**. Even when styles or formats differ, each artifact should demonstrate **intentional alignment with the portfolio's purpose**, reinforcing both academic coherence and scholarly depth.

To ensure that portfolio dissertations or capstones remain cohesive, purposeful, and academically rigorous, faculty should require students to submit a **comprehensive portfolio proposal early in the process**. This document serves as both a planning tool and a point of alignment between the student and their committee, helping everyone involved understand how the various components will come together to form a coherent dissertation or capstone. A strong proposal demonstrates the student's ability to think strategically about their scholarly voice, intended impact, and the relationship between diverse research outputs. The proposal should include:

- **A Clearly Articulated Overall Research Goal or Central Question**. This defines the thematic anchor for the portfolio and explains how the selected artifacts will contribute to a unified line of inquiry.
- **A Detailed Description of Each Intended Artifact and Its Primary Audience**. For example, one product may target academic scholars through a journal article, while another addresses practitioners through a policy brief or curriculum guide.
- **A Justification for the Selected Formats and Mediums**. Students should explain why each product form is appropriate for the content, audience, and goals of the research, including how nontraditional formats (e.g., videos, datasets, or digital tools) support dissemination and impact.
- **A Production and Integration Timeline**. This includes anticipated dates for drafting, feedback, revision, and synthesis, ensuring the student is thinking proactively about workload, coherence, and scholarly framing across artifacts.

By embedding this proposal into the dissertation or capstone process, faculty set the stage for **intentional, interdisciplinary, and ethically grounded scholarship** - one that mirrors the realities of knowledge work in the 21st century.

Example Framework:

- **Theme**: *Equitable access to education in rural communities*
- **Components**:
    - *Quantitative article on policy outcomes.*
    - *Podcast featuring local educators.*
    - *Toolkit for rural administrators.*
    - *Final synthesis essay tying together implications and methods.*

---

2. Coach Students on Genre-Specific Rigor

Each product in a portfolio dissertation or capstone must **adhere to the standards of its respective genre**, whether it is an academic manuscript, a policy report, a curriculum guide, or a multimedia artifact. This means meeting expectations for rigor, clarity, audience engagement, and evidence-based argumentation - without compromising scholarly integrity.

Faculty play a key role in helping students **balance innovation with academic quality**, ensuring that creative formats still uphold ethical practices, disciplinary norms, and the overall coherence of the dissertation or capstone.

Example Coaching Points:

- **For a Podcast**: *"Is the narrative coherent?" "Are sources cited in notes?" "Is the tone appropriate for the intended audience?"*
- **For a Digital Tool**: *"Does it function as intended?" "Is it accessible and ethically designed?"*

Encourage students to **collaborate with experts in media, data visualization, or design** when their portfolio includes formats that require specialized technical or creative skills. These collaborations can greatly enhance the quality, accessibility, and impact of nontraditional dissertation or capstone components - especially when visual storytelling, digital interactivity, or user-centered design are involved. Faculty should support these interdisciplinary partnerships by helping students maintain scholarly coherence and ensuring that such collaborations are integrated ethically and transparently into the dissertation or capstone process.

---

3. Emphasize Integration and Scholarly Contribution

Faculty should guide students in crafting a **final synthesis chapter** that brings coherence to the entire portfolio and clearly articulates the intellectual trajectory of the work. This chapter should not merely summarize each artifact, but rather demonstrate how the components collectively contribute to a broader research question or field of practice. It is also a critical opportunity to **situate the work within scholarly discourse**, reflect on the student's development as a researcher, and identify future directions for inquiry or application.

Key Questions to Guide Synthesis

The synthesis chapter serves as the intellectual **bridge that unifies the portfolio**, helping students move beyond description to reflection, integration, and scholarly positioning. Rather than treating each product as a standalone achievement, this chapter invites students to critically explore how their body of work functions as a **coherent and evolving contribution to knowledge**. Faculty can use the following guiding questions to help students construct a synthesis that is both reflective and field-relevant:

- **How do These Pieces Speak to One Another?** Identify conceptual, methodological, or thematic connections across artifacts and explain how they build toward a unified research narrative.
- **What Cumulative Insight do They Provide?** Articulate the overall significance of the portfolio as a whole - what it reveals that no single product could capture in isolation.
- **What Tensions or Contradictions Emerged?** Acknowledge conflicting findings, shifts in perspective, or unexpected challenges that shaped the work and contributed to deeper learning.

- **What Does this Work Contribute to Your Field?** Position the portfolio within the broader disciplinary or professional landscape, highlighting its relevance, originality, and potential for future impact.

This chapter plays a vital role in **reinforcing the coherence** of the portfolio by drawing explicit connections between its individual components. It helps the reader understand how each artifact contributes to a unified scholarly narrative, rather than functioning as isolated outputs. Additionally, the synthesis chapter enhances the **academic depth of the dissertation or capstone**, demonstrating the student's ability to think critically across formats, reflect on methodological and thematic integration, and articulate their unique contribution to the field.

---

4. Prepare Committees and Institutions

Institutions may need to **revise existing dissertation or capstone policies** to accommodate and legitimize non-traditional formats such as portfolios, multimedia products, or practice-based research. Without clear guidelines and support, faculty committees may struggle to fairly evaluate work that diverges from the conventional five-chapter structure. As such, institutions should consider offering **targeted training for dissertation or capstone committees**, ensuring they are equipped to assess diverse forms of scholarly contribution with consistency, rigor, and respect for innovation.

Faculty Leadership in Supporting Portfolio Dissertations or Capstones

Faculty play a crucial role in leading the cultural and structural shifts necessary to support non-traditional dissertation or capstone formats. As experienced mentors and stewards of academic standards, faculty can advocate for policies and practices that embrace scholarly diversity while preserving rigor. Their leadership ensures that innovation in dissertation or capstone design is **not only permitted but meaningfully supported** across departments and programs. Faculty leadership may include:

- **Helping Departments Define Acceptable Formats for Portfolio or Alternative Dissertations or Capstones**. This involves working collaboratively to clarify what constitutes an academically sound portfolio, establish expectations for scope and quality, and ensure that diverse outputs (e.g., digital tools, creative work, applied reports) are formally recognized as legitimate scholarly contributions.
- **Creating or Adapting Rubrics that Assess Both Individual Components and the Portfolio's Overall Coherence**. Rubrics should balance specificity and flexibility, offering clear criteria for evaluating rigor, relevance, integration, and reflective synthesis - so that assessors can fairly evaluate both traditional and non-traditional elements within a unified framework.
- **Offering Workshops or Reading Groups for Committees Evaluating First-Time Portfolio Submissions**. These professional learning opportunities help committee members build confidence and shared understanding around assessing alternative formats, discuss case examples, and explore how to uphold academic integrity while honoring innovation.

Faculty Tip: Encourage committee members to focus on the **intent and scholarly contribution** of each portfolio component, rather than judging it solely by how closely it mirrors a traditional dissertation or capstone chapter. This shift in perspective allows for a more **nuanced and equitable evaluation** of diverse formats, especially those tailored to professional, creative, or community-based contexts. By prioritizing the **purpose, rigor, and relevance** of each piece, committees can uphold high academic standards while embracing innovative forms of doctoral scholarship.

Example Portfolio Dissertation or Capstone Structure

Section	Description
Introductory Chapter	Presents the central question, rationale for the format, and literature background
Article 1 (Peer-Reviewed)	Traditional academic manuscript
Product 2 (Digital Report)	Applied product with explanation and citations
Product 3 (Podcast/Media)	Public-facing output with transcript and context
Synthesis Chapter	Integrates findings, reflects on process, outlines future work

---

Section Reflection: Embracing the Portfolio Dissertation or Capstone as a Model of Scholarly Relevance and Rigor

This section offers a compelling and pragmatic vision of the portfolio dissertation or capstone as a 21st-century alternative to the traditional five-chapter model - one that honors scholarly rigor while expanding the definition of what counts as academic contribution. In an era of multimodal communication, real-world application, and AI-supported inquiry, the portfolio model provides much-needed flexibility for students whose research spans disciplines, engages diverse audiences, and calls for dissemination beyond the academic monograph.

By framing the portfolio dissertation or capstone not as a dilution of scholarly standards but as a **reimagination of form**, this section positions faculty as both gatekeepers of academic integrity and champions of innovation. It highlights how a cohesive, well-framed collection of scholarly artifacts - whether peer-reviewed articles, policy briefs, digital tools, or creative outputs - can serve as powerful evidence of a student's ability to conduct meaningful, field-relevant research. Through clear scaffolds such as synthesis chapters, reflection components, and unified thematic narratives, the model ensures coherence, depth, and impact across varied outputs.

Importantly, the section equips faculty with concrete strategies for mentoring students through this format, including the development of proposals, genre-specific coaching, and integration of reflective practice. It also addresses institutional implications, urging departments and committees to adapt policies and rubrics that legitimize diverse scholarly formats without compromising evaluative rigor.

Ultimately, this section reaffirms that the future of doctoral scholarship lies not in rigid adherence to tradition, but in responsive, thoughtful design - where students demonstrate intellectual growth, methodological expertise, and societal relevance across multiple platforms. By supporting the portfolio dissertation or capstone, faculty help redefine excellence in ways that honor both academic standards and the complexity of contemporary knowledge production.

Section 3: Design-Based and Practice-Oriented Dissertations or Capstones

---

In applied doctoral programs - such as education, business, nursing, healthcare leadership, public administration, and social work - students are often less interested in contributing to abstract theory than in **solving problems in practice**. These students are practitioner-scholars: educators redesigning curriculum for multilingual learners, hospital administrators testing workflow systems, or business leaders piloting new DEI frameworks. The traditional five-chapter dissertation or capstone often struggles to capture the **messy, iterative, and contextual nature** of this work.

Design-based and practice-oriented dissertation or capstone models offer an alternative that aligns more closely with the **realities of practice-based research**. These formats emphasize **development, implementation, evaluation, and refinement of interventions in real-world settings**. Their products are not only research outputs, but **tools for change** - curriculum plans, strategic models, policy recommendations, or organizational frameworks.

This section introduces faculty to the **core principles and structural features** of design-based research (DBR) and action research - two methodologies rooted in iterative inquiry and real-world problem solving. These approaches emphasize the co-creation of knowledge through **cycles of implementation, reflection, and refinement**, often in collaboration with practitioners, communities, or organizational stakeholders. Faculty will gain practical strategies for supervising dissertations or capstones that **prioritize innovation and measurable impact**, while still upholding the standards of **academic rigor, methodological transparency, and scholarly contribution**.

What Is Design-Based and Practice-Oriented Research?

Design-based research (DBR) and action research are **cyclical, intervention-focused, and practice-centered** methodologies that seek to generate solutions to real-world problems while contributing to scholarly knowledge. Both approaches emphasize **iterative development**, where insights from each cycle of implementation inform the next, allowing for continuous refinement of interventions or practices. Unlike traditional linear research models, DBR and action research are inherently **responsive and collaborative**, making them especially well-suited for contexts where change, complexity, and stakeholder engagement are central.

- **Design-Based Research (DBR).** Rooted in the fields of education and the learning sciences, design-based research involves the **systematic design, implementation, and iterative refinement** of interventions in authentic, real-world settings. The goal is not only to solve complex, context-specific problems but also to generate **theoretical insights** that can inform broader educational or organizational practices. By operating at the intersection of **design and research**, DBR contributes to both **practical innovation and scholarly advancement**, making it a powerful methodology for impact-oriented dissertations or capstones (McKenney & Reeves, 2018; F. Wang & Hannafin, 2005).
- **Action Research.** Widely used in the social sciences and professional fields such as education, healthcare, and organizational leadership, action research emphasizes **collaborative, participatory problem solving**. In this approach, the practitioner serves as both the **researcher and the change agent**, engaging directly with the context to enact and study meaningful improvements. Grounded in principles of **reflection, empowerment, and iterative inquiry**, action research is especially well-suited for dissertations or capstones that seek to bridge theory and practice through **localized, real-time impact** (Kemmis & McTaggart, 2007).

Key Characteristics Shared by Design-Based Research and Action Research

Although Design-Based Research (DBR) and Action Research emerge from different disciplinary traditions, they share a **core set of methodological and philosophical commitments** that distinguish them from more traditional, linear dissertation or capstone models. Both approaches prioritize **real-world relevance, iterative inquiry, and practitioner engagement**, making them especially valuable for students conducting research in dynamic, applied settings. Faculty guiding these dissertations or capstones should understand the following foundational elements that unite these two approaches:

- **Iterative Cycles of Inquiry (Plan - Act - Observe - Reflect - Refine)**. Both methodologies follow a cyclical process in which interventions are tested, evaluated, and revised across multiple rounds. This iterative design allows the research to evolve in response to findings, stakeholder feedback, and contextual changes, strengthening both rigor and relevance.
- **A Central Focus on Solving a Real-World Problem**. DBR and action research are driven by practical challenges that arise within authentic contexts - such as classrooms, clinics, or organizations - where the goal is to develop meaningful, actionable solutions that can be sustained or scaled.
- **A Strong Emphasis on Stakeholder Involvement**. Collaboration with key participants - such as teachers, administrators, patients, or community members - is fundamental. These stakeholders are not passive subjects but **co-constructors of knowledge**, shaping both the research questions and the implementation of interventions.
- **Research that is Situated in a Specific, Local Context**. Unlike generalized studies that seek universal laws, these methodologies are rooted in the **particularities of place**,

acknowledging that meaningful change often depends on context-sensitive understanding and responsiveness.

- **Outcomes that may Include Artifacts, Systems, or Process Improvements**. In addition to academic insights, the products of DBR and action research often include **tangible outputs** - such as instructional models, digital tools, workflows, or leadership strategies - that have immediate value in the field.
- **The Researcher Plays an Active, Embedded Role in the Process**. Rather than maintaining distance or neutrality, the researcher is a **participant and collaborator**, using reflection-in-action to adapt the study in real time and contribute to both practice and theory.

Supervising the Practice-Based Dissertation or Capstone: Key Considerations

---

1. Define the Problem Context Clearly

The first and most critical step in a **practice-oriented dissertation or capstone** is identifying a clearly defined, contextually grounded **problem of practice**. Unlike abstract theoretical inquiries, these problems emerge from **authentic challenges faced by organizations, communities, or professional environments**, and they serve as the anchor for designing, testing, and refining solutions. A well-framed problem of practice provides clarity of purpose, aligns stakeholders, and allows for meaningful, measurable progress within the scope of a dissertation or capstone project. A strong problem of practice should be:

- **Specific Enough to be Addressed Within a Single Project Cycle**. It should be narrow in scope, with clearly defined boundaries and a manageable scale that enables the student to implement, observe, and refine an intervention within the dissertation or capstone timeline.
- **Grounded in Stakeholder Needs and Local Realities**. The problem should reflect real-world concerns as expressed by those most affected - such as students, practitioners, patients, or community members - and be situated in the particular **social, cultural, or institutional context** in which the research will occur.
- **Informed by Prior Literature or Theory**. Even when rooted in practice, the problem should be supported by a **review of relevant research and conceptual frameworks**, ensuring that the project is not only locally responsive but also **academically situated and theoretically informed**.

Example:

- *A student in an EdD program identifies high student disengagement in 9th-grade math. They design and pilot a gamified learning module aligned with district standards.*

Faculty Strategy: Supporting Students in Framing Actionable Research Questions

Faculty play a crucial role in helping students **translate real-world concerns into researchable, academically sound inquiries**. In practice-oriented dissertations or capstones - such as those using design-based research (DBR) or action research - this translation is not always intuitive. The student must balance the complexity of real-world challenges with the constraints of time, scope, and academic rigor. Faculty can guide this process by offering structure, asking critical questions, and reinforcing methodological discipline from the very beginning. Key strategies include:

- **Help Students Connect Real-World Problems to Focused Research Questions**. Encourage students to move from broad concerns (e.g., "teacher burnout" or "access to health care") to **targeted, researchable questions** that can be explored through data collection, stakeholder engagement, and reflective analysis. This often involves identifying leverage points - specific moments, populations, or practices that are ripe for intervention.
- **Emphasize Clarity of Scope: One Site, One Intervention, One Cycle**. Students should be guided to frame their project within **a single setting**, testing one intervention or strategy through **a clearly bounded cycle of inquiry**. This promotes methodological coherence, feasibility, and depth of analysis, ensuring that the project remains manageable while still yielding meaningful insights.

---

2. Scaffold the Research Design Around Iteration

Unlike traditional, linear dissertations or capstones that move sequentially from problem statement to conclusion, **Design-Based Research (DBR) and action research evolve through dynamic, iterative cycles**. These cycles typically involve planning, implementing an intervention, collecting data, reflecting on outcomes, and refining both the intervention and the research design. This recursive process allows for **continuous learning and adaptation**, making these approaches especially suited to complex, real-world contexts where solutions must be responsive to changing conditions.

Common Structure for DBR Dissertation or Capstone Chapters

Design-Based Research (DBR) dissertations or capstones follow a structure that mirrors the **cyclical and adaptive nature of the methodology** itself. Unlike the rigid five-chapter format of traditional dissertations or capstones, DBR structures are intentionally flexible, emphasizing **problem-solving through design, implementation, and reflection** in real-world contexts. The chapter sequence below provides a framework that balances scholarly rigor with the **practical realities of iterative intervention**:

- **Introduction and Problem Statement**. Presents a clearly defined and contextually grounded problem of practice, including background, significance, and the rationale for choosing a DBR approach.
- **Literature Review and Theoretical Framing**. Synthesizes relevant research and positions the study within theoretical frameworks that inform both the problem space and the intervention design.
- **Intervention Design and Rationale**. Details the structure, function, and intent of the proposed intervention, explaining how it addresses the identified problem and aligns with both theory and practice.

- **Implementation and Data Collection**. Describes the real-world enactment of the intervention, the stakeholders involved, and the data collection strategies used during each cycle.
- **Analysis and Iterative Refinement**. Analyzes collected data and outlines how the intervention and/or research design evolved in response to findings - highlighting the recursive nature of DBR.
- **Reflection, Implications, and Future Directions**. Offers a reflective synthesis of lessons learned, discusses practical and theoretical contributions, and proposes next steps for continued innovation and study.

This structure supports students in **narrating their design journey**, emphasizing not just outcomes but the **learning, adaptation, and reasoning** that occurred throughout the process.

Assignment Example:

- *Students submit a* ***"Design Iteration Log"*** *that tracks all changes made to their intervention, research methods, or focus across each cycle. The log includes before-and-after snapshots of materials (e.g., revised lesson plans, workflows, or protocols), rationales for each change, and reflections on how data or stakeholder feedback informed decisions.*

This assignment emphasizes learning through adaptation and helps students articulate the scholarly value of iterative refinement.

Faculty Tip: Encourage students to **systematically document the changes** made to their intervention, methods, or focus as the project evolves. These iterations are not signs of failure or indecision - they are essential to the integrity and learning embedded in design-based or action research. Remind students that the process of refining ideas in response to data and stakeholder input is itself a **valuable scholarly contribution**, offering insight into both the complexity of real-world practice and the responsiveness of thoughtful inquiry.

---

3. Focus on Methodological Transparency

Because interventions in design-based and action research are often **context-specific and variable**, it is crucial that students maintain **rigorous documentation** throughout the research process. Detailed records of implementation steps, stakeholder interactions, contextual conditions, and iterative changes help ensure transparency and allow others to understand how and why decisions were made. This level of documentation not only strengthens the **credibility and trustworthiness** of the research but also enables future adaptation and replication in similar or evolving settings.

Example Requirements for Documenting a Practice-Based Intervention

In practice-oriented dissertations or capstones such as Design-Based Research (DBR) or Action Research, students must go beyond describing outcomes - they need to **capture the full arc of design, implementation, and refinement**. This involves providing rich, transparent documentation that allows readers to trace the evolution of the intervention and understand the decisions that shaped it. Clear documentation enhances **credibility, reproducibility, and**

scholarly contribution, particularly in context-specific and adaptive research models. Key documentation components may include:

- **A Detailed Description of the Intervention Itself**. This might include curriculum materials, professional development modules, instructional strategies, leadership models, or technology tools. The student should describe not only what was designed, but also the rationale behind key design choices.
- **Clear Participant Roles and Site Characteristics**. Students should explain who was involved (e.g., teachers, students, staff), in what capacity, and under what conditions. Contextual factors - such as setting type, institutional norms, and demographic characteristics - are critical for understanding both implementation and findings.
- **Data Collection Methods Aligned with Each Cycle of Inquiry**. Students must outline how evidence was gathered - through observation, surveys, interviews, focus groups, or artifact analysis - and how each method informed decisions or refinements in the project.
- **An Explanation of Decision Points and Pivots Throughout the Design Process**. Rather than presenting a polished narrative, students should highlight where adjustments were made, why changes occurred, and how those changes enhanced the intervention's effectiveness or contextual fit.

By including these elements, students ensure that their dissertation or capstone captures **not just the outcomes of their project but rather the full depth of the research process itself**. This includes how knowledge was developed, tested, and refined through cycles of action, reflection, and adaptation - hallmarks of practice-based methodologies. As a result, the dissertation or capstone becomes a **transparent record of inquiry**, demonstrating scholarly rigor through iterative design rather than linear execution.

Assignment Example:

- *Students submit an "Intervention Brief" with visual models, decision logs, and stakeholder maps before implementing changes.*

---

4. Assess Scholarly Contribution Through Practical Impact

Traditional dissertations or capstones often emphasize the production of **generalizable knowledge** - findings that can be applied broadly across settings, populations, or theoretical frameworks. In contrast, **practice-oriented research** prioritizes **actionable knowledge**, aiming to generate insights and interventions that address specific, real-world problems. While the scope may be narrower, the impact can be immediate and meaningful, offering **practical guidance for future efforts in similar contexts** and contributing to a cycle of applied innovation and reflection.

Example Contributions from Practice-Oriented Dissertations or Capstones

Unlike traditional dissertations or capstones that often focus on theory development or generalized empirical findings, practice-oriented dissertations or capstones aim to produce **tangible, context-sensitive solutions** that respond directly to community, organizational, or field-based needs. These contributions reflect the intersection of **rigor and relevance**, advancing both scholarly understanding and professional practice. The examples below illustrate the kinds of innovations that can emerge from design-based or action research models:

- **A New Advisory Model for Community College Retention**. Developed in collaboration with academic counselors and student support staff, this model integrates real-time data analytics and student feedback loops to reduce dropout rates and increase student engagement.
- **An AI-Driven Rubric for Equity-Based Hiring in HR Departments**. This tool supports fair and inclusive hiring practices by using machine learning to detect language bias in job descriptions and rank candidates based on transparent, mission-aligned criteria.
- **A Participatory Planning Framework for Rural Health Access**. Created through engagement with rural healthcare providers and residents, this framework supports collaborative decision-making around resource allocation, transportation, and culturally responsive care.

Each of these contributions represents a **scholarly intervention within real-world systems**, designed not only to solve pressing problems but to generate insights grounded in practice. While their primary value may be localized, these interventions offer **immediate utility** to stakeholders and provide a foundation for **adaptation or replication** in similar environments. Though they may not yield universally generalizable truths, they produce **transferable lessons, adaptable models, and evidence-informed frameworks** that can inform future efforts in comparable settings (T. Anderson & Shattuck, 2012).

---

5. Prepare for Ethical Complexity in Real-Time Research

Unlike lab-based studies that often occur in controlled environments with limited variables, **design-based dissertations or capstones unfold within live systems**, where complexity, unpredictability, and human relationships shape every stage of the research. These settings - such as schools, clinics, or community organizations - introduce **real-world constraints and opportunities**, requiring students to navigate stakeholder dynamics, institutional cultures, and ethical considerations. As a result, the research carries **authentic consequences**, making the findings not only academically valuable but also immediately relevant to those involved.

Common Ethical Challenges in Practice-Oriented and Iterative Research

Design-based and action research dissertations or capstones often require students to operate within **dynamic, real-world environments** where ethical challenges can evolve rapidly. Unlike one-time data collection projects, these dissertations or capstones involve **ongoing interaction with participants**, shifting contexts, and recursive cycles of engagement - all of which introduce unique ethical considerations. Faculty advisors must help students anticipate, document, and navigate these dilemmas with care, transparency, and accountability. Common ethical challenges include:

- **Shifting Consent Dynamics**. In long-term or cyclical studies, participants may change roles, leave the organization, or experience evolving relationships to the project. This requires students to revisit and re-establish **informed consent** - especially when new responsibilities or power dynamics emerge (e.g., a student becomes a peer mentor mid-study).

- **Power Imbalances Between Researcher and Participants**. When the student-researcher holds a position of authority (e.g., as a supervisor, instructor, or facilitator), there is a risk that participation may not feel fully voluntary. Students must be guided to implement safeguards - such as anonymous feedback channels or third-party facilitators - to **protect autonomy and reduce coercion**.
- **Participant Fatigue from Repeated Data Collection**. Iterative cycles often involve multiple rounds of surveys, interviews, or observations, which can exhaust participants and reduce engagement or data quality over time. Researchers must design data collection with **efficiency and respect**, balancing scholarly goals with participants' time, attention, and emotional labor.

Faculty Role in Supporting Ethical Practice Throughout the Dissertation or Capstone

In practice-oriented dissertations or capstones - such as design-based research (DBR) and action research - **ethical complexity unfolds across time**, not just at the start of the study. Faculty advisors play a vital role in helping students develop the **ethical reflexivity and procedural rigor** required to work within dynamic, relational environments. Because interventions often impact real people, systems, and decision-making structures, faculty must model and support ethical scholarship that evolves with the project. Key responsibilities include:

- **Guide Students in Preparing Robust Ethical Protocols**. Help students anticipate both standard and emergent ethical concerns by crafting protocols that are **responsive, flexible, and context-sensitive**. This includes contingency planning for shifting roles, data ownership, and long-term participant impact - issues often underexplored in conventional IRB templates.
- **Encourage Ongoing Reflective Journaling to Navigate Dilemmas**. Recommend or require reflective writing throughout the dissertation or capstone process to help students surface and document ethical tensions as they arise. This habit not only fosters **ethical self-awareness** but also provides a valuable audit trail that can be referenced during synthesis and defense.
- **Reinforce the Need for Member Checks and Participant Voice**. Remind students that ethical research is **dialogic**, not extractive. Encourage strategies such as member checking, collaborative data interpretation, and feedback loops to ensure that participant voices are respected, validated, and woven into the final narrative with integrity.

Tangible Outputs in Practice-Based Dissertations or Capstones

Unlike traditional dissertations or capstones that culminate in a theoretical manuscript or empirical report, **practice-based dissertations or capstones often produce concrete, use-oriented deliverables** designed to inform, guide, or improve professional practice. These outputs demonstrate the student's ability to translate research into **actionable knowledge** - knowledge that meets stakeholder needs, supports implementation, and generates impact beyond the academic setting. These products not only enrich the scholarly contribution but also serve as enduring tools for the field, organization, or community involved in the study. Common tangible outputs may include:

- **Instructional Modules**. Curriculum units, professional development sessions, or learning activities that can be implemented in schools, universities, or workplace training environments.
- **Toolkits**. Collections of resources - such as templates, checklists, and process guides designed to help practitioners replicate or adapt an intervention in similar contexts.
- **Dashboards**. Data visualization tools or digital platforms that synthesize and display key performance metrics, stakeholder feedback, or progress indicators to support real-time decision-making.
- **Strategic plans**. Research-informed planning documents that guide organizational change, program development, or resource allocation in alignment with evidence-based priorities.
- **Implementation Guides**. Step-by-step instructions that detail how an intervention or innovation can be launched, sustained, and evaluated within a specific setting.
- **Policy Briefs**. Concise, research-backed documents written for decision-makers that outline the implications of findings and recommend actionable next steps for policy or governance.

These outputs position the student not only as a **scholar capable of rigorous inquiry** but also as a **practical contributor who understands how to translate research into usable tools and strategies**. By creating deliverables that have direct relevance for practitioners, policymakers, or community stakeholders, the student demonstrates an ability to engage with the world beyond academia. In doing so, they emerge as a **knowledge mobilizer - someone equipped to lead change, inform practice, and bridge the gap between theory and action in real-world settings**.

Example Dissertation or Capstone Structure: Action Research in Public Health

Chapter	Purpose
Introduction	Define the problem of practice (e.g., vaccine hesitancy in rural clinics)
Literature Review	Summarize theory, interventions, and prior work
Methodology	Action research design and ethical approach
Intervention Cycle	Plan - Act - Observe - Reflect - with data analysis and narrative
Implications	What worked, what did not, next steps
Appendices	Survey instruments, stakeholder summaries, materials developed

---

Section Reflection: Embracing Iteration, Impact, and Ethical Practice in Practice-Oriented Dissertations or Capstones

This section makes a persuasive case for the legitimacy, rigor, and relevance of design-based and practice-oriented dissertation or capstone models - especially in professional doctoral programs where the goal is not only to **understand** the world, but to **change** it. As research increasingly unfolds in dynamic, real-world contexts - schools, hospitals, businesses, and communities - traditional linear structures and theory-centric frameworks often fall short. This section affirms that methodologies such as Design-Based Research (DBR) and Action Research are not only appropriate but essential for capturing the complexity, messiness, and innovation of practice-based inquiry.

By breaking from rigid, one-size-fits-all formats, these approaches foreground **iterative design, stakeholder collaboration, and applied problem-solving**. The section emphasizes that scholarly rigor is not sacrificed when research is responsive and embedded - it is simply reframed around contextual relevance, reflective refinement, and tangible contribution. Faculty are encouraged to guide students in articulating clear problems of practice, documenting cycles of intervention and learning, and demonstrating how change is developed, tested, and evaluated over time.

The emphasis on **ethical complexity** is particularly compelling. Unlike static data collection, practice-oriented dissertations or capstones require ongoing ethical discernment as roles shift, relationships evolve, and interventions unfold in lived systems. The section offers faculty concrete tools - from reflective journals to member checks - to help students navigate these complexities with integrity.

Ultimately, this section reframes scholarly contribution as both **rigorous and responsive**. It positions faculty not just as evaluators of methods, but as co-designers of inquiry that bridges theory and action. In doing so, it reaffirms that impact, innovation, and integrity can - and must - coexist in the future of doctoral scholarship.

Section 4: Multimodal and Digital Dissertations or Capstones - Expanding the Medium of Scholarship

---

In a world where ideas are now communicated through podcasts, infographics, interactive websites, and real-time simulations, the traditional dissertation or capstone - built exclusively on text - can feel increasingly out of sync with how knowledge is shared and consumed. Students entering doctoral programs today are not just writers; they are **designers, coders, filmmakers, data storytellers, and digital educators**. Their research questions often demand multimodal responses - formats that can **show, simulate, visualize, and narrate** as well as argue.

The multimodal or digital dissertation or capstone embraces this evolution. It allows doctoral candidates to present their research through **a blend of media** - including video essays, digital archives, podcasts, animations, data dashboards, and AI-generated content - while pairing these artifacts with **rigorous reflection, theoretical grounding, and critical**

analysis. This approach honors not only what students are researching, but **how they are positioned to share their work with multiple audiences** (Ball, 2004; Palmeri, 2012).

What Is a Multimodal Dissertation or Capstone?

A multimodal dissertation or capstone is an **integrated scholarly project** that weaves together multiple forms of media - such as audio, video, images, or interactive platforms - to examine and communicate a research problem. While it still includes traditional written components such as a proposal, literature review, methodology section, and analytic commentary, these are often complemented by or framed around **non-textual artifacts** that serve as primary sites of meaning-making. In this format, the central argument or contribution may be most powerfully expressed through **visual, performative, or digital modes**, allowing for a broader and more inclusive range of scholarly expression.

Examples of Multimodal Components in Dissertations or Capstones

Multimodal dissertations or capstones allow students to engage with research questions through **diverse media forms**, expanding the possibilities for analysis, representation, and dissemination. These components are not supplementary; they are **central to the argument and scholarly contribution**, offering alternative ways to construct and communicate meaning. Below are examples of multimodal elements that may serve as primary artifacts within a dissertation or capstone project:

- **A video essay analyzing visual culture**. Combines images, narration, and cinematic editing to critically explore how cultural identities are portrayed in film, advertising, or digital platforms - offering a form of analysis that is itself visual and temporal.
- **An interactive map showing migration patterns and AI-predicted changes**. Uses geospatial data, overlays, and user-controlled features to visualize historical and projected migration flows, making complex relationships more accessible and engaging for both academic and public audiences.
- **A podcast series capturing oral histories with community stakeholders**. Integrates storytelling, interviews, and sound design to document lived experiences related to the research topic, while amplifying underrepresented voices and promoting knowledge co-construction.
- **A digital tool or app built to test a pedagogical theory**. Translates theoretical insights into a usable product - such as a classroom simulator, game-based learning module, or adaptive assessment tool - providing both a testing ground and a demonstration of impact.
- **A data visualization dashboard that reveals public health disparities**. Presents aggregated datasets through interactive charts and graphs, allowing users to explore trends, compare regions, and uncover inequities - supporting data-informed advocacy and policy work.

These components, when thoughtfully designed and grounded in academic rigor, have the potential to **transform the dissertation or capstone into a more experiential and participatory scholarly artifact**. By incorporating media that engage different senses, modalities, and user interactions, students can reach broader audiences and align their work with **contemporary forms of knowledge production and dissemination**. The key is that **form must follow function** - the chosen media should meaningfully advance the research question, enhance understanding, or offer analytical depth, rather than acting as decoration or mere storytelling.

Why Use a Multimodal or Digital Format?

---

1. To Match Method to Medium

Some research questions are **inherently multimodal or applied in nature**, requiring methods of exploration and expression that extend beyond conventional academic prose. These inquiries may involve visual analysis, interactive data modeling, digital tool creation, or community-based storytelling - approaches that are better suited to **non-textual or hybrid outputs**. In such cases, traditional writing alone may constrain the researcher's ability to fully represent the complexity, context, or **practical application** of the work, making alternative formats not only appropriate but essential.

Example:

- *A doctoral candidate in digital rhetoric investigates how TikTok videos are used for mental health advocacy. Rather than describing the content, she creates an interactive video essay analyzing tone, gesture, and audience engagement - paired with scholarly citations and commentary.*

This format allows her to **critically engage with the medium of study - such as film, sound, or interactive technology - in its native form**, creating a more authentic and immersive mode of scholarly analysis. By using the medium itself as a vehicle for argumentation and insight, she can explore nuances, patterns, and meanings that may be flattened or lost in purely textual explanations. In this way, the multimodal format becomes not just a method of presentation but rather a **core component of the research process**, enabling deeper intellectual engagement than text alone can offer.

---

2. To Reach Broader and More Diverse Audiences

Multimodal formats are often **more accessible and engaging** than traditional, text-heavy dissertations or capstones, particularly for audiences beyond academia. By incorporating visual, auditory, or interactive elements, these projects can **communicate complex ideas in ways that are culturally resonant and emotionally impactful**, reaching communities, practitioners, and stakeholders who may not regularly engage with academic prose. This expanded reach not only democratizes knowledge but also increases the potential for **real-world application and public relevance**, strengthening the societal value of doctoral research.

Example:

- *A student in public health creates a GIS-enabled web map of clean water access in tribal communities, with embedded community interviews and resource guides. The project is designed for community leaders, not just dissertation or capstone committees.*

This approach reflects a growing shift in doctoral education from **knowledge preservation - storing findings in static, archived documents - toward knowledge mobilization**, which emphasizes making research accessible, usable, and impactful across multiple contexts. Multimodal dissertations or capstones align with this shift by enabling students to **actively disseminate their work through diverse formats and platforms**, increasing its visibility and utility beyond the academy. This evolution challenges institutions to rethink traditional notions of scholarly communication and embrace formats that **foster engagement, participation, and broader societal relevance** (Estima, 2020).

---

3. To Support Creative and Culturally Responsive Scholarship

Students from Indigenous, diasporic, multilingual, or artistic backgrounds often bring with them **cultural and epistemological traditions** that do not fit neatly within the rigid structure of the traditional dissertation or capstone. Their ways of knowing and expressing may involve storytelling, performance, visual symbolism, or multilingual code-switching - **genres that resist standard academic prose** and linear argumentation. Multimodal and portfolio formats create space for these scholars to **honor their identities and intellectual traditions**, while still engaging in rigorous, reflective, and impactful research.

Example:

- *A Māori doctoral student in education designs a bilingual storytelling archive featuring elders' knowledge in audio and video, accompanied by reflections on epistemology and educational theory.*

Multimodal formats can empower students to **represent their communities in ways that are both culturally grounded and intellectually rigorous**, allowing for more authentic engagement than traditional text-based formats often permit. These formats offer flexibility for integrating **storytelling, visual art, oral history, or ceremonial practice** - approaches deeply rooted in Indigenous, diasporic, or non-Western epistemologies. By creating space for these diverse expressions, multimodal dissertations or capstones honor **alternative ways of knowing and being**, supporting students in conducting research that is relational, reflective, and respectful of their community's knowledge systems (Ball, 2004; Kovach, 2021).

Faculty Strategies for Supporting Multimodal Dissertations or Capstones

---

1. Guide Students in Justifying the Format

Faculty must ensure that students' choices of media are **driven by the research question, theoretical framework, and intended audience**, rather than by novelty or aesthetic appeal alone. This means guiding students to select formats that **enhance the analysis, communication, or accessibility** of their work, rather than distract from or dilute its scholarly value. When media choices are grounded in research logic, multimodal components become **intentional tools for meaning-making**, reinforcing both academic rigor and the relevance of the work across contexts.

Students engaging in multimodal or practice-based dissertation or capstone work should be encouraged to think critically and intentionally about the media they choose to represent their research. Faculty can support this reflection by asking questions that align creative decision-making with **scholarly purpose, methodological soundness, and audience awareness**. These prompts help ensure that media choices are not simply aesthetic or technological preferences, but are instead deeply connected to the goals and values of the research itself. Students should be asked:

- **Why is This Medium the Best Tool for Your Inquiry?** This question prompts students to justify their choice based on how the medium uniquely captures, conveys, or explores their topic in ways that text alone may not.
- **How does it support Your Research Question or Audience Needs?** Students must consider the fit between form and function, ensuring that their media choice enhances clarity, accessibility, or impact for the intended audience or stakeholders.
- **How Will You Ensure Scholarly Rigor within This Format?** This encourages students to articulate how they will embed academic standards - such as transparency, critical reflection, theoretical grounding, and methodological integrity - into nontraditional or creative formats.

Assignment Example:

- *Require a **Multimodal Justification Memo** early in the dissertation or capstone proposal stage to help students critically plan and defend the use of nontraditional formats. This 2–3 page memo should outline and explain how each media component supports the research aims, aligns with theoretical frameworks, and maintains scholarly rigor. By requiring this justification upfront, faculty can assess feasibility, anticipate resource needs, and ensure that creative choices are grounded in methodological logic - not novelty.*

The Memo Should Include:

- **Intended Digital or Non-Textual Outputs**. *A list and description of the proposed multimodal elements (e.g., podcast episodes, interactive dashboards, short films, curriculum guides) that will function as core components of the dissertation or capstone.*
- **Rationale for Each Medium**. *A clear explanation of why each selected medium is appropriate for the research question, theoretical lens, and target audience - highlighting how the medium enhances insight, communication, or accessibility.*
- **Tools and Platforms Required**. *A list of any specialized tools, software, or platforms (e.g., ArcGIS, Adobe Premiere, StoryMaps, Anchor.fm) the student will need, along with their plan for learning, access, and technical support.*

- **Accessibility and Ethics Plan**. *An outline of how the student will ensure that all digital/media components are accessible to intended users (e.g., captions, alt text, multilingual formats) and how ethical concerns such as data privacy, cultural sensitivity, or participant representation will be addressed in the multimodal elements.*

This assignment reinforces intentional design and provides a **roadmap for faculty feedback**, ensuring that multimodal dissertations or capstones begin with academic alignment and institutional support.

---

2. Pair Media With Analytic and Theoretical Commentary

Digital products - while powerful vehicles for engagement and innovation - must be **grounded in scholarly explanation** to ensure that their academic merit is clear and assessable. Faculty should require students to accompany any non-textual or multimedia output with written or oral components that **contextualize the work within traditional academic frameworks**. These explanatory elements help translate the creative or applied dimensions of the project into a form that allows for critical review, committee assessment, and disciplinary contribution. These accompanying components should clearly explain:

- **Research Design**. A detailed account of the methodology used to plan, develop, and implement the digital product, including data sources, cycles of inquiry, and evaluation strategies.
- **Theoretical Framing**. A clear articulation of the conceptual and scholarly foundations that informed the product's design and purpose, showing how the work engages with or extends existing literature and paradigms.
- **Ethical Considerations**. An account of how the student addressed privacy, representation, consent, cultural sensitivity, and accessibility within the creation and dissemination of the digital product.
- **Contribution to Scholarship**. A discussion of what the product adds to the field, whether by offering a new model, generating applied insight, challenging dominant narratives, or demonstrating the value of multimodal forms of inquiry.

This practice ensures that digital scholarship is not only **visually or technically compelling** but also firmly rooted in academic expectations and scholarly accountability. By requiring a clear explanation of methods, theory, and ethical considerations, it brings structure and **credibility** to creative or applied formats that might otherwise be misunderstood or undervalued. In doing so, it positions multimodal work as a legitimate and **rigorous form of doctoral research**, capable of advancing both knowledge and practice.

Assignment Example:

- *A student creates a 15-minute interactive documentary and pairs it with a 25-page written analysis situating the work within feminist media studies and participatory design frameworks.*

This ensures the **project meets institutional expectations for scholarly depth**, while enabling expressive range.

3. Support Technical Skill Development

Students may need **technical support and training** to effectively implement the tools and platforms required for their multimodal or digital dissertation or capstone components. From podcast editing and sound mixing to interactive dashboard creation and data visualization coding, these platforms often require **skills that fall outside traditional academic preparation**. Faculty and institutions should be prepared to guide students toward appropriate resources - such as digital scholarship labs, instructional technologists, or online tutorials - to ensure that **technological challenges do not limit the quality or feasibility** of their scholarly work.

Faculty Support Options for Multimodal Dissertation or Capstone Work

Supporting students through the technical and conceptual complexities of multimodal scholarship requires faculty to adopt **proactive, collaborative, and flexible strategies**. Because many digital formats involve unfamiliar tools and workflows, thoughtful faculty mentorship can make the difference between student frustration and innovative, impactful research. Below are several concrete ways faculty can provide meaningful support:

- **Encourage Collaboration with Instructional Designers, Media Labs, or Academic Librarians**. Faculty should help students connect with on-campus or virtual support networks that specialize in instructional technology, digital scholarship, or multimodal production. These collaborators can assist with software tutorials, platform recommendations, media accessibility standards, and best practices for managing digital assets.
- **Include Digital Tool Planning in Early Supervision Meetings**. Rather than treating technical execution as an afterthought, supervisors should discuss tool requirements and capabilities during the proposal or design phase. This ensures that students choose platforms that align with their goals, skillsets, and available resources, minimizing delays or overreach later in the process.
- **Offer Flexibility in Timelines to Accommodate Learning Curves and Production Demands**. Faculty should recognize that digital production - especially when new tools or formats are involved - often takes more time than traditional writing. Offering grace in deadlines, building in checkpoints for technical support, and adjusting expectations as needed will empower students to maintain both **academic rigor and creative excellence**.

Faculty Tip: Encourage students to begin their multimodal work with **low-barrier, user-friendly tools** such as Canva for design, Twine for interactive storytelling, StoryMaps for spatial narratives, or Audacity for audio editing. These platforms are intuitive, widely supported, and often free, allowing students to focus on **content creation and conceptual clarity** without being overwhelmed by steep technical learning curves. Once students build confidence and establish the purpose of their media components, they can gradually explore more **advanced platforms** if needed, ensuring that the technology serves the scholarship - not the other way around.

4. Address Assessment, Archiving, and Accessibility

Committees may struggle to evaluate **non-traditional dissertation or capstone forms**, especially if members are accustomed to assessing work based on established norms such as linear argumentation, chapter-based structure, and dense academic prose. Multimodal, digital, or practice-based outputs can challenge expectations about what constitutes rigor, originality, and scholarly contribution. To support fair and informed evaluation, committees may need **guidance, rubrics, or professional development** that helps them appreciate how innovation and academic integrity can coexist across diverse scholarly formats.

Faculty Should Consider the Following When Supporting and Evaluating Multimodal Dissertations or Capstones

As the boundaries of scholarly communication expand to include digital and non-textual forms, faculty play a pivotal role in **ensuring academic integrity, accessibility, and sustainability**. Supporting multimodal scholarship requires intentional planning, clear evaluation frameworks, and collaboration with institutional partners. The following practices can help faculty guide students effectively while maintaining high standards of inclusivity and rigor:

- **Develop Rubrics Tailored to Multimodal Criteria**. Traditional evaluation tools may fall short when assessing creative or digital components. Faculty should create or adapt rubrics that account for **conceptual coherence, technical execution, audience engagement, and scholarly contribution**, ensuring that all forms of expression are held to rigorous, discipline-appropriate standards.
- **Ensure that Digital Projects Meet ADA Accessibility Standards**. To uphold principles of equity and inclusivity, faculty should ensure that all media components - videos, audio recordings, infographics, and interactive interfaces - include **captions, transcripts, alt-text, and keyboard navigation options**. Collaborating with accessibility specialists or campus disability services can help identify gaps and provide tools for compliance.
- **Work with Institutional Repositories to Ensure Long-Term Archival Stability**. Unlike static PDFs, digital projects may rely on external platforms, evolving file formats, or interactive media that pose challenges for archiving. Faculty should help students coordinate with university libraries or digital scholarship offices to **preserve their work in open-access repositories** or through sustainable file management practices that maintain scholarly visibility and integrity over time.

Example Rubric Criteria for Evaluating Multimodal Dissertations or Capstones

When reviewing dissertations or capstones that include digital, visual, or other non-traditional formats, committees must assess both **academic substance and media effectiveness**. A well-designed rubric helps ensure consistency, fairness, and clarity in the evaluation process, while also validating diverse scholarly contributions. Below are expanded examples of criteria commonly used in multimodal dissertation or capstone assessment:

- **Research Coherence Across Modes**. Evaluates how well the various components - textual, visual, auditory, or interactive - work together to support a unified research question or argument. Strong coherence indicates that each medium contributes meaningfully to the overall scholarly narrative rather than standing alone or distracting from the research focus.

- **Media Quality and Purpose Alignment**. Assesses whether the selected media forms are technically sound and intentionally chosen to serve the research goals. This includes clarity of visuals, sound quality, interactive design, and whether the form enhances rather than diminishes the message being conveyed.
- **Scholarly Integration and Insight**. Measures the depth of analysis, theoretical grounding, and academic contribution across all formats. High scores reflect original thinking, critical engagement with relevant literature, and the ability to **synthesize ideas across modalities**.
- **Accessibility and Usability**. Examines whether the project is designed with inclusivity in mind, including features such as alt-text, captions, transcripts, logical navigation, and compatibility with assistive technologies. This criterion ensures that the work adheres to **ethical and institutional accessibility standards**.
- **Reflective and Critical Depth**. Looks for evidence of metacognition and thoughtful engagement with the research process, media choices, and ethical implications. This may be demonstrated through written commentaries, design memos, or process documentation that articulate the rationale behind creative decisions and the challenges encountered.

A rubric using these criteria can help **bridge the gap between creative expression and scholarly rigor**, offering a clear framework for evaluating non-traditional dissertation or capstone formats. It provides committees with the language and structure needed to assess diverse outputs without defaulting to conventional benchmarks that may not apply. In doing so, it helps **balance innovation with academic accountability**, ensuring that multimodal dissertations or capstones are assessed both fairly and constructively - honoring their originality while upholding the standards of doctoral scholarship.

Example Structure: Multimodal Dissertation or Capstone in Digital Humanities

Component	Purpose
Introductory Chapter	Research questions, justification for multimodal form, and literature framing
Media Artifact #1	Data visualization dashboard with public interface
Media Artifact #2	Video documentary with participant co-authorship
Written Commentary	30-page essay theorizing aesthetics and public engagement strategies
Conclusion Chapter	Reflection on impact, implications, and future research
Appendix	Platform specs, source data, and digital ethics consent documentation

Section Reflection: Expanding Scholarly Possibility Through Multimodal and Digital Dissertations or Capstones

This section makes a powerful case for reimagining the dissertation or capstone as a flexible, media-rich artifact capable of communicating complex research across multiple platforms, languages, and audiences. By positioning multimodal and digital dissertations or capstones as rigorous, reflective, and inclusive alternatives to the traditional monograph, it affirms that **how** research is expressed is increasingly as important as **what** is being studied.

Rather than marginalizing non-textual forms as creative add-ons, the section reframes them as **central components of scholarly contribution**. Video essays, podcasts, data dashboards, web archives, and interactive maps are treated not as novelty, but as valid vehicles for meaning-making - especially in fields where communication, participation, and public impact are essential. Through examples and scaffolded structures, faculty are shown how to mentor students toward intentional, ethically grounded media choices that align with research questions and disciplinary norms.

Crucially, the section underscores that rigor in multimodal work is achieved not through adherence to form, but through transparency, coherence, accessibility, and critical framing. By requiring analytic commentary, reflective justifications, and media-specific evaluation rubrics, it demonstrates how academic integrity and creative expression can coexist. Additionally, it addresses the institutional responsibilities of archiving, assessment, and accessibility, reinforcing that supporting multimodal scholarship demands systemic readiness, not just individual enthusiasm.

Ultimately, this section reframes multimodal dissertations or capstones not as exceptions, but as emerging exemplars - models of 21st-century scholarship that honor diverse epistemologies, communicate across audiences, and make research visible, impactful, and deeply human. It challenges faculty to meet this moment by guiding students beyond the page and into the future of scholarly storytelling.

Section 5: Interdisciplinary and Transdisciplinary Dissertation or Capstone Designs

The most urgent and complex challenges of the 21st century - climate change, social justice, misinformation, healthcare access, and ethical AI - do not exist within the borders of a single discipline. They are **boundary-crossing, context-sensitive, and multidimensional**. Increasingly, doctoral students are turning to **interdisciplinary and transdisciplinary research** to address these challenges - combining tools from sociology and engineering, drawing insights from education and public health, or merging design theory with political science.

Yet the traditional dissertation or capstone structure, grounded in discipline-specific logics, often fails to support the **synthetic reasoning, methodological diversity, and epistemological**

pluralism that such projects demand. Faculty must be equipped to guide students through this more complex terrain - where research is not just about mastering one field, but about **navigating and integrating multiple intellectual worlds** (Klein, 2010; Repko & Szostak, 2020).

Key Definitions: Interdisciplinary and Transdisciplinary Research

Understanding the distinction between interdisciplinary and transdisciplinary research is essential for supervising or conducting dissertations or capstones that **cross or transcend traditional academic boundaries**. Both approaches challenge the limitations of single-discipline inquiry by embracing complexity, collaboration, and innovation - but they differ in scope, purpose, and process.

- **Interdisciplinary Research**. Interdisciplinary research involves the **purposeful integration of theories, methods, and conceptual frameworks** from two or more academic disciplines to address a shared research question or problem. Rather than merely borrowing from other fields, interdisciplinary work aims to synthesize perspectives to generate **new insights or solutions** that would not emerge within the confines of a single discipline. It is especially valuable for addressing multifaceted issues such as climate change, education reform, or public health, where multiple lenses are required to fully understand and respond.
- **Transdisciplinary Research**. Transdisciplinary research goes a step further by **transcending traditional disciplinary boundaries altogether**, often involving collaboration between academic researchers and **non-academic stakeholders** - such as community members, industry leaders, activists, or policymakers. The goal is to **co-produce knowledge** that is not only theoretically rich but also **immediately actionable and contextually grounded**. Rooted in complexity theory and systems thinking, this approach reflects a commitment to inclusivity, social relevance, and the democratization of knowledge (Nicolescu, 2002)

Why Inter- and Transdisciplinary Dissertations or Capstones Matter

---

1. Addressing Wicked Problems with Collaborative Thinking

Example: Interdisciplinary Approach to Urban Food Insecurity

- *A doctoral student investigates the* ***complex issue of food insecurity in urban neighborhoods****, approaching it through an interdisciplinary lens that brings together multiple academic and community-based perspectives. This research not only identifies the problem's root causes but also explores how structural, environmental, and social factors intersect to shape lived experiences of food access.*

The Student Draws On:

- **Geography**. *Uses spatial analysis and Geographic Information Systems (GIS) to* ***map food deserts****, revealing patterns of limited grocery store access in relation to income, transportation routes, and population density.*
- **Public Health**. *Examines the* ***nutritional and health outcomes*** *associated with limited food access, such as higher rates of obesity, diabetes, and cardiovascular disease in under-resourced communities.*
- **Policy Analysis**. *Analyzes* ***municipal zoning laws, licensing practices, and subsidy programs*** *to understand how local policies may unintentionally restrict the development of healthy food infrastructure in certain areas.*
- **Community Engagement**. *Conducts* ***interviews with local organizers, residents, and food justice advocates*** *to incorporate lived experience, build trust, and identify culturally relevant strategies for improving access.*

By weaving these strands together, the student produces a dissertation or capstone that is **analytically rich and deeply contextualized**, blending empirical evidence with lived experience to create a multidimensional understanding of the issue. Grounded in theory yet attuned to real-world conditions, the work offers both **scholarly contributions to academic discourse** and **practical insights for policymakers, practitioners, and community stakeholders**. Such projects **cannot be adequately addressed through a single disciplinary lens** - they demand the convergence of expertise, the integration of diverse methods, and a collaborative framework that values both academic and community knowledge systems.

---

2. Expanding Scholarly Imagination and Social Impact

Interdisciplinary designs allow students to **explore complex problems through multiple lenses**, enabling them to ask richer, more nuanced research questions that go beyond the scope of any single field. By drawing from diverse disciplines, students are empowered to **imagine broader, more innovative solutions** that reflect the complexity of real-world challenges. This approach also enhances the relevance and reach of their work, allowing them to **engage multiple audiences** - from academic peers and policymakers to practitioners and community stakeholders - with research that is both intellectually robust and socially impactful.

Example:

- *A student examining the ethics of AI surveillance draws from philosophy (deontology vs. utilitarianism), law (privacy protections), and computer science (algorithmic bias). The dissertation or capstone includes both a normative ethics framework and a prototype bias audit tool.*

Faculty Strategies for Supporting Inter- and Transdisciplinary Research

---

1. Help Students Frame a Coherent Research Question Across Domains

Interdisciplinary questions must strike a careful balance between **focus and expansiveness**, allowing for depth of analysis while remaining open to diverse perspectives.

They need to be **specific enough to guide data collection, analysis, and methodological rigor**, yet broad enough to invite the integration of theories, frameworks, and insights from multiple disciplines. This balance enables researchers to explore **complex, layered phenomena in meaningful ways**, fostering both analytical precision and intellectual flexibility.

Guiding Questions for Designing Interdisciplinary Research

Developing a strong interdisciplinary research design requires clarity, intentionality, and a willingness to synthesize rather than simply combine disciplinary insights. These guiding questions help students identify the **core problem**, determine which fields will contribute to its understanding, and plan for meaningful integration across intellectual boundaries.

- **What is the Central Issue Being Addressed?** Students should clearly define the phenomenon or problem at the heart of their inquiry. This includes identifying the real-world relevance of the issue, its scope, and why it warrants an approach that extends beyond a single field.
- **Which Disciplines Offer Valuable Insights - and Why?** Rather than pulling from disciplines arbitrarily, students must articulate how each field contributes something essential to the research. This might include theoretical frameworks, methodological tools, or contextual understanding that together enrich the overall analysis.
- **How Will These Perspectives be Integrated (not just Juxtaposed)?** Integration is what distinguishes interdisciplinary research from multidisciplinary work. Students should describe how they plan to synthesize disciplinary viewpoints - through shared concepts, cross-referenced analyses, or blended methods - to produce a coherent and unified contribution to knowledge.

These questions serve as the foundation for designing interdisciplinary dissertations or capstones that are **academically rigorous**, ensuring that each disciplinary contribution is methodologically sound and conceptually grounded. At the same time, they promote work that is **intellectually expansive**, encouraging students to reach beyond conventional boundaries to explore more complex, layered understandings of their topic. By addressing these guiding questions early in the research process, students are better equipped to produce **cohesive, innovative scholarship** that speaks to diverse audiences and challenges traditional ways of knowing.

Example Prompt:

- *"What problem are you trying to solve - and what does each discipline help you see that the others cannot?"*

---

2. Support Theoretical and Epistemological Integration

Students undertaking interdisciplinary research must learn to **navigate competing ontologies and epistemologies**, as different disciplines often hold fundamentally different assumptions about what counts as knowledge and how it should be produced. For instance, a field such as anthropology may prioritize **subjective experience, context, and narrative**, while another field such as public health may emphasize **quantifiable metrics, standardized**

measures, and generalizability. Bridging these philosophical and methodological tensions requires not only technical skill but also **intellectual humility, reflexivity, and a commitment to synthesis over simplification**.

Faculty Role in Supporting Interdisciplinary Integration

Faculty play a vital role in helping students successfully navigate the **philosophical, methodological, and practical challenges** that arise when combining multiple disciplinary perspectives. Effective mentorship in interdisciplinary dissertations or capstones goes beyond advising on content - it involves guiding students through the complex process of **negotiating divergent ways of knowing**, while fostering clarity, coherence, and intellectual confidence. Faculty should:

- **Help Students Articulate the Assumptions of Each Discipline**. Encourage students to name and examine the foundational beliefs, preferred methods, and evidentiary standards that each discipline brings to the research. This awareness allows students to better understand **where tensions might arise** and how each perspective contributes uniquely to the inquiry.
- **Model How to Negotiate Tensions Rather than Force False Consensus**. Rather than flattening disciplinary differences or seeking artificial agreement, faculty can demonstrate how to hold multiple viewpoints in productive tension. This includes modeling strategies such as **side-by-side comparison, layered analysis, or methodological complementarity**, which allow disciplines to dialogue without collapsing into uniformity.
- **Encourage Transparency in Reasoning and Synthesis**. Urge students to be explicit about how and why they are integrating different forms of evidence or reasoning. Statements like, *"Here is how I am combining qualitative and quantitative reasoning, and here is why that makes sense for this problem"* help readers follow the logic and **trust the rigor** of the interdisciplinary process.

This kind of faculty support not only strengthens the quality of the dissertation or capstone by ensuring coherence, rigor, and intellectual depth across multiple domains - it also equips students to **confidently engage with diverse ways of thinking and problem-solving**. Through mentorship that embraces disciplinary differences rather than erasing them, students develop the ability to **translate ideas across boundaries, synthesize conflicting perspectives, and collaborate with experts in other fields**. In doing so, they build true **interdisciplinary fluency** - a vital skill set for scholars, educators, and practitioners who must navigate and lead within today's increasingly complex, interconnected systems.

Example:

- *A student combines feminist theory (interpretivist) and behavioral economics (positivist) to study gender bias in hiring. They present two theoretical lenses side-by-side, then synthesize insights through a reflective methodology section.*

---

3. Align and Educate the Dissertation or Capstone Committee

Interdisciplinary committees often include faculty from **multiple academic departments**, each bringing their own disciplinary standards, traditions, and assumptions about what constitutes a strong dissertation or capstone. These differences can lead to **divergent expectations** around methodological rigor, preferred formats, theoretical grounding, and the nature of scholarly contribution. Navigating these varied perspectives requires clear communication, shared understanding, and a commitment to **collaborative evaluation**, ensuring the student's work is assessed fairly and in alignment with its interdisciplinary intent.

Faculty Strategy for Interdisciplinary Committee Alignment

When guiding an interdisciplinary dissertation or capstone, it is essential that faculty take an active role in ensuring **early and ongoing alignment among committee members**. Because interdisciplinary work often spans divergent traditions and expectations, even well-intentioned feedback can become confusing or contradictory if committee members are not operating with a shared understanding of the project's scope and standards. Proactive alignment fosters **coherent mentorship, constructive evaluation, and a unified support system** for the student. Faculty should:

- **Hold a Committee Alignment Meeting Early in the Dissertation or Capstone Process.** Schedule a meeting during or shortly after the proposal stage where all committee members can discuss the purpose, structure, and interdisciplinary goals of the project. This ensures that everyone begins with a **shared framework for expectations**, reducing the risk of midstream disagreements.
- **Discuss Expectations for Methodology, Format, Evaluation Criteria, and Publication Goals**. Use this time to clarify how methodological rigor will be demonstrated, what scholarly contributions are expected, whether nontraditional formats (e.g., multimodal or portfolio) are acceptable, and how the student might publish or share their work post-graduation. Alignment here builds trust and **reduces ambiguity for the student**.
- **Clarify Roles and Areas of Mentorship**. Establish who will serve as the primary content expert, who will guide research design and methodology, and who will mentor integration, writing, or reflective components. This division of labor helps the student know where to turn for specific guidance and ensures that **committee strengths are used strategically**.

Faculty Tip: Consider including an **external reader or community partner** on the dissertation or capstone committee when the research involves public engagement, applied impact, or transdisciplinary collaboration. These individuals can offer **real-world insight, practical feedback, and context-specific expertise** that enrich the scholarly process and ensure that the research is responsive to the needs of its intended audience. Including voices beyond the academy also reinforces the value of **co-produced knowledge**, helping students navigate the complexities of stakeholder engagement while grounding their work in relevance, reciprocity, and ethical practice.

---

4. Guide Students in Selecting a Flexible Structure

Traditional five-chapter dissertation or capstone formats - while useful for structuring linear, discipline-specific research - often need to be **adapted or reimagined** when students pursue interdisciplinary inquiry. These projects frequently require a more flexible structure to accommodate **multiple theoretical frameworks, blended methodologies, or collaborative components** that do not fit neatly into rigid chapter boundaries. Reworking the format allows students to better reflect the **complexity, integration, and intellectual synthesis** that define high-quality interdisciplinary scholarship.

Alternative Structures for Interdisciplinary Dissertations or Capstones

When working across disciplines, traditional chapter models may not fully capture the complexity or integrative nature of the research. Alternative structures can offer greater flexibility, enabling students to organize their work in ways that reflect **multiple perspectives, modes of analysis, and intended audiences**. These formats honor the unique demands of interdisciplinary scholarship while maintaining academic rigor and coherence.

- **Sectioned by Theme**. In this structure, the dissertation or capstone is organized around key themes or dimensions of the central problem - such as "Social Impacts," "Technical Dimensions," and "Policy Implications." This allows the student to synthesize insights from multiple disciplines under unified headings, showing how different perspectives contribute to a fuller understanding of the issue.
- **Parallel Analysis**. This format dedicates separate chapters to different disciplinary lenses, each applying its own methodology and theoretical grounding to the same central question. A final integration chapter then brings these strands together, highlighting convergence, divergence, and new insights generated by the interdisciplinary approach.
- **Hybrid Formats**. These dissertations or capstones include traditional academic chapters - such as a literature review, methodology, and synthesis - alongside **practice-oriented deliverables** such as a practitioner toolkit, curriculum design, multimedia product, or policy brief. This format is particularly effective for students aiming to produce scholarship that is both academically robust and **immediately applicable in real-world contexts**.

Each of these structures empowers students to **design a dissertation or capstone that reflects the unique contours of their research questions, disciplinary integrations, and intended audiences**. Rather than forcing the project into a rigid five-chapter format, students are encouraged to make structural choices that enhance clarity, coherence, and scholarly contribution. This flexibility not only supports more authentic and meaningful inquiry but also models the kind of **adaptive, purpose-driven thinking** that is essential for complex, interdisciplinary scholarship.

Example: Structuring an Interdisciplinary Dissertation or Capstone on Rural Education Policy

- *A student investigating rural education policy opts for a* ***three-part structure*** *that aligns with the interdisciplinary and applied nature of the research. This format allows the student to combine* ***historical, empirical, and design-based approaches*** *to generate both scholarly insight and practical recommendations. The structure reflects the* *student's intent to move beyond analysis toward impact, offering a comprehensive view of both the problem and possible solutions.*

- **Historical Analysis of Policy**. *This section traces the evolution of rural education legislation and funding over the past 50 years, using policy analysis methods from public administration and educational history. It identifies systemic patterns and policy shifts that have shaped access, equity, and infrastructure in rural schools.*
- **Qualitative Interviews with Teachers**. *Drawing on educational research and sociological methods, this section presents in-depth interviews with rural educators about their lived experiences, challenges, and insights. Themes are analyzed to surface the everyday implications of policy decisions on classroom practice and teacher well-being.*
- **Design Proposal for Rural School Support Networks**. *Informed by both historical patterns and stakeholder perspectives, the final section offers a research-based proposal for a community-driven school support model. The design includes implementation guidelines, stakeholder roles, and sustainability strategies, bridging theory and practice through applied innovation.*

This example demonstrates how an alternative dissertation or capstone structure can **seamlessly integrate multiple disciplinary methods**, allowing the student to engage with a research problem from historical, empirical, and design-oriented perspectives. By aligning each section of the dissertation or capstone with a specific purpose - analysis, stakeholder voice, and applied innovation - the structure supports both intellectual depth and practical relevance. As a result, the dissertation or capstone becomes **not only academically rigorous**, meeting scholarly standards across fields, but also **socially actionable**, offering tangible solutions that can inform real-world practice and policy.

---

5. Coach for Integration, Not Just Aggregation

Faculty must push students to move beyond merely placing disciplines side by side - what is often referred to as multidisciplinary juxtaposition - and instead, guide them toward **true interdisciplinary synthesis**. This means encouraging students to actively integrate theories, methods, and perspectives in ways that **generate original insights or frameworks**, rather than presenting separate analyses that never fully intersect. By fostering this level of intellectual integration, faculty help students create work that is **greater than the sum of its parts**, demonstrating both scholarly rigor and innovative thought across disciplinary boundaries.

Reflection Questions to Deepen Interdisciplinary Integration

As students work across disciplinary boundaries, it is essential that they engage in ongoing **critical reflection** about the intellectual, methodological, and personal dimensions of integration. These questions are designed to help students **surface the complexities, challenges, and transformative learning** that often accompany interdisciplinary research. They also support transparency and self-awareness in the dissertation or capstone, demonstrating how synthesis was achieved and why it matters.

- **What Tensions or Contradictions Emerged Between Perspectives?** This question invites students to reflect on philosophical, methodological, or practical conflicts they encountered - such as differing definitions of evidence, conflicting assumptions about causality, or incompatible stakeholder expectations. Articulating these tensions helps clarify where intellectual negotiation was required.

- **What Insights were only Possible Through Integration?** Here, students identify the unique contributions that emerged from combining disciplines - whether it was a novel framework, a richer understanding of a complex problem, or an unexpected solution that no single field could have produced alone. This showcases the added value of interdisciplinarity.
- **How Has your Thinking Evolved as a Result of Working Across Boundaries?** This prompts metacognitive reflection on how the student's assumptions, analytic habits, or theoretical preferences shifted over the course of the project. It reinforces the idea that interdisciplinary research is not only an academic process but also a **form of intellectual growth and identity formation**.

These questions can be used in reflective memos, dissertation or capstone chapters, or oral defenses to help students **demonstrate the intellectual rigor, decision-making, and synthesis strategies** embedded in their interdisciplinary journey. By articulating how they navigated and integrated multiple disciplinary perspectives, students not only showcase the depth of their research but also provide evidence of their **metacognitive growth and adaptability as scholars**. To further enhance this process, faculty should encourage the use of **visual tools - such as concept maps, Venn diagrams, or integration matrices** - which make the synthesis process more explicit, traceable, and accessible to both academic and non-academic audiences.

Sample Dissertation or Capstone Title and Structure

Title: *Designing Inclusive AI Literacy: A Transdisciplinary Approach to Ethical Education*

Section	Disciplinary Lens
Chapter 1: Introduction & Problem	Education, Philosophy
Chapter 2: Literature Review	Education, CS, Ethics
Chapter 3: Participatory Design	Design Thinking, Community Research
Chapter 4: Pilot Program Results	Mixed Methods: Surveys + Reflective Logs
Chapter 5: Discussion	Integrated Framework + Policy Implications

---

Section Reflection: Guiding Integration and Innovation in Inter- and Transdisciplinary Dissertations or Capstones

This section offers a compelling and comprehensive guide for faculty navigating the growing demand for interdisciplinary and transdisciplinary dissertation or capstone designs. In a world where pressing societal challenges defy traditional disciplinary silos, doctoral research must increasingly reflect the **complexity, intersectionality, and collaborative potential** of real-world inquiry. This section shows that faculty can no longer mentor research solely within the confines of singular epistemologies - they must now help students **bridge, synthesize,** and **transform** ideas across domains.

By clearly distinguishing between interdisciplinary and transdisciplinary work, the section equips educators with a critical lens for understanding not just **what** knowledge is being combined, but **how** and **why**. The emphasis on framing coherent research questions, supporting theoretical integration, and navigating epistemological tensions demonstrates that rigorous interdisciplinary scholarship is not additive - it is **generative**, producing insights only possible through purposeful integration.

Practical strategies - such as early committee alignment, alternative dissertation or capstone structures, stakeholder engagement, and reflective integration prompts - position faculty to support both innovation and accountability. Importantly, the section challenges educators to coach students toward **synthesis**, not aggregation. This reframing helps students produce work that is methodologically sound, socially responsive, and intellectually bold.

Ultimately, this section reinforces that the future of doctoral research lies in preparing scholars who are **boundary-crossers** - able to think across disciplines, speak to multiple audiences, and contribute actionable knowledge in a complex, interconnected world. By embracing interdisciplinary and transdisciplinary approaches, faculty uphold scholarly rigor while expanding what academic inquiry can - and must - become.

Section 6: AI-Augmented Dissertations or Capstones - Integrating Generative Tools with Integrity

As generative AI tools such as ChatGPT, Claude, and Perplexity become increasingly accessible and powerful, they are rapidly reshaping the research process. Doctoral students are using AI to assist with **idea generation, literature synthesis, coding of qualitative data, statistical modeling, language refinement, and even visualization design**. These tools, when used responsibly, can expand a student's cognitive and analytical reach - but they also introduce new challenges related to **authorship, integrity, and scholarly rigor**.

The rise of the AI-augmented dissertation or capstone demands a fundamental shift in the role of faculty - from **passive gatekeepers of academic tradition to proactive mentors of ethical and innovative scholarship**. As AI tools increasingly influence how students gather, analyze, and present knowledge, faculty must be equipped to guide them in using these technologies with **transparency, discernment, and academic integrity**. This includes helping students maintain clear intellectual authorship, understand the limitations and biases of AI-generated content, and reflect critically on the broader implications of using intelligent tools in scholarly work.

This section offers a comprehensive roadmap for supervising AI-augmented dissertations or capstones, equipping faculty with the tools and frameworks needed to **support innovation without compromising academic integrity**. It provides guidance on ethical practices - such as disclosure, attribution, and critical reflection - as well as **evaluative strategies** tailored to dissertations or capstones that involve generative or analytical AI tools. By highlighting institutional considerations and real-world examples, the section shows how AI can be used to **deepen scholarly inquiry**, foster original thinking, and enrich the research process rather than diminish it.

What Is an AI-Augmented Dissertation or Capstone?

An AI-augmented dissertation or capstone incorporates **generative or analytical AI tools - such as ChatGPT, Claude, Elicit, or Copilot - as active collaborators** in various stages of the research process, including literature review, data analysis, writing, or visualization. However, these tools are not replacements for scholarly thinking; rather, they serve as support that enhances efficiency, creativity, or depth when used with **intentionality and critical oversight**. Central to this model is the preservation of **student ownership, original insight, and ethical transparency**, ensuring that the human researcher remains the primary intellectual driver and ethical steward of the work.

How AI Can Support the Dissertation or Capstone Process

Artificial intelligence tools are reshaping the landscape of academic research by providing new forms of **cognitive scaffolding and technical assistance**. When used responsibly, AI can streamline time-consuming tasks, uncover patterns, and prompt new insights - allowing students to focus more deeply on interpretation, synthesis, and critical reflection. Below are several ways AI may serve as a meaningful partner throughout the dissertation or capstone process (Bailey et al., 2023):

- **Generating Research Questions or Narrowing Focus Areas.** AI language models can assist students in brainstorming potential research topics, identifying knowledge gaps, and refining overly broad ideas into targeted, researchable questions - especially during the exploratory phase.
- **Summarizing and Organizing Literature.** Tools such as Elicit or Scite can summarize academic articles, group sources by theme, and extract key findings or methods, helping students manage large bodies of literature and identify conceptual threads more efficiently.
- **Coding Qualitative Data or Performing Sentiment Analysis**. AI-powered platforms can aid in identifying recurring themes, tagging categories, or analyzing emotional tone in interviews or open-ended responses - supporting the early stages of qualitative analysis while still requiring human interpretation and validation.
- **Creating Preliminary Drafts or Rephrasing Sections**. Generative AI tools such as ChatGPT can assist students in organizing thoughts, rephrasing awkward language, or drafting introductory paragraphs, which students can then refine and personalize. This use supports fluency without outsourcing authorship.
- **Visualizing Data Trends or Creating Interactive Charts**. AI tools can be used to generate graphs, dashboards, or interactive visualizations that make complex data sets more understandable, especially in projects involving large-scale or multidimensional datasets.

- **Simulating Models (e.g., Economic, Behavioral, Policy-Based).** In more advanced dissertations or capstones, AI and machine learning algorithms can simulate various real-world scenarios - such as the impact of policy changes or behavioral shifts - providing predictive insight that enhances the analytical depth of the research.

These applications demonstrate that AI, when integrated thoughtfully and ethically, can serve as a **powerful augmenting tool that enhances engagement, fosters innovation, and upholds scholarly rigor** - not a shortcut to avoid critical thinking. While AI can assist with summarization, analysis, or drafting, it does **not replace human judgment, insight, or responsibility**. The student remains the central agent in the research process, fully accountable for **decisions, interpretations, and the originality of scholarly contributions**.

Supervising AI Use Across the Dissertation or Capstone Lifecycle

---

1. Idea Generation and Literature Review

AI can help students generate potential research topics, identify recurring themes across articles, and quickly summarize large volumes of scholarly sources - especially during the early stages of the dissertation or capstone process. These capabilities can increase efficiency and help students focus their inquiry by highlighting key debates or gaps in the literature. However, AI-generated summaries may be **inaccurate, outdated, or lack the depth and nuance** found in human-authored synthesis, making it essential for students to verify sources, read full texts, and engage critically with the material.

Faculty Strategy for Guiding AI Use in Literature Engagement

To ensure that AI serves as a **complement rather than a substitute for scholarly rigor**, faculty should provide structured guidance on how students use generative and research-oriented AI tools during the literature review process. This involves cultivating habits of verification, comparison, and critical reflection to prevent overreliance on machine-generated content and promote academic integrity. Faculty can implement the following strategies:

- **Require Students to Cross-Verify AI Summaries with Original Texts.** Instruct students to read and annotate full articles after reviewing AI-generated summaries, checking for **misrepresentations, missing context, or oversimplified claims**. This encourages direct engagement with the literature and helps students develop a more accurate and critical understanding of their field.
- **Encourage the use of Tools such as Elicit or Scite.ai Alongside Traditional Databases.** While AI platforms can assist with efficiency and organization, they should be used in tandem with **established academic databases** (e.g., JSTOR, PubMed, ERIC, or ProQuest). This blended approach supports broader search coverage, enhances source credibility, and trains students in both emerging and conventional research practices.
- **Assign a "Literature Audit" Where Students Compare AI-Curated Bibliographies to Peer-Reviewed Indexes.** This assignment challenges students to evaluate the **completeness, relevance, and scholarly quality** of AI-recommended sources. By

comparing outputs from AI tools with results from Scopus, Web of Science, or Google Scholar, students learn to assess algorithmic biases and develop a more intentional approach to source selection.

These strategies reinforce the principle that **AI should function as a support system - not a substitute - for human intellectual work**, especially in the context of graduate-level research. By requiring verification, critical comparison, and thoughtful integration, faculty ensure that students remain actively engaged in evaluating and synthesizing information rather than passively accepting machine-generated content. Ultimately, this approach empowers students to maintain **scholarly responsibility and academic integrity** while gaining fluency in emerging technologies that will shape the future of research and knowledge production.

Example Prompt:

- *"Explain how the AI tool supported your literature review. Which suggestions were most helpful, and which did you disregard or revise?"*

---

2. Methodology and Data Analysis

In an AI-augmented dissertation or capstone, the methodology and data analysis sections are particularly important for demonstrating transparency, academic integrity, and intellectual ownership. Students must clearly articulate not only what methods were used, but also how AI tools were integrated at each stage - whether for data organization, pattern recognition, or visual representation. Faculty play a vital role in helping students distinguish between AI as a **technical assistant** and the researcher's own **interpretive responsibility**, ensuring that the analytical process remains grounded in scholarly rigor and thoughtful decision-making.

AI Support for Data Analysis in Dissertations or Capstones

As AI capabilities expand, students are increasingly incorporating intelligent tools into the data analysis phase of their dissertation or capstone work. While these tools can offer efficiency, accuracy, and enhanced visualization, it is essential that their use be **transparent, methodologically appropriate, and critically evaluated**. Faculty can guide students to use AI not to replace their analytical thinking, but to deepen it through pattern recognition, model testing, and visual storytelling. Students may use AI to assist with:

- **Thematic Coding**. Students conducting qualitative research can use tools such as NVivo with built-in AI features, or prompt ChatGPT to identify potential patterns in cleaned interview transcripts. These tools can surface frequently mentioned themes, tag recurring language, or even suggest tentative codes - but students must still interpret, validate, and contextualize findings within the broader theoretical framework.
- **Statistical Modeling**. For quantitative research, students may use GPT plug-ins, Python notebooks, or Copilot to assist with conducting regression analyses, calculating correlations, or running simulations. These tools can help generate code snippets, correct syntax errors, or test assumptions, but faculty should ensure students understand the **underlying statistical rationale** and do not treat outputs as infallible.
- **Data Visualization**. Students may use AI tools to enhance the presentation of complex datasets, such as generating **interactive dashboards, dynamic charts, or heat maps**

that reveal trends more intuitively. These visualizations can improve accessibility and engagement, but should still be **anchored in accurate data interpretation** and accompanied by thoughtful narrative explanation.

These AI-assisted strategies allow students to redirect their time and energy from repetitive or technical tasks toward **higher-order thinking, interpretation, and synthesis**. By automating elements such as basic coding, data formatting, or preliminary categorization, AI creates more space for students to explore patterns, challenge assumptions, and draw meaningful conclusions. This shift empowers students to engage more deeply with their research questions, resulting in **insightful, conceptually grounded analyses** that reflect their own intellectual contributions.

Faculty Role in AI-Augmented Methodology and Data Analysis

Faculty play a critical role in ensuring that students use AI as an analytical aid - not as a substitute for **scholarly reasoning, methodological rigor, or ethical accountability**. As AI becomes more embedded in research workflows, faculty must help students remain active stewards of their research process, understanding not only what the AI tool did, but why and how its output was incorporated. Thoughtful faculty guidance ensures that the final dissertation or capstone reflects not just automated functionality, but genuine **intellectual authorship and critical insight**. Faculty should:

- **Ensure Students Retain Control Over Codebook Development, Interpretation of Statistical Findings, and Final Visual Decisions**. AI may help generate initial themes or statistical outputs, but students must remain responsible for confirming their relevance, defining analytic categories, and explaining data relationships in context. Faculty should emphasize that **AI suggestions are starting points - not conclusions**.
- **Require Detailed Documentation of AI Workflows and Model Parameters**. Students should clearly describe which AI tools were used, how they were prompted, what default models or settings were applied, and at which stages of the analysis the tools contributed. This documentation ensures **replicability, transparency, and integrity** - core tenets of sound research methodology.
- **Ask Reflective Evaluation Questions**. Faculty can encourage deeper accountability by prompting students to answer questions such as:
    - *"How was the AI prompted?"*
    - *"What assumptions did it make about your data?"*
    - *"How did you evaluate, adapt, or reject its outputs?"*

These questions help students become **critical interpreters of the AI tools** they use, encouraging them to move beyond passive reliance and toward intentional, reflective engagement. By asking students to consider how AI was prompted, what assumptions underpinned its output, and how they adapted or challenged those results, faculty foster deeper awareness of the **epistemological and methodological implications** of AI-assisted research. This reflective practice ensures that AI tools are used to **enhance the rigor, clarity, and originality** of the dissertation or capstone - without undermining the student's authorship or the scholarly integrity of the final product.

Ethical Note: Protecting Participant Privacy in AI-Assisted Research

AI tools should never have access to personally identifiable participant data unless the information has been **fully anonymized and reviewed by an Institutional Review Board (IRB)** or equivalent ethics committee. Even seemingly minor identifiers - such as location details, job titles, or indirect references - can pose privacy risks when shared with third-party AI platforms, especially those operating on cloud-based or proprietary servers. Faculty must emphasize that ethical use of AI includes **not only how the tools are applied, but also what data they are exposed to**, reinforcing the researcher's responsibility to uphold participant confidentiality, data security, and compliance with institutional and legal standards.

---

3. Drafting and Language Refinement

AI can assist with improving **clarity, grammar, flow, and stylistic coherence**, offering valuable support to students - particularly multilingual writers - who may face additional linguistic challenges in academic writing. These tools can help students express their ideas more effectively, reduce the cognitive load of surface-level editing, and build confidence in their written voice. However, this involvement must be **clearly documented and transparently disclosed**, ensuring that the line between technical support and intellectual authorship remains visible and ethically maintained throughout the dissertation or capstone.

Faculty Recommendation for Supervising AI-Assisted Writing

As AI tools become increasingly integrated into the writing process, faculty must adopt a clear, ethical, and supportive stance that distinguishes between **responsible assistance and inappropriate delegation of intellectual labor**. Accepting AI-assisted writing support - especially for clarity and surface-level refinement - can foster accessibility and confidence for students, but boundaries must be drawn to preserve the authenticity of scholarly work. Faculty should:

- **Accept AI-Assisted Writing Support as Legitimate, but Distinguish Between Polishing and Ghostwriting**. Clarify that using AI to improve grammar, flow, or sentence structure is acceptable when students remain in control of content, argumentation, and original insight. In contrast, having AI generate entire sections or ideas without revision or reflection crosses into **unauthorized authorship**, especially if not disclosed.
- **Require Version Comparison: Initial Student Draft vs. AI-Suggested Revision vs. Final Version**. Encourage students to submit multiple drafts that show the evolution of their writing, including what they retained, revised, or rejected from AI suggestions. This practice reinforces **metacognitive awareness, ownership of voice**, and the development of intentional, iterative writing habits - core elements of doctoral-level scholarship.

Sample Disclosure Statement:

- *"I used ChatGPT to refine paragraph structure in Chapters 2 and 5. All ideas, citations, and conceptual framing were developed independently."*

Evaluating AI-Augmented Work: What to Look For

1. Indicators of Responsible AI Use in Dissertation or Capstone Writing and Analysis

As AI becomes a more common element in the research process, it is essential to develop shared indicators of what constitutes **ethical, responsible, and academically sound integration** of these tools. Responsible use of AI is not defined solely by what the tool does, but by how the student exercises **judgment, transparency, and critical reflection** in using it. The following indicators can guide both student practice and faculty supervision in AI-augmented dissertations or capstones:

- **Clear Disclosure of When and How AI was Used**. The student explicitly states which tools were used (e.g., ChatGPT, Grammarly, Scite), what functions they supported (e.g., summarizing, editing, generating code), and at which stages of the research process they were integrated.
- **Critical Evaluation of AI Outputs**. Rather than accepting AI-generated content at face value, the student reviews, questions, and validates outputs - identifying inaccuracies, inconsistencies, or oversights and correcting them through informed decision-making.
- **Evidence of Intellectual Ownership in Framing and Interpretation**. The student demonstrates that the ideas, arguments, conclusions, and interpretations presented are the product of their own thinking, even when AI tools were used to refine expression or organize information.
- **Transparent Rationale for Integrating (or Rejecting) AI-Suggested Elements**. The student explains why certain AI-generated content was retained or modified, showing an active role in curating the final form of the work. This includes articulating how AI support aligned - or conflicted - with disciplinary standards or project goals.
- **Reflexive Commentary on the Benefits, Risks, and Ethical Trade-Offs**. The student reflects on the role AI played in shaping their work, acknowledging its advantages (e.g., efficiency, clarity, inspiration) while also grappling with concerns such as potential bias, loss of voice, or over-reliance.

These indicators offer a robust framework for evaluating **academic integrity in an era where AI tools are becoming commonplace in research and writing**. They help distinguish between superficial use of technology and thoughtful, ethical integration that reflects the student's understanding, authorship, and critical engagement. By applying these indicators, faculty can ensure that AI use **enhances the scholarly credibility and originality** of a dissertation or capstone - rather than obscuring the student's intellectual voice or diminishing the rigor of the work.

2. Red Flags in AI-Augmented Dissertation or Capstone Work

While AI can enhance productivity and clarity, improper or undisclosed use can undermine the **integrity and credibility** of a dissertation or capstone. Faculty must be vigilant in identifying signs that suggest **overreliance on AI tools or a lack of student authorship**, especially when the final product appears polished but lacks intellectual substance. The following red flags can indicate potential misuse or underdeveloped critical engagement with AI-assisted research:

- **Perfect Grammar but No Depth of Analysis**. Writing may be fluent and free of errors, but if the content lacks critical reasoning, contextual nuance, or disciplinary insight, it may indicate that AI was used to generate or heavily revise the material without sufficient human interpretation or ownership.
- **Inability to Explain or Justify Key Claims**. When questioned during supervision meetings or oral defenses, the student struggles to articulate the rationale behind major arguments, methodological choices, or interpretations - suggesting that AI outputs were accepted without reflection or understanding.
- **Fabricated or Unverifiable Citations**. The bibliography includes sources that do not exist, are misattributed, or are irrelevant to the topic. This can result from relying on AI-generated citations without cross-checking them through credible academic databases.
- **Lack of Versioning or Process Documentation**. The student cannot provide earlier drafts, AI prompts, or revision notes that demonstrate the evolution of their thinking and writing. This absence of process transparency raises concerns about authorship and academic honesty.

By recognizing these warning signs early, faculty can take a **proactive and supportive approach** to guiding students back toward ethical, engaged scholarship. Rather than treating red flags as grounds for punishment, faculty can use them as opportunities for reflection, discussion, and re-alignment of expectations. Through thoughtful intervention, faculty can help students **correct course, reestablish intellectual ownership, and use AI as a tool for deeper learning** - not as a shortcut that diminishes the quality or integrity of their academic work.

---

3. Faculty Tip: Use Process Artifacts to Assess Depth of Engagement

Evaluating a student's final submission alone may not fully capture the depth of their thinking or the authenticity of their contributions - especially in an AI-augmented research environment. To gain clearer insight into how students are interacting with AI tools and shaping their work over time, faculty should request and review **process artifacts** that document the evolution of the dissertation or capstone.

- **Prompt logs** can reveal how students formulated and refined questions to AI tools, offering a window into their reasoning, specificity, and iterative inquiry.
- **Annotated drafts** allow students to highlight where AI suggestions were implemented, revised, or rejected - providing evidence of critical engagement and metacognitive decision-making.
- **AI output transcripts** show what the tool generated in response to prompts, giving faculty a reference point for assessing what content was AI-generated versus human-authored.

These artifacts make the student's learning process **visible and traceable**, giving faculty a clearer view of how ideas developed, how tools were used, and how decisions were made across the stages of research and writing. By focusing on the evolution of the work - not just the final draft - faculty can assess the student's **intellectual effort, critical thinking, and engagement with both human and machine-generated content**. Additionally, the use of process artifacts fosters a habit of **self-reflection and ethical reasoning**, reinforcing the message that AI should be used with purpose, transparency, and scholarly integrity throughout the dissertation or capstone journey.

Institutional Considerations

---

1. AI Use Policies in Dissertations or Capstones: Institutional Guidance for Clarity and Integrity

As AI tools become increasingly embedded in academic research and writing, institutions must develop **clear, consistent, and forward-looking policies** that define acceptable practices and protect the integrity of the dissertation or capstone process. Without explicit guidelines, students may either misuse AI unknowingly or avoid helpful tools out of fear or confusion. Thoughtful institutional policy not only reduces ambiguity but also **supports responsible innovation**, encouraging transparency and ethical scholarship in an evolving digital landscape. Institutions should begin crafting guidance that addresses the following key areas:

- **What Constitutes Acceptable AI Use**? Define specific scenarios where AI tools may be used (e.g., for grammar checking, summarizing articles, generating visualizations) and where use is discouraged or prohibited (e.g., generating whole chapters, fabricating citations). This clarity helps faculty and students distinguish between **supportive augmentation and academic misconduct**.
- **When and How Students Must Disclose Assistance**? Institutions should require students to **explicitly document how AI tools were used**, at what stages, and for what purposes. This disclosure may appear in a methods section, an appendix, or a standalone "AI Use Statement," reinforcing the value of transparency as a scholarly norm.
- **Citation Standards for AI Tools (e.g., MLA, APA, Chicago Now Include Examples)**. As style guides continue to evolve, institutions should adopt and promote consistent formatting for citing AI-generated content. Whether referencing a ChatGPT-generated summary or acknowledging the use of Copilot for code generation, **proper attribution signals academic honesty** and aligns student work with current scholarly conventions.
- **Criteria for Authorship vs. Collaboration**. Institutions must help students and faculty understand that **AI tools cannot be listed as co-authors**, but their contributions should be acknowledged appropriately. Clear criteria should be established to differentiate between **student-generated insight and tool-generated assistance**, helping committees fairly evaluate student work and uphold standards of academic authorship.

Developing and disseminating these policies sends a powerful message: **AI belongs in the academy, not as a threat to scholarship, but as a tool that must be engaged with thoughtfully and transparently**. By outlining expectations for disclosure, attribution, and ethical use, institutions demonstrate their commitment to **academic integrity in a rapidly changing research landscape**. These policies also empower students and faculty to explore

AI's potential responsibly - ensuring that its use enhances the scholarly process rather than compromising the credibility of the work.

Sample Policy Language:

- *"Students may use AI tools for research assistance, language refinement, or data exploration. Any use must be disclosed in writing within the methodology or acknowledgments section. Final scholarly judgments must remain the student's own."*

---

2. Repository and Archiving Standards

Some institutions may be hesitant to archive AI-generated content within dissertations or capstones due to **ongoing uncertainties around authorship, ownership rights, and intellectual contribution**. Concerns also arise regarding the ability to verify the **originality of AI-generated text** and to trace how it was created, especially when metadata and prompt histories are not easily accessible or reproducible. Until clearer standards and technical infrastructure are developed, these challenges may lead institutions to adopt **cautious or restrictive policies** around the permanent inclusion of AI-generated material in official academic repositories.

Faculty Action Steps for Archiving AI-Augmented Dissertations or Capstones

As the use of AI tools becomes more common in the dissertation or capstone process, faculty play a key role in ensuring that both the final product and its supporting materials are **ethically documented, academically sound, and institutionally archivable**. Clear faculty guidance helps bridge the gap between evolving student practices and institutional standards for scholarly preservation. Faculty should take the following steps:

- **Encourage Students to Submit Both the Final Dissertation or Capstone and Any Digital Appendices, Including AI Prompt Logs or Tool Specifications**. By archiving not only the polished text but also accompanying materials - such as prompt histories, plugin settings, AI-generated outputs, or version comparisons - students provide a transparent record of how AI was used throughout the research process. This documentation enhances **accountability, reproducibility, and future scholarly interpretation**.
- **Ensure All Files are Accessible and Meet Long-Term Repository Guidelines**. Faculty should work with students to format materials in ways that are compatible with institutional repositories, including the use of open file formats (e.g., PDF/A, CSV, TXT), ADA-compliant accessibility features (e.g., captions, alt text), and clear metadata. Doing so supports the **long-term preservation, discoverability, and usability** of AI-augmented dissertations or capstones by future researchers and readers.

These actions help create a culture of **transparency and academic responsibility**, where the use of AI tools is not hidden or minimized, but openly acknowledged and critically documented. By guiding students to preserve prompt logs, tool settings, and annotated drafts, faculty reinforce the idea that the research process - **not just the final product - matters** in scholarly evaluation. Ultimately, these efforts ensure that AI-enhanced dissertations or capstones are held to the same standards of **archival rigor, intellectual integrity, and long-term academic credibility** as their traditional counterparts.

---

3. Publication and Co-Authorship Implications

Some publishers are now requiring authors to include **AI disclosure statements** as part of the manuscript submission process, reflecting growing concerns about transparency and authorship in scholarly communication. These policies ask researchers to specify whether generative tools were used for tasks such as drafting, editing, translation, or data analysis, and to clarify the extent of AI involvement. This shift signals an evolving standard in academic publishing - one that prioritizes **ethical clarity, proper attribution, and accountability** in the use of emerging technologies.

As AI tools become increasingly integrated into research and writing workflows, faculty must prepare students to meet the evolving expectations of scholarly publishers. This includes helping students navigate the **complexities of disclosure, authorship, and justification** when submitting AI-augmented work for peer review. Clear faculty mentorship at this stage supports not only ethical publishing but also the student's ability to position their work with confidence and transparency in academic discourse. Faculty should coach students on:

- **Whether their Manuscript Includes AI-generated Content**. Help students reflect critically on their writing and research process to determine if AI played a substantive role - such as generating text, suggesting structure, summarizing literature, or conducting data analysis - that should be disclosed to editors and readers.
- **How to Acknowledge AI Tools Without Assigning Authorship**. Guide students in writing disclosure statements that **credit the tool's role without attributing co-authorship**, following emerging norms in publishing. For example: *"Portions of this manuscript were revised using ChatGPT for clarity and grammar. All substantive content was generated and verified by the author."*
- **How to Justify AI-Supported Methodologies for Peer-Reviewed Submission**. When AI tools are used for analytical tasks (e.g., text mining, data visualization, or sentiment analysis), students should explain **why the tool was chosen, how it was validated, and how human oversight ensured rigor**. This prepares students to respond to reviewer concerns and meet the documentation standards of reputable journals.

By addressing these topics proactively, faculty equip students to navigate the complexities of AI use in scholarly publishing with **clarity, confidence, and ethical awareness**. This guidance not only reinforces the importance of academic integrity but also helps students develop the professional skills needed to meet the evolving expectations of editors, peer reviewers, and disciplinary communities. In doing so, faculty ensure that students are not merely completing a dissertation or capstone - they are being prepared to **contribute responsibly and credibly to the broader academic and professional conversation.**

Note: AI should never be listed as an author, as it cannot take responsibility for the content, decisions, or ethical implications of a scholarly work (Nature Editorial, 2023). Authorship requires the ability to exercise judgment, be accountable for the accuracy and integrity of the research, and respond to peer review - capacities that AI tools do not possess.

Instead, any substantive use of AI should be clearly disclosed in an acknowledgment or methods section, ensuring transparency without attributing authorship where it cannot apply rightfully.

Example: AI-Augmented Dissertation or Capstone in Educational Leadership

Title: *Using Generative AI to Support Inclusive Curriculum Design in Multilingual Classrooms*

Section	AI Use
Chapter 1: Introduction	Brainstormed framing language via Claude; edited by the student
Chapter 2: Literature Review	Used Elicit to surface studies, and manually validated all entries
Chapter 3: Methodology	Thematic coding assisted by GPT-5; codebook reviewed and adapted
Chapter 4: Findings	Charts created with Perplexity's visualization tool
Chapter 5: Discussion	AI-assisted drafts for structure only; the student rewrote sections
Appendix	Prompt log, AI-generated summaries with student annotations

---

Section Reflection: Stewarding Integrity and Innovation in AI-Augmented Dissertations or Capstones

This section offers a timely and comprehensive roadmap for supervising doctoral research in an era increasingly shaped by generative AI tools. Rather than viewing AI as a threat to scholarly integrity, it reframes these technologies as powerful - but ethically complex - tools that can support deeper insight, greater efficiency, and novel forms of inquiry. The central theme is clear: **AI should augment, not replace human judgment, authorship, or responsibility**.

By detailing how tools such as ChatGPT, Elicit, and Copilot can contribute meaningfully to every stage of the dissertation or capstone process - from idea generation to drafting to data visualization - this section positions AI as a legitimate academic partner when used transparently. Equally important, however, is the insistence on safeguards: clear documentation, disclosure, critical reflection, and evaluative rigor. These principles ensure that AI is integrated into research with care and intentionality, not as a shortcut that bypasses intellectual labor.

The section also outlines actionable faculty strategies, such as using annotated drafts, prompt logs, and AI use statements to make student thinking visible and traceable. These process artifacts allow advisors to assess student growth, authorship, and ethical reasoning over time - offering a more robust and equitable evaluation framework than product-based assessments alone.

At its core, this section redefines the faculty role in AI-augmented research: not as gatekeepers of tradition, but as mentors of **transparent, adaptive, and critically engaged scholarship**. It empowers institutions to develop forward-thinking policies while equipping students to produce work that is ethically grounded and technologically fluent. In doing so, it models how academic integrity can be preserved - not by resisting change, but by guiding it with vision, structure, and trust.

Section 7: Collaborative Dissertations or Capstones - Redefining Authorship and Contribution

---

The image of the dissertation or capstone as a solo scholarly act - a lone student toiling away on a monograph to prove independent competence - is rooted in an older academic tradition. But in today's research culture, the most pressing questions increasingly demand **collaborative, interdisciplinary, and stakeholder-engaged approaches**. Whether in science, social justice, public health, or education, impactful research is often **co-created**, **team-based**, and **dialogic**.

The **collaborative dissertation or capstone** acknowledges this reality by allowing students to work in formal partnership with other students, faculty, community members, or professional practitioners to develop, implement, and disseminate research. These dissertations or capstones retain individual accountability while embracing **shared authorship**, **distributed data collection**, and **joint intervention design**. When well-structured, they do not dilute academic rigor - they **reframe scholarly contribution** for the interconnected, team-oriented world of modern inquiry (Golde & Walker, 2006; Repko & Szostak, 2020).

This section outlines key structures, supervision strategies, and ethical considerations for supporting **collaborative dissertations or capstones - projects in which two or more students contribute to a shared body of work**. As collaborative models gain traction in disciplines such as the arts, public health, education, and digital humanities, faculty must know how to guide joint inquiry while ensuring that **each student demonstrates independent intellectual rigor and scholarly accountability**. When designed thoughtfully, collaborative dissertations or capstones can foster deeper learning, innovative outcomes, and authentic teamwork - honoring both **individual excellence and collective contribution** in a way that reflects the realities of 21st-century research and professional collaboration.

Why Collaborative Dissertations or Capstones Matter

---

1. Reflecting the Realities of Team-Based Research

Many research projects in fields such as health sciences, environmental studies, education, and engineering are inherently collaborative - requiring teams to **co-design studies, collect and interpret data together, and co-author findings for diverse audiences**. These disciplines often mirror real-world challenges that cannot be addressed in isolation, demanding input from multiple perspectives and areas of expertise. Preparing doctoral students for careers in these fields means going beyond individual scholarship; it requires **intentional training in teamwork, interdisciplinary communication, and the ability to navigate group dynamics** while contributing meaningfully to complex, shared intellectual endeavors.

Example:

- *A doctoral candidate in public health collaborates with two peers on a multi-site COVID-19 vaccine equity study. One leads data collection in rural clinics, another designs a GIS mapping tool, and the third coordinates community interviews. Each writes a standalone dissertation or capstone component, integrated through shared findings and methods.*

---

2. Advancing Equity Through Participatory Partnerships

Community-based participatory research (CBPR) and participatory action research (PAR) are research models that emphasize **equity, co-ownership, and mutual learning** between academic researchers and community members. Unlike traditional top-down approaches, these models center the **co-creation of knowledge with stakeholders** - including teachers, patients, students, and activists - who contribute critical experiential and contextual expertise that might otherwise be overlooked. By valuing these lived perspectives alongside academic frameworks, CBPR and PAR challenge conventional power dynamics and foster research that is not only **more inclusive and grounded** but also more likely to generate meaningful, actionable outcomes for the communities involved.

Example:

- *An EdD student partners with a local high school to co-develop a restorative justice curriculum. Youth, administrators, and teachers all contribute to the design and evaluation. The student documents process, outcomes, and reflection, positioning the community as **co-researchers**, not subjects.*

---

3. Enabling Complex, Interdisciplinary Inquiry

Some research questions are inherently too broad, complex, or multifaceted for a single scholar to explore thoroughly on their own. These types of inquiries often span disciplines, involve diverse populations, or require the integration of multiple data sources and methods - making them ideal candidates for collaborative dissertation or capstone models. In such cases, **a team-based approach allows for deeper, more nuanced investigation**, enabling each student to bring their expertise to bear while contributing to a shared, cohesive body of work.

Example:

- *In an interdisciplinary doctoral program on climate adaptation, three students focus on different dimensions of resilience - policy, infrastructure, and communication. Each writes an individual dissertation or capstone chapter, but they share data collection protocols and present joint publications as appendices.*

Faculty Strategies for Supervising Collaborative Dissertations or Capstones

---

1. Clarify the Model Early

Faculty and students must clearly define the type and boundaries of collaboration to ensure fairness, clarity, and academic integrity throughout the dissertation or capstone process. This includes outlining what aspects of the project will be developed jointly - such as data collection instruments, shared frameworks, or group analyses - and which elements will reflect each student's independent contribution. Establishing these expectations early helps avoid confusion, prevent overlap in responsibilities, and **support a balanced approach where both collaboration and individual scholarship are meaningfully represented**.

Faculty and students must clarify the exact structure and expectations of the collaborative dissertation or capstone to ensure transparency and academic accountability. Important questions to consider include:

- **Is the dissertation or capstone co-authored**, meaning a single document jointly written and defended by multiple students?
- Or is the dissertation or capstone **co-designed but individually written**, where students work together on the study design, instruments, or data collection, but produce separate dissertations or capstones reflecting their unique analysis and perspectives?
- Alternatively, is the dissertation or capstone a model where students use **shared data but conduct distinct analyses**, demonstrating their ability to apply different theoretical lenses or methodological approaches to a common dataset?

Each of these collaborative dissertation or capstone formats carries distinct implications for **authorship, evaluation criteria, and academic credit**, which must be thoughtfully considered by both faculty and institutional leadership. Without clear guidelines, students and committees may face confusion or inconsistency in how individual contributions are assessed, raising concerns about fairness, transparency, and academic standards. To prevent misunderstandings and uphold scholarly integrity, the chosen structure and expectations should be **explicitly documented in both departmental policies and each student's dissertation proposal**, ensuring that all parties are aligned from the outset.

Suggested Models for Collaborative Dissertations or Capstones

As institutions begin to recognize the value of collaboration in doctoral education, several emerging models offer flexible structures that balance **individual scholarly accountability with collective inquiry and impact** (Kamler, 2008). These models can accommodate diverse epistemologies, stakeholder participation, and interdisciplinary research needs while still maintaining academic rigor. Below are three applicable and adaptable formats that institutions and faculty may consider:

- **Paired Dissertation or Capstone Projects**. In this model, two students work on **interconnected but independently authored dissertations or capstones**. They may share a research site, data collection instruments, or theoretical framework - such as studying different grade levels in the same school district or evaluating related interventions within a healthcare system. Each student retains full responsibility for their own analysis, writing, and defense, while benefiting from peer collaboration and intellectual synergy.
- **Team-Based Dissertations or Capstones**. Multiple students co-author a single dissertation or capstone document that presents a unified project. To ensure clarity and accountability, the work includes an **explicit contribution breakdown**, detailing which student led or contributed to each section (e.g., literature review, methodology, data analysis). This model is especially well-suited for interdisciplinary or applied fields where joint authorship reflects real-world collaborative practice, but it requires **strong committee oversight and clearly defined evaluation standards**.
- **Community-Engaged Projects**. In this format, one doctoral student authors the dissertation or capstone while **non-academic partners** - such as educators, activists, or local residents - are meaningfully involved as co-designers, co-researchers, or co-presenters. Though not listed as co-authors, these collaborators are credited for their contributions and may be included in dissemination efforts such as presentations or reports. This model honors **participatory values and contextual expertise**, particularly in Community-Based Participatory Research (CBPR) and Participatory Action Research (PAR) frameworks.

Each of these models supports a different balance of **autonomy, collaboration, and scholarly impact**, offering students and faculty the flexibility to tailor the dissertation or capstone format to the specific needs of the research question and disciplinary context. Whether emphasizing independent authorship, shared authorship, or partnership with external stakeholders, these structures allow for meaningful engagement while preserving academic standards and clarity of contribution. By thoughtfully selecting a model that aligns with **scholarly goals, community realities, and institutional policies**, faculty can help students produce work that is both academically rigorous and socially relevant.

Faculty Tip: Require a Collaboration Agreement for Clarity and Accountability

To ensure that collaborative dissertation or capstone projects run smoothly and maintain academic integrity, faculty should require students to develop a **Collaboration Agreement** at the outset of the project (Brodin & Avery, 2020). This agreement serves as a formal, written roadmap that outlines expectations, fosters mutual accountability, and helps prevent misunderstandings or disputes later in the process. It also provides faculty and committees with a clear framework for evaluating both individual and collective contributions. A strong **Collaboration Agreement** should include:

- **Individual Roles and Responsibilities**. Clearly define what each student is responsible for across all phases of the project - such as literature review, data collection, analysis, writing, or community engagement - so that contributions are balanced and traceable.

- **Shared Milestones and Deliverables**. Establish a timeline with mutually agreed-upon checkpoints and shared outputs (e.g., IRB approval, draft submissions, presentations) to ensure coordination and progress toward completion.
- **Conflict Resolution Mechanisms**. Anticipate potential disagreements and outline procedures for resolving them constructively, including when and how faculty advisors or department chairs will be involved.
- **Authorship Expectations for Publications**. Clarify how future publications or presentations emerging from the project will be credited - whether co-authored or individually attributed - and what criteria will determine order of authorship.

By requiring this type of agreement, faculty help students build essential **professional competencies in collaboration, communication, and shared decision-making** - skills that are critical for success in both academic and applied research settings. These agreements create a shared foundation of expectations, reducing ambiguity and minimizing potential conflict as the project evolves. At the same time, they reinforce core academic values such as **transparency, fairness, and ethical responsibility**, ensuring that each participant's contribution is recognized and that the integrity of the collaborative dissertation or capstone is upheld.

---

2. Maintain Individual Accountability

While collaborative dissertations or capstones encourage shared inquiry and joint production, each student must still demonstrate **independent doctoral-level mastery** to meet academic expectations and earn the degree. Collaboration does not dilute scholarly rigor; rather, it requires that each student contribute a **clearly identifiable and intellectually robust component** that reflects their unique academic development and expertise. Evaluation should focus on both the collective coherence of the project and the **individual's capacity to contribute meaningfully to the field**. Each student must demonstrate doctoral-level competence in the following areas:

- **Framing Questions**. Students should be able to articulate research questions that are original, significant, and situated within relevant disciplinary and contextual frameworks - even when developed within a team or in conversation with collaborators.
- **Designing or Adapting Methods**. Each student must contribute to the research design, demonstrating methodological fluency by justifying their approach, adapting tools to specific contexts, and aligning methods with both ethical standards and research objectives.
- **Interpreting Findings**. Analysis and interpretation should reflect the student's independent thinking, offering insights that go beyond surface-level observations to engage with theoretical, empirical, or practical implications.
- **Contributing to Literature/Theory**. Students must engage deeply with existing scholarship and clearly articulate how their work advances, challenges, or complements ongoing academic conversations in their field.

- **Ethical Reflection**. Beyond meeting IRB or institutional requirements, students should reflect critically on the ethical dimensions of their work, including power dynamics, representation, and the responsibilities that come with co-producing knowledge.

By holding each student accountable for these core competencies, faculty ensure that collaborative dissertations or capstones are more than just joint efforts - they are platforms for **demonstrating individual scholarly growth and excellence**. This approach affirms that meaningful collaboration does not replace personal mastery, but rather enhances it by requiring each student to articulate, defend, and apply their own thinking within a broader research context. As a result, collaborative dissertations or capstones maintain **intellectual depth, academic rigor, and clear evidence of individual contribution**, while also modeling the interdisciplinary and team-based approaches increasingly valued in both academic and professional settings.

Assessment Strategy for Collaborative Dissertations or Capstones

To ensure fairness, transparency, and academic rigor in collaborative dissertation or capstone projects, institutions and faculty must adopt clear and intentional assessment strategies that account for both **shared outcomes and individual scholarly development**. These strategies not only support evaluation but also reinforce student accountability, encourage self-reflection, and validate each participant's academic voice within the collaboration. Faculty should consider the following assessment practices:

- **Require each Student to Submit a Reflection Chapter Articulating Their Specific Contributions and Learning**. This chapter should detail the student's intellectual journey, highlighting their role in shaping the project's design, analysis, and interpretation. It offers an opportunity to demonstrate critical thinking, ethical awareness, and the evolution of their scholarly identity within a collective framework.
- **Conduct Individual Defenses Even for Joint Projects**. While the research may be shared, each student should defend their understanding of the full project and explain their specific contributions. This allows committees to assess individual mastery of the content, clarity of insight, and readiness for scholarly independence.
- **Ask: What Unique Scholarly Contribution Did you Make?** During the defense or in written documentation, students should be able to clearly articulate how their work advanced the overall project and contributed new knowledge or perspective to the field. This question reinforces the expectation that **each student must bring something original and substantial to the research effort**.

These assessment strategies ensure that collaborative dissertations or capstones uphold the **highest standards of doctoral scholarship**, emphasizing the importance of intellectual rigor, individual contribution, and reflective engagement even within a shared project framework. By requiring individualized reflections, personal defenses, and clear articulation of each student's unique scholarly role, these practices **preserve academic integrity while embracing the complexity and innovation of collaborative inquiry**. In doing so, they validate the evolving nature of research in today's world - one where team-based, interdisciplinary, and community-engaged approaches are not only encouraged but essential to solving real-world problems with depth and nuance.

3. Coordinate Committee Expectations

Committees evaluating collaborative dissertations or capstones may hold divergent views on what constitutes **rigor, originality, and authorship** in a shared research context. Some members may come from disciplines that traditionally emphasize solo scholarship, while others may be more accustomed to co-authored or applied research models - leading to different expectations about contribution, evaluation, and credit. Without clear guidelines and alignment conversations, these differing perspectives can create confusion or tension, making it critical for faculty and institutions to **foster shared understanding and establish consistent evaluation criteria** across all committee members.

Faculty Advisors as Key Facilitators of Collaborative Dissertation or Capstone Success

Faculty advisors play a pivotal role in ensuring the success and integrity of collaborative dissertations or capstones by serving as **mediators, mentors, and methodological guides**. In contexts where multiple students, disciplines, or committee members are involved, the advisor becomes the central figure who helps maintain clarity, consistency, and academic standards throughout the process.

- **Facilitating Alignment Conversations**. Advisors should initiate early and ongoing discussions among committee members and collaborators to establish shared expectations about contribution, authorship, methodology, and evaluation. These alignment conversations help prevent misunderstandings and ensure that everyone involved is working from a **common framework of rigor and responsibility**.
- **Defining Acceptable Structures and Assessment Standards**. In collaboration with the department or graduate school, advisors help determine which formats are acceptable for collaborative dissertations or capstones (e.g., co-authored, parallel studies, shared data) and what standards must be met to assess individual mastery within those structures. This guidance ensures **consistency and fairness across student experiences**.
- **Assisting in Navigating Disciplinary Differences**. When collaborative projects span multiple fields or research traditions, advisors help students and committees navigate contrasting views on what counts as valid evidence, contribution, or rigor. By translating expectations across disciplines and helping to integrate multiple perspectives, advisors support students in crafting dissertations or capstones that are both **interdisciplinary and academically sound**.

With strong faculty leadership, collaborative dissertations or capstones can become powerful models of **innovative, engaged, and high-impact research** that mirror the realities of professional and academic collaboration. When advisors set clear expectations, foster communication, and uphold rigorous standards, students are empowered to navigate complex group dynamics while making meaningful individual contributions. In this way, collaborative dissertations or capstones not only reflect the best of modern research practice - interdisciplinary, participatory, and problem-oriented - but also **honor the foundational principles of doctoral education: Intellectual independence, ethical responsibility, and scholarly contribution.**

Example:

- *Two students co-author a design-based intervention and submit separate, integrated dissertations or capstones. The committee agrees on common rubrics but evaluates each student's document independently for coherence, contribution, and reflection.*

---

4. Navigate Institutional Policy with Flexibility

As doctoral research evolves to reflect the realities of interdisciplinary teamwork, digital scholarship, and community engagement, faculty have a critical role in helping institutions **modernize policies and perceptions** around dissertation or capstone authorship and structure. Rather than seeing collaboration as a threat to academic rigor, faculty can serve as champions for models that are **both innovative and intellectually demanding**. Faculty should:

- **Advocate for Policy Revisions that Allow for Structured Collaboration**. Faculty can work with graduate schools, academic senates, or dissertation or capstone committees to propose changes that permit co-authorship, shared datasets, or creative outputs - provided that each student's contribution is clearly defined and individually assessed. These efforts ensure that institutional frameworks **keep pace with evolving research practices**.
- **Document Precedents and Outcomes to Support Future Students**. By recording the structures, evaluation methods, and results of successful collaborative dissertations or capstones, faculty can help establish institutional memory and provide examples that justify future projects. This documentation can serve as a **template for policy development and a guide for faculty new to supervising collaborative work**.
- **Emphasize that Collaborative Does Not Mean "Less Rigorous" - it Means Differently Rigorous**. Faculty should actively dispel the myth that shared work is synonymous with diluted standards. Instead, they can articulate how collaborative dissertations or capstones require a **high level of coordination, individual mastery, and joint accountability**, making them no less demanding than traditional formats - just more reflective of how knowledge is created in the real world.

Through these actions, faculty contribute not only to the success of individual students but also to a broader **institutional culture shift that recognizes the evolving nature of scholarship**. By advocating for inclusive policies, documenting effective practices, and modeling flexible approaches to rigor, faculty help create systems that are both academically sound and responsive to the demands of interdisciplinary, collaborative, and technology-enhanced research. In doing so, they position their institutions as leaders in doctoral education - **honoring the traditions of scholarly excellence while embracing the innovation and relevance required for impact in a rapidly changing world**.

Sample Policy Language:

- *"Collaborative dissertations or capstones are permitted with committee approval. Each student must demonstrate independent contribution and submit documentation of authorship distribution, process reflection, and ethical responsibility."*

Examples of Collaborative Dissertation or Capstone Designs

Model A: Shared Data, Separate Interpretations

Student A	Quantitative analysis of school equity policy impact
Student B	Qualitative interviews with teachers about implementation
Shared Output	Methodology chapter, executive summary for district stakeholders

Model B: Co-Authored Intervention

Students	Jointly design and implement a professional development curriculum
Dissertations or Capstones	Each focuses on a different analytic lens (e.g., teacher learning, organizational)
Shared Component	Published guidebook, co-presented at conference

Model C: Community-Based Collaborative

Student	Works with a grassroots housing coalition to co-develop data visualization tools
Community Partner	Attend defense, co-author a reflective chapter or publication
Dissertation or Capstone	Documents process, theory of change, and impact analysis

Section Reflection: Collaborative Dissertations or Capstones as Models of Shared Scholarship

This section redefines doctoral research as a collaborative endeavor that aligns more authentically with the realities of 21st-century scholarship. Moving beyond the solitary dissertation or capstone model, it presents a compelling case for collaborative dissertations or capstones as rigorous, innovative, and socially engaged forms of inquiry. Whether rooted in team-based design, participatory action, or interdisciplinary integration, collaborative dissertations or capstones reflect how knowledge is increasingly created - through partnerships that bridge students, faculty, disciplines, and communities.

The section offers faculty practical models - paired projects, co-authored interventions, and community-engaged frameworks - while emphasizing the necessity of maintaining individual scholarly accountability. By advocating for clear collaboration agreements, structured reflection, and individualized defenses, it upholds academic rigor without sacrificing the benefits of co-creation. Importantly, it positions faculty as facilitators of alignment across students, committees, and institutions, helping to clarify authorship, ensure fair evaluation, and support policy evolution.

Ultimately, this section frames collaboration not as a dilution of doctoral standards, but as a form of "**different rigor**" - one that demands high-level communication, ethical engagement, and integrative thinking. It equips institutions to embrace models of scholarship that are inclusive, practice-relevant, and attuned to the complexity of real-world problems, while also ensuring that doctoral students emerge as both independent thinkers and capable contributors to collaborative knowledge production.

Section 8: Institutional Support and Policy for Dissertation or Capstone Innovation

---

As doctoral research evolves to include AI-augmented workflows, digital and multimodal products, interdisciplinary structures, and collaborative formats, a new challenge emerges: **the innovation in practice often outpaces institutional policy**. Faculty and students may envision creative, rigorous dissertations or capstones - but without supportive infrastructure, those ideas can be stalled or even blocked by outdated guidelines, rigid templates, or unclear approval pathways.

In this final section, we turn our attention to the **institutional scaffolding required to sustain and legitimize dissertation or capstone innovation**. This includes **graduate school policies**, **formatting requirements**, **committee expectations**, and **archiving protocols**. Faculty who want to support non-traditional dissertations or capstones must not only mentor students in creative scholarship - they must also **engage with policy structures to normalize and sustain innovation** (Golde & Walker, 2006; Walker et al., 2009).

Why Institutional Policy Matters

While academic freedom grants faculty and students a degree of flexibility in shaping the design, content, and structure of dissertations or capstones, doctoral degrees are ultimately conferred by institutions - and as such, they are governed by **centralized standards, administrative protocols, and legacy expectations** (Altbach, 2007). These institutional frameworks shape not only what is considered academically legitimate but also how innovation is received and assessed within formal review processes. Without clear alignment between faculty innovation and institutional policy, even well-intentioned flexibility can result in unintended friction or rejection. These standards influence:

- **What Counts as an Acceptable Dissertation or Capstone Format**. Institutions may limit dissertations or capstones to traditional five-chapter models, discouraging alternative formats such as portfolios, multimodal projects, or community-engaged designs - regardless of their scholarly rigor or disciplinary relevance.
- **How Proposals are Evaluated**. Departments may lack standardized rubrics or guidelines for evaluating non-traditional designs, leading to inconsistency across reviewers or confusion at proposal hearings.
- **Who can Serve on Committees**? Rigid criteria may exclude qualified interdisciplinary or practitioner experts who bring essential insight to collaborative, applied, or community-based work.
- **What is Preserved in Institutional Repositories**? Digital, multimedia, or co-authored components may fall outside repository guidelines, making it difficult to archive the full scope of the student's scholarly contribution.

- **Whether students Face Delays at Defense or Graduation**. If a project does not conform to institutional definitions of originality, format, or authorship, students may encounter late-stage resistance - jeopardizing their ability to defend or graduate on time.

Without **proactive and inclusive policy reform**, even the most promising and pedagogically sound dissertation or capstone innovations may be deemed **noncompliant at the eleventh hour**, leaving students vulnerable to delays, revision requests, or outright denial. Institutions must therefore recognize that innovation in doctoral education requires not only **faculty creativity and student ambition**, but also **administrative flexibility and policy alignment** to ensure fairness, transparency, and academic progress.

Key Areas for Institutional Alignment and Faculty Advocacy

---

1. Graduate School Policies and Format Guidelines

Graduate schools typically publish detailed formatting and content requirements that serve as **gatekeepers to dissertation or capstone approval and degree conferral**. These guidelines establish institutional norms for what constitutes an acceptable dissertation or capstone and are often embedded in student handbooks, graduate catalogs, or electronic thesis and dissertation or capstone (ETD) submission portals. While these standards are designed to promote consistency, clarity, and academic rigor, they may also unintentionally limit innovation (Kamler, 2008) - especially as new forms of scholarship emerge in response to digital tools, interdisciplinary inquiry, and community engagement. Graduate school requirements often include:

- **Accepted Dissertation or Capstone Formats**. These may be limited to traditional monographs or article-based compilations, with little room for portfolios, collaborative projects, or multimodal outputs.
- **Chapter Structure**. Many handbooks specify a five-chapter model (introduction, literature review, methodology, results, and discussion), even when the research design does not align with that structure.
- **Formatting Guidelines**. Technical details such as page numbering, margin width, font size, and citation style are rigidly enforced, often through institutional repositories or ProQuest submission systems.
- **Expectations for Originality and Authorship**. Policies typically assume a single author working independently, which can create tension for students pursuing co-authored, participatory, or AI-integrated projects.

Faculty Strategy

To ensure that innovation in doctoral work is not inadvertently blocked by outdated policies, faculty can play a vital role in shaping institutional change (Kelly, 2016):

- **Propose Language Updates that Include Emerging Formats**. Faculty committees can recommend revisions to dissertation or capstone guidelines that explicitly allow for

portfolio, multimodal, practice-based, or collaborative models, providing definitions and eligibility criteria.

- **Provide Model Templates for Common Alternatives**. To make adoption smoother, faculty can offer sample structures and exemplars for alternative dissertation or capstone formats, helping students and committees understand how rigor can be maintained across diverse approaches.
- **Collaborate with Graduate Deans to Codify Flexibility Within a Framework of Rigor**. Faculty can advocate for a policy framework that preserves academic standards while encouraging innovation, such as establishing approval pathways for non-traditional formats or adding reflective justification sections to proposal and defense documents.

By proactively engaging with graduate school policies, faculty ensure that **doctoral education remains responsive, inclusive, and aligned with the realities of contemporary scholarship and professional practice**.

Example Policy Addition:

- *"Dissertations or capstones may include multimodal, practice-based, collaborative, or AI-supported elements, subject to committee and program approval. All formats must include a rationale for structure, documentation of the research process, and alignment with doctoral learning outcomes."*

---

2. Proposal and Defense Approval Processes

Innovative dissertations or capstones often encounter institutional resistance - not because they lack quality or merit, but because they challenge **entrenched assumptions about what a dissertation or capstone "should" look like** (Gravett, 2021). This resistance is particularly common during the **proposal approval stage or pre-defense review**, when faculty committees may be unfamiliar with non-traditional formats such as design-based research, collaborative projects, community-engaged inquiry, or multimodal outputs. Without established frameworks for evaluating these emerging models, committees may default to traditional standards, inadvertently stalling progress and disempowering students who are working at the cutting edge of scholarship. To ensure innovative dissertation or capstone formats are given fair and constructive review, faculty and graduate programs can implement the following **best practices**:

- **Create Proposal Templates for Different Dissertation or Capstone Types**. Provide structured templates tailored to formats such as **design-based dissertations or capstones, community-engaged research, portfolio models, or digital/multimodal projects**. These templates help students frame their proposals clearly while giving committees a roadmap for evaluating diverse methodologies and outputs.
- **Develop a Rubric for Assessing Innovation**. Establish a proposal and dissertation or capstone assessment rubric that prioritizes **coherence, intellectual rigor, and scholarly contribution**, rather than strict adherence to traditional formats. Rubrics can include criteria such as innovation alignment with research goals, ethical integrity, transparency of process, and contextual relevance.

- **Host Cross-Departmental Proposal Development Workshops**. Facilitate collaborative spaces where faculty from different disciplines can share perspectives and expectations around dissertation or capstone innovation. These workshops not only support students during the proposal stage but also **build shared faculty understanding**, reducing institutional friction when novel approaches are introduced.

By proactively preparing both students and faculty to support and evaluate diverse dissertation or capstone models, institutions can **foster a culture of thoughtful experimentation**, ensuring that innovation is not stifled by tradition but rather elevated through intentional, rigorous academic practice.

Example:

- *A doctoral student proposes a podcast-based dissertation or capstone on language revitalization. The proposal includes sample episodes, a theoretical framework, an access plan for participants, and a reflection strategy. The defense committee uses a rubric tailored for public scholarship and multimodal inquiry.*

---

3. Committee Composition and Preparation

Dissertation or capstone committees are typically composed based on disciplinary expertise, institutional affiliation, and methodological fit. However, **innovative dissertation or capstone projects - particularly those involving multimodal design, AI integration, practice-based inquiry, or community engagement - often require expertise that extends beyond traditional academic boundaries**. When committee members lack familiarity with non-traditional outputs or interdisciplinary methods, they may struggle to assess the work fairly, despite its scholarly merit (Baptista et al., 2015). This mismatch can create unnecessary hurdles for students and undermine the potential of boundary-crossing research.

Faculty Considerations

To ensure that innovative dissertations or capstones receive informed and equitable evaluation, faculty should take proactive steps in broadening the evaluative capacity of committees:

- **Invite Outside Experts or Community Collaborators to Serve in Advisory Roles**. Including **technical experts, media producers, policymakers, or community leaders** as advisors (even if not voting committee members) provides essential insight into the project's relevance, accuracy, and impact beyond the academy. Their perspectives enrich the scholarly process and honor the real-world orientation of applied research.
- **Train Committee Members in Evaluating Non-Traditional Products**. Faculty and programs should offer workshops or discussion sessions focused on assessing emerging forms of scholarship, such as **interactive tools, AI-generated artifacts, documentary films, public-facing reports**, or collaborative action research. These trainings help align expectations and reduce disciplinary bias in evaluation.
- **Create Guidelines for Assessing Interdisciplinary and Multimodal Scholarship**. Clear rubrics or departmental memos can outline criteria for rigor, coherence,

contribution, and originality across diverse formats. These guidelines ensure consistency in how innovation is judged, regardless of the form it takes.

Together, these strategies equip dissertation or capstone committees to engage meaningfully with innovative projects, creating space for **ethical, impactful, and forward-looking doctoral research**.

Institutional Tip: Encourage doctoral programs to offer committee members continuing education credits or workshops in emerging research paradigms. By institutionalizing professional development for faculty - whether through pedagogy centers, graduate schools, or interdisciplinary working groups - universities not only support more effective supervision but also **signal their commitment to evolving definitions of scholarly excellence**.

---

4. Documentation, Citation, and Archiving

For innovation in doctoral research to be **sustainable and institutionally recognized**, students must be equipped not only to create novel forms of scholarship but also to **document, cite, and preserve** their work in ways that uphold academic standards. This is especially important as dissertations or capstones increasingly include **generative AI contributions, collaborative authorship with community partners or practitioners, and multimodal outputs** that go beyond traditional text. Without clear records of authorship, tool usage, or formatting standards, even the most innovative projects risk being misunderstood, under-evaluated, or rendered inaccessible for future scholarship. **To ensure sustainability, students must be able to**:

- **Document their Process Clearly**. Students using AI tools or engaging in collaborative authorship must be able to trace their development process - from prompt inputs to revision histories to conceptual pivots. This transparency protects both academic integrity and intellectual ownership.
- **Cite Digital or AI Contributions Responsibly**. As tools such as ChatGPT, Perplexity, or Midjourney become common in dissertation or capstone development, students must know how to attribute machine-generated outputs, software tools, and datasets according to current scholarly standards (e.g., APA 7th Edition, MLA 9th Edition, or Chicago Style updates).
- **Preserve Their Work in Accessible, Future-Proof Formats**. Non-traditional outputs - such as interactive dashboards, podcasts, digital portfolios, and web-based tools - must be deposited in formats that will remain accessible and archivable through institutional repositories or external platforms, ensuring **scholarly durability**.

Faculty Support Includes:

- **Advising Students to Keep Prompt Logs, Draft Versions, and Tool Metadata**. Faculty can encourage students to archive each iteration of AI-generated work, including **prompt history, timestamps, versioning notes, and tool specifications**. These records not only support evaluation but also create replicable research practices.

- **Recommending Citation Standards**. Faculty should stay current with evolving guidance from major style manuals and encourage students to cite AI tools, datasets, images, and software properly. This includes both **in-text attribution and appendices that disclose tool parameters and decision-making**.
- **Working with Libraries to Ensure Repositories Can House Non-Textual Content**. Faculty and departments should partner with institutional librarians and digital scholarship offices to develop repository workflows that can **ingest and preserve multimedia content**, such as audio files, video documentaries, interactive maps, or web-based visualizations.

By embedding these practices into dissertation or capstone advising and program requirements, faculty ensure that innovation is not only possible - but **sustainable, transparent, and preserved for future generations of scholarship**. This alignment between creativity and accountability is essential for building a doctoral culture that embraces both rigor and relevance.

Example: Preserving an Interactive Dissertation or Capstone Artifact

- *Consider a doctoral student whose research explores* ***educational equity across school districts****, using large-scale demographic and performance data. Instead of limiting their findings to static tables and narrative discussion, the student creates an* ***interactive data dashboard*** *that allows users - such as policymakers, educators, or fellow researchers - to explore equity indicators by region, school type, or funding levels. This digital artifact is not an add-on but a core part of the scholarly contribution, offering both* ***analytical depth and public engagement****.*
- *To ensure the dashboard is preserved, ethically attributed, and academically evaluated, the student includes the following components in their institutional repository submission:*
    - **Screenshots of Dashboard Functionality**. *A series of annotated images captures the structure, filters, and user interface of the dashboard, providing a visual record in case the live version becomes inaccessible.*
    - **Link to an Archived Version**. *A static version of the dashboard is hosted on an institutional server or a platform such as Zenodo, Figshare, or GitHub Pages, ensuring long-term accessibility even if third-party tools change or expire.*
    - **Written User Guide**. *A downloadable PDF explains how the dashboard works, who the intended users are, and what data is represented - ensuring the tool is understandable without needing technical training.*
    - **AI Code Documentation**. *If AI tools (e.g., Copilot, GPT-powered Python scripts, or Tableau with AI integration) were used to clean, analyze, or visualize the data, the student includes clear documentation of prompts, model parameters, and decision points - supporting both reproducibility and ethical disclosure.*
    - **Accompanying Dissertation or Capstone Chapter Explaining the Research Narrative**. *A traditional text-based chapter provides the* ***theoretical framing, literature context, and critical interpretation*** *of the findings displayed in the dashboard, situating the digital product within a rigorous scholarly argument.*

This example demonstrates how digital tools and AI-enhanced workflows can **enhance, not diminish, academic quality** - as long as their contributions are properly contextualized, cited, and preserved. Faculty can use this model to guide students in producing non-traditional artifacts, helping them balance **technical creativity with scholarly accountability**.

---

5. External Review and Dissemination Norms

Innovative dissertations or capstones often push beyond the traditional academic audience to engage **public, professional, or practitioner communities**. Whether through policy briefs, podcasts, documentary films, instructional modules, or digital tools, these components are frequently designed with **real-world application and public engagement in mind**. While this enhances the impact and accessibility of doctoral research, it also introduces **complex questions** around academic timing, evaluation, and dissemination norms - especially when scholarly and non-scholarly outputs are integrated. This raises questions about:

- **Peer Review**. *"What forms of review are appropriate or required for public-facing components?" "Should a policy brief reviewed by a school district, or an AI tool tested by a community organization, be considered equivalent to a peer-reviewed academic publication?"*
- **Pre-Defense Dissemination**. *"Can students share portions of their dissertation or capstone publicly - such as presenting a workshop, publishing a podcast, or submitting a video series - before their final defense?" "If so, how does this impact originality claims or intellectual property ownership?"*
- **Public Scholarship Versus Traditional Scholarly Publishing**. *"Should work developed for broader audiences (e.g., op-eds, community reports, interactive media) be evaluated differently than traditional chapters or journal articles?" "How can institutions ensure that public scholarship is **rigorously evaluated and meaningfully credited**?"*

Institutional Solutions

To support students engaging in innovative, outward-facing scholarship, universities and doctoral programs should develop clear structures and protections that uphold both **academic integrity and scholarly relevance**:

- **Create Clear Policies on Pre-Publication and External Collaboration**. Institutions should offer guidance on what kinds of outputs can be shared or published before the dissertation or capstone is complete, under what conditions external partners can be acknowledged or co-credited, and how public engagement aligns with academic expectations.
- **Recognize and Credit Peer-Reviewed Creative Work or Applied Contributions**. Dissertation or capstone committees and graduate schools must be encouraged to value outputs such as **policy impact, professional adoption, or artistic exhibition**, especially when such work undergoes external peer or stakeholder review. This legitimizes broader forms of contribution and reflects the growing emphasis on applied impact in doctoral training.
- **Support Students in Navigating Journal Policies, Intellectual Property Rights, and Open-Access Considerations**. Faculty and librarians should help students

understand the nuances of **preprint servers, embargo periods, Creative Commons licensing, and IRB permissions** - especially when work involves community partners, minors, or sensitive content.

By anticipating and addressing these questions, institutions not only protect students but also **affirm the value of doctoral research that reaches beyond the ivory tower**. Supporting public- and practice-facing scholarship as part of the dissertation or capstone recognizes that impact is not limited to peer-reviewed publications - it can also live in classrooms, policies, communities, and interactive platforms that reflect the evolving nature of scholarly contribution.

Faculty Leadership in Shaping Culture

While updating institutional policy is critical, **policy alone cannot transform the doctoral landscape**. Lasting change requires a parallel shift in academic culture - one that redefines what counts as rigorous, meaningful, and impactful scholarship in an era shaped by interdisciplinary inquiry, community engagement, and digital innovation. Faculty play a central role in driving this cultural transformation, not just as supervisors, but as **visible leaders, advocates, and collaborators** who shape norms and expectations across departments and institutions. Faculty must:

- **Serve as Models and Mentors for Innovation**. Faculty who embrace nontraditional formats in their own scholarship or who supervise students through creative, practice-based, or AI-augmented dissertations or capstones demonstrate that **academic excellence and innovation are not mutually exclusive**. Modeling curiosity, transparency, and critical engagement helps normalize these approaches for students and peers alike.
- **Advocate for Institutional Alignment at Department, College, and Graduate School Levels**. Culture change begins in local contexts but must scale through coordinated action. Faculty can influence dissertation or capstone policies, format approvals, and committee composition by **advocating for consistency and clarity across governance levels**, ensuring students do not face mixed messages or last-minute rejection of innovative work.
- **Support One Another in Navigating Discomfort with Nontraditional Forms**. Innovation often provokes uncertainty, especially when faculty are asked to evaluate outputs or methods outside their disciplinary comfort zones. **Peer dialogue, co-supervision, and professional development** can help build collective confidence and reduce the risks of bias or inequity in dissertation or capstone review processes.

Leadership Actions to Drive Change

- **Form Task Forces on Dissertation or Capstone Reform**. Department chairs and program directors can launch faculty working groups or joint committees to **audit existing guidelines**, examine best practices across peer institutions, and propose recommendations that reflect contemporary scholarly needs.
- **Collaborate with Academic Affairs to Update Handbooks and Rubrics**. Faculty leaders should work with graduate deans, assessment offices, and digital scholarship

teams to **integrate flexible, transparent standards** into official documents - ensuring consistency in how traditional and alternative formats are assessed.

- **Showcase Successful Alternative Dissertations or Capstones in Orientations or Research Showcases**. Visibility is powerful. Hosting panels, exhibitions, or digital showcases of **portfolio, collaborative, community-based, or multimodal dissertations or capstones** helps normalize their legitimacy and provides templates for future students. Faculty can also feature these models in orientation sessions or publish them in open-access repositories.

By taking proactive leadership roles, faculty not only support student success - they help cultivate a doctoral culture that is **bold, reflective, and responsive to the real challenges of our time**. Leadership in this context means shaping not just rules, but **values and visions** - ensuring that doctoral education evolves to meet the moment while preserving its foundational commitment to intellectual rigor and scholarly contribution.

Institutional Models and Resources

In recent years, some universities and colleges have begun to explore structured support for alternative dissertation or capstone formats. These approaches recognize that scholarly excellence can be expressed through multiple structures and media - not just the traditional monograph. By formalizing policies, guidelines, and templates for multimodal, practice-based, or community-engaged work, institutions can broaden the scope of academic contribution while maintaining rigor, relevance, and inclusivity.

Examples of Potential Institutional Innovation Models

- **Guidelines for Non-Traditional Formats**. A graduate school could publish explicit guidance for multimedia, creative, or community-based dissertation or capstone projects. Such guidelines might encourage students to align the form of their work with the nature of their research while collaborating closely with supervisory committees to ensure both scholarly quality and clarity of purpose.
- **Support for Digital and Experimental Scholarship**. An academic support office might offer resources for projects that include software, websites, interactive platforms, or other digital artifacts. Guidance could address preservation strategies, intellectual property considerations, and peer-review processes suitable for non-traditional outputs.
- **Archival Standards for Multimodal Work**. A university library could establish processes for archiving digital and interactive components - such as podcasts, video essays, or data visualizations - alongside written documentation. This might include templates for metadata, long-term storage requirements, and instructions for depositing projects in institutional repositories.
- **Templates for Applied and Practice-Based Research**. A doctoral college could create standard templates and rubrics for dissertations or capstones that result in tangible outputs such as instructional prototypes, strategic plans, toolkits, or design-based interventions. These templates might include criteria for evaluating both the product and the reflective analysis accompanying it.

Why These Models Matter

Such frameworks show that systemic support for dissertation or capstone innovation is both achievable and scalable. They address not only questions of format and content but also the equally important dimensions of preservation, evaluation, and ethical standards.

Faculty and administrators seeking to expand alternative pathways for advanced scholarly work can use these models as starting points - adapting them to local disciplinary strengths, technological capacities, and student needs. As advanced education evolves, implementing adaptable policies of this kind ensures that groundbreaking work is not dismissed due to outdated procedural norms.

Section Reflection: Building the Infrastructure for Innovation

This final section powerfully reframes dissertation or capstone reform as not only a pedagogical shift but also a structural imperative. It highlights that even the most creative and rigorous student work can be undermined by outdated institutional policies, rigid templates, and unclear approval pathways. By shifting the lens from individual initiative to systemic readiness, the section challenges faculty to become institutional architects - proactively shaping policies, formats, and evaluation systems that legitimize diverse, future-facing forms of scholarly contribution.

The section emphasizes that true innovation in doctoral education requires alignment between practice and policy. It identifies five critical leverage points for faculty leadership: revising graduate school formatting rules, preparing committees to assess emerging formats, modernizing archiving and documentation practices, establishing fair standards for public-facing work, and advancing a culture of dissertation or capstone innovation through policy, mentorship, and visibility. These strategies move beyond rhetorical support for nontraditional dissertations or capstones, offering concrete, scalable models of institutional change.

Ultimately, this section makes clear that faculty have a dual role: to empower students to produce bold, ethically engaged scholarship and to advocate for the conditions that allow such work to be formally recognized, evaluated, and preserved. When institutions are willing to evolve, doctoral education becomes not only a site of knowledge reproduction, but a launchpad for transformation - capable of responding to urgent societal needs, technological shifts, and the diverse epistemologies of emerging scholars.

Chapter 6 Conclusion: Leadership in Practice - Modeling the Human Center of AI-Enhanced Education

Chapter 6 explored the evolving role of faculty in an academic landscape reshaped by generative AI - not merely as faculty, but as **leaders by example**. In a time of pedagogical uncertainty and accelerating automation, the behaviors, boundaries, and choices modeled by educators become some of the most powerful forms of guidance students receive. This chapter has argued that **responsible faculty modeling is not optional - it is foundational to shaping a culture of ethical, intentional, and transparent AI use in higher education**.

In **Section 1**, the chapter opened with a clear claim: **modeling is leadership**. As students confront ambiguous messages about AI's legitimacy, they look to faculty for cues - not just in what is taught, but in what is **practiced**. Faculty who hide their own AI use while policing students' behavior undermine a culture of trust; those who narrate, critique, and disclose their use of AI tools normalize integrity as a shared process.

Section 2 built on this foundation by highlighting **how faculty use AI in preparation, communication, and brainstorming**. When faculty disclose that a syllabus was first drafted with ChatGPT but revised for tone and clarity, they demystify AI while affirming the **human editorial role**. This kind of modeling distinguishes between tool use and tool dependence, reinforcing the importance of human oversight.

Section 3 encouraged **open dialogue with students**, positioning transparency not just as an individual act, but as a pedagogical method. When educators share their AI learning journeys and invite students to co-create course policies, they cultivate **shared accountability and collective agency** - both essential for ethical AI integration.

Section 4 focused on **modeling limitations**. Faculty who openly acknowledge the flaws in AI-generated outputs - whether oversimplified arguments or hallucinated citations - teach students that **critical engagement** is an ongoing process. This kind of modeling fosters **intellectual humility** and shows that technological fluency includes knowing when ***not*** to trust the machine.

In **Section 5**, the emphasis turned to **values-based transparency**. Faculty who explain **why** they use or avoid AI in particular instructional tasks help students understand that AI use is not just procedural - it is **ethical**. These conversations make visible the faculty member's internal compass, inviting students to develop one of their own.

Section 6 introduced **public-facing modeling**, showing how faculty can extend their influence beyond the classroom. Whether through committee leadership, blog posts, or campus panels, faculty who reflect publicly on AI use signal that **ethical scholarship is a civic responsibility**, not just a private reflection.

Section 7 provided examples across teaching, research, communication, and policy work, reinforcing that modeling can - and should - be embedded at every level of professional activity. These diverse touchpoints illustrate that **faculty modeling is not a singular event but a pervasive presence** in academic culture.

Finally, **Section 8** connected responsible modeling to institutional transformation. When faculty behaviors are **recognized, supported, and systematized**, a culture of thoughtful AI engagement emerges - not driven by policy alone, but by **visible, human-centered practice**. Institutional structures that support this modeling through syllabi, workshops, and promotion criteria help scale ethical AI integration from individual innovation to **collective identity**.

Together, these eight sections converge on a central conclusion: **Faculty who model responsible AI use are not just navigating change - they are defining the ethical infrastructure of education in the AI era**. They show that leadership is not found in knowing all the answers about technology, but in demonstrating how to ask the right questions - honestly, visibly, and in community with students.

The chapter's enduring theme is clear: **Modeling is not about mastery - it is about mentorship. In the age of generative AI, the most lasting faculty influence may come not from the content we deliver, but from the example we set**.

Chapter 7: Mentorship Models that Work - Balancing Personalization with Accountability

Mentorship in the AI era demands more than access and encouragement. It now requires intentional redesigns of structure, process, and relationship dynamics to meet the challenges and opportunities of a rapidly evolving academic environment. Traditional mentorship models - centered on one-on-one, hierarchical guidance - often fall short in contexts where artificial intelligence reshapes knowledge production, academic writing, and research collaboration (Bailey et al., 2023; Han, 2025). In this new terrain, **transparency, collaboration, and iterative evaluation** become essential attributes of effective mentorship. This chapter introduces **scalable and inclusive mentorship frameworks** that better reflect the distributed, interdisciplinary, and AI-augmented nature of academic work today.

Section 1: The Evolution of Academic Mentorship - From Patronage to Partnership

---

For centuries, mentorship in academia has been rooted in hierarchical models of patronage, where access to expertise, opportunity, and advancement depended largely on the discretion and favor of a powerful faculty advisor. This "master-apprentice" model - originating in medieval guild systems and persisting through the early formation of Western universities - reflected a rigid structure of intellectual gatekeeping (Barker, 2011).

Over time, especially during the 20th century, this model gave way to a more informal style of apprenticeship characterized by personalized but often unstandardized support. Yet even then, mentorship remained largely a **privatized, personality-driven process**: successful outcomes often depended on compatibility, proximity, and unspoken rules rather than transparent structures or inclusive design (Paglis et al., 2006).

In the contemporary context - shaped by digital learning, increased diversity, and the emergence of AI-augmented research - such models are no longer sufficient. Today's mentorship must shift from being hierarchical and opaque to **collaborative, inclusive, and ethically grounded**. The dominant model is evolving toward mentorship as **partnership**, where both mentor and mentee engage in a **co-constructed, reciprocal learning relationship** that promotes not just academic success but long-term professional formation (Austin & McDaniels, 2006; W. B. Johnson & Griffin, 2024).

Historical Trajectory of Mentorship in Doctoral Education

---

1. The Patronage Era

During the early phases of higher education, **mentorship functioned more as patronage than as a developmental relationship**. Senior scholars - often white, male, and institutionally powerful - would selectively sponsor junior scholars into elite academic circles, favoring mentees who mirrored their own values, backgrounds, and dispositions. These relationships were rooted in **social compatibility and perceived intellectual promise**, but the criteria were deeply subjective and often biased by race, gender, and class norms (Walker et al., 2009). Advancement through doctoral study was typically **unstructured**, with progress monitored informally and decisions about scholarly readiness left to the mentor's sole discretion. In this model, the mentor's endorsement was both **gatekeeper and guarantor**, leaving little room for transparency or challenge.

This **gatekeeping logic** systematically excluded many capable individuals from full participation in the academic community. **Women, students of color, and nontraditional learners** - including first-generation students, older adults, and those from working-class or immigrant backgrounds - were often perceived as outsiders to the dominant scholarly identity and thus **denied access to the mentoring relationships that conferred legitimacy and advancement** (Austin, 2002; Barker, 2011). The absence of culturally responsive mentorship and the lack of racial representation among faculty further **deepened feelings of isolation and marginalization**. Mentorship, rather than serving as a bridge to academic integration, often reinforced structural inequities that shaped who was welcomed into scholarly communities - and who was left out (Byars-Winston & Dahlberg, 2019).

Only in recent decades has this paradigm begun to shift toward more inclusive, developmental, and reflexive mentorship models that actively recognize and seek to dismantle the exclusionary dynamics embedded in the history of higher education.

---

2. Informal Apprenticeship

As graduate education expanded in the post–World War II era - driven by increased federal funding, the GI Bill, and a growing demand for advanced research and professional expertise - the mentorship paradigm began to shift. While no longer rooted in overt patronage systems, mentorship remained an **informal and highly variable practice**, shaped largely by institutional culture and individual faculty inclinations (Gardner, 2008). The expectation was that students would **"figure it out" through academic osmosis** - by observing their advisors, mimicking disciplinary norms, and absorbing implicit rules of academic conduct without structured guidance or clear benchmarks for success. Formal mentorship training was rare, and written expectations around milestones, feedback, or intellectual development were often absent.

This **laissez-faire approach to mentorship**, while occasionally effective for self-directed students with well-matched advisors, introduced significant inconsistencies into the graduate experience. **Access to meaningful mentorship was contingent on faculty availability, interest, and mentoring style**, leading to wide disparities even within the same program or department. Students who were unfamiliar with academic culture - especially first-generation students, international students, and students of color - were more likely to misinterpret expectations or be overlooked in environments that privileged insider knowledge and cultural familiarity (Austin, 2002; Barker, 2011).

A critical limitation of this evolving but still unstructured model was its **vulnerability to bias, inconsistency, and over-reliance on faculty goodwill**, particularly in large or under-resourced programs. Without systems of accountability or developmental scaffolding, faculty members were often unequipped to mentor effectively across lines of difference or provide sustained support amid heavy workloads. As a result, students from underrepresented backgrounds frequently experienced mentorship as **transactional, opaque, or even exclusionary**, reinforcing longstanding inequities in access, belonging, and scholarly advancement within doctoral education (Byars-Winston & Dahlberg, 2019; Sanczyk et al., 2021).

To address these limitations, modern reform efforts have emphasized structured mentorship models, cultural competence training, and program-level oversight mechanisms aimed at making mentorship more **equitable, transparent, and responsive** to student needs.

---

3. Mentorship as Partnership in the 21st Century

The emerging **"mentorship as partnership"** model signals a significant shift in the philosophy and practice of graduate supervision. Moving beyond the traditional view of faculty as hierarchical gatekeepers to academic knowledge and success, this model reframes mentors as **facilitators, co-learners, and professional allies**. In doing so, it aligns mentorship with the values of inclusivity, equity, and adaptability that define 21st-century higher education.

Rather than assuming a one-way transmission of expertise, this approach is grounded in the recognition that today's graduate students are not passive apprentices. **They enter doctoral programs with diverse lived experiences, professional backgrounds, disciplinary fluency, and global perspectives** - assets that enrich scholarly dialogue and redefine what it means to contribute to knowledge. For students of color, international scholars, first-generation college graduates, and others from historically marginalized groups, the partnership model offers a more affirming and empowering experience - one that honors identity as integral to intellectual growth (Barker, 2011; Pfund et al., 2016).

This evolving model also reflects a broader transformation in the research enterprise itself. **Contemporary scholarship is increasingly interdisciplinary, applied, and AI-integrated**, requiring mentors and mentees alike to continuously navigate unfamiliar tools, emerging methodologies, and new ethical landscapes (Bailey et al., 2023; Caillaud & Skec, 2024). In this context, mentorship becomes a **collaborative endeavor** in which both parties engage in mutual learning, co-creation of knowledge, and shared professional development.

At its core, the mentorship-as-partnership paradigm is **bidirectional**. It is not simply that students learn from faculty; it is that mentors also learn from their students. Whether through exposure to novel technologies, fresh perspectives on societal challenges, or lived experiences that challenge dominant narratives, students help faculty **expand their own intellectual and cultural horizons**. As Pfund et al. (2016) emphasized, effective mentorship in this model includes shared goal-setting, open communication, and reciprocal feedback - all anchored in a relationship of **respect, trust, and growth**.

Importantly, this model does not diminish the mentor's responsibility - it reorients it. Faculty are still expected to guide, challenge, and support their mentees, but they do so **within**

a framework of relational accountability rather than positional authority. By embracing mentorship as a partnership, institutions can better prepare scholars - both faculty and students - to thrive in a research environment defined by complexity, diversity, and rapid change.

Key Features of Mentorship as Partnership

---

1. Mutual Accountability

In the 21st-century mentorship paradigm, **mutual accountability** is foundational to a successful and equitable relationship. Unlike traditional models where responsibility for communication and progress rested primarily with the student - or was shaped by the mentor's availability and disposition - this approach emphasizes that **both mentor and mentee share responsibility** for the relationship's success. Accountability is no longer unidirectional; instead, it is **reciprocal, intentional, and transparent**.

Both parties are expected to **maintain regular and open communication**, honor agreed-upon timelines, and actively reflect on goals, progress, and challenges. This shared responsibility ensures that expectations remain aligned over time and that neither party carries the burden of managing the relationship alone. It also creates space for course correction, constructive feedback, and mutual learning - particularly critical in complex, fast-evolving research contexts where timelines and methods may shift.

For students of color and others from historically marginalized backgrounds, mutual accountability also serves as a **corrective structure against potential mentoring imbalances**, including power dynamics, implicit bias, or unspoken assumptions about availability, productivity, or scholarly identity (Barker, 2011; Byars-Winston & Dahlberg, 2019). When accountability is jointly held, the mentoring relationship becomes a space of **respectful partnership**, not supervision by default.

Example Practice:

- *One effective way to establish mutual accountability is to develop a* ***written mentorship agreement*** *early in the relationship. This agreement can outline:*
    - ***Meeting frequency and scheduling protocols.***
    - ***Decision-making expectations*** *(e.g., authorship, project scope).*
    - ***Milestones and timeline benchmarks.***
    - ***Preferred methods and turnaround time for feedback.***
    - ***Conflict resolution pathways.***
    - ***Communication norms,*** *including availability and modes of contact.*

Such agreements help normalize clear boundaries and expectations without implying distrust. They can be revisited and updated regularly to reflect changes in research focus, life circumstances, or team structure. Ultimately, this approach fosters a mentoring culture grounded in **clarity, respect, and mutual investment** - qualities that are especially crucial in an era of interdisciplinary research and accelerated change.

---

2. Developmental Dialogue, Not One-Way Instruction

In the mentorship-as-partnership model, **faculty are no longer positioned merely as evaluators or disciplinary gatekeepers**, but as **thought partners** - collaborators who walk alongside students in their intellectual and professional development. This redefined role emphasizes **dialogue over direction, inquiry over instruction**, and mutual engagement over hierarchical oversight. Thought partnership reflects a mentoring approach grounded in curiosity, humility, and co-investment in growth.

As thought partners, faculty create space for **critical reflection**, **challenge untested assumptions**, and **affirm the evolving scholarly identities** of their students. This role requires deep listening, the ability to ask probing questions, and a willingness to engage with ambiguity and emergence - particularly relevant in research that is exploratory, interdisciplinary, or AI-integrated. Such mentorship supports not just technical competence, but the development of **scholarly confidence, ethical grounding, and personal voice** (Brookfield, 2017; W. B. Johnson & Griffin, 2024).

For students from underrepresented backgrounds, including students of color and first-generation scholars, this model provides a more inclusive and empowering form of mentorship. Rather than demanding assimilation into dominant academic norms, it recognizes identity as central to knowledge creation and **validates the student's lived experience as a source of scholarly insight**.

Prompt Example:

- *"What did you learn from this analysis - and what are you still unsure about? Let us think through it together."*

This type of prompt exemplifies the thought partner stance. It invites the student to reflect critically, identify uncertainties, and engage in collaborative meaning-making with their mentor. By framing the discussion as a joint intellectual journey, the mentor signals that **vulnerability is welcome, growth is nonlinear, and shared inquiry is the hallmark of rigorous scholarship**. Ultimately, when faculty serve as thought partners, mentorship becomes a **transformative experience** - one in which both mentor and mentee sharpen their thinking, deepen their values, and expand their capacity to navigate complexity together.

---

3. Mentorship Responsibilities in the Age of Generative AI

In the era of generative artificial intelligence, the mentor's role extends beyond traditional academic guidance to include **digital ethics, critical literacy, and reflective practice**. As AI tools such as ChatGPT, Copilot, and discipline-specific generators become embedded in scholarly workflows, mentors are now tasked with helping students navigate not just what these tools **can** do, but what they **should** do. This demands a more deliberate, values-driven form of mentorship - one that bridges technological fluency with scholarly integrity.

Mentors must begin by **guiding students in the ethical and responsible use of generative AI**. This includes raising awareness about issues of authorship, attribution, bias, data privacy, and the distinction between legitimate support and academic misconduct (Reiss, 2021; Selwyn, 2019). Faculty should help students understand that while AI can accelerate productivity, it can also introduce risks - such as plagiarism, hallucinated sources, or overreliance on surface-level synthesis - that compromise the rigor and originality of academic work.

Second, mentors are responsible for **supporting students in balancing machine-generated output with human insight**. The power of generative AI lies in its ability to assist, not replace, human reasoning. Mentors can help students cultivate a mindset in which AI serves as a **springboard for deeper inquiry** rather than a shortcut to conclusions. This includes discussions about when and how to interrogate AI-generated text, how to integrate AI suggestions into authentic thinking processes, and how to retain student voice and intent in academic writing (Bailey et al., 2023; Nikolopoulou, 2025).

Third, effective mentorship in this era requires **modeling transparent and critical engagement with digital tools**. Faculty themselves must be willing to share their own uses - and misuses - of AI in research, publishing, or administrative tasks. By modeling openness and critical reflection, mentors foster an environment where students feel safe to experiment, question, and evolve their own digital practices without fear of judgment (Brookfield, 2017).

Faculty Tip:

- *Regularly ask students to reflect on their use of AI in research, writing, and feedback processing. For example, prompt them with questions like:*
    - *"How did AI assist you in this task?"*
    - *"What decisions did you make after reviewing the AI's suggestions?"*
    - *"Where did you disagree with the AI, and why?"*

These reflective check-ins not only build **AI literacy and ethical self-regulation**, but also cultivate metacognitive habits that prepare students for a future in which human-machine collaboration is the norm. By embracing these new mentoring responsibilities, faculty can ensure that **technological advancement enhances, rather than diminishes, academic integrity, student agency, and the core values of scholarly inquiry**.

The Evolving Role of Faculty Mentors

---

1. From Content Expert to Learning Architect

In today's dynamic academic landscape, faculty are undergoing a profound professional evolution - from **content experts who transmit knowledge**, to **learning architects who design experiences that cultivate intellectual agility, critical inquiry, and lifelong adaptability**. This shift reflects not only the ubiquity of digital information and generative AI but also the increasing complexity of the problems students are expected to understand and address in their academic and professional lives.

Faculty are still expected to possess deep disciplinary expertise, but **expertise alone is no longer sufficient**. With information readily accessible online and generative technologies capable of producing instant summaries, definitions, and even literature reviews, students no longer look to faculty solely for facts. Instead, they need faculty to **curate, contextualize, and scaffold learning** - to help them make sense of what information matters, how to evaluate it, and how to apply it meaningfully across domains (Austin, 2002; Brookfield, 2017). This transformation into a **learning architect** involves several critical functions:

- **Curating Resources, not Just Delivering Content.** Faculty must now design environments that emphasize quality over quantity, guiding students toward credible, diverse, and thought-provoking materials. This includes integrating peer-reviewed literature, multimedia tools, open-access resources, and AI-generated content - all while modeling critical source evaluation. The goal is not to inundate students with information, but to **help them discern, connect, and prioritize** what matters most.
- **Teaching Students How to Navigate Ambiguity.** In an era marked by uncertainty - technological disruption, competing truth claims, and fast-changing research methods - faculty must cultivate students' tolerance for complexity. This includes helping them frame good questions, embrace failure as part of learning, and **develop flexible thinking skills** that extend beyond disciplinary silos. Faculty should create assignments and discussions that resist easy answers and encourage iterative exploration, reflection, and revision (Gardner, 2009; Mercer & Howe, 2012).
- **Helping students Synthesize Information Across Disciplines and Modalities.** Today's challenges - climate change, AI ethics, global health - require integrative thinking. Faculty must help students learn how to **draw connections across academic fields, personal experiences, and digital tools** to generate original insights and solutions. This includes fostering multimodal literacy, interdisciplinary reasoning, and collaborative problem-solving skills that transcend traditional academic boundaries (Brodin & Avery, 2020; Repko & Szostak, 2020).

By embracing this new role, faculty move from being the **sole purveyors of knowledge** to becoming **designers of intellectual ecosystems** - ecosystems that encourage curiosity, foster independence, and empower students to navigate the unknown. As learning architects, faculty are not just teaching **what** to know, but modeling **how** to learn, unlearn, and relearn in an age defined by change.

---

2. From Evaluator to Coach

In reimagining mentorship for the AI era, one of the most important transformations is the shift **from evaluator to coach**. While evaluation remains a necessary component of graduate education, mentors who rely solely on critique risk reinforcing power hierarchies and undermining student confidence. In contrast, the coaching model emphasizes **growth, partnership, and forward momentum**, offering feedback not as a final judgment, but as a catalyst for development (Nicol & Macfarlane-Dick, 2006).

A coach-style mentor focuses not only on identifying what needs improvement, but also on **guiding students through the cognitive, emotional, and strategic work** of making those improvements. This approach fosters a **safe environment for learning**, where students are encouraged to take intellectual risks, reflect on their decisions, and develop resilience in the face of complex academic tasks. Coaching shifts the mentor's tone from gatekeeping to empowerment, from **"what is wrong"** to **"what is next."**

This is especially important for students who may feel uncertain or underprepared - such as first-generation scholars, students of color, or those engaging with interdisciplinary or AI-integrated research for the first time. Coaching builds **academic confidence alongside competence**, promoting a sense of agency and ownership in the research process (Brookfield, 2017; Byars-Winston & Dahlberg, 2019).

Example Practice:

- *Rather than simply annotating a dissertation or capstone chapter with a vague critique such as "unclear," a coach-minded mentor might say:*
    - *"This section is promising - how might you link it more directly to your theoretical (or conceptual) framework?"*

This Feedback Approach Accomplishes Several Things:

- **Affirms progress**, which builds motivation.
- **Poses a question**, which invites reflection and dialogue.
- **Provides direction**, which helps the student move forward with clarity.

Coaching also aligns with principles of **formative assessment**, where feedback is embedded throughout the learning journey rather than delivered only at the end. Effective mentors **check in regularly**, use rubrics collaboratively, and co-develop revision plans. They also encourage students to **self-assess and articulate their learning needs**, modeling the metacognitive skills essential to long-term academic and professional success (Carless & Boud, 2018; Zimmerman, 2002).

Ultimately, coaching reframes mentorship as **an evolving partnership focused on growth**, not perfection. It enables mentors to challenge students rigorously while supporting them compassionately - a dual responsibility at the heart of meaningful, equitable graduate education.

---

3. The Case for Institutionalizing Partnership Mentorship

As graduate education adapts to the complexities of the 21st century - characterized by interdisciplinary challenges, digital research ecosystems, and increasing attention to equity and wellbeing - the need to institutionalize **mentorship as partnership** is both urgent and strategic. While traditional mentorship often depended on the goodwill and informal practices of individual faculty, **systemic, programmatic support** is required to ensure that effective mentorship is **equitable, sustainable, and scalable** across entire institutions.

Programs that embrace partnership-based mentorship models are shown to **increase doctoral completion rates**, a critical metric of graduate program success. Research by Golde (2005) highlighted that one of the most significant predictors of attrition is the quality of the mentoring relationship. When students feel guided, respected, and included - rather than isolated or under-supported - they are far more likely to persist through the intellectual and personal challenges of doctoral study.

Moreover, such programs actively **reduce feelings of isolation and marginalization**, particularly among students from underrepresented backgrounds. Partnership mentorship recognizes the full humanity of the student, acknowledging their cultural identity, lived experience, and evolving scholarly goals as integral to the mentoring process. This holistic and inclusive approach counters the alienation and invisibility that many students - especially students of color, first-generation students, and women in STEM - have historically reported in graduate settings (Sanczyk et al., 2021).

Beyond improved retention and belonging, institutionalized mentorship programs also **prepare students for collaborative, interdisciplinary careers beyond the academy**. As research and employment trends increasingly value teamwork, cross-sector fluency, and ethical adaptability, students must develop the skills to engage in complex, diverse, and evolving knowledge communities. Partnership mentorship cultivates these competencies by encouraging **dialogue, co-learning, and mutual accountability** - qualities foundational to leadership and innovation in both academic and non-academic professions.

Crucially, institutionalization also signals that **mentorship is not a mystical or innate trait possessed only by "naturally gifted" advisors**, but a **teachable, assessable professional skill**. Just as faculty are trained to conduct research and teach effectively, they must also be supported in learning how to mentor effectively. Institutions that adopt this view can provide faculty with mentorship training, reflection tools, peer learning circles, and evaluation criteria - ensuring that mentorship quality does not depend on individual personality or style but is guided by shared values and evidence-based practices (Pfund et al., 2016).

In summary, institutionalizing partnership mentorship is not merely a pedagogical enhancement - it is a **strategic investment in academic excellence, student success, and workforce readiness**. It aligns with equity commitments, responds to changing research landscapes, and strengthens the relational infrastructure that undergirds graduate education.

Section Reflection: Redefining Mentorship as a 21st-Century Partnership

This opening section offers a sweeping and deeply necessary reexamination of the historical foundations and evolving future of academic mentorship. It traces the transformation from hierarchical patronage to developmental partnership, underscoring that traditional models - however well-intentioned - are no longer sufficient in an era defined by diversity, digital disruption, and AI-augmented inquiry. The shift toward mentorship as partnership is framed not as a softening of standards but rather as a recalibration of power, responsibility, and shared growth between faculty and doctoral students.

The section powerfully dismantles the outdated notion of mentorship as a privatized or personality-driven endeavor, emphasizing instead the need for intentional, inclusive, and structured support - particularly for students from historically marginalized backgrounds. By introducing concepts such as mutual accountability, developmental dialogue, and mentorship responsibilities in the age of AI, it paints a compelling vision of mentorship not as one-way transmission, but as a co-learning relationship grounded in respect, reflexivity, and ethical guidance.

Importantly, the section elevates faculty as evolving professionals - no longer just content experts or evaluators, but also learning architects and academic coaches. This reconceptualization expands the mentor's role to include curating intellectual ecosystems, fostering synthesis across disciplines, and modeling transparent digital literacy in increasingly complex research environments. The call to institutionalize mentorship as a strategic practice - not an individual act of goodwill - makes clear that systemic change is essential for equitable, effective doctoral education.

In summary, this section reframes mentorship as a cornerstone of graduate transformation - where students are not shaped to fit old academic molds, but supported to become adaptive, ethical, and collaborative scholars in a rapidly shifting world.

Section 2: Personalized Mentorship in Diverse Learning Contexts

---

Doctoral education is no longer the exclusive domain of traditionally aged, full-time students on tenure-track pathways. Today's learners represent an expanding mosaic of **identities, life stages, professional goals, and cognitive styles**. Students may be career changers, caregivers, multilingual researchers, first-generation scholars, or working professionals returning for applied degrees. Others may be neurodivergent or managing invisible disabilities while navigating academic expectations.

In this richly diverse landscape, the one-size-fits-all mentorship model fails. Personalized mentorship offers a responsive, equity-minded approach - where faculty tailor support to a student's developmental needs, scholarly trajectory, and sociocultural context - while still upholding **academic rigor and accountability** (W. B. Johnson & Griffin, 2024; Sanczyk et al., 2021).

This section offers **practical strategies and illustrative examples** to help faculty implement personalized mentorship models that honor the individuality of each student. By meeting students where they are - academically, culturally, and emotionally - faculty can foster relationships that are responsive, inclusive, and developmentally appropriate. These models aim to **guide students toward becoming confident, capable, and critically engaged scholars** who are prepared to thrive in diverse academic and professional environments.

What Is Personalized Mentorship?

Personalized mentorship involves the intentional adaptation of guidance and support to align with each student's distinct learning journey. This includes responding to **individual learning styles and feedback preferences**, recognizing that some students thrive with detailed written commentary while others benefit more from real-time dialogue or visual modeling. It also requires attentiveness to a student's **cultural and linguistic background**, which may shape their communication style, interpretation of academic expectations, and comfort in seeking feedback or expressing uncertainty.

Mentors must also consider differences in **academic preparation and confidence levels**, particularly among students who may be returning to higher education after time away, navigating unfamiliar research cultures, or entering programs with nontraditional backgrounds.

A personalized approach helps these students build competence without being penalized for where they begin. In addition, mentorship should be aligned with the student's **career trajectory and long-term goals**, recognizing that not all doctoral candidates aspire to academic careers, and that guidance should reflect diverse professional pathways, including those in industry, policy, entrepreneurship, or interdisciplinary domains.

Crucially, this approach includes an awareness of **mental health, neurodiversity, and accessibility needs** - factors that profoundly shape the capacity to engage, persist, and thrive. Personalized mentorship does not mean lowering standards or making exceptions; rather, it means **removing avoidable barriers** that disproportionately affect students who do not conform to traditional academic molds. When faculty offer scaffolded, contextualized, and humanized mentorship, students are empowered not only to meet high standards but to **exceed them with clarity, dignity, and support** (Zellers et al., 2008).

Key Strategies for Personalizing Mentorship

---

1. Begin with a Diagnostic Mentorship Conversation

Effective personalization begins not with assumptions, but with **listening deeply and intentionally**. Before mentors can tailor their guidance, they must first understand the student's unique academic history, motivations, needs, and communication preferences. This process can be initiated through a **diagnostic mentorship conversation** - a structured, open-ended dialogue designed to elicit key insights about the student's starting point, aspirations, and working style.

Rather than launching immediately into task-oriented guidance, mentors can use this conversation to explore the student's **prior educational and research experiences**, identifying foundational knowledge, research exposures, and any gaps that might affect future progress. It is also an opportunity to learn about the student's **individual strengths**, areas of uncertainty, and personal goals. Understanding **preferred communication styles** - such as whether a student thrives in synchronous verbal discussion or needs time for asynchronous, written feedback - can dramatically improve the clarity, timeliness, and receptivity of mentor guidance.

Equally important, this conversation allows space for the student to articulate **short-term needs and long-term ambitions**, whether oriented toward academia, industry, public service, or interdisciplinary fields. It also creates a respectful opening for students to share **lived experiences and identity-based factors** - including cultural background, first-generation status, or prior experiences of marginalization - that may shape how they engage with institutional structures and expectations. When approached with humility and genuine interest, these conversations can build trust and position the mentor as a collaborator in the student's holistic development.

Example Conversation Prompts:

- *"Tell me about your academic journey so far."*
- *"What aspects of research excite you most - and which ones feel intimidating?"*

- *"How do you prefer to receive feedback - formally, informally, in real-time?"*

These kinds of questions are not merely introductory - they are **diagnostic tools** that help the mentor locate the student's **current zone of development** and respond with intentional, developmentally appropriate support (Brookfield, 2017). In doing so, mentors lay the foundation for a partnership that is both rigorous and responsive - one that evolves in sync with the student's emerging identity as a scholar.

---

2. Balancing the Three Core Mentorship Functions

According to Kram (1988), effective mentorship can be understood as encompassing three interconnected functions - **developmental, instrumental, and psychosocial** - each of which plays a vital role in supporting doctoral student success. These functions are not fixed in proportion or sequence; rather, they must be **intentionally adapted to the evolving context, identity, and needs of each student**. Faculty who recognize these dimensions and apply them responsively create more inclusive, empowering mentorship experiences that foster both scholarly growth and personal resilience.

The **developmental function** centers on cultivating students' academic capacities: strengthening critical thinking, academic writing, research design, and engagement with complex theoretical frameworks. This role is particularly essential when students are developing scholarly voice, navigating literature synthesis, or transitioning from practitioner mindsets to academic rigor (Austin, 2002; Brodin & Avery, 2020). The **instrumental function** involves supporting students in navigating the logistical and procedural demands of graduate study - such as time management, meeting institutional deadlines, understanding proposal processes, and establishing professional networks. This is especially important for first-generation students or those unfamiliar with academic norms, who may lack the implicit knowledge necessary to advance efficiently (Golde, 2005; W. B. Johnson & Griffin, 2024).

Equally important is the **psychosocial function**, which attends to the student's emotional well-being, identity affirmation, and sense of belonging. This aspect of mentorship provides **relational stability and encouragement**, particularly critical for students from marginalized or underrepresented groups who may face heightened levels of imposter syndrome, stereotype threat, or cultural mismatch within academic spaces (Barker, 2011; Sanczyk et al., 2021). Psychosocial mentoring affirms the student's humanity and lived experience as integral to their scholarly potential, creating space for authenticity and reflection in environments that are often implicitly exclusionary.

Example:

- *A first-generation doctoral student may benefit most from **instrumental mentoring** to understand how to prepare for a dissertation or capstone proposal defense, communicate with committee members, or interpret institutional expectations.*
- *In contrast, a mid-career student returning to academia from industry may need **developmental support** to sharpen their academic writing or reorient toward peer-reviewed scholarship.*

- *Meanwhile, a student of color navigating a predominantly white academic environment may require* ***psychosocial support*** *to feel valued, validated, and safe - particularly in fields where they may be one of few.*

Faculty Tip: These mentoring roles should not be treated as static responsibilities. As students move through the phases of doctoral training - from coursework and candidacy to dissertation or capstone completion and post-graduation planning - the balance among these functions will shift. Faculty are encouraged to **revisit and recalibrate their mentoring approach regularly**, using reflective dialogue and collaborative check-ins to ensure alignment with student needs and aspirations (W. B. Johnson & Griffin, 2024; Pfund et al., 2016).

---

3. Adapting Feedback to Student Differences

Students receive and process feedback in highly individual ways, shaped by a complex interplay of **cognitive preferences, cultural background, neurodiversity, and previous experiences with academic gatekeeping**. For many, feedback is not simply instructional - it can also be emotionally charged, reinforcing either a sense of capability or, conversely, a feeling of exclusion or inadequacy. Effective mentors recognize that a one-size-fits-all approach to critique may unintentionally hinder learning or exacerbate anxiety, particularly for students who have previously experienced marginalization within academic systems (Brookfield, 2017; Sanczyk et al., 2021).

To ensure that feedback is **constructive, accessible, and empowering**, faculty can employ a range of differentiated strategies. For example, offering **visual scaffolds** - such as flowcharts, checklists, or concept maps - can be especially helpful for students with ADHD or executive function challenges, enabling them to better organize their thinking and plan revisions in manageable steps (Carless & Boud, 2018). For students who process **spoken language more fluently than written text**, audio-recorded or screen-capture feedback allows for greater nuance and relational tone, making critique feel more collaborative and less impersonal. These methods also benefit students with visual processing difficulties or those who speak English as an additional language, for whom tonal cues can clarify intent and reduce misinterpretation.

Another key approach is providing **strength-based feedback**, especially when mentoring students from underrepresented backgrounds who may have internalized deficit-based academic messaging. Leading with what is working - such as conceptual clarity, original framing, or reflective insight - can build momentum and resilience before introducing areas for improvement. This technique is not about sugar-coating critique but about framing feedback in a way that **preserves the student's sense of agency and scholarly potential** (Byars-Winston & Dahlberg, 2019; Nicol & Macfarlane-Dick, 2006).

Example:

- *A multilingual doctoral student drafting their literature review receives two distinct tiers of feedback: the first round focuses on the* ***structure, coherence, and logical flow*** *of ideas, while the second round - delivered only after the foundational framework is sound - offers suggestions on* ***word choice, tone, and academic language****.*
- *By sequencing the feedback in this way, the mentor avoids overwhelming the student, supports a sense of accomplishment, and builds confidence for more nuanced revision.*

Personalized feedback strategies not only enhance learning outcomes - they also affirm the mentor's role as a responsive, adaptive educator who is attuned to the **whole student**, not just the written product. In an increasingly diverse and digitally mediated academic environment, this level of intentionality is no longer optional - it is essential to equitable, effective mentorship.

---

4. Honoring Identity-Rooted Scholarship through Personalized Mentorship

Personalized mentorship also includes **affirming and supporting students' desire to pursue research topics that reflect their communities, languages, and lived experiences**. For many students - particularly those from historically marginalized, immigrant, Indigenous, or multilingual backgrounds - research is not simply an academic exercise; it is a form of advocacy, cultural preservation, or community accountability. When mentors validate these commitments and treat them as legitimate scholarly contributions, they create conditions in which students can pursue **authentic, meaningful, and socially relevant scholarship** without having to detach from their identities (Kovach, 2021; Sanczyk et al., 2021).

This commitment requires faculty to go beyond technical advising and engage in mentorship practices that challenge dominant norms of what counts as "rigorous" or "objective." For example, faculty must be willing to **recognize and support nontraditional methodologies**, such as Indigenous inquiry, participatory action research, or arts-based research, not as exceptions but as **equally valid epistemological approaches** grounded in deep theoretical and ethical traditions (Candy & Edmonds, 2018; Repko & Szostak, 2020). Mentors must also **coach students in navigating academic gatekeeping** - such as biased peer review, institutional skepticism, or narrowly defined dissertation or capstone expectations - while helping them preserve the integrity and authenticity of their work. In doing so, mentors act as cultural brokers and academic allies, offering students the language, strategy, and institutional insight to move their work forward without erasure or compromise.

Advocating for inclusive committee composition is another critical practice. Students conducting identity-embedded or community-centered research often benefit from having committee members who bring **lived experience, cultural knowledge, or methodological expertise** aligned with the work. Mentors can play a vital role in ensuring that the committee is not only diverse in expertise but also inclusive in worldview - thereby protecting the student from isolation and affirming the scholarly legitimacy of the research.

Example:

- *A doctoral student designs a study involving* ***bilingual interviews with undocumented youth****, aiming to capture stories in both English and Spanish to preserve narrative authenticity.*
- *Her mentor actively supports her IRB application by helping her articulate how* ***linguistic equity and cultural confidentiality*** *are not just ethical imperatives but central to the rigor and trustworthiness of the study.*
- *In parallel, the mentor helps her frame the project's* ***scholarly contribution****, positioning it as a vital intervention in both the field of education and the broader discourse on immigration and representation.*

By honoring identity-rooted scholarship, mentors uphold the principle that academic research should **reflect the complexity and diversity of the world it seeks to understand**. This not only empowers individual students - it also expands the intellectual boundaries and ethical horizons of the academy itself.

---

5. Mentoring Beyond the Professoriate

In today's academic landscape, **not all doctoral students are preparing for careers within the professoriate** - nor should they be expected to. While traditional faculty roles remain one pathway, an increasing number of doctoral students are pursuing careers in **policy, nonprofit leadership, educational consulting, industry research, entrepreneurship, and other applied or interdisciplinary fields**. Faculty mentorship must evolve to reflect this professional diversity, providing students with the guidance, flexibility, and resources they need to prepare for futures that may extend far beyond the boundaries of the academy (Austin, 2002; Golde & Walker, 2006).

One important responsibility of the mentor is to help students **map their existing and emerging skills onto potential career trajectories**, including transferable competencies such as research design, data analysis, writing, presentation, collaboration, and ethical reasoning. This process requires regular, open dialogue about the student's goals and a willingness to integrate professional development into academic planning. In some cases, this may include **customizing the dissertation or capstone format** itself. Alternatives to the traditional monograph - such as **portfolio dissertations or capstones, practice-based inquiries, or design-based prototypes** - allow students to produce work that is both academically rigorous and professionally relevant (Kamler, 2008; McKenney & Reeves, 2018).

Mentors should also support students in **exploring public and applied dissemination pathways**, such as publishing policy briefs, contributing to professional blogs, developing instructional resources, or presenting findings to stakeholder communities. These forms of scholarship extend the impact of doctoral research while helping students develop the communication and engagement skills valued in many sectors beyond academia (Ball, 2004; Barker, 2011).

Example:

- *A doctoral student with a professional background in **user-experience (UX) design** chooses to integrate **multimodal design thinking and a prototype evaluation process** into their dissertation or capstone.*
- *Their mentor not only supports the scholarly justification for this methodological approach but also helps the student articulate its value to **employers in the tech sector**.*
- *Together, they curate a professional portfolio that includes research documentation, annotated design artifacts, and reflection pieces - demonstrating both academic rigor and industry readiness.*

By mentoring beyond the professoriate, faculty affirm that **doctoral education is not a one-track endeavor**, but a flexible, evolving platform for preparing scholars, innovators, and change agents across a wide range of domains. This shift not only empowers students to define their own success - it also expands the relevance and reach of the doctorate itself.

Sample Personalized Mentorship Agreement

Category	Student Need	Mentor Support Strategy
Learning Preferences	Written feedback with visual structure	Annotated examples, checklists, and clear rubrics
Communication Style	Biweekly email check-ins + monthly Zoom calls	Scheduled in advance with the student's agenda
Research Context	Bilingual community engagement methodology	Ethics and methods coaching, committee advocacy
Career Alignment	Public education advocacy	Policy brief co-writing and presentation coaching

Section Reflection: Personalized Mentorship as a Foundation for Equity and Student Thriving

This section powerfully expands the mentorship conversation by reframing personalization not as a luxury but more so as a necessity in today's increasingly diverse doctoral education landscape. It argues persuasively that in a system no longer defined by homogeneity - of age, background, neurotype, career goal, or cultural experience - effective mentorship must move beyond uniform strategies and instead meet students where they are. Personalized mentorship, as described here, becomes an act of equity: a way of scaffolding rigor while honoring difference, context, and individual trajectory.

The section outlines five deeply actionable strategies that operationalize this equity-minded model. It begins with the diagnostic mentorship conversation - presented as a critical first step in building trust, clarifying support needs, and surfacing lived experiences that might otherwise remain invisible. It continues by introducing the three functions of mentorship - developmental, instrumental, and psychosocial - and shows how their balance must evolve as students are progressing. Particularly compelling is the section's attention to feedback: how faculty can adapt both form and tone to accommodate cognitive difference, linguistic diversity, and prior experiences with exclusion.

Equally important is the call to honor identity-rooted scholarship and to support career paths beyond the professoriate. These two elements represent some of the most forward-looking contributions in this section. By affirming nontraditional epistemologies and co-creating professional relevance, personalized mentorship is positioned as a force for both academic transformation and real-world impact.

Ultimately, this section reframes the mentor's role as an intentional, reflexive guide - one who helps students cultivate scholarly confidence without demanding assimilation. It invites faculty to reimagine mentorship not as dispensing identical advice, but as shaping a relationship where each student is fully seen, supported, and challenged in ways that align with their unique potential. In doing so, it models what truly inclusive, future-ready graduate education can become.

Section 3: Co-Mentoring Models - Shared Responsibility, Expanded Insight

---

The demands of modern doctoral research - characterized by interdisciplinarity, applied relevance, and digital complexity - have outgrown the traditional model of one-to-one faculty mentorship. No single advisor can realistically meet the full spectrum of needs for students working at the intersection of multiple domains, especially in fields involving AI, participatory research, or policy translation. In response, graduate programs are increasingly turning to **co-mentoring models**, where **two or more advisors share mentoring responsibilities**, each contributing complementary strengths (Austin, 2002; Kochan & Trimble, 2000).

When implemented effectively, co-mentoring improves both **depth and breadth** of scholarly guidance, helps students learn to **synthesize varied perspectives**, and distributes the mentoring burden more equitably among faculty (Pfund et al., 2016). This section provides faculty with practical frameworks and protocols to implement co-mentoring systems that are structured, ethical, and empowering - for both students and mentors.

Why Co-Mentoring Matters

---

1. Supporting Interdisciplinary Research Through Co-Mentoring

As the boundaries between academic disciplines continue to blur, many doctoral students are conducting research that **integrates multiple methods, theories, and epistemologies**. These projects often bridge traditionally siloed domains - for example, using artificial intelligence to analyze cultural narratives, applying ethnographic techniques to algorithmic decision-making, or blending statistical modeling with participatory design. While such **interdisciplinary inquiry reflects the complexity of real-world challenges**, it also introduces unique intellectual demands. Students must learn to navigate divergent vocabularies, methodological expectations, and validation standards across fields - an undertaking that can quickly lead to **epistemological overload** without thoughtful mentorship (Brodin & Avery, 2020; Repko & Szostak, 2020).

Co-mentoring provides a powerful structure to support this kind of complexity. By engaging **two or more faculty mentors from distinct but complementary disciplines**, students can draw upon specialized expertise without being forced to flatten or oversimplify the tensions between methods or paradigms. Each mentor contributes depth in their area of focus, while also modeling how to negotiate interdisciplinary boundaries with intellectual humility and rigor. This approach reinforces the idea that synthesis is not the absence of disciplinary fidelity, but a **careful negotiation among frameworks** in service of deeper insight (McKenney & Reeves, 2018; Walker et al., 2009).

Importantly, co-mentoring also promotes **relational balance and identity safety**, particularly for students whose research may challenge established disciplinary conventions or whose lived experience informs their scholarly lens. With diverse mentors offering both content expertise and epistemic validation, students are better equipped to pursue ambitious research agendas without feeling pressure to conform to a single academic mold.

Example:

- *A doctoral student researching **urban health inequalities** develops a project that combines **GIS mapping with community-based qualitative interviews**. To support this hybrid design, one mentor is a geographer specializing in spatial analytics, and the other is a public health expert experienced in participatory research.*
- *Together, they help the student **balance the technical precision required in geospatial data analysis with the ethical and relational dynamics of conducting fieldwork** in historically marginalized communities.*
- *The co-mentoring team ensures that the student's work maintains methodological rigor while honoring the lived realities of the populations being studied.*

By institutionalizing co-mentorship for interdisciplinary projects, programs send a clear message: **complex questions deserve complex mentorship**. This model not only strengthens research outcomes but also equips students with the collaborative and adaptive capacities essential for scholarly and professional success in an increasingly interconnected world.

---

2. Addressing Mentor Capacity and Burnout

As faculty navigate increasingly complex workloads - ranging from teaching and research to service, administration, and student advising - the challenge of providing sustained, individualized mentorship to doctoral students has become more acute. This is especially true in programs experiencing **enrollment growth, increased dissertation or capstone supervision demands, or heightened expectations for diversity, equity, and inclusion in mentorship**. While most faculty are committed to supporting their students, the reality is that no single mentor can be expected to offer **comprehensive expertise, emotional labor, and logistical oversight** across every phase of doctoral training without risk of overload or burnout (Austin & McDaniels, 2006; Pfund et al., 2016).

In this context, **co-mentoring emerges not only as a pedagogical enhancement, but as a structural safeguard** - one that allows for the strategic distribution of mentorship responsibilities across multiple faculty. By pairing or grouping mentors with complementary strengths, programs can ensure that students receive timely, well-rounded support in areas such as research design, writing development, fieldwork, career preparation, and well-being, without placing undue pressure on a single advisor. This model enhances faculty sustainability by creating **mentoring ecosystems**, where relational and intellectual labor is shared rather than siloed.

Moreover, co-mentoring allows faculty to **focus on their strengths and capacities**, whether those lie in theoretical framing, methods instruction, professional networking, or psychosocial support. This not only improves the quality of mentorship for students - it also increases faculty satisfaction and retention by affirming that effective mentorship is a

collaborative endeavor, not a heroic individual performance (Boud & Falchikov, 2006; W. B. Johnson & Griffin, 2024).

By addressing mentor capacity through structural solutions rather than relying solely on personal resilience, institutions demonstrate a commitment to **sustainable graduate education** - one in which both students and faculty can thrive. Co-mentoring is not just a kindness to overburdened advisors; it is a strategic investment in the long-term health of doctoral programs and the scholars they produce.

---

3. Modeling Scholarly Dialogue and Navigating Diverse Feedback

One of the most valuable aspects of working with multiple mentors is the opportunity it provides for students to **experience and engage with the pluralism that defines academic life**. No single scholar holds a monopoly on truth, and in environments where knowledge production is increasingly interdisciplinary, methodological diversity and theoretical disagreement are not only common - they are essential to robust inquiry. Co-mentoring structures expose students to **varied intellectual traditions, evaluative standards, and feedback styles**, allowing them to develop a more sophisticated and agile approach to academic dialogue (Pfund et al., 2016; Walker et al., 2009).

Through this process, students learn how to **integrate conflicting viewpoints** without capitulating to every suggestion, fostering the capacity to make reasoned, defensible choices about their research direction. They also learn to **justify methodological and conceptual decisions** in light of differing disciplinary expectations - skills that are critical not only for dissertation or capstone defense, but also for publishing, grant writing, and collaboration in diverse research settings. This requires what might be called **intellectual diplomacy**: the ability to listen actively, respond thoughtfully, and make principled choices even amid disagreement or ambiguity (Brodin & Avery, 2020; Brookfield, 2017).

In addition to strengthening academic judgment, co-mentoring builds students' **leadership capacity**, particularly in relation to project management, communication, and negotiation. Students who learn to balance input from multiple advisors are better prepared to **lead interdisciplinary teams, synthesize stakeholder perspectives, and communicate across professional or cultural differences** - all essential competencies in both academic and applied research environments. This mentorship model reflects the realities of modern scholarship, where collaborative, adaptive, and context-sensitive thinkers are in high demand.

By modeling scholarly dialogue and helping students navigate diverse feedback with clarity and confidence, co-mentoring does more than enrich academic development - it **prepares students for the complexity and diversity of intellectual life beyond the dissertation or capstone**.

Co-Mentoring Models in Practice

---

1. Content–Methodology Pairing

One highly effective co-mentoring strategy is **content–methodology pairing**, in which a student is guided by both a **domain expert** and a **methodological specialist**. This approach ensures that the dissertation or capstone is not only conceptually rich and contextually grounded, but also **methodologically rigorous and technically sound**. As research questions grow more complex - often involving large datasets, digital tools, or cross-disciplinary inquiry - students increasingly require mentorship that can support both the **substantive depth of their topic and the analytical demands of their chosen methods** (McKenney & Reeves, 2018; Repko & Szostak, 2020).

In such arrangements, the domain expert typically offers guidance on **theoretical framing, literature engagement, and disciplinary relevance**, helping the student situate their research within ongoing scholarly conversations. Meanwhile, the methodological mentor focuses on the **technical execution of research design**, supporting areas such as statistical analysis, computational modeling, experimental design, or qualitative rigor, depending on the chosen approach. This division of labor does not fragment the project; rather, it promotes **cross-functional coherence**, encouraging students to think integratively while drawing on the highest standards of both content and method.

Example:

- *A student writing a dissertation or capstone on **misinformation dynamics on social media platforms** is supported by two mentors: a **communications scholar**, who advises on the theoretical underpinnings of media influence, ethical concerns around digital manipulation, and the sociopolitical contexts of disinformation; and a **data scientist**, who helps the student build and refine sentiment analysis models using Python and conduct large-scale scraping of social media data.*
- *The result is a project that is both **conceptually insightful and methodologically robust**, meeting the standards of multiple scholarly communities and producing findings with interdisciplinary relevance.*

By pairing content and methodology expertise, mentors create a **collaborative scaffolding** that supports students in developing as both scholars and researchers. This model exemplifies what rigorous, future-facing doctoral education can look like - **intellectually integrative, methodologically fluent, and responsive to the demands of real-world complexity**.

---

2. Faculty–Practitioner Hybrid Model

For students pursuing **applied, translational, or design-based dissertations or capstones**, the **faculty–practitioner hybrid model** offers a powerful mentoring structure that bridges the gap between academic inquiry and real-world implementation. In this model, a traditional academic mentor is paired with a **field-based expert**, such as a clinical leader, industry professional, or community partner. The result is a mentorship team that can guide both the **scholarly integrity of the research and its contextual relevance and feasibility** in practice-based environments (W. B. Johnson & Griffin, 2024; McKenney & Reeves, 2018).

Academic mentors provide critical support in **formulating research questions, aligning with disciplinary frameworks, navigating institutional requirements, and maintaining methodological rigor**. Meanwhile, practitioner mentors bring firsthand insight into

organizational dynamics, stakeholder expectations, policy constraints, and end-user needs - elements that are often overlooked in purely academic settings but are crucial for real-world applicability. This dual perspective helps students design research that is not only theoretically grounded but also implementable, scalable, and aligned with the conditions of practice.

Example:

- *A Doctor of Nursing Practitioner (DNP) student piloting a* ***patient-centered care model*** *in a regional hospital is co-mentored by a* ***nursing faculty member*** *and a* ***hospital director****. The faculty mentor supports the student in refining their intervention design, applying outcome evaluation frameworks, and navigating the IRB process.*
- *Simultaneously, the hospital director provides access to institutional resources, advises on implementation logistics, and ensures that the research fits within the operational flow and patient care priorities of the healthcare setting.*
- *Together, they help the student produce a dissertation or capstone that is both* ***academically rigorous and institutionally relevant****, exemplifying the goals of translational scholarship.*

This hybrid model is particularly valuable in professional doctorate programs - such as education (EdD), nursing (DNP), or public health (DPH) - where the ultimate goal is to produce **scholar-practitioners capable of driving innovation in real-world systems**. It reinforces the notion that rigor and relevance are not competing values, but mutually reinforcing dimensions of high-impact research (Boud et al., 2023).

---

3. Mentorship Pods or Teams

For students engaged in complex, interdisciplinary, or high-impact dissertation or capstone projects, a **mentorship pod** - also known as a mentoring team - offers a comprehensive and collaborative approach to academic guidance. Rather than relying on a single mentor to provide support across all domains, this model **strategically distributes responsibility** among a small group of 3 to 4 mentors, each offering **distinct expertise and perspectives**. This structure acknowledges the multifaceted nature of contemporary research and reflects the collaborative environments that students will likely encounter in their postdoctoral or professional careers (Pfund et al., 2016; Walker et al., 2009).

Each member of the pod assumes a clearly defined role that contributes to the student's development across scholarly, technical, ethical, and applied dimensions of the research. The **chair** typically provides overarching guidance and ensures coherence across contributions, serving as the central point of integration and programmatic accountability. A **methodologist** - quantitative, qualitative, or mixed methods - offers deep support in research design, data analysis, and methodological alignment. A **content expert** ensures disciplinary rigor and relevance, helping the student remain anchored in the central debates and theoretical conversations of the field. Finally, an **external stakeholder** - such as a practitioner, policymaker, or community representative - provides insight into the real-world implications, usability, or ethical considerations of the research in practice-based settings (Austin & McDaniels, 2006; Repko & Szostak, 2020).

Example Structure:

Role	Focus
Chair	Oversight and integration
Methodologist	Quantitative/qualitative rigor
Content Expert	Field-specific knowledge
External Stakeholder	Practitioner/community-based input

This structure ensures that **no aspect of a complex dissertation or capstone is unsupported**, while also modeling the collaborative intellectual environments that increasingly define academic and professional research. Students not only benefit from a broader range of expertise - they also learn to **coordinate feedback, negotiate competing priorities, and synthesize diverse forms of input** into a coherent scholarly product. These are essential skills for managing grants, leading teams, and engaging in interdisciplinary inquiry well beyond the dissertation or capstone stage (Brodin & Avery, 2020; Carless & Boud, 2018).

Mentorship pods reinforce the idea that academic success is not an isolated pursuit but a **collective and negotiated process**, one that prepares students to lead with intellectual flexibility, strategic communication, and collaborative acumen.

Best Practices for Structuring Co-Mentorship

---

1. Establish a Shared Mentoring Plan

In any co-mentoring or team-based mentorship structure, **clarity of roles and expectations is essential**. Without a shared plan, students may receive **conflicting advice, unclear feedback, or uneven support**, leading to confusion, frustration, and lost momentum. Faculty, too, may unintentionally duplicate efforts, make assumptions about one another's roles, or disengage if responsibilities are not clearly defined. To prevent such pitfalls, it is important to **establish a shared mentoring plan early in the relationship** - a flexible, collaboratively developed document that outlines responsibilities, communication norms, and shared expectations (Pfund et al., 2016; Zellers et al., 2008).

A shared mentoring plan serves multiple purposes: it provides a **roadmap for collaboration**, creates **accountability among mentors**, and empowers the student to navigate the mentorship structure with confidence. At minimum, the plan should specify each mentor's **domain of responsibility** - such as theory development, methods advising, institutional navigation, or career planning - and outline expectations for how frequently each party will communicate. It should also include a **protocol for joint decision-making**, such as when and how to convene joint meetings, how feedback will be synthesized, and how final guidance will be communicated to the student. Just as importantly, the plan should articulate **a strategy for resolving disagreements**, offering a non-punitive framework for addressing differing opinions or misaligned expectations within the mentoring team (Austin & McDaniels, 2006).

Example Clause:

- *"Mentor A will lead the review of literature and theoretical framing; Mentor B will guide all aspects of data analysis. The student will prepare synthesis questions in advance of monthly joint meetings and maintain a shared mentoring log to track progress and decisions."*

Such language provides structure without rigidity and promotes transparency in ways that benefit both student and mentors. As mentorship needs evolve over the course of the doctoral journey, the plan can and should be **reviewed and revised**, allowing the mentorship structure to remain responsive to new challenges and opportunities.

By proactively establishing a shared mentoring plan, doctoral programs foster not only smoother collaboration - but also a culture of **intentionality, professionalism, and mutual respect** in the mentoring process. This contributes to more sustainable advising relationships and more successful doctoral outcomes overall.

---

2. Support Student Synthesis and Agency

In mentoring arrangements that involve multiple faculty - whether in co-mentoring dyads, pods, or committee structures - students are often exposed to **divergent ideas, preferences, and evaluative standards**. While such diversity enriches intellectual development, it can also create pressure to appease competing voices, particularly when mentors offer **contradictory feedback or implicitly assert disciplinary authority**. In these situations, mentors must be careful not to "pull" the student in different directions, but rather to **cultivate the student's ability to synthesize feedback and assert scholarly agency** (Pfund et al., 2016; Walker et al., 2009).

One strategy for fostering agency is to invite students to **prepare reflective memos prior to mentoring meetings**, outlining their current thinking, questions, or dilemmas. These memos promote metacognition and allow the student to engage with feedback not just reactively, but **proactively and critically**. Faculty can also encourage the **triangulation of ideas and approaches**, helping students explore multiple pathways or interpretations rather than defaulting to one mentor's perspective. This process teaches students to identify common threads, weigh trade-offs, and develop an integrated line of reasoning that reflects both **rigor and authenticity** (Brookfield, 2017).

Most importantly, mentors should help students learn to **articulate rationales for their decisions**, especially when navigating differences among advisors. Rather than seeking to please everyone, students must develop the confidence and language to defend their choices - methodological, theoretical, or stylistic - while remaining open to revision. This skill is central to scholarly identity formation and prepares students for the intellectual negotiations that characterize peer review, collaborative research, and leadership in interdisciplinary spaces (Barker, 2011; Brodin & Avery, 2020).

Example Prompt:

- *"You have received differing advice from both of us - how do you propose to resolve the tension while preserving your scholarly voice?"*

This kind of prompt signals trust in the student's judgment while reinforcing that synthesis is their responsibility - not something to outsource or avoid. Over time, students who are coached in this way develop not only a stronger dissertation or capstone - they emerge as **self-directed scholars capable of navigating complexity with clarity, diplomacy, and integrity**.

---

3. Hold Joint Meetings When Possible

In co-mentoring arrangements, even brief **joint meetings between the student and multiple mentors** can significantly enhance clarity, alignment, and relational trust. While individual check-ins are often necessary and valuable, periodic **triadic or team-based conversations** help ensure that mentors are working from a shared understanding of the student's progress, goals, and challenges. These sessions reduce the risk of miscommunication or contradictory advice by allowing the mentoring team to **surface tensions, coordinate feedback, and model collaborative scholarly discourse** in real time (Pfund et al., 2016; Zellers et al., 2008).

Joint meetings also serve an important developmental purpose. When mentors engage in dialogue with one another in the presence of the student, they demonstrate how **academic disagreement can be constructive, respectful, and generative** - rather than hierarchical or competitive. Students witness firsthand how scholars from different traditions negotiate meaning, justify decisions, and adjust their perspectives, providing a live model of interdisciplinary collegiality and intellectual humility (Brookfield, 2017; Repko & Szostak, 2020). This modeling is especially valuable for students who are learning to navigate complex mentorship structures or manage competing forms of authority.

Faculty Tip: To further reinforce student leadership and scholarly ownership, consider **rotating facilitation roles** between mentors and explicitly inviting students to set the agenda for each meeting. This might include identifying key questions, selecting which feedback to prioritize, or outlining discussion goals in advance. Such practices not only make meetings more efficient - they also position the student as an **active agent in their own scholarly development**, rather than a passive recipient of guidance (Carless & Boud, 2018; Zimmerman, 2002).

Over time, regular joint meetings promote a mentoring culture characterized by **transparency, coherence, and mutual respect**. They remind everyone involved that doctoral education is not just about content mastery - it is about learning how to work productively across differences, an essential skill for academic and professional life alike.

Case Study: Co-Mentoring in a Multimodal Dissertation or Capstone

Student Project. This case study illustrates how a **co-mentoring structure can support a multimodal, interdisciplinary dissertation or capstone**, enabling a student to integrate diverse methodologies and epistemologies while cultivating agency and scholarly depth. The student's project focused on **climate activism in the digital age**, specifically analyzing how grassroots environmental movements mobilize on Instagram. The dissertation or capstone combined **visual content analysis of social media posts, in-depth interviews with activists, and GIS-based digital cartography** of protest networks and climate impact zones.

Mentor Roles. To support this complex design, the student worked with a three-person mentorship team, each offering domain-specific expertise. A **digital media scholar** provided guidance on visual methods, narrative theory, and social critique, helping the student frame Instagram content within contemporary debates on digital activism and representation (Ball, 2004; Brookfield, 2017). An **environmental scientist** served as the subject matter expert, ensuring the student's interpretations of climate data and policy contexts were scientifically grounded. A **GIS specialist** advised on the use of digital mapping tools, helping the student transform location data into compelling spatial visualizations that complemented the narrative findings (McKenney & Reeves, 2018).

Structure. The mentorship structure was intentionally designed to support integration and agency. All mentors had access to a **shared digital folder** for drafts, annotated comments, and methodological resources, promoting transparency and asynchronous collaboration. The team held **monthly meetings**, with facilitation responsibilities rotating among mentors to balance leadership and highlight different perspectives. In addition, the student submitted **quarterly reflection logs**, documenting their decisions, challenges, and synthesis efforts. These logs not only helped the student track their intellectual evolution - they also prompted valuable mentoring conversations about navigating epistemological tensions and managing multi-modal research demands (Pfund et al., 2016; Repko & Szostak, 2020).

Outcome. The outcome was a dissertation or capstone that demonstrated a **sophisticated, interdisciplinary research framework**, bridging critical theory, environmental science, and geospatial analysis. The student co-authored and published two peer-reviewed articles with different mentors - one in a media studies journal and another in an applied environmental science outlet - reflecting the project's dual academic relevance. Just as significantly, the student reported increased confidence in **navigating methodological complexity, integrating diverse feedback, and articulating their scholarly identity across disciplines**.

This case underscores the transformative potential of co-mentoring when paired with a **clear structure, intentional communication, and responsive mentorship design**. It affirms that multimodal dissertations or capstones - once considered difficult to supervise - can flourish when supported by a collaborative, student-centered mentoring team.

Section Reflection: Co-Mentoring as a Model for Collaborative, Future-Ready Doctoral Education

This section reframes mentorship as a shared intellectual endeavor, arguing persuasively that the complexities of 21st-century doctoral research demand more than a single mentor can provide. Through clear structure and compelling examples, it positions co-mentoring not as a luxury or workaround, but as a high-impact, equity-centered model of academic supervision. In doing so, it shifts the narrative from mentorship as solitary guidance to mentorship as distributed expertise - fostering richer dialogue, deeper interdisciplinarity, and more sustainable faculty engagement.

The section's strength lies in its multidimensional argument: co-mentoring supports **students** by bridging epistemic divides and promoting intellectual agency; it supports **faculty** by reducing the burdens of solitary mentorship and enabling specialization; and it supports **institutions** by modeling the kinds of collaborative, adaptive learning environments that define modern scholarship and workforce expectations. Particularly noteworthy is the emphasis on **intellectual pluralism**: students not only receive richer academic guidance but also learn to navigate disagreement, synthesize diverse inputs, and lead interdisciplinary conversations with confidence.

The three co-mentoring models - content–methodology pairing, faculty–practitioner hybrid, and mentorship pods - offer grounded, adaptable frameworks that graduate programs can implement immediately. These are not theoretical ideals - they are implementable structures aligned with diverse student needs, applied contexts, and emerging forms of scholarship. The section's guidance on best practices - such as developing a shared mentoring plan, supporting student synthesis, and holding joint meetings - ensures that co-mentoring is not only ambitious, but coherent and functional.

Ultimately, this section contributes a powerful reframing of doctoral mentorship for the AI-integrated, interdisciplinary, socially engaged research era. It calls for faculty to embrace co-mentorship not as an admission of limits, but as a model of humility, collaboration, and systemic care. It shows that mentoring, when reimagined as shared work, can become more sustainable, more inclusive, and more intellectually generative - preparing students not just to complete a dissertation or capstone, but to thrive in the collaborative knowledge ecosystems that await them beyond it.

Section 4: Building Scalable Mentorship Systems for Programmatic Success

Mentorship is widely recognized as a cornerstone of doctoral success, yet many graduate programs still rely on informal, mentor-dependent practices that create inconsistency and inequity across cohorts. As doctoral education becomes more interdisciplinary, diverse, and digitally mediated, programs must shift from isolated, mentor-centered relationships to **scalable mentorship systems** that are sustainable, inclusive, and systematically structured (Walker et al., 2009; Zellers et al., 2008).

A scalable mentorship system ensures that all students receive **high-quality, intentional, and developmentally appropriate guidance**, regardless of their background, mode of enrollment (e.g., online or hybrid), or chosen research methodology. Such systems not only support student retention and achievement but also help balance faculty workloads and elevate institutional culture around mentoring (Austin, 2002; Pfund et al., 2016).

This section outlines a set of **proven models, digital tools, and accountability structures** designed to help institutions move beyond ad hoc advising toward the intentional cultivation of **mentorship ecosystems**. In contrast to mentorship as an isolated faculty responsibility, ecosystems are institutional frameworks that embed mentoring into the very fabric of doctoral education - aligning policy, practice, and culture around shared values of **adaptability, equity, and sustainability** (Austin & McDaniels, 2006; Zellers et al., 2008).

At the heart of this approach is the recognition that mentoring excellence is **not the result of individual charisma or innate talent**, but of structured support, reflective training, and distributed leadership. Models such as co-mentoring teams, faculty–practitioner partnerships, and interdisciplinary pods offer students layered, complementary support while expanding institutional capacity. **Digital tools** - from shared feedback platforms and scheduling systems to mentorship logs and reflection templates - facilitate coordination, transparency, and timely communication across mentoring relationships. When paired with **accountability structures** such as mentoring plans, periodic check-ins, and institutional recognition programs, these tools create a foundation for mentoring that is both flexible and responsible.

The goal is to design systems that not only meet students where they are, but also evolve as students are progressing - ensuring that mentorship remains **developmentally appropriate, culturally responsive, and academically rigorous** throughout the doctoral journey. By investing in these scalable, evidence-informed structures, institutions affirm that **effective mentorship is a collective, strategic priority** - not a peripheral task, but a cornerstone of long-term student and faculty success (W. B. Johnson & Griffin, 2024; Pfund et al., 2016).

Why Systematize Mentorship?

---

1. Preventing Inequity and Isolation

One of the most pressing challenges in doctoral education is the **uneven distribution of mentorship**, which often mirrors broader structural inequalities within academia. Research has shown that **students from ethnic backgrounds, first-generation scholars, and those engaged in interdisciplinary or online programs** are disproportionately affected by mentorship gaps (Sanczyk et al., 2021; Zellers et al., 2008). When institutions fail to provide systemic mentorship infrastructure, advising becomes a **matter of luck or privilege** - contingent on informal networks, faculty availability, or cultural proximity, rather than equity or intentionality.

In such unstructured environments, the absence of regular, engaged mentorship can lead to **academic drift, professional uncertainty, and heightened feelings of isolation**. These effects are compounded for students who may already feel marginalized within their programs or institutions, whether due to race, gender, language background, disability, or geographic distance. The result is a stratified mentoring landscape in which some students receive robust, high-touch support, while others are left to navigate complex academic systems without adequate guidance (Barker, 2011; W. B. Johnson & Griffin, 2024).

Example:

- *A Black doctoral student enrolled in an online leadership program reports going* ***six months without any substantive meeting*** *with their advisor - no check-ins, no feedback, no direction.*
- *Meanwhile, another student in the same cohort, but with stronger personal access to a faculty member, receives* ***weekly coaching sessions*** *and tailored career advice. The discrepancy is not rooted in merit or effort, but in the absence of institutional mechanisms to ensure equitable access to mentorship.*
- *A* ***structured mentorship system,*** *with calendared check-ins, shared advising expectations, and centralized tracking, would help close these gaps - ensuring that* ***every student receives consistent support,*** *regardless of informal connections or unspoken hierarchies.*

Preventing inequity in mentorship requires institutions to **move from reactive to proactive systems**, embedding expectations for regular engagement, transparency, and feedback into doctoral program design. Doing so not only supports student retention and completion - it affirms that **inclusive excellence in graduate education depends not on happenstance, but on deliberate, systemic design**.

---

2. Distributing Mentorship Responsibilities to Prevent Burnout and Promote Equity

In many doctoral programs, a **small number of committed faculty absorb the bulk of mentoring duties**, often without formal recognition or compensation. This concentration of labor leads to **chronic burnout, diminished mentoring quality, and widespread inequities in service distribution** - particularly for women faculty, faculty of color, and those with reputations for being "student-centered" or "approachable" (Austin & McDaniels, 2006; W. B. Johnson & Griffin, 2024). Over time, this imbalance not only undermines faculty well-being but also limits the institution's capacity to provide consistent, high-quality mentorship to all students.

To address this issue, institutions must adopt systems that **intentionally distribute mentorship across departments, cohorts, and mentoring models**. Rather than treating mentorship as a personal favor or invisible labor, universities should **embed it into faculty workload models**, ensuring that mentoring is recognized as a core component of scholarly contribution - on par with teaching and research. This includes **formally crediting mentorship in promotion and tenure evaluations**, where it is too often categorized as peripheral or undervalued, despite its centrality to graduate education (Pfund et al., 2016; Zellers et al., 2008).

A further strategy is to **rotate mentorship roles annually**, especially within co-mentoring teams or cohort-based advising structures. This approach prevents overreliance on a few individuals, diversifies the mentoring voices available to students, and fosters a broader culture of collective responsibility. When mentorship is widely shared and institutionally supported, it becomes not just a burden to be managed but rather a **professional responsibility to be cultivated and celebrated**.

To establish faculty strategies, incorporate mentorship into **formal workload allocation** to make it visible and valued. Ensure it is **counted in promotion and tenure decisions** as a key form of faculty impact. And implement **rotational mentoring assignments** - whether by year, cohort, or role - to avoid burnout, increase inclusivity, and broaden student exposure to diverse mentoring styles. By institutionalizing these strategies, programs can **maximize faculty capacity for meaningful mentoring engagement**, while signaling a commitment to equity, sustainability, and excellence in doctoral education.

Core Elements of a Scalable Mentorship System

---

1. Programmatic Mentorship Models

While individualized mentoring relationships remain central to doctoral education, institutions must also develop **program-level structures that are scalable, equitable, and aligned with both institutional goals and student needs**. Effective mentorship systems are not accidental - they are **built on clear, replicable models** that ensure every student has access to consistent guidance, regardless of background, discipline, or personal network. These models must be flexible enough to adapt across contexts, yet structured enough to foster accountability, continuity, and a shared culture of mentoring excellence (Pfund et al., 2016; Zellers et al., 2008).

A. Cohort-Based Mentorship

Cohort-based mentorship structures group students into defined learning communities, often supported by **a mentoring team composed of faculty, advanced peers, or professional advisors**. This approach promotes **social learning, peer accountability, and a sense of shared journey**, reducing feelings of isolation - especially in online, part-time, or interdisciplinary programs. Mentors in these models often serve as facilitators of academic development and community-building, creating spaces for structured reflection, milestone planning, and cross-cohort knowledge transfer (Austin & McDaniels, 2006).

Example:

- *A doctoral program in nursing launches a **"Mentorship Circle"** in which each incoming cohort is assigned one **lead mentor** responsible for general academic oversight and multiple **content-specific advisors** who support research design, clinical alignment, and policy translation.*
- *Students receive support tailored to both their developmental stage and disciplinary focus while building trust and connection within a community of practice.*

B. Rotational Mentorship

Rotational mentorship allows students - typically in their first year - to **cycle through multiple faculty mentors**, exposing them to different advising styles, research perspectives, and disciplinary subcultures before selecting a long-term advisor. This model reduces pressure on students to prematurely commit to a mentoring relationship and ensures **greater fit between mentor and mentee**, especially in programs with diverse faculty strengths and research agendas.

Students who engage in rotational models report greater agency in choosing mentors, and faculty benefit from **shared advising responsibility** during early-stage doctoral onboarding. Structured rotation plans should include reflection tools to help students articulate what they value in a mentor and what type of support they need to succeed.

This model aligns with findings by Pfund et al. (2016), which emphasized that students are more likely to thrive when they have early exposure to **multiple mentorship modalities** before committing to a primary advisor.

C. Career-Aligned Tracks

As doctoral students pursue increasingly diverse career trajectories, mentorship must reflect that diversity. Career-aligned mentorship models group students into **advising tracks based on intended professional outcomes** - such as academic research, industry leadership, policy work, educational consulting, or entrepreneurship. Within each track, students are paired with mentors who can provide **domain-specific insights, relevant networking opportunities, and guidance on translating doctoral research into practice** (W. B. Johnson & Griffin, 2024).

This model supports alignment between dissertation or capstone work and long-term goals while reducing the misalignment that can occur when traditional academic mentorship is applied to non-academic pathways. It also helps students understand the distinct expectations, deliverables, and forms of scholarly communication associated with different sectors.

Example:

- *Consider a university's interdisciplinary doctoral program in public policy, which offers three mentorship tracks:* ***academic****,* ***applied policy****, and* ***nonprofit/advocacy****.*
- *Each track includes faculty and external mentors who co-develop individualized development plans with students, including publication goals, internship placements, and dissemination strategies tailored to their future career context.*

When implemented strategically, these **programmatic mentorship models** serve as the scaffolding for robust and inclusive doctoral education. They balance structure with flexibility, institutional vision with individual agency, and create **scalable pathways to high-quality, purpose-driven mentorship** for all students.

---

2. Mentorship Training for Faculty

High-quality mentorship does not emerge solely from disciplinary expertise or goodwill. It requires **intentional preparation, reflective practice, and sustained institutional investment**. As doctoral education becomes more diverse, interdisciplinary, and digitally mediated, faculty must be equipped not only to supervise research but also to navigate **complex mentoring relationships that span cultures, modalities, and power differentials**. Formal mentorship training plays a vital role in developing this capacity and ensuring consistency across programs and departments (Deneen & Boud, 2014; Pfund et al., 2016).

Effective mentorship training should extend beyond basic advising protocols to include competencies in **culturally responsive mentoring** - helping faculty recognize how race, gender, language, socioeconomic status, and historical marginalization shape the student experience. This is especially important for supporting students from underrepresented groups, who often report lower access to relational support and role models within doctoral programs (Barker, 2011; Sanczyk et al., 2021). In addition, training should address the use of **digital and hybrid engagement tools**, such as collaborative feedback platforms, video-based check-ins, and asynchronous advising spaces - critical in remote or part-time doctoral programs where mentoring often occurs across time zones and technologies (Holmes et al., 2022; W. B. Johnson & Griffin, 2024).

Faculty must also be prepared to **navigate differences in background, power, and institutional role** - whether mentoring international students, adult learners returning from industry, or first-generation scholars with limited exposure to academic norms. In the AI era, mentors must further learn how to **guide students through AI-integrated workflows**, including the use of generative tools in literature reviews, data analysis, and writing, while modeling ethical judgment and transparency (Kacena et al., 2024; Mienye & Swart, 2025). To meet these needs, institutions can offer **multi-modal training formats**:

- **Asynchronous modules** for accessibility and self-paced engagement.
- **Peer mentoring discussions** to promote shared reflection and institutional learning.
- **Case-based workshops** that use real scenarios to explore difficult mentoring moments, power dynamics, or cross-cultural misunderstandings.

When implemented consistently, mentorship training enables faculty to develop a **shared language and set of expectations** around mentoring quality, engagement, and equity. It also affirms that effective mentorship is a **discipline of its own - teachable, improvable, and essential to doctoral success**.

---

3. Digital Infrastructure to Support Mentoring

As graduate programs grow in size, complexity, and delivery modality, the need for **robust digital infrastructure to support mentorship** has become increasingly urgent. In many programs, mentoring relationships remain undocumented, decentralized, or dependent on informal communication patterns - leaving students vulnerable to inconsistent support and institutions unable to track or evaluate mentoring outcomes. Digital platforms offer a scalable solution by **systematizing mentoring interactions**, facilitating communication, and ensuring that no student falls through the cracks (Pfund et al., 2016; Zellers et al., 2008).

The most effective systems are **not one-size-fits-all**, but flexible tools that align with program culture and mentoring models. **Mentorship CRMs (Customer Relationship Management platforms)** such as *Chronus* or *Mentorloop* allow programs to track student–mentor pairings, log meeting notes, document progress toward academic milestones, and set reminders for follow-up actions. These systems provide visibility for program directors and reduce overreliance on memory or individual initiative to maintain mentoring continuity.

Learning Management Systems (LMS) such as *Canvas* or *Moodle* can also be adapted to serve mentorship purposes by hosting **mentorship contracts, check-in forms, resource libraries, and threaded discussions** between mentors and mentees. These platforms help students keep all related materials in one place and make the mentoring relationship more structured and transparent. LMS-integrated mentorship hubs also offer opportunities for peer-to-peer mentoring, reflective journaling, and documentation of co-mentoring input.

Increasingly, programs are experimenting with **AI-powered assistants** that can automate meeting scheduling, provide summaries of mentor feedback, or flag incomplete mentorship logs for administrative follow-up. These tools enhance administrative efficiency while also supporting equity - ensuring, for example, that **students in online or asynchronous programs receive the same level of tracking and outreach as those on campus** (Holmes et al., 2022; Reiss, 2021).

Example:

- *A doctoral program in educational leadership integrates a custom* ***mentorship dashboard*** *linked to the institution's student information system.*
- *The platform sends an automatic alert to the graduate program director if a student* ***has not logged a mentor meeting within 45 days****.*
- *This trigger prompts an outreach - first to the mentor, then to the student - to assess whether support is needed or re-engagement is required.*
- *This* ***proactive infrastructure ensures that no student is inadvertently neglected*** *due to workload, turnover, or miscommunication.*

By investing in digital infrastructure, institutions move beyond reactive advising models and toward a **mentorship culture rooted in accountability, equity, and transparency**. These systems not only support the mentoring relationship - they also provide the institutional backbone for data-informed decision-making, continuous improvement, and student success across diverse program contexts.

---

4. Standardized Mentorship Agreements and Feedback Loops

Sustainable, equitable mentorship cannot rely solely on goodwill or informal understanding. To ensure clarity, consistency, and accountability, doctoral programs must adopt **standardized mentorship agreements** - formal yet flexible documents that define the scope, structure, and expectations of the mentoring relationship. When paired with **regular feedback loops**, these agreements form the backbone of a mentoring culture that is **transparent, student-centered, and open to continuous improvement** (Deneen & Boud, 2014; Zellers et al., 2008). At their core, mentorship agreements provide an **explicit framework** for communication and collaboration. Key components should include:

- **Frequency and mode of meetings** (e.g., monthly Zoom calls, in-person check-ins, asynchronous exchanges).
- **Milestones and deliverables**, including target dates for proposal submission, data collection, drafts, or presentations.
- **Roles and responsibilities** in research, writing, and publication, such as expectations around co-authorship, feedback turnaround, and intellectual contribution.
- **AI use and authorship guidelines**, addressing how tools such as ChatGPT or citation generators may or may not be incorporated into scholarly workflows.

- A clearly defined **conflict resolution protocol**, outlining steps for mediation, escalation, or reconfiguration of the mentoring relationship if needed.

While a mentorship agreement formalizes expectations, it is not static. Regular **feedback loops** are essential to monitor satisfaction, identify emerging needs, and adjust mentoring practices over time (Brookfield, 2017; Pfund et al., 2016). Effective tools include:

- **Anonymous semester-end evaluations**, which allow students to reflect honestly on their mentoring experience.
- **Self-assessments** enabling students to articulate their progress, challenges, and evolving support needs.
- **Mentor development surveys**, where faculty reflect on their own mentoring strategies and receive feedback for growth.

Example:

- *A doctoral program in the social sciences introduces a biannual* ***"Mentoring Satisfaction Survey"****, completed anonymously by all graduate students.*
- *The results are aggregated by department and shared - confidentially and constructively - during faculty meetings.*
- *These data are used to inform* ***faculty development workshops****, highlight emerging concerns, and* ***celebrate exemplary mentoring practices*** *through annual recognition awards.*
- *Over time, this process normalizes mentorship as a shared, assessable responsibility rather than an invisible or private labor.*

By grounding mentorship in agreements and supported by structured feedback, institutions move toward a **culture of shared expectations, professional learning, and trust**. This model promotes not only individual student success but also a departmental climate where **mentorship is visible, valued, and improved in the community**.

Example: Implementing a Three-Tier Mentorship Program in a Dissertation or Capstone Program

The following example illustrates one possible way a university could design and implement a **three-tiered mentorship model** to support doctoral students. It is not based on any single existing institution, but rather draws on widely recognized best practices in doctoral education (Austin & McDaniels, 2006; Pfund et al., 2016) to demonstrate how such a system might operate in practice.

Purpose

In many doctoral programs, students balance academic work with professional and personal commitments, making sustained, equitable mentorship essential. A single mentor cannot fully address every academic, developmental, and career need. In this model, mentoring responsibilities are distributed across three coordinated roles, ensuring guidance in **research development**, **peer support**, and **career planning**.

Model Structure

Tier	Focus	Mentor Role	Suggested Frequency
Tier 1	Research Mentoring	Faculty Chair	Biweekly
Tier 2	Peer Mentoring	Advanced Doctoral Student	Monthly
Tier 3	Professional Mentoring	Career Advisor or Program Alum	Once per semester

Tier 1: Research Mentoring

A faculty chair serves as the primary academic guide, meeting biweekly with the student to provide direction on research design, literature engagement, and dissertation or capstone milestones. This relationship ensures continuity and intellectual rigor throughout the dissertation or capstone process, with the chair acting as the anchor for the student's scholarly growth.

Tier 2: Peer Mentoring

Each student is paired with an advanced doctoral candidate who has completed core program milestones. Monthly meetings with this peer mentor focus on navigating program requirements, problem-solving, and normalizing challenges. This role also provides emotional support, helping to reduce feelings of isolation and build a sense of community, particularly for part-time or online learners (Byars-Winston & Dahlberg, 2019; Sanczyk et al., 2021).

Tier 3: Professional Mentoring

A career advisor or program alum meets with the student once per semester to help align academic work with long-term professional goals. This guidance may include strategies for publishing or presenting work, networking in professional circles, and translating research findings into practitioner or policy contexts (W. B. Johnson & Griffin, 2024).

Implementation Notes

- **Coordination**. A program coordinator manages mentor assignments, tracks meeting schedules, and provides resources to all mentors.
- **Training**. Each mentor tier receives role-specific training to ensure clarity of expectations and effectiveness of support.
- **Documentation**. Meetings are logged through a shared platform to facilitate communication among mentors and track student progress.

- **Evaluation**. Annual surveys and feedback sessions inform ongoing refinement of the program.

Anticipated Outcomes

When applied consistently, this model can:

- Increase student engagement and sense of belonging.
- Reduce time-to-degree delays by providing consistent checkpoints.
- Strengthen academic identity and career readiness.
- Improve faculty efficiency by sharing mentoring responsibilities across multiple tiers.

This example demonstrates how a university could implement a scalable, coordinated mentorship system that addresses the **full arc of doctoral development**. By aligning multiple mentorship inputs, institutions can ensure that doctoral programs remain both academically rigorous and responsive to students' professional futures.

Section Reflection: Systematizing Mentorship for Equitable and Sustainable Doctoral Success

This section marks a pivotal evolution in how doctoral mentorship must be reimagined - not as a series of isolated faculty–student relationships, but as a robust, institutionalized system of support that ensures equity, consistency, and developmental responsiveness across programs. It skillfully argues that excellence in doctoral mentorship is no longer about individual charisma or discretionary goodwill, but about strategic design: scalable models, structured feedback, digital infrastructure, and collective accountability.

By positioning mentorship as a **systemic responsibility**, the section makes a compelling case for transitioning from luck-based access to intentional equity. Through examples of rotational mentorship, cohort-based structures, and career-aligned advising tracks, it illustrates how programs can provide high-touch, high-quality mentorship to **all** students - especially those from underrepresented backgrounds, nontraditional pathways, or remote learning contexts. These models offer both the personalization students need, and the scalability institutions require.

Crucially, the section does not ignore faculty realities. It directly confronts the issue of burnout and labor imbalance, highlighting that meaningful mentorship must be distributed, recognized, and formally embedded in promotion and tenure processes. By normalizing training, incentivizing engagement, and offering flexible delivery methods, the section promotes faculty growth alongside student support. It affirms that mentorship is not just a student need - it is a professional competency that institutions must develop in their faculty.

The integration of digital tools and feedback systems is particularly noteworthy. From CRM-style mentorship dashboards to standardized mentoring agreements and AI-assisted scheduling, the section shows how digital innovation can improve communication, close accountability gaps, and track progress without adding bureaucratic burden. These insights are vital as programs expand hybrid and online offerings.

The institutional case study at the end serves as a concrete model, reinforcing the argument that structured, multi-tiered mentorship - faculty, peer, and professional - can not only scale but enhance quality, reduce attrition, and increase student agency. It demonstrates how thoughtful system design leads to higher engagement, faster degree completion, and more confident scholarly identity formation.

Ultimately, this section transforms mentorship from a vulnerable point in doctoral education to a resilient, strategic strength. It offers not just a critique of status quo inequities, but a blueprint for transformation - one that aligns mentorship with the future of interdisciplinary, inclusive, and impact-driven scholarship.

Section 5: Integrating AI into the Mentorship Relationship

As generative artificial intelligence becomes increasingly embedded in research, writing, and learning, doctoral mentorship must evolve to include **intentional, ethical, and pedagogically sound uses of AI within the mentoring relationship**. Rather than viewing AI as a threat to human-centered guidance, this section introduces **practical strategies for leveraging AI as a tool to enhance - not replace - academic mentorship**. Approaches such as **co-prompting, shared exploration, guided reflection, and collaborative feedback planning** offer mentors and students new ways to engage with content, process complexity, and co-construct knowledge, while remaining grounded in **scholarly integrity and human judgment** (Kacena et al., 2024; Mienye & Swart, 2025).

Co-prompting involves the mentor and student collaboratively developing prompts for AI tools - whether to explore theoretical contrasts, generate literature summaries, or prototype outlines - thereby turning AI into a **thinking partner rather than a surrogate**. This shared design process helps students learn how to ask better academic questions and critically evaluate machine-generated responses, while mentors retain visibility into the student's reasoning and voice. Similarly, **shared exploration** can include reviewing AI-generated content together in real-time, modeling scholarly critique, and distinguishing between helpful suggestions and flawed or biased output (Floridi & Chiriatti, 2020; Reiss, 2021).

Guided reflection using AI can be structured through journaling tools or transcript summaries that help students analyze feedback across drafts, track their intellectual development, or identify recurring gaps in reasoning. In these instances, AI augments metacognition, but mentors remain essential in helping students **interpret patterns and maintain epistemic self-awareness**. Additionally, **AI-assisted feedback planning** - such as organizing reviewer comments, summarizing meeting notes, or mapping revision priorities - can streamline the logistics of mentorship while reinforcing student ownership of the research process.

Throughout these applications, it is critical to preserve the **student's scholarly voice, uphold academic authorship standards, and foreground human judgment**. Mentors must help students distinguish between process support and content outsourcing, ensuring that AI use does not displace critical engagement or ethical responsibility (Boud et al., 2023; Slimi &

Carballido, 2023). When guided effectively, AI becomes a **scaffold for inquiry and communication**, not a substitute for intellectual labor or mentorship relationships.

This section offers strategies that position AI not as a shortcut, but as a catalyst for **deeper, more reflective, and more inclusive mentorship practices**, reinforcing the centrality of human mentorship even in an era of machine-generated assistance.

Why Integrate AI into Mentorship?

---

1. Transparency Builds Trust and Reduces Ethical Risk

In an era where generative AI tools are readily available and increasingly powerful, **avoiding conversations about AI in doctoral mentorship can have unintended - and often harmful - consequences**. When faculty do not explicitly acknowledge or guide AI use, students are left to **experiment privately**, often without clear ethical boundaries or institutional guidance. This silence may inadvertently foster **covert or inconsistent AI use**, increasing the risk of **accidental plagiarism, inappropriate overreliance, or misrepresentation of authorship** (Reiss, 2021; Slimi & Carballido, 2023).

Students, particularly those early in their doctoral journey or from educational systems with different norms, may not know whether using AI to generate text, summarize sources, or rephrase ideas is considered legitimate assistance or academic dishonesty. In the absence of open mentorship, they may either **hide their use of AI entirely** or fail to engage critically with its outputs - relying on machine-generated language without the necessary analysis, synthesis, or attribution (Mienye & Swart, 2025; Weber-Wulff et al., 2023). Both scenarios undermine not only the student's learning, but the integrity of the dissertation or capstone process itself.

By contrast, **proactive engagement around AI fosters a culture of transparency, reflection, and scholarly accountability**. When mentors initiate these conversations with openness and curiosity, they signal that AI is a tool to be evaluated - not a shortcut to be shamed or a danger to be ignored. Framing the dialogue around inquiry rather than enforcement empowers students to **ask thoughtful questions about process, ethics, and authorship**, strengthening their academic agency and decision-making.

Example:

- *A mentor begins a dissertation or capstone advising session with the question, "Have you experimented with any AI tools for this section? Let us review what it gave you and see where we need to deepen the analysis."*
- *This simple prompt opens a nonjudgmental space for disclosure and discussion. The student gains insight into what aspects of their work need human refinement - such as theoretical coherence or voice consistency - while the mentor can coach them in* ***transforming AI output into genuine scholarly work****.*

Such moments are critical for **building trust, promoting intellectual honesty, and teaching responsible engagement with emerging technologies**. Faculty who normalize these conversations help demystify AI use and prevent the kind of ambiguity that often leads to reactive enforcement or accusations of misconduct (Bailey et al., 2023; Fishman, 2009). In summary, the choice is not whether AI will be used in graduate work - it already is. The real question is whether **mentorship will step forward to shape how it is used**, anchoring that use in integrity, critical inquiry, and shared responsibility.

---

2. Modeling Humility and Co-Learning in AI-Enhanced Mentorship

In many cases, today's doctoral students arrive with greater fluency in emerging technologies - especially generative AI - than their faculty mentors. Rather than perceiving this as a challenge to authority or expertise, such moments should be seen as **valuable opportunities to model intellectual humility, reciprocal learning, and collaborative inquiry**. Faculty who embrace co-learning signal that scholarship is not about omniscience, but about **curiosity, adaptability, and mutual growth** - especially in a rapidly evolving technological landscape (Brodin & Avery, 2020; Brookfield, 2017).

This dynamic also helps disrupt hierarchical mentoring structures that may unintentionally suppress innovation or silence student initiative. When faculty position themselves as **co-investigators rather than gatekeepers**, they create space for students to contribute meaningfully to the academic conversation - not only through content, but also through method and tool selection. This is particularly important in interdisciplinary research or practice-based doctoral programs, where students often bridge scholarly inquiry with evolving professional practices and digital platforms (Ball, 2004; Holmes et al., 2022).

Example:

- *In one mentorship interaction, a doctoral student presents how they used **Perplexity.ai** to generate a preliminary synthesis of emerging literature on algorithmic bias. Rather than dismissing the tool, the mentor expresses curiosity and asks the student to walk through their process.*
- *Together, they explore the **limitations of AI-generated summaries**, including surface-level conceptual mapping, unreliable citation practices, and the risk of reinforcing dominant narratives.*
- *The mentor then provides **disciplinary context and theoretical depth**, helping the student situate the AI-assisted summary within the broader epistemological debates in the field.*

This co-learning exchange not only strengthens the student's research - it also enhances the mentor's own understanding of the tools students are using and encourages **critical engagement rather than passive consumption of AI output** (Floridi & Chiriatti, 2020; Weber-Wulff et al., 2023). Over time, such interactions foster a **mentorship culture defined by curiosity, shared exploration, and trust**, where both parties contribute to a deeper understanding of what it means to do ethical, rigorous, and forward-looking scholarship. In embracing co-learning, faculty reaffirm that the heart of mentorship is not knowing everything - but **knowing how to learn together**, especially in an era where the boundaries between human and machine intelligence are being constantly redefined.

Sample Mentorship Use Cases with AI

---

1. Using AI to Scaffold Early Idea Generation and Scholarly Refinement

Generative AI can be a powerful tool for helping students **overcome the blank page**, brainstorm new angles, or identify emerging themes. However, without critical guidance, students may mistake surface-level suggestions for academically sound starting points. Mentors play a crucial role in ensuring that AI-assisted ideation becomes a **launchpad for deeper inquiry**, not a shortcut to diluted thinking. The key is to integrate AI use into the mentoring conversation - **treating it as a collaborative artifact to be examined, questioned, and improved** (Floridi & Chiriatti, 2020; Reiss, 2021).

In this approach, students use AI to generate **preliminary inputs** - such as research questions, topic clusters, or conceptual comparisons - which are then brought into the mentoring space for **joint critique and refinement**. This method not only accelerates early-stage thinking but also promotes **intellectual ownership**, as students learn to move from machine-generated suggestions to human-driven insight. It fosters a metacognitive process in which students **learn how to evaluate, challenge, and strengthen their own thinking** in alignment with disciplinary standards (Brookfield, 2017; Carless & Boud, 2018).

Mentorship Strategy. Ask the student to prompt an AI tool with an open-ended query - for example: *"Generate research questions about AI use in public health policy."* The student then brings the generated list to a scheduled mentoring meeting. During the session, mentor and student collaboratively:

- **Identify questions that are overly broad, methodologically vague, or ethically problematic**, such as those that assume technological neutrality or ignore policy complexity.
- **Rewrite selected questions** for clarity, precision, and originality - ensuring that the research inquiry aligns with the student's epistemological stance and program expectations.
- **Analyze embedded assumptions** in the AI's phrasing, surfacing implicit biases, gaps in framing, or oversimplified dichotomies. This critical analysis sharpens the student's conceptual lens and helps them internalize the values of their academic discipline (Benjamin, 2023; Slimi & Carballido, 2023).

This practice not only strengthens idea generation - it also models how to **engage productively with imperfect tools**, reinforcing the importance of human judgment, disciplinary rigor, and ethical reflexivity in scholarly development. Rather than treating AI as either forbidden or flawless, mentors guide students in using it **strategically and reflectively**, helping them distinguish between convenience and insight. By framing AI use as part of an iterative, collaborative thinking process, faculty cultivate in students the capacity to **move from machine output to meaningful academic contribution** - a skill that will remain essential across future scholarly and professional contexts.

---

2. Using AI to Scaffold Structure and Thematic Organization

Generative AI tools can serve as powerful scaffolds in the **early stages of academic writing**, especially for students struggling to impose structure on complex or expansive ideas. When used intentionally, these tools can generate **sample outlines, thematic groupings, or domain-based hierarchies** that offer students a visual or conceptual entry point into the task of organizing their literature review, argumentation, or analysis. Crucially, the purpose is not to adopt these outputs uncritically, but to **treat them as provisional artifacts** - starting points for scholarly dialogue, critique, and refinement within the mentoring relationship (Floridi & Chiriatti, 2020; Reiss, 2021).

This practice supports students in developing **organizational awareness and theoretical alignment**, helping them move from surface-level categorization to a more purposeful academic structure. For students unfamiliar with disciplinary conventions - or working in interdisciplinary spaces where organizational models are less prescriptive - AI-generated outlines can illuminate gaps or tensions that may otherwise remain implicit. With the mentor's guidance, these outlines become tools for **critical engagement rather than passive templates** (Boud et al., 2023; Brookfield, 2017).

Co-Prompting Example:

- *A mentor and student co-create the following prompt:*
    - o *"Create a literature review outline on equity in digital learning environments. Include sections on access, teacher preparedness, and student outcomes."*
- *The AI returns a structured outline with three main sections, each populated with bullet-pointed subthemes.*

Together, Mentor and Mentee:

- ***Evaluate the outline for conceptual gaps*** *- e.g., "Where are the foundational equity frameworks such as culturally responsive pedagogy, digital justice, or universal design for learning?"*
- ***Reorganize the content*** *to prioritize theoretical and contextual coherence, such as foregrounding structural barriers before diving into educator practice or student impact.*
- ***Develop nuanced transitions and connective logic****, moving the student from a list of topics to a structured academic narrative that flows with intention and clarity* (Nicol & Macfarlane-Dick, 2006; Repko & Szostak, 2020).

In this process, AI is positioned as a **generative assistant**, not a decision-maker. Its output provides scaffolding, but the intellectual labor of synthesis, critique, and prioritization remains the student's responsibility, supported by the mentor's disciplinary insight. The co-prompting process itself becomes a teaching moment, reinforcing **the epistemological values of the field**, the importance of framing, and the art of scholarly argumentation. Ultimately, by guiding students through the act of transforming machine-generated scaffolds into coherent academic architecture, mentors help cultivate essential habits of **critical discernment, conceptual rigor, and structural fluency** - skills that remain foundational across research genres and academic contexts.

3. Mentoring Students Who Use AI for Conceptual Clarification

As generative AI tools become increasingly accessible, many students are turning to them as a **first-pass explainer for dense theoretical or methodological concepts**. Tools such as ChatGPT or Claude can provide accessible summaries of unfamiliar ideas, breaking down jargon-heavy texts into more digestible language. While this can reduce cognitive overload and offer an entry point into complex material, these explanations are often **overly simplified, decontextualized, or framed through generalized assumptions** that miss key disciplinary nuances (Floridi & Chiriatti, 2020; Mienye & Swart, 2025).

For novice scholars or students entering new theoretical terrain, the danger lies in mistaking AI-generated summaries for authoritative interpretations. These outputs may omit epistemological underpinnings, elide field-specific controversies, or fail to engage with the historical evolution of a concept. Over time, reliance on such simplified explanations can **impede deeper conceptual mastery** and lead to vague or superficial scholarship if not accompanied by critical interrogation and mentorship support (Brookfield, 2017; Holmes et al., 2022).

Mentorship Response Example:

- *Mentors can respond constructively by* ***acknowledging the utility of AI as a learning scaffold****, while also coaching students to recognize its limitations.*
- *Encourage students to* ***use AI as a starting point*** *- to break down dense ideas or generate working definitions - but to bring those outputs to mentoring sessions for discussion, refinement, and contextualization.*

In the Mentoring Session, the Faculty Member Might:

- ***Ask the student to restate the AI's explanation in their own words****, assessing comprehension and identifying gaps.*
- ***Test the student's understanding*** *through follow-up questions that require application or critique - e.g., "How would this concept apply to your research context?" or "What might this explanation leave out from a critical theory perspective?"*
- ***Introduce field-specific debates or contrasting interpretations****, offering published sources or canonical thinkers that provide depth and scholarly lineage.*
- ***Highlight misinterpretations or conceptual conflations*** *in the AI output, helping the student learn to distinguish between simplification and distortion* (Nicol & Macfarlane-Dick, 2006; Repko & Szostak, 2020).

This process not only supports conceptual mastery - it also fosters metacognitive habits and academic humility. Students begin to see that knowledge is not merely a product to be retrieved, but a **conversation to be entered**, critiqued, and built upon. The role of the mentor in this context is to **bridge the gap between algorithmic efficiency and disciplinary depth**, ensuring that the use of AI does not undermine the slow, rigorous process of scholarly formation. By scaffolding student learning in this way, faculty help students transition from passive consumers of information to **critical participants in their field's intellectual debates** - a shift that lies at the heart of doctoral education.

4. Using AI to Support Feedback Processing and Revision Planning

One of the most cognitively demanding aspects of the doctoral journey is learning how to **process, prioritize, and integrate feedback** - especially when it comes from multiple mentors, committee members, or peer reviewers. Students often encounter diverse or even conflicting suggestions, and without guidance, they may struggle to translate commentary into a coherent revision plan. In such moments, generative AI tools can offer a productive assistive function by **organizing feedback thematically**, thereby reducing overwhelm and enabling more focused academic conversations (Brookfield, 2017; Nicol & Macfarlane-Dick, 2006).

When used with intention and transparency, AI can help students **summarize, sort, and analyze written feedback** across categories such as structure, clarity, argumentation, methods, or source use. These tools do not replace the student's interpretive responsibility, but they can streamline the often-scattered process of managing multiple sets of margin comments, tracked changes, or conflicting email responses. The goal is not to automate revision, but to scaffold student thinking - helping them **see patterns, anticipate mentor priorities, and identify areas requiring further discussion or clarification** (Ball, 2004; Carless & Boud, 2018).

Example:

- *A doctoral student receives extensive feedback on a dissertation or capstone chapter from two mentors.*
- *To make sense of the input, the student* ***copies the comments into ChatGPT*** *and asks it to produce a* ***bullet-point summary sorted by thematic focus*** *- for instance: structural coherence, clarity of theoretical framing, integration of primary sources, and tone.*
- *The resulting list highlights both overlapping concerns and unique feedback points from each reviewer.*
- *The student brings this summary to their next mentoring session, where they and the faculty mentor* ***collaboratively develop a revision plan****, deciding which issues to address first, where deeper discussion is needed, and how to reconcile divergent perspectives.*

This strategy models **intentional AI use as part of the revision process**, reinforcing that while AI can help with logistical organization, the higher-order decisions - how to interpret feedback, what to revise, and how to maintain authorial voice - remain with the student. Mentors play a critical role in guiding this transition from sorting to synthesis, helping students weigh trade-offs, recognize implicit feedback, and formulate **a coherent path forward that reflects scholarly maturity and project alignment** (Pfund et al., 2016; Repko & Szostak, 2020).

Incorporating AI into the feedback process in this way encourages **agency, organization, and strategic thinking**, while also demystifying the often-unspoken labor of scholarly revision. It reminds students that engaging with critique is not a solitary task, but a **dialogical, iterative process** - one that is strengthened when supported by both human mentors and thoughtfully used digital tools.

Best Practices for Ethical and Reflective AI Use in Mentorship

1. Clarifying Boundaries for AI Use in Academic Writing and Authorship

As generative AI becomes an increasingly common component of student research workflows, faculty mentors must take proactive steps to **establish clear boundaries between acceptable exploration and areas where human authorship must remain exclusive**. Without these boundaries, students may unintentionally compromise academic integrity by relying on AI tools in ways that obscure authorship, misrepresent originality, or violate ethical standards. Establishing "green zones" for exploratory support and "red zones" for protected authorship helps students navigate this evolving terrain with confidence, accountability, and clarity (Mienye & Swart, 2025; Slimi & Carballido, 2023).

Green zones may include using AI to generate **initial outlines, suggest counterarguments, brainstorm keywords, or summarize secondary literature** - activities that help scaffold early thinking or organize information. However, these uses must be **accompanied by critical reflection, source verification, and faculty oversight** to ensure alignment with scholarly standards and research goals.

Conversely, faculty must articulate **"red zones" where AI use is categorically inappropriate**, either due to ethical risks, evaluative expectations, or the need for authentic human expression and interpretation. These include:

- **Writing positionality statements or reflective sections**, where authenticity, voice, and introspection are central to the purpose of the text. These sections require the student to articulate their values, experiences, and research worldview - elements that cannot be ethically or meaningfully generated by a machine.
- **Interpreting original data or coding qualitative results**, particularly in grounded theory, ethnographic, or phenomenological work. AI may be able to summarize patterns, but it lacks the lived contextual understanding required to engage in the sense-making processes that qualitative research demands (Boud et al., 2023; Candy & Edmonds, 2018).
- **Composing final dissertation or capstone abstracts, published journal articles, or grant proposals without proper disclosure.** These outputs carry institutional and scholarly weight, and undisclosed AI authorship compromises transparency, authorship ethics, and the peer-review process (Slimi & Carballido, 2023; Weber-Wulff et al., 2023).

Faculty should explicitly discuss these boundaries in early mentoring conversations and include them in mentorship agreements or program-wide guidelines. Doing so not only protects academic integrity but also **builds student awareness of the ethical, rhetorical, and epistemological dimensions of authorship** in the AI era (Fishman, 2009; Reiss, 2021).

By defining and reinforcing these boundaries, mentors help students learn that AI is not a substitute for scholarly labor - but a tool that must be used **within a clear framework of responsibility, transparency, and intellectual ownership**. This distinction is essential to preserving the trustworthiness and human depth of academic work.

2. Encouraging Transparent Documentation of AI Use

As AI tools become more integrated into the scholarly workflow, students must be equipped not only to use them ethically but also to **track and reflect on their use with intentionality**. Documenting AI engagement is not merely a compliance measure - it is a pedagogical opportunity. When students are encouraged to record how and why they used generative tools, they develop **critical awareness, ethical sensitivity, and intellectual ownership** of their work. This process fosters **metacognition** - the ability to think about one's own thinking - and reinforces academic integrity through transparent authorship practices (Brookfield, 2017; Nicol & Macfarlane-Dick, 2006).

Faculty can guide this practice by asking students to **maintain a log or reflection journal** that captures key elements of their interaction with AI tools. Entries may include:

- **What Prompt was Used?** Documenting the exact phrasing helps students understand how prompt design shapes the output and reflects their intent. It also reinforces the student's role as the initiator of the inquiry, not just a passive recipient.
- **What Output did AI Provide?** Describing the output allows for a clear comparison between what was generated and what was ultimately used. It also supports later discussions about accuracy, depth, and relevance.
- **What was Kept, Changed, or Discarded?** By analyzing which parts of the output were incorporated or rejected, students begin to engage in **critical evaluation**, applying disciplinary standards and personal judgment to the material.
- **Why was That Decision Made?** This step moves beyond technical reporting into reflective justification, encouraging students to articulate how their choices align with theoretical frameworks, methodological rigor, or authorial voice.

This form of documentation does more than create a paper trail - it teaches students how to **trace their scholarly decision-making**, something essential in an academic climate that increasingly values transparency and reproducibility. It also provides mentors with a window into the student's thinking process, allowing for more targeted feedback, deeper conversations about epistemology, and early detection of potential ethical missteps (Boud & Falchikov, 2006; Floridi & Chiriatti, 2020).

Furthermore, in disciplines or institutions where AI use must be disclosed in formal submissions (e.g., dissertation or capstone acknowledgments, or journal articles), this documentation provides a reliable source for crafting transparent and precise statements of tool engagement. It supports a culture where AI use is not hidden or stigmatized, but **critically examined and academically situated**. By embedding this reflective practice into the mentoring relationship, faculty empower students to become **responsible, self-aware scholars** - not only capable of using advanced tools, but also of understanding and justifying how those tools shape their thinking, writing, and research.

---

3. Modeling Transparency: Mentor Disclosure of AI Use

As students experiment with generative AI across their academic work, faculty play a critical role in **modeling what ethical, thoughtful, and bounded AI use looks like**. This includes not only setting expectations for student engagement, but also being transparent about their own use of AI in mentorship contexts. When mentors **disclose their use of AI tools - whether for administrative efficiency, cognitive scaffolding, or content brainstorming - they demystify the technology, reduce stigma, and signal that reflective use is both acceptable and accountable** (Floridi & Chiriatti, 2020; Reiss, 2021).

Importantly, this kind of modeling does not portray AI as an intellectual authority or a shortcut for scholarly work. Instead, it shows students how to use AI **in support of - not as a substitute for - human judgment, disciplinary expertise, and relational engagement**. Transparency also helps reinforce the distinction between mechanical assistance and scholarly authorship, a line that can otherwise become blurred in the absence of clear faculty leadership (Boud et al., 2023; Slimi & Carballido, 2023). Mentors might disclose their AI use in the following contexts:

- **Drafting syllabus content** or brainstorming discussion prompts, where AI offers administrative support or generative ideas to be revised and tailored.
- **Summarizing or organizing feedback** across multiple drafts or student cohorts to improve clarity and consistency in advising.
- **Synthesizing meeting notes or action items** after complex discussions allows mentors to focus on the strategic direction of mentorship rather than documentation alone.

Example Disclosure:

- *"I used ChatGPT to summarize our last meeting notes and clarify action items - but all review of your text was mine, line by line."*

This kind of statement offers **clarity, reassurance, and boundary-setting**. It helps students understand where AI fits in the mentor's workflow and where human expertise takes over. Such disclosures can also prompt productive conversations about **the appropriate use of AI in academic settings**, creating space for shared norms to evolve across the mentoring relationship (Brookfield, 2017; Holmes et al., 2022).

By openly sharing their own AI practices, mentors build a foundation of **trust, integrity, and co-learning**, showing that AI is not a secret advantage or a source of academic anxiety, but a tool to be wielded with care and clarity. This approach normalizes exploration while emphasizing the continued centrality of human insight in scholarly development.

Example: AI-Integrated Mentorship Workflow

To illustrate how generative AI can be thoughtfully woven into the doctoral mentoring process, the following example outlines a **four-week AI-integrated mentorship workflow**. In this model, AI is not positioned as a replacement for human mentorship but as a **supplementary tool** - used strategically to support cognitive scaffolding, organization, and iteration. The mentor remains central throughout, guiding the student in making decisions, deepening critical thinking, and reinforcing academic integrity.

This approach exemplifies **co-use and co-interpretation**, in which students learn not only how to use AI but also how to **evaluate its outputs, interrogate its assumptions, and align its suggestions with disciplinary norms** (Brookfield, 2017; Reiss, 2021). Each week's activity involves a discrete phase of the writing process, paired with both student action and intentional mentor engagement.

Stage	AI Tool Use	Mentor Role
Week 1: Brainstorming	Student uses AI (e.g., ChatGPT, Perplexity) to generate a list of potential research questions related to their topic.	Mentor reviews the questions, assesses **scope, clarity, and originality**, and helps the student refine or prioritize lines of inquiry based on theoretical framing and research feasibility.
Week 2: Literature Outline	AI generates a **preliminary thematic structure** for the literature review, clustering sources or concepts by keyword or domain.	Mentor evaluates the logic of the organization, adds **key missing perspectives or citations**, and helps realign the outline with the student's conceptual framework (Floridi & Chiriatti, 2020).
Week 3: First Draft Review	Student pastes mentor feedback into AI to generate a **summary of revisions by theme** (e.g., structure, clarity, evidence).	Mentor co-develops a **revision plan** with the student, ensuring alignment with academic standards and voice while emphasizing reflective processing of feedback (Nicol & Macfarlane-Dick, 2006).
Week 4: Reflection	Student maintains a log of **AI prompts used, what outputs were kept or discarded, and why.**	Mentor reviews the log and offers **meta-level guidance** on judgment, authorship, and future AI use - encouraging ethical reflection and strategic thinking (Slimi & Carballido, 2023).

This workflow highlights the importance of **sequencing AI use**, ensuring that each phase builds student agency rather than diminishing it. By embedding AI into the process rather than outsourcing core intellectual work, students develop the capacity to **discern when, how, and why to use these tools**, reinforcing their role as scholars - not just tool users.

At the same time, the mentor's role remains irreplaceable: offering **disciplinary depth, ethical grounding, and relational support** that AI cannot replicate. The ultimate goal is to cultivate a **hybrid workflow** that is not only efficient but deeply reflective, preparing students to navigate a research ecosystem where human-machine collaboration will be the norm.

Section Reflection: Humanizing Mentorship in the Age of AI-Augmented Inquiry

This section offers a compelling, future-facing vision for doctoral mentorship - one that neither resists nor romanticizes generative AI, but rather integrates it ethically, transparently, and pedagogically into the mentor–mentee relationship. Far from displacing the human core of mentorship, the strategies outlined here elevate it, positioning faculty as ethical co-navigators who scaffold students' intellectual development amid an increasingly AI-mediated research environment.

By introducing approaches such as co-prompting, shared AI critique, guided reflection, and feedback planning, the section demonstrates that AI can act not as a shortcut to academic production but as a cognitive scaffold that invites deeper inquiry. The mentor's role is reaffirmed - not as an information gatekeeper, but as a reflective partner who helps students interrogate, contextualize, and refine the outputs of generative tools. The ethical emphasis on preserving voice, authorship, and critical discernment ensures that the tools serve the scholar, not the other way around.

Moreover, this section reframes mentorship as a **co-learning relationship**, where students often bring technological fluency and mentors contribute disciplinary depth and ethical perspective. In doing so, it models intellectual humility and dialogic pedagogy. The AI-integrated workflow example at the end offers a powerful synthesis: mentorship that is structured, iterative, and ethically anchored in human reasoning, not automation.

Ultimately, this section expands on what it means to mentor in the 21st century. It equips faculty to embrace AI not as a threat to scholarly rigor, but as a pedagogical opportunity to cultivate discernment, ownership, and academic integrity in the scholars of tomorrow. In doing so, it preserves the heart of mentorship - relationship, growth, and trust - while adapting it to the complex demands of AI-augmented doctoral education.

Section 6: Accountability Structures - Monitoring Progress Without Micromanaging

While effective mentorship must be flexible and responsive, it also requires **structured accountability mechanisms** to support sustained progress, reduce drift, and create shared visibility into the student's development. Without clear checkpoints or expectations, even well-intentioned mentoring relationships can become uneven, reactive, or inadvertently neglectful - especially when layered atop demanding faculty workloads or complex student schedules. At the same time, accountability must be **collaboratively constructed**, not imposed in ways that strip students of their autonomy or diminish their ownership of the scholarly process (Brookfield, 2017; Nicol & Macfarlane-Dick, 2006).

This section outlines **practical strategies for building accountability structures** that are clear, supportive, and growth-oriented. These strategies are designed to **align with students' evolving needs**, providing structure without rigidity and guidance without surveillance. They promote a culture in which students are encouraged to **self-direct their progress while remaining embedded in a relational web of support and visibility** (Carless & Boud, 2018; Zellers et al., 2008). Examples of such strategies include:

- **Collaboratively developed milestone maps**, where students and mentors co-create timelines for key dissertation or capstone phases, regularly revisiting and adjusting them to reflect new developments, delays, or discoveries.
- **Monthly reflection memos or check-in forms**, where students document recent work, identify challenges, and outline next steps. These tools help shift accountability from reactive status updates to proactive metacognition and planning.
- **Shared digital dashboards or tracking tools**, such as those embedded in LMS platforms or mentorship CRMs, which provide both student and mentor with a clear, visual summary of meeting dates, feedback cycles, and deliverables (Holmes et al., 2022).
- **Scheduled feedback loops**, including structured meetings at critical junctures - proposal submission, literature review completion, data analysis launch - that function as accountability touchpoints and opportunities for recalibration.

These strategies foster **a transparent and collaborative mentoring environment** in which both student and mentor share responsibility for momentum and clarity. Importantly, accountability here is framed not as punitive oversight but as **a developmental tool that scaffolds independence**. Students are not held to arbitrary timelines; rather, they are supported in learning how to set realistic goals, reflect on progress, adapt to complexity, and communicate their evolving needs (Austin & McDaniels, 2006; Boud & Falchikov, 2006). When implemented with care, these accountability structures strengthen the mentoring relationship, reduce misunderstandings, and equip students with **lifelong skills in project management, self-regulation, and scholarly resilience** - essential attributes for academic and professional success.

The Multiple Functions of Accountability Structures in Doctoral Mentorship

---

Effective accountability structures in doctoral mentorship serve more than administrative or scheduling purposes - they are **multi-functional tools that support academic progress, emotional resilience, and scholarly identity development**. When thoughtfully designed and implemented, these structures offer far-reaching benefits for both students and mentors by creating rhythm, transparency, and opportunities for timely intervention. Crucially, they help align expectations and support systems, reducing the likelihood of isolation, miscommunication, or burnout - common contributors to doctoral attrition (Golde, 2005; Walker et al., 2009).

One core function is to **track progress toward clearly defined academic and developmental goals**. Whether outlined in a mentorship agreement, milestone map, or shared dashboard, goal-tracking structures offer visibility into the student's trajectory. They help identify not only whether progress is being made, but also when timelines need to be adjusted due to unforeseen challenges or evolving research directions.

Equally important is the capacity of accountability tools to **trigger structured reflection on process and decision-making**. Through mechanisms such as progress memos, milestone check-ins, or guided discussion prompts, students are encouraged to pause, evaluate their own work habits and scholarly reasoning, and articulate next steps. This promotes **metacognition and intellectual autonomy**, helping students become more self-aware and proactive in navigating complexity (Brookfield, 2017; Nicol & Macfarlane-Dick, 2006).

Accountability structures also play a **preventative function**, reducing the risk of last-minute crises around dissertation or capstone deliverables, submission deadlines, or committee meetings. By setting up interim goals and feedback checkpoints, mentors and students can **catch misunderstandings, underdeveloped ideas, or workload bottlenecks** early - before they escalate into high-stakes emergencies.

Perhaps most significantly, these systems can **surface hidden struggles that may otherwise go unspoken**, such as imposter syndrome, procrastination, burnout, or unreflective overuse of AI tools. When students are asked to report not only on outputs but also on process and well-being, they may feel more comfortable disclosing confusion, overwhelm, or gaps in confidence. This opens the door for mentors to respond with empathy, coaching, or referrals to additional support - whether that involves refining scholarly focus, managing expectations, or addressing emotional barriers to progress (Barker, 2011; Sanczyk et al., 2021).

Finally, accountability systems help **clarify expectations and reduce ambiguity**, which research has shown is essential to reducing anxiety and increasing retention among doctoral students. Many students - particularly first-generation, international, or part-time learners - report struggling not with the difficulty of the work, but with the **opacity of academic norms and unspoken performance standards**.

Transparent structures provide guidance not only on what must be done, but on how to approach it, when to ask for help, and what excellence looks like in practice (Golde, 2005; Walker et al., 2009). By serving these layered functions, accountability structures become more than bureaucratic tools - they function as **developmental scaffolds**, supporting student growth, scholarly resilience, and a more humane and responsive culture of doctoral education.

Key Strategies for Constructive Accountability

---

1. Co-Designing a Visual Roadmap for the Dissertation or Capstone Journey

Doctoral work unfolds over an extended, often nonlinear timeline that can easily overwhelm students with its scope, ambiguity, and competing demands. One way to anchor this complexity is through the **co-design of a visual roadmap** - a collaboratively developed, phase-based representation of the dissertation, capstone, or research journey. When mentors and students work together to map out key stages, deliverables, and reflection points, they create a **shared framework for tracking progress, adjusting expectations, and maintaining momentum**. This practice transforms a daunting process into a series of tangible, manageable steps, while reinforcing the student's agency in shaping their path (Gardner, 2008; Nicol & Macfarlane-Dick, 2006). The roadmap can be customized based on the program structure, the student's pace, and project design. It typically includes:

- **Monthly or quarterly milestones**, such as proposal drafts, ethics approvals, data collection launches, and chapter submissions.

- **Explicit checkpoints** for major research phases: formulating research questions, literature synthesis, methodological design, data analysis, writing and revision cycles, and final submission.
- **Intentional buffer zones** for rest, setbacks, and reflection - recognizing that the doctoral process is as much about sustainability and adaptation as it is about productivity (Austin & McDaniels, 2006; Brookfield, 2017).

This roadmap serves multiple purposes. It enhances **transparency and predictability**, especially for students unfamiliar with academic rhythms or unwritten expectations. It creates a **non-punitive structure** for accountability, enabling both mentor and student to revisit timelines, acknowledge progress, and adjust plans in light of evolving data, insights, or personal circumstances. It also **normalizes detours and delays**, which are inevitable in complex intellectual work, and frames them as part of the scholarly process rather than signs of failure or inadequacy (Boud & Falchikov, 2006; Zellers et al., 2008).

Example Tool:

- *A student and mentor use a **shared Notion workspace** or **Trello board** to create a project board with visual cards labeled by phase - e.g., "Draft Chapter 2," "Submit IRB," "Conduct Interviews," "Preliminary Data Analysis," "Revise Based on Committee Feedback."*
- *Each card includes due dates, checklists, and embedded documents or links. Both parties can leave notes, track revisions, or flag areas that require discussion.*
- *The board becomes a living mentorship tool - part project manager, part reflective journal - that evolves alongside the dissertation or capstone itself.*

Visual roadmaps such as these help manage the **temporal ambiguity and cognitive load** inherent in doctoral work, offering a psychologically grounded mechanism that supports student motivation and mentor visibility. They also serve as **boundary objects** - shared representations that facilitate communication, alignment, and shared understanding across the mentoring relationship (Holmes et al., 2022; Repko & Szostak, 2020). By investing in co-designed timelines, mentors do more than improve project management - they model how to **navigate complexity with intentionality, reflection, and relational support**, qualities that serve students long after the dissertation or capstone is complete.

---

2. Using Monthly Reflection Reports to Sustain Momentum and Support

In the context of long-term research projects such as dissertations or capstones, mentorship often hinges on periodic, high-stakes meetings - proposal defenses, chapter reviews, or committee check-ins. Yet, much of the doctoral journey unfolds **between these formal touchpoints**, where students may struggle with uncertainty, isolation, or decision paralysis. Monthly reflection reports offer a **low-stakes, high-impact strategy** to sustain progress, encourage self-regulation, and foster continuous communication between mentors and mentees, even in the absence of live meetings (W. B. Johnson & Griffin, 2024; Pfund et al., 2016).

These brief reports function as a **structured yet flexible self-assessment tool**, giving students a recurring opportunity to track their work, voice concerns, and clarify upcoming goals. When built into the culture of the mentoring relationship, they create a **non-punitive rhythm of reflection**, reducing the psychological barriers that often prevent students from reaching out or acknowledging difficulty. This is especially critical for students navigating imposter syndrome, academic fatigue, or uncertainty about next steps (Brookfield, 2017; Sanczyk et al., 2021). A recommended format consists of **3–5 reflective questions**, designed to encourage both cognitive and emotional awareness:

- **What Did you Work On this Month?** Promotes accountability and allows mentors to understand the student's workflow and time management.
- **What Went Well? What was Difficult?** Invites recognition of small wins and normalizes challenges, creating space for supportive conversations rather than reactive troubleshooting.
- **What Feedback or Support do you Need?** Encourages proactive help-seeking, particularly useful for students reluctant to admit confusion during formal meetings.
- **Did you Use Any Tools (e.g., AI, Writing Apps)? How?** Surfaces students' engagement with digital tools and enables ethical discussion around AI integration, revision support, or writing enhancement (Mienye & Swart, 2025; Reiss, 2021).
- **What is your Next Goal?** Reinforces intentional planning and helps mentors assess alignment with broader project milestones.

Delivery Options are adaptable to institutional and student preference:

- **Google Forms** with automated reminders and shared summaries.
- **Email check-ins** with attached reflections or shared documents.
- **Learning Management System (LMS) portals** allow submissions to be archived and accessed by mentoring teams.

These tools are especially valuable in programs with **distributed cohorts, asynchronous formats, or large advising loads**, as they keep lines of communication open and reduce the likelihood that students will disengage unnoticed. They also **shift mentorship from reactive to developmental**, providing mentors with a consistent window into the student's process, not just their output (Carless & Boud, 2018; Nicol & Macfarlane-Dick, 2006).

Over time, the monthly reflection practice becomes more than a reporting mechanism - it serves as a **scaffold for metacognition, emotional awareness, and scholarly identity formation**. Students learn to track their own rhythms, name their needs, and take ownership of their learning journey, while mentors gain the insight needed to offer timely, personalized support.

---

3. Using Technology for Visibility, Not Surveillance, in Mentorship

As doctoral mentoring increasingly occurs across time zones, modalities, and platforms, the strategic use of digital tools can greatly enhance **shared visibility, collaboration, and mutual accountability**. However, the purpose of technology in the mentoring relationship must be clearly defined: **it should support - not supplant - dialogue, trust, and scholarly**

autonomy. When used well, technology provides a structure for co-navigation of the doctoral journey, offering mentors and students a shared lens on goals, progress, and process. When misused, it risks becoming a tool of **micromanagement or passive oversight**, eroding the relational core of effective mentorship (Brookfield, 2017; Nicol & Macfarlane-Dick, 2006).

The key is to **leverage technology not for surveillance, but for visibility** - ensuring that both mentor and mentee can access a shared record of what has been planned, discussed, and completed. These tools foster **transparency without intrusion** and encourage students to reflect on and take ownership of their workflows, timelines, and evolving needs (Carless & Boud, 2018; Holmes et al., 2022). Popular tools for mentorship support include:

- **Trello or Asana** for visual task tracking, where research milestones (e.g., "Submit IRB," "Draft Chapter 3") are represented as cards or to-do items that move through customizable phases.
- **Notion** for collaborative goal-setting, embedded meeting notes, shared literature logs, and document archiving - an all-in-one workspace that supports project integration and reflection.
- **Canvas or Moodle** for structured progress tracking in programs that offer modular milestones or require regular submission of reflective assignments or professional development logs.
- **Slack** or similar platforms for low-stakes, informal updates that reduce email fatigue while maintaining relational momentum - ideal for brief questions, encouragement, or sharing small wins.

Mentor Practice: Rather than prescribing a tool unilaterally, **invite students to select the platform** that aligns with their own organizational preferences, cognitive styles, or learning rhythms. This empowers students to take the lead in shaping how mentoring support is organized and accessed, reinforcing their agency and professional identity (Austin & McDaniels, 2006; W. B. Johnson & Griffin, 2024). When students co-select the technological scaffolds used in the mentoring relationship, they are more likely to engage meaningfully and consistently.

Caution: Technology should never replace conversation. Tools such as checklists or progress dashboards should be viewed as **conversation starters**, not evaluative monitors. Mentors must avoid the temptation to use these platforms to micromanage student behavior, as this can undermine trust and promote compliance over critical engagement. The most effective digital mentorship strategies integrate regular check-ins, feedback loops, and reflective dialogue - ensuring that **human connection remains central** even as digital scaffolds evolve (Brookfield, 2017; Zellers et al., 2008).

When used with care, digital tools can **enhance clarity, reduce uncertainty, and support students in managing complex tasks** - without compromising the core relational and developmental values of doctoral mentorship. The result is a technology-supported ecosystem where structure and autonomy coexist, and where both mentor and student are fully visible to each other as co-participants in a meaningful scholarly journey.

---

4. Accountability as a Lens for Support, Not Surveillance

While accountability in doctoral mentorship is often associated with tracking deliverables - chapter drafts, IRB approvals, or milestone completions - its most transformative function lies in its capacity to **surface the deeper challenges that often go unspoken**. Effective mentors recognize that behind missed deadlines or stalled progress often lie **internal barriers** such as perfectionism, fear of failure, unacknowledged confusion, or silent disengagement. When approached with care and intention, accountability becomes not just a system for monitoring output, but a **diagnostic lens** for understanding and responding to what a student might be struggling to articulate (Brookfield, 2017; Sanczyk et al., 2021). Key signals of these deeper struggles may include:

- **Perfectionism or procrastination**, where the student continually revises without submitting, delays meeting preparation, or sets unrealistic standards that impede momentum.
- **Overreliance on AI**, using generative tools to produce text without fully understanding, integrating, or critiquing the material - resulting in superficially polished drafts that lack depth or original thought (Mienye & Swart, 2025; Slimi & Carballido, 2023).
- **Avoidance behaviors**, such as canceling meetings, going silent over email, or disengaging from peer support structures are often a sign of academic anxiety or feelings of inadequacy.
- **Submission of polished writing** that reads well on the surface but reveals, upon closer review, **conceptual gaps, weak synthesis, or misalignment with research goals**.

In these moments, mentors must practice **relational accountability** - holding space for vulnerability while gently probing the process beneath the product. The aim is not to punish or pressure, but to restore momentum through **dialogue, scaffolding, and empathetic reframing** (Boud & Falchikov, 2006; Nicol & Macfarlane-Dick, 2006).

Mentor Tip: Ask **direct yet compassionate questions** to help students surface internal barriers:

- *"What part of this process feels most challenging right now?"*
- *"Are there areas where you are unsure or avoiding because they feel overwhelming?"*
- *"Is there anything you feel hesitant to share about how you have approached this draft?"*

Such questions invite the student to **name the obstacle** - be it conceptual confusion, motivational fatigue, or misalignment between expectations and capacity. Once the challenge is visible, mentors can offer **responsive scaffolding**, such as:

- **Co-working sessions** to reduce isolation and normalize iterative drafting.
- **Alternate formats** (e.g., audio brainstorming, visual mapping, bullet-point outlines) to reduce cognitive load and stimulate flow.
- **Revisiting foundational concepts or threshold theories** helps the student reconnect with the conceptual architecture of their work (Carless & Boud, 2018; Gardner, 2009).

By anchoring accountability in compassion rather than compliance, mentors help students shift from shame to agency. They reinforce that struggling is not a failure, but a **signal for**

strategic support - one that, when addressed with skill and care, often catalyzes deeper understanding, renewed confidence, and sustained progress.

---

5. Redefining Accountability in AI-Enhanced Academic Work

As generative AI becomes more integrated into student workflows - from literature review summaries and brainstorming to data structuring and prose refinement - **traditional models of academic accountability must evolve**. In addition to tracking timelines and deliverables, mentors must now help students account for **how AI tools were used**, **what judgments were applied**, and **how authorship was preserved** throughout the process. Accountability in this context is not punitive - it is **an opportunity to foster critical awareness, ethical engagement, and scholarly ownership** in an era of rapidly shifting writing and thinking practices (Selwyn, 2019; Slimi & Carballido, 2023).

To achieve this, mentors should guide students in **making their engagement with AI tools visible and reflective**, not hidden or assumed. The use of AI in academic work is not inherently problematic; what matters is **how thoughtfully, transparently, and ethically it is applied**. Structured reflection - whether through written logs, mentorship conversations, or collaborative review of AI-generated content - helps students move from passive use to active, critical engagement. Key elements of AI-specific accountability include:

- **How the Tools were Used**. *"What prompt was entered?" "Was it for brainstorming, summarizing, outlining, or rephrasing?"*
- **Whether Outputs were Verified and Critically Assessed**. *"Did the student cross-check AI content with primary sources?" "Did they identify errors, gaps, or superficial treatments?"*
- **How Authorship was Preserved**. *"What portion of the final output reflects the student's original reasoning, synthesis, or voice?" "How were AI-generated contributions transformed through human interpretation?"*

Reflection Prompt for Logs or Meetings:

- *Describe any AI tools you used this week. "What did they help with?" "What did you change or reject, and why?"*

This question invites the student to **analyze the process**, not just the product - shifting focus from output to intention, evaluation, and revision. It also reinforces that students are responsible not only for the originality of their ideas but also for **the integrity of the tools they use to shape them** (Floridi & Chiriatti, 2020; Weber-Wulff et al., 2023).

From a mentorship perspective, these conversations deepen the mentor-student relationship by creating space to **discuss epistemology, ethics, and scholarly identity**. They reinforce that AI-generated text is only as valuable as the human intellect that **questions, reshapes, and contextualizes it**. Students need not only permission to use AI - but also **coaching on when to trust it, when to doubt it, and how to preserve the reflective and generative aspects of academic work** (Benjamin, 2023; Selwyn, 2019). By integrating AI-specific accountability into reflective practice, mentors foster the development of **responsible, discerning scholars** -

those who can leverage technological tools without relinquishing the depth, complexity, and ethical consciousness that define doctoral-level thinking

---

Sample Accountability Structure: The 4-Touchpoint Model

In the context of doctoral mentorship, accountability is most effective when it is **relational, reflective, and rhythmically structured**. The 4-Touchpoint Model offers a practical framework that balances **predictable check-ins with deeper reflective practices**, ensuring students remain supported without being micromanaged. By combining structured interactions with opportunities for open dialogue and ethical inquiry, this model fosters a culture of **trust, transparency, and sustained scholarly momentum** (W. B. Johnson & Griffin, 2024; Nicol & Macfarlane-Dick, 2006).

Touchpoint	Purpose	Frequency
Check-In Meeting	Relationship maintenance, informal updates, address emerging questions or concerns	Biweekly
Milestone Review	Assess progress on predefined tasks and dissertation or capstone benchmarks; adjust timelines as needed	Monthly
Progress Report	Written reflection on recent accomplishments, challenges, and upcoming goals	Monthly (written)
AI-Use Reflection	Document and evaluate generative tool use, ethical decisions, and learning outcomes	Quarterly (written)

- **Check-In Meeting (Biweekly)**. These informal, low-stakes conversations serve as the **relational glue** of the mentoring partnership. They help normalize small updates, reduce isolation, and create space for adaptive support. Importantly, check-ins allow mentors to detect subtle shifts in engagement, confidence, or wellbeing - before issues escalate into larger obstacles (Austin & McDaniels, 2006; Brookfield, 2017).
- **Milestone Review (Monthly)**. In these slightly more formal conversations, mentor and student review **progress against the dissertation or capstone roadmap**. These reviews provide accountability without rigidity and allow for recalibration of timelines in response to life changes, data delays, or evolving research directions. They reinforce the mentor's role as a partner in project management, not just a content advisor (Carless & Boud, 2018; Gardner, 2008).
- **Progress Report (Monthly – Written)**. Written reflections give students the opportunity to **pause, take stock, and articulate their own narratives of growth and challenge**. Prompts such as *"What went well this month?"* or *"What roadblocks did you encounter?"* foster metacognition and increase students' ability to self-regulate, ask for support, and recognize patterns in their work habits (Nicol & Macfarlane-Dick, 2006; Zimmerman, 2002).

- **AI-Use Reflection (Quarterly – Written)**. This touchpoint invites students to **critically assess their engagement with AI tools**, promoting ethical awareness and scholarly accountability. Questions such as *"What did AI help you do?"* and *"What did you revise or reject?"* encourage students to treat generative technologies not as neutral tools, but as **catalysts for intentional decision-making and authorship reflection** (Reiss, 2021; Slimi & Carballido, 2023). These reflections can also inform mentor conversations about where deeper conceptual or methodological guidance is needed.

Outcome: The 4-Touchpoint Model provides a **balanced mentoring rhythm** - combining conversational presence with structured documentation, and logistical tracking with intellectual reflection. It helps students feel seen and supported without overwhelming them with reporting obligations. It also helps mentors remain engaged, informed, and better equipped to provide **timely, responsive, and developmentally appropriate guidance**. By integrating this model, programs reinforce that accountability is not synonymous with pressure - it is a **scaffold for progress, agency, and partnership** throughout the doctoral journey.

Section Reflection: Reframing Accountability as Supportive Structure in Doctoral Mentorship

This section offers a transformative redefinition of accountability in doctoral education - shifting it from a paradigm of oversight and compliance to one of visibility, shared responsibility, and developmental scaffolding. By reframing accountability as a tool for progress rather than a mechanism of control, the section empowers mentors and institutions to adopt structured systems that support student autonomy while ensuring sustained momentum and scholarly rigor.

Through practical strategies such as milestone roadmaps, monthly reflection reports, digital dashboards, and the 4-Touchpoint Model, the section shows how structure can coexist with flexibility. These tools foster metacognitive growth, normalize struggle, and bring process-based mentoring to the forefront, particularly for students navigating complexity, isolation, or nontraditional learning trajectories. Importantly, accountability is positioned not as a bureaucratic demand but as an ethical and pedagogical act - one that surfaces hidden challenges, encourages transparency in AI use, and promotes intellectual resilience.

By integrating reflection, relational dialogue, and ethical inquiry into routine mentoring practices, the section affirms that doctoral progress is not merely a sequence of deliverables - but a journey shaped by adaptive structure, intentional mentorship, and empowered student engagement. In doing so, it helps build a culture of doctoral education that is not only efficient but also humane, inclusive, and profoundly responsive to the evolving realities of research and learning in the AI era.

Section 7: Navigating Difficult Mentoring Scenarios and Misalignment

---

Even the most thoughtfully structured and well-intentioned mentorship relationships can encounter turbulence. Whether it is unmet expectations, communication breakdowns, cultural disconnects, or mismatched personalities, misalignment in doctoral advising is not only common - it is predictable. Yet many faculty feel underprepared to manage these tensions constructively, often fearing that conflict signals failure. In reality, difficult mentoring moments offer opportunities for **recalibration, reflection, and modeling professional resilience** (W. B. Johnson & Griffin, 2024; Pfund et al., 2016).

As doctoral education becomes more diverse and digitally mediated, mentoring conflicts are further complicated by **asynchronous communication, AI tool use, and cross-cultural dynamics** (Sanczyk et al., 2021; Slimi & Carballido, 2023). Students may misinterpret feedback as personal criticism, over-rely on AI tools to mask uncertainty, or simply disengage silently. Faculty may feel frustration, helplessness, or guilt when mentees fail to progress as expected. This section provides faculty with **practical strategies and mindsets** to navigate misalignment and restore constructive mentoring relationships.

Common Mentorship Challenges

---

1. Navigating Resistance to Feedback with Empathy and Dialogue

In the doctoral journey, critical feedback is essential for intellectual development, but it is not always easily received. Students may push back - **defensively, passively, or through disengagement** - when critique challenges their understanding, disrupts their sense of competence, or exposes uncertainty in their work. This resistance should not be interpreted as defiance; it is often a **protective response rooted in deeper emotional, cultural, or cognitive dynamics** that mentors must learn to recognize and address with care (Brookfield, 2017; Nicol & Macfarlane-Dick, 2006). Common sources of resistance include:

- **Imposter syndrome**, where students internalize critique as confirmation that they are not intellectually capable or do not belong in the academic space. Even constructive feedback can be interpreted as a threat rather than an opportunity (Sanczyk et al., 2021).
- **Cultural communication norms** that shape how students interpret and respond to feedback. For example, students from cultures that value deference to authority may avoid asking questions or expressing disagreement, while others from assertive communication cultures may feel the need to defend their position immediately - either of which can be misread by faculty as resistance rather than a cultural mismatch (Barker, 2011; Byars-Winston & Dahlberg, 2019).
- **Over-reliance on AI-generated content**, where students present drafts that are linguistically polished but **conceptually shallow or misaligned**, leading them to believe their work is "done" when in fact it lacks theoretical or methodological depth. When critique exposes this gap, it could feel destabilizing - especially if students believed they were producing high-quality work based on the tool's output (Reiss, 2021; Slimi & Carballido, 2023).

Mentor Strategy: The mentor's task is to **reframe feedback as dialogic rather than declarative** - an invitation to reflect, not a verdict to absorb. By using language that emphasizes collaboration, curiosity, and growth, mentors reduce defensiveness and foster scholarly agency.

Example Approach:

- *"This section has real potential - can you walk me through your thinking here? Let us explore how to deepen the analysis together."*

This response validates effort while inviting the student into a **co-inquiry process**. Rather than positioning the mentor as the arbiter of correctness, it casts both parties as intellectual partners working to develop clarity and rigor. Additionally, mentors can scaffold feedback by:

- Asking the student to **respond in writing** to key pieces of critique before revising, prompting reflection rather than reaction.
- Offering **tiered feedback**, starting with strengths and high-level guidance before delving into detailed edits - especially for students early in the writing process.
- **Co-analyzing AI-generated sections** together, encouraging the student to explain choices, challenge assumptions, and make revisions based on disciplinary expectations (Floridi & Chiriatti, 2020; Holmes et al., 2022).

By approaching critique as a shared endeavor, mentors help students move beyond defensiveness and develop **intellectual resilience - the ability to sit with uncertainty, revise meaningfully, and grow through iterative engagement**. Over time, this not only improves the work - it transforms how students understand their own role as scholars in dialogue with both human mentors and machine-generated outputs.

---

2. Understanding and Responding to Disengagement in the Mentoring Relationship

In doctoral mentoring, delays in communication, missed meetings, or sudden disengagement are often viewed as warning signs - but they are rarely signs of laziness or indifference. More often, they signal **overload, fear, or disconnection**, particularly when students are grappling with the invisible pressures of doctoral life. Mentees may underestimate the time required for **ethical research approvals, qualitative coding, or multiple rounds of revision**, and feel overwhelmed when their internal timelines no longer match the demands of their work. These patterns of delay are frequently **symptoms of deeper distress** - not just logistical hurdles (Gardner, 2008; Golde, 2005). Underlying causes may include:

- **Mental health challenges** such as anxiety, depression, or burnout, which may be undiagnosed, unspoken, or stigmatized within academic settings.
- **Work/life imbalance**, particularly for students balancing caregiving responsibilities, full-time employment, or geographic separation from institutional support.
- **Shame from falling behind**, leading students to delay communication for fear of disappointing their mentor or appearing inadequate - a dynamic that compounds isolation and inaction.
- **A perceived lack of belonging**, especially among first-generation, international, or marginalized students who may interpret their struggles as confirmation that they do not belong in academia (Byars-Winston & Dahlberg, 2019; Sanczyk et al., 2021).

In these moments, the mentor's response is critical. **Replacing reprimand with compassionate curiosity** preserves the relationship and opens the door to re-engagement. A question such as …

- *"Is there something outside of our meetings that is affecting your timeline? How can we adjust expectations without losing momentum?"*

… shifts the focus from compliance to care, from disappointment to problem-solving. It signals to the student that they are seen not as a failing project, but as a whole person navigating a complex journey.

Mentor Practice: Rather than assuming resistance or disengagement, explore possibilities such as:

- **Introducing a short pause** in deadlines to allow the student to regroup without punitive consequences.
- **Redistributing or sequencing the workload**, perhaps focusing on reflective writing or smaller-scale goals while capacity is restored.
- **Connecting students to institutional or community resources**, including counseling, accessibility services, writing support, or peer mentoring networks.

This approach models a mentoring philosophy rooted in **academic humanism - one that values scholarly excellence, but not at the expense of wellbeing**. It acknowledges that progress is nonlinear and that sustainable doctoral work requires flexibility, attunement, and caring. Over time, this kind of relational accountability builds trust and reinforces the idea that **asking for help is not a sign of weakness, but a core competency of scholarly life**. Mentors who respond to disengagement with empathy, inquiry, and adaptive support contribute not only to individual success but to a more inclusive, compassionate academic culture.

---

3. Culturally Responsive Mentorship Across Lines of Difference

Mentoring across cultural lines brings both opportunity and complexity. While globalized doctoral programs enrich scholarship through linguistic, epistemological, and experiential diversity, they also present **cross-cultural challenges that, if unacknowledged, can lead to misunderstanding, misalignment, or unintended marginalization**. In particular, mentoring relationships that span national, linguistic, or epistemic boundaries may contain **unspoken differences in communication norms, academic expectations, and the mentor–mentee power dynamic** (Barker, 2011; Sanczyk et al., 2021). Common areas of misalignment include:

- **Tone and Formality**. Students from high-context cultures may use indirect or deferential language, which can be misinterpreted as passive or disengaged. Conversely, students from low-context, assertive cultures may offer critique in ways perceived as abrupt or disrespectful by mentors from different backgrounds.
- **Definitions of Originality or "Appropriate" Academic Writing**. Norms around paraphrasing, citation, and textual ownership vary globally. What counts as plagiarism or "voice" in one system may not align with another's norms, potentially leading to unfair judgments or unintentional violations (Fishman, 2009; Sutherland-Smith, 2016).

- **The Role of Questioning and Critique**. In many Western academic traditions, critique is a sign of engagement, and disagreement - even with authority - is encouraged. But in other cultural contexts, questioning a mentor's suggestion may be viewed as insubordinate or personally offensive.

When these cultural differences remain unspoken, students may feel confused, unsafe, or judged, while mentors may interpret caution or reticence as a lack of initiative. To prevent these misalignments, faculty must engage in **culturally responsive mentorship** - a practice that centers **self-awareness, empathy, and mutual meaning-making** (Byars-Winston & Dahlberg, 2019; Gay, 2018).

Response Strategy: Mentors can use **reflective dialogue** to uncover assumptions and create space for difference without imposing assimilation. Consider normalizing cultural variation with a statement such as:

- *"In some cultures, critiquing an advisor's suggestion may feel disrespectful. I want you to know that I value your thinking - can we practice pushing back productively?"*

This kind of language creates **psychological safety**, affirms the student's cultural experience, and invites a shared learning process. It positions the mentor not as a gatekeeper of academic norms, but as a **bridge-builder between traditions** - someone willing to help the student adapt without erasing their voice or background (Brookfield, 2017; Kovach, 2021). Additional culturally responsive strategies include:

- **Discussing epistemological traditions openly**, including how authority, knowledge, and critique function in different academic cultures.
- **Co-analyzing writing samples** to surface embedded norms about voice, structure, and argumentation.
- **Encouraging students to reflect on their educational background** and how it shapes their understanding of feedback, authorship, or participation.

By embracing this approach, mentors cultivate an environment where **difference is seen not as a deficit, but as a source of insight and richness**. They help students become bicultural academic navigators - capable of engaging across traditions, meeting institutional expectations, and developing scholarly identities that are both authentic and adaptable.

---

4. Bridging the Output–Understanding Gap in AI-Enhanced Learning

As generative AI tools become increasingly integrated into students' research and writing processes, mentors face a new pedagogical challenge: **ensuring that polished outputs reflect genuine understanding rather than surface-level completion**. Tools such as ChatGPT, Perplexity.ai, or Scite.ai can generate outlines, synthesize literature, and rephrase confusing passages with impressive fluency. But when students rely on these tools without critical reflection, they may inadvertently **bypass the very cognitive processes that foster deep learning, conceptual clarity, and scholarly development** (Selwyn, 2019; Slimi & Carballido, 2023). This disconnect between output and comprehension manifests in several ways:

- Students may **submit structurally sound drafts** without being able to explain their organizational choices or defend their theoretical framing.
- Literature reviews may summarize existing work **without demonstrating analytical synthesis** or disciplinary alignment.
- Responses to mentor feedback may appear "fixed" at the sentence level, while the underlying conceptual misunderstanding remains unresolved.

Such patterns can be particularly difficult to detect, as AI-generated content often looks credible - until mentors probe for **reasoning, connection, and authorship**. To address this, faculty must move beyond surface evaluation and implement strategies that **illuminate the process alongside the product**.

Mentor Strategy: Invite students to **document and articulate their AI usage** as a tool for transparency and metacognition. A process-oriented prompt might include:

- *"Show me how you used the AI tool, what you kept, and what you changed. How did it influence your thinking?"*

This question shifts the focus from **"Did you use AI?"** to **"How did you engage with it?"** - prompting the student to reflect on their intellectual agency in the midst of technological assistance. It also allows mentors to detect conceptual gaps and offer targeted guidance without stigmatizing tool use. To build this reflective habit over time, students can maintain **critical AI reflection logs**, as discussed in Section 5, where they:

- Identify specific tasks AI supported (e.g., outlining, rewording, summarizing),
- Describe which elements were accepted, adapted, or discarded,
- Justify changes made and note how the interaction informed their understanding of the material.

These reflective practices foster a **recursive learning process** - where the tool becomes a site of inquiry, not a shortcut around it. Over time, students begin to distinguish between **technical fluency and scholarly depth**, and develop the judgment to know when AI can assist, and when it must be paused in favor of deeper reading, reasoning, or dialogue. By building in process accountability and reflection, mentors help students reclaim authorship and develop the habits of **critical engagement, epistemic awareness, and intellectual ownership** that define meaningful doctoral education in the AI era.

---

5. Navigating Mentorship Misalignment and Transitions

While effective mentorship is foundational to doctoral success, not every mentor–mentee pairing is destined to thrive. Sometimes, despite best intentions, the relationship is marked by **persistent misalignment in communication styles, research priorities, or interpersonal dynamics**. These challenges may emerge gradually or become evident early in the relationship, but when left unaddressed, they can compromise not only progress but also the student's confidence, wellbeing, and sense of belonging in the academic community (Byars-Winston & Dahlberg, 2019; Walker et al., 2009).

Mentorship misalignment is not necessarily the result of misconduct or negligence - it often stems from **incompatibility in advising approaches, expectations, or scholarly worldviews**. For example, a student who values collaborative feedback and iterative dialogue may feel stifled by a mentor with a directive, top-down style. Conversely, a mentor expecting high levels of self-direction may misinterpret a student's need for structure as lack of initiative. Cultural factors, generational gaps, or differing views on the role of technology - particularly around AI integration - can also add friction to the mentoring relationship (Brookfield, 2017; Sanczyk et al., 2021).

When to Consider Reassigning Mentors:

- If the relationship has become **adversarial or unproductive**, marked by frequent conflict, miscommunication, or mutual frustration.
- If **either party feels consistently unsafe, dismissed, or unheard**, including situations involving identity-based marginalization, power imbalances, or lack of cultural responsiveness.
- If **progress has stalled despite multiple efforts to repair the relationship**, such as facilitated conversations, clarified expectations, or revised communication patterns.

In such cases, it is important for departments to have a **clear, confidential, and non-punitive process for mentor reassignment**, ensuring that students can seek a change without fear of retaliation or professional damage. Faculty advisors and graduate program directors should receive training on how to recognize early signs of mentoring misfit and **support transitions with transparency and professionalism** (W. B. Johnson & Griffin, 2024; Zellers et al., 2008).

Faculty Practice: Normalize mentorship transitions as a **routine and sometimes necessary part of graduate education**, rather than a sign of failure or personal inadequacy. Just as academic interests evolve, so too do mentoring needs - and allowing room for realignment is a sign of a mature, student-centered mentoring culture. A supportive conversation might begin with:

- *"Mentorship is about fit as much as it is about expertise. If you feel that this pairing is not working for your growth, we can explore options that better align with your needs and learning style."*

When handled with care, a mentor reassignment can be **a restorative turning point**, allowing the student to re-engage with their work and the faculty member to redirect their mentoring energy more effectively. It also sends an important institutional message: that **doctoral mentorship is relational and dynamic**, and that student wellbeing, agency, and scholarly development take precedence over rigid advising assignments.

Tools and Techniques for Navigating Conflict

---

1. Fostering Structured Reflection to Strengthen the Mentoring Relationship

Effective mentorship is not solely about giving feedback - it also involves **listening, recalibrating, and growing alongside the mentee**. One of the most powerful tools in sustaining a healthy and responsive mentoring relationship is **structured reflection**. When mentors invite students to reflect explicitly on the mentoring dynamic itself - not just on their research - it models vulnerability, builds trust, and enhances the mutuality of the academic partnership (Brookfield, 2017; Nicol & Macfarlane-Dick, 2006).

Structured reflection creates space for the mentee to express what may otherwise remain unsaid: frustration, confusion, unmet needs, or even appreciation. It moves the relationship from a one-directional advising model to a **reciprocal dialogue grounded in trust and transparency**. Especially in feedback-intensive environments, reflection helps mentees process critical input, develop resilience, and understand their own emotional and cognitive responses to challenge. Prompts to facilitate this kind of reflection may include:

- **"What Do You Need More of From Me as a Mentor?"** This opens the door for students to articulate unmet expectations - such as more timely feedback, clearer guidance, or affirmation - without fear of overstepping.
- **"What Has Been Most Challenging About Our Meetings?"** Acknowledges that mentoring conversations can be emotionally complex and gives students permission to voice discomfort, uncertainty, or disconnect constructively.
- **"How Do You Prefer to Receive Critique?"** Encourages a conversation about tone, modality, and sequencing - factors that can deeply influence how feedback is perceived and internalized, especially across lines of cultural difference or power.

These questions are not only relational - but they are also **developmental**. They support the growth of metacognition, self-advocacy, and professional identity, all of which are critical for doctoral success and post-graduate leadership (W. B. Johnson & Griffin, 2024; Zimmerman, 2002). Mentors can incorporate these prompts into scheduled check-ins, reflection logs, or mid-semester feedback sessions. The key is to approach the questions with **genuine openness** - not as performative gestures, but as invitations for realignment and shared improvement.

When students feel safe to reflect honestly on their mentoring experience, they are more likely to **persist, engage deeply, and grow into confident, discerning scholars**. And when mentors welcome that reflection with curiosity and humility, they reinforce a mentoring culture that is not only effective, but also truly transformational.

---

2. Holding a Mentorship Reset Conversation: Rebuilding Clarity, Trust, and Momentum

In any sustained mentoring relationship, moments of misalignment, drift, or miscommunication are not only common - they are natural. Whether caused by shifting timelines, evolving research questions, mismatched expectations, or personal challenges, such moments often benefit from a **"reset" conversation**: a deliberate, structured dialogue to **reestablish expectations, reaffirm boundaries, and recalibrate the mentoring partnership**. A reset conversation does not signal failure - it reflects **maturity, accountability, and a commitment to mutual growth** (Brookfield, 2017; Walker et al., 2009).

The purpose of a reset is to create a safe space for both mentor and mentee to **surface concerns, clarify assumptions, and co-create a refreshed roadmap for communication and collaboration**. This process is especially valuable at transitional points in the doctoral journey - such as moving from coursework to dissertation or capstone, entering fieldwork, or navigating an interdisciplinary pivot. It is equally important when responding to tension, disengagement, or evolving mentorship needs. Template topics for a reset conversation include:

- **Communication Preferences**. Discuss **how, when, and through what channels** communication should occur. For example, some students may prefer asynchronous email updates, while others thrive with scheduled Zoom check-ins or informal Slack messages. Discuss tone as well - "*Do students want detailed line edits or higher-level conceptual framing?"* Clarifying expectations on **responsiveness, accessibility, and formality** reduces ambiguity and prevents misread intentions (W. B. Johnson & Griffin, 2024).
- **Feedback Cycles**. Establish a rhythm for **when feedback will be given and how quickly students are expected to respond**. This includes turnaround times for draft reviews, expectations for revisions, and how to signal when a deliverable is ready for critique. Students benefit from predictability, while mentors benefit from boundaries that manage workload equitably (Boud & Falchikov, 2006; Nicol & Macfarlane-Dick, 2006).
- **AI Tool Use and Reflection**. Explore **how generative tools are being used** in the student's workflow, and set shared expectations for documentation, authorship boundaries, and ethical reflection. Clarify what constitutes appropriate use for brainstorming or outlining, and where human reasoning and original voice must take precedence (Reiss, 2021; Slimi & Carballido, 2023).
- **Career Alignment and Long-Term Goals**. Revisit the student's **professional aspirations and how the dissertation or capstone - and mentoring process - can better align with those aims**. This ensures that mentorship remains not just academically rigorous, but **strategically relevant** for the student's trajectory - whether in academia, policy, industry, or a hybrid role (Austin & McDaniels, 2006; Gardner, 2008).

A reset conversation might begin with a mentor offering language such as:

- *"As we move into this next phase, I want to make sure we are still aligned. Can we take time to revisit what is working well and what might need adjusting in terms of communication, feedback, or support?"*

By inviting shared authorship of the mentoring dynamic, mentors shift from a hierarchical model to a **collaborative and adaptive structure**, reinforcing the student's agency and voice within the relationship. These conversations are not one-time events - they can be repeated as needed, serving as **relational tune-ups that prevent misalignment from escalating into disengagement** (Sanczyk et al., 2021). When approached with openness and trust, reset conversations foster **renewed clarity, strengthened connection, and a revitalized commitment to shared success**.

3. When Misalignment Persists: Documentation and Third-Party Support

Despite thoughtful efforts to recalibrate the mentoring relationship through reset conversations, clarified expectations, and increased transparency, **some mentorship misalignments may persist**. In such cases - especially when communication has broken down, academic progress is at risk, or psychological safety is compromised - it is essential to move from informal troubleshooting to **formal documentation and structured support**. This transition is not punitive; it is a form of scholarly and relational due diligence, designed to protect both mentor and mentee while creating space for resolution, redirection, or reassignment (Walker et al., 2009; Zellers et al., 2008). Documentation serves several key purposes:

- It ensures that **both parties have a clear record of what was discussed, agreed upon, and attempted** - including communication adjustments, revised timelines, or division of responsibilities.
- It provides an evidence-based account, should additional support be required from program administrators.
- It models **professionalism and accountability**, reinforcing that mentorship, such as research, is a relationship that benefits from reflection, iteration, and structure (Brookfield, 2017; Byars-Winston & Dahlberg, 2019).

Documentation can take the form of brief follow-up emails, shared meeting summaries, or a written action plan. Each entry should:

- **Identify the concern or point of misalignment.**
- **Summarize the conversation held to address it.**
- **List specific next steps and timelines.**
- **Clarify who is responsible for which actions.**

If these steps do not lead to resolution, it is appropriate - and often necessary - to **involve a third party**. Depending on institutional structures, this may include:

- A **graduate program director or academic department chair** who can facilitate dialogue, mediate expectations, or initiate a formal reassignment process.
- An **ombudsperson** who offers a confidential and impartial space for addressing concerns, particularly in cases involving perceived bias, power imbalance, or communication breakdown.
- A **graduate student support office or professional development center**, which may offer additional advising, coaching, or mental health resources.

Escalating a mentorship concern should be **normalized as a responsible act**, not a sign of failure or interpersonal dysfunction. Graduate programs that offer clear, compassionate pathways for addressing misalignment reduce student attrition, mitigate faculty burnout, and signal that mentorship is a **relational process worthy of institutional investment and care** (Austin & McDaniels, 2006; Gardner, 2008). Ultimately, when persistent challenges arise, the goal is not to assign blame - but to **center the student's academic progress and wellbeing**, while ensuring that faculty mentors have the support they need to mentor effectively, or step back when a better fit is required.

4. Responding to Tension: Prioritizing Emotional Regulation and Dignity

Tension is inevitable in mentoring relationships - especially in high-stakes environments such as doctoral education, where the pressures of productivity, identity formation, and intellectual rigor intersect. Moments of strain may arise around feedback, missed expectations, conflicting worldviews, or unresolved miscommunication. When these tensions surface, mentors must act not as enforcers, but as **models of emotional intelligence, self-regulation, and professional maturity** - skills students will need as they navigate future collaborations, peer review, and interdisciplinary dialogue (Brookfield, 2017; Pfund et al., 2016).

Rather than escalating or retreating, effective mentors **hold space for discomfort** while maintaining mutual dignity. This begins with **regulating one's own affect** - monitoring tone, body language, and pacing in the moment - and attending to the emotional subtext beneath the content of the conversation. In high-pressure academic cultures, students often experience critical feedback as personal judgment or existential threat. The mentor's task is to create a climate in which **honest dialogue can occur without emotional harm** (Nicol & Macfarlane-Dick, 2006; Sanczyk et al., 2021). Language examples for de-escalation and reconnection:

- ***"Let us pause and come back to this with fresh eyes."*** Acknowledges tension without assigning blame. It allows for a moment of regrouping that preserves the relationship and the work.
- ***"I can hear that this feedback landed hard. Let us talk through it."*** Signals empathy and invites reflection, shifting the conversation from reaction to inquiry.

These responses communicate that tension is not failure - it is **a shared human response to vulnerability, uncertainty, and challenge**. They also model how to engage in disagreement without rupture, a skill that becomes essential in professional settings where collaboration often includes conflict. Mentors may also choose to:

- **Schedule a short follow-up conversation**, allowing emotions to settle and creating space for deeper reflection.
- **Ask the student to write a short reflection** on how the exchange felt and what questions it raised.
- **Own any missteps**, such as a poorly phrased comment or moment of impatience, reinforcing that mentors, too, are learning and growing in the relationship.

By treating moments of tension as **teachable opportunities**, faculty mentors reinforce that professionalism is not defined by perfection, but by how we respond when communication falters. These moments offer students powerful lessons in how to navigate difficult conversations, receive critique without collapsing, and advocate for themselves with composure and clarity. In this way, conflict is not merely managed - it is transformed into **a site of growth, ethical modeling, and relational repair**, reinforcing the core values of doctoral mentorship in a humanizing, emotionally intelligent academic culture.

5. Facilitating a Constructive Mentor Transition

Despite efforts to recalibrate expectations, repair communication, and realign priorities, there are times when a mentoring relationship **cannot or should not be sustained**. In these cases, the most responsible action a mentor can take is to help facilitate a **respectful, well-supported transition** to a new advisor - one who is better aligned with the student's evolving research focus, working style, or professional needs. Ending a mentoring relationship need not be a failure. When handled with care, it can be **a generative act of academic stewardship** - one that preserves the student's momentum, dignity, and sense of belonging within the scholarly community (Byars-Winston & Dahlberg, 2019; Walker et al., 2009).

The first step in this process is to help the student **clarify what they need** moving forward. This may involve reflecting on the mentoring styles, disciplinary orientations, or project expertise that would best support their work. The mentor should then assist the student - either directly or in coordination with a graduate program director - in identifying potential faculty members who align with those criteria. When possible, **mentors should make the introduction or provide context**, signaling professionalism and a shared commitment to the student's success. Key practices for a clean and constructive transition include:

- **Transferring mentorship documentation**, such as feedback logs, progress reports, or milestone records, with the student's consent. This provides continuity and reduces the need for the student to start over or re-explain their project in full.
- **Leaving the door open for future collaboration**, especially if the mismatch was contextual rather than personal. A parting message might include:
    - *"Although our mentoring styles did not fully align, I admire your work and would welcome the chance to collaborate or support you in another capacity moving forward."*
- **Avoiding disparagement**, even if tensions have been significant. Professionalism requires that both parties preserve the student's standing and reputation in the department and wider academic circles (Austin & McDaniels, 2006; Zellers et al., 2008).

Mentorship transitions should also be **normalized at the program level**. Graduate education is developmental by nature, and it is reasonable that a student's intellectual needs or working style may shift during a multi-year project. Institutions that frame advisor changes as a **routine and supported part of academic life**, rather than as stigmatized exceptions, contribute to more flexible and student-centered mentoring cultures (Gardner, 2008; W. B. Johnson & Griffin, 2024).

Ultimately, a well-executed handoff affirms that the mentor's role is not to possess or control the student's trajectory, but to **support their scholarly growth - wherever that journey leads**. By treating transitions with empathy, clarity, and care, mentors reinforce the values of academic integrity, relational respect, and collective responsibility that define doctoral education at its best.

Section Reflection: Mentoring Through Misalignment - Repair, Recalibration, and Resilience

This section reframes mentoring conflict not as a failure, but as a developmental inevitability and a generative opportunity. It offers faculty a compassionate, structured approach for navigating the difficult but common challenges that emerge in doctoral advising - resistance to feedback, disengagement, cross-cultural misunderstanding, AI-related misalignments, and irreconcilable mentor–mentee mismatches. By situating these tensions within the evolving realities of doctoral education, the section emphasizes that sustainable mentorship requires emotional intelligence, cultural humility, and a readiness to adapt as needs evolve.

Rather than defaulting to avoidance or escalation, the section equips mentors with practical tools for de-escalation, reset conversations, structured reflection, and mentor transitions. It also highlights how difficult moments - when approached with curiosity, dialogue, and transparency - can become pivotal growth opportunities for both students and faculty. Importantly, the section reinforces that fostering psychological safety, maintaining dignity, and upholding student agency are not ancillary to academic progress; they are the conditions that make progress possible.

Ultimately, the section underscores that resilient mentorship is not defined by the absence of misalignment but by the ability to navigate complexity with clarity, care, and shared accountability. It positions mentors not just as academic advisors, but as relational leaders capable of modeling repair, conflict navigation, and inclusive scholarly partnership in an age of increasing diversity and digital mediation.

Section 8: Cultivating a Culture of Mentorship Within and Beyond Academia

---

While much attention in doctoral education is often focused on the individual mentor–mentee relationship, sustainable success in both research and professional growth requires a broader cultural transformation. **Mentorship must shift from being seen as a personal act of generosity or responsibility to being recognized as a collective, institutional value that is embedded across the academic ecosystem**. A true culture of mentorship is one in which supportive, ethical, and reciprocal learning relationships are normalized, made visible, formally rewarded, and expected as part of professional practice - not treated as siloed or optional commitments (W. B. Johnson & Griffin, 2024; Pfund et al., 2016).

In today's academic landscape, **shaped by digital transformation, generative AI, and increasingly diverse pathways to scholarly and societal impact, mentorship must evolve into a community-based infrastructure**. This infrastructure must prepare all scholars not only to succeed as lifelong learners but also to step into roles as future mentors, capable of sustaining the cycle of knowledge and care. This section, therefore, explores practical strategies for embedding mentorship into departmental policy, faculty development initiatives, student life, and professional ecosystems, while modeling equity, inclusion, and innovation as cornerstones of the mentoring experience.

---

1. Institutionalizing Mentorship: Moving Beyond Isolated Excellence

While individual faculty members may demonstrate exceptional skill, care, and dedication in their mentorship practices, **isolated excellence is not enough** to ensure broad, equitable student success. Research consistently shows that **structured, institutionalized mentorship systems** - those that are formalized, coordinated, and evaluated at the program or department level - yield significantly better outcomes in terms of **doctoral retention, engagement, sense of belonging, and timely completion**, particularly for students from historically underrepresented or structurally marginalized groups (Byars-Winston & Dahlberg, 2019; Sanczyk et al., 2021).

Informal or idiosyncratic approaches to mentorship often reinforce inequities, privileging students who know how to "work the system," access informal networks, or secure especially attentive advisors. In contrast, institutional models that include **transparent mentorship policies, clear expectations, structured onboarding, and periodic review** help standardize access to high-quality mentoring across diverse student populations. Such systems **reduce the variability and ambiguity that often contribute to student attrition**, especially among first-generation, international, or minoritized doctoral scholars (Golde, 2005; Zellers et al., 2008).

Example:

- *A mid-sized research department implemented a **formal mentorship framework** that included:*
    - *Structured mentor–mentee matching based on shared interests and communication styles.*
    - *Required mentor orientation and annual mentorship workshops.*
    - *A written mentorship agreement template outlining expectations, meeting frequency, and authorship roles.*
    - *A feedback and review system, including student satisfaction surveys and faculty development resources.*

For instance, consider a department that implemented a formal mentorship framework. Over a three-year period, such a program could plausibly yield a 20% increase in four-year doctoral completion rates and a measurable rise in student satisfaction, particularly around advising clarity and program support.

Institutionalized mentorship does not mean rigid uniformity - it means providing a **coherent scaffolding** that departments can adapt while upholding shared principles of accessibility, accountability, and care. When mentorship becomes **a structural priority rather than an individual burden**, it signals to both students and faculty that advising is **central to the mission of doctoral education**, not an invisible labor or optional skill. By embedding mentorship into the infrastructure of graduate programs - through policy, evaluation, and resource allocation - institutions create the conditions for **sustainable, inclusive, and consistently excellent doctoral training**, where every student has access to the guidance they need to thrive.

2. Redefining Mentorship in the AI-Augmented Era

As artificial intelligence continues to automate routine tasks and reshape how knowledge is accessed, produced, and communicated, the role of doctoral mentorship must evolve accordingly. Traditional models of mentorship - centered on **in-person advising, content transmission, and fixed disciplinary pathways** - are no longer sufficient to prepare students for a research and professional landscape defined by **constant change, digital collaboration, and machine-assisted cognition** (Reiss, 2021; Selwyn, 2019). In this new context, effective mentorship is not simply about guiding a student through a dissertation or capstone - it is about **equipping them to lead, adapt, and mentor others in an increasingly hybrid academic world**. Modern mentorship is:

- **Distributed Across Modalities**. Faculty now engage with students through a variety of platforms - Zoom for synchronous discussions, Slack for informal check-ins, and LMS dashboards for milestone tracking and resource sharing. These tools **decentralize the mentoring relationship**, allowing for more frequent touchpoints, greater flexibility, and expanded access across time zones, career stages, and life contexts (Holmes et al., 2022). The shift requires faculty to **maintain presence and relational depth even in asynchronous or technologically mediated environments**.
- **Focused on Navigating Change**. As disciplines intersect and AI challenges traditional research workflows, students need mentorship that helps them **interpret uncertainty, explore emerging questions, and remain grounded in evolving contexts**. The mentor's job is no longer to simply transmit a static body of knowledge - it is to model **intellectual agility**, invite iterative thinking, and support students as they confront ambiguity with purpose and creativity (Repko & Szostak, 2020; Walker et al., 2009).
- **Essential for Fostering Judgment, Ethics, and Adaptability**. In an era where AI can generate fluent text, summarize data, and produce arguments at scale, students must learn to **discern when automation is appropriate, how to verify machine-generated content, and how to preserve their own voice and integrity** in hybrid workflows. Mentors play a crucial role in cultivating this discernment - not by policing tool use, but by **teaching students to ask better questions, surface ethical dilemmas, and evaluate the implications of their choices** (Floridi & Chiriatti, 2020; Slimi & Carballido, 2023).

Faculty Role. Today's mentors must broaden their scope. It is no longer enough to teach students how to complete a dissertation or capstone, or publish an article. Faculty must **prepare doctoral candidates to become mentors themselves**, able to guide others in diverse learning ecosystems, communicate across generational and cultural divides, and model responsible knowledge practices in an AI-augmented world. This includes developing skills in:

- **Cross-modal communication**, balancing empathy, structure, and clarity across in-person, virtual, and hybrid platforms.
- **Generational translation**, helping students interpret and critique both analog and digital academic traditions.
- **Mentorship modeling**, offering transparency about one's own uncertainties, tools, and thought processes to demystify leadership and scholarly discernment.

In this evolving landscape, **mentorship can no longer be understood as a static transfer of knowledge - it must be seen as a dynamic, co-constructed apprenticeship in judgment, ethics, and adaptability**. Faculty who embrace this expanded role help students learn how to navigate uncertainty, interrogate the assumptions behind technological and disciplinary practices, and cultivate resilience in the face of change. By doing so, they contribute not only to their students' immediate academic success but also to building a future academy that is grounded in inclusivity, reflective practice, and informed integration of new technologies.

Institutional Strategies for Cultivating Mentorship Culture

---

1. Recognizing Mentorship as Scholarly Work, Not Invisible Labor

Despite its central role in doctoral education, mentorship is often undervalued in institutional reward structures - frequently treated as an informal service responsibility rather than as a core component of academic labor. This marginalization contributes to **burnout, inequitable workloads, and underinvestment in mentoring development**, especially among faculty who already carry disproportionate service burdens, including women, faculty of color, and those with reputations for student-centered care (Walker et al., 2009; Zellers et al., 2008). If mentorship is to be taken seriously as a transformative force in graduate education, it must be **recognized, evaluated, and rewarded as scholarly work** - on par with teaching, research, and public service.

Institutions can implement policy strategies that elevate mentorship from invisible labor to a visible, measurable academic contribution that is formally recognized in evaluations. This requires embedding mentorship into promotion and tenure criteria, workload policies, and teaching awards so that the time and care invested in guiding students is treated as core scholarly work rather than peripheral service. By institutionalizing these commitments, universities signal that mentorship is not only valued but essential to the health, equity, and future of academic life. These include:

- **Including Mentorship Contributions in Promotion and Tenure Guidelines**. Faculty dossiers should explicitly request documentation of mentoring impact, such as successful student completions, co-authored publications, dissertation or capstone advising, and evidence of developmental support. Criteria should distinguish between mere advising and **intentional, relational mentorship** - valuing quality and equity, not just quantity.
- **Rewarding Co-Authorship, Grant Collaboration, and Mentorship Awards**. Faculty who mentor students into co-authorship, especially those from underrepresented backgrounds, should receive formal credit for their role in developing emerging scholars. Similarly, mentoring roles in **student-focused grant applications, conference support, or interdisciplinary mentoring networks** should be recognized as research-aligned labor, not extra-curricular activity (Austin & McDaniels, 2006; Byars-Winston & Dahlberg, 2019).
- **Incorporating Mentorship Values into Faculty Hiring and Evaluation Rubrics**. Departments should include mentoring commitments in **job postings, interview**

protocols, and annual reviews, ensuring that the institution attracts and retains faculty who view mentorship as integral to scholarly life. Highlighting mentorship expectations early in the hiring process helps **cultivate a culture where mentoring is part of academic identity, not optional enrichment**.

Example Language for a Job Posting:

- *"Successful candidates will demonstrate a sustained commitment to mentoring diverse doctoral students through personalized, ethical, and evidence-informed approaches."*

This phrasing signals that mentorship is not a soft skill - it is a **scholarly, ethical, and pedagogical responsibility**, central to institutional mission and doctoral success. Moreover, when institutions publicly value mentorship, they send a message to students that their development matters - and to faculty that mentoring is a respected domain of academic labor worthy of training, time, and recognition. By embedding mentorship into the **infrastructure of academic evaluation and advancement**, universities create the conditions for a more sustainable, inclusive, and generative research culture - one in which **mentoring excellence is not exceptional, but expected, resourced, and celebrated.**

---

2. Vertical and Horizontal Peer Mentoring: Building Multidimensional Support Networks

While faculty mentorship is central to doctoral success, peer mentoring provides a **complementary and equally essential layer of support** - fostering academic resilience, belonging, and confidence among graduate students. Peer mentoring operates along two key dimensions: **vertical mentoring**, which connects students across stages (e.g., first-years with advanced doctoral candidates or postdocs), and **horizontal mentoring**, which cultivates relationships among peers navigating similar milestones. Together, these layered relationships create a **relational scaffolding** that supplements faculty mentorship and promotes **collective learning, mutual accountability, and identity-affirming community** (Byars-Winston & Dahlberg, 2019; Pfund et al., 2016).

Peer mentoring encourages metacognitive growth by providing spaces where students can **articulate uncertainty, share strategies, and normalize the nonlinear nature of doctoral work**. In contrast to hierarchical faculty–student relationships, peer spaces often feel **less evaluative and more dialogic**, allowing students to voice confusion, test ideas, or seek validation without fear of judgment (Brookfield, 2017). These networks are especially critical for students from historically marginalized groups, who may experience feelings of isolation, stereotype threat, or imposter syndrome within predominantly white or highly competitive academic environments (Barker, 2011; Sanczyk et al., 2021). Models of vertical and horizontal peer mentoring include:

- **Year-Ahead Peer Mentors for Incoming Cohorts**. Assigning new students a mentor from the class ahead helps demystify the transition into doctoral study and provides real-time insight into expectations, milestones, and departmental culture.
- **Dissertation or Capstone Writing Accountability Groups**. Peer-led writing circles provide structure, shared motivation, and a low-pressure environment for feedback and

goal setting. These groups encourage transparency about writing challenges and foster momentum through collective accountability (Nicol & Macfarlane-Dick, 2006).

- **Identity-Based Mentorship Circles**. Affinity-based groups - such as BIPOC doctoral collectives, LGBTQ+ scholar networks, or international student support pods - create affirming spaces for discussing the intersection of scholarly identity, institutional culture, and lived experience. These spaces center mentorship around shared context, cultural validation, and collective wisdom (Byars-Winston & Dahlberg, 2019; Gay, 2018).

Example:

- *An online STEM doctoral program implements a three-tier peer mentoring model in which each first-year student is paired with both a second-year doctoral peer mentor and a senior doctoral candidate in their dissertation or capstone phase.*
- *The second-year mentor provides guidance on transitioning into the program, managing online coursework, and navigating digital academic tools, while the senior student offers support around research design, dissertation or capstone proposal development, and preparing for comprehensive exams.*
- *This vertically integrated structure ensures that students receive layered, stage-relevant support, while also building community across cohorts and offering visibility into different phases of the doctoral journey.*

These multidimensional networks not only reduce reliance on a single advisor - they also promote distributed expertise, emotional reciprocity, and community-based resilience that no one individual can provide. By weaving together peer-to-peer relationships, faculty guidance, and professional connections, they create a support system that mirrors the collaborative reality of scholarly and professional life. **When intentionally designed and supported by institutional infrastructure, peer mentoring becomes a powerful mechanism for cultivating a more inclusive, collaborative, and insightful doctoral experience that sustains both academic success and personal well-being**.

---

3. Building Mentorship Capacity in Faculty and Students

Mentorship is not an innate skill - it is a **scholarly, relational, and developmental practice** that can and must be cultivated over time. To build a sustainable mentoring culture, institutions must invest in both **faculty mentorship development and student mentorship preparation**, creating a community of practice in which mentoring is viewed not as peripheral labor but rather as a core academic competency. When faculty and students are both equipped to mentor thoughtfully, they reinforce one another's growth and contribute to a **more inclusive, reflective, and generative academic environment** (Austin & McDaniels, 2006; Brookfield, 2017).

For Faculty: Cultivating Mentorship as a Professional Practice.

- **Offer regular mentorship training** that addresses practical and ethical dimensions of mentoring, including how to give feedback, engage across lines of identity difference, and navigate AI-assisted workflows. These workshops should include discussion-based formats, invite interdisciplinary perspectives, and **bridge theory with applied case examples** (W. B. Johnson & Griffin, 2024; Sanczyk et al., 2021).

- **Include mentorship case studies in teaching and learning workshops**, allowing faculty to collaboratively explore dilemmas such as mentoring across cultural lines, managing stalled student progress, or responding to students' overreliance on AI-generated text. These conversations surface implicit assumptions and strengthen faculty's capacity to **mentor with intentionality, humility, and discernment** (Byars-Winston & Dahlberg, 2019).
- **Require a mentoring philosophy statement in annual reviews or promotion files**, prompting faculty to articulate their mentoring approach, reflect on areas for growth, and connect their mentoring to institutional goals around equity and excellence. Such statements elevate mentorship to a **visible, assessable dimension of scholarly life**, reinforcing its importance across career stages and disciplines.

For Students: Developing as Emerging Mentors.

Doctoral education is not only about becoming a researcher - it is also about learning to **mentor others**, including undergraduates, interns, and future peers. Providing students with structured opportunities to develop mentorship skills enhances **knowledge retention, leadership capacity, and professional identity formation** (Brookfield, 2017; Gardner, 2008).

- **Offer mentoring training for students**, particularly those in teaching assistantships or peer mentorship programs. This training can cover **developmental advising, inclusive feedback, boundary-setting, and mentoring across difference**, giving students tools to mentor with care and confidence.
- **Integrate mentorship responsibilities into TAships, fellowships, and research assistant roles**, encouraging students to see themselves as **collaborators in the development of others**, not just recipients of guidance. This reinforces metacognition, communication skills, and ethical decision-making.
- **Encourage students to keep "mentorship-in-practice" logs or journals**, where they document how they support peers, guide undergraduates, or reflect on their own mentoring experiences. These logs promote **intentionality and reflective practice**, reinforcing that mentoring is not incidental but integral to the life of a scholar.

Scholarly Rationale: Preparing students to mentor strengthens their own learning by requiring them to clarify, teach, and actively apply the knowledge they have acquired, transforming passive understanding into articulated expertise. At the same time, the process deepens empathy and accountability in academic relationships, as students begin to recognize the responsibilities of guiding others through challenges similar to their own. Simultaneously, **mentoring others contributes to professional identity formation, helping students imagine themselves not only as knowledge producers, but as educators and stewards of the discipline** who carry forward its intellectual and ethical traditions (Austin & McDaniels, 2006; Brookfield, 2017).

---

4. Extending Mentorship Culture Beyond Graduation

A robust mentorship culture does not end at dissertation or capstone defense. As the boundaries of doctoral education evolve to include **public engagement, interdisciplinary collaboration, and non-academic career pathways**, mentorship must expand beyond traditional timelines and institutional walls. Preparing students to contribute meaningfully beyond the academy requires **longitudinal, networked mentorship structures** - ones that extend into postdoctoral life, professional practice, and civic engagement. In doing so, doctoral programs affirm that **mentorship is not transactional, but relational and developmental across the arc of a scholar's career** (Austin & McDaniels, 2006; W. B. Johnson & Griffin, 2024). To institutionalize this broader vision, doctoral programs can:

- **Partner with alumni to offer career mentoring**, drawing on graduates working in academia, industry, government, and nonprofit sectors. Alumni mentors can provide critical insights into life after graduation, support students through career transitions, and help demystify diverse professional landscapes. These relationships **anchor the doctoral experience in real-world trajectories**, expanding what mentorship can mean at different stages of scholarly and professional development (Byars-Winston & Dahlberg, 2019).
- **Connect students to community-based or industry mentors**, especially when their work addresses applied problems or marginalized populations. For example, students pursuing research in environmental justice, public health, or digital equity may benefit from mentoring relationships with practitioners or community leaders who offer contextual expertise and accountability to those directly affected by the research (Gay, 2018; Holmes et al., 2022).
- **Recognize public, entrepreneurial, and policy-focused mentorship as legitimate forms of academic mentorship**, worthy of institutional support and scholarly credit. When students are mentored in shaping white papers, founding startups, or delivering public workshops, those mentoring efforts should be acknowledged alongside traditional dissertation or capstone advising. Doing so **expands institutional definitions of scholarship and leadership** (Ball, 2004; Walker et al., 2009).

Example:

- *A doctoral student completing a dissertation or capstone on **AI ethics in algorithmic decision-making** co-facilitates a **community tech justice workshop** in partnership with a local civic organization.*
- *Faculty advisors support the student not only in organizing the event but also in writing a **reflective policy brief** and preparing a cross-platform dissemination strategy - including academic conference presentations, practitioner blogs, and a social media campaign.*
- *This mentoring relationship affirms the student's identity as both a scholar and a public educator, and demonstrates how mentorship can support **impact-driven scholarship that moves across academic and civic domains**.*

By cultivating mentorship networks that bridge academic and public worlds, doctoral programs equip students with the tools to lead, collaborate, and mentor others long after graduation, extending their influence beyond the academy into civic and professional spheres. This practice reinforces the idea that **advanced education should not end at the dissertation or capstone defense, but should prepare graduates to translate their expertise into**

meaningful contributions across communities, industries, and policy contexts. At its core, this approach reflects a deeper institutional commitment: that doctoral education is not simply about credentialing - it is about developing ethical, engaged, and adaptive leaders capable of thriving in a complex and interdependent world.

---

5. Creating a Culture Where Mentorship Thrives

High-quality mentorship is not sustained solely through policy or training - it is rooted in **academic cultures that value, elevate, and celebrate relational labor as an essential part of scholarly life**. In institutions where mentorship is visible, rewarded, and embedded in community practice, both students and faculty come to understand it not as an individual favor or institutional checkbox, but as a **shared academic responsibility and form of leadership**. Over time, these cultural signals shape how students experience graduate education and how future faculty approach their roles as scholars and mentors (Byars-Winston & Dahlberg, 2019; Walker et al., 2009). Mentorship thrives in environments that:

- **Treat mentoring as leadership**, recognizing that guiding others is not an extracurricular activity but a central mode of academic influence, especially when it includes capacity-building, ethical modeling, and boundary-crossing collaboration.
- **Share stories of mentor–mentee success**, including co-authored publications, joint public engagement, or transformative advising experiences. Storytelling humanizes mentorship and provides models for others to emulate.
- **Encourage collaboration over competition**, promoting mentoring networks, writing groups, and team-based advising as the norm rather than the exception - especially in interdisciplinary and applied programs (Austin & McDaniels, 2006).
- **Use language that reflects care, not just compliance**, framing mentorship as relationship-building and intellectual partnership, rather than as supervision, oversight, or "service."

To cultivate this kind of culture, academic leaders and graduate programs can take **concrete actions** that align structure with values:

- **Host annual mentorship showcases**, where faculty and students present case studies of collaborative projects, mentoring innovations, or lessons learned in cross-cultural advising. These events celebrate mentorship as an evolving practice and foster cross-departmental learning.
- **Fund small grants for co-authored work between faculty and students**, such as collaborative articles, policy briefs, community engagement projects, or digital exhibits. These opportunities provide resources and visibility for mentoring relationships that extend beyond the dissertation or capstone.
- **Celebrate mentors across disciplines and career stages**, including junior faculty, adjunct faculty, staff advisors, and peer mentors - not just full professors or long-tenured scholars. This reinforces the idea that **mentorship is a collective endeavor and a culture-shaping force**, not the domain of a few exemplary individuals (Brookfield, 2017; Zellers et al., 2008).

Cultural Impact: When mentorship is visible, resourced, and honored, students begin to **see it not as charity or obligation**, but as a **core responsibility of scholarly citizenship**. They internalize the idea that knowledge is relational, that growth happens in community, and that leadership is measured not only by output, but by **how one nurtures and supports the development of others**.

Such a culture extends the impact of mentorship far beyond any single pairing, transforming it from an isolated relationship into a collective and enduring academic practice. It becomes a living ethos woven into the daily fabric of academic life, shaping how faculty, students, and colleagues support one another in inquiry, reflection, and growth. Over time, **this ethos carries forward across generations of scholars and into every field of professional practice, ensuring that mentorship remains not just an activity but a legacy of shared responsibility and intellectual stewardship**.

Illustrative Model: Designing a Mentorship Fellows Program to Advance Institutional Culture

To move beyond fragmented or informal mentoring efforts, graduate schools should consider establishing a **Mentorship Fellows Program** - a structured initiative that positions both faculty and advanced doctoral students as co-leaders in cultivating a culture of intentional, inclusive, and evidence-informed mentorship. Such a program can serve as a **catalyst for institutional change**, embedding mentorship into the broader framework of scholarly development, equity, and leadership preparation. In this model, a cohort of Mentorship Fellows would be selected annually, representing a cross-section of disciplines and mentoring experiences. Fellows would engage in a one-year cycle that includes:

- **Co-developing mentorship workshops** focused on topics such as identity-aware feedback, mentoring across modalities, AI-integrated supervision, and culturally responsive advising.
- **Documenting their mentoring practices**, including reflective journals, peer case studies, and mentorship philosophy statements, which would contribute to a growing institutional resource hub.
- **Serving as mentorship ambassadors**, leading peer-to-peer learning in their departments, offering mentorship consultations, and building capacity through mentorship circles and interdisciplinary panels.

By treating mentorship as a public, collaborative practice - not a private or invisible labor - such a program would **normalize mentoring excellence across faculty ranks and student cohorts**, while offering ongoing support and visibility for mentoring as a core element of graduate education. **Anticipated outcomes** of this kind of initiative would include:

- **Stronger cross-disciplinary collaboration**, as faculty and students jointly design mentoring frameworks that are transferable across research domains.
- **Improved mentoring effectiveness**, measured through student satisfaction surveys, increased clarity in advising relationships, and greater confidence among mentees.
- **Early identity formation among future faculty and professionals**, as Student Fellows reflect on and practice mentoring before assuming formal supervisory roles

post-graduation (Austin & McDaniels, 2006; Brookfield, 2017; Byars-Winston & Dahlberg, 2019).

This model affirms that mentorship development should not be left to happenstance or the personality of individual faculty members, as that approach risks inconsistency and inequity across programs. Instead, **it should be institutionalized as a recognized scholarly and civic responsibility, embedded in departmental policies, professional development structures, and assessment frameworks**. In doing so, doctoral education prepares students not only to complete their dissertations or capstones but rather to emerge as ethical, adaptive, and relational leaders who can sustain meaningful mentorship within and beyond the academy.

Section Reflection: Institutionalizing Mentorship as a Cultural Ethos

This final section broadens the lens from individual mentoring practice to the systemic and cultural foundations required to sustain mentorship excellence across academic and professional contexts. It reframes mentorship not as a discretionary act of goodwill, but as a shared institutional value - one that must be resourced, recognized, and embedded across the structures and rhythms of doctoral education. Drawing on research, policy strategies, and real-world examples, the section demonstrates how mentorship can be cultivated as both a scholarly commitment and a relational practice - one that shapes academic identity, supports equity, and prepares students to mentor others across diverse fields and futures.

Importantly, this section also confronts the realities of the AI-augmented research landscape, emphasizing that mentorship in the 21st century must adapt to new technologies, expanded modalities, and dynamic student pathways. Faculty are no longer just content experts - they are ethical guides, cross-modal communicators, and professional role models in hybrid, digitally mediated environments. By outlining strategies such as mentorship training, peer mentorship models, post-graduation networks, and Mentorship Fellows Programs, the section provides a roadmap for creating an ecosystem where mentorship thrives - not by chance, but by design.

Ultimately, this section affirms that when mentorship is visible, honored, and collectively enacted, it becomes a living culture - one that nourishes scholarly growth, professional formation, and intergenerational leadership. It invites institutions to see mentorship not as ancillary labor, but as the heartbeat of academic life.

Chapter 7 Conclusion: Designing for Discernment - Reimagining Learning Goals in an AI-Augmented World

Chapter 7 argued that as artificial intelligence becomes a ubiquitous force in academic and professional life, faculty must take proactive responsibility for designing learning goals that prepare students not only to **use** AI tools, but to collaborate with them **ethically, reflectively, and creatively**. The chapter challenged traditional learning design that centers solely on independent mastery, instead proposing a richer framework - one that prioritizes **discernment, process transparency, and judgment** as the new hallmarks of student success.

In **Section 1**, the case was made for **AI-responsive learning outcomes**. Rather than asking if students can complete a task without assistance, faculty should now ask: ***"Can students use AI tools in ways that preserve voice, context, and ethical clarity?"*** This reframe repositions AI not as a threat to student authorship, but as a prompt for deeper metacognitive engagement.

Section 2 built on this reorientation by mapping AI-infused learning goals to **Bloom's Taxonomy and digital literacy frameworks**, showing how students can evolve from simply recognizing AI outputs to analyzing, evaluating, and eventually co-creating with them. These stages align well with the development of **higher-order thinking**, reinforcing that AI collaboration must be taught as a process of **strategic decision-making**, not passive usage.

In **Section 3**, the chapter extended these ideas into **career and civic readiness**, highlighting that real-world success will increasingly depend on the ability to work **with** intelligent systems - without being overruled or misled by them. Whether designing for fields such as journalism, nursing, marketing, or education, the learning goal is the same: **to use AI with awareness, empathy, and ethical foresight**.

Section 4 introduced assessment strategies that reward **transparency, iteration, and reflection**. Faculty are urged to evaluate not just the end product of student work, but the **process of engagement** - how students prompted the AI, revised its output, justified their choices, and recognized disciplinary standards. This shift, first outlined in Chapter 4, affirms that in AI-enhanced work, **intellectual agency lies in the margins, not just the message**.

In **Section 5**, the chapter offered the **AI Use Portfolio** as a model of assessment that centers **documentation, annotation, and synthesis** - asking students to make their collaboration with AI tools visible and accountable. This model turns AI from a silent assistant into a co-learner whose contributions must be negotiated, explained, and ethically framed.

Section 6 reminded us that **faculty modeling** is essential to successful learning design. Students will only internalize these goals if they see their faculty navigating AI with thoughtfulness - sharing prompts, questioning outputs, and acknowledging missteps. This modeling reinforces a shared academic culture where **reflection trumps automation**.

Section 7 added that these goals must be **flexible across disciplinary contexts**. In technical fields, AI might support code or data analysis. In the arts and humanities, it might challenge creative boundaries or amplify critique. What matters is that **AI integration aligns with field-specific standards for credibility, voice, and interpretation** - a point that ensures equity and relevance in learning design.

Finally, **Section 8** closed with a call to embed AI-aligned goals into **institutional structures**, including syllabi, assessment rubrics, general education standards, and accreditation narratives. If these goals remain isolated to individual classrooms, the larger academic system will continue to evaluate students using outdated benchmarks that no longer reflect how learning actually happens.

The central message of Chapter 7 is this: **Effective learning in the AI era is not defined by whether a student can work without AI - but by how responsibly, critically, and creatively they work with it.** Learning goals must evolve from measuring **isolation** to measuring **discernment**.

To design for the future, faculty must center **judgment over automation, transparency over polish, and ethical use over tool fluency**. Only then will students be equipped to shape AI - not just be shaped by it.

Chapter 8: Developing AI Literacy Across Disciplines

AI is not just for STEM fields. From history to education, nursing to business, AI is reshaping how evidence is gathered, synthesized, and interpreted. This chapter helps faculty from **all** disciplines understand how to integrate AI literacy into their curricula - and how to prepare students to think critically about AI's influence on knowledge itself.

Section 1: What Is AI Literacy? A Cross-Disciplinary Imperative

---

In an era where generative AI systems can produce essays, diagnose diseases, generate code, and influence public discourse, the need for **AI literacy** has become universal. Once confined to computer science or data analytics departments, understanding AI is now a baseline competency for citizenship, professional engagement, and critical inquiry (Long & Magerko, 2020; Southworth et al., 2023). Whether students are studying sociology or nursing, graphic design or theology, they will inevitably encounter and interact with systems shaped by artificial intelligence.

Yet "AI literacy" is often narrowly interpreted as knowing how to code or deploy AI systems. In reality, AI literacy is **multidimensional**: it includes **understanding, using, evaluating, and reflecting** on AI and its social impact. This section introduces a **four-part framework - functional, applied, critical, and reflective** - to help faculty across disciplines infuse AI literacy into their teaching in meaningful, ethically grounded ways.

What Is AI Literacy?

As artificial intelligence reshapes the landscape of research, communication, and intellectual labor, **AI literacy is quickly becoming a foundational academic and civic skill.** Such as earlier calls for digital or information literacy, this next frontier demands not only operational fluency, but also **critical reflexivity, ethical discernment, and disciplinary grounding**. As Lee (2008) emphasized, AI literacy must prepare individuals not merely to interact with AI tools, but to **navigate their ethical, political, and epistemological implications** with clarity and confidence. At its core, **AI literacy encompasses four key capacities** that together support responsible and empowered engagement with artificial intelligence:

- **Understanding the Core Principles of AI Systems**. This includes basic knowledge of how AI models are trained, how algorithms process and predict outputs, and how data shapes those predictions. For graduate students and faculty alike, understanding these principles is essential to interpreting AI's role in research and education, including the risks of bias, hallucination, and data misrepresentation (Floridi & Chiriatti, 2020; Selwyn, 2019).

- **Using AI Tools Effectively and Responsibly**. AI literacy also includes the ability to identify which tools are appropriate for which tasks - whether it be brainstorming, summarizing, outlining, or querying data - and to engage with them **in ways that support learning, integrity, and originality**. Responsible use entails not only disclosure, but a clear understanding of **where human reasoning must remain central** in the research process (Mienye & Swart, 2025; Slimi & Carballido, 2023).
- **Evaluating the Outputs and Consequences of AI**. Students and scholars must learn to interrogate AI-generated content critically. This includes recognizing what is **missing, misrepresented, or artificially smoothed over**, and evaluating AI suggestions against disciplinary standards, methodological rigor, and epistemological frameworks. Such critical engagement is vital to preventing the **outsourcing of thinking** to tools that may reproduce normative bias or epistemic shallowness (Rciss, 2021; Weber-Wulff et al., 2023).
- **Reflecting on AI's Influence in Specific Disciplines and Society at Large**. Finally, AI literacy requires scholars to situate their tool use in **broader cultural, social, and disciplinary contexts**. For instance, *"How do AI writing tools reshape expectations in qualitative research?" "What are the implications of predictive analytics in healthcare or education?" "Who is excluded or misrepresented in the data sets AI learns from?"* These reflections underscore that AI is not neutral - it is **shaped by values, embedded in systems of power, and entangled in global dynamics of knowledge production and labor** (Benjamin, 2023; Binns, 2018; Noble, 2018).

In doctoral education and faculty mentorship, fostering AI literacy means **equipping scholars to be both competent users and thoughtful stewards** of AI technologies. This involves integrating AI ethics and functionality into research methods courses, offering structured opportunities for reflection, and modeling responsible use in writing, teaching, and supervision. It also demands **culturally responsive and epistemically inclusive approaches**, recognizing that AI systems often marginalize perspectives outside of dominant data regimes and linguistic patterns (Birhane et al., 2022; Gulya, 2023).

AI literacy is not a technical elective - it is a **core scholarly competency**, necessary for those who will shape the next generation of knowledge, policy, and public discourse. To develop it is to commit not just to using AI, but to **understanding, questioning, and reshaping the environments in which it operates**.

Four Dimensions of AI Literacy (Across All Disciplines)

---

1. Functional AI Literacy: Equipping Scholars with Foundational Understanding

At the foundation of any meaningful engagement with artificial intelligence lies **functional AI literacy** - the ability to understand how AI systems work, what they are capable of, and what their limitations are. This level of literacy is not about technical mastery or coding fluency. Rather, it is about enabling students and faculty across disciplines to **engage critically**

and confidently with AI tools by understanding their underlying mechanisms and conceptual vocabulary (Bender et al., 2021; Floridi & Chiriatti, 2020). Functional AI literacy includes the ability to grasp and explain concepts such as:

- **Algorithms, Training Data, and Machine Learning**. Understanding how AI models "learn" by identifying patterns in vast amounts of labeled or unlabeled data, and how that learning is guided - or distorted - by the structure of training inputs and model architecture.
- **Bias in Data and Model Development**. Recognizing that AI models are not objective - they reflect the biases, omissions, and dominant perspectives embedded in the data they are trained on, which can reinforce social inequalities, epistemic exclusion, and algorithmic harm (Binns, 2018; Birhane et al., 2022; Noble, 2018).
- **Terminology such as "Large Language Models" (LLMs), "Tokens," "Black Box," and "Hallucination."** These terms describe critical AI functions and challenges. For example:
    - **LLMs** refer to models such as GPT-5 that predict language based on probabilistic associations in vast corpora of text.
    - **Tokens** are the building blocks of input and output, which may fragment words or alter interpretive meaning.
    - **Black Box** denotes the opacity of AI decision-making, even to developers.
    - **Hallucination** describes the confident generation of false or fabricated information by AI systems.

These concepts help scholars move beyond surface-level usage of AI tools and toward **informed, critical interaction** - a necessary step in ensuring ethical, transparent, and intellectually responsible research and writing practices (Reiss, 2021; Selwyn, 2019).

Example in Literature:

- *In an undergraduate English seminar, a professor introduces students to* ***how GPT-5 predicts text based on statistical patterns*** *in its training data.*
- *Students are then asked to compare this predictive process to human literary authorship, exploring questions such as: "What distinguishes machine-generated prose from creative intention?" "How does statistical association differ from metaphor, allusion, or thematic resonance in literature?"*
- *The result is a rich discussion about* ***authorship, creativity, and the boundaries between mimicry and meaning****, grounded in both computational insight and humanistic critique* (Bender et al., 2021; Gulya, 2023).

Faculty Tip: Functional AI literacy does not require faculty to **teach code or understand deep technical models**. What matters is the ability to guide students through key distinctions - such as **prediction versus comprehension**, or **pattern recognition versus conceptual reasoning**. Faculty across the humanities, social sciences, and STEM fields can anchor these conversations in domain-specific contexts, demonstrating how AI tools **shape and reflect the values, assumptions, and limits** of each discipline (Buckingham-Shum et al., 2019; Holmes et al., 2022). By embedding functional AI literacy into coursework, research training, and mentorship, institutions equip scholars not only to use AI tools - but to **critique their impact,**

interrogate their claims, and contextualize their role within broader conversations about knowledge, power, and creativity.

---

2. Applied AI Literacy: Developing Critical Engagement Through Practice

Whereas functional AI literacy involves understanding the concepts that underlie artificial intelligence systems, **applied AI literacy focuses on hands-on engagement** - developing students' capacity to use AI tools in real-world academic and professional contexts while maintaining critical awareness. This layer of literacy moves beyond theoretical knowledge to emphasize **practical usage, evaluation, and adaptation**, ensuring that students do not simply accept AI outputs at face value but **interrogate them with discernment and purpose** (Floridi & Chiriatti, 2020; Selwyn, 2019). Applied AI literacy includes the ability to:

- **Use Common AI Tools Strategically and Transparently**. This includes language models such as *ChatGPT* and *Perplexity* for brainstorming and summarization; research tools such as *Scite* for citation tracing and credibility scoring; visual generators such as *DALL·E* for data storytelling or design; and revision tools such as *Grammarly* for clarity enhancement. Each tool offers distinct affordances - and limitations - depending on the discipline, task, and desired learning outcome (Mienye & Swart, 2025; Reiss, 2021).
- **Understand the Limits of AI-Generated Content**. Students must learn to question whether AI summaries are **superficial, biased, or misleading**, especially when nuance, context, or cultural understanding is essential. This is particularly important in disciplines such as history, ethics, or the arts, where meaning is not reducible to pattern recognition alone (Bender et al., 2021; Noble, 2018).
- **Differentiate Between Human-Authored and AI-Assisted Outputs**. Applied AI literacy means being able to identify how a tool shaped the structure, tone, or vocabulary of a piece of writing, and to reflect on whether the final product preserves **the student's own reasoning, authorship, and disciplinary voice** (Slimi & Carballido, 2023; Weber-Wulff et al., 2023).

Example in Nursing:

- *In a graduate nurse practitioner course, a faculty member assigns students to interact with an* ***AI-powered patient chatbot****, asking them to simulate a range of health communication scenarios (e.g., delivering test results, responding to patient anxiety, managing cross-cultural misunderstandings).*
- *Students then critique the chatbot's* ***accuracy, tone, and equity implications****, evaluating whether it reflects ethical care practices, biases in health literacy, or insensitivity to patient diversity. This applied exercise bridges clinical training with* ***AI ethics and health informatics*** (Chen & Decary, 2020; Fiske et al., 2019).

Example in Education:

- *Teacher education students use a generative AI tool to* ***create a lesson plan on a chosen topic****.*

- *After generating the plan, students reflect on what the AI may have omitted - such as **culturally responsive pedagogy, student differentiation, classroom management strategies**, or equity-based assessment practices.*
- *This activity fosters reflection on what it means to teach responsibly and critically in a technology-enhanced environment, and where **human insight must intervene to shape truly inclusive and student-centered practice*** (Gay, 2018; Ray & Ray, 2024).

These types of applied assignments **build metacognition, ethical reasoning, and disciplinary ownership**. They show students that AI is not a shortcut, but a collaborator that must be guided, constrained, and challenged. Applied AI literacy thus supports the broader goal of **scholarly empowerment**: enabling students to shape, rather than be shaped by, the technologies they encounter. By embedding applied AI literacy into curricula and mentoring conversations, educators foster the next generation of scholars and professionals who can **use AI effectively while remaining grounded in disciplinary ethics, civic responsibility, and human-centered judgment**.

---

3. Critical AI Literacy: Interrogating Power, Justice, and the Politics of Technology

Beyond functional and applied skills, doctoral students and scholars must cultivate **critical AI literacy** - the ability to interrogate how artificial intelligence is embedded within **larger systems of power, inequity, and cultural meaning**. This dimension of literacy is not about how AI works or how to use it, but **how it shapes - and is shaped by - social, political, and epistemological forces**. It requires scholars to approach AI not merely as a tool, but as a product of human choices, institutional logics, and historical legacies (Benjamin, 2023; Eubanks, 2018). Critical AI literacy includes exploration of topics such as:

- **Algorithmic Bias and Structural Discrimination**. AI systems trained on biased or incomplete data may reproduce existing inequalities. From hiring algorithms to image recognition systems, critical AI literacy requires students to understand how **statistical predictions may reflect sociopolitical patterns** rather than neutral logic (Birhane et al., 2022; Noble, 2018).
- **Data Privacy and Surveillance**. Many AI applications depend on massive datasets - often collected without informed consent or clear boundaries. Understanding how AI intersects with **state surveillance, corporate data collection, and predictive tracking** is essential to evaluating its implications for civil liberties and digital autonomy (Eubanks, 2018; O'neil, 2017).
- **Who Builds AI - and Who is Left Out**. The tech industry and AI research fields remain homogenous, raising concerns about whose values, needs, and epistemologies shape the systems being built. Critical literacy involves asking not only how AI functions, but **who is at the table in its design, and who is affected by its use** (Binns, 2018; Slimi & Carballido, 2023).
- **How AI Reinforces or Challenges Dominant Ideologies**. Whether in education, media, or governance, AI can both stabilize and disrupt power. Many systems embed and reproduce dominant cultural norms - such as Eurocentric perspectives, heteronormativity, or technocratic efficiency - under the guise of neutrality. At the same time, these tools can open new possibilities for resistance, alternative knowledge

frameworks, and more inclusive forms of meaning-making and narrative justice (Benjamin, 2023; Gulya, 2023).

Example in History or Sociology:

- *In a seminar on the sociology of technology, students analyze the history and function of predictive policing algorithms, such as COMPAS or facial recognition tools used in urban surveillance.*
- *They are asked to connect these tools to broader historical patterns of surveillance, neighborhood mapping, and the expansion of carceral infrastructures.*
- *Through critical discussion, students* ***challenge the myth that data-driven systems are objective or impartial, interrogating the institutional assumptions and systemic priorities embedded in their design*** (Bender et al., 2021; Eubanks, 2018).

These exercises cultivate a deeper understanding that AI is not only a technical innovation - it is a site of social reproduction, contestation, and accountability. By interrogating AI's embedded politics, students learn to ask: "*Whose knowledge is centered?" "Whose interests are prioritized?" "Who benefits from this automation - and who bears the risk?"*

Incorporating critical AI literacy into all levels of education is essential for **developing students and scholars who can lead not just technologically, but ethically and relationally**. It prepares all learners to contribute to the development of AI systems and research agendas that are **just, inclusive, and aligned with human dignity and social responsibility**.

---

4. Reflective AI Literacy: Cultivating Meta-Awareness and Epistemic Humility

The most advanced dimension of AI literacy - **reflective AI literacy** - requires students to move beyond operational knowledge or critical analysis to engage in **meta-level reflection**. This form of literacy invites scholars to ask: *"How is AI reshaping the way we create, validate, and value knowledge in my field?"* It prompts inquiry not only into what AI does, but into **how it is changing the architecture of meaning-making itself** - from authorship and creativity to reasoning, interpretation, and authority (Floridi, 2019; Selwyn, 2019).

Reflective AI literacy positions students not just as tool users or critics, but as **thoughtful co-creators of disciplinary futures**. It requires epistemic humility - the acknowledgment that one's field, methods, and norms are not fixed but evolving under technological influence. It also fosters **intellectual adaptability**, enabling students to recalibrate their approaches in response to emerging possibilities, tensions, and ethical questions raised by machine-augmented scholarship. This dimension can be meaningfully engaged across disciplines:

Example in Business:

- *In a business ethics or strategic management course, students reflect on how AI tools are transforming* ***hiring practices, financial forecasting, and decision-making at scale****.*
- *Through case studies, they explore questions such as:*
    - *"What happens when algorithms shape who gets hired?"*
    - *"When do predictive tools determine investment strategies?"*

- *"When chatbots make frontline customer decisions?"*
- *Students are then asked to revisit traditional business ethics frameworks - based on human accountability, rational actors, or fiduciary duty - and* ***consider how these frameworks must evolve in AI-mediated environments*** *(Gulya, 2023; Reamer, 2023).*

Example in Theology or Philosophy:

- *In a seminar on philosophy of mind or theological anthropology, students debate whether AI can simulate or even approximate* ***moral reasoning, compassion, or spiritual insight****.*
- *They consider questions such as:*
  - *"Can an AI system be taught to recognize ethical nuance?"*
  - *"What does it mean for human agency or moral responsibility when machines participate in decision-making?"*
- *This leads to* ***deeper inquiry into personhood, consciousness, and the boundaries of the human****, encouraging students to grapple with long-standing philosophical commitments in light of emerging realities (Bender et al., 2021; Benjamin, 2023).*

Reflective AI literacy also fosters an awareness of how academic traditions and disciplinary structures might **resist, absorb, or be transformed by AI integration**. For example:

- In literary studies, *"What does it mean when AI generates poetry or pastiche in the style of canonical authors?"*
- In STEM, *"How does reliance on automated modeling tools shape what is deemed a valid hypothesis?"*
- In qualitative research, *"How do AI-assisted transcription, coding, or summarization alter the interpretive relationship between researcher and data?"*

Rather than prescribing definitive answers, reflective AI literacy encourages **ongoing inquiry**. It positions students to think relationally - about how human and machine intelligences interact, how boundaries shift over time, and how professionals might take **intentional, values-driven roles in guiding the future of knowledge and innovation** (Brookfield, 2017; Holmes et al., 2022). In cultivating this kind of literacy, faculty mentors play a vital role. By modeling reflective questioning, posing epistemological challenges, and creating space for exploratory dialogue, mentors foster students who are not only skilled, but **wise - able to navigate the complexities of AI not just with technical fluency, but with moral imagination and intellectual depth**.

Disciplinary Dimensions of AI Literacy: Reframing Knowledge, Power, and Practice

---

As artificial intelligence becomes embedded in the core practices of nearly every field, AI literacy must be approached not only as a technical competency but as a **disciplinary imperative**. The influence of AI is not uniform - it intersects with the methods, values, and epistemologies of each domain in **distinct and often disruptive ways**. As Long and Magerko (2020) argued, the task of AI literacy is not merely to prepare students to interact with machines, but to help them critically examine how those machines are **shaping human creativity, authority, and meaning** across the spectrum of knowledge-making.

AI is not neutral. Its outputs are structured by the **data it consumes, the goals it is optimized to achieve, the assumptions embedded in its design**, and the socio-political contexts in which it is deployed (Benjamin, 2023; Slimi & Carballido, 2023). For this reason, AI literacy cannot remain the sole responsibility of computer science or engineering departments. Rather, it must become **a shared responsibility across the academy**, equipping students in every discipline to **understand, critique, and engage AI as both a technological tool and a cultural force** (Byars-Winston & Dahlberg, 2019; Noble, 2018). The questions that AI raises vary by field - and so do the literacies required to address them:

- **In Literature**. AI is already being used to generate poems, short stories, and entire novels. Students and scholars must ask: "*What does this mean for authorship, originality, and the human creative voice?*" "*Can a machine be considered a co-author?*" "*How do we assign intellectual ownership in a text co-produced by an algorithm and a human prompt?*" These questions intersect with **copyright law, aesthetics, and literary ethics** (Bender et al., 2021; Gulya, 2023).
- **In Law**. AI systems can now draft contracts, summarize legal cases, or assist in predictive sentencing. Legal professionals must grapple with issues of **fairness, transparency, and accountability**. "*Who is liable when an AI-generated contract contains errors or biases?*" "*How do we ensure that legal decisions informed by AI do not reproduce systemic injustice?*" These dilemmas require **procedural clarity and normative frameworks** grounded in legal ethics and civil rights traditions (Binns, 2018; O'neil, 2017).
- **In Public Health**. AI models predict disease outbreaks, allocate health resources, and even assist in diagnostics. Yet these systems often rely on **incomplete or biased datasets**, which may lead to underrepresentation of vulnerable populations or overgeneralization of findings. Students in public health must learn to **assess not just model accuracy, but equity and harm** - recognizing the stakes of data omission in life-and-death scenarios (Chen & Decary, 2020; Eubanks, 2018).
- **In Education**. AI tutors and personalized learning platforms are increasingly positioned as supplements - or even alternatives - to human teachers. This raises critical questions: "*How do we evaluate the quality and equity of AI-generated instruction?*" "*Can adaptive learning truly recognize and respond to the cultural, emotional, and developmental dimensions of learning?*" Teacher education programs must prepare future educators to **integrate, monitor, and critique AI-enhanced instruction**, ensuring that technology enhances rather than erodes pedagogical care (Holmes et al., 2022; Ray & Ray, 2024).

These examples underscore that AI literacy is **field-specific and context-dependent**. Each discipline must ask: "*How is AI changing what we know, how we know it, and who gets to participate in that knowledge?*" Faculty mentors play a crucial role in guiding these inquiries, encouraging students to explore **not only how AI can support their work, but how it may challenge their discipline's values, norms, and boundaries**.

Incorporating AI literacy across disciplines fosters students who are not just consumers of AI-generated content but **ethical stewards and critical co-creators**. They learn to engage AI with skepticism, imagination, and care - equipped to question what is automated, challenge what is unjust, and shape what comes next.

Practical Strategies for Integrating AI Literacy into Teaching and Course Design

Developing AI literacy across disciplines requires not only top-down curriculum design, but also **faculty-level experimentation and integration**. Faculty - regardless of field - can take meaningful steps to embed AI literacy into their syllabi, assignments, and classroom discourse. These strategies center on transparency, reflection, and interdisciplinary collaboration, helping students engage AI not passively, but as a **tool for inquiry, critique, and creative problem-solving** (Holmes et al., 2022; Selwyn, 2019). Here are four actionable entry points:

---

1. Audit Your Syllabus

"Where might AI tools already be influencing student work?" "Could you surface this influence through class discussion or reflection prompts?"

Many students already use AI - whether to generate ideas, paraphrase text, summarize readings, or check grammar - yet these interactions often go unacknowledged. Begin by reviewing your assignments through the lens of AI exposure. "*Could students be tempted to use generative tools in place of original analysis or reflection?" "Where might AI help support scaffolding without replacing authentic learning?"* Use this audit as a springboard for class conversation. Prompt students to reflect on:

- *"When do you turn to AI in your academic workflow?"*
- *"How does it support or interfere with your understanding?"*
- *"What norms should govern AI use in this course?"*

These conversations build **transparency and shared norms**, demystifying AI while reinforcing academic integrity (Slimi & Carballido, 2023; Weber-Wulff et al., 2023).

---

2. Integrate Low-Stakes Assignments

Ask students to use an AI tool and reflect on its usefulness, limitations, and ethical dimensions.

Low-stakes assignments allow students to **experiment, make mistakes, and reflect** without fear of grade penalties. Examples might include:

- Using ChatGPT to generate a preliminary outline, then rewriting it based on critique.
- Asking Perplexity.ai to summarize a scholarly article, then fact-checking it for omissions or inaccuracies.
- Using an AI image generator (e.g., DALL·E) to visualize a literary or historical concept, followed by a critique of cultural bias or aesthetic flattening.

Each activity should be paired with reflection prompts such as:

- *"What did the AI do well?"*
- *"What was problematic, misleading, or ethically concerning?"*
- *"How did using this tool influence your own thinking?"*

These exercises foster **applied and critical AI literacy**, encouraging students to engage the technology with **awareness, curiosity, and caution** (Mienye & Swart, 2025; Ray & Ray, 2024).

---

3. Collaborate Across Departments

Pair humanities with data science courses, or education with ethics seminars, to co-teach interdisciplinary approaches to AI.

AI is not a single-field phenomenon. Its ethical, methodological, and cultural dimensions demand an **interdisciplinary response**. Consider developing co-taught modules, cross-listed seminars, or joint assignments between:

- Literature and computer science (e.g., narrative structure and text generation).
- Education and philosophy (e.g., adaptive learning and moral reasoning).
- Environmental science and data ethics (e.g., AI modeling and planetary justice).

Such pairings allow students to **see AI through multiple lenses** - technical, humanistic, ethical, and social - promoting the kind of **integrative thinking** necessary for responsible innovation (Benjamin, 2023; Binns, 2018; Brookfield, 2017).

---

4. Use AI as a Thinking Partner - Not a Shortcut

Model this in your own writing and class design, narrating where AI helped and where it fell short.

Faculty play a crucial role in shaping students' expectations around AI use. By openly sharing your own experiments with generative tools - whether for brainstorming, editing, or resource discovery - you demystify the technology and model **critical engagement over dependence**. Example practices:

- Annotate your own AI-assisted drafts in class to show revision thinking.
- Explain how you used AI to prototype an assignment prompt, but ultimately reworked it for clarity and tone.
- Demonstrate how an AI summary helped identify gaps, but required triangulation with peer-reviewed sources for academic rigor.

These modeling practices foster **reflective AI literacy**, helping students develop the **judgment and discernment to use tools responsibly** - as collaborators in thought, not as substitutes for learning (Bender et al., 2021; Floridi & Chiriatti, 2020). By embedding these practices into your pedagogy, you help students not only **understand what AI is**, but also **who they are becoming in relation to it**. This is the essence of AI literacy: not fluency in prompts alone, but **ethical, contextual, and adaptive participation in a rapidly shifting knowledge ecosystem**.

Section Reflection: Reframing AI Literacy as a Core Scholarly Competency

This opening chapter establishes AI literacy not as a technical add-on but instead as an essential scholarly capacity that transcends disciplines and redefines what it means to be an engaged academic, educator, and professional in the AI era. It makes the compelling case that AI literacy is not merely about knowing how to use tools, but about cultivating a critical, ethical, and reflective stance toward artificial intelligence's growing role in shaping knowledge, power, and human expression.

The four-part framework - **functional, applied, critical, and reflective** - provides a scaffold for integrating AI literacy into any field, from literature to law, theology to nursing. Each dimension deepens the reader's understanding of AI not only as a computational system but as a social, cultural, and epistemological force. Importantly, the chapter highlights that the disciplinary relevance of AI varies widely, and that faculty must guide students in navigating AI's promises and pitfalls in ways that are context-specific, justice-oriented, and intellectually rigorous.

The reflection also emphasizes that fostering AI literacy is not optional - it is a pedagogical responsibility. Faculty are called not just to teach **about** AI, but to model transparency, humility, and critical judgment **with** AI, offering students the tools to reflect on their roles as both users and future mentors in AI-integrated environments.

In reframing AI literacy as a cross-disciplinary imperative, the chapter lays the groundwork for an institutional culture where generative technologies are not feared or blindly adopted - but interrogated, shaped, and stewarded with care.

Section 2: Teaching AI in the Humanities - Language, Meaning, and Creativity

Few academic traditions are more attuned to the nuances of language, authorship, identity, and interpretation than the humanities. Fields such as literature, philosophy, linguistics, and cultural studies have long explored how meaning is created, contested, and transformed. Today, these same disciplines face a profound and urgent question: "*What happens to language and meaning when machines write?*"

Large language models such as ChatGPT, Claude, and Gemini now generate full essays, poems, translations, and even ethical arguments - instantly and fluently. For humanists, this represents both a **challenge to traditional interpretive practices** and a **new domain of critical inquiry**. Rather than viewing AI as a threat to creativity or humanistic thought, this section frames AI as an opportunity to **expand and deepen conversations** about authorship, originality, narrative structure, cultural bias, and epistemological limits (Bender et al., 2021; Benjamin, 2023).

AI in the Humanities: Cultural Artifact, Not Just Utility

In humanities disciplines - where interpretation, context, and voice are central to meaning-making - **AI-generated content must be examined not simply for what it produces, but for what it reveals**. While tools such as ChatGPT or Claude may be used to draft summaries, mimic literary styles, or answer philosophical prompts, their outputs are not neutral nor fully autonomous. They are **cultural artifacts**, trained on vast corpora of human-generated language, and embedded with the assumptions, omissions, and ideologies of their training data.

As Bender et al. (2021) argued, large language models do not "understand" meaning in any human sense. Rather, they statistically model patterns of word usage, syntax, and association. This process allows them to mimic fluency without comprehension, generating text that **sounds authoritative while lacking the intentionality, context sensitivity, or ethical discernment of human discourse**. In doing so, they raise a central question for humanities scholars:

- *"What do AI-generated texts reflect - and obscure - about how machines approximate, distort, or mechanize human meaning?"*

To answer this question, scholars must move beyond the use of AI as a functional writing aid and instead treat it as a **textual object** worthy of close reading, critique, and cultural analysis. This approach reframes AI not as an invisible backend utility, but as a **participant in contemporary meaning systems**, with implications for authorship, knowledge legitimacy, and aesthetic value (Benjamin, 2023; Gulya, 2023; Noble, 2018).

Pedagogical Approach: Treat AI Output as a Text to Analyze

In literature, history, cultural studies, philosophy, and other interpretive fields, faculty can create powerful learning opportunities by asking students to **critique AI-generated outputs as they would a work of fiction, a political speech, or a media artifact**. Sample critical questions might include:

- **What Assumptions Underlie this Response?** *"Does the model privilege certain genres, epistemologies, or rhetorical strategies?" "What ideological or discursive norms are reproduced?"*
- **Whose Voices are Present, and Whose are Absent?** *"Are particular cultural or gendered perspectives amplified or omitted?" "How does the model's training data shape whose knowledge is represented as "standard" or "neutral?"*
- **How Does this Text Reflect or Erase Historical and Cultural Context?** *"In mimicking consensus patterns, does the AI flatten complexity, overlook dissent, or erase marginalized histories?"*

These questions foster **critical AI literacy within a humanistic frame**, where the goal is not merely to determine whether a text is useful, but to interrogate **what kind of knowledge it performs, what it leaves behind, and how it circulates in broader power structures** (Eubanks, 2018; Slimi & Carballido, 2023).

Example in Literary Studies:

- *A comparative literature seminar asks students to analyze a short story generated by an AI tool in the style of a canonical author such as Octavia Butler.*
- *Students examine how the AI mimics surface elements of style - tone, rhythm, imagery - while failing to reproduce deeper layers of thematic critique, narrative innovation, or conceptual complexity.*
- *Discussion centers on where the AI achieves fluency without meaning, where its reliance on statistical patterning erases authorial voice, and how its outputs reflect the training data's blind spots.*

This reflective approach encourages students to become interrogators of **form, voice, and underlying assumptions** rather than passive recipients of machine-generated content. It reinforces the value of humanistic insight in an AI-saturated world - demonstrating that context, interpretation, and ethical complexity remain profoundly human skills. In summary, the humanities are not peripheral to the AI conversation - they are central to understanding what AI-generated texts reveal about authorship, creativity, and the cultural futures we imagine.

Key Pedagogical Applications in Humanities Classrooms

---

1. Assignment Spotlight: Comparing Human and AI Interpretations of Literature

As artificial intelligence tools become more accessible and more fluent in generating academic-style prose, humanities educators face both a challenge and an opportunity: how to help students distinguish between **mechanical fluency and human interpretation**. One powerful strategy is to **situate AI not as a surrogate author, but as a rhetorical foil** - a way to sharpen students' own critical thinking and literary analysis by **contrasting their work with that of the machine**. This assignment invites students to **examine critically the differences between human and AI-authored literary interpretation**, reinforcing not only content knowledge but also **authorship awareness, stylistic discernment, and epistemological reflection** (Brookfield, 2017; Floridi, 2019).

Assignment Idea: Comparative Literary Analysis Using AI

- ***Step 1**: Students select or are assigned a poem - preferably one rich in metaphor, layered in historical or political meaning, or emotionally nuanced (e.g., Gwendolyn Brooks, W. B. Yeats, or Mahmoud Darwish). Students write a **short literary analysis**, drawing from their understanding of poetic devices, historical context, and critical frameworks.*
- ***Step 2**: Students then **prompt ChatGPT (or another AI language model)** with a similar task:*
    - *"Write a literary analysis of [Poem Title] focusing on theme, imagery, and symbolism."*

- ***Step 3***: *In class, students bring both versions for side-by-side comparison. The activity is guided by structured discussion prompts designed to foster deeper critical engagement and* ***meta-awareness of textual interpretation***.

Discussion Prompts:

- **What does the Machine "Understand" about the Poem?** *"Where does the AI perform well in identifying motifs, structure, or surface meaning?"*
- **Where does it Falter in Emotional Nuance or Ideological Critique?** *"Does the AI miss subversive elements, ambiguity, or irony?" "Does it overgeneralize, flatten, or avoid politicized themes?"*
- **How do its Limitations Reflect its Training Data?** *"Are certain canonical or Western interpretive frameworks overrepresented? What cultural or affective elements are lost?"*
- **What does Your Own Analysis Reveal that the AI cannot Replicate?** *"Where do intuition, lived experience, or theoretical depth come into play?"*

Learning Outcome: Through this assignment, students learn to **defend their interpretive choices**, critique AI-generated prose, and recognize that fluency is not equivalent to insight. They are empowered to see their own role not only as analysts, but as **meaning-makers** - capable of perceiving nuance, contradiction, and context in ways that language models cannot.

This process demystifies AI, helping students see where it is **useful, where it is limited, and where human judgment remains essential** (Bender et al., 2021; Slimi & Carballido, 2023). This activity can also be easily adapted across genres - applied to visual analysis, rhetorical criticism, or comparative philosophy - and can serve as an anchor for broader discussions about **machine authorship, digital ethics, and the role of humanistic inquiry in an AI-mediated world**.

---

2. Reframing Authorship in the Age of AI: A Humanities-Based Inquiry

Few academic disciplines are better positioned than the humanities to grapple with the philosophical and ethical implications of AI-generated writing. Long before generative models emerged, scholars were already interrogating the **instability of authorship, the multiplicity of textual meaning, and the tension between intention and interpretation**. Seminal works such as Roland Barthes' *"Death of the Author"* (Barthes, 1985) and Michel Foucault's *"What Is an Author?"* (Foucault, 2003) challenged the idea of the autonomous, authoritative writer, emphasizing instead the discursive systems through which texts acquire meaning.

Now, the rise of AI-generated content - produced without consciousness, intention, or lived experience - compels us to **revisit those foundational debates** in light of new technological realities. If authorship has always been a construct, AI raises the stakes by introducing **entities that write without subjectivity**, yet can mimic authorial voice with startling fluency (Bender et al., 2021; Slimi & Carballido, 2023). The result is a powerful pedagogical opportunity: to re-engage students in **an evolving inquiry into what it means to create, attribute, and interpret writing** in a machine-augmented world.

Assignment Idea: Authorship Across Human and Machine Texts

- *In this assignment, students are invited to explore authorship not as a static identity, but as a* ***contested and evolving social, philosophical, and ethical construct****. Through readings, debate, and textual comparison, students are prompted to think critically about authorship in the age of AI.*

Assignment Steps:

- *Students read excerpts from* ***Barthes (1985)*** *and* ***Foucault (2003)*** *to ground the discussion in poststructuralist theories of authorship.*
- *They are introduced to* ***contemporary ethical guidelines*** *on AI authorship, such as those from academic publishers, journals, and professional associations (Reiss, 2021; Weber-Wulff et al., 2023).*
- *Students analyze or produce* ***two types of text*** *- one human-authored (e.g., a reflective essay, article excerpt, or poem) and one AI-generated (on a similar topic or in the same genre).*
- *Using these sources, students debate questions such as:*
    - *"Is AI-generated writing 'original' if it synthesizes existing patterns but lacks intentionality?"*
    - *"Should AI tools be credited as co-authors, or merely acknowledged as instruments - like a spellchecker or search engine?"*
    - *"What does authorship mean when 'the writer' does not possess subjectivity, bias, or agency?"*
    - *"How do intellectual property laws and institutional guidelines uphold or challenge older models of authorship?"*

Discussion Goals and Learning Outcomes:

- Students learn to **contrast traditional and emerging frameworks of authorship**, connecting literary theory with practical, real-time questions facing academia and publishing.
- Students develop a **nuanced understanding of intentionality, voice, and authorship ethics** - recognizing that authorship is not merely about who typed the words, but about who shaped the meaning, accepted responsibility, and engaged in dialogue with readers.
- Students come away with the tools to **participate in ongoing debates about citation, attribution, and co-authorship in the age of AI**, informed by both critical theory and professional norms (Benjamin, 2023; Floridi & Chiriatti, 2020).

Supporting Texts to Include:

- *"The Death of the Author"* (Barthes, 1985).
- *"What Is an Author?"* (Foucault, 2003).
- *"On the Dangers of Stochastic Parrots"* (Bender et al., 2021).
- Selected journal ethics policies and publisher statements on AI use and attribution.
- Recent essays or op-eds debating AI and intellectual labor (e.g., Gulya, 2023; Noble, 2018).

By engaging with these materials, students are encouraged to think of authorship not as a relic of the past, nor as a legal checkbox, but as an **ongoing cultural negotiation** - shaped by technologies, ideologies, and shifting standards of knowledge production. AI, in this context, becomes not just a disruptor but instead a **mirror reflecting the values and contradictions already embedded in how we define authorship itself**.

---

3. Bias in AI: Humanities Perspectives on Data, Power, and Justice

Artificial intelligence systems are not built in a vacuum. They are trained on **massive datasets - often extracted from the internet, institutional archives, and commercial platforms - that mirror the hierarchies, exclusions, and inequities of human society**. These systems absorb not only linguistic patterns, but also **ideological norms, cultural assumptions, and structural biases** embedded in the data they consume. As a result, AI tools are prone to **reinforcing gender and cultural stereotypes**, often under the guise of objectivity or efficiency (Benjamin, 2023; Eubanks, 2018). For humanities, which have long examined how meaning, power, and representation shape human experience - this raises urgent questions:

- *"Whose voices and identities are centered or erased in algorithmic systems?"*
- *"What forms of knowledge are privileged?"*
- *"How do AI systems reproduce or resist the very injustices critical scholars seek to uncover?"*

These questions are not just theoretical. They have real implications for how AI shapes discourse in education, healthcare, employment, policing, and beyond. As such, they belong squarely in the humanities classroom, where **critical analysis of language, culture, and ideology** is foundational.

Example Assignment: Interrogating Bias Through Prompt Analysis

- *This assignment invites students to engage directly with generative AI tools as **objects of critical inquiry**.*
- *Rather than treating AI as a neutral assistant, students learn to examine its outputs for the **coded ideologies and implicit hierarchies** they reveal.*

Assignment Steps:

- *Students use a tool such as ChatGPT or Perplexity.ai to generate definitions or descriptions of abstract concepts - for example:*
    - *"What makes a great leader?"*
    - *"Define intelligence."*
    - *"Describe a successful entrepreneur."*
- *Students then **analyze the output through the lens of race, gender, nationality, and cultural bias**, drawing from frameworks in critical theory, feminist studies, postcolonial analysis, or media ethics.*
- *Guiding questions include:*
    - *"What patterns emerge in the AI's descriptions?"*
    - *"Are specific demographics, cultural values, or Western ideals consistently prioritized?"*
    - *"How do these representations compare with humanistic visions of justice, equity, and inclusivity?"*

- *Students produce a short analytical reflection or group presentation that identifies key themes, critiques the outputs, and proposes how more equitable training and prompt design might shift the results.*

AI in the Media Ecosystem: As generative AI becomes more embedded in the production and circulation of digital content, students must be equipped to recognize AI not simply as a **technical tool**, but as an **active participant in media ecosystems**. AI systems now play a growing role in shaping public narratives, amplifying ideological framings, and **intervening in the flow of cultural meaning** - from political messaging to internet humor to viral storytelling. Understanding these dynamics is essential to developing **critical AI literacy that engages both technological function and cultural impact** (Binns, 2018; Noble, 2018).

Students can extend their critical lens to examine how **AI-generated content contributes to misinformation ecosystems, meme culture, and platform logics**, exploring not only how AI creates content, but **how that content circulates, is perceived, and is weaponized or monetized**. Key areas of inquiry:

- **Deepfakes, Political Propaganda, and Algorithmic Amplification**. Generative AI enables the creation of **highly realistic fake videos, synthetic images, and seemingly credible news content**, which can be weaponized in political campaigns or disinformation efforts. Students can study the **life cycle of AI-generated falsehoods**: how they are produced, where they are shared, and how algorithmic platforms **prioritize, amplify, or suppress them**. This analysis prompts discussion of **media trust, truth construction, and democratic vulnerability** (Eubanks, 2018; Reiss, 2021).
- **Meme Culture and Ideological Normalization**. Students may explore how **AI-generated memes or viral text snippets** reinforce dominant ideologies or trivialize serious social issues. Through automation, meme culture accelerates the spread of **humor, misogyny, cultural appropriation**, or political mockery under the guise of satire. Analyzing meme aesthetics, language, and virality allows students to interrogate **how humor, speed, and replication obscure bias and ethical impact** (Bender et al., 2021; Gulya, 2023).
- **Platform Design and the Politics of Virality**. Beyond content itself, students can examine **how platforms such as TikTok, YouTube, Reddit, and X (formerly Twitter)** deploy recommendation algorithms that influence **which AI-generated content becomes visible, trusted, or monetized**. This includes investigating:
  - *"What kinds of AI-produced stories or visuals are more likely to go viral?"*
  - *"How do engagement metrics (clicks, shares, likes) intersect with misinformation dynamics?"*
  - *"What responsibility do platforms have for moderating synthetic content - and whose interests shape those policies?"*

Pedagogical Implications: Incorporating this interdisciplinary extension into AI literacy curricula enables students to:

- Engage with **critical media studies, digital ethics, and platform governance**;
- Develop **analytical frameworks for tracing power, influence, and discourse in AI-mediated environments**;

- Examine how AI contributes to epistemic instability while simultaneously becoming **a source of cultural legitimacy**.

Assignments might include:

- Tracing the trajectory of a viral AI-generated meme or deepfake.
- Comparing how different platforms rank or moderate synthetic content.
- Reflecting on their own consumption of AI-generated media and its effect on perception.

Scholarly Rationale: By approaching AI as a **media actor**, not just a content generator, students begin to see how technologies participate in **constructing public consciousness and shaping sociopolitical imagination** (Binns, 2018; Gulya, 2023; Noble, 2018). They are challenged not only to identify misinformation or bias but to ask:

- *"What ideologies are rendered invisible?"*
- *"Whose narratives are deplatformed or algorithmically sidelined?"*
- *"What kinds of AI outputs are made profitable, and what values do they reinforce?"*

Learning Outcome: Through this assignment, students develop both **critical AI literacy and ethical media analysis** skills. They learn to trace how **data histories, power structures, and cultural norms are encoded in algorithmic outputs**, and to evaluate how these outputs align - or conflict - with the ideals of justice, dignity, and inclusivity central to humanistic inquiry.

This analysis reveals that **AI is not just producing content - it is entangled in the political economy of attention**. It participates in shaping what people believe, fear, ridicule, or desire. This level of inquiry deepens students' understanding of **AI's cultural role and ethical stakes**, preparing them to navigate digital life with **awareness, skepticism, and a commitment to equity in information systems**. By centering these conversations in humanities education, faculty equip students not just to recognize AI bias, but to **imagine alternatives - to ask what an equitable, culturally responsive AI could look like, and what role humanists might play in shaping it**.

---

4. Exploring AI and Creativity: A Philosophical and Artistic Inquiry

As generative AI becomes increasingly adept at producing poems, screenplays, and visual compositions, educators in the arts and humanities are confronted with a powerful - and often unsettling - question:

- *"If AI can write a convincing poem, does that make it creative?" "Why or why not?"*

This philosophical prompt opens rich space for intellectual exploration across disciplines. It challenges students not only to reflect on **what AI can do**, but to articulate **what it means to create**, to feel, to risk, and to express. It draws directly on foundational questions in aesthetics, authorship, and the philosophy of mind - while remaining deeply relevant to contemporary debates in literature, media, ethics, and digital humanities (Bender et al., 2021; Floridi, 2019).

Discussion Framework: Key Questions for Exploration

- **What Constitutes Creativity?** *"Is creativity defined by novelty alone, or does it also require intentionality, emotional resonance, contextual awareness, or the capacity to take risks?" "Does surprise equal artistry, or is creative value contingent on deeper symbolic engagement?"*
- **Can Creativity Exist Without Consciousness?** *"If a machine lacks subjectivity, self-awareness, or emotional interiority, can its outputs still be considered 'creative'?" "Or is creativity inextricably tied to lived experience and the impulse to communicate meaning?"*
- **What Distinguishes Human Expression from Machine Synthesis?** *"Does the ability to generate language that mimics human patterns equate to authorship?" "Or are there aspects of human expression - ambiguity, vulnerability, memory, identity - that cannot be mechanized?"*

Application in Arts and Performance Education: In creative writing, theater, media studies, and digital humanities, faculty can design experiential assignments that allow students to engage AI as a **creative stimulus, foil, or remix partner**, while preserving the student's role as the meaning-maker. Here is a suggested assignment sequence:

- ***Generate***: *Students prompt a generative AI tool to produce a poem, short dramatic monologue, screenplay excerpt, or translation of a literary passage.*
- ***Compare***: *Students conduct a close reading of the AI-generated work alongside a human-authored counterpart, analyzing formal features, emotional tone, thematic coherence, and artistic choices. Guiding questions might include:*
  - *"What feels 'human' about this work, and what does not?"*
  - *"What emotional or cultural depths are missing or mimicked?"*
  - *"Where does the AI capture pattern, but miss meaning?"*
- ***Respond or Remix***: *Students then compose a creative response - whether in the form of a parody, inversion, continuation, or commentary - that engages critically with the AI text. This invites students to assert* ***voice, perspective, and purpose****, making visible what the AI cannot access: identity, memory, vulnerability, or embodied knowledge.*
- ***Reflect***: *Students write a brief statement addressing:*
  - *"How did engaging with AI change or clarify your understanding of creativity?"*
  - *"What limitations or possibilities do you see in machine-generated art?"*
  - *"Where do you locate human authorship within algorithmic influence?"*

Pedagogical Rationale and Outcome: This kind of assignment fosters **reflective AI literacy, creative agency, and aesthetic discernment**. Students learn that creativity is not only a product - but a **process of exploration, failure, refinement, and intention**. They experience firsthand that while AI can replicate the scaffolding of a genre, it cannot replicate the **why** behind the work - the emotional stakes, cultural inheritance, or ethical purpose.

This exploration encourages students to develop **philosophical nuance, aesthetic judgment, and cultural self-awareness**, prompting them to position AI not only as a technological development but as a **provocative interlocutor in longstanding debates about art, originality, and human nature** (Benjamin, 2023; Brookfield, 2017). By situating AI at the intersection of art, philosophy, and authorship, educators empower students to become

critical makers and reflective interpreters - equipped to engage with emerging technologies not as replacements for human creativity, but as **examiners that clarify what it means to create in a machine-augmented world**.

Sample Interdisciplinary Unit: "Interpreting the Machine"

Consider this five-week interdisciplinary unit, titled *"Interpreting the Machine,"* which is designed to engage students from the humanities, arts, social sciences, and emerging technology studies in a sustained exploration of artificial intelligence as a **cultural, philosophical, and rhetorical phenomenon**. Rather than approaching AI solely through technical or utilitarian lenses, this unit invites students to reflect on how AI technologies are reshaping core humanistic concerns: **authorship, bias, creativity, intelligence, and ethical imagination**. Drawing on a blend of foundational texts, contemporary case studies, and hands-on digital exploration, the unit cultivates **critical AI literacy** while modeling the kind of integrative, values-centered inquiry that the humanities do best (Benjamin, 2023; Selwyn, 2019).

Week 1, Introduction to Generative AI, Demonstration of ChatGPT or Perplexity.ai

- Discuss Bender et al. (2021), *"On the Dangers of Stochastic Parrots"*
- **Reflection Journal**: *"What do I assume AI can and cannot do?"*

Week 2, Language and Bias, Students Generate Prompts on Terms such as "Leader," "Immigrant," or "Success"

- Analyze outputs for implicit gendered or national biases.
- Read excerpts from Noble (2018) and Eubanks (2018) on algorithmic discrimination.
- Class discussion: *"Is algorithmic bias a technical flaw or a social mirror?"*

Week 3, Authorship and Creativity, Debate: "Can AI be a co-author?"

- Read Barthes (1985) and Foucault (2003), and examine publisher AI authorship policies.
- Analyze AI-generated poetry or essays in contrast with student-authored texts.
- Write a brief position paper on the meaning of originality in AI-generated work.

Week 4, Philosophy of Intelligence, Read Excerpts from John Searle's "Chinese Room Argument," Daniel Dennett on Consciousness, and Ada Lovelace's Letters on Mechanical Computation

- **Seminar Discussion**: *"Is AI intelligent, or just elaborate mimicry?"*
- **Reflective Writing**: *"What distinguishes human thinking?"*

Week 5, Reflective Final Project, Students Draft a Personal or Collective Manifesto Titled "The Humanities in the Age of AI"

- Share manifestos through creative formats (e.g., zine, podcast script, digital collage, open letter).

- Peer review and group discussion on where responsibility and imagination belong in the future of AI.

Learning Objectives: By the end of the unit, students will be able to:

- **Critically analyze AI-generated content** using humanistic frameworks of authorship, creativity, and ethical accountability.
- Articulate when and how **bias, data curation, and social values** shape AI's outputs and uses.
- Debate philosophical questions related to **intelligence, intention, and machine agency**.
- Reflect on the evolving role of the humanities in interpreting and shaping technological systems.

Pedagogical Rationale: This 5-Week unit positions students not merely as consumers or critics of AI, but as **interlocutors and co-authors in an unfolding dialogue** about knowledge, power, and machine cognition. Through interdisciplinary texts and interactive exercises, they develop the skills to question what appears fluent, to surface what is hidden, and to reclaim humanistic inquiry as a vital resource for the AI age (Brookfield, 2017; Floridi, 2019). By culminating in a creative, reflective manifesto, the unit honors both **the academic and the imaginative**, affirming that education in the humanities is not just about interpreting the world - but about **redefining how we live, learn, and create within it**, even as machines enter the conversation.

Section Reflection: Reclaiming Meaning-Making in the AI Era

This section situates the humanities at the very heart of the AI conversation - not as passive observers of technological change, but as active interpreters, critics, and co-creators of meaning in a machine-augmented world. Rather than retreating from generative AI, the chapter encourages humanities educators to lean in - treating AI not only as a tool to be used or resisted, but as a cultural text to be analyzed, contested, and taught through.

By framing AI outputs as artifacts embedded with bias, ideology, and rhetorical intent, the section powerfully expands the scope of humanities pedagogy. It introduces strategies that transform AI from an opaque writing assistant into a catalyst for deeper inquiry into authorship, originality, and the politics of language. Through side-by-side text analysis, authorship debates, creative remixing, and examinations of bias, students develop not just functional competence with AI, but ethical discernment, cultural critique, and reflective judgment.

Ultimately, this chapter underscores a transformative truth: AI may generate language, but it cannot replicate meaning. Meaning arises from intention, context, memory, and lived experience - all of which remain deeply human. As the humanities guide students through this evolving landscape, they assert their enduring relevance and ethical purpose: to help society interpret, imagine, and shape a future where language is not only automated - but understood, valued, and owned with care.

Section 3: AI in the Social Sciences - Data, Decision-Making, and Power

Artificial intelligence systems are not neutral tools of efficiency; they are deeply entwined with the ways institutions govern, distribute resources, and define legitimacy. For students in sociology, political science, economics, anthropology, criminology, and communication studies, **AI literacy is therefore not just about learning technical concepts, but about interrogating the institutional logics and social consequences of algorithmic decision-making** (Benjamin, 2023; Eubanks, 2018; Noble, 2018).

In these disciplines, AI shapes who receives bail, how job applications are filtered, which neighborhoods are policed, what news circulates, and how financial credit is granted. Social science education must prepare students to move beyond asking whether AI is accurate or efficient and instead ask deeper questions: *"Whose priorities are embedded in this system?" "What assumptions structure its decisions?" "Who benefits, and who is made invisible?"*

This section adapts the four-part framework of AI literacy introduced in Section 1 - functional, applied, critical, and reflective - specifically for the social sciences. It will show how:

- **Functional literacy** enables students to grasp core concepts such as predictive modeling, risk scoring, or recommendation algorithms as they operate in policy and institutional contexts.
- **Applied literacy** develops through hands-on projects where students experiment with real-world datasets and examine how small changes in variables alter outcomes.
- **Critical literacy** asks students to analyze the power dynamics and institutional goals embedded in systems such as predictive policing, hiring platforms, or media recommendation engines.
- **Reflective literacy** prompts students to consider how AI is reshaping governance, accountability, and what it means to be a citizen in algorithmically mediated societies.

By framing AI literacy in this way, social science faculty can equip students not just to critique AI outputs, but to interrogate the systems and assumptions behind them. This positions students as future researchers, policymakers, and civic leaders who are prepared to challenge, reform, and reimagine how intelligent systems are used in public life.

---

1. Functional AI Literacy in the Social Sciences

At its foundation, functional AI literacy equips social science students with the conceptual vocabulary and technical grounding needed to critically analyze how AI systems operate within governance, economics, and society. This is not about turning sociology majors into coders or political scientists into machine learning engineers. Instead, it is about giving students the tools to ask **how these systems work, what assumptions they encode, and how those assumptions shape institutional outcomes** (Floridi & Chiriatti, 2020; Selwyn, 2019).

Core Concepts for Social Science Contexts

Students must be introduced to key terms and mechanisms, but always situated in policy and institutional practice:

- **Predictive Modeling.** Many systems in criminal justice, healthcare, and finance rely on statistical models that forecast future behavior (e.g., likelihood of recidivism, probability of loan default). Functional literacy requires students to see predictive scores not as "facts," but as probabilistic estimates built on past data.
- **Risk Scoring.** Tools such as credit scoring or school accountability metrics assign individuals or organizations numerical "risk" labels. Students must understand both how these numbers are generated and how they shift responsibility from human actors to automated systems.
- **Training Data.** AI outputs are only as representative as the data they learn from. In social systems, training data often excludes marginalized groups or encodes institutional bias (Benjamin, 2023; Eubanks, 2018). Understanding this helps students critique "neutral" systems that reproduce inequality.
- **The Black Box Problem.** In deep learning and other complex systems, even developers cannot always explain how an algorithm arrived at a given output. Students need to grapple with the implications for transparency, accountability, and due process (Doshi-Velez & Kim, 2017).

Example (Criminology):

- *In a criminal justice technology seminar, students examine how a bail decision system produces a numerical "risk of reoffending" score* (Angwin et al., 2022).
- **The Instructor Walks Them Through**:
  - ***"What Data are Used?"*** *Prior arrests, employment status, and housing history.*
  - ***"How are Those Features Weighted?"*** *Certain patterns are emphasized, while others are ignored.*
  - ***"What Assumptions are Baked In?"*** *Past contact with law enforcement predicts future behavior, regardless of context.*
  - ***"Who is Accountable if the System is Wrong?"*** *Judges may defer to the algorithm, even when it contradicts their own judgment.*
- Through this exercise, students see that the problem is not simply whether the system is "accurate" or not, but how institutional design choices shift accountability from humans to machines, and what that means for justice.

Example (Political Science):

- *In a public policy course, students analyze an AI model designed to predict which neighborhoods should receive additional policing resources.*
- *By examining the training data, they discover it was drawn primarily from historical arrest records.*
- **This Sparks Discussion**:
  - *"Does the model truly predict crime?" or*
  - *"Does it reproduce the geography of past enforcement?"*
- **Such Inquiry Reframes AI from a Question of Accuracy to a Question of Institutional Goals**:
  - *"Is the tool optimizing safety?" or*

- *"Optimizing efficiency within an already unequal system?"*

Why This Matters: Functional literacy in the social sciences is not simply about teaching the language of algorithms. It is about giving students the tools to connect the mechanics of AI to the **policies and power structures that deploy it.** In this way, students learn to interrogate not just outputs, but design choices: *"Why was this model trained in this way?" "What institution benefits from its predictions?" "Who loses visibility or voice?"*

By embedding this approach into introductory and advanced coursework, faculty help students see that AI is not a mysterious black box operating "out there." It is a set of technical and institutional choices that they, as future policymakers, advocates, or analysts, will one day have the power to critique, contest, or redesign (Boyd & Crawford, 2012; O'Neil, 2017).

---

2. Applied AI Literacy in the Social Sciences

While functional AI literacy provides students with the conceptual grounding to understand **how** systems operate, applied AI literacy places them in direct interaction with those systems. The aim is not to make students passive users of AI tools, but to help them experience firsthand how institutional assumptions and data design shape algorithmic outputs. By working with simplified models, datasets, and public-facing AI applications, students can move beyond theoretical critique and grapple with the concrete ways that algorithmic choices alter decisions in finance, health, governance, and media (Boyd & Crawford, 2012; O'Neil, 2017).

From Tools to Contextual Experiments

Applied literacy in the social sciences involves carefully structured exercises where students use AI outputs as case studies for critical reflection:

- **Experimentation with Real-World Data.** Students should manipulate simplified datasets to see how altering inputs changes results. For example, adjusting variables such as neighborhood income levels or educational attainment can reveal how predictive models embed particular assumptions about risk and opportunity.
- **Cross-Tool Comparisons.** By comparing the same query across multiple AI systems - such as ChatGPT, Perplexity, or domain-specific policy dashboards - students can identify where outputs diverge and ask why.
- **Simulation of Institutional Scenarios.** Students can role-play as policymakers, judges, or journalists who must decide whether to trust or contest an AI tool's recommendation. This bridges technical critique with civic accountability.

Example (Political Science or Public Policy)

- *In a policy analysis course, students use a simplified housing application dataset in Google Colab or Orange.*
- **Students Run a Predictive Classification Model**:
  - *"Who will be approved for affordable housing when altering one variable at a time?"*
    - *ZIP code.*
    - *Household income.*

        - *Education level.*
        - *Occupation.*
- **Observe**:
    - *"How does the model shift eligibility predictions?"*
- **Debrief Questions**:
    - *"Does the model reward certain demographics over others?"*
    - *"Are predictions about 'eligibility' actually predictions about social worthiness?"*
    - *"Who benefits if these outputs guide resource allocation, and who is systematically excluded?"*
- This exercise reframes accuracy as only one part of the story; **the more important insight lies in recognizing how institutional logic shapes model design**.

Example (Communication Studies)

- *In a media literacy class, students generate AI summaries of trending political stories using a conversational AI tool.*
- **Students Then**:
    - *Compare the AI summary to original reporting from multiple outlets.*
    - *Identify which perspectives were foregrounded or erased.*
    - **Analyze the Stylistic Neutrality of the AI Output**:
        - *"Does 'neutral tone' itself conceal particular institutional values?"*
- **Through This Applied AI Literacy Work**:
    - *Students begin to see AI not only as a tool for speed, but as a cultural actor shaping how publics interpret political reality* (Noble, 2018; Crawford, 2021).

Example (Economics)

- *In an applied econometrics seminar, students examine an algorithm designed to forecast loan default risk.*
- **Students Discover:**
    - *The training dataset overrepresents certain industries while underrepresenting others.*
- **The Instructor Prompts Students to Ask**:
    - *"Is this truly a model of 'risk,' or a proxy for institutional confidence in specific economic sectors?"*
    - *"How do omissions in data availability alter predictions about borrowers?"*
    - *"What policy interventions might address these gaps before relying on such a tool in practice?"*
- **Applied AI Literacy Positions Students**:
    - *To connect technical modeling to broader questions of equity, accountability, and institutional responsibility* (Floridi & Chiriatti, 2020).

Why This Matters: Applied literacy demonstrates that **AI systems are not simply "right or wrong," but contextually constructed**. Students learn to critique outputs as artifacts of design, training, and institutional purpose. By embedding structured experimentation into coursework, faculty help students develop the capacity to interrogate automation not as an external inevitability, but as a series of choices made by institutions - choices that can, and must, be scrutinized, revised, or resisted.

3. Critical AI Literacy in the Social Sciences

Critical AI literacy asks students to move beyond **how AI works** or **how to use it** toward examining how AI reshapes systems of power, decision-making, and accountability. **In the social sciences, this means situating AI technologies within broader structures of governance, economics, and knowledge production**. Students must recognize that AI is not neutral: it encodes institutional assumptions, serves particular interests, and often shifts responsibility away from human actors onto seemingly "objective" models (Benjamin, 2023; Eubanks, 2018; Noble, 2018).

By cultivating this literacy, faculty help students interrogate AI as both a technical system and a political actor. **The aim is to teach learners not simply to critique outputs, but to ask deeper questions about design, oversight, and the narratives institutions construct around "efficiency" and "objectivity."**

Interrogating Algorithmic Bias as Systemic Design

Bias in AI is not just a data issue - it reflects design choices and institutional priorities. Social science students must be taught to ask: "*Whose values shaped the algorithm?*" "*Which outcomes were prioritized?*" "*Whose risks were deemed acceptable?*"

Example (Criminology Course):

- *Students analyze a pretrial risk assessment tool such as COMPAS* (Angwin et al., 2022).
- *Rather than only debating disparities in false positives, students focus on the institutional goals the tool was designed to optimize:*
    - *Reducing jail populations.*
    - *Cutting costs.*
    - *Minimizing recidivism risk.*
- **Students Then Ask**:
    - *Whether these goals align with broader commitments to justice and accountability or*
    - *Whether they sideline community well-being in favor of efficiency* (Angwin et al., 2022; O'Neil, 2017).

This reframes critique **away from focusing narrowly on whether an individual AI output is "right" or "wrong." Instead, the emphasis shifts toward examining the broader systems, assumptions, and institutional goals embedded in the technology**. In doing so, the conversation becomes less about isolated errors and more about structural accountability - how algorithms shape decisions, distribute consequences, and reinforce particular values.

Examining Surveillance and Data Governance

AI systems in social sciences often involve surveillance: predictive policing, welfare monitoring, or media tracking. These technologies raise questions not only about accuracy, but about legitimacy and consent.

Example (Political Science or Public Policy):

- *Students explore how city governments use predictive analytics to allocate police patrols.*
- **Next, Students**:
    - *Map the institutional assumptions behind "high-risk" areas.*
    - *Examine whose data is collected.*
    - **And Ask**:
        - *"Who governs the governors?"*
        - *"What checks exist to prevent mission creep?"*
        - *"How transparent is the logic to the public?"*

AI literacy in public policy extends far beyond improving technical models or collecting cleaner datasets - it is fundamentally about protecting civic rights and ensuring democratic accountability. Policymakers and students must learn to ask not only whether an algorithm is efficient, but also whether it is transparent, equitable, and aligned with public values (Crawford, 2021). By framing AI as a civic issue rather than merely a technical one, this lens highlights the responsibility of democratic institutions to safeguard fairness, accountability, and citizen trust in an increasingly automated society (Floridi, 2019).

AI as a Force in Shaping Public Discourse

In communication and sociology courses, students can explore how recommendation algorithms set the agenda for news, culture, and politics. Here, critical literacy emphasizes not whether content is factually correct, but how algorithmic amplification alters what citizens see, trust, and act upon.

Example (Communication Studies):

- *Students use tools such as CrowdTangle or Hoaxy to analyze how AI-driven recommendation systems spread AI-generated misinformation.*
- **The Exercise Asks**:
    - *"Who benefits financially from virality?"*
    - *"Whose perspectives are silenced when content moderation algorithms mislabel legitimate speech?"*
    - *"What institutional pressures shape which 'truths' are amplified?"*

This reframes media critique beyond the narrow lens of fact-checking, shifting attention to how AI systems structure visibility, attention, and influence online. Rather than asking only whether a claim is true or false, students must interrogate how algorithms amplify certain voices, suppress others, and shape public discourse itself (Cinelli et al., 2021). In doing so, AI literacy becomes a study of governance and media power - revealing the institutional and structural dynamics that determine not just what information circulates, but whose knowledge is legitimized or erased (Noble, 2018).

Fostering Civic and Ethical Agency

Critical AI literacy ultimately means teaching students that they are not passive recipients of technology. They are stakeholders, advocates, and future decision-makers who can demand different design principles and accountability structures. Faculty can foster this by:

- Assigning **policy memos** that critique current AI use and propose reforms.
- Hosting **structured debates** where students inhabit the roles of policymakers, data scientists, and citizens.
- Encouraging **reflection papers** that connect algorithmic critique to professional codes of ethics in law, public health, or journalism.

Through these practices, students come to recognize that engaging critically with AI is not a peripheral skill but a foundational responsibility of modern scholarship. They see that democratic participation and professional integrity both require the ability to interrogate how systems work, whose interests they serve, and what assumptions they embed (Brookfield, 2017). In this way, questioning AI becomes not an optional add-on to learning, but a core practice for sustaining ethical, reflective, and socially accountable engagement in every sphere of life (Selwyn, 2019).

From Neutrality Myth to Accountability Practice

Critical AI literacy reframes the social sciences' role in AI education: not to teach algorithms as neutral tools, but to interrogate them as contested sites of power and policy. Students leave with the capacity to ask:

- *"Whose goals are these systems designed to serve?"*
- *"Whose harms are overlooked in the name of efficiency?"*
- *"Where should human judgment override machine prediction?"*

By embedding these questions directly into curricula, **educators shift the frame from passive use of AI toward active scrutiny of its design and deployment**. Students begin to recognize that what often feels like **an untouchable "black box" is in fact a system created, maintained, and shaped by human choices and institutional priorities**. This reframing gives learners the agency to hold AI accountable, not just as future professionals but as informed citizens capable of questioning power and advocating for ethical alternatives.

---

4. Reflective AI Literacy in the Social Sciences

Reflective AI literacy invites students to step back from immediate critiques of bias or functionality and instead ask meta-level questions: *"How is AI reshaping the very way knowledge, authority, and responsibility are defined in society?"* In the social sciences, this means examining AI not only as a technical innovation but rather as a force that reconfigures epistemology, professional practice, and democratic governance (Floridi, 2019; Selwyn, 2019).

This reflective stance cultivates epistemic humility - recognizing that the categories, values, and judgments embedded in AI may shift the boundaries of entire disciplines. Students are encouraged to interrogate not only what AI does, but what it does **to** social science inquiry itself.

AI and the Redefinition of Evidence

One reflection point for the social sciences is the status of evidence itself. When algorithms generate insights by detecting statistical patterns across massive datasets, the definition of what counts as valid social evidence begins to shift away from traditional methods of observation, ethnography, or small-sample analysis. **This raises critical questions for students and researchers:** *"Are correlations discovered by machines equivalent to causal explanations, and how should they be weighed against the contextual depth and interpretive nuance that human-centered methods provide?"*

Example (Sociology Course):

- *Students compare an ethnographic study of urban poverty with an AI-generated predictive model of housing insecurity.*
- **They Ask**:
  - *"Which realities are visible in the quantitative model?"*
  - *"Which experiences are erased?"*
  - *"What assumptions about causality or human behavior does each method reinforce?"*

This comparison emphasizes that reflective AI literacy is about more than "accuracy." It is about how disciplines define legitimate knowledge and what consequences arise when machine-driven proxies replace human narratives (Benjamin, 2023; Eubanks, 2018).

Authority and Delegated Judgment

AI also challenges traditional notions of authority in law, economics, and governance. When decision-making is delegated to algorithms, reflective literacy requires students to ask: "*Who is ultimately accountable for choices made by systems?" "How do institutions shift responsibility from human actors to technological proxies?"*

Example (Public Policy Seminar):

- *Students analyze a case where an automated benefits eligibility system denies access to public services.*
- **The Reflection Exercise Asks**:
  - *"Is the government official, the vendor, or the algorithm itself responsible for the decision?"*
  - *"What does this outsourcing reveal about how institutions understand authority and accountability?"*

By exploring these questions, students learn that AI literacy extends far beyond the mechanics of spotting system errors or inaccuracies. They begin to **understand that institutions adopt AI tools not only to streamline tasks but also to reshape authority, decision-making processes, and the boundaries of professional responsibility.** This awareness positions students to critically evaluate how AI alters institutional roles and to engage in discussions about accountability, transparency, and the values embedded in organizational choices.

Reflecting on Social Science Methodologies

AI is increasingly used to analyze social behavior through sentiment analysis, network mapping, and predictive analytics. Reflective AI literacy asks: "*What is lost when human meaning-making is translated into machine-readable patterns?" "What aspects of social life resist algorithmic capture?"*

Example (Anthropology Course):

- *Students compare a machine-generated sentiment analysis of protest slogans with anthropological field notes from the same event.*
- **They Reflect On**:
    - o *How cultural nuance, irony, and embodied experience disappear when filtered through an algorithm.*

This activity underscores the importance of disciplinary reflexivity by drawing attention to how AI tools shape the research process itself. **Students come to recognize that the influence of AI extends beyond producing results - it alters the framing of inquiry, determining which questions are even considered valid.** By reflecting on this dynamic, learners develop a deeper awareness of how technology can silently redirect intellectual focus, highlighting the need for ongoing critical vigilance.

Teaching Reflective Inquiry as a Civic Skill

Ultimately, reflective AI literacy prepares students not just as scholars, but as citizens. **By examining how AI reframes evidence, accountability, and authority, they develop the capacity to critique institutions and demand transparency**. Reflection turns AI from a technical concern into a civic issue, positioning students as actors who can question not just outputs, but the design of systems that increasingly govern public life (Brookfield, 2017; Selwyn, 2019).

Reframing Reflective Knowledge in an AI Era

Reflective AI literacy in the social sciences moves beyond evaluating whether AI outputs are "right" or "wrong." Instead, it emphasizes asking:

- *"How is AI reshaping what counts as knowledge?"*
- *"Whose authority is being transferred to machines?"*
- *"How do institutions use AI to reinforce or redefine their goals?"*

By equipping students with these reflective skills, **educators cultivate scholars who can see AI not only as a technical instrument but instead as a cultural and political force that demands interrogation**. This prepares students to become critical stewards of knowledge - capable of holding systems accountable, while reimagining what just, inclusive, and human-centered decision-making might look like in the algorithmic age.

Pedagogical Pathways for Social Science AI Education

Teaching AI literacy in the social sciences requires more than abstract critique; it demands structured pedagogical strategies that help students connect theory to practice, and reflection to action. Faculty can create learning environments where students not only examine the assumptions and institutional goals embedded in AI systems but also test their insights through applied projects, collaborative problem-solving, and ethical self-examination.

This part of Section 3 introduces three complementary approaches for embedding AI literacy into social science curricula. First, **Applied Strategies for Teaching AI Literacy in**

Social Science Classrooms explores concrete teaching practices that bring algorithmic systems into everyday assignments and discussions. Second, **Capstone and Project-Based Learning in the Social Sciences** highlights ways for students to engage AI through deeper, integrative projects that connect technical critique with policy and civic impact. Finally, **Reflective Practices and Ethical Self-Awareness in Social Science AI Education** emphasizes the importance of cultivating critical reflection and ethical responsibility, ensuring that students see themselves not just as analysts of AI, but as future stewards of its role in society.

---

1. Applied Strategies for Teaching AI Literacy in Social Science Classrooms

Integrating AI literacy into the social sciences requires more than theoretical lectures; it demands practice-based learning that situates AI tools within the lived realities of governance, economics, media, and civic life. Applied strategies invite students to use, critique, and redesign AI systems while continually asking: *"Whose goals are encoded?" "What assumptions drive these outputs?" "How do institutions leverage AI to shift accountability?"*

These exercises move beyond teaching whether AI outputs are "true" or "false." They instead emphasize that **AI must be understood as a system of institutional power, designed with particular goals, constraints, and assumptions that shape its outcomes**. By reframing AI this way, students learn to interrogate not just the accuracy of outputs but the broader social consequences, governance structures, and design logics that underpin algorithmic decision-making.

Strategy 1: Case-Based Policy Analysis

Case studies give students an opportunity to evaluate how AI shapes public decision-making in concrete, contextualized ways. By analyzing scenarios in which algorithms influence policy, resource distribution, or civic life, students begin to see the practical stakes of technological design. This process transforms abstract critiques of AI into applied inquiries about governance, accountability, and social responsibility.

Example (Political Science):

- *Students review a predictive policing case where an algorithm allocates patrol resources.*
- *Rather than asking only if the algorithm was "accurate"*
- **They Analyze**:
  - *"Which institutional goals drove its design?"*
  - *"Who benefits from its implementation?"*
  - *"What accountability structures exist when errors occur?"*

Assignments culminate in a short policy memo where students move from critique to constructive reform, linking theoretical analysis to actionable proposals. **This exercise demonstrates that responsible AI literacy extends beyond measuring accuracy or technical performance; it requires grappling with the institutional and societal contexts in which AI systems operate**. By situating their recommendations within broader policy frameworks, students learn that real accountability comes from shaping governance structures, not simply from debugging algorithms (Boyd & Crawford, 2012; O'Neil, 2017).

Strategy 2: Algorithmic Systems Mapping

System maps help students move beyond abstract critiques and into a visual analysis of how AI operates within broader institutional networks. By mapping out the actors, data flows, and accountability gaps, students can see how decisions are distributed across organizations rather than residing in a single algorithm. This practice fosters a deeper understanding of the layered complexity behind AI decision-making, encouraging students to identify where human oversight, policy intervention, or ethical review might be most urgently needed.

Example (Economics or Public Policy):

- *Students build a flow diagram of an unemployment benefits algorithm.*
- **They Identify**:
    - *Data inputs (employment history, demographic details).*
    - *Institutional actors (government agencies, software vendors, claimants).*
    - *Decision points where accountability shifts from human oversight to automated logic.*

Assignments require students to write reflective essays that move beyond surface critique. In these essays, students are prompted to ask questions such as: "*What values are embedded in this system?*" "*Where are citizens most vulnerable to error or misclassification?*" By engaging with these questions, students learn to uncover the hidden assumptions behind algorithmic design and to recognize the ways automation encodes institutional priorities. This process makes visible the non-neutral architecture of AI, highlighting that every model reflects choices about data, values, and power (Benjamin, 2023; Selwyn, 2019).

Strategy 3: Cross-Tool Comparison Projects

Different AI tools embed different institutional assumptions, reflecting the goals, values, and constraints of the organizations that design them. For instance, a hiring algorithm may prioritize efficiency and cost reduction, while a medical triage system might emphasize risk minimization and liability protection. By designing assignments that compare and critique outputs across tools, students can uncover these hidden assumptions and develop a more nuanced understanding of how institutional priorities shape algorithmic behavior.

Example (Communication Studies):

- *Students run the same political news prompt through ChatGPT, Perplexity.ai, and Google's AI-powered search.*
- **They Then Compare**:
    - *What narratives were emphasized or excluded?*
    - *How authority was framed (citations, tone, confidence).*
    - *Which assumptions about credibility shaped each tool's design?*

Debrief discussions emphasize that **AI outputs should not be viewed simply as the results of "better" or "worse" algorithms. Instead, they must be understood as reflections of the institutional priorities, commercial incentives, and regulatory environments that shape how data is collected, filtered, and applied**. By surfacing these structural influences, students learn to see AI systems as deeply entangled with broader political economies of technology, rather than as neutral computational tools (Crawford, 2021).

Strategy 4: Role-Play and Stakeholder Debate

Role-play simulations teach students to see AI not as a detached technical process, but as part of larger institutional ecosystems. In these exercises, participants assume roles such as policymakers, administrators, or affected citizens, which highlights the competing priorities and values that shape how AI is deployed. By navigating these tensions in a structured scenario, students come to recognize that AI operates within contested environments where accountability, power, and institutional assumptions are always in play.

Example (Anthropology or Criminology):

- *In a classroom debate, students adopt the roles of a policymaker, community activist, software engineer, and journalist responding to an algorithmic fraud detection system in welfare programs.*
- **Each Must Argue**:
  - *For or against continued use focusing on the trade-offs of:*
    - *Efficiency.*
    - *Transparency.*
    - *Accountability.*

This exercise surfaces tensions between values such as justice, efficiency, and privacy, showing students that AI systems rarely optimize for all priorities at once. By requiring them to weigh competing perspectives, it highlights the trade-offs that lie at the heart of public decision-making and algorithmic design. In doing so, **students practice the kind of critical balancing that defines social science inquiry, where complexity, nuance, and conflicting goals must be navigated rather than reduced to simple answers** (Brookfield, 2017.

Strategy 5: Reflexive Journaling and Ethical Inquiry

Applied work must be paired with ongoing reflection to prevent critique from remaining at the surface level. Without structured opportunities for students to pause, document their reasoning, and question their assumptions, assignments risk becoming mere technical exercises. Reflection deepens the learning process, transforming practical engagement with AI into a critical inquiry about its institutional goals, ethical implications, and broader social impact.

Example (Sociology):

- *Students maintain journals responding weekly to prompts.*
- **Such As**:

- *"When did you notice AI shifting responsibility from humans to systems?"*
- *"What assumptions did the AI outputs reflect about human behavior?"*
- *"If you redesigned the system, what institutional goals would you prioritize differently?"*

This reflection builds the habit of interrogating AI as a socio-technical actor, reminding students that algorithms are not neutral but shaped by human choices, institutional goals, and data histories. **By questioning how systems are designed and deployed, students learn to see AI less as an authority and more as a participant in shaping social processes**. Over time, this habit cultivates a disposition of skepticism and inquiry, equipping learners to challenge assumptions rather than accept outputs at face value (Slimi & Carballido, 2023).

---

2. Capstone and Project-Based Learning in the Social Sciences

Capstone projects and long-term applied assignments provide one of the richest opportunities for students to grapple with AI's role in governance, economics, and public life. Unlike short exercises, capstone work allows them to connect theory, data, and real-world systems, while practicing the habits of accountability and critical interrogation that AI literacy demands. **The aim is to move beyond** *"Can the model make accurate predictions?"* **and instead focus on** *"Whose interests are encoded in the model's design?" "What institutional structures does it serve?" "How should accountability be distributed when harm occurs?"*

Model 1: Algorithmic Impact Audits

Students conduct semester-long audits of AI systems currently deployed in public institutions, workplaces, or media platforms. These audits require them to analyze not just technical functionality, but also the institutional goals, data sources, and governance structures that shape how the system operates. By sustaining this work across a full term, **students learn to see AI not as a one-off output generator, but as an ongoing socio-technical actor with long-term consequences for decision-making, accountability, and civic life**.

Example (Criminology/Public Policy):

- *Teams analyze a risk-assessment algorithm used in pretrial detention.*
- **Their Deliverables Include**:
  - *Mapping stakeholders (judges, defendants, policymakers, software vendors).*
  - *Identifying embedded assumptions about "risk."*
  - *Proposing accountability measures, such as independent oversight boards or mandatory audit reports.*

This mirrors the kinds of impact assessments that professionals are increasingly required to conduct in fields such as public policy, social services, and corporate governance. By engaging in these structured evaluations, **students learn to critique AI not only for its technical bias but also for the broader institutional consequences it produces - shaping equity, accountability, and access to resources** (Eubanks, 2018; Selwyn, 2019). In this way, classroom assignments begin to function as training grounds for real-world oversight, preparing students to hold both technologies and the organizations that deploy them to account.

Model 2: Policy Toolkit Development

Capstone projects can also produce practical resources that extend beyond the classroom, offering policymakers, nonprofits, or community organizations tangible tools for decision-making. For example, students might design ethical auditing frameworks, create public-facing guides on algorithmic accountability, or compile policy briefs that synthesize academic research with community concerns. **These outputs not only demonstrate applied mastery but also position students as contributors to civic knowledge and institutional practice, bridging academic inquiry with real-world impact.**

Example (Political Science/Sociology):

- *Students design a "Community Toolkit for Algorithmic Transparency."*
- **Students Include:**
    - Plain-language guides to how credit scoring or housing algorithms work.
    - Templates for community organizations to request algorithmic disclosures.
    - Policy recommendations for improving transparency in local governance.

Such projects push students to move beyond critique alone by emphasizing the importance of proposing workable alternatives. In doing so, they learn that responsible AI literacy involves not only identifying institutional flaws but also imagining how those systems might be reshaped to better serve public needs. **This coupling of critique with reform situates their learning within a broader framework of civic engagement and professional responsibility, preparing them to contribute constructively to debates about AI's role in society** (Brookfield, 2017; Noble, 2018).

Model 3: Cross-Disciplinary Research Collaborations

Capstone projects can pair social science students with peers in computer science or data science to combine critique with design. **When interdisciplinary teams collaborate, they not only identify institutional consequences of AI but also experiment with practical alternatives that embody more ethical design principles**. This dual emphasis ensures that graduates leave with the ability both to interrogate existing systems and to envision responsible, innovative replacements that serve civic and professional goals (Brookfield, 2017; Slimi & Carballido, 2023).

Example (Economics + Data Science):

- *Mixed teams redesign a financial loan evaluation algorithm. Some students will be Economists; some will be Data Scientists.*
- *Economists surface fairness and accessibility issues.*
- *Data Scientists adjust variables and weighting.*
- **Together, They Propose a System With**:
    - *Built-in oversight mechanisms.*
        - *Transparency dashboards.*
        - *Applicant appeals processes.*

These collaborations highlight the epistemological friction that arises when different disciplines approach the same AI-related problem from distinct angles. For instance, a computer scientist might emphasize model efficiency and technical precision, while a sociologist prioritizes equity, governance, and lived experience. By working through these tensions, students see that accountability in **AI cannot be reduced to one framework - it requires negotiation across disciplinary perspectives, integrating technical accuracy with social responsibility** (Floridi et al., 2018; Benjamin, 2023).

Model 4: Public-Facing Capstones

Students present their findings not only to faculty but also to authentic audiences, such as community partners, nonprofit organizations, or policy groups. **This practice reinforces accountability by requiring students to explain their critiques in clear, accessible language and to engage with stakeholders who may be directly affected by algorithmic systems**. Presenting beyond the classroom turns AI literacy projects into public-facing scholarship, bridging academic analysis with civic impact and professional responsibility.

Example (Communication Studies):

- A team studying algorithmic misinformation develops a public webinar explaining how AI shapes election coverage on social media.
- The event includes live demonstrations of content amplification and a Q&A session with local journalists and community members.

This public-facing dimension emphasizes that AI literacy cannot remain confined within classrooms or academic silos. **When students present their work to community members, policymakers, or nonprofit leaders, they practice translating complex critiques of automation into language that informs civic debate and decision-making**. In doing so, they come to understand AI literacy as both an academic competency and a civic responsibility: the obligation to **help society recognize, question, and hold accountable the systems** that increasingly shape collective life (Gulya, 2023).

Assessment and Reflection

Capstone assessments should move beyond evaluating the final product to emphasize the **process of critical engagement**. In AI literacy projects, what matters is not only whether students can identify system flaws, but whether they can interrogate the institutional contexts, values, and consequences shaping those systems. Assessment, therefore, must highlight four dimensions:

- **Transparency in documenting how AI was analyzed.** Students should clearly show the prompts, outputs, data sources, and evaluative steps they used. Transparency makes their reasoning traceable and prevents the temptation to present critique without evidence.
- **Depth of stakeholder and institutional critique.** Strong projects identify which institutions designed or deployed the system, whose interests were prioritized, and

whose needs were overlooked. This requires connecting technical outputs to broader organizational goals and incentives.

- **Practicality of reform proposals.** Students should be challenged to translate critique into action. This may include policy recommendations, institutional guidelines, or design adjustments that address the issues identified. Proposals need not be fully implementable, but they should be feasible, specific, and attuned to disciplinary and civic realities.
- **Reflexivity.** Perhaps the most important dimension is the student's capacity to reflect on how their own assumptions evolved through the project. *"Did they begin by assuming the system was neutral, only to realize its embedded politics?" "Did they underestimate the difficulty of balancing efficiency with fairness?"* Reflexivity demonstrates that students have grown not only as analysts but as professionals preparing to engage responsibly with AI systems.

Final reflection essays can serve as a culminating assessment tool. Prompts might include:

- *"What institutional goals did the system serve?"*
- *"Where should accountability be placed - on the designer, the deployer, the regulator, or the user?"*
- *"What role should you, as a future professional, play in shaping or resisting such systems?"*

By asking these questions, the reflection shifts assessment away from a narrow evaluation of technical accuracy and toward an exploration of ethical responsibility and civic agency. **Students leave not only with stronger disciplinary knowledge but also with the habit of interrogating automation as a socio-technical actor** - an approach that prepares them for leadership in both professional and democratic contexts (Brookfield, 2017; Selwyn, 2019; Eubanks, 2018).

Capstones as Training for Accountability

Capstone and project-based learning make visible what shorter assignments cannot: the structural nature of AI systems. **By requiring students to map institutions, design reform proposals, and communicate findings beyond the classroom, these projects reframe AI literacy as accountability training.** Students graduate not as passive evaluators of "accuracy," but as critical thinkers prepared to navigate and reshape the systems that will govern their professions and communities.

---

3. Reflective Practices and Ethical Self-Awareness in Social Science AI Education

If capstone projects allow students to interrogate AI systems at the institutional level, reflective practices bring the work inward - helping students surface their own assumptions, biases, and ethical positioning as participants in an algorithmic society. Reflection transforms AI literacy from a technical skillset into a civic and professional disposition: the habit of pausing, questioning, and articulating values before acting on machine-generated suggestions. At its core, reflective practice pushes students to ask: *"What role do I play in shaping how AI is used?" "How does my positionality affect what I see in an algorithm?" "Where am I complicit in accepting convenience over accountability?"*

Journaling as Metacognitive Practice

Structured journaling provides students with an ongoing record of their engagements with AI tools, allowing them to track both successes and challenges over time. This continuity encourages students to revisit earlier reflections, compare them with later entries, and recognize patterns in their learning and ethical growth. **By treating the journal as a living document, students build a habit of critical observation and accountability**, deepening their awareness of how AI systems influence their choices, assumptions, and professional development.

Example (Political Science Course):

- *Students maintain a weekly "AI Reflection Log" in which they document:*
  - *The AI tools they used for coursework or research.*
  - *Where outputs aligned with their goals and where they failed.*
  - *What institutional assumptions did they notice (e.g., about what counts as "risk," "efficiency," or "objectivity")?*
  - *How they decided whether to trust or reject the output.*

Over the semester, these journals evolve into more than simple logs of activity - they become mirrors of students' growing ethical awareness and capacity for self-critique. Each entry provides evidence of how their thinking shifts when confronted with the tensions between human judgment and machine output, helping them articulate not only what they did but why they made particular choices. In this way, **reflective journaling reinforces that AI literacy is not just about tool proficiency but about *thinking about thinking* in the presence of machine partners, cultivating metacognitive habits essential for ethical and responsible practice** (Brookfield, 2017).

Reflexive Essays on Assumptions and Accountability

Short reflective essays provide a structured space for students to pause and reconsider their own relationship with AI. Rather than limiting their focus to whether a system "worked well" or "performed poorly," these essays encourage them to interrogate deeper epistemic questions, such as: *"What counts as evidence when algorithms are involved?" "Who decides what is trustworthy knowledge?" "What are the broader implications of delegating decision-making to machines?"* By moving beyond surface-level evaluations, these essays **help students connect their individual experiences with AI to larger issues of knowledge construction, disciplinary values, and institutional accountability**. In doing so, reflection becomes not just a record of use but a practice of critical inquiry - pushing students to articulate how AI is reshaping the very foundations of knowledge and authority in their field.

Example (Anthropology or Sociology):

- *Students write a midterm essay responding to the prompts:*

   - *"What assumptions about human behavior are embedded in the AI systems you have studied this semester?"*
   - *"Who benefits from these assumptions, and who bears the risk if they are wrong?"*

This approach encourages students to push their analysis beyond the technical accuracy of outputs, asking instead what cultural assumptions, institutional priorities, or political values shaped the system in the first place. **By linking technical systems to broader disciplinary critiques of power, culture, and design, students learn that AI always encodes a worldview - even when presented as neutral or objective** (Selwyn, 2019; Benjamin, 2023). **The critical shift, then, is not in asking** *"Was the AI right?"* **but in recognizing the deeper question:** *"What worldview does this AI assume - and do I accept, challenge, or reframe it?"* This reframing positions AI literacy as an exercise in civic and ethical judgment, where students must locate themselves as participants in shaping, questioning, and contesting automated systems.

Dialogic Reflection: Structured Conversations

Reflection can also take collective form. When structured as facilitated dialogues, it allows students to bring their private reflections into conversation with others, testing assumptions in a shared space. **These discussions deepen learning by exposing students to divergent perspectives, revealing blind spots, and encouraging them to refine their reasoning in response to peer critique and collaborative inquiry**.

Example (Economics or Communication Studies):

- *Small groups use a structured protocol:*
   - *Each student brings one AI-generated output (e.g., a model-generated market analysis or a misinformation example from social media).*
   - *They present their critique, then peers respond by asking:*
      - *"What assumptions do you think the model made?"*
      - *"Who gains from this framing?"*
      - *"What data might have been left out?"*

The goal in these dialogues is not to force agreement, but to create practice in recognizing and articulating divergent viewpoints. By engaging multiple interpretations of the same algorithmic event, **students learn that AI systems can be understood through many lenses - technical, cultural, institutional, and ethical**. This emphasis on interpretive multiplicity reinforces the value of plural perspectives and prepares students to navigate complexity without reducing it to a single "correct" conclusion (Cox, 2004; Noble, 2018).

Public or Professional Reflection Statements

To prepare for civic and career contexts, students can be asked to articulate their stance on AI use within their chosen field. This exercise challenges them to move beyond abstract critique and connect technological issues to professional standards, workplace responsibilities, and societal expectations. By practicing how to clearly state, defend, and refine their positions, students strengthen both their ethical reasoning and their capacity for professional advocacy in AI-mediated environments.

Example (Criminology or Public Policy Capstone):

- *As a final assignment, students draft a "**Professional AI Use Statement**" in which they:*
  - *Outline how they plan to engage AI in their future work.*
  - *Define boundaries for responsible and irresponsible uses.*
  - *Identify principles (e.g., transparency, equity, accountability) that they will uphold when faced with algorithmic decisions.*

This kind of statement echoes the structure and intent of professional codes of ethics, reminding students that ethical commitments are not confined to the classroom but extend into their careers. By aligning personal reflections on AI with broader disciplinary standards, students begin to see themselves as future leaders responsible for shaping professional norms. In this way, **the exercise strengthens the bridge between academic reflection and long-term leadership development,** fostering habits of integrity and accountability that endure well beyond graduation (Byars-Winston & Dahlberg, 2019).

Assessment Considerations

Assessment of reflective practices should prioritize **depth, honesty, and growth** rather than superficial accuracy or formulaic answers. Reflection is valuable precisely because it surfaces complexity and ambiguity, allowing students to grapple with tensions rather than simply resolve them. Faculty should emphasize that the goal is not a "perfect" position on AI use, but the cultivation of intellectual humility and ethical discernment over time (Brookfield, 2017; Slimi & Carballido, 2023).

Key Rubric Dimensions May Include:

- **Evidence of Identifying Assumptions or Institutional Logics.** Strong reflections reveal that students have recognized underlying patterns - such as efficiency biases in automated decision-making or institutional priorities embedded in algorithms - rather than simply describing tool functionality.
- **Clarity in Articulating One's Own Values and Choices.** Assessments should highlight how students make visible their stance toward AI use, including where they choose to accept, modify, or reject machine outputs based on professional ethics, disciplinary norms, or civic responsibility (Benjamin, 2023).
- **Willingness to Question Initial Trust in AI Outputs.** Reflection is most powerful when it demonstrates a willingness to revise one's own assumptions. Students who acknowledge moments of misplaced trust, error, or uncritical adoption show evidence of growth and critical self-awareness (Noble, 2018; Reiss, 2021).
- **Ability to Connect Personal Reflection to Disciplinary or Societal Stakes.** Faculty should reward students who situate their reflections within broader contexts - for example, linking their personal skepticism of an AI summary to wider debates about misinformation, or connecting their critique of an algorithm to structural consequences in healthcare, education, or governance (Crawford, 2021; Selwyn, 2019).

By assessing reflective practice through these dimensions, faculty move evaluation away from compliance checklists and toward **ethical and intellectual development**. Students come to see reflection as a site of scholarly rigor, not as a soft or secondary exercise, and faculty position AI literacy as integral to disciplinary growth and civic accountability.

Reflection as Accountability

By embedding reflection into AI literacy education, faculty remind students that accountability begins not in the algorithm but in the interpreter. The most powerful questions are not whether the system produced the "right" answer, but: *"Whose values shaped this tool?" "What assumptions am I carrying into my own use of it?" "What responsibilities do I hold as a scholar and future professional?"*

Through journaling, essays, dialogues, and professional statements, students cultivate the ethical self-awareness needed to resist passive automation and embrace active, values-driven engagement with AI systems. These reflective practices push learners to articulate their evolving relationship with technology, making explicit the assumptions they hold, the responsibilities they accept, and the boundaries they wish to set in their professional roles. In this way, **reflection is not treated as an optional add-on, but as a central pillar of social science education in the algorithmic age** - ensuring that students graduate not only with analytic skills, but with the moral imagination to challenge automation when it undermines justice, equity, or human dignity.

How Universities Themselves Model and Enforce Responsible AI Practice

---

1. Building Institutional Accountability into Social Science AI Education

If students are expected to critique AI systems for their embedded assumptions and institutional logics, then universities themselves must model the same accountability. Faculty cannot teach AI literacy effectively if their institutions adopt generative technologies in opaque or contradictory ways. Social science education is therefore strengthened when students see that the very institutions training them are also willing to interrogate, disclose, and adapt their use of AI.

Institutional accountability requires clear communication about how AI tools are being used in teaching, administration, and research support - and a willingness to surface the same ethical questions that students are asked to consider in class: *"Who benefits from this use of AI?" "What assumptions are shaping its design?" "What risks must be acknowledged, and how will they be mitigated?"*

---

2. Transparency in Institutional AI Use

Universities increasingly adopt AI for admissions screening, plagiarism detection, advising dashboards, or workload analytics, presenting these systems as tools for efficiency and scale.

Yet, in practice, these technologies often operate behind the scenes, shaping major decisions without student awareness or faculty oversight. **This lack of transparency raises critical questions about accountability, fairness, and consent - reminding us that the integration of AI in higher education is as much an ethical challenge as it is a technical one**.

Practice Example (Education Administration):

- *A political science department adopts an AI advising platform to help students select courses.*
- *Instead of deploying it silently, the department:*
  - *Publishes documentation of how the tool works.*
  - *Shares data on error rates and flagged risks.*
  - *Provides opt-out options for who students that are uncomfortable with automated guidance.*

This practice reinforces the principle that transparency and accountability apply to all participants in the academic community. **When faculty openly disclose their own use of AI - whether for preparing course materials, drafting communications, or analyzing data - they model the same reflective responsibility expected of students**. In doing so, they demonstrate that ethical engagement with AI is not only a classroom expectation but also a professional standard of integrity and trustworthiness (Slimi & Carballido, 2023).

---

3. Policy Development as Pedagogical Practice

AI literacy gains legitimacy when it is shaped not only by administrators or technologists, but by those most directly affected: faculty and students. When their perspectives are included in the drafting of policies - whether about disclosure, assessment, or ethical use - the result is a framework that reflects classroom realities as well as institutional goals. **This shared authorship fosters buy-in, enhances credibility, and demonstrates that AI governance is a collaborative process rather than a top-down mandate**.

Example (Sociology Program):

- *Before implementing AI-based plagiarism detection, a curriculum committee invites student representatives, faculty, and technologists to co-develop guidelines.*
- **What is Considered**:
  - *Students analyze bias concerns.*
  - *Faculty consider pedagogical impact.*
  - *Administrators weigh logistical needs.*

By opening the policy-making process to faculty, students, and staff, **institutions demonstrate that transparency is not just a principle to demand of AI systems but also of governance itself**. When participants can see how decisions are made and influence the outcomes, accountability shifts from being a one-directional critique of tools to a shared responsibility for shaping the systems in which those tools operate. This participatory design models reflexivity in practice, reminding all stakeholders that **responsible innovation requires continuous dialogue, ethical questioning, and collective ownership** (Brookfield, 2017; Selwyn, 2019).

4. Auditing AI for Institutional Bias and Assumptions

Universities increasingly adopt AI for admissions screening, plagiarism detection, advising dashboards, and workload analytics, embedding automation into core educational processes. Yet **these tools often function behind the scenes, hidden from those most affected - students and faculty - who may remain unaware of how decisions are being shaped on their behalf**. This opacity underscores the urgent need for transparency and accountability, ensuring that institutional reliance on AI does not bypass ethical scrutiny or democratic oversight.

Example (Institutional Research Office):

- *Faculty and graduate students co-lead an audit of an AI-driven learning analytics dashboard.*
- **Together They Ask**:
  - *"Does the system equate high grades with engagement?"*
  - *"Does it disproportionately flag students from non-traditional backgrounds as at risk?"*
  - *"How are the categories of 'success' and 'failure' being defined by the system?"*

This type of inquiry highlights that the tools of critique taught in social science classrooms are not merely theoretical exercises, but practical skills with immediate relevance. When students apply their frameworks of power analysis, ethics, and institutional critique to the AI systems operating within their own universities, they see how classroom methods translate directly into lived governance. In doing so, they recognize that **critical AI literacy is not optional - it must extend into the evaluation of institutional practices themselves** (Benjamin, 2023; Eubanks, 2018).

5. Feedback Loops Between Students and Institutions

Accountability cannot be reduced to a single audit or report - it must be sustained as a living process that evolves alongside the technology. Institutions should establish ongoing structures, such as annual forums, advisory councils, or digital feedback portals, where students share their experiences with campus AI systems and raise concerns. **When administrators respond to these reflections with transparency and action, accountability shifts from a compliance exercise to a genuine dialogue that fosters trust, equity, and institutional learning**.

Practice Example (Criminology and Public Policy Students):

- *Students draft policy memos critiquing the university's adoption of AI-based proctoring software.*
- *Their reflections on privacy, equity, and student trust are compiled and shared with the provost's office.*
- *The administration, in turn, publishes a response explaining changes to practice, clarifications of policy, or reasons for continuing the current approach.*

Accountability is not achieved through a single report or one-off review, but through a continuous, iterative process. When institutions create structured avenues - such as regular surveys, reflective forums, or digital feedback dashboards - students can share their experiences with campus AI systems, and administrators can respond with tangible adjustments. **This ongoing dialogue reinforces that accountability is a living practice**, ensuring that AI systems evolve in step with the needs, concerns, and values of the academic community.

Section Reflection: AI in the Social Sciences - Beyond Surface Accuracy to Systemic Accountability

This section underscores that AI must be understood not merely as a technical innovation, but as an institutional and political force that directs how opportunities, risks, and decisions are distributed. By situating AI literacy within the frameworks of sociology, political science, economics, anthropology, criminology, and communication studies, students learn to critique not whether an AI is "right" or "wrong," but how its design reflects deeper assumptions about efficiency, authority, and control. Pedagogical strategies such as policy memo writing, system mapping, debate simulations, and reflective journaling move students past surface-level outcomes into structured interrogation of algorithms' institutional goals.

If social science education calls students to critique AI systems by interrogating assumptions, goals, and consequences, then institutions must hold themselves to the same standard. Faculty and administrators cannot credibly teach "critical AI literacy" while deploying opaque, unexamined technologies in their own operations. By embracing transparency, participatory policy design, and institutional audits, universities model what democratic AI governance looks like in practice. When institutions practice accountability alongside students, they reinforce the idea that AI literacy is not about catching errors or debating who is "most at risk," but about learning to see systems clearly, challenge their hidden assumptions, and insist on ethical design.

Ultimately, this section reframes the social sciences as central to AI education, not as external observers but as active sites of accountability and design. By interrogating the hidden logics of automation and challenging their supposed neutrality, students learn that integrity in AI is not about surface correction - it is about questioning the systems that define truth, risk, and value in the first place. In this way, AI becomes a field of civic engagement and ethical stewardship, preparing graduates to influence institutions - academic, corporate, or governmental - with clarity, responsibility, and care.

Section 4: AI in the Arts and Design - Co-Creation and Aesthetic Innovation

---

Generative AI is reshaping the landscape of creative practice. Tools such as DALL·E 2, Midjourney, RunwayML, Adobe Firefly, and ChatGPT now generate visual artwork, video edits, poems, song lyrics, and UX mockups in seconds. This moment of innovation brings not only **new tools**, but **new paradigms of making** - where AI systems serve as *co-creators, provocateurs, and aesthetic filters* (McCormack et al., 2019; Miller, 2019).

For art and design educators, this is both a thrilling opportunity and a conceptual challenge. *"How do we* ***evaluate originality*** *in the age of neural style transfer?" "What does* ***authorship*** *mean when a prompt generates a painting?" "What happens to* ***critical making*** *when cultural datasets drive outputs we cannot fully control?"* This section offers frameworks, assignments, and discussion models to help faculty teach AI literacy through **experimental creation, critique, and reflection** - ensuring students remain not just tool users, but ethical, imaginative **shapers of emerging media ecologies** (Goldschmidt, 2019; Manovich, 2018).

AI Literacy Through Artistic Co-Creation

---

1. Understanding AI as a Design Material: Toward Algorithmic Material Literacy

In design education, materials are not passive elements; they are **active collaborators** in the creative process. Designers are trained to explore the **affordances, constraints, and expressive potential** of media such as wood, metal, textiles, light, and typography. Each material shapes the outcome through its inherent properties: its grain, its resistance, its resonance. In this context, artificial intelligence - particularly generative AI - can be introduced not as a black-box tool or abstract innovation, but as a **design material in its own right** (Candy & Edmonds, 2018).

This reframing of AI as a **conceptual and procedural medium** invites students to explore how its patterns, probabilities, and training data behave under manipulation. Such as other materials, AI systems have **tendencies and limits** - they respond differently to ambiguity, metaphor, repetition, or contradiction. They express particular aesthetics, produce certain textures of output, and reveal internal logics that can be shaped but not fully controlled. Teaching AI in this way cultivates **material awareness of algorithms**, helping students move from surface-level prompt engineering to **critical design experimentation** informed by insight into data, bias, and machine representation.

Studio Exercise: Prompt Iteration and Reverse-Engineering Visual Logics

Assignment Title: *"Sculpting a Visual Identity with a Machine"*

Objective: Students are asked to explore a text-to-image generation model (e.g., DALL·E, Midjourney, Stable Diffusion) by attempting to create a **cohesive visual identity** - such as for a fictional brand, public campaign, or speculative future project. The goal is not to perfect a product, but to **engage critically with how the system interprets language into visual form**.

Steps:

- **Prompt Generation**. Students begin with a phrase or concept - e.g., *"Feminist Urbanism," "Climate Resilience in South Asia," or "Joyful Resistance."* Students input a series of increasingly refined prompts into the model to generate images.

- **Iteration and Documentation**. Students record each prompt used, the visual outputs, and their observations. *"How did changing a word alter the result?" "What styles or tropes emerge automatically?"*
- **Reverse-Engineering the Logic**. Students analyze what the system seems to prefer - *"Does it flatten metaphor into cliché?" "Does it default to Eurocentric imagery or gendered stereotypes?"*
- **Critical Reflection**. Students respond to the following prompts:
  - *"What kinds of images does this model favor?" "What happens when I introduce ambiguity, contradiction, or irony?" "How do the visual patterns reveal the system's underlying assumptions?"*

Deliverables:

- A curated series of image iterations.
- A written or visual "map" of system behaviors and biases.
- A reflection on the experience of working with AI as a material: *"Where did it surprise, resist, misread, or inspire?"*

Pedagogical Impact: From Technique to Awareness:

This studio exercise fosters what might be called **algorithmic material literacy** - the ability to treat AI not as a mysterious black box but as a design material to be studied, tested, and shaped. Just as students once learned the grain of wood or the malleability of clay, **here they learn the "grain" of algorithmic systems: their tendencies, resistances, and hidden preferences**. In doing so, they cultivate intentionality and inquiry, recognizing that working with AI requires the same creative discipline and critical awareness applied to any medium of design or scholarship. It encourages students to:

- See **AI outputs as shaped by underlying training data**, not as spontaneous acts of creativity.
- Understand that **machine aesthetics are not neutral**, but structured by cultural preferences, economic imperatives, and platform design.
- Move beyond surface prompt manipulation into **iterative, reflective, and critical design practice**, akin to traditional sketching or prototyping (Benjamin, 2023; Gulya, 2023).

Rather than teaching AI as a tool to be mastered, this approach reframes it as a **co-author** whose contributions must be examined with the same rigor as any collaborator. **Students learn to study the system's internal logic - its assumptions, gaps, and defaults** - not to replicate its patterns, but to identify where human creativity and ethical reasoning must intervene. In this way, AI becomes a partner to be challenged and repurposed, ensuring that student agency is exercised not through passive use but instead through critical engagement and deliberate reorientation of machine outputs.

Designing With, Not Just Through, AI

When AI is treated as a material, students learn to **negotiate with its tendencies** rather than merely react to its outputs. They begin to ask not just **what** the machine can make, but **why** it makes what it does - and what it resists, ignores, or amplifies. This shift promotes design literacy that is not only technical, but **critical, ethical, and imaginative**, preparing students to create in - and critique - the hybrid design landscapes of the AI age.

---

2. Teaching the History of Generative and Procedural Art: Tracing Lineages of Machine-Mediated Creativity

While the rise of generative AI has sparked debates over originality, authorship, and artistic intent, it is not the aesthetic rupture it is often made out to be. Rather, generative AI emerges from a **long tradition of proceduralism, rule-based composition, and human-machine co-creation** - a lineage that spans conceptual art, algorithmic drawing, and computational aesthetics throughout the 20th and early 21st centuries. Teaching AI-generated art within this historical continuum enables students to **understand contemporary machine creativity not as unprecedented, but as an extension - and complication - of long-standing artistic inquiries into authorship, process, and control** (Galanter, 2003; McCormack et al., 2019).

Key Historical Anchors in the Genealogy of Generative Art:

- **Sol LeWitt**. A pioneer of conceptual art, LeWitt's *Wall Drawings* (1968–2000s) were composed not by the artist's hand, but by teams following written instructions. In LeWitt's paradigm, **the idea becomes the machine that makes the art** - an early inversion of the artist's role as executor in favor of procedural authorship.
- **Harold Cohen's AARO.** A groundbreaking AI art program developed in the 1970s and continually refined for decades, AARON was an **autonomous system that generated figurative and abstract drawings**, designed by Cohen not to simulate human creativity, but to interrogate its boundaries.
- **Casey Reas and the Processing Platform**. As a co-creator of the open-source visual language Processing, Reas helped democratize access to **code-based aesthetics**, emphasizing that procedural logic itself could be a **primary material for artistic composition**. His "Software Structures" directly referenced LeWitt and foregrounded **machine instruction as an artistic medium**.

These precedents offer students both historical and conceptual grounding, showing that prompt-based generative AI did not emerge in isolation but builds on earlier traditions of rule-based creativity. **By situating AI within the lineage of systems such as procedural art, conceptual instruction, and algorithmic design, learners see how human–machine collaboration has always evolved through structured constraints and imaginative delegation**. This framing helps them recognize AI not as a rupture, but as part of a broader continuity in the evolution of human tools, creative partnerships, and interactive systems.

Example Lecture Pairing: Proceduralism Then and Now

Visual Pairing:

- **Midjourney** (or DALL·E) outputs based on prompts such as "a surrealist dreamscape in the style of René Magritte."
- **Sol LeWitt's Wall Drawing #797**. Instructions such as "Draw a 10-inch square. Within it, draw ten thousand straight lines, using a hard pencil."

Discussion Questions:

- *"Is a text prompt the new 'instruction set?'"*
- *"Where is authorship located - in the prompt, the algorithm, the training data, or the output?"*
- *"How do generative constraints shape aesthetic outcomes?"*
- *"Is procedural art about relinquishing control or refining it in new forms?"*

Student Insight: Through this juxtaposition, students explore how both conceptual and computational artists have long challenged traditional notions of creativity - by **foregrounding process, minimizing direct authorship, and inviting the machine or the system to co-generate form**. They come to understand that **AI art inherits this tradition**, even as it introduces new questions of scale, ethics, and black-box opacity.

Learning Outcomes: By teaching AI art through the lens of generative and procedural history, students will:

- **Develop a critical framework for understanding prompt-based creation** within a broader aesthetic lineage.
- Analyze how **conceptualism, automation, and abstraction** have been used historically to interrogate creativity.
- Reflect on how **authorship and intentionality evolve** in machinic contexts.
- Recognize the **continuities and ruptures** between pre-digital algorithmic thinking and contemporary AI-driven generation.

Beyond Hype - Reframing AI as Part of an Artistic Legacy

Generative AI is not merely a product of 21st-century technological acceleration - it is part of a longer history in which artists have relied on rules, systems, and machines to probe the boundaries of authorship and creative expression. By connecting AI to earlier traditions of instruction-based art and computational design, students can develop a historically grounded perspective that situates today's tools within a broader continuum of experimentation. **This lens resists the hype of novelty and instead frames AI as both a descendant of past practices and a disruptor that forces us to reconsider what creativity, originality, and authorship mean in the present**.

---

3. Critical Making: Ethics of Data and Representation in Generative AI

As generative AI continues to permeate visual culture - from social media filters to concept art, branding, and digital storytelling - it raises urgent questions about **how machines learn to "see" and what visual legacies they inherit**. Creative AI systems such as Midjourney, DALL·E, and Stable Diffusion are trained on **massive image corpora scraped from the internet**. These training datasets often contain a broad, unsorted mix of copyrighted works, culturally sensitive imagery, and content shaped by **Western-centric visual norms**. As a result, these models reproduce and amplify biases present in the source material, leading to critical concerns about **artistic theft, cultural appropriation, and racialized aesthetics** (Benjamin, 2023; Crawford & Paglen, 2021; Noble, 2018).

In visual art, design, and digital humanities classrooms, these issues present a powerful opportunity for **critical making** - a practice that merges material engagement with conceptual critique. Students are invited not only to study AI's outputs but to **create through and against them**, using design, writing, and visual analysis as forms of cultural interrogation.

Project Idea: "Is Midjourney Stealing Art?"

Assignment Options:

- **A Position Paper**. Students write a short essay (800–1200 words) that argues for or against the ethical legitimacy of image-generating AI systems, grounded in research and visual evidence.
- **A Visual Critique Poster or Zine**. Students design a digital or print-based artifact that communicates a critical perspective on Midjourney, addressing ethical questions through the language of design itself.

Research Tasks:

- Investigate how Midjourney and similar platforms train their models (e.g., use of LAION-5B datasets or other scraped corpora).
- Analyze examples of alleged **image mimicry, uncredited reproduction, or visual stereotyping**.
- Study the language of the platform's user agreements, terms of service, or image moderation policies.

Critical Themes to Explore:

- **Intellectual Property and Artistic Labor**. *"What does it mean for a model to be trained on copyrighted or uncredited artist work?" "Is style replicable or ownable?" "What protections (if any) exist for digital artists whose work is absorbed into training data without consent?"*
- **Cultural Appropriation and Visual Erasure**. *"How do generative models reproduce* ***clichés, caricatures, or exoticized depictions*** *of marginalized communities?" "What happens when sacred symbols or traditional dress are transformed into aesthetic tropes for prompt-driven consumption?"*
- **Aesthetic Homogenization and Eurocentrism**. *"Are certain facial features, lighting styles, or design motifs overrepresented in AI outputs?" "How do* ***Western standards of beauty, composition, and realism*** *become default in datasets scraped from predominantly English-language or Euro-American platforms?"*

Key Readings and Sources for AI in the Arts and Design:

Faculty and students engaging with AI in the creative disciplines benefit from sources that situate generative technologies within histories of aesthetics, systems of power, and ongoing debates over authorship and representation. The following readings and resources provide both theoretical grounding and contemporary critique, offering multiple entry points for classroom integration and student inquiry.

Core Texts:

- **Crawford and Paglen (2021), *Excavating AI: The Politics of Images in Machine Learning Training Sets*.** This work exposes how visual datasets used in machine learning are rarely neutral. It provides a detailed critique of "dataset opacity" and how categories, images, and metadata embed social and aesthetic hierarchies. For students in design and visual studies, it offers a concrete lens for interrogating the unseen infrastructures of image-making systems.
- **Benjamin (2023), *Race After Technology*.** Benjamin demonstrates how technological systems - visual recognition tools included - can encode and reinforce social hierarchies under the guise of neutrality. While not limited to the arts, her analysis provides a critical foundation for students to examine how AI-generated images, museum databases, or recognition technologies intersect with power, inclusion, and cultural representation.
- **Noble (2018), *Algorithms of Oppression*.** Noble's examination of search engines shows how algorithmic design shapes cultural visibility and invisibility. For arts and media students, this translates into questions of aesthetic exclusion - whose styles, traditions, and voices are amplified, and whose are erased in the algorithmic curation of creative content.

Supplementary Perspectives:

- **Artistic Resistance and Activist Movements.** Artist-led projects such as **Spawning** (an opt-out initiative for creators) represent a growing movement against uncompensated dataset use. These resources highlight how artists are asserting agency over their work, modeling forms of advocacy students can study or replicate.
- **Legal and Policy Debates.** Current copyright battles over whether AI-generated works can be protected as original creations introduce essential conversations for arts, design, and intellectual property curricula. Faculty can incorporate case law and policy updates as living documents of how society is renegotiating authorship in real time.
- **Historical Precedents in Generative and Procedural Art.** Readings from Harold Cohen (on *AARON*), Sol LeWitt (instruction-based works), and Casey Reas (Processing and code art) provide necessary historical grounding. These precedents help students see that generative AI is not an unprecedented rupture, but a continuation of system-driven creativity (Galanter, 2003; McCormack et al., 2019).

Pedagogical Application: When paired together, these sources help faculty craft assignments that move beyond evaluating the "quality" of AI-generated art. Instead, students are taught to interrogate:

- How training data defines what images are possible.
- How institutional logics shape what aesthetics are privileged.
- What new responsibilities do artists, designers, and scholars hold in an era when creative labor is distributed across humans and machines?

Learning Outcomes: By engaging in this assignment, students will:

- **Analyze the ethical dimensions of data-driven creativity**, including issues of consent, authorship, and systemic bias.

- Understand how generative AI platforms **mediate cultural memory and visual representation**.
- Develop **visual and textual literacy** to express critique through both scholarly writing and creative composition.
- Practice **critical AI literacy through a humanistic and design-based lens**, linking theory to visual culture and public discourse.

Instructor Tip: Encouraging students to share their final visual pieces in a gallery walk, online publication, or public forum transforms their work from a private classroom exercise into a public-facing dialogue. This act reframes critique as both a creative and civic practice, positioning students not only as makers but also as contributors to cultural conversation. In doing so, they learn that visual culture is a site of dialogue, resistance, and ethical intervention - where artistic practice can question systems, amplify marginalized perspectives, and imagine alternative futures.

AI as a Medium of Representation and Contestation

Teaching generative AI through the lens of critical making helps students see that machine-produced images are not neutral outputs, but acts of cultural reproduction that carry embedded assumptions and exclusions. **By unpacking the data infrastructures and power dynamics behind these visuals, students gain critical tools to question algorithmic authority and resist the illusion of objectivity**. In turn, this equips them to center underrepresented voices and imagine more equitable, justice-oriented forms of visual expression in an age increasingly shaped by synthetic media.

---

4. Process-Based Assignments with Reflection Logs: Centering Iteration, Judgment, and Creative Intent

In an era where AI-generated outputs often appear visually polished, there is a growing risk that students - and educators - may confuse surface fluency with creative depth. Tools such as DALL·E, Midjourney, and Adobe Firefly can produce sleek imagery in seconds, yet the **learning and authorship emerge not from the instant result, but from how students revise, critique, and contextualize that output**. In design education and digital media programs, it is therefore essential to emphasize **process over product**, encouraging students to treat AI as a **provocative partner** in an evolving creative dialogue - not a one-click solution (Candy & Edmonds, 2018; Paul, 2002).

Process-based assignments that integrate **reflection logs** help students develop **metacognitive awareness** of their decision-making: *"How are choices being shaped by the tool?" "When do students accept what the model gives them, and when do they intervene, correct, or resist?"* Through structured iterations and annotations, students begin to see themselves not as passive users, but as **intentional, reflective creators** who engage AI critically, strategically, and ethically.

Assignment Idea: AI Triptych + Reflection Log

Title: *"Tracing the Conversation Between Artist and Algorithm"*

Objective: Students will create a **three-panel triptych** that documents their engagement with a generative AI image model. Each panel captures a distinct stage of the creative process, and the final submission is accompanied by a **written reflection log**.

Triptych Components:

- **Panel 1: Initial Prompt and Raw AI Output**. Students input a creative prompt (e.g., *"A Utopian Eco-Tech Cityscape"*) into a generative model and document the unedited image.
- **Panel 2: Modified Output with Human Edits**. Using image-editing tools (e.g., Photoshop, Procreate, Figma), students revise or remix the AI-generated work - adjusting composition, layering new elements, or integrating text and symbolism.
- **Panel 3: Annotated Breakdown of Decisions**. Students create a visual or textual annotation highlighting:
    - *"What aspects of the AI output they retained (and why)?"*
    - *"What they altered, removed, or enhanced?"*
    - *"Where the AI succeeded in reflecting the prompt - and where it misrepresented or oversimplified it?"*

Reflection Log Prompt:

- *"How did the AI influence your decision-making?"*
- *"Did it spark new ideas or lead you into aesthetic dead ends?"*
- *"In what ways did you assert authorship or challenge the machine's assumptions?"*

Encourage students to reflect on their **intentionality**, not just the visual result: *"Were they surprised by the output?" "Did the tool force them to confront assumptions about composition, symbolism, or visual hierarchy?"*

Pedagogical Outcomes and Theoretical Rationale:

- **Metacognitive Design Awareness**. Students learn to think about thinking - to observe how their own creative judgment evolves across iterations (Brookfield, 2017; Nicol & Macfarlane-Dick, 2006).
- **Intentional Use of AI Tools**. Rather than defaulting to the most visually "impressive" output, students develop criteria for **evaluating alignment with purpose, meaning, and context**.
- **Recognition of AI's Limitations**. Through editing and reflection, students discover where the model lacks nuance, introduces clichés, or replicates dominant aesthetics - insights that support **critical AI literacy** (Crawford & Paglen, 2021; Gulya, 2023).
- **Framing AI as Medium, Not Author**. The triptych format positions AI output as a starting point, not an endpoint - reinforcing that authorship lies in **curation, transformation, and interpretive framing** (Candy & Edmonds, 2018; Paul, 2002).

Extension Possibilities:

- Host a **class critique session** where students present their triptychs and discuss the creative dialogue they experienced with the AI model.
- Invite students to **revisit their original prompt** and refine it based on what they learned - highlighting how prompt design becomes a form of composition.

- Archive triptychs in a shared digital gallery or zine, emphasizing **process transparency and iterative thinking** as central values in AI-era creativity.

Designing Through the Algorithm

This assignment positions AI not as a shortcut to finished design, but as a material with friction, capable of both sparking inspiration and demanding negotiation. Students quickly discover that AI outputs are rarely perfect; instead, they often reveal unexpected gaps, biases, or stylistic limitations that require human intervention. **By grappling with these imperfections, learners come to see the creative process as a dialogue with the machine, one in which human intention, judgment, and values remain indispensable**.

Through the combination of iterative practice and reflective analysis, students gain insight into their own creative values, the assumptions embedded in AI tools, and the evolving role of the human artist in computational design ecosystems. Each round of revision pushes students to ask not only **what** the machine produced, but **why** it produced it, and what that reveals about the underlying data or algorithm. In this way, design education shifts from producing polished products to cultivating critical inquiry, aesthetic agility, and the capacity to work thoughtfully within hybrid human–machine environments.

By centering the process, faculty empower students to become critically aware, aesthetically agile, and ethically grounded designers - ready to shape, question, and reimagine creativity in an AI-mediated world. **This orientation emphasizes that the future of art and design is not about replacing the artist, but about expanding the boundaries of what artistic practice can be when paired with intelligent systems.** Graduates leave not only with technical proficiency but with the moral imagination to guide creative work in ways that are responsible, inclusive, and transformative.

Integrating AI Literacy into the Creative Curriculum: From Tool Use to Critical Practice

As generative AI systems increasingly influence creative industries - design, writing, filmmaking, and curation, they also demand thoughtful integration into **arts and creative education**. Yet AI literacy in the creative disciplines must extend beyond technical competence. It should empower students to become **intentional, critical, and reflective makers** who understand not just how to use AI, but how to **question its aesthetics, interpret its biases, and reshape its outputs** through their own voice and vision (Benjamin, 2023; Candy & Edmonds, 2018).

The table below outlines sample AI-integrated assignments across creative disciplines, with a focus on **tool-specific application, conceptual learning goals, and critical engagement**. These examples illustrate how AI can be leveraged as a **medium of making, a prompt for inquiry, and a site of reflection.**

Creative Curriculum Integration: Assignment Models by Discipline

Discipline	Assignment Example	AI Tool(s)	Learning Focus
Graphic Design	Brand Identity Prototyping via Prompt Iteration	Midjourney, Adobe Firefly	Visual affordances, stylistic iteration, prompt engineering
Animation/Film	Storyboard-to-Video Experiment Using Text-to-Video Generator	RunwayML	Narrative pacing, frame continuity, visual logic
Creative Writing	Generate and Revise AI-Composed Poems or Dialogues	ChatGPT, Sudowrite	Voice, metaphor, poetic structure, human revision process
Art History	Curate an "AI Imaginary Exhibition" and Write a Critical Essay	DALL·E, Stable Diffusion	Dataset transparency, historical erasure, aesthetic bias in AI-generated visuals

---

Expanded Descriptions and Pedagogical Aims

---

1. Graphic Design: Brand Identity Prompt Iteration

Students use AI image generators to rapidly explore design directions for a speculative brand, iterating across prompts to generate **typography, color palettes, and visual motifs**. Through reflection, they evaluate:

- *"What kinds of aesthetics does the tool default to?"*
- *"How are non-Western styles, vernacular design, or experimental compositions represented or misrepresented?"*

The emphasis is on material literacy and stylistic authorship: the student must curate, critique, and reconfigure AI outputs rather than passively accept them. This means **learning to treat AI-generated work as raw material - something to be shaped, challenged, and contextualized within human-driven frameworks of meaning**. By positioning themselves as authors rather than consumers, students preserve agency, develop aesthetic judgment, and learn to assert voice and values in the face of algorithmic fluency.

---

2. Animation/Film: Text-to-Video Storyboarding

In a motion design or film studio course, students use tools such as RunwayML to generate short visual sequences from textual storyboards. They then evaluate:

- How well the tool interprets pacing, character coherence, or tonal shifts.
- Where cinematic conventions are reinforced or undermined.
- What editing or frame sequencing is required to achieve narrative cohesion?

This introduces students to how machines interpret story structure, offering a unique window into the logic and limitations of algorithmic creativity. By engaging with AI-generated scripts, visual prompts, or narrative outlines, students can compare automated structures with human approaches, recognizing both overlaps and blind spots. **This opens a broader dialogue on AI's role in pre-visualization, collaborative scripting, and mood boarding - highlighting where it can spark imagination and where human perspective must refine or resist machine patterns**.

---

3. Creative Writing: Human Revision of AI-Generated Texts

Students prompt a generative language model to compose a poem or scene, then **revise it manually** - enhancing metaphor, refining voice, or correcting tonal mismatches. They reflect on:

- Where they "intervened" as authors.
- What creative decisions were prompted or resisted by the AI's suggestions?
- How authorship shifts when language is co-produced.

This assignment reinforces that revision is where true authorship emerges, underscoring that the act of rewriting, reframing, or reorganizing is central to human creativity. By critically engaging with AI outputs, **students learn that they are not bound to machine structures** but retain the agency to reinterpret, subvert, or transform them into something uniquely their own. In doing so, **they see revision not as correction of error but as a powerful site of meaning-making, where human intention reshapes automated patterns into authentic expression** (Bender et al., 2021; Paul, 2002).

---

4. Art History: Curatorial Critique of the AI Imagination

Students curate a virtual "AI Imaginary Exhibition" by generating images via a prompt series on a chosen theme - e.g., "Renaissance portraiture reimagined by AI" or "Global mythologies in synthetic art." They then write a **curatorial essay critiquing**:

- The visual logic and historical accuracy of the outputs.
- Aesthetic bias, omission, or distortion in the model's interpretations.
- The training data's influence on visual cultural assumptions (Crawford & Paglen, 2021; Noble, 2018).

This helps **students recognize that AI-generated art is not only about creating images but also about exposing the structures that shape artistic canons and exclusions**. By analyzing how training data privileges certain aesthetics while erasing others, students learn that machine creativity is entwined with art history's biases and narratives. In turn, this fosters critical awareness, showing that **engaging with AI means engaging with the deeper epistemologies and value systems that guide cultural production**.

Building Creative AI Literacy Through Practice and Reflection

These discipline-specific assignments demonstrate that **AI belongs within creative education not as a mere productivity tool, but as a cultural medium that requires shaping, interrogation, and reflection**. By experimenting with prompts, revising machine-generated drafts, curating outputs, and engaging in speculative storytelling, students learn to navigate AI's limits and possibilities with both creativity and critique. This dual focus ensures that technical agility is paired with intellectual discernment, anchoring artistic practice in thoughtful engagement rather than passive consumption.

They also come to understand that **AI does not complete the act of creativity - it begins it**. Machine outputs serve as raw material that demand reinterpretation, ethical decision-making, and imaginative redesign by human authors. In this way, students recognize that authorship in the AI era lies not in generating fluent outputs but rather in how one reclaims agency, embeds values, and shapes culture through collaboration with machines.

Section Reflection: Centering Human Agency in AI-Augmented Artistic Practice

This section reclaims the arts and design fields as essential spaces for rethinking human creativity in an AI-saturated world. Rather than casting generative AI as a threat to originality or as a simple production tool, the section offers a sophisticated framework for treating AI as a co-creative material - something to be experimented with, shaped, critiqued, and ultimately understood as both medium and message.

The most powerful insight here is the reframing of AI as a **design material**, one with expressive tendencies, cultural baggage, and embedded biases - much like any other artistic substrate. Students are not trained merely to "prompt" AI, but to **dialogue** with it. This approach cultivates material intelligence, critical literacy, and aesthetic discernment, grounding creative process in ethical, conceptual, and historical awareness.

By incorporating process-based reflections, critical making assignments, and historical lineages of procedural and conceptual art, this section situates AI within a continuum of artistic inquiry - demystifying it without diminishing its potential. The pedagogical focus on iteration, curation, and intentional authorship ensures that students retain creative agency while engaging critically with generative technologies.

Ultimately, the section offers a roadmap for cultivating **critical creative AI literacy: the ability to use, question, and reimagine AI through a deeply human lens**. It empowers emerging artists and designers to become not just skilled creators in an AI world, but thoughtful cultural stewards who know when to collaborate with the machine - and when to resist its logic.

Section 5: AI in Health, Education, and the Helping Professions

In professions centered on care, service, and equity, the arrival of artificial intelligence is both a **technological disruption** and an **ethical reckoning**. From clinical decision support systems in nursing to adaptive learning platforms in education, AI is being used to diagnose, triage, personalize, and intervene - often in **contexts where lives, learning, and dignity are on the line** (Selwyn, 2019; Topol, 2019).

Yet practitioners and students in these fields often feel **underprepared** to evaluate, critique, or even understand how AI systems function. A study by Mesko et al. (2018) found that few nursing and medical students received formal training in AI-related tools, despite their increasing prevalence in patient-facing settings. Similar gaps are documented in education (Luckin et al., 2016), counseling (Fiske et al., 2019), and social work (Reamer, 2023).

This section offers practical strategies for integrating AI literacy into helping-profession curricula - **not through coding**, but through **ethics, human-centered design, and critical decision-making**.

Why AI Literacy Matters in Care and Service Fields

In care and service professions - including **healthcare, education, counseling, social work, and community advocacy** - artificial intelligence is increasingly positioned as a solution for overburdened systems. AI triages patients, generates lesson plans, flags behavioral concerns, and scores eligibility for benefits. Yet the introduction of automated systems into human-centered fields raises urgent questions about **trust, bias, and the irreducibility of relational care**. In these domains, **AI literacy is not a technical convenience - it is an ethical imperative**.

Educators preparing students for careers in healthcare, social work, education, or other service-oriented professions **must prioritize more than technical competency with AI systems**. They need to ensure that graduates can critically assess how these tools are designed, what assumptions they embed, and how their use shapes decision-making and access to resources. Just as importantly, students must be trained to preserve the human judgment, empathy, and advocacy that distinguish professional care, ensuring that **automation enhances rather than erodes the ethical commitments at the heart of these fields** (Benjamin, 2023; Eubanks, 2018; Javed et al., 2023).

Three Core Concerns That Make AI Literacy Essential in Care and Service Fields

---

1. Trust Is Fragile

In healthcare, education, and social services, **client trust forms the backbone of every professional relationship**, and once compromised, it is difficult to rebuild. When practitioners turn to algorithmic systems to make recommendations - whether suggesting a medical treatment plan, flagging a student for intervention, or approving social benefits - **the opacity of these systems can make clients feel disempowered or overlooked**. To safeguard trust in these high-stakes environments, professionals must be able to clearly explain how such decisions were generated, identify the limitations of the system, and demonstrate where human judgment intervened to ensure fairness and accountability.

AI systems are often "black boxes," producing outputs with little transparency. Without a working understanding of how algorithms function - what data they use, what assumptions they encode, and how they are optimized - professionals risk **delegating authority to tools they cannot justify or defend**. Worse, when outcomes are harmful or discriminatory, they may be **unable to intervene effectively** or reassure those in their care (Javed et al., 2023; Pasquale, 2015). AI literacy helps future professionals ask:

- *"What is this system prioritizing? What am I being asked to trust - and why?"*

---

2. Bias Harms

Automated systems, even when designed with the intention of fairness, frequently encode inequities tied to race, gender, language, socioeconomic status, or ability. Predictive risk scores in social services, facial recognition in healthcare, and automated grading tools in education have repeatedly been shown to replicate and reinforce historical injustices. What is most concerning is that these outcomes often appear under the guise of objectivity or efficiency, masking deeply embedded structural biases behind the authority of machine-generated results (Benjamin, 2023; Eubanks, 2018; Noble, 2018).

In care-oriented professions - where decisions can determine access to resources, shape life opportunities, or even affect survival - these algorithmic harms are not abstract. They result in real consequences for individuals and communities, disproportionately impacting those already marginalized by social, economic, and institutional structures. **Far from being neutral, AI becomes a new mechanism through which old inequalities are reinscribed, making literacy in these issues not just an academic goal but an ethical necessity for future professionals**.

AI literacy in this context enables students to move beyond surface critiques of whether a tool "works" and instead investigate whose needs the tool serves, whose data it relies upon, and whose perspectives it systematically erases. **By tracing these harms back to their structural origins, students learn to recognize that bias is not simply a technical flaw - it is an institutional and political choice embedded within design and deployment**. Equipped with this awareness, they can begin to imagine, propose, and advocate for alternatives rooted in principles of equity, inclusion, and justice.

Students must be empowered to ask probing, reflective questions that shift attention away from algorithmic performance alone and toward broader accountability. For example:

- *"Whose needs were prioritized in the design of this tool?"*
- *"Whose experiences were omitted?"*
- *"Who benefits from its use, and who bears the costs of its errors?"*

By cultivating this line of questioning, educators equip students to recognize that AI is not an unquestionable authority, but a system designed with human goals, assumptions, and limitations. **Instead of passively accepting outputs as neutral or definitive, students learn**

to interrogate where the tool may oversimplify, exclude, or reinforce institutional priorities. In doing so, they embrace a form of values-driven engagement that balances technical fluency with ethical responsibility, ensuring that technology serves human purposes rather than dictating them.

---

3. Empathy Is Irreplaceable

Despite rapid advances in natural language processing, affective computing, and predictive diagnostics, **AI cannot replicate therapeutic rapport, culturally responsive pedagogy, or trauma-informed care**. These forms of relational practice extend far beyond information transfer; they rely on attunement to subtle cues, the capacity to engage in emotional labor, and the ability to adapt in ways that reflect cultural and historical context. **Human connection in these settings is shaped by lived experience and trust, qualities that no algorithm can authentically reproduce**.

In service professions, empathy is not an optional trait but a central mechanism for healing, learning, and empowerment. AI may serve as a support tool by providing scaffolding for communication, data insights, or task efficiency, but it cannot replace the presence and flexibility of human interaction. **True care requires ethical judgment, narrative responsiveness, and an embodied commitment to human dignity that only people can provide** (Brookfield, 2017; Reamer, 2023). Students in these fields must learn to ask:

- *"How can AI assist - but not replace - my professional judgment, advocacy, and relational practice?"*

Review of Educational Imperative: Teaching AI Literacy with Relational Ethics

Faculty in education, social work, nursing, psychology, and allied fields must prepare students not just to use AI tools, but to **think critically and ethically about their integration**. This means:

- Incorporating **scenario-based learning** where students role-play how they would explain an AI-generated diagnosis or recommendation to a patient or student.
- Assigning **case studies** in which algorithmic harm has occurred, and asking students to design ethical interventions.
- Creating **reflective writing prompts** where students explore the emotional and ethical boundaries of delegating care to machines.

By grounding AI literacy in the values of equity, autonomy, and relational accountability, educators ensure that students understand technology as more than just a tool for efficiency. They **learn to see AI within the context of human dignity, cultural responsiveness, and ethical responsibility, recognizing that every automated process has real consequences for people's lives**. In doing so, students are prepared to work confidently with AI systems while never losing sight of the human beings at the center of their professional practice.

Pedagogical Strategies for Applied AI Literacy in Care and Service Fields

Applied AI literacy in care and service professions - such as education, nursing, social work, counseling, and allied health - requires more than familiarity with technological systems. It demands that future practitioners develop the ability to **contextualize algorithmic outputs, recognize bias, exercise professional judgment, and preserve human dignity** in AI-augmented environments.

To meet these goals, faculty must embed AI literacy through pedagogical strategies that are experiential, ethically grounded, and socially situated. The following five approaches foster **judgment, empathy, critical analysis, and interdisciplinary collaboration**, positioning students as reflective, relational professionals who can engage AI critically rather than deferentially.

---

1. Case-Based Ethical Reasoning: Navigating AI Authority and Human Context in Care Professions

As artificial intelligence becomes more prevalent in healthcare and service environments, professionals are increasingly expected to interpret or implement machine-generated recommendations within complex, high-stakes human contexts. Case-based ethical reasoning offers a pedagogical strategy that places students in **realistic, nuanced scenarios** where they must practice balancing **algorithmic authority with human-centered care**, **institutional policy with ethical discernment**, and **data-driven logic with social complexity**.

Rather than abstract discussion, these case studies immerse students in scenarios where **decision-making unfolds within constraints** - of time, bureaucracy, and conflicting obligations. This approach builds the **situational fluency, reflective judgment, and moral courage** necessary to responsibly navigate AI-mediated work in education, healthcare, and social services (Brookfield, 2017; Reamer, 2023).

Example Case: AI Discharge Planning in Nursing

Scenario: An AI system implemented by a hospital is designed to optimize discharge planning by analyzing risk factors for readmission. Based on clinical indicators, it identifies a patient as "low risk" and flags them for expedited discharge. However, the attending nurse knows the patient is unstably housed, lacks access to transportation, and has no family support.

Student Challenge: The student must decide whether to endorse the discharge, delay it, or escalate concerns to a supervisor - **balancing institutional pressure for efficiency with ethical concerns about post-discharge safety**.

Discussion Prompts for Critical Analysis:

- **What Non-Medical or Structural Factors Might the Algorithm Have Failed to Include?** For example, housing status, food insecurity, access to primary care, or community support systems. This highlights the **limitations of clinical data** in capturing social determinants of health (Eubanks, 2018; Noble, 2018).
- **Who is Accountable if the Patient is Discharged and Suffers Harm?** This raises critical questions about **distributed responsibility** in AI-augmented decisions. "*Is it*

the nurse, the algorithm developer, the hospital administrator, or all three?" Students explore **legal, institutional, and moral forms of accountability** (Floridi et al., 2018; Javed et al., 2023).

- **How can the Nurse Ethically Push Back Against the System While Working Within Institutional Constraints?** This prompts students to consider strategies for **ethical resistance**, including documentation, advocacy, escalation procedures, or appeal to professional codes of conduct (W. B. Johnson & Griffin, 2024; Reamer, 2023).

Learning Outcomes: Through this kind of case-based reasoning, students develop:

- **The capacity to challenge AI recommendations** when they conflict with lived realities or social justice concerns - **a critical skill as algorithmic systems increasingly inform clinical, educational, and social service decisions** (Chen & Decary, 2020; Topol, 2019).
- **A deeper appreciation of relational ethics**, especially in fields where trust, empathy, and context sensitivity cannot be reduced to data points or predictive scores (Benjamin, 2023; Byars-Winston & Dahlberg, 2019).
- **The ability to articulate their professional obligations**, drawing on ethical frameworks, codes of practice, and the long-standing values of care and accountability in their field.

Faculty Implementation Tips:

- **Rotate roles** during discussion - have students inhabit not only the practitioner's perspective but also that of the patient, hospital administrator, or AI designer.
- **Pair the case with professional ethics literature**, such as nursing or counseling codes of conduct, to ground discussion in real-world accountability standards.
- **Extend the case with a written assignment**, asking students to draft a short "moral case report" that justifies their decision path, cites ethical frameworks, and reflects on institutional dynamics.

Ethics at the Interface of AI and Human Judgment

Case-based ethical reasoning transforms AI literacy from a technical competence into **an embodied, relational practice of responsibility**. It trains students to see **not only what AI recommends, but what it misses** - and to act with integrity when those omissions have consequences for safety, dignity, and equity. As data-driven systems become more deeply embedded in care environments, such scenarios help future professionals **develop the judgment and voice to center the human in algorithmic landscapes**.

---

2. Role-Play and Simulation: Practicing AI-Informed Communication with Empathy and Judgment

In professional fields where interpersonal communication is central - such as education, healthcare, counseling, and social work - AI increasingly enters the room not through autonomous decisions, but through **dashboards, scores, and algorithmic labels** that practitioners are expected to interpret, explain, and act upon. Yet these systems rarely speak with nuance or contextual awareness. **Role-play and simulation** exercises offer a pedagogical approach that allows students to explore what happens when **algorithmic output collides with real-world emotion, cultural complexity, and relational stakes**.

Unlike traditional case studies, role-play requires students to **embody the ethical tensions** inherent in AI-augmented practice. They must engage with both **data and dialogue**, practicing how to **balance technical interpretation with human connection**. These simulations develop students' fluency in navigating **the limits of AI's authority** while preserving professional trust and rapport.

Example (Education): Simulated Parent-Teacher Conference

Scenario: Students participate in a role-play of a **parent-teacher meeting**. The teacher is presented with a **learning analytics dashboard** that categorizes a student as "underperforming" based on test scores, engagement metrics, and assignment completion rates.

Role Assignments:

- One student plays the teacher.
- One student plays the parent.
- A third student may serve as observer or facilitator, taking notes on communication strategies.

The Teacher Must:

- Interpret and explain the dashboard findings.
- Address the parents' concerns and questions.
- Integrate **observations about the student's motivation, participation, and learning style**.
- Make a recommendation (e.g., intervention, referral, or support plan).

The Parent May Raise Issues Such as:

- Cultural or linguistic bias in the assessment tools.
- Socioeconomic challenges affecting homework completion.
- Concerns about labeling and its impact on the student's confidence.

Learning Objectives:

- **Integrating Data with Human Judgment**. Students learn that **quantitative outputs must be interpreted in light of lived experience**, pedagogical insight, and individual variability (Brookfield, 2017; Nicol & Macfarlane-Dick, 2006).
- **Practicing Ethical Restraint**. Students consider when it is appropriate to **question or contextualize AI data**, rather than uncritically accepting algorithmic claims about performance or risk (Holmes et al., 2022; Noble, 2018).
- **Cultivating Relational Intelligence**. Students develop the **empathic communication skills** needed to deliver complex information in a way that honors dignity, trust, and shared problem-solving (Brookfield, 2017; Gay, 2018).

Pedagogical Benefits:

- **Real-Time Decision-Making Under Social Pressure**. The simulation recreates the immediacy and emotional dynamics of professional conversations, pushing students to **balance fidelity to data with responsiveness to human needs**.
- **Role Reversals and Perspective-Taking**. Students who play the parent or client role gain **insight into how AI-based labels feel when communicated without care or context**, reinforcing the importance of trauma-informed and culturally responsive communication (Benjamin, 2023; Sanczyk et al., 2021).
- **Deconstructing AI Objectivity**. Facilitators can guide post-roleplay discussions to unpack **how and why the AI system produced its recommendation**, and where it may have missed relevant, non-quantifiable dimensions of the student's life (Binns, 2018; Eubanks, 2018).

Extension Possibilities Across Disciplines:

- **Social Work**. Simulate an intake interview where an AI system flags a client as "noncompliant." Students must decide whether to question the label or integrate it into care planning.
- **Nursing**. Role-play a patient consultation in which an AI risk score suggests early discharge despite signs of emotional distress or caregiver absence.
- **Counseling**. Simulate a session debrief in which an AI sentiment analysis misinterprets affective tone, prompting a conversation about **human nuance in therapeutic work**.

Practicing Judgment in the Gray Areas of AI Use

Role-play and simulation provide a space to **rehearse the ethical tensions** that arise when AI enters human-centered professions. These exercises emphasize that **data must be translated, mediated, and often challenged** before it can inform responsible practice. By practicing communication that **honors the complexity of clients, students, and patients**, learners become not just literate in AI systems, but **professionally fluent in the art of data-informed, human-first care**.

---

3. Technology Policy and Equity Audits: Ethical Accountability in Applied AI Systems

As AI systems increasingly mediate access to mental health care, social services, and educational support, future professionals in counseling, social work, and related fields must be prepared to critically examine the systems that shape their clients' experiences. **Equity audits offer a structured, ethically grounded method for students to interrogate the assumptions, exclusions, and systemic impacts embedded in AI tools**. These audits bridge technical analysis with professional ethics, providing a practical model for holding technology accountable to the values of inclusion, justice, and human dignity (Benjamin, 2023; Eubanks, 2018; Reamer, 2023).

AI tools deployed in the care professions - such as mental health chatbots, digital intake forms, and triage algorithms - often present themselves as efficient, scalable solutions to underfunded systems. Yet these tools also risk **reproducing systemic inequities under the guise of objectivity**, particularly when they are trained on biased datasets, designed without inclusive consultation, or deployed without transparency (Binns, 2018; Crawford & Paglen, 2021; Noble, 2018). An equity audit invites students to **step into the role of critical evaluators**, assessing both the technical mechanics and the sociocultural implications of these systems.

Assignment: Equity Audit of a Mental Health Chatbot or Intake System

Context: Students select a publicly available or institutionally approved digital tool currently in use by a healthcare provider, nonprofit organization, or mental health platform. Examples may include AI-powered intake screeners, chatbots for anxiety and depression, or decision support tools used in crisis triage.

Audit Process: Using a structured framework grounded in **professional codes of ethics** - such as those from the National Association of Social Workers (NASW), American Counseling Association (ACA), or American Psychological Association (APA) - students examine the tool across four key dimensions:

Equity Audit Criteria:

- **Language Use and Framing**.
  - *"Are questions phrased in a* ***trauma-informed, culturally responsive, and non-stigmatizing manner****?"*
  - *"Are assumptions about family, identity, or pathology embedded in normative language?"*
  - *"How might phrasing reflect unconscious bias or marginalize certain experiences?"*
- **Accessibility and Inclusivity**.
  - *"Does the system accommodate users with* ***limited English proficiency****, neurodiverse processing styles, visual or hearing impairments, or limited literacy?"*
  - *"Are multilingual interfaces available?"*
  - *"Are alternative formats (audio, visual, text simplification) supported?"*
- **Informed Consent and Data Transparency**.
  - *"Is* ***informed consent clearly explained in accessible language****?"*
  - *"Does the user understand what data is collected, how it is stored, and whether it will be used for training or third-party analysis?"*
  - *"Are there meaningful options for opting out?"*
- **Representation and Systemic Blind Spots**.
  - *"Does the system reflect* ***Western-centric clinical norms****, or does it account for diverse cultural models of mental health and well-being?"*
  - *"Which populations are implicitly centered in the design - and who is erased or 'othered?'"*
  - *"Is the model trained on* ***inclusive datasets****, or does it replicate historical exclusions?"* (Benjamin, 2023; Gulya, 2023).

Student Deliverables:

- A written **audit report** that synthesizes findings, contextualizes them in ethical frameworks, and identifies risks and opportunities.

- A set of **concrete reform recommendations** - for example: adjusting language to reduce harm, expanding accessibility features, enhancing consent disclosures, or advocating for participatory co-design with marginalized users.
- Students may also present their findings in class to model **interdisciplinary advocacy and communication**.

Learning Outcomes: Through this assignment, students develop:

- **Applied ethical reasoning skills**, linking theoretical ethics to real-world digital tools (Brookfield, 2017; Reamer, 2023).
- **Awareness of algorithmic harm and potential for equity enhancement**, depending on design, implementation, and use (Eubanks, 2018; Noble, 2018).
- **Confidence in voicing critiques**, grounded not only in social justice but also in **the professional standards that define good practice** in their field (NASW, ACA, APA).

Pedagogical Rationale: This assignment reinforces that **ethical responsibility does not end at the point of tool adoption**. Practitioners must be prepared to assess whether AI systems **align with or undermine the values of care, justice, and autonomy** - and to advocate for reform when they do not. Equity audits help students understand that **data systems are never neutral** and that their role as professionals includes **active, ongoing evaluation of the technologies that structure their practice** (Crawford & Paglen, 2021; Floridi et al., 2018; Sanczyk et al., 2021).

From Tool Use to Tool Accountability

Technology policy and equity audits transform AI literacy into a **form of ethical vigilance and professional leadership**. They empower students to move beyond passive tool use and into **critical engagement with the infrastructures that shape access, representation, and care**. In doing so, students learn that their voice matters - not only in how they use AI, but in how they shape its development, critique its failures, and champion its reform for more just and inclusive futures.

---

4. Interdisciplinary Collaboration Assignments: Building AI Literacy Through Cross-Domain Dialogue

In the rapidly evolving landscape of AI development and implementation, no single discipline holds all the necessary expertise. **Technologists understand the algorithms, but may overlook context. Practitioners understand human needs, but may not grasp system design. Policymakers shape regulations, but rely on evidence from both domains.** To prepare students for real-world environments in which AI systems are created and deployed collaboratively, educators must foster **interdisciplinary literacy** - the ability to **translate between fields, engage in mutual critique, and co-create solutions** grounded in shared accountability.

Interdisciplinary collaboration assignments teach students that ethical, effective AI design requires **more than technical accuracy or professional empathy in isolation**. It requires both, simultaneously, in conversation. These projects simulate the real-world challenge of working across epistemological boundaries - between clinical insight and code architecture, policy frameworks, and user experience design - so that students develop the **collaborative fluency** essential to responsible AI deployment (Barocas et al., 2023; Floridi et al., 2018).

Example Assignment: Nursing + Computer Science Collaboration

Context: Students from nursing and computer science programs are paired in interdisciplinary teams to evaluate and redesign a **symptom-checker interface** - a tool increasingly used in telemedicine, urgent care triage, and mobile health applications.

Team Roles:

- **Nursing students** bring expertise in patient needs, empathy-based communication, cultural competency, and clinical judgment. They evaluate:
  - Whether the interface **uses inclusive language**.
  - How clearly it communicates risk.
  - Whether it supports **diverse health literacy and accessibility needs**.
  - How it may generate **patient anxiety or false reassurance**.
- **Computer science students** explain:
  - How the **algorithm ranks symptoms** and determines urgency.
  - What data sources and training sets were used?
  - How variables (e.g., age, sex, preexisting conditions) are **weighted**.
  - What **assumptions** are embedded in the model's logic?

Collaborative Design and Discussion Process: The teams work together to:

- Identify **misalignments** between algorithmic reasoning and patient-centered priorities.
- Propose **interface changes** that preserve clinical accuracy while improving trust, clarity, and usability.
- Evaluate **trade-offs** between model precision and user comprehension, such as simplifying risk language without sacrificing critical detail.
- Draft a **shared design memo** outlining their recommendations and explaining how the revised tool reflects **fairness, transparency, and patient empowerment**.

This collaboration requires students to negotiate differences in disciplinary language, values, and evidentiary standards, pushing them to recognize that what counts as "valid knowledge" can vary widely between fields. For example, a computer scientist may prioritize statistical accuracy and model optimization, while a social worker emphasizes relational ethics and human trust. By learning to balance explainability with predictive complexity, or numerical rigor with contextual nuance, students gain the capacity to integrate multiple perspectives into more ethical and accountable uses of AI.

Learning Outcomes: By participating in this assignment, students develop:

- **Cross-disciplinary translation skills**, learning to explain domain-specific insights to peers from different fields (Brookfield, 2017; Byars-Winston & Dahlberg, 2019).
- A grounded understanding of how **AI system design is shaped by professional norms, institutional pressures, and cultural assumptions** (Benjamin, 2023; Binns, 2018).
- The ability to engage in **constructive critique and revision**, a key part of both ethical design and collaborative practice (Floridi et al., 2018; W. B. Johnson & Griffin, 2024).

- A realistic appreciation of the **epistemic friction** that arises when different kinds of expertise meet - and how to navigate it productively (Barocas et al., 2023).

Pedagogical Considerations:

- **Scaffolding is Essential.** Provide students with shared vocabulary tools and briefings on each other's fields to reduce initial barriers to collaboration.
- **Assign Rotating Roles.** Let students alternate between facilitator, explainer, and documenter to reinforce shared responsibility and reduce disciplinary hierarchy.
- **Include Reflection.** Ask students to write individual reflections on what was difficult, surprising, or illuminating about working across domains.

Extension Possibilities: This model can be adapted across fields:

- **Education + Data Science**. Co-develop predictive tools for identifying students in need of support, balancing data accuracy with educational equity.
- **Public Health + Ethics**. Design vaccine distribution algorithms informed by epidemiological data and social justice frameworks.
- **Social Work + Policy Analysis**. Audit algorithmic triage tools in child protective services through both computational fairness and trauma-informed care lenses.

Each version reinforces that **AI is never "just a tool" but a socially constructed system**, shaped by institutional priorities, design choices, and cultural assumptions. **What gets built - and just as importantly, what gets left out - depends on who participates in its creation, whose voices are amplified, and whose perspectives are excluded** (Crawford & Paglen, 2021; Noble, 2018). By surfacing these dynamics, students learn to see AI not as neutral infrastructure, but as a reflection of social power that demands critical interrogation and ethical accountability.

Ethics Through Collaboration

Interdisciplinary assignments cultivate AI literacy by immersing students in the messy, collaborative reality of applied design. In doing so, they move beyond isolated competence and toward **shared ethical agency** - learning not only how to build or use AI, but how to **co-create technologies that center fairness, usability, and care**. This is not just preparation for future employment - it is training for democratic participation in shaping AI systems that increasingly govern public life.

---

5. Reflective Writing and Process Journals: Cultivating Ethical and Emotional Awareness in AI-Augmented Practice

In care and service fields where **relational intelligence, moral discernment, and contextual sensitivity** are foundational, students must be encouraged not only to understand how AI systems work but also to reflect on how those systems affect their professional development and identity. Reflective writing and process journals serve as essential tools for developing this awareness. These activities create intentional pauses within an otherwise fast-paced, decision-oriented educational environment - spaces in which students can **make sense**

of their own reactions to AI, surface ethical tensions, and identify moments of discomfort or uncertainty (Brookfield, 2017; Zimmerman, 2002).

As AI technologies increasingly intersect with clinical decisions, educational assessments, and social service recommendations, students may find themselves **silently deferring to machine outputs or grappling with doubts they do not yet have the language to express**. Reflection provides a structure for these internal conversations to emerge. It supports **metacognition**, helping students become more aware of how they think, feel, and decide. More importantly, it fosters **ethical agency** - the confidence to question systems, express unease, and remain attuned to human complexity even when protocols or algorithms suggest otherwise (Byars-Winston & Dahlberg, 2019; Reamer, 2023).

Structure: Ongoing Reflective Practice in Field or Classroom Settings

Students are encouraged to maintain a **weekly or biweekly journal** throughout the semester, especially when engaged in fieldwork, simulation-based learning, or assignments that involve interacting with AI systems.

Suggested Prompts Might Include:

- **What decisions did I make this week that were shaped by AI-generated data?** This helps students trace the influence of digital systems on their professional practice, often in subtle or habituated ways.
- **When did I trust the system's recommendation? When did I question it - and why?** This cultivates awareness of their internal thresholds for deference and skepticism, prompting them to articulate when intuition or ethical concern overrode algorithmic suggestion.
- **What emotional responses did I observe in others - clients, students, and patients when AI was introduced into the interaction?** This builds students' capacity for **empathic observation**, especially around fear, confusion, or resistance to technology, and helps them assess the **relational consequences of automation**.
- **Did I notice moments of ethical uncertainty or dissonance? What were they, and how did I respond?** Encourages moral clarity and reflection on **power, autonomy, and care obligations**.

Examples of Implementation Across Fields:

- **In Counseling.** A student reflects on using a mood-tracking AI tool that suggests depressive trends in a client's responses. The student wrestles with whether the tool's suggestion aligns with their clinical impression and writes about how they brought it up - if at all - in the session.
- **In Nursing.** A student logs their experience of receiving an early warning score for patient deterioration generated by an AI triage system. They note their hesitation to act on it, given other contextual signs, and explore how institutional culture pressures them to trust the system.
- **In Education.** A preservice teacher uses AI-generated student performance data to prepare a parent-teacher conference, but reflects afterward that the conversation felt more "mechanical" than relational. The journal helps them unpack that discomfort and imagine alternative framings.

Learning and Development Outcomes:

- **Ethical Attunement.** Students develop the capacity to recognize moral tensions that might otherwise remain suppressed or rationalized in the face of institutional norms or data-driven workflows (Floridi et al., 2018; Reamer, 2023).
- **Metacognitive Growth.** Journaling encourages students to identify patterns in their own learning, biases, and evolving professional values - essential for lifelong reflective practice (Nicol & Macfarlane-Dick, 2006; Zimmerman, 2002).
- **Emotional Literacy.** Writing about emotional responses to AI (both their own and others') strengthens students' ability to recognize and respond to the **affective dimensions of digital systems**, particularly in sensitive or vulnerable settings (Benjamin, 2023; Sanczyk et al., 2021).
- **Professional Identity Formation.** Through reflection, students begin to articulate **what kind of practitioner they want to be** - and what boundaries they will draw when technology appears to conflict with care ethics or social justice (Brookfield, 2017; Byars-Winston & Dahlberg, 2019).

Pedagogical Tips:

- **Keep it Low-Stakes.** Journals should not be graded for grammar or structure but assessed for depth of reflection. This encourages vulnerability and honesty.
- **Invite Optional Sharing.** Allow students to bring journal excerpts into class discussions or peer groups if they choose. This can foster community, normalize uncertainty, and elevate often-silenced concerns.
- **Model Reflective Transparency.** Faculty can share anonymized examples or their own reflections on using AI, demonstrating that **ethical questioning is part of professionalism, not a failure of understanding**.

Reflection as Resistance and Renewal

In systems increasingly defined by automation, speed, and metrics, reflective writing becomes a **form of resistance** - a way to center human meaning, complexity, and moral discernment. Process journals do not merely document reactions; they help students **construct a coherent, ethically grounded professional identity** in an AI-mediated world. Through sustained reflection, students learn to ask not only, *"What does the system say?"* but also, *"What do I believe, and what does this moment require of me as a human being?"*

Humanizing AI Through Pedagogy

In care and service education, applied AI literacy must go beyond functional use. It must empower students to engage AI systems **ethically, reflectively, and relationally**. Whether interpreting a dashboard, challenging a predictive score, or co-designing a better interface, students need tools to **navigate complexity with humility and professional clarity**.

These five strategies positioned AI not as a detached technological challenge, but as a **relational, institutional, and ethical concern**. They ensure that future professionals do not become technicians of automation, but **human-centered stewards of systems** that increasingly shape well-being, equity, and trust.

Sample Discussion Themes Across Professions: Mapping AI Literacy to Practice Realities

Artificial intelligence is no longer a distant horizon in care and service professions - it is embedded in the tools practitioners use, the decisions they make, and the systems that govern their work. However, AI's role and impact are not uniform across fields. Each profession encounters AI in different forms, framed by its **ethos, regulatory structures, relational expectations, and epistemic traditions**. Educators must therefore align AI literacy instruction with the **specific technological applications and ethical tensions** that shape each discipline's landscape.

The table below outlines a set of **field-specific discussion themes**, designed to help students engage with AI not as a generic innovation, but as a **socio-technical system that reflects and reshapes the values, priorities, and risks of their chosen profession**.

Sample Discussion Themes Across Professions

Field	Common AI Applications	AI Literacy Focus Areas
Nursing	Triage tools, diagnostic decision support	Accountability, explainability, clinical bias, cultural humility
Education	Adaptive learning platforms, grading AI	Data ethics, personalization vs. standardization, transparency in algorithmic feedback
Counseling	Chatbots, digital therapy apps	Relational boundaries, empathy limits, algorithmic misinterpretation of affect
Social Work	Child welfare risk prediction systems	Surveillance, data patterns, informed consent, structural injustice

Nursing: Clinical Accuracy Meets Contextual Ethics

AI-powered triage tools and decision support systems are being rapidly adopted in hospitals to flag deterioration risk, prioritize care, and recommend diagnostic pathways. While such systems may enhance efficiency and predictive accuracy, they often struggle to capture **non-clinical indicators**, such as language barriers, socioeconomic precarity, or trauma history (Chen & Decary, 2020; Topol, 2019).

Key Discussion Themes:

- *"What should a nurse do when the AI suggests early discharge, but the patient lacks safe housing?"*
- *"How do nurses assert their* ***epistemic authority*** *when AI contradicts lived observation?"*

- *"What accountability mechanisms exist when harm occurs due to AI-guided decisions?"*

AI Literacy Goals: Building student capacity for explainability means ensuring they can clearly articulate how AI systems reach conclusions, particularly in contexts where trust and clarity are essential. Alongside this, **students must be trained to recognize the limitations of models, including their tendencies toward bias, omission, or overgeneralization, so they can identify when human judgment should override machine output**. Finally, in interprofessional settings - such as healthcare teams - students should learn to navigate accountability structures, positioning themselves as advocates who safeguard patient well-being while responsibly mediating between algorithmic recommendations and human needs (Benjamin, 2023; Reamer, 2023).

Education: Data-Driven Personalization vs. Student Dignity

In schools, AI tools are increasingly used to deliver adaptive learning pathways, automate grading processes, and flag students for intervention based on detected behavioral or performance patterns. **While these technologies are often marketed as tools that enhance personalization, they simultaneously introduce risks such as intensified data surveillance, reliance on algorithmic labels, and the possibility of narrowing pedagogical approaches to what machines can measure**. As a result, educators must critically evaluate whether these systems truly support student growth or inadvertently compromise equity, privacy, and the flexibility needed for meaningful, human-centered learning (Holmes et al., 2022; Noble, 2018).

Key Discussion Themes:

- *"How do adaptive platforms decide what content a student sees - and what do they fail to notice?"*
- *"Can AI fairly assess motivation, creativity, or emotional development?"*
- *"How transparent are these systems in communicating to students and families?"*

AI Literacy Goals: Fostering critical thinking about **algorithmic transparency requires helping students ask not only what an AI system produces, but how and why its conclusions are generated**. This approach strengthens student agency by ensuring they do not passively accept personalization features but instead question the ethical trade-offs, hidden assumptions, and accountability gaps embedded in the tools. Such reflection is especially vital in communities historically marginalized by standardized metrics, where **unexamined personalization risks reinforcing inequity rather than supporting inclusive learning opportunities** (Brookfield, 2017; Sanczyk et al., 2021).

Counseling: Empathy and the Edges of Automation

AI-based mental health apps, including **chatbots and mood monitors**, are increasingly marketed as scalable solutions to broaden access to care in overburdened health systems. Yet, **these technologies typically simulate affective responses without true comprehension, creating an appearance of empathy that can mask their inability to respond to deeper**

psychological or cultural needs. This absence of nuance - particularly in relation to trauma sensitivity, cultural contexts, and the therapeutic value of silence - **raises serious questions about whether such tools enhance care or risk trivializing the complexity of human mental health** (Benjamin, 2023; Slimi & Carballido, 2023).

Key Discussion Themes:

- *"When might an AI system misread a crisis or de-escalation need?"*
- *"What are the limits of 'empathetic' language when it is produced by predictive patterning?"*
- *"Where should the boundary lie between augmentation and replacement of therapeutic work?"*

AI Literacy Goals: Supporting student reflection on algorithmic empathy gaps **encourages learners to critically assess where machine responses fail to capture the complexity of human emotions**. These exercises also prompt students to examine professional boundaries, ensuring they understand the risks of outsourcing deeply relational work to automated systems. Ultimately, reflection reinforces **the necessity of human presence in emotionally charged or high-risk scenarios, where trust, judgment, and ethical responsibility cannot be delegated to machines** (Brookfield, 2017; Zimmerman, 2002).

Social Work: Risk Scoring, Systemic Bias, and Client Trust

Child welfare agencies and social service providers are increasingly adopting predictive analytics to flag families that may be at higher risk of maltreatment or neglect. While these systems are intended to allocate resources more efficiently, they are often built from incomplete, outdated, or administratively biased datasets. As a result, they can inadvertently amplify systemic inequities, compromise due process, and reduce trust between social workers and the communities they serve (Crawford & Paglen, 2021; Eubanks, 2018).

Predictive models in social work present both technical and ethical challenges. They risk shifting professional judgment away from human expertise and toward opaque scores that may not capture the complexity of family dynamics or community contexts. For social workers, the reliance on such systems raises questions about accountability, informed consent, and whether algorithmic surveillance aligns with the core values of advocacy, dignity, and relational trust that define the profession (Binns, 2018; Gulya, 2023).

Key Discussion Themes:

- *"Should predictive models ever be used in decisions as consequential as family separation, or should they remain advisory tools?"*
- *"How might risk scores alter the trust and transparency in relationships between social workers and their clients?"*
- *"What data sources are used in these systems, and what forms of harm or misclassification might they encode?"*
- *"How can social workers advocate for AI designs that reflect participatory input from the communities most impacted?"*

AI Literacy Goals: Students of social work should learn to:

- Identify structural and institutional biases embedded in datasets and algorithms.
- Evaluate the ethical costs of predictive surveillance in contexts where human well-being is at stake.
- Develop strategies to challenge over-reliance on algorithmic scoring and advocate for participatory, human-centered alternatives in policy and practice.
- Articulate how transparency, professional judgment, and equity can serve as safeguards against the misuse of predictive tools (Byars-Winston & Dahlberg, 2019; Slimi & Carballido, 2023).

Contextualizing AI Literacy Within Professional Practice

AI literacy must be tailored to reflect the ethical questions, data regimes, and interpersonal dynamics unique to each profession. For a nurse, this may mean explaining a triage alert that prioritizes one patient over another, while for a teacher, it might involve interpreting adaptive learning scores that claim to measure student progress. A social worker, meanwhile, may confront a predictive risk assessment that flags families for intervention. In each of these scenarios, accuracy alone is not enough; **students must learn to interrogate what these outputs mean for human relationships, professional authority, and social responsibility**.

These discussions underscore that AI systems are never neutral. **Every model encodes assumptions about what counts as evidence, which outcomes are valued, and whose needs are prioritized**. In healthcare, such assumptions might reflect efficiency over empathy; in education, they may privilege standardized learning over creativity; in social services, they might emphasize prediction at the expense of trust. By surfacing these embedded logics, students learn to see AI not as an objective decision-maker, but as a system shaped by institutional goals and cultural frameworks.

To engage ethically and effectively with AI, students must therefore **become fluent across multiple dimensions of practice**. They need **technical fluency to understand how algorithms work, emotional intelligence to navigate the human impacts of AI-mediated decisions, and systemic awareness to evaluate the broader implications of automation in their field**. When faculty integrate these dimensions into professional training, they prepare students to do more than critique AI - they prepare them to engage with it reflectively, responsibly, and with a commitment to human-centered care and justice.

Section Reflection: Reclaiming Humanity in AI-Augmented Care

This section elevates AI literacy in the helping professions from a technical necessity to a moral obligation. It powerfully asserts that in fields where trust, empathy, and human dignity are central - such as healthcare, education, counseling, and social work - AI systems cannot be accepted uncritically. Instead, they must be interrogated, contextualized, and challenged through the lens of relational ethics, equity, and professional responsibility.

By anchoring AI literacy in the realities of care-based work, the section expands the definition of competence to include emotional intelligence, ethical fluency, and institutional awareness. It foregrounds three non-negotiables: trust must be earned, bias must be exposed, and empathy must remain irreplaceable. The pedagogical strategies offered - ranging from role-play simulations and reflective journals to interdisciplinary audits and ethical case analyses - are not only innovative but essential for preparing students to lead with integrity in AI-mediated environments.

What emerges most clearly is the call to **prepare future professionals not merely to use AI, but to steward it**. These students must become translators, advocates, and gatekeepers - capable of mediating between algorithmic recommendations and the human lives those recommendations affect. This section does not ask whether AI can improve care; it asks what care demands of AI, and how educators can prepare students to uphold those demands with courage and clarity.

In an era of rapid automation, this vision offers a vital humanizing countercurrent that centers people, not just processes. It reminds us that ethical AI literacy in the helping professions is not about resisting technology itself, but about questioning how automation is deployed and what values it elevates. **The true concern is not efficiency versus inefficiency, but whether the pursuit of efficiency erodes care, context, and justice** - the very elements that define professions built on empathy, trust, and human dignity.

Section 6: AI in STEM - Beyond Tool Use to Conceptual Understanding

In computer science, engineering, data science, and biological modeling, **AI is most often introduced as a technical craft: how to build models, train neural networks, fine-tune parameters, and deploy classifiers into production systems**. Students learn the mechanics of TensorFlow, PyTorch, or R with fluency, yet many still struggle to explain in plain language what their models actually do, what assumptions drive their predictions, and what broader effects their work may have once deployed in the world (Barocas et al., 2023). Technical expertise alone can inadvertently leave graduates with blind spots about the deeper meaning of their practice.

This functional emphasis on tool mastery, while undeniably powerful, risks presenting AI as a neutral optimizer - as though its sole role were to minimize loss functions or increase efficiency. Such framing neglects the reality that **AI is a sociotechnical system, shaped by the quality of its training data, the contexts of its deployment, the labor that sustains it, and the energy costs of scaling it** (Crawford, 2021; Pasquale, 2015). By ignoring these forces, students may come to see AI as purely mathematical, rather than as a technology entangled with human values, economic incentives, and environmental trade-offs.

This section, therefore, calls for a pedagogical shift: moving from "how to use" AI toward "what it means to build." Instead of stopping at technical proficiency, educators must integrate ethics, sustainability, fairness, and systems-level thinking into technical curricula. By doing so, students not only learn to code effectively, but also to grapple with the institutional goals, cultural assumptions, and social consequences embedded in every line of code and every dataset. **The aim is to prepare a new generation of scientists and engineers who can pair technical brilliance with ethical foresight** - building systems that are not only accurate, but also just, accountable, and sustainable.

Key AI Literacy Themes for STEM Education

---

1. The Black-Box Problem and Interpretability: Navigating Opacity in AI-Driven Decision-Making

As machine learning systems become more deeply embedded in **safety-critical environments** - such as healthcare diagnostics, criminal risk assessments, autonomous vehicles, and credit scoring - their **opacity has become a major point of ethical, legal, and operational concern**. The so-called *black-box problem* arises when a system's internal decision-making logic is **so complex, non-linear, or poorly documented** that even its designers cannot fully explain why it produces a particular output (Doshi-Velez & Kim, 2017). This undermines **trust, accountability, and justifiability**, especially when the stakes include life, liberty, or access to essential services (Floridi et al., 2018; Topol, 2019).

The problem is most acute in **deep learning models**, which achieve high performance through massive training data and layered abstraction - but at the cost of human interpretability. In response, explainable AI (XAI) has emerged as a subfield devoted to making these models **more transparent, auditable, and communicable**, especially to non-technical stakeholders. However, **interpretability often involves trade-offs** with predictive accuracy or speed, and these trade-offs must be **evaluated in context**, not as abstract technical exercises.

Assignment Idea (Computer Science or Data Science): Comparative Model Interpretability in Healthcare

Scenario: Students are tasked with developing two machine learning models to **predict heart disease risk** based on a standard dataset (e.g., UCI Cleveland dataset):

- A **decision tree model** or logistic regression, which allows for straightforward interpretation of variable importance and path-based reasoning.
- A **neural network model**, which may achieve higher predictive performance but lacks intuitive traceability for non-technical audiences.

Role Play Setup: Students present their models to a **mock clinical review board** composed of classmates, faculty, or health professionals acting as physicians, hospital administrators, and patient advocates. Each team must justify its model's use, explain its recommendations, and respond to stakeholder concerns.

Discussion Focus Areas:

- **Which Model is More Explainable - and To Whom?** Students must reflect on **audience-specific interpretability**, distinguishing between what is understandable to data scientists versus clinicians, patients, or regulators (Barocas et al., 2023; Doshi-Velez & Kim, 2017).

- **How do you Justify Predictions to Stakeholders?** Teams must translate technical outputs into **ethically communicable and actionable recommendations**, modeling the responsibility of AI developers to engage with the **relational and epistemic dimensions of trust** (Byars-Winston & Dahlberg, 2019; Reamer, 2023).
- **Where does Transparency Outweigh Performance - and Where Might it not?** Students evaluate scenarios in which **a marginal gain in accuracy** might be unacceptable if it leads to **opaque decision-making**, especially when explainability is legally or morally necessary (Eubanks, 2018; Floridi et al., 2018).

Learning Outcomes:

- **Appreciate the Interpretability–Performance Tradeoff**. Students learn that model selection is **not merely technical**, but contingent on **stakeholder needs, domain constraints, and the consequences of misinterpretation**.
- **Practice Ethical Communication**. Presenting models to non-technical actors teaches students to **translate algorithmic reasoning into accessible, trustworthy language** - a crucial competency in interdisciplinary AI work (Benjamin, 2023; Brookfield, 2017).
- **Engage in Socio-Technical Decision-Making**. Students confront the reality that **the best model is not always the most accurate one**, but the one that balances performance with **fairness, transparency, and contextual appropriateness** (Binns, 2018; Gulya, 2023).

Pedagogical Extensions:

- Introduce tools such as **LIME, SHAP, or model cards** to explore post-hoc explanation techniques.
- Assign complementary readings from **Crawford and Paglen (2021)** on dataset legibility or **Slimi and Carballido (2023)** on interpretability in educational contexts.
- Add a reflective writing component. *"When should a model's decision be overruled by human professionals - and why?"*

Interpretability as a Professional and Ethical Imperative

Understanding and addressing the black-box problem is essential for students who will work at the intersection of AI and public life. In domains where **opacity threatens autonomy, safety, or fairness**, interpretability is not a bonus - it is a **precondition for trust and ethical governance**. This assignment challenges students to think beyond metrics, asking not only *"What works best?"* but also, *"What can be justified, explained, and defended - ethically and socially - in the real world?"*

---

2. Algorithmic Fairness and Bias Mitigation: Embedding Equity into the Model Lifecycle

Artificial intelligence systems increasingly influence decisions in hiring, lending, criminal justice, education, and healthcare - domains already marked by systemic inequities. When AI models are trained on historical data that reflect these inequities, or when developers fail to account for **contextual, cultural, and demographic variation**, the result is not neutral automation but **amplified injustice** (Barocas et al., 2023; Noble, 2018). In many cases, algorithmic harm emerges **not from malicious intent, but from omissions in design and evaluation** - blindness to how race, gender, class, disability, or language shape access and outcomes.

Algorithmic fairness education must therefore go beyond abstract theory. It must prepare students to **audit datasets for skewed representation**, test for **performance disparities across protected groups**, and apply **remediation strategies** that reflect ethical reasoning, not just statistical parity (Benjamin, 2023; Binns, 2018). Fairness must become a **pre-deployment mindset**, not a post-hoc add-on.

Lab Exercise (Data Science or AI Ethics Course): Auditing and Mitigating Bias

Assignment Context: Students are provided with a widely studied, real-world dataset known for fairness controversies - such as the **COMPAS recidivism dataset** (used in pretrial risk scoring), or a **facial recognition benchmark dataset** such as the PPB (Pilot Parliaments Benchmark).

Part 1: Baseline Audit. Students begin by training a predictive model - e.g., a logistic regression classifier for COMPAS or an image classifier for face identification. They evaluate:

- **Accuracy and false positive/negative rates** across subgroups (e.g., race, gender).
- **Calibration errors** between groups.
- **Disparate impact ratios** or ROC curves segmented by demographic labels.

Part 2: Bias Mitigation. Students apply **post-processing fairness interventions** using libraries such as Fairlearn or AIF360. Examples include:

- **Equalized odds**, where false positive and false negative rates are balanced across groups.
- **Demographic parity** that ensures equal prediction rates regardless of group membership.
- **Threshold shifting**, to equalize decision boundaries while tracking performance trade-offs.

Visualization and Communication: Students produce comparative plots to show how fairness techniques changed the model's behavior - and where tensions emerged between equity and performance.

Reflective Prompt: Ethics Beyond Metrics. After completing the technical component, students write a brief reflection in response to prompts such as:

- *"Did improving fairness reduce accuracy? Should that be acceptable?"*
- *"Which kinds of harm are we trying to prevent - and for whom?"*
- *"Would your fairness decision change if the model were used for university admissions versus targeted advertising? Why?"*

These reflections encourage students to engage not just with statistical measures, but with **contextual ethics, real-world impact, and social positionality** (Floridi et al., 2018; Gulya, 2023; Reamer, 2023).

Learning Outcomes: By the end of this assignment, students will be able to:

- Identify **how dataset composition affects model equity**, including over- and under-representation.
- Diagnose **disparities in model performance** across protected groups and interpret what these disparities mean in human terms.
- Apply fairness interventions while **critically analyzing trade-offs** - not just mathematically, but ethically.
- Recognize that fairness is **domain-sensitive**, and that what counts as "acceptable" trade-off in one field (e.g., marketing) may be unacceptable in another (e.g., healthcare or criminal justice) (Binns, 2018; Eubanks, 2018).

Pedagogical Integration Tips:

- **Interdisciplinary pairing:** Invite students from ethics, sociology, or law to join data science teams to discuss **non-technical fairness dimensions** during debrief.
- **Policy translation task:** Ask students to write a short policy brief for a hypothetical agency - e.g., a city police department or healthcare provider - explaining the ethical implications of their fairness strategy.
- **Use real-world case precedents:** Complement the lab with readings on **COMPAS deployment controversies** or **facial recognition bans**, showing how model decisions affect lives (Benjamin, 2023; Crawford & Paglen, 2021).

From Technical Tuning to Ethical Commitments

Fairness cannot be outsourced to math alone. As this lab illustrates, **statistical parity is not ethical sufficiency**, and mitigation strategies must be understood not just as optimization tools, but as **expressions of professional and civic responsibility**. When students learn to see fairness as embedded in **data history, social context, and institutional power**, they become better equipped to build AI systems that **promote justice rather than replicate harm**.

---

3. Ecological and Labor Impacts of AI Systems: Revealing the Infrastructure Beneath "Intelligence"

Much of AI education focuses on system performance, algorithmic innovation, and interface design - rarely interrogating the **material and human infrastructure** that sustains the illusion of automated intelligence. Yet every AI system is built atop layers of energy consumption, data extraction, and **invisible labor**. Training a single large language model (LLM), for instance, requires **massive computational resources**, contributing significantly to global carbon emissions (Strubell et al., 2020). At the same time, the data used to fine-tune AI systems is often annotated, flagged, or cleaned by **precarious workers in the Global South**, many of whom are paid subsistence wages to make AI seem "intelligent" (Crawford, 2021; Gray & Suri, 2019).

This hidden scaffolding constitutes what Crawford (2021) described as **AI's extractive logic** - a socio-technical pipeline that draws from environmental, cognitive, and emotional resources without transparency or accountability. For students to fully grasp what it means to design or deploy AI responsibly, they must move beyond abstraction and into an understanding of **AI as a planetary and labor system**, not just a computational one (Bender et al., 2021; Benjamin, 2023).

Assignment Idea (Engineering Ethics or Human-Centered AI): Computational Cost and Design Trade-offs

Part 1: Energy Analysis of LLM Training and Deployment. Students examine published studies on the **energy consumption of large models**, such as GPT-5. Using carbon accounting tools or estimates from cloud providers, they:

- Calculate the energy use associated with training versus inference.
- Compare local (edge-device) inference to cloud-based querying.
- Discuss regional disparities in **energy sourcing and environmental impact** (e.g., coal-powered data centers vs. renewable regions).

Discussion Questions:

- *"What trade-offs emerge between model size, latency, and energy draw?"*
- *"How might model design be adapted to* ***prioritize sustainability without compromising equity of access or critical functionality****?"*

Deliverable: A proposal outlining **design revisions or deployment strategies** - e.g., smaller distillation models, use-case throttling, or intelligent caching - that reduce environmental impact while preserving function for users in varied socio-economic settings.

Follow-Up Seminar: Hidden Labor and Ghost Work

Assigned Readings:

- Gray and Suri (2019), *Ghost Work: How to Stop Silicon Valley from Building a New Global Underclass.*
- Crawford (2021), *The Atlas of AI: Power, Politics, and the Planetary Costs of Artificial Intelligence* (chapter on data annotation and human-machine entanglement).

Seminar Themes:

- *"Who trains, labels, and moderates the content used by large-scale AI systems?"*
- *"What labor protections (if any) exist for these workers?"*
- *"How do narratives of automation* ***erase or undervalue the human effort*** *embedded in AI performance?"*

Student Reflection Prompt:

- *"What does it mean to call a system 'automated' when it is supported by thousands of microtask workers?"*
- *"How should ethical AI design include these workers?"*

Students are encouraged to research data annotation platforms, such as Amazon Mechanical Turk or Appen, and examine how these platforms depend on low-paid, often invisible labor to sustain AI development. **By analyzing who performs this work, under what conditions, and for whose benefit, they begin to see that ethical AI is not only about technical accuracy but also about fair labor practices**. Including questions of worker dignity and equity as a core element of responsible AI design helps students connect algorithmic performance to the human systems that make it possible, shifting ethics from an afterthought to an integral design principle.

Learning Outcomes:

By engaging with these activities, students will:

- Recognize the **ecological footprint of computation**, particularly in scaling deep learning architectures (Strubell et al., 2020).
- Evaluate the **global distribution of resource costs** - including energy, hardware extraction, and data processing labor (Crawford, 2021).
- Critically reflect on how AI narratives obscure dependency on **low-wage, human-in-the-loop infrastructure** (Bender et al., 2021; Gray & Suri, 2019).
- Begin to integrate **ecological sustainability and labor ethics** as core design principles, not optional considerations (Floridi et al., 2018).

Pedagogical Rationale: Beyond Model-Centric Thinking

Most AI curricula train students to optimize for **performance metrics**: accuracy, precision, speed. These assignments reframe the question toward **externalities**: "*What does AI cost the environment, and who pays with their labor to make 'automation' possible?*" In doing so, students are challenged to reconceive their role **not only as system optimizers but also as stewards of complex, interdependent socio-technical ecosystems** (Gulya, 2023; Noble, 2018).

Designing for Visibility, Justice, and Sustainability

AI systems are not immaterial abstractions - they are extractive, infrastructural, and labor-intensive. To educate ethical technologists and AI-literate professionals, we must **illuminate what is typically hidden**: the carbon footprints buried in data centers, and the human fingerprints on every "automated" decision. When students learn to account for these impacts, they begin to design with **responsibility, reciprocity, and long-term sustainability** in mind.

---

4. Project-Based Learning with Ethical and Systems Focus: Designing for Responsibility, Not Just Results

Traditional AI and engineering curricula often emphasize technical mastery through tightly scoped problem sets or proof-of-concept demonstrations. While this approach cultivates precision and rigor, it risks training students to see design challenges as **isolated optimization problems**, disconnected from their broader human, ecological, and political contexts. **Project-based learning (PBL) infused with ethical and systems thinking** offers a powerful alternative. By asking students to design AI solutions with embedded attention to stakeholder needs, long-term impact, and social accountability, educators help cultivate **reflective, multidisciplinary problem-solvers** equipped to work in real-world, high-stakes domains (Brookfield, 2017; Floridi et al., 2018).

Incorporating **ethics and systems analysis** into the full lifecycle of design work ensures that responsibility is treated not as an add-on, but as a **core design constraint - like latency,**

efficiency, or cost. This helps students move beyond technical minimalism toward **anticipatory and participatory design paradigms**, where the implications of a system matter as much as its performance (Benjamin, 2023; Binns, 2018).

Example Capstone Project: Urban Waste Optimization Algorithm

Scenario: A team of students is tasked with designing an AI-based system to optimize **municipal waste collection routes** and reduce landfill overflow through predictive analytics. Instead of treating this as a purely logistical challenge, they are required to embed **ethical and systemic considerations** into the design process.

Deliverable Components:

- **Data Source Evaluation.** Students must analyze the datasets used to train the model, assessing:
    - **Coverage**. *"Do datasets include low-income or underserved districts?"*
    - **Quality**. *"Are the sensors used in various neighborhoods equally calibrated?"*
    - **Consent**. *"Were residents informed or consulted when their waste data were collected?"*

This cultivates awareness of dataset politics and embedded bias at the point of input, reminding students that what goes into a model is never neutral (Bender et al., 2021; Crawford & Paglen, 2021). Students learn to see that **every dataset carries assumptions about what is included, what is excluded, and how categories are defined, shaping the kinds of outputs the model will later produce**. By engaging with these questions early, students begin to understand that bias does not just appear in algorithmic results - it is structured from the very start through data collection, labeling, and selection practices.

- **Bias Risk Assessment**.
    - Teams must identify how their model may unintentionally **prioritize certain communities over others**, such as underserved areas with less complete data or over-policing "overflow" neighborhoods.
    - They simulate **impact disparities** and consider fairness interventions (e.g., demographic parity adjustments) (Barocas et al., 2023; Eubanks, 2018).
- **Energy Usage Estimation**.
    - Students calculate the **computational and energy costs** of model training and continuous inference, especially if deployed at a city scale.
    - They propose trade-offs such as model compression or edge deployment to **balance accuracy with sustainability** (Gulya, 2023; Strubell et al., 2020).
- **Community Stakeholder Feedback Plan**.
    - Teams must create a mechanism to **collect input from residents, sanitation workers, and environmental justice organizations**.
    - They draft **pre-deployment community consultation plans** and **post-deployment communication strategies**, emphasizing **participatory accountability** (Benjamin, 2023; Sanczyk et al., 2021).
- **Post-Deployment Monitoring Proposal**.
    - The project concludes with a framework for **ongoing evaluation**, including:
        - Performance auditing.
        - Fairness tracking across demographic segments.

- A protocol for addressing unintended consequences (e.g., over-scheduling in specific neighborhoods or neglect of edge cases).

This component affirms that responsible AI does not end at launch - it requires continuous social and technical responsiveness to ensure that systems remain accountable in dynamic contexts (Floridi et al., 2018; Reamer, 2023). **Students learn that models deployed in real-world environments must be revisited, audited, and adjusted as new data, ethical concerns, or unintended impacts emerge**. In this way, AI is reframed not as a static product, but as an evolving sociotechnical practice that demands ongoing stewardship, reflection, and reform.

Learning Outcomes: Students who complete such a capstone project will be able to:

- Conduct **integrated stakeholder analysis**, identifying who is affected, how, and with what consequences.
- Evaluate design choices through **multi-dimensional ethical lenses**, including distributive justice, environmental sustainability, and procedural fairness (Binns, 2018; Noble, 2018).
- Balance performance metrics with broader **social and ecological constraints**, moving from isolated optimization to systems thinking.
- Produce **design documentation that is legible to non-technical actors**, enhancing transparency and accountability in public-facing systems (Byars-Winston & Dahlberg, 2019).

Pedagogical Considerations:

- **Scaffold Early**. Introduce each component (e.g., data ethics, environmental impact, stakeholder theory) in prior modules to prepare students for integration.
- **Engage Cross-Disciplinary Mentors**. Bring in advisors from policy, urban planning, or community advocacy to review student work from diverse standpoints.
- **Assess Process as Well as Outcome**. Evaluate how well students **navigated ethical ambiguity, interdisciplinary collaboration, and iterative feedback**, not just their technical artifact.

Designing AI with Social Imagination

Project-based learning that centers **ethical foresight and systemic responsibility** does more than prepare students to build better tools - it prepares them to **ask better questions**. By embedding considerations of equity, energy, and human impact into the full lifecycle of design, students learn that **innovation without reflection is not neutral - it is negligence**. The future of AI education depends on developing not only competent technologists but instead **ethically agile systems thinkers** who can navigate the complexity of building for a shared world.

---

5. Interdisciplinary Collaboration in STEM Courses: Embedding Ethics Through Value-Sensitive Design

STEM education often emphasizes abstraction, modularity, and optimization - qualities essential for precision, but frequently insufficient for anticipating the **social, cultural, and**

ecological dimensions of technology deployment. To develop AI systems that support not only efficiency but also equity, sustainability, and human dignity, students must learn to **design with values in mind**, not just metrics. This requires moving beyond disciplinary silos and engaging with **interdisciplinary collaboration** as a core mode of responsible AI practice.

Value-sensitive design (VSD) provides one such framework. Developed by Friedman et al. (2013), VSD emphasizes the integration of **human values - such as privacy, justice, ecological stewardship, and respect for cultural traditions - into the design and evaluation of technology**. In practice, this means involving diverse stakeholders, anticipating unintended consequences, and foregrounding ethical reflection from the outset of a project.

In STEM classrooms, VSD-oriented collaboration encourages students to work not only with fellow engineers or data scientists but also with **social scientists, artists, Indigenous knowledge holders, educators, and policy experts**. These partnerships enable more **holistic, pluralistic AI design practices**, attuned to both local needs and global consequences (Benjamin, 2023; Brookfield, 2017).

Example: AI-Driven Conservation Monitoring with Indigenous Collaboration

Project Context: A cross-disciplinary student team from **biology and computer science** is tasked with designing an AI system for **wildlife conservation monitoring** using drones and sensor networks. Rather than building in isolation, they partner with **Indigenous land stewards**, who bring deep cultural, ecological, and spiritual knowledge of the territory.

Interdisciplinary Process:

- **Computer science students** develop object recognition algorithms to track species movement.
- **Biology students** validate data inputs and assess ecological baselines.
- **Indigenous collaborators** offer insight into **place-based values, traditional ecological knowledge, and community priorities** that should inform deployment and data interpretation.
- **Social scientists or ethicists** help structure deliberation around **data sovereignty, consent, and long-term governance** of the system.

Discussion Themes and Design Tensions:

- **Whose Definition of "Environmental Success" Guides the Project?** Students must reconcile scientific measures of biodiversity with Indigenous knowledge systems that emphasize **relational accountability, reciprocity, and spiritual stewardship** (Benjamin, 2023; Tuck & Yang, 2014).
- **What are the Risks of Surveillance, Data Misuse, or Territorial Encroachment?** Students must address the ethical implications of deploying AI systems on traditional lands - especially in light of **historical extractivism and technological colonization** (Crawford, 2021; Noble, 2018).
- **How is Power Shared Across Disciplinary and Cultural Boundaries?** The project challenges students to create structures for **ongoing dialogue, shared governance, and respectful disagreement** - a critical skill in participatory AI work (Binns, 2018; Sanczyk et al., 2021).

Learning Outcomes: Students participating in such projects develop:

- **Cross-disciplinary translation fluency**, learning to communicate and collaborate across technical, cultural, and epistemological boundaries (Byars-Winston & Dahlberg, 2019).
- The ability to identify **value conflicts and negotiate ethical trade-offs**, rather than relying on reductive metrics or convenience-based optimization.
- Deepened understanding of **how AI systems can either reinforce or challenge existing power asymmetries**, depending on their design, deployment, and governance (Floridi et al., 2018; Gulya, 2023).
- A stronger commitment to **long-term relational accountability**, recognizing that ethical design is not just a phase, but an ongoing practice.

Pedagogical Recommendations:

- **Co-teach with faculty from non-STEM fields** to model collaborative inquiry and value-centered reasoning.
- Scaffold collaboration with readings on **decolonial methodologies, participatory design, and data sovereignty** (Crawford & Paglen, 2021; Gray & Suri, 2019).
- Include **consent protocols, stakeholder interviews, and feedback loops** in grading criteria to underscore process, not just product.

Reimagining Design Through Interdisciplinary Dialogue

Interdisciplinary collaboration is not ancillary to responsible AI - it is foundational. When STEM students learn to **co-create with, rather than build for**, communities and collaborators with different forms of knowledge, they move beyond problem-solving and toward **ethical world-making**. Value-sensitive design offers a generative model for AI education that is **inclusive, context-aware, and deeply human** - equipping students to design systems not just with technical excellence, but with **cultural humility and ecological wisdom**.

Key Teaching Strategies: Infusing Ethics into AI and Data Education

To prepare students for AI development and deployment in a world shaped by social inequity, ecological fragility, and contested values, ethics cannot be confined to a standalone lecture or optional unit. Instead, it must be **interwoven into the core of technical instruction**, treated as an ongoing lens for decision-making, critique, and self-awareness. The following strategies provide **practical, replicable entry points** for embedding ethical reasoning across labs, projects, and classroom dialogue - transforming AI education from performance-driven to **consequence-aware and relationally grounded** (Benjamin, 2023; Brookfield, 2017; Floridi et al., 2018).

---

1. Ethics-Infused Lab Prompts: The "Consequence Paragraph"

Strategy: In every coding or modeling assignment, students are required to write a **brief reflection paragraph** answering questions such as:

- *"What populations could be harmed or excluded if this model were deployed?"*
- *"What assumptions does my model make about fairness, privacy, or access?"*
- *"Who would need to approve or audit this system before real-world use?"*

Purpose: This strategy builds the habit of **ethical anticipation** - training students to consider **the social life of their code**, not just its functional correctness. It also prepares them to explain their design choices in public-facing, stakeholder-centered ways (Binns, 2018; Reamer, 2023).

---

2. Cross-Functional Reflection Logs: Decision-Making in Context

Strategy: Throughout technical labs or team-based projects, students maintain **personal or shared reflection logs** documenting:

- Design decisions and rationales.
- Trade-offs between performance, explainability, fairness, or efficiency.
- Moments of uncertainty, disagreement, or value conflict.

Purpose: These logs serve as **metacognitive tools**, helping students recognize that **technical development is always situated within a web of professional, political, and moral concerns** (Byars-Winston & Dahlberg, 2019; Zimmerman, 2002). Logs can also form the basis for ethical case presentations or portfolio narratives.

---

3. Comparative Model Evaluation: Beyond Accuracy

Strategy: Rather than selecting the highest-performing model by default, students must compare multiple models using **multi-dimensional evaluation criteria**, such as:

- *"Which model is most **interpretable** to non-expert users?"*
- *"Which model has the **lowest variance across demographic subgroups**?"*
- *"Which model is more **sustainable or scalable** given environmental or institutional constraints?"*

Purpose: This trains students to think **critically and contextually** about model selection, emphasizing that **accuracy is not a stand-in for impact** - especially in fields such as healthcare, education, and criminal justice where transparency, fairness, or latency may be more urgent than a marginal improvement in F1 score (Doshi-Velez & Kim, 2017; Strubell et al., 2020).

---

4. Embedded Reading Discussions: Theory Meets Code

Strategy: Alongside technical instruction, integrate curated readings from critical AI literature, such as:

- Ruha Benjamin's *Viral Justice* (Benjamin, 2023).
- Kate Crawford's *Atlas of AI* (Crawford, 2021).

- Safiya Noble's *Algorithms of Oppression* (Noble, 2018).
- Virginia Eubanks' *Automating Inequality* (Eubanks, 2018).

Pair these with coding assignments and ask students to reflect:

- *"How do the authors' critiques apply to the tool we are building?"*
- *"What blind spots might we replicate if we ignore their warnings?"*
- *"What structural changes might make our designs more just or inclusive?"*

Purpose: This strategy connects **code to critique**, grounding students in the lived, systemic realities that AI systems may obscure. It fosters **intellectual humility and epistemic plurality**, encouraging students to see that social knowledge is just as essential to ethical design as technical skill (Benjamin, 2023; Crawford & Paglen, 2021).

---

5. Invite Practitioners: Applied Q&A with AI Stakeholders

Strategy: Bring in professionals who work at the intersection of technology and accountability, including:

- **AI auditors** who assess bias, explainability, or safety.
- **Ethicists and policy advisors** who shape regulatory frameworks.
- **Impact analysts** who study how technologies affect users and communities.

Discussion Topics:

- *"What ethical dilemmas arise in industry vs. academia?"*
- *"How are social consequences measured and communicated to leadership?"*
- *"What does ethical dissent look like in real-world teams?"*

Purpose: Hearing from practitioners demystifies ethical practice and reveals the tensions, politics, and negotiations that shape real-world deployment, showing students that decisions are rarely simple or neutral. These practitioner insights ground abstract ethical principles in lived experience, helping students see how trade-offs between efficiency, fairness, and accountability actually play out in professional settings (Barocas et al., 2023; Gulya, 2023). They also reinforce that **ethics is not an optional add-on to technical work, but a core dimension of professional responsibility that must guide every stage of design, implementation, and evaluation**.

Ethics as Practice, Not Abstraction

By embedding these five strategies across instruction, educators move beyond treating ethics as a separate or peripheral concern and instead frame it as an everyday practice of design, reflection, and accountability. This approach emphasizes that **ethical considerations are not something to add after a model is built, but part of the very fabric of technical decision-making**. In doing so, students begin to see that their projects exist within larger social systems, where every line of code or design choice carries consequences for how others will interact with, question, and live alongside the technologies they create.

As students practice navigating ambiguity, engaging critique, and documenting their ethical reasoning, they gain skills that extend far beyond technical mastery. These practices prepare them to create not only high-performing models but also ones that embody responsibility, transparency, and care. Ultimately, **this equips students to contribute meaningfully to shaping a future for AI that is more just, inclusive, and sustainable** - where innovation and ethical stewardship are inseparable parts of the same professional identity.

Section Reflection: Designing AI Literacy for Ethical Technologists

This section delivers a compelling transformation of STEM-based AI education - from a narrow focus on technical proficiency to a broader commitment to ethical, contextual, and systems-aware understanding. It powerfully reframes AI literacy in STEM not as the ability to build performant models, but as the capacity to interrogate, communicate, and design with accountability. **The shift from "how it works" to "what it means" is evident across the pedagogical strategies, case studies, and interdisciplinary integrations offered**.

At its core, the section insists that ethical competence in STEM must be practiced, not just professed. Assignments such as comparative model justification, fairness audits, energy and labor cost analyses, and value-sensitive co-design projects ask students to confront the real-world implications of their work. These experiences cultivate engineers and data scientists who are not only technically capable, but socially literate - able to negotiate trade-offs, anticipate harm, and communicate decisions across disciplinary, cultural, and civic boundaries.

What stands out most is the insistence that design is never neutral. Every AI model is built on assumptions, trained on histories, and deployed into contexts shaped by power, inequality, and human fragility. **The section emphasizes that STEM educators must normalize ethical reflection as part of everyday instruction** - infusing labs with consequence paragraphs, encouraging cross-functional reflection logs, and positioning practitioners as guides for real-world accountability.

Ultimately, this section calls for AI literacy that **prepares students to be stewards of complex systems - not just builders of optimized code**. By grounding learning in justice, sustainability, and dialogue, it charts a new path forward for engineering and computer science education - one where the integrity of AI is measured not just in performance metrics, but in its capacity to serve the public good.

Section 7: Designing Interdisciplinary AI Modules for General Education

---

General education (Gen Ed) curricula serve as the **intellectual commons** of the undergraduate experience. Gen Ed is where students learn to think critically, communicate clearly, and engage with contemporary issues across disciplinary lines. Given AI's widespread influence on public life, labor, information, and communication, general education is a

strategic gateway for building broad, interdisciplinary AI literacy (Byars-Winston & Dahlberg, 2019; Long & Magerko, 2020).

This section offers a practical roadmap for faculty who want to design short, transferable AI-infused modules that can be seamlessly embedded into existing courses in ethics, media literacy, writing, communication, global studies, and first-year seminars. Rather than requiring technical expertise, **these modules emphasize inquiry, reflection, storytelling, and societal relevance, ensuring that both students and faculty can engage critically with AI regardless of backgroun**d. By focusing on accessible practices, the approach democratizes AI literacy, positioning it as a shared responsibility across the curriculum rather than a specialized skill confined to computer science or engineering.

Why General Education Is Essential for AI Literacy

While much of AI education is housed in specialized technical majors - such as computer science, data science, or engineering - the ethical, social, and epistemological challenges posed by AI systems are **universal in scope**. These systems influence everything from hiring and housing to policing, pedagogy, and public health. As such, AI literacy cannot remain siloed within technical domains. It must become a **generalizable civic competency**, cultivated across the entire undergraduate experience. **General Education (Gen Ed)** - often a student's first and most interdisciplinary academic exposure - offers a powerful, underutilized space for building this foundation.

---

1. Universal Reach: Engaging Every Undergraduate

General education courses are required for all students, regardless of major, making them one of the few curricular spaces with truly universal reach. This breadth provides institutions with a unique opportunity to ensure that every student - whether they are preparing to become a nurse, artist, teacher, or entrepreneur - has the capacity to think critically about AI and its implications. By embedding AI literacy in Gen Ed, educators signal that understanding and questioning algorithmic systems is not a specialized skill but a civic and cultural necessity for all learners.

Importantly, Gen Ed is often the only point of contact many non-STEM majors will have with structured conversations about data, algorithms, or digital ethics. In this context, AI literacy should not be equated with technical training or coding proficiency; instead, it means cultivating habits of inquiry and skepticism toward technologies that increasingly shape public and private life. Students are asked to confront questions such as:

- *"Who designs these systems?"*
- *"What goals and values are embedded in them?"*
- *"How do they shape the way knowledge, opportunity, and power are distributed?"*

Embedding AI literacy at the Gen Ed level ensures that future decision-makers, voters, and civic actors are equipped to engage with AI as both users and subjects of its influence

(Benjamin, 2023; Selwyn, 2019). **By encountering these questions early in their academic journey, students begin to recognize how algorithmic systems shape public discourse, economic opportunity, and civic life**. This preparation fosters not only technical awareness but also ethical and political responsibility, positioning graduates to approach AI with critical judgment rather than passive acceptance.

---

2. Cross-Disciplinary Relevance: AI as a Social Force

General education courses often explore themes of civic engagement, media analysis, identity formation, and social change. These topics are not peripheral to AI - they are already being reshaped by it. **Algorithmic systems now curate the news that frames public debate, mediate patterns of policing and surveillance, influence how students are assessed in classrooms, and determine eligibility for essential public benefits** (Eubanks, 2018; Noble, 2018). Far from being abstract technologies, these systems intersect directly with the core human concerns that Gen Ed courses address, making AI literacy central to understanding the contemporary civic and cultural landscape. For example:

- **Media Literacy Course**. Instead of simply noting that AI blurs fact and fabrication, the course could analyze **deepfake journalism** and AI-generated "news" images circulated during elections. Students could trace how these artifacts shape public trust, examine who funds their distribution, and debate how platforms should regulate their spread. This goes beyond truth/falsehood into questions of power, credibility, and governance.
- **Political Science Course**. Rather than just exploring polarization, students might investigate how **algorithmic microtargeting** affects voter mobilization and issue salience. A class exercise could compare campaign ads delivered to different demographic groups via recommender systems, then ask: *"Whose voices are amplified?" "Whose concerns are ignored?"* This situates AI within broader concerns about democratic participation and institutional accountability.
- **Sociology Course**. Instead of focusing narrowly on racial logics, students could examine how **predictive risk scoring in welfare or education** redefines what counts as "at-risk" populations. They could map how such systems shift decision-making authority from frontline workers to automated dashboards, highlighting how definitions of vulnerability, responsibility, and trust are institutionally constructed. This reframes AI not just as a bias problem but as a reshaping of social categories themselves.

By integrating AI literacy into these courses, faculty move beyond abstract discussion of algorithms and tie them to the lived realities students encounter in media, politics, education, and daily life. This approach highlights that **AI systems are never purely technical - they are embedded in cultural assumptions, institutional logics, and political economies that shape how decisions are made and whose interests are served**. In doing so, students come to understand that data systems are contested terrains of power, requiring critical inquiry and civic responsibility rather than passive acceptance (Crawford, 2021; Gulya, 2023).

---

3. Formation of Habits of Mind: Building Reflective Thinkers

Perhaps most crucially, General Education is where students first begin shaping the intellectual habits that carry them throughout life - **habits such as curiosity, the willingness to ask questions even when answers are uncertain**. It is also where skepticism is cultivated, as **students learn to weigh evidence, recognize bias, and challenge surface-level claims with deeper analysis**. Just as importantly, Gen Ed courses nurture ethical reasoning and the capacity to hold tension between multiple perspectives, preparing students to navigate complexity with both humility and critical confidence. These cognitive dispositions are **foundational to AI literacy**, which demands:

- Comfort with uncertainty (e.g., probabilistic outputs, imperfect models).
- The capacity to ask good questions (e.g., *"What counts as 'fair'?" "Whose data were used?"*).
- The willingness to **challenge technical authority** when it obscures harm or inequity.

In this sense, General Education is more than a vehicle for transmitting subject matter - **it constructs the intellectual scaffolding students need to navigate an AI-saturated world**. By teaching them to question assumptions, evaluate evidence, and reflect on ethical consequences, Gen Ed provides the foundation for responsible engagement with technology. In doing so, it builds the very infrastructure that AI-literate citizenship depends on, ensuring students are equipped to participate thoughtfully in democratic, professional, and cultural life (Brookfield, 2017; Selwyn, 2019).

General Education as the Cornerstone of Ethical AI Engagement

If artificial intelligence is to be understood not merely as a computational tool but as a structural force that shapes knowledge, power, and identity, then its study must begin in the most accessible, universal space of higher education: the general education curriculum. **Restricting AI literacy to upper-level electives or technical programs risks creating a divide where only a small segment of students gain the ability to question, critique, and responsibly apply these technologies**. General education ensures that every student, regardless of major or intended profession, has the opportunity to engage with AI's ethical, cultural, and civic dimensions.

By embedding AI into Gen Ed, institutions create a shared foundation of inquiry and responsibility. This approach reframes AI not as a specialized technical skill, but as a civic competency - akin to writing, information literacy, or critical thinking - that prepares students to live and work in an AI-mediated world. When first-year writing seminars analyze AI-generated texts for authorship, or global studies courses examine the geopolitics of data, **students learn that AI is not just shaping industries, but also shaping identity, opportunity, and democracy itself**.

Most importantly, integrating AI into Gen Ed democratizes access to critical reflection on technology, ensuring that engagement with AI is not the privilege of a few but the responsibility of all. **By encountering AI early and often in their educational journey, students develop the awareness and skills to see themselves not as passive recipients of algorithmic influence, but as active participants in shaping the systems that increasingly govern their**

lives. In this way, general education becomes the cornerstone of ethical AI engagement, equipping graduates across all disciplines to lead with discernment, justice, and care.

Design Principles for Effective AI Modules in Gen Ed

---

1. Center Social Relevance, Not Just Technology: Beginning with What Students Already Know

For many students - especially those outside of STEM fields - artificial intelligence can feel abstract, opaque, or intimidating. They may see AI as the domain of coders and engineers, not as something they are qualified or invited to critique. Yet these same students interact with AI-driven systems every day: through personalized playlists, content moderation algorithms, auto-graded quizzes, and AI-generated responses in their own coursework. **The challenge for educators is not to introduce AI from scratch, but to reveal that students are already living inside algorithmic environments - and that their experiences offer a valuable starting point for inquiry.**

By anchoring AI education in questions that directly connect to students' digital, social, and academic lives, faculty create entry points that feel personally meaningful rather than abstract. **This immediacy sparks emotional engagement, encouraging students to see their own identities, choices, and communities reflected in the stakes of technological change**. In turn, these connections transform students from passive observers of distant innovation into active participants who recognize their role in shaping how AI will influence knowledge, culture, and society.

Sample Questions That Spark Relevance and Reflection:

- **"Why did TikTok Recommend that Video?"** This opens a conversation about **recommendation algorithms**, surveillance capitalism, and the dynamics of attention capture. Students can explore how **engagement metrics**, prior viewing patterns, and demographic profiling shape what they see - and what remains invisible (Crawford, 2021; Noble, 2018). It also raises questions of agency: *"Are we curating our feeds, or are they curating us?"*
- **"Who Decides What is Flagged as Fake News?"** This question delves into the **politics of content moderation**, misinformation labeling, and algorithmic credibility scoring. It invites exploration of **platform governance**, third-party fact-checking systems, and the blurred line between automation and editorial judgment (Cinelli et al., 2021; Gulya, 2023). Students begin to ask not just *"What is true?"* but *"Who decides what is visible, credible, and shareable?"*
- **"Can ChatGPT do My Homework - and Should It?"** Here, students grapple with the implications of **AI-assisted writing tools** and the evolving boundaries of academic integrity. Discussions can examine not only detection and enforcement, but deeper questions about **authorship, effort, and the meaning of learning** in a machine-assisted age (Selwyn, 2019; Slimi & Carballido, 2023).

Each of these questions foregrounds the ethical tensions that sit at the heart of AI use, ensuring that students are not only analyzing functionality but grappling with values and consequences. By **tying abstract algorithmic processes to emotional investment and everyday experiences, the questions draw students into a personal stake in the inquiry**. This grounding opens pathways into deeper explorations of algorithm design, bias, transparency, and the broader sociopolitical forces that shape how AI systems are built, deployed, and interpreted.

Pedagogical Impact: From Passive Learning to Personal Inquiry. When students begin with a question that connects directly to their lived experience, they are more likely to engage with curiosity, sustain attention, and recognize the relevance of abstract concepts. Such grounding transforms AI from a distant technological issue into a personal and social one, making critical reflection feel necessary rather than optional. In turn, this fosters a deeper commitment to inquiry, encouraging students to see themselves as active participants in shaping how technology intersects with their own lives. Students are more likely to:

- **Articulate what they already know**, even if tacitly, about how AI operates in their lives;
- **Feel authorized to critique systems**, recognizing that expertise includes observation, intuition, and embodied knowledge - not just technical skill;
- **Pose their own follow-up questions**, moving from curiosity to inquiry and eventually to systemic critique.

This approach reflects a student-centered epistemology, where the starting point of teaching is not abstract disciplinary frameworks but the lived realities of learners. Paulo Freire described this as **the "thematic universe" of the student - the constellation of concerns, experiences, and cultural references that shape how they make meaning of the world** (Brookfield, 2017). By beginning with these themes, educators honor student agency and create conditions where academic content becomes dialogical, connected, and transformative rather than detached or imposed.

Relevance as the Doorway to AI Literacy

Too often, AI is taught as a set of technical capabilities to be admired or feared. But students do not need to start with neural networks - they can start with TikTok. The key to equitable and meaningful AI literacy is **to meet students where they already are**, and then scaffold upward toward complexity, criticality, and co-creation. By beginning with questions rooted in social experience, educators signal that AI is not just a technology - it is a mirror, a mediator, and a force shaping how students **learn, connect, and make sense of the world**.

---

2. Emphasize Inquiry and Critique Over Mastery: Teaching AI as a Lens, Not a Toolset

In the age of rapidly evolving generative systems, black-box models, and proprietary platforms, technical mastery is always provisional. New tools emerge faster than course syllabi can adapt. What persists, however, is the need for students to **develop a way of thinking about technology** - a mindset rooted in **critical inquiry, ethical reflection, and social analysis**. In general education and non-STEM courses especially, the goal is not to produce AI developers, but to cultivate **AI-literate citizens** who can evaluate systems, ask hard questions, and engage with automated technologies as informed thinkers, not passive users.

This means shifting emphasis from teaching the functionality of specific tools to interrogating their design, impact, and embedded values. The goal is not to master Python libraries, API calls, or neural network architectures in isolation, but to cultivate the ability to ask: ***"Who designed this system, with what goals, and using which data?"*** By foregrounding these deeper questions, students learn that AI literacy is less about technical mastery and more about understanding how algorithms shape knowledge, influence decision-making, and redistribute power in society. By centering **inquiry and critique over mastery**, educators prepare students to become **flexible, critical interpreters of AI**, capable of adapting to new systems while holding them accountable to human values and democratic norms (Benjamin, 2023; Brookfield, 2017; Selwyn, 2019).

Key Capacities to Prioritize in AI-Integrated Learning

- **Critical Thinking**. Students learn to **evaluate claims, identify fallacies, trace assumptions**, and distinguish correlation from causation in algorithmic outputs. This is especially important in media environments where AI-generated summaries, deepfakes, or filter bubbles shape public discourse (Cinelli et al., 2021; Noble, 2018).
- **Media Literacy**. AI plays a central role in determining what students see, believe, and share. Students must learn to **analyze digital systems as producers of meaning** - not just as tools for access, but as **actors in the construction of reality** (Crawford, 2021; Gulya, 2023).
- **Ethical Reasoning**. What is considered "efficient" or "optimal" in AI systems may not align with fairness, dignity, or accountability. Students must explore **moral trade-offs** and consider competing values - e.g., privacy vs. personalization, transparency vs. complexity (Floridi et al., 2018; Reamer, 2023).
- **Cultural Interpretation**. AI systems do not operate in a vacuum - they **mediate language, representation, and identity**. Students should examine how AI platforms reflect, reinforce, or resist dominant narratives, norms, and ideologies (Benjamin, 2023; Binns, 2018; Noble, 2018).

Faculty Example: Media Inquiry in a Communications Course

Assignment: A communications instructor asks students to investigate how two algorithmically driven platforms - such as **YouTube and TikTok** - surface content related to climate change.

Process: Students conduct a side-by-side search and analyze:

- *"Which videos are prioritized?"*
- *"What creators or sources dominate?"*
- *"How do thumbnails, hashtags, or engagement metrics affect visibility?"*

Interpretive Framework: Students apply **agenda-setting theory** to understand how platform design shapes public attention. They explore:

- *"How do algorithms act as **gatekeepers** of public knowledge?"*

- *"In what ways does commercial incentive (e.g., ad revenue) intersect with climate narratives?"*
- *"What structural forces influence which voices are amplified or suppressed?"*

Outcome: Rather than merely identifying platform differences, students build **a vocabulary of critique** - one they can apply to future technological systems across contexts.

Pedagogical Implications: When students are taught to **think with and about AI systems**, rather than simply use them, they develop lasting competencies:

- They become **adaptive learners** who can critically evaluate new technologies.
- They grow into **informed citizens** who can participate meaningfully in debates about automation, privacy, and policy.
- They cultivate the confidence to ask: *"Whose knowledge is being valued here - and what is at stake?"*

This approach recognizes that **AI is not just a subject of instruction - it is a subject of interpretation, power, and ethics** (Bender et al., 2021; Brookfield, 2017; Selwyn, 2019). To treat AI responsibly means teaching students to question not only how it works, but also whose assumptions it encodes and whose interests it serves. In doing so, **educators shift the focus from technical fluency alone to a broader form of literacy that includes cultural critique, ethical reasoning, and democratic accountability**.

Building Inquiry-Centered AI Literacy Across the Curriculum

Building inquiry-centered AI literacy across the curriculum means equipping students to see artificial intelligence not only as a technical instrument, but as a cultural and political force that shapes how knowledge is produced and how authority is distributed. In a world where generative systems influence public discourse, policy, and everyday decision-making, **students need more than tool fluency - they need the critical capacity to ask how systems are designed, whose interests they serve, and what consequences they produce**. By prioritizing inquiry and critique over narrow mastery, educators cultivate learners who are not only digitally competent, but also ethically awake, socially grounded, and intellectually agile - ready to navigate and reshape an AI-mediated society with responsibility and vision.

---

3. Use Narrative and Case-Based Pedagogy: Making AI Human Through Stories

For many students, the implications of artificial intelligence remain abstract until they are situated in **personal, emotional, and ethical contexts**. Data flows, model architectures, and training sets often feel removed from everyday experience. **Narrative and case-based pedagogy** bridge this gap by using storytelling to make AI **legible, tangible, and morally engaging**. Stories do not just explain how a system works - they prompt students to **inhabit the lived consequences of automation**, revealing how technical systems intersect with trust, power, and vulnerability (Brookfield, 2017; Reamer, 2023).

Whether drawn from real-world headlines or fictionalized dilemmas, narrative-based approaches help students explore **multiple perspectives** within complex AI scenarios. They encourage ethical reflection not as an abstraction, but as a **felt tension between human values and machine logic**. Students begin to ask not only what a system does, but what it means, whom it serves, and what could go wrong (Benjamin, 2023; Binns, 2018).

Sample Case Study: AI and Academic Integrity

Scenario: An instructor receives an alert from a campus-integrated AI system designed to detect AI-generated writing. The system flags a student's paper as likely written by a language model due to stylistic patterns and linguistic complexity. The student firmly denies the allegation, insisting they authored the paper independently.

Role-Play Setup: Students are assigned roles in a simulated academic hearing:

- The **instructor**, tasked with determining how to proceed.
- The **student**, defending their work.
- A **dean or committee representative**, upholding institutional policy.
- A **technical expert**, explaining the system's confidence score and limitations.

Discussion Focus:

- **Trust in Automation**. *"How much weight should an instructor give to an AI-generated suspicion?" "Should it be treated as evidence or merely a prompt for further inquiry?"* Students explore the dangers of over-reliance on automated decision support (Bender et al., 2021; Noble, 2018).
- **Due Process and Procedural Fairness**. *"What safeguards should be in place to ensure students have a fair opportunity to respond?" "How do institutions balance academic integrity with the presumption of student good faith?"*
- **Bias in Training Data**. *"Could the system's algorithm disproportionately flag students based on language variety, ESL status, or unconventional prose?" How do stylistic norms get encoded as "suspicious," and who decides what "authentic" student writing looks like?"* (Crawford, 2021; Slimi & Carballido, 2023).
- **Human vs. Machine Judgment**. *"Where should the boundary lie between **machine detection** and **human discretion**?" "What is lost when faculty defer ethical and pedagogical decisions to technical systems?"*

Learning Outcomes: Students leave the case with a deeper appreciation for:

- The **ethical ambiguity of automated enforcement**.
- The emotional and reputational risks of **false positives**.
- The institutional responsibilities to balance **efficiency with empathy**.
- The broader societal implications of **outsourcing judgment to machines**.

This case also prepares students to navigate real-world interactions with AI-powered surveillance and decision systems by grounding their learning in scenarios that mirror credit scoring, job hiring, or public benefits screening. In working through these examples, **students strengthen not only their technical critique but also their ethical literacy, learning to identify where fairness, transparency, or due process may be compromised**. By combining scenario analysis with values-based reflection, the exercise equips them to engage AI systems as informed professionals and civic actors, capable of questioning automation rather than simply complying with its outputs (Eubanks, 2018; Floridi et al., 2018).

Pedagogical Recommendations:

- **Use Diverse Narrative Formats**. Mix case studies with multimedia storytelling, documentary excerpts, or first-person testimonials from those impacted by AI systems (e.g., students, workers, patients).
- **Introduce Competing Narratives**. Present the same event from multiple viewpoints - e.g., the flagged student, the AI engineer, the faculty member under institutional pressure - to illustrate **how power and knowledge shape perception** (Benjamin, 2023; Gulya, 2023).
- **Invite Students to Write Their Own Cases**. Have students develop fictionalized AI dilemmas based on current events, incorporating plausible technical and ethical challenges.

Ethics Through Embodied Dialogue

Narrative and case-based pedagogy turns AI from an abstract topic into a **relational and moral experience**. By stepping into roles, facing uncertainty, and defending positions, students learn that ethics is not about memorizing rules - it is about **negotiating complexity in community**. Stories allow students to rehearse the hard choices they may one day face as users, builders, or critics of AI systems. And in doing so, they become not only better learners, but more responsible and **empathetic participants in the AI-mediated world**.

---

4. Make Modules Short, Adaptable, and Portable: Designing for Scalability and Impact

As institutions seek to democratize AI literacy across general education, the key to success lies not in comprehensive overhauls or highly specialized courses, but in **modular, flexible content** that can be infused into a variety of learning environments. **Short, adaptable, and portable modules** make it possible to integrate AI ethics, critical data studies, and algorithmic literacy into courses across disciplines - without requiring faculty to become AI experts or radically rework their syllabi. These modules are most effective when they are:

- **Tightly scoped** (1–2 class sessions).
- **Interdisciplinary-friendly**, able to "plug in" to humanities, social sciences, STEM, or professional programs.
- **Supported by open-source, accessible materials** that reduce barriers to adoption (Benjamin, 2023; Brookfield, 2017).

This microcurriculum model also encourages pedagogical experimentation by giving faculty permission to begin small, test approaches in low-stakes contexts, and refine them over time. In doing so, **faculty can adapt AI-focused modules to align with their own disciplinary themes while still reinforcing broader competencies such as ethical reasoning, media literacy, and socio-technical critique** (Floridi et al., 2018; Gulya, 2023). Over the long term, this iterative approach builds confidence and creates a culture of innovation, showing that AI literacy is best cultivated not through rigid prescriptions but through flexible, context-sensitive teaching practices.

Sample Module Titles That Spark Curiosity and Dialogue

The most effective entry points into AI literacy begin with curiosity. Well-crafted module titles can act as invitations - provoking questions, surfacing tensions, and signaling to students that the topic is both relevant and urgent. Each of the examples that follows is designed not just to inform, but to open dialogue, encouraging students to explore AI as a cultural force, an ethical dilemma, and a site of personal and civic responsibility:

---

1. "ChatGPT and the Future of Thinking"

Disciplinary Fit: Writing studies, philosophy, education, communication.

Focus:

- How generative AI affects authorship, originality, and the purpose of education.
- The difference between producing ideas and understanding them.
- Whether AI can think - or whether it mirrors us back to ourselves.

Pairings:

- **Reading**. Excerpt from Selwyn (2019) or Slimi and Carballido (2023) on AI and education.
- **Activity**. Students compare their own writing to AI-generated output.
- **Reflection**. *"What does using ChatGPT teach me about how I think - and what I value in learning?"*

---

2. "Who Controls Your Feed?"

Disciplinary Fit: Media studies, political science, psychology, sociology.

Focus:

- Platform algorithms and the personalization of reality.
- Filter bubbles, agenda setting, and AI-driven misinformation.
- Agency and power in mediated attention economies (Cinelli et al., 2021; Crawford, 2021).

Pairings:

- **Reading**. Selections from *Atlas of AI* (Crawford, 2021) or Noble (2018).
- **Activity**. Students audit their own social media feeds and reflect on what they notice/do not see.
- **Discussion**. *"Is the algorithm reflecting my interests - or shaping them?"*

---

3. "Can an Algorithm Be Racist?"

Disciplinary Fit: History, law, sociology, ethnic studies.

Focus:

- Structural bias in training data and model design.
- Disparate impact in hiring, policing, health, and finance.
- The difference between intent and outcome in automated systems (Benjamin, 2023; Eubanks, 2018).

Pairings:

- **Reading**. Excerpts from *Algorithms of Oppression* (Noble, 2018) or *Viral Justice* (Benjamin, 2023).
- **Activity**. Students review a real-world case of algorithmic harm (e.g., COMPAS, facial recognition).
- **Prompt**. *"If a system produces racist outcomes - even without racist intent - who is responsible?"*

---

4. "What Would a Fair AI Look Like?"

Disciplinary Fit: Ethics, computer science, business, public policy.

Focus:

- Competing definitions of fairness (e.g., demographic parity vs. equalized odds).
- Trade-offs between accuracy, interpretability, and equity (Barocas et al., 2023; Binns, 2018).
- Participatory design and community accountability.

Pairings:

- **Reading**. Floridi et al. (2018) on AI governance.
- **Activity**. Students simulate a design team tasked with revising a biased system.
- **Debrief**. *"Is fairness something you can compute - or something you must negotiate?"*

Pedagogical Value: High-Impact, Low-Lift Integration

These modules:

- **Require minimal technical knowledge** to teach or engage with.
- Foster **authentic student curiosity**, grounded in lived digital experience.
- Support a **culture of critical questioning**, rather than passive consumption.
- Can be taught **individually or bundled**, forming the basis of an AI literacy track, certificate, or interdisciplinary minor.

They also demonstrate that faculty from the humanities, social sciences, arts, and professional programs can contribute meaningfully to AI pedagogy without needing to master technical coding or system design. **By engaging AI through the lenses of ethics, culture, and civic responsibility, faculty model for students how to interrogate technology's social**

implications alongside its computational power. In doing so, they reinforce the idea that AI literacy is less about technical fluency and more about cultivating a capacity for ethical reasoning, democratic accountability, and cultural critique (Reamer, 2023; Selwyn, 2019).

Building AI Literacy One Question at a Time

Short, portable modules empower institutions to **mainstream AI literacy** across the curriculum without waiting for structural overhaul. When designed around compelling questions, interdisciplinary readings, and accessible activities, these modules cultivate **intellectual curiosity, ethical reflection, and democratic imagination**. They show students that understanding AI is not just about knowing how it works - but about asking what kind of world we want it to build.

Examples of Interdisciplinary General Education AI Modules: Teaching AI Literacy Across the Curriculum

General education (Gen Ed) provides a unique opportunity to introduce students from all majors to the **ethical, cultural, and political dimensions of artificial intelligence**. Because Gen Ed courses are broad in scope and foundational in purpose, they serve as ideal platforms for **interdisciplinary AI modules** that build critical capacities - not by teaching students how to build AI systems, but by helping them understand how such systems shape the world around them.

The table below outlines sample **portable, discipline-aligned AI modules** that embed AI literacy into a wide range of Gen Ed offerings. Each module emphasizes **skills development**, real-world relevance, and pedagogical flexibility - supporting faculty in meeting existing course objectives while integrating AI-focused content (Benjamin, 2023; Brookfield, 2017; Selwyn, 2019).

Sample Interdisciplinary AI Modules for General Education

Module Title	Embedded In	Core Skills Developed
ChatGPT and Critical Thinking	First-Year Writing Seminar	Argument analysis, rhetorical awareness, authorship reflection
AI, Race, and Algorithms	Sociology / Cultural Studies	Data bias, systemic inequality, algorithmic discrimination
Algorithms and Free Speech	Media or Communications	Platform governance, content moderation, digital rights
AI and Global Inequality	Global Studies / Ethics	Data colonialism, transnational labor, surveillance geopolitics

Module Title	Embedded In	Core Skills Developed
When Machines Judge	Philosophy / Criminal Justice	Moral reasoning, due process, procedural fairness

1. ChatGPT and Critical Thinking

Course Fit: First-Year Writing or Introduction to Composition.

Focus: This module introduces students to AI-generated writing by having them compare human- and machine-authored arguments. Students analyze:

- Logical coherence and rhetorical devices.
- Use of evidence and citation.
- Audience awareness and tone.

Activity:

- Students prompt ChatGPT to write a short argumentative essay and then critique its strengths and weaknesses, asking:
  - *"What is missing when a machine writes an argument?"*
  - *"What does critical thinking require beyond fluent language?"*

Learning Outcome:

- Students develop **metacognitive awareness** about their own thinking, build discernment in evaluating AI output, and reflect on the evolving meaning of authorship and academic integrity (Selwyn, 2019; Slimi & Carballido, 2023).

---

2. AI, Race, and Algorithms

Course Fit: Sociology, African American Studies, Cultural Anthropology.

Focus: This module explores how seemingly neutral algorithms may reproduce structural racism, classism, and ableism. Students examine case studies such as:

- Predictive policing tools (e.g., COMPAS).
- Discriminatory mortgage or hiring algorithms.
- Bias in facial recognition software (Benjamin, 2023; Eubanks, 2018).

Activity:

- Students read selections from *Algorithms of Oppression* (Noble, 2018) and *Viral Justice* (Benjamin, 2023), then conduct a media analysis of a potential AI-biased incident.

Learning Outcome:

- Students learn to identify **how power and inequality are encoded into digital infrastructures**, connecting technical systems to broader histories of discrimination and resistance (Binns, 2018; Crawford, 2021).

3. Algorithms and Free Speech

Course Fit: Media Studies, Communications, Journalism.

Focus: Students explore how content recommendation algorithms on platforms such as YouTube, Facebook, and TikTok influence freedom of expression, public discourse, and media polarization (Cinelli et al., 2021; Gulya, 2023).

Activity:

- Simulate a platform policy team responding to public backlash about deplatforming or algorithmic amplification. Students debate:
    - *"What speech should be flagged or downranked?"*
    - *"Who defines 'harmful' or 'misleading' content?"*
    - *"What role should AI play in moderation?"*

Learning Outcome:

- Students build **media literacy**, understand platform governance dynamics, and confront **tensions between moderation, regulation, and expression** (Brookfield, 2017; Noble, 2018).

---

4. AI and Global Inequality

Course Fit: Global Studies, International Relations, Environmental Ethics.

Focus: This module interrogates the **geopolitics of AI** - who controls its infrastructure, who does its invisible labor, and who bears the costs of its environmental and economic impact (Crawford, 2021; Gray & Suri, 2019).

Activity:

- Students trace the life cycle of a large AI system, from data collection to model training to deployment - mapping:
    - The environmental toll of training (Strubell et al., 2020).
    - The hidden labor of content moderation and annotation.
    - The global flow of data, profit, and regulation.

Learning Outcome:

- Students develop a **systems view of AI** and critically reflect on **data colonialism, extractive labor, and digital sovereignty** (Bender et al., 2021; Floridi et al., 2018).

---

5. When Machines Judge

Course Fit: Philosophy, Criminal Justice, Political Theory.

Focus: Students examine **automated decision-making in the justice system**, such as algorithmic sentencing, risk scores, and surveillance tools.

Activity:

- Role-play a bail hearing where students must evaluate whether to use an AI-risk assessment tool. They analyze:
    - Issues of bias, transparency, and due process.
    - Moral dilemmas between safety and fairness.
    - Competing definitions of justice and accountability.

Learning Outcome:

- Students sharpen **ethical reasoning**, confront real-world moral complexity, and question **whether machines can or should make consequential decisions** (Doshi-Velez & Kim, 2017; Reamer, 2023).

General Education as a Portal for Critical AI Citizenship

Each of these five modules above illustrated how **AI literacy can be integrated seamlessly into general education courses**, aligning with core learning goals while preparing students to live, learn, and lead in an AI-mediated world. Rather than teaching technical fluency alone, these modules cultivate **critical judgment, civic awareness, and ethical reflection** - the foundations of democratic engagement in the algorithmic age.

Faculty Development and Institutional Models: Scaling AI Literacy Across General Education

Successfully integrating AI literacy across general education requires more than high-quality content - it demands **sustained faculty support, cross-departmental collaboration, and institutional alignment**. Most educators, particularly those outside STEM, are eager to engage students in conversations about AI's social and ethical dimensions but may lack the technical background or pedagogical models to do so confidently. Likewise, institutions may recognize the urgency of preparing students for an AI-mediated world, yet struggle to identify scalable, inclusive strategies for implementation.

To meet this challenge, institutions must move away from treating AI education as the niche domain of computer scientists or technologists and instead position it as a shared academic responsibility. **This shift requires intentional investment in professional development, the creation of resource hubs that make assignments and case studies accessible across disciplines, and policies that reward values-driven curriculum innovation**. When AI is embedded institution-wide - as a matter of pedagogy, ethics, and civic preparation - it signals to both faculty and students that the institution is committed to shaping not just technical competence, but reflective, responsible, and socially grounded engagement with intelligent systems (Brookfield, 2017; Floridi et al., 2018; Selwyn, 2019).

Key Institutional Strategies to Support AI Literacy in Gen Ed

---

1. Offer Modular Faculty Workshops on AI Concepts and Pedagogy

Strategy: Design short, modular faculty development sessions that demystify AI systems and explore ways to integrate AI literacy into existing courses. Workshops should:

- Introduce basic AI concepts (e.g., machine learning, algorithmic bias, generative AI).
- Showcase interdisciplinary teaching examples.
- Model ethical discussion strategies using AI case studies.
- Provide reusable activities, assignments, and assessment tools.

Rationale:

- Workshops lower the barrier to entry and build faculty confidence, especially in fields where technology is not typically foregrounded.
- Faculty leave not as AI experts, but as **ethically empowered educators** capable of teaching AI's social consequences (Byars-Winston & Dahlberg, 2019; Reamer, 2023).

---

2. Fund Interdisciplinary Curriculum Fellowships

Strategy: Provide funding and course release for faculty to collaboratively design interdisciplinary AI modules that bridge STEM and non-STEM departments. Teams may include:

- A computer science professor and a writing instructor are designing a "ChatGPT and Rhetoric" module.
- A sociology faculty member and an engineering colleague are co-developing a module on "Algorithmic Fairness in Urban Systems."

Rationale:

- Fellowships incentivize **team teaching, knowledge exchange, and curricular innovation**, creating durable collaborations that can seed ongoing programmatic change (Benjamin, 2023; Floridi et al., 2018).

---

3. Create Repositories of AI Assignments Categorized by Discipline, Duration, and Learning Outcomes

Strategy: Develop an open-access institutional (or consortial) repository where faculty can:

- Browse AI-related assignments and modules by field (e.g., philosophy, biology, media studies).
- Filter by time commitment (e.g., one class session, one week, full unit).
- Align materials with Gen Ed learning goals (e.g., ethical reasoning, critical thinking, intercultural competence).

Rationale:

- Such repositories make it easy for faculty to adopt and adapt AI content **without reinventing the wheel**.
- Over time, these shared assets foster **a community of practice**, enabling faculty to iterate on, reflect upon, and co-own the teaching of AI literacy (Brookfield, 2017; Gulya, 2023).

---

4. Embed AI Literacy into General Education Learning Outcomes

Strategy: Formally integrate AI literacy into Gen Ed learning outcomes by mapping it to existing institutional goals, such as:

- **Digital literacy** (understanding how technologies shape knowledge).
- **Ethical reasoning** (evaluating algorithmic decisions and fairness).
- **Civic responsibility** (engaging critically with AI's social impact).
- **Lifelong learning** (navigating emerging tools with curiosity and critique).

Rationale:

- Embedding AI literacy into **institution-wide outcomes legitimizes its place in the curriculum**, ensures sustained faculty attention, and provides a basis for assessment and accreditation alignment (Benjamin, 2023; Reamer, 2023; Selwyn, 2019).

Institutionalizing Ethical, Interdisciplinary AI Education

If AI literacy is to be a universal competency rather than a technical elective, institutions must create the **pedagogical and structural conditions for scalable, inclusive engagement**. Faculty development, cross-disciplinary incentives, and outcome alignment are not peripheral supports - they are essential design features of an ethical and future-ready general education curriculum.

By equipping faculty with the tools, time, and community to embed AI critically in their teaching, colleges and universities help ensure that AI is not just a technical challenge for specialists, but a **shared civic concern addressed through interdisciplinary learning**. The goal is not to teach every student to build AI - but to prepare every student to **question, understand, and shape the AI systems that increasingly shape them**.

Student Reflection Questions (Cross-Disciplinary): Cultivating AI Literacy Through Ethical Self-Inquiry

AI literacy is not only about understanding technologies - it is about examining the **assumptions, values, and consequences** embedded in those technologies. Reflection is central to that process. Across disciplines, thoughtfully designed reflection questions invite students to connect **personal experience, professional identity, and civic responsibility** to the systems that increasingly shape their lives.

Whether in a writing seminar, a sociology class, a media studies course, or an engineering lab, reflection prompts can help students grapple with **ethical ambiguity, structural complexity, and personal agency** in the AI age. They also support **metacognitive growth**, allowing students to name what they know, notice what they have internalized, and surface what they may have previously overlooked (Brookfield, 2017; Byars-Winston & Dahlberg, 2019; Zimmerman, 2002). Below are four reflection questions that can be adapted across general education settings to foster **critical thinking, civic dialogue, and ethical action**.

---

1. "What does it Mean to Trust a Machine with a Decision About You?"

This prompt invites students to consider the **emotional, philosophical, and practical dimensions of algorithmic decision-making**, particularly when those decisions are consequential - such as job applications, healthcare triage, or academic surveillance.

Discussion Themes:

- *"What does trust look like in a machine-human relationship?"*
- *"What are the conditions under which trust is earned - or misplaced?"*
- *"Have you ever experienced (or feared) being misclassified by a system?"*

Learning Goal:

- Encourage students to reflect on the **relational and ethical stakes of algorithmic governance** (Eubanks, 2018; Reamer, 2023), recognizing that efficiency alone does not justify automation.

---

2. "How does an Algorithm Define 'Truth'?"

This question challenges students to interrogate the epistemologies baked into AI systems:

- *"What does it mean for a machine to 'know' something?"*
- *"How are labels such as 'true,' 'relevant,' or 'credible' determined?"*

Discussion Themes:

- *"Who selects the training data, and what is omitted?"*
- *"How do recommender systems shape perceptions of truth?"*
- *"Can truth be ranked, predicted, or optimized?"*

Learning Goal:

- Promote **media literacy and epistemic humility**, helping students explore how AI systems **prioritize certain worldviews while suppressing others** - often under the guise of neutrality (Cinelli et al., 2021; Crawford, 2021; Noble, 2018).

---

3. "Where do you see AI Shaping Your Future Profession?"

This question encourages students to link AI literacy to their **aspirations, responsibilities, and disciplinary norms**. It personalizes the conversation and frames AI not as something "out there," but as **integrated into their field's evolving toolkit**.

Discussion Themes:

- *"How is AI being used in your discipline today?"*
- *"What tasks might be automated - and what cannot (or should not) be?"*
- *"How might you advocate for ethical use of AI in your profession?"*

Learning Goal:

- Foster **discipline-specific critical foresight**, prompting students to consider both the opportunities and challenges of AI in professional practice (Benjamin, 2023; Gulya, 2023; Selwyn, 2019).

---

4. "What can You Do to Ensure AI is Fair and Accountable?"

This question activates student agency. It pushes beyond critique into **design thinking, advocacy, and democratic participation**.

Discussion Themes:

- *"What role can users, students, or citizens play in shaping AI norms?"*
- *"How might you engage with policies, institutions, or communities to promote transparency?"*
- *"What values would you center if you were designing an AI system?"*

Learning Goal:

- Help students recognize that AI is not inevitable or unchangeable - it is built, deployed, and governed by people. Reflection leads to action when students see themselves as **co-stewards of technological futures** (Binns, 2018; Brookfield, 2017; Floridi et al., 2018).

Section Reflection: AI Literacy as a Foundational Dimension of General Education

This section presents a bold and necessary reimagining of general education as a critical site for cultivating AI literacy - not through technical mastery, but through ethical inquiry, interdisciplinary analysis, and civic engagement. It argues persuasively that the stakes of artificial intelligence are too profound - and too far-reaching - to be confined to STEM classrooms. Instead, AI must become a shared concern across the undergraduate curriculum, embedded in the questions, habits of mind, and critical competencies that general education is uniquely positioned to foster.

The section reframes AI not as a technological abstraction, but as a lived and social system - one that students already encounter through content feeds, grading algorithms, generative tools, and predictive profiling. By foregrounding narrative, inquiry, and reflection, it positions students as co-analysts of their digital environments, equipping them with the vocabulary, confidence, and ethical frameworks to interrogate how these systems shape knowledge, power, and identity. The emphasis on short, portable modules ensures that integration is scalable and inclusive, inviting faculty across disciplines to contribute without requiring technical expertise.

Perhaps most significantly, this section emphasizes the transformative potential of general education to democratize AI literacy. Through accessible assignments, interdisciplinary modules, and thoughtfully designed reflection prompts, it cultivates not just informed users, but ethically attuned and critically literate citizens - students who are capable of recognizing, questioning, and ultimately shaping the algorithmic systems that increasingly shape them. In doing so, it offers a powerful vision of general education as the ethical backbone of higher education's AI era.

Section 8: Building Faculty Confidence and Collaboration in Teaching AI Literacy

---

Despite widespread interest in AI and its societal implications, many faculty feel underprepared to teach AI literacy in meaningful ways. **A persistent barrier is the misconception that one must be a coder, data scientist, or machine learning expert to contribute to AI-related instruction**. In reality, effective AI education requires not technical mastery but ethical curiosity, critical thinking, and pedagogical adaptability - skills faculty across disciplines already possess and can build upon (Long & Magerko, 2020; Reiss, 2021).

This section offers strategies for building faculty confidence and fostering interdisciplinary collaboration, ensuring AI literacy emerges as a shared institutional capability rather than an isolated burden on a few specialists. It emphasizes that **the most effective AI education happens when faculty work together, pooling disciplinary expertise to interrogate both technical systems and their broader cultural implications**. Ultimately, AI education should be framed as a collective journey - best traveled with colleagues, shared tools, and mutual support - where responsibility and innovation are distributed across the academic community.

Barriers to Faculty Engagement: Addressing Fear, Disciplinary Distance, and Pedagogical Uncertainty

As institutions push to integrate AI literacy into general education, the **engagement and confidence of faculty** become critical variables. Yet for many faculty - particularly those outside of STEM - AI feels **unfamiliar, intimidating, and professionally risky**. While administrators may envision seamless integration, many faculty members silently wrestle with doubt:

- *"Am I qualified to teach this?"*
- *"Will I sound uninformed?"*
- *"What if my students know more than I do?"*

These concerns are not trivial - they reflect **deep pedagogical vulnerability**, shaped by gaps in training, time constraints, and the pace of technological change. Addressing them requires more than providing information; it requires **creating cultures of safety, trust, and mutual learning**. Below are four common barriers to faculty engagement in AI education, along with institutional strategies for **meeting faculty where they are** (Brookfield, 2017; Byars-Winston & Dahlberg, 2019).

---

1. "I Do Not Understand How AI Works Well Enough to Teach It."

This is perhaps the most widespread concern among faculty - and also one of the easiest to misinterpret. Many assume that teaching AI literacy requires fluency in machine learning, programming languages, or algorithm design, which can feel intimidating or outside their expertise. In reality, **most interdisciplinary AI modules emphasize critical thinking, social context, and ethical reasoning**, enabling faculty from any discipline to contribute meaningfully without needing advanced technical development skills.

Reframing Strategy:

- Faculty do not need to teach how AI works - they need to teach **how to think about AI**: how it affects knowledge, relationships, power, and values.
- Institutions can offer **nontechnical workshops, modular readings, and prebuilt case studies** that allow faculty to engage AI conceptually without being experts (Floridi et al., 2018; Reamer, 2023).

Support Tip: Invite faculty to co-teach or guest-lecture with a STEM colleague, modeling cross-disciplinary fluency and shared authority. **This collaboration not only demystifies technical content for non-STEM students but also shows how ethical, cultural, and professional perspectives enrich technical discussions**. By making these partnerships visible, institutions signal that AI literacy thrives when expertise is shared across boundaries rather than siloed within disciplines.

---

2. "My Discipline is Not Technical - What Could I Possibly Contribute?"

Faculty in the arts, humanities, and social sciences may assume that AI is "not their domain." Yet these very fields offer the interpretive, ethical, and humanistic tools most needed to evaluate AI's social impacts, from questions of authorship and creativity to issues of governance and justice. By engaging these perspectives, **institutions ensure that AI literacy is not reduced to technical training alone**, but is enriched by the cultural critique and ethical insight that only these disciplines provide.

Reframing Strategy:

- Historians can teach thc lineage of automation and labor.
- Literature faculty can explore authorship, voice, and machine-generated text.
- Sociologists can unpack structural bias in datasets.
- Artists can interrogate aesthetic norms in generative models.

Support Tip: Highlight that **AI is not just a tool - it is a cultural artifact, shaped by language, ideology, and design choices** (Benjamin, 2023; Noble, 2018). Understanding this dimension requires the interpretive and critical skills that nontechnical faculty bring, as they are trained to analyze meaning, context, and systems of representation. That is precisely where their expertise excels: in uncovering how AI reflects cultural values, reproduces social assumptions, and influences how knowledge and authority are constructed.

---

3. "What if My Students Know More Than I do?"

Faculty often fear being "kicked out" as less technically fluent than their students. This fear, while valid, reflects not only concerns about digital skill gaps but also deeper anxieties about authority, credibility, and maintaining classroom control. Left unaddressed, such worries can discourage experimentation and transparency, even though modeling curiosity and humility around AI can actually strengthen trust and foster collaborative learning environments.

Reframing Strategy:

- Use this dynamic as an opportunity to **model intellectual humility and co-learning**.
- Let students contribute their digital fluency while faculty guide critical reflection, historical context, and ethical debate.

Support Tip: Normalize "teaching through inquiry" - posing questions, facilitating dialogue, and allowing students to lead in unpacking AI systems (Brookfield, 2017; Gulya, 2023). **This approach shifts the classroom dynamic from one of expert delivery to shared exploration**, where uncertainty becomes a pedagogical strength rather than a weakness. By foregrounding inquiry, faculty empower students to practice critical thinking, engage diverse perspectives, and see themselves as active participants in shaping knowledge about A.

---

4. "Where Do I Even Start?"

Even motivated faculty often feel paralyzed by the absence of clear entry points, vetted resources, or institutional guidance. Without reliable models or curated tools, **the sheer volume of information about AI can overwhelm rather than empower, leaving faculty unsure where to begin**. The issue is not resistance - it is cognitive overload, a challenge that requires structured pathways, scaffolded training, and peer support to transform uncertainty into confident experimentation.

Reframing Strategy:

- **Start Small**. One discussion, one reading, one reflection prompt.
- Use prebuilt modules with flexible implementation options (e.g., a one-day unit on ChatGPT and academic integrity).

Support Tip: Institutions should create discipline-sorted repositories, peer mentorship networks, and opt-in teaching circles for shared experimentation and reflection (Byars-Winston & Dahlberg, 2019). **Such structures reduce the burden on individual faculty by offering curated resources that feel relevant to their disciplinary norms and contexts**.

They also foster a culture of collective growth, where faculty see themselves not as isolated learners but as participants in a community of inquiry and practice.

Strategies to Build Faculty Confidence and Capacity: Scaffolding Interdisciplinary AI Pedagogy

Empowering faculty to teach AI literacy - especially within general education - requires more than offering content expertise. It involves **cultivating confidence, fostering collaboration, and reimagining teaching as a collective, interdisciplinary endeavor**. Most faculty already possess the tools to engage AI meaningfully: they understand how to lead discussions, frame ethical questions, and situate content within larger cultural and civic conversations. What they often lack is not capacity, but a **clear, supported pathway into unfamiliar terrain**. The following six strategies highlight how **cross-disciplinary co-design** can serve as a powerful entry point for AI literacy integration - lowering barriers, distributing expertise, and modeling the very kind of collaborative, multifaceted thinking that AI systems demand from the societies they shape (Brookfield, 2017; Byars-Winston & Dahlberg, 2019).

---

1. Start with Cross-Disciplinary Co-Design

Rationale: AI is not a purely technical phenomenon - it is a **socio-technical system** with political, historical, ethical, and communicative dimensions. Teaching AI effectively often requires **more than one lens**. Co-designing modules across disciplinary lines allows faculty to **bring their strengths to the table without needing to master everything alone**. This approach invites faculty to form **teaching partnerships** where each person contributes domain expertise. It also allows students to see how knowledge is constructed through dialogue, synthesis, and interpretive plurality - mirroring the way real-world AI challenges unfold across sectors (Benjamin, 2023; Floridi et al., 2018).

Illustrative Example: Co-Creating a Module on "AI in Elections"

A multidisciplinary faculty team creates a unit exploring the role of artificial intelligence in shaping electoral processes, civic participation, and political discourse. Each faculty member contributes from their disciplinary standpoint:

- **Political Science Professor**. Introduces democratic theory and ethical frameworks for civic technology. Facilitates analysis of how algorithmic systems affect **voter manipulation, polarization, and public trust**.
- **Computer Science Professor**. Provides a nontechnical explanation of how recommender systems and machine learning models **analyze user behavior to target ads or spread misinformation**. Explains concepts such as data profiling, model drift, and content amplification.
- **Communications or Media Studies Professor**. Leads students in analyzing how AI-powered platforms influence **agenda-setting, framing, and media virality**. Guides students in examining platform governance and content moderation.

Together, the faculty designs a unit that includes:

- A **case study** on algorithmic bias in political advertising.
- A **simulation** of targeted campaign messaging using AI-generated profiles.
- A **reflective discussion** on civic ethics and the future of democratic participation.

Benefits of Co-Design:

- **Lowered Faculty Anxiety.** Each educator contributes from a position of strength, **minimizing the fear of "not knowing enough" about AI**.
- **Greater Student Engagement.** Students encounter AI from **multiple, intersecting vantage points**, reinforcing its relevance and complexity.
- **Scalable Integration.** Co-designed modules can be **adapted across departments**, forming the foundation for interdisciplinary minors, certificates, or pathways in AI and society.
- **Modeled Collaboration.** Students observe faculty modeling **intellectual humility, collaborative inquiry, and disciplinary negotiation** - key capacities in a world increasingly shaped by cross-sector AI challenges.

Pedagogical Considerations:

- **Time-Efficient Design:** Modules can be developed through short summer working groups or faculty learning communities.
- **Shared Credit:** Co-teaching or module exchange can be recognized in promotion and workload agreements.
- **Institutional Support:** Mini-grants or curriculum fellowships can incentivize participation and pilot development (Byars-Winston & Dahlberg, 2019).

---

2. Use Open-Access, Ready-to-Adapt AI Literacy Modules: Reducing Barriers and Increasing Equity

One of the most effective ways to scale AI literacy across general education is by equipping faculty with **modular, high-quality, open-access teaching resources**. These resources - many developed by globally respected institutions - are specifically designed for flexible use by educators across disciplines and experience levels. They address a common faculty concern: *"Where do I start, and how can I do this without becoming an AI expert?"*

Open-access AI literacy modules not only reduce **development time and instructional overhead**, but they also promote **equity in curricular access** - allowing institutions of all sizes and resource levels to participate meaningfully in AI education. These materials often include full lesson plans, slides, activities, and assessments - enabling faculty to **focus on contextual adaptation and facilitation**, rather than technical content creation (Brookfield, 2017; Byars-Winston & Dahlberg, 2019).

Featured Open-Access Sources for AI Literacy Modules

- **MIT RAISE (Responsible AI for Social Empowerment and Education)**
    - Focuses on making AI education accessible to diverse learners across K–12 and postsecondary settings.

- Offers modules on **machine learning, algorithmic bias, fairness, and transparency**.
- Includes both **unplugged activities** (no coding required) and **interactive AI tools** for classroom demonstration.

- **AI4ALL Teacher Toolkits**
  - Designed for high school and undergraduate educators seeking to introduce AI through **ethics, identity, and community engagement**.
  - Features case studies on **AI in healthcare, criminal justice, and environmental justice**.
  - Emphasizes inclusive pedagogy and **representation in AI careers**, making it well-suited for equity-focused classrooms.
- **Stanford Human-Centered AI (HAI) Resource Hub**
  - Provides **research-grounded teaching materials**, including lectures, discussion guides, and policy-oriented readings.
  - Encourages interdisciplinary exploration of AI's impact on democracy, labor, global inequality, and mental health.
  - Excellent for faculty teaching **media studies, political science, public policy, and ethics**.
- **OpenAI Educator Resources**
  - Includes resources such as **"AI for K–12 Educators," "ChatGPT on Campus," and classroom prompt libraries**.
  - Offers guidance on **AI-assisted writing, academic integrity, and student engagement** with tools such as ChatGPT.
  - Useful for faculty teaching in **writing, communications, or first-year seminars**.

Faculty Practice: Start with One Adaptable Activity

Faculty do not need to design an entire unit from scratch. A **single activity or case study** from one of these repositories can serve as a meaningful launch point:

Examples:

- Adapt an AI bias case study from AI4ALL to facilitate discussion in a sociology or criminal justice course.
- Use a "prompt comparison" activity from OpenAI's ChatGPT educator kit to explore authorship and originality in a writing seminar.
- Integrate a fairness-focused exercise from MIT RAISE to help science students reflect on how model outputs vary across demographic data.
- Use a Stanford HAI news literacy simulation to explore **algorithmic amplification and misinformation** in a media studies course.

Follow-Up Strategy: Use the initial activity to spark curiosity and discussion. Then, **scaffold complexity** - by adding a reflection assignment, assigning a relevant reading, or inviting students to redesign the system using human-centered principles.

Benefits of Open-Access Modules:

- **Pedagogical Accessibility.** Materials are structured for faculty with no prior AI training.

- **Disciplinary Flexibility.** Modules are designed to be contextually adaptable across general education courses - from humanities and social sciences to STEM.
- **Scalability.** Activities can be used as one-day conversations or extended into multi-week units.
- **Equity and Inclusion.** These resources often foreground **ethics, fairness, and representation**, supporting the development of **justice-oriented AI literacy** (Benjamin, 2023; Gulya, 2023; Noble, 2018).

---

3. Join or Create Faculty Learning Communities (FLCs): Building Collaborative Capacity for AI Pedagogy

As institutions explore how to embed AI literacy across general education, one of the most effective strategies for building faculty capacity is to cultivate **Faculty Learning Communities (FLCs)** - voluntary, interdisciplinary groups that meet regularly to explore shared pedagogical challenges, experiment with new practices, and engage in collaborative reflection. When thoughtfully facilitated, FLCs offer faculty a **low-stakes, peer-supported space** to engage with unfamiliar material - like AI ethics, generative tools, or algorithmic systems - without the pressure of expert performance.

Originally conceptualized by Cox (2004), FLCs function as a form of **grassroots professional learning**. They operate on the principle that meaningful change in teaching arises not through top-down mandates or one-off workshops, but through **ongoing, collegial dialogue and shared inquiry**. For AI literacy initiatives, FLCs serve as a **laboratory for interdisciplinary integration**, enabling faculty from diverse disciplines to co-develop modules, share classroom experiences, and align AI instruction with broader institutional values (Brookfield, 2017; Byars-Winston & Dahlberg, 2019).

3.1 Reading Groups. Faculty meet monthly to discuss shared readings that explore the technical and ethical critiques, systemic perspectives on education, and current research articles for immediacy dimensions of AI. Suggested sources may include:

- **The Ethical Algorithm** (Kearns & Roth, 2019). A practical introduction to balancing innovation with fairness, privacy, and accountability in AI systems.
- **Weapons of Math Destruction** (O'neil, 2017). A critical look at how predictive algorithms amplify inequality and risk in education, finance, and justice.
- **Artificial Unintelligence** (Broussard, 2019). An accessible critique of AI hype, encouraging reflection on what machines can and cannot do compared to human judgment.
- **Artificial Intelligence in Education** (Holmes et al., 2022). Research on how higher education can embed AI literacy and prepare students for ethical engagement with intelligent systems.
- **Peer-reviewed articles** on topics such as generative AI in teaching and assessment, sustainability in AI, or cross-disciplinary AI pedagogy (e.g., Weber-Wulff et al., 2023; Ray & Ray, 2024).

Benefits: Encouraging reflective, theory-informed dialogue allows participants to pause and think critically about how AI intersects with both disciplinary practices and larger societal forces. **By grounding conversations in theoretical frameworks, faculty and students can connect their immediate experiences with AI to enduring debates about power, ethics, and knowledge**. This process fosters interdisciplinary bridges, ensuring that AI is not treated as a narrow technical subject but as a phenomenon situated within - and shaped by - broader social, cultural, and institutional systems.

3.2. Teaching Clinics. Faculty observe one another's AI-related lessons - either live or through short recorded micro-teaching sessions - and then engage in structured, collegial peer feedback. This process not only provides immediate insights into classroom strategies but also normalizes vulnerability and experimentation in teaching with emerging technologies. Clinics can also include collaborative lesson redesign, small-group reflection exercises, and shared resource mapping, creating a supportive cycle of observation, critique, and collective improvement. Clinics can also include:

- Module-sharing workshops.
- "What worked / what flopped" roundtables.
- Live walkthroughs of AI tools in classroom use.

Benefit: Creates a culture of pedagogical transparency and iterative improvement, where faculty learn by doing and reflecting together (Brookfield, 2017). This shared process helps normalize experimentation with AI-related teaching, turning uncertainty into a collective opportunity for growth rather than an individual burden. Over time, **such collaboration fosters a supportive environment in which faculty model reflective practice for one another**, reinforcing the very habits of inquiry and adaptation they seek to instill in their students.

3.3. Hackathons and "AI Pedagogy Jam Sessions." Short, intensive design sprints in which faculty collaborate to co-create assignments, case studies, reflection prompts, or ethics activities that integrate AI into their courses provide a dynamic entry point into curriculum innovation. **These sessions allow faculty from diverse disciplines to rapidly prototype ideas, test them against peer feedback, and refine them into classroom-ready modules**. By concentrating time and energy in a collaborative, creative burst, design sprints transform experimentation into tangible teaching resources while also cultivating cross-disciplinary trust and shared ownership of AI pedagogy.

Sample Prompts:

- *"Design a 1-day lesson for non-majors on algorithmic bias."*
- *"Draft a student reflection prompt on ChatGPT and original thinking."*
- *"Map AI use cases in your discipline and brainstorm teaching interventions."*

Benefit: Rapid, collaborative ideation promotes collective creativity by allowing faculty to pool diverse disciplinary perspectives, generating richer and more innovative approaches than any one individual could design alone. **These sessions distribute ownership of AI integration, ensuring that responsibility and expertise are shared across the institution**

rather than concentrated in a few early adopters. Over time, this collective model fosters a culture of experimentation, where faculty feel empowered to test, revise, and co-create AI-infused pedagogy as part of a broader academic community.

Case Example: "Teaching with ChatGPT Week" at a Liberal Arts College

Consider at a liberal arts college with a faculty learning community dedicated to digital pedagogy that organized a themed week called **"Teaching with ChatGPT."** The event featured:

- Lightning talks from writing, chemistry, and philosophy faculty.
- Classroom experiments with AI co-writing, feedback summarization, and ethical reflection.
- A panel on student perceptions and misuse of generative AI tools.
- A community whiteboard where faculty posted "AI surprises," "AI challenges," and "AI questions we still have."

Benefits: Faculty reported increased confidence, new assignment ideas, and a shift from fear to **critical curiosity**. Importantly, the week **centered on diverse disciplines** and framed AI not just as a tech issue, but as a humanistic and educational one.

Why FLCs Work for AI Literacy:

- **Normalize Uncertainty.** Faculty can admit confusion, raise questions, and test ideas in a **supportive, non-evaluative space**.
- **Leverage Peer Expertise.** Faculty from different fields bring different lenses - philosophical, technical, cultural - fostering richer approaches to AI pedagogy.
- **Support Just-In-Time Learning.** Instead of large-scale retraining, FLCs offer **incremental, embedded growth**, scaffolded by community and shared experimentation.
- **Model Collaboration for Students.** When faculty collaborate across disciplines, they demonstrate **interdisciplinary thinking in action**, a key component of AI-informed education.

---

4. Normalize Faculty-as-Learner Models: Modeling Inquiry in the Age of AI

One of the most generative pedagogical shifts in AI-integrated education is the movement from faculty-as-expert toward **faculty-as-inquirer**. In a landscape where tools, capabilities, and norms change rapidly - and where students often arrive with lived fluency in emerging technologies - **professors do not need to perform mastery to facilitate meaningful engagement**. Instead, they can model something even more valuable: **disciplined curiosity, ethical uncertainty, and intellectual humility**. As Brookfield (2017) has argued, when educators authentically engage as learners, they signal that knowledge is not a fixed asset to be delivered, but a shared and iterative process of discovery. In the context of generative AI, this model is especially resonant. No one has all the answers - because the questions themselves are still evolving.

Normalizing **faculty-as-learner** does not mean surrendering authority. Rather, it means **reframing authority as relational and reflective**, grounded in the ability to ask good questions, contextualize technological shifts, and navigate complexity alongside students. This approach not only reduces barriers to faculty participation in AI pedagogy - it also **builds trust, authenticity, and collaborative agency in the classroom** (Byars-Winston & Dahlberg, 2019; Reiss, 2021). Faculty can embrace their role as co-learners through structured exercises in which they **learn with and from students**. These do not require deep technical knowledge - only a willingness to frame inquiry as collective. Here are three adaptable co-learning strategies:

Practice Tip 1. Prompt Exploration Lab: "Tuning the Machine Together"

Activity: Students and faculty collaboratively experiment with prompt engineering in tools such as ChatGPT or Claude. They compare:

- How small changes in wording alter tone, specificity, or bias.
- How different disciplines might ask the same question in different ways - and yield different results.

Discussion Questions:

- *"What kinds of prompts produce thoughtful, misleading, or superficial responses?"*
- *"Whose voice is being echoed - and whose is missing?"*

Outcome: Students see that **AI output is shaped by human framing**, and faculty model the process of **learning through iteration and reflection** (Reamer, 2023; Slimi & Carballido, 2023).

Practice Tip 2. Bias Identification Sprint: "Where is the Pattern - and Where is the Problem?"

Activity: Together, faculty and students review a set of algorithmic recommendations (e.g., search results, social media feeds, Spotify suggestions). They identify:

- Patterns in visibility or exclusion;
- Discrepancies across demographic variables;
- Moments that provoke discomfort or raise ethical questions.

Discussion Questions:

- *"What values seem to drive the algorithm?"*
- *"How might bias enter through training data or design assumptions?"*

Outcome: Students practice **critical AI literacy**, while faculty validate emergent critique and co-construct ethical language around digital systems (Benjamin, 2023; Crawford, 2021).

Practice Tip 3. Discipline Futures Workshop: "How Is AI Reshaping Our Field?"

Activity: Students and faculty collectively map how AI is changing their discipline - from research methods and labor roles to epistemological assumptions.

Discussion Questions:

- *"What parts of our field are most affected by automation or augmentation?"*
- *"What capacities will be more - or less - valued in an AI-integrated future?"*
- *"What should our profession advocate for?"*

Outcome: The class becomes a site of **disciplinary imagination**, where uncertainty is not a threat, but an opportunity for collaborative inquiry and shared authorship of the future (Floridi et al., 2018; Gulya, 2023).

---

5. Share and Curate Assignment Repositories: Enabling Scalable, Collaborative AI Pedagogy

As AI literacy becomes a general education imperative, institutions must shift from isolated experimentation to **sustainable, shared curricular ecosystems**. One of the most impactful strategies for scaling this shift is the creation of **open, curated assignment repositories** - centralized collections of teaching materials that empower faculty to adopt, adapt, and iterate on AI-integrated instruction across disciplines.

These repositories reduce redundancy, celebrate faculty innovation, and **lower the activation threshold** for faculty new to AI pedagogy. Just as importantly, they model a **culture of scholarly generosity**, where ideas circulate freely across departments and disciplines - reinforcing that teaching AI is a collective endeavor, not a competitive one (Brookfield, 2017; Byars-Winston & Dahlberg, 2019).

Key Components of a Robust Assignment Repository: Effective repositories include more than just lesson plans. They are structured to support both **practical implementation and pedagogical reflection**. Core components may include:

- **AI Literacy Syllabi**. Complete or partial syllabi organized by field, level (introductory, intermediate, advanced), and instructional format (in-person, hybrid, online).
- **Sample Assignments by Discipline**. Categorized by general education area (e.g., ethics, composition, media studies, data science), use case (e.g., prompt engineering, bias detection), and assignment type (e.g., essay, project, simulation, group work).
- **Student Reflection Prompts**. Curated prompts focused on **trust, authorship, fairness, disciplinary change**, and the **emotional and cognitive dimensions** of engaging with AI.
- **Tool Comparison Charts**. Visual guides to help faculty and students compare AI platforms (e.g., ChatGPT vs. Perplexity, DALL·E vs. Midjourney) based on criteria such as accuracy, transparency, accessibility, and data sourcing.
- **Capstone Project Models**. Final project blueprints that integrate **technical reasoning, ethical inquiry, and civic engagement** - ranging from policy briefs to AI audits, digital portfolios, and speculative design proposals.

Case Example: Institutional Repository with Taxonomic Tagging

Consider, at one university, a cross-disciplinary AI curriculum team launches an internal platform where faculty can upload and browse AI-integrated teaching materials. Each contribution is:

- **Categorized by Bloom's Taxonomy level** (e.g., "Apply," "Analyze," "Evaluate").
- Linked to specific **general education outcomes** (e.g., ethical reasoning, digital literacy, critical thinking).
- Filtered by **course level**, from first-year seminars to senior capstones.

Impact: Contributors receive credit for participation, and materials are peer-reviewed within the institution to ensure **adaptability, inclusivity, and relevance across disciplines**. This initiative not only increases faculty adoption of AI content, but also fosters **peer-to-peer mentorship, pedagogical dialogue, and interdisciplinary alignment** - turning scattered innovation into institutional infrastructure.

Benefits of Assignment Repositories

- **Scalability**: Enables rapid dissemination of AI pedagogy across departments without reinventing curricula.
- **Efficiency**: Reduces prep time, particularly for faculty integrating AI content for the first time.
- **Adaptability**: Provides modular entry points - allowing faculty to adopt a single activity or entire units.
- **Equity**: Levels the instructional playing field by offering high-quality materials to faculty at all levels of technical familiarity.
- **Recognition**: Creates formal mechanisms to **acknowledge teaching innovation** as a scholarly contribution.

Curation and Governance Recommendations

- **Assign editorial stewards** by discipline or teaching center;
- Include filters for **disciplinary lens, institutional context, technical intensity**, and **student learning goals**;
- Encourage faculty to include **reflection memos** describing what worked, what did not, and what evolved - turning the repository into a **living archive of instructional insight**;
- Consider open-sharing options with **Creative Commons licensing** to extend the repository's impact beyond campus.

---

6. Advocate for Institutional Support Structures: Embedding AI Literacy into the Core of Higher Education

While classroom innovation often begins with individual faculty members, **long-term, equitable, and scalable AI literacy** depends on sustained institutional investment. Without structural support - professional development, funding, recognition, and policy alignment - AI pedagogy risks becoming a **boutique experiment**: available only in isolated courses, overburdening the willing few, and absent from the broader curriculum. To fulfill the promise of general education as a space for civic and intellectual formation, colleges and universities must build **infrastructures of support** that position AI literacy as a shared, institution-wide responsibility.

Crucially, this advocacy must be **strategically framed**. AI literacy should not be reduced to a coding competency or an emerging tech elective. It must be understood as a **core 21st-century capacity**, on par with writing, critical thinking, and digital citizenship - one that prepares students to navigate, critique, and shape the intelligent systems that now mediate knowledge, identity, labor, and power (Byars-Winston & Dahlberg, 2019; Long & Magerko, 2020).

Integrating AI literacy into general education requires more than individual initiative - it demands **institutional vision, policy alignment, and structural support**. Faculty can experiment, innovate, and lead, but without systemic reinforcement, even the most promising efforts risk remaining isolated or unsustainable. To embed AI literacy as a lasting, cross-disciplinary competency, colleges and universities must develop **infrastructure that normalizes, funds, and rewards pedagogical engagement with AI**.

The four strategies that follow offer a practical roadmap for institutionalizing AI literacy at scale. Together, they provide a framework for supporting faculty, incentivizing interdisciplinary curriculum development, embedding AI into strategic priorities, and fostering a campus-wide culture of ethical, critical engagement with intelligent technologies:

- **Embed AI into teaching and learning center offerings**
- **Provide mini-grants for interdisciplinary course development**
- **Offer faculty retreats focused on AI pedagogy**
- **Include AI literacy in strategic plans and general education learning outcomes**

Each strategy can be implemented flexibly and incrementally, but collectively they signal a powerful shift: from AI as a specialized topic to **AI literacy as a core institutional commitment**.

6.1 Embed AI Into Teaching and Learning Center Offerings

Action: To scale and sustain AI literacy across general education, institutions should ensure that **Centers for Teaching and Learning (CTLs)** actively incorporate AI-related topics into their ongoing professional development programming. This integration sends a clear signal: **AI pedagogy is not an isolated or experimental pursuit - it is part of the evolving instructional landscape** that all educators are invited to shape.

Rather than treating AI as a specialized technical concern, CTLs can frame it as **a pedagogical, ethical, and curricular opportunity**, relevant across disciplines and teaching modalities. Through **recurring workshops, 1:1 consultations, curated resource hubs, and faculty learning communities**, CTLs can offer faculty accessible entry points into AI-enhanced teaching - regardless of technical background or disciplinary home. Topics might include:

- **"Teaching with Generative AI: Pedagogy, Policy, and Possibility"** to explore how tools such as ChatGPT or DALL·E can support or challenge traditional teaching goals; address concerns about plagiarism, authorship, and automation.
- **"Designing Reflective Assignments in an AI-Enhanced Classroom"** helps faculty craft activities that ask students to document, question, and critique their use of AI tools, encouraging metacognitive growth and academic integrity.
- **"Ethics and Explainability for Non-STEM Faculty"** offer accessible frameworks for understanding algorithmic bias, black-box models, and socio-technical critique - empowering humanities and social science faculty to engage AI without needing to teach code.

Rationale: Incorporating AI into existing CTL infrastructure does more than build technical familiarity - it helps **normalize AI pedagogy as an inclusive, institution-wide priority**. Faculty who might never attend a discipline-specific AI workshop may be more likely to engage through trusted CTL offerings, where pedagogy - not performance - is the primary focus. Moreover, aligning AI instruction with broader faculty development efforts ensures that it is **contextualized within existing teaching values**: inclusive practice, learner-centered design, assessment transparency, and critical reflection (Brookfield, 2017). It helps demystify AI, reduces fear, and positions faculty as **co-creators of an ethical AI learning culture** - not late adopters struggling to catch up.

6.2 Provide Mini-Grants for Interdisciplinary Course Development

Action: To encourage the integration of AI literacy across disciplines and course levels, institutions should offer **competitive seed funding** in the form of mini-grants to faculty teams committed to piloting AI-infused modules or redesigning existing general education courses. These mini-grants serve as a tangible investment in pedagogical experimentation - especially for **cross-functional collaborations that foreground ethics, equity, and student-centered learning**. Grant-funded teams may include:

- Two or more faculty from different departments (e.g., computer science + philosophy; sociology + data science).
- A librarian or instructional designer who contributes digital literacy expertise.
- A graduate assistant or undergraduate learning partner supporting testing and reflection.

Suggested Grant Features:

- **Funding range**. **$1,000–$5,000 per team**, based on scope and deliverables.
- **Grant term**. 1–2 semesters for design, pilot, and reflection.
- **Use of funds**. Faculty stipends, student co-researchers, course materials, event hosting, or tool licenses.
- **Deliverables**. Shareable course materials such as **revised syllabi, annotated lesson plans, sample assignments, AI ethics cases, or student reflection data**.
- Final contribution to an institutional repository or showcase event to promote dissemination and visibility.

Rationale: Mini-grants reduce common structural barriers to innovation: time, compensation, and institutional permission. For many faculty, the lack of release time or summer salary inhibits deep curricular redesign. Micro-funding **signals institutional value** and provides material support to explore uncharted pedagogical territory.

Incentivizing interdisciplinary teaching further addresses the **siloed nature of AI education**, where technical and ethical knowledge often remain artificially separated. These grants foster **collaborative design thinking**, where faculty jointly develop modules that integrate algorithmic literacy with real-world implications - helping students think not just about how AI works, but what it means and whom it impacts (Benjamin, 2023; Floridi et al., 2018). Critically, embedding **equity and ethics as core grant criteria** ensures that course innovations do not merely reproduce dominant narratives of progress or efficiency, but instead surface **questions of justice, access, and power** - essential for meaningful AI literacy in a general education context (Byars-Winston & Dahlberg, 2019; Noble, 2018).

Extended Impact:

- **Peer-modeled innovation.** Grantees become early adopters whose materials and reflections can serve as peer-reviewed exemplars for others across campus.
- **Scalable design.** Projects can begin as one-week modules, but later expand into full courses, first-year experiences, or interdisciplinary certificates.
- **Communities of practice.** Faculty teams may continue collaboration beyond the grant term, helping seed longer-term faculty learning communities or joint research on teaching and learning.

6.3 Offer Faculty Retreats Focused on AI Pedagogy

Action: To cultivate sustained and thoughtful integration of AI into the undergraduate curriculum, institutions should host **faculty retreats focused on AI literacy, pedagogy, and interdisciplinary module development**. Whether offered in summer, during intersession, or as part of an annual professional development series, these retreats provide **protected time and collaborative space** for faculty to explore the implications of AI for teaching, learning, and disciplinary transformation.

Structured as intensive, immersive gatherings, retreats can be designed for faculty from a broad range of departments - whether STEM, humanities, social sciences, or professional fields. They support **curiosity-driven exploration, community-building, and the co-creation of adaptable curriculum** that foregrounds ethics, inclusion, and pedagogical creativity. Core retreat elements may include:

- **Hands-on exploration of AI tools** such as ChatGPT, Claude, Perplexity.ai, DALL·E, or discipline-specific systems (e.g., clinical decision tools, writing tutors, citation managers). Faculty examine outputs, identify strengths and risks, and consider classroom applications.
- **Showcases of classroom experiments** from faculty who have piloted AI-integrated activities, offering insights into what worked, what surprised them, and how students responded.

- **Collaborative module design sprints**, in which faculty teams co-develop new syllabi units, reflection assignments, or co-teaching proposals aligned to general education outcomes.

Optional Features to Deepen Impact:

- **Guest speakers** from AI ethics, technology policy, design justice, or algorithmic bias fields to provide critical framing and global context (e.g., representatives from Stanford HAI, Data & Society, or AI4ALL).
- **Emotional and ethical labor sessions** that acknowledge AI pedagogy often induce discomfort, uncertainty, or institutional tension. Reflection circles and faculty storytelling build resilience and trust (Brookfield, 2017; Reiss, 2021).
- **Cohort formation and sustained engagement**, such as creating follow-up writing groups, teaching partnerships, or curriculum fellowships to ensure the work continues beyond the retreat.

Rationale: In a field marked by **rapid technological shifts and social complexity**, faculty need not only content knowledge but **intellectual room to pause, reflect, and design with intention**. Unlike short-form workshops or asynchronous training modules, retreats offer a **temporal and relational reprieve from routine pressures** - enabling deeper inquiry, interdisciplinary synthesis, and future-facing curriculum design.

They also provide an **emotionally intelligent response** to the pedagogical stressors introduced by AI - uncertainty about academic integrity, fear of being outpaced by students, or concerns about equity and surveillance in the classroom. These are not purely technical concerns - they are **relational and moral** ones, best addressed in community (Byars-Winston & Dahlberg, 2019; Reiss, 2021).

Extended Outcomes:

- Development of **cross-disciplinary module templates** that can be adopted or adapted across departments.
- Growth of an internal **faculty leadership cohort** equipped to mentor peers, run learning communities, or advise on AI-related academic policy.
- Strengthened alignment between **AI integration and institutional mission values**, including equity, digital citizenship, and lifelong learning.

6.4 Include AI Literacy in Strategic Plans and Gen Ed Learning Outcomes

Action: To ensure the long-term relevance and sustainability of AI integration efforts, academic institutions should **embed AI literacy explicitly into core curricular frameworks, strategic planning documents, and program assessment structures**. This involves working closely with curriculum committees, accreditation liaisons, teaching and learning centers, and senior academic leadership to **codify AI-related competencies** into the foundational architecture of undergraduate education. At a minimum, institutions should:

- **Explicitly name AI literacy, algorithmic awareness, or data ethics** in general education outcomes and digital fluency rubrics.

- Position AI literacy alongside existing general education priorities such as **information literacy, civic engagement, ethical reasoning, and global citizenship**.
- Incorporate AI-related objectives into **strategic planning**, program review templates, and accreditation narratives (e.g., for regional or disciplinary accrediting bodies).

Strategic Language Examples:

- *"Graduates will demonstrate the ability to critically analyze the social and ethical dimensions of algorithmic systems and artificial intelligence."*
- *"Students will engage with emerging technologies through interdisciplinary inquiry, addressing questions of bias, authorship, data justice, and civic responsibility."*
- *"Faculty across the curriculum will be supported in integrating AI tools and frameworks that advance inclusive, reflective, and adaptive learning."*

Rationale: Elevating AI Literacy from Innovation to Imperative

When AI literacy is institutionalized through formal curricular structures, it transitions from a **niche innovation** - reliant on a few early adopters - into a **recognized curricular imperative**, aligned with the university's broader mission to prepare graduates for ethical leadership in a digitally saturated world. This alignment creates several benefits:

- **Clarity for Faculty**. Naming AI literacy within general education frameworks signals that **all disciplines are welcome and needed** in this work - not just computer science or engineering. It gives faculty permission to engage and a shared vocabulary to do so (Brookfield, 2017; Selwyn, 2019).
- **Consistency for Students**. When AI learning goals are embedded across departments, students encounter these competencies **multiple times, from multiple perspectives**, reinforcing their importance and supporting interdisciplinary synthesis (Floridi et al., 2018).
- **Legitimacy for Funding and Staffing**. Codifying AI literacy at the institutional level supports the case for **dedicated grants, new course development, professional development initiatives, and staffing needs** (e.g., instructional designers or ethics specialists focused on emerging technology).
- **Accreditation Readiness**. As regional and professional accrediting bodies increasingly emphasize digital literacy, global awareness, and ethical preparedness, AI literacy **enhances institutional standing** by demonstrating curricular responsiveness to societal transformation.

Extended Impact:

- Enables **vertical and horizontal curriculum mapping** of AI outcomes across programs and course levels.
- Encourages academic units to **develop AI-infused minors, certificates, or pathways**, further integrating ethics, critical thinking, and digital fluency.
- Supports assessment and continuous improvement processes by aligning AI pedagogy with measurable outcomes, such as **student reflection, civic reasoning, or technology critique** (Byars-Winston & Dahlberg, 2019; Gulya, 2023).

Strategic Framing for Campus Advocacy: Repositioning AI Literacy as a Shared Institutional Priority

Successfully advocating for AI literacy across departments, committees, and institutional leadership requires more than enthusiasm - it requires a **strategic reframing of what AI education is, who it serves, and why it matters for all learners**. Faculty champions, teaching center directors, and curriculum leaders must make the case that AI literacy is not a fleeting trend or purely technical add-on, but a **foundational academic and civic competency**, necessary for life in an increasingly automated and algorithmically mediated world.

This reframing work is essential to gaining traction with colleagues who may see AI as irrelevant to their field, and with administrators balancing innovation against finite resources. The following advocacy frames can be tailored to different stakeholders - faculty, provosts, deans, trustees, and curriculum committees - to position AI literacy as **mission-aligned, equity-centered, and future-oriented** (Benjamin, 2023; Brookfield, 2017).

---

1. AI Literacy as a Civic Competency

Argument: AI literacy should be understood as central to **democratic participation** and **civic responsibility** in the 21st century. Just as information literacy prepares students to evaluate sources and claims, AI literacy enables them to **interrogate and navigate algorithmic systems** that shape public discourse, allocate resources, and influence decision-making.

Examples:

- *Understanding how predictive policing systems affect civil liberties.*
- *Evaluating the transparency of recommendation algorithms during elections.*
- *Interpreting health risk scores or loan application outcomes produced by black-box models.*

Message for Leaders: This is not about coding - it is about preparing students to **engage critically and ethically with the AI-driven systems that govern education, law, medicine, media, and governance** (Noble, 2018; Selwyn, 2019).

---

2. AI Literacy as a Workplace Necessity

Argument: Across sectors, students will increasingly be expected to **interact with, critique, or build upon AI systems** - whether in nursing documentation systems, marketing automation, arts-based creation, or logistics and operations. AI literacy is not a tech-sector specialization; it is **a cross-sector professional fluency**.

Examples:

- *Nurses using AI-based triage systems must balance machine guidance with patient context.*
- *Designers using generative visual tools must address questions of originality and bias.*

- *Business professionals working with AI-driven analytics must understand how outputs are produced - and where they might be misleading.*

Message for Leaders: Embedding AI literacy supports **career readiness, lifelong learning, and interdisciplinary fluency**, aligning with institutional goals for graduate employability and adaptability (Gulya, 2023; Reamer, 2023).

---

3. AI Literacy as a Humanistic Skillset

Argument: AI literacy is not just about knowing how tools work - it is about knowing how they affect meaning, identity, ethics, and society. Faculty in the humanities and social sciences play a crucial role by teaching students to **interpret AI systems as cultural artifacts**, to ask who they serve, and to interrogate whose voices they amplify or erase.

Examples:

- *Exploring authorship and originality in machine-generated poetry.*
- *Analyzing bias in facial recognition systems through a critical race lens.*
- *Debating moral agency and accountability in automated decision-making.*

Message for Leaders: AI literacy aligns with long-standing liberal arts goals: **critical inquiry, ethical reasoning, and civic imagination**. It reinforces - not replaces - the mission of higher education as a humanizing force (Benjamin, 2023; Binns, 2018; Brookfield, 2017).

Bridge Topic

From Peripheral Innovation to Core Curricular Commitment

When framed as a **civic responsibility**, a **professional imperative**, and a **humanistic inquiry**, AI literacy transcends departmental boundaries. It becomes a **shared curricular foundation**, supporting democratic learning, ethical leadership, and critical adaptability in the face of accelerating technological change.

Strategic framing helps move the conversation from *"Should we teach AI?"* to *"How can we ensure all students are prepared to live and lead in an AI-shaped world?"* The answer, increasingly, must be **through interdisciplinary, values-informed general education** - backed by institutional vision and cross-campus collaboration.

Examples of Empowered Faculty Collaboration: Catalyzing AI Pedagogy Through Shared Practice

Faculty collaboration is one of the most powerful accelerants for institutional AI literacy. When faculty move beyond isolated experimentation and engage in **purpose-driven collaboration**, they generate not only stronger teaching - but also **shared language, ethical reflexivity, and scalable models** for curriculum design. Below are four examples of faculty-led initiatives that exemplify empowered, interdisciplinary, and justice-aware AI pedagogy. These four models (presented as an initiative, description, and impact) illustrate how institutions can foster meaningful innovation without requiring large-scale restructuring or excessive technical retraining.

Initiative 1: AI Across the Curriculum (AAC)

A cross-college task force convenes faculty from diverse disciplines - philosophy, business, biology, computer science, media studies - to design **modular, co-taught units** that embed AI topics into existing general education courses. Faculty rotate through shared workshops where they explore how AI is transforming knowledge production, civic systems, and disciplinary methods. Outputs include:

- A shared repository of adaptable syllabi and readings.
- AI case studies aligned to each major's learning goals.
- "Faculty pairing" models that match STEM and non-STEM faculty for team-taught segments.

Impact: Creates long-term capacity for interdisciplinary AI teaching, with shared responsibility and peer-supported implementation. Promotes **horizontal alignment** across curriculum.

Initiative 2: ChatGPT Reflection Studio

During a designated teaching week, faculty gather to test generative AI tools such as ChatGPT in a lab-style format. Participants collaboratively:

- Craft assignments involving AI output analysis.
- Compare classroom experiences across disciplines.
- Refine reflection prompts that encourage student metacognition.

Impact: Normalizes vulnerability and experimentation in AI pedagogy. Contributors receive credit for participation, and materials are peer-reviewed within the institution to ensure **adaptability, inclusivity, and relevance across disciplines**. Encourages **faculty-as-learners** (Brookfield, 2017), fostering a culture of **iterative design, transparency, and ethical responsiveness**.

Initiative 3: Generative AI Showcase Symposium

A cross-campus event where students and faculty present **AI-enhanced coursework**, including:

- Literature reviews written with prompt-augmented synthesis.
- Visual arts projects created with DALL·E or Midjourney.
- Debate prep using Perplexity.ai to identify counterarguments.
- Ethics papers analyzing risks in AI deployment.

Impact: The symposium features panel reflections, tool demonstrations, and dialogue on **authorship, originality, and accountability** across disciplines. Elevates student and faculty experimentation to institutional visibility. Reinforces that AI pedagogy is not just a set of tools - it is a space of **critical inquiry and creative collaboration**.

Initiative 4: Ethical AI Teaching Incubator

A semester-long faculty cohort composed of faculty from STEM, humanities, and education who:

- Explore readings on AI ethics, surveillance, labor, and epistemology (e.g., Benjamin, 2023; Crawford, 2021).
- Audit existing syllabi to identify sites of ethical tension.
- Design and peer-review one AI-integrated unit with embedded reflection and positionality.

Impact: The incubator meets monthly and includes guest visits from ethicists, librarians, and technologists. Builds **philosophical fluency, peer mentorship, and curricular coherence** around complex AI issues. Encourages faculty to **center equity, justice, and transparency**, especially in technical or tool-centric classrooms.

Section Reflection: From Hesitation to Leadership - Empowering Faculty in the AI Literacy Movement

This section reframes faculty discomfort around teaching AI not as a deficit, but as an invitation to reimagine what it means to be an educator in the algorithmic age. It recognizes that most faculty are not machine learning experts - and do not need to be. What they bring instead are essential skills in ethical reasoning, contextual framing, critical interpretation, and learner-centered pedagogy. The section makes a compelling case that interdisciplinary collaboration, shared curricular infrastructure, and institutional support are the keys to transforming AI literacy from a niche experiment into a broad-based, mission-aligned priority.

Rather than relying on top-down mandates or technical retraining, the section emphasizes confidence-building through community: co-teaching, open-access resources, learning communities, and reflection-centered pedagogy. Faculty are invited to take part in a shared cultural and civic project, where their existing strengths - curiosity, relational care, storytelling, and ethical inquiry - are indispensable. The section champions a "faculty-as-learner" model that humanizes both the subject matter and the teaching process, reminding institutions that humility, collaboration, and vulnerability are not obstacles to AI pedagogy - they are its most powerful assets.

Ultimately, this section argues that institutional transformation does not begin with content mastery, but with shared courage and mutual trust. When institutions invest in collaborative infrastructure - through mini-grants, retreats, repositories, and aligned learning outcomes - they empower faculty to become co-creators of AI education that is inclusive, interdisciplinary, and justice-driven. Faculty are not expected to master AI in isolation. Instead, they are invited to lead - together - in building the pedagogical imagination and ethical capacity that this moment demands.

Chapter 8 Conclusion: Legacy Through Leadership - Building Ethical Academic Culture in the AI Era

Chapter 8 expanded the focus from classroom practice to institutional influence, arguing that faculty are not only faculty responding to change, but **ethical leaders shaping it**. In a time when generative AI challenges traditional norms of authorship, feedback, assessment, and authority, educators are uniquely positioned to create a legacy that goes beyond adaptation - and toward intentional transformation. The eight sections of this chapter outlined pathways for faculty to act as co-architects of AI-ready institutions, rooted in the values of **equity, transparency, collaboration, and civic responsibility**.

In **Section 1**, the chapter called for a **mindset shift** - from passive tool adoption to active infrastructure design. It emphasized that AI is no longer confined to isolated classroom tools; it is becoming embedded in institutional systems that affect grading, advising, and decision-making. Faculty, therefore, must help design these systems, not merely respond to them.

Section 2 made this tangible through the creation of **AI governance and ethics committees**. These cross-functional groups ensure that AI is implemented with pedagogical intent and ethical oversight, allowing faculty to raise questions about fairness, accountability, and student impact before systems are institutionalized. This structure also affirms faculty as **guardians of educational values**, not just end users of technology.

Section 3 shifted to **cross-disciplinary curriculum councils**, where faculty design AI-infused learning pathways across general education and majors. Here, leadership involves preparing all students - not just tech majors - to understand AI's societal, ethical, and cultural implications. By infusing AI literacy across the curriculum, institutions avoid creating a digital elite and instead cultivate an informed, justice-oriented student body.

Section 4 introduced **co-design studios and hackathons** as participatory spaces where faculty, students, and staff collaboratively prototype AI tools, assignments, or grading systems. These labs of innovation allow communities to imagine **ethical applications before they are imposed**, giving agency to those most impacted by AI decisions.

In **Section 5**, the chapter emphasized the importance of **feedback loops**. Faculty must be involved not only in the creation of AI-related policies, but in their ongoing review and revision. When institutions build transparent mechanisms for reflection and course correction, faculty trust increases - and innovation becomes sustainable.

Section 6 celebrated **public scholarship** as a form of academic leadership. Faculty who write, speak, and organize around AI's societal impact extend their influence beyond campus, modeling how intellectual expertise can guide public understanding and policy. This outward-facing engagement transforms ethical leadership into civic stewardship.

Section 7 distilled these pathways into **five guiding principles for faculty-centered AI design**: transparency, inclusion, agency, ethical stewardship, and reflexivity. These principles offer a blueprint for institutions seeking to align AI integration with humanistic values - ensuring that innovation is accountable to those it serves.

Finally, **Section 8** argued that **legacy is built through culture**. Faculty shape not just individual student experiences, but the norms, expectations, and values that guide future cohorts. Whether through mentoring practices, curriculum design, committee leadership, or public dialogue, educators play a foundational role in defining what kind of academy - and what kind of society - we are co-creating with AI.

The concluding theme of Chapter 8 is this: **Ethical leadership in the AI era is not a position - it is a practice.** Faculty who act with foresight, integrity, and collaboration will leave a legacy that outlasts any single tool or policy. In a moment of profound change, their leadership will help determine whether AI in higher education becomes a force of empowerment - or a driver of inequality. By embracing this role, educators do more than respond to AI - they redefine what it means to teach, lead, and build a university worthy of the future.

Chapter 9: Faculty Development for the AI Future

Higher education must invest in its faculty if it hopes to responsibly integrate AI into teaching and research. This chapter outlines the institutional supports, professional development frameworks, and peer-learning initiatives that can help educators stay ahead of the curve. Topics include AI policy development, training strategies, and incentivizing innovation across departments. This chapter focuses on helping institutions and individual educators prepare for long-term professional growth by cultivating the mindsets, skills, and support systems needed to adapt to ongoing AI evolution.

Section 1: Rethinking Faculty Development in an Age of Acceleration

---

The pace of AI advancement - from generative tools such as ChatGPT and Claude to automated assessment platforms and intelligent tutoring systems - has outstripped traditional models of faculty development. While instructional design centers have long offered workshops on course design, learning technologies, and digital pedagogy, these offerings were typically **periodic, elective, and skills-based**. In contrast, the AI era requires **adaptive, embedded, and interdisciplinary models** of professional growth - ones that respond not only to new tools but to **new ways of knowing, teaching, and assessing** (Byars-Winston & Dahlberg, 2019; Slimi & Carballido, 2023).

Why Traditional Faculty Development Models Fall Short: Rethinking Professional Learning in the Age of AI

For decades, faculty development programs have been built on well-established but increasingly outdated assumptions: that teaching tools change slowly, that expertise is cumulative and stable, and that pedagogical transformation unfolds in **gradual, iterative cycles**. In this model, faculty are offered **episodic training sessions**, often centered on familiar platforms (e.g., LMS features, rubrics, course design), with the expectation that once adopted, instructional strategies will remain relevant for several years.

But in an educational ecosystem reshaped by generative AI and rapidly evolving automation tools, **these legacy models no longer suffice**. The scale and speed of technological disruption - not to mention its **ethical ambiguity and social complexity** - demand a fundamentally new paradigm for faculty development: one that centers **continuity, co-learning, and critical reflection**, rather than occasional technical training alone (Brookfield, 2017; Reiss, 2021).

Outdated Assumptions in Legacy Faculty Development Models

- **Faculty Need Occasional Tool Training, Not Conceptual Reframing**. Traditional models prioritize **how to use a tool** (e.g., click paths, grading functions), but often fail to address **why the tool matters**, how it redefines learning, and what risks or values are embedded in its design. In the case of AI, this is especially insufficient - because the most pressing challenges are not mechanical, but **epistemological and ethical**.
- **Expertise Is Static Rather Than Evolving**. Faculty development has long been grounded in the assumption that once an instructor masters a pedagogical strategy or platform, it remains valid over time. However, in the AI era, expertise is **provisional, fluid, and co-constructed**. Faculty must continuously revisit and re-evaluate their own assumptions about authorship, assessment, and authenticity - as models change monthly and norms evolve in real time (Slimi & Carballido, 2023).
- **Change Happens Incrementally, Not Exponentially**. AI shifts the terrain faster than traditional professional development cycles can accommodate. A single semester may bring significant advances in generative modeling, changes in student behavior, or the emergence of new tools that **disrupt classroom practice, institutional policy, and disciplinary expectations** - requiring agile, ongoing faculty dialogue (Farooq, 2025).

The New Terrain Faculty Must Navigate

- **Rapid Technological Change**. From GPT-5 to Claude to platform integrations in tools such as Microsoft Copilot or LMS-native AI assistants, educators must contend with **frequent updates and shifting capabilities**, often without guidance from centralized IT or academic affairs.
- **Shifting Epistemologies**. Concepts such as **originality, authorship, cognitive effort, and rigor** are being redefined. Faculty must decide how to **assess work influenced by AI**, how to preserve meaningful human learning, and how to recognize or reward creativity in a hybrid human-machine context (Brookfield, 2017; Reamer, 2023).
- **Student Usage That Outpaces Policy**. Students are already using generative AI to brainstorm, summarize, co-write, and respond to feedback. Institutional policy often lags behind student behavior - leaving faculty to improvise, negotiate, or silently disengage when official guidance feels insufficient (Reiss, 2021).

The Emotional Cost of Pedagogical Dislocation

Without structured and ongoing institutional support, many faculty experience the AI transformation not as a promising opportunity but instead as a source of anxiety, disorientation, or even disengagement from their teaching practice. **This reaction often stems from uncertainty about what counts as "responsible" use of AI in the classroom, as well as fear of being outpaced by students who adopt tools more quickly**. In this climate, common concerns emerge around workload expectations, disciplinary relevance, and the erosion of academic authority in the face of rapidly evolving technologies. Common faculty concerns include:

- *"My students know more about this than I do."*
- *"What counts as cheating anymore?"*
- *"I do not want to fall behind, but I do not know where to begin."*

This emotional burden is not a reflection of inadequacy - it is a natural response to **paradigm-level disruption**. As Brookfield (2017) noted, when educators are asked to change not just their tools, but their assumptions about knowledge, authority, and meaning-making, **support must include reflection, solidarity, and co-construction - not just skills acquisition**.

Bridge Topic

From Transactional Training to Transformational Support

The age of AI requires a faculty development model grounded in intellectual humility, interdisciplinary dialogue, and critical inquiry. Rather than positioning faculty as passive recipients of technical training, **institutions must recognize that teaching with AI demands ongoing adaptation and a willingness to admit uncertainty**. This means replacing one-off tool demonstrations with long-term learning communities, iterative design labs, and faculty-as-learner spaces that make experimentation and reflection part of the culture of pedagogy.

AI is not merely an instructional aid - **it is a catalyst for rethinking what it means to teach, learn, and know**. When faculty are supported in treating AI as both a tool and a subject of inquiry, they can model curiosity, critical reflection, and ethical reasoning for their students. Development models that honor this complexity empower educators not simply to cope with AI but to lead its ethical, inclusive, and human-centered integration into higher education.

A Framework for AI-Responsive Faculty Growth: Reimagining Professional Development for the Algorithmic University

The acceleration of AI technologies in education demands a fundamental shift in how institutions **support, equip, and engage faculty**. Traditional models of faculty development - episodic workshops, static training modules, and one-size-fits-all pedagogical guidance - are poorly suited to the **dynamic, ethically fraught, and discipline-spanning challenges** that AI brings to higher education. What is needed is a development framework that is not only responsive to new tools but also **grounded in critical inquiry, professional identity, and collaborative meaning-making** (Brookfield, 2017; Reiss, 2021).

The following four-part framework outlines key principles for building a future-ready approach to **AI-responsive faculty development**. Each dimension is accompanied by practical illustrations that translate theory into action across diverse institutional contexts.

Framework 1. Agile: Responsive to Rapid Technological Change

In an environment where AI tools evolve monthly - and student adoption often outpaces faculty training - **professional development must be designed with flexibility and speed at**

its core. Faculty need opportunities that are adaptive to different disciplines, modular enough to be integrated into busy schedules, and responsive to the latest technological developments. Most importantly, **these learning opportunities must be available on demand**, so faculty can access just-in-time support when new tools or student practices surface in their classrooms.

Example Practice:

- Rather than relying solely on annual workshops, centers for teaching and learning (CTLs) launch **monthly "AI Labs"** - informal, drop-in sessions where faculty experiment with emerging features (e.g., GPT-5 multimodal input, auto-citation tools), share classroom applications, and surface collective concerns.
- Each lab has a thematic anchor (e.g., "AI and Feedback," "AI and Assessment Equity") and is co-facilitated by faculty across disciplines.

Outcome: Agile development cultivates a habit of pedagogical inquiry, encouraging faculty to continually ask how their teaching should evolve in response to new technologies rather than offering a one-time fix. **This iterative approach provides institutions with the flexibility to integrate AI into curricula gradually, ensuring that adaptation feels manageable rather than overwhelming**. In doing so, agile practices help align rapid tool evolution with sustainable faculty development, creating a culture of curiosity and responsiveness instead of fear or resistance (Farooq, 2025).

Framework 2. Continuous and Iterative: Growth as a Career-Long Practice

AI is not a single topic to master - it represents a continuous transformation in how we teach, assess, and engage with knowledge itself. Because of this, faculty development cannot be framed as a one-time training session but must be reimagined as an ongoing, iterative journey of learning and adaptation. Such upskilling should be aligned with each educator's unique disciplinary context, personal values, and evolving professional roles, ensuring that growth in AI literacy remains meaningful, sustainable, and ethically grounded.

Example Practice: Institutions offer **stackable micro-credentials or digital badges** on AI-related teaching topics such as:

- *"Prompt Engineering for Educators."*
- *"AI Ethics and Equity in the Classroom."*
- *"Designing Generative Assessments."*
- *"Interpreting Algorithmic Tools in Professional Fields."*

These credentials are housed within a centralized faculty development dashboard, ensuring they are visible and accessible for both individual faculty and institutional leadership. By linking them to tenure and promotion portfolios, teaching awards, or public showcases, the institution underscores that AI pedagogy and reflective practice are recognized as legitimate markers of professional growth. **This visibility not only motivates faculty to pursue ongoing development but also builds a culture where innovation and ethical engagement with AI are celebrated as part of academic excellence**.

Outcome: Faculty receive recognition for their intellectual engagement with emerging technologies, which validates their efforts and reinforces the importance of innovation in academic life. **At the same time, institutions benefit by building a record of distributed, discipline-specific experiments and practices that showcase adaptability and creativity across departments**. This dual outcome creates a virtuous cycle where individual contributions are rewarded, while the broader academic community gains a growing repository of approaches to guide sustainable integration of AI into teaching and scholarship (Byars-Winston & Dahlberg, 2019).

Framework 3. Collaborative Across Disciplines: Teaching as a Cross-Functional Practice

AI is not the domain of any one department, because its influence extends across the sciences, humanities, and professional fields alike. It raises questions that span technical coding and ethical responsibility, creative authorship and logical design, as well as automation and human identity. **Faculty development must therefore embrace this complexity, creating spaces where diverse disciplines come into shared dialogue** - ensuring that AI is examined not only as a technical tool, but as a cultural, civic, and ethical force that touches every area of knowledge.

Example Practice: A co-led workshop series titled **"ChatGPT in the Studio, the Seminar, and the Lab"** pairs faculty from:

- **Studio Art**. Exploring AI as co-creator in visual design.
- **Philosophy**. Interrogating authorship and personhood.
- **Biology**. Examining AI-assisted lab reporting.

Sessions emphasize how disciplinary norms shape the way AI tools are used, critiqued, and resisted, reminding faculty that **AI integration is always filtered through the assumptions of their fields**. When students see faculty from different disciplines - such as a computer scientist and a philosopher - jointly unpack an AI case study, they learn that expertise is collaborative and shaped by dialogue. **This modeling deepens student understanding of AI while showing that critical inquiry across disciplines is as valuable as technical fluency**.

Outcome: Cross-disciplinary collaboration breaks the siloed logic of tool training and instead fosters a rich ecology of perspectives, where technical, ethical, cultural, and social insights intersect. This diversity is essential for preparing students to navigate AI in real-world contexts that are pluralistic, contested, and shaped by multiple forms of expertise (Benjamin, 2023; Floridi et al., 2018). **By engaging voices across fields, collaboration ensures that students learn not only how AI works, but also how it impacts people, institutions, and democratic life in ways no single discipline could fully capture**.

Framework 4. Reflective and Conceptual: Space to Interrogate Values and Roles

AI integration is not just technical - it is also moral, emotional, and pedagogical, touching the very heart of what it means to educate in a rapidly changing world. **Faculty need structured opportunities not only to learn new tools, but also to critically examine how these tools affect their roles as teachers, mentors, and evaluators**. In this way, professional development becomes less about keeping up with technology and more about shaping a thoughtful, values-driven vision of teaching in an AI-augmented future.

Example Practice: A facilitated dialogue series invites faculty to respond to the prompt:

- *"What aspects of my teaching practice should never be automated - and why?"*

Participants write reflective statements, share them in small groups, and collaboratively explore the boundaries of machine-assisted learning. Sessions are framed with readings from Brookfield (2017), Benjamin (2023), and Reiss (2021), connecting reflection to scholarly discourse.

Outcome: Participants write reflective statements, then share them in small groups where they collaboratively explore the boundaries and possibilities of machine-assisted learning. This collective exchange not only surfaces individual insights but also creates space for dialogue about tensions, uncertainties, and opportunities in AI-integrated education. Sessions are anchored with readings from Brookfield (2017), Benjamin (2023), and Reiss (2021), ensuring that student and faculty reflections foster **epistemic humility, pedagogical integrity, and emotional literacy** - all essential for navigating AI not just as a set of tools, but as a **transformational force** (Gulya, 2023; Reamer, 2023).

Bridge Topic

Building a Responsive, Ethical, and Human-Centered Faculty Culture

This four-part framework - **Agile, Continuous, Collaborative, Reflective** - offers institutions a blueprint for faculty development that is not only technologically relevant but also deeply educational and ethically grounded. By weaving together adaptability, sustained learning, cross-disciplinary exchange, and reflective inquiry, **the model ensures that faculty are not simply reacting to technological disruption but shaping it with intention**. In doing so, it prepares educators not just to adapt, but to lead - to model curiosity, accountability, and care in an era where intelligent systems increasingly influence academic life.

As AI continues to reshape higher education, the aim is not to transform every faculty member into a technologist or coder. Instead, **the goal is to cultivate educators who can act as thoughtful stewards of human learning, guiding students to navigate a machine-shaped world with integrity, creativity, and discernment**. In this vision, faculty become anchors of ethical reasoning and pedagogical care, ensuring that human values remain central even as digital systems evolve around them.

Practical Development Strategies for Institutions

Strategy 1. Just-in-Time Learning Platforms: Supporting Flexible, Autonomous Faculty Engagement

In an AI-driven academic environment where new tools, risks, and classroom dynamics emerge rapidly, faculty cannot wait for semesterly workshops or formal certification programs to gain the insight they need. Instead, they require **on-demand, accessible, and relevant learning opportunities** that respond to questions as they arise - whether in the middle of course prep, while reviewing student submissions, or in departmental conversations about academic integrity. **Just-in-time learning platforms** meet this need by offering **curated, modular, self-paced resources** that faculty can consult as needed. These platforms shift the paradigm from top-down instruction to **self-directed, inquiry-based faculty development**, allowing faculty to find what they need when they need it - without the cognitive overhead of navigating dense technical documentation or theoretical texts (Brookfield, 2017; Reiss, 2021).

Key Components of a Just-in-Time AI Literacy Hub. A well-designed repository should include short, focused materials - categorized by instructional scenario, topic area, and tool type - ensuring **immediacy, clarity, and relevance**. Suggested content includes:

- **Short How-To Videos on AI Tools**. Demonstrations of platforms such as DALL·E, ChatGPT, Claude, or Adobe Firefly, focusing on educational use cases (e.g., "How to use text-to-image generation for visual storytelling assignments").
- **Reading Primers on Algorithmic Bias**. Concise, accessible summaries of key texts such as *Algorithms of Oppression* (Noble, 2018) or *Atlas of AI* (Crawford, 2021), paired with classroom application ideas.
- **Case Studies on AI in Assessment and Grading**. Real or fictional classroom scenarios exploring issues such as AI-assisted writing, automated scoring systems, or prompt-inflated originality - each accompanied by discussion prompts and ethical analysis frameworks (Slimi & Carballido, 2023).
- **Ethics Simulation Toolkits**. Downloadable role-play activities and reflection templates for facilitating classroom debates on topics such as algorithmic fairness, surveillance, data consent, or generative creativity (Benjamin, 2023; Floridi et al., 2018).

Platform Options and Accessibility Considerations. Effective just-in-time platforms should be lightweight, searchable, and easy to maintain. Common institutional tools include:

- **Canvas Commons**. Useful for embedding modules directly into course shells or cross-listing across departments.
- **Google Sites**. A user-friendly option for creating hyperlinked pages with embedded documents, videos, and reflection forms.
- **Notion**. Offers a modular, interactive design space with tagging, search, and collaborative editing.
- **LMS-Integrated Hubs**. Institutions may build an AI pedagogy portal within Blackboard, Moodle, or D2L, ensuring content is **housed where faculty already work**.

Platforms Should Be:

- **Mobile-friendly** for access on the go.
- **Metadata-tagged** for quick navigation by topic or discipline.
- **Updated regularly** by a teaching center, faculty fellows, or designated AI pedagogy stewards.

Institutional Benefits:

- **Scalability**. A single resource can serve dozens of departments, especially when curated by theme (e.g., AI and writing, AI and data ethics, AI and student well-being).
- **Faculty Empowerment**. Just-in-time platforms support **agency and autonomy**, especially for faculty seeking a low-stakes entry point into AI pedagogy.
- **Equity and Inclusion**. Materials can be adapted for **adjuncts, part-time faculty, and graduate faculty**, ensuring broader access to innovation regardless of rank or tech fluency.

Strategy 2. Faculty Fellowships and Incentivized Innovation: Rewarding Leadership in AI Pedagogy

Sustainable AI integration across the curriculum will not emerge from isolated volunteerism or unfunded mandates. It requires **intentional investment in faculty leadership, time for thoughtful experimentation, and recognition for pedagogical innovation**. Faculty fellowships offer a high-impact model for doing just that - providing **protected time, compensation, peer visibility, and institutional support** for faculty leading the way in AI-integrated teaching.

Rather than relying solely on top-down implementation, a fellowship model empowers faculty to **co-design, test, and model responsible AI pedagogy** in their own disciplines. It acknowledges that developing thoughtful, ethics-centered, and discipline-relevant curriculum takes time - time that must be institutionally supported if AI education is to be inclusive, reflective, and durable (Brookfield, 2017; Byars-Winston & Dahlberg, 2019).

Program Example: AI Pedagogy Fellows

Overview: A university launches a semester-long **AI Pedagogy Fellows Program**, open to faculty from all colleges and disciplines. Each fellow receives a stipend, access to instructional design support, and participation in a cross-departmental learning community.

Fellow Responsibilities:

- **Prototype AI-integrated syllabi or course modules** relevant to their field (e.g., algorithmic bias in sociology, generative writing prompts in English, AI-assisted lab analysis in biology).
- **Pilot and assess modules in their classrooms**, gathering student feedback and iterating based on results.
- **Lead peer learning events**, such as faculty showcases, panel discussions, or workshops, to disseminate insights and promote campus-wide dialogue on AI teaching strategies.

Deliverables Might Include:

- Annotated syllabi and assignment guides.
- Reflection memos on pedagogical challenges and breakthroughs.
- Contributions to an institutional AI pedagogy repository.
- Optional white papers or articles for teaching and learning journals.

Fellowship Benefits and Institutional Rationale:

- **Time and Compensation for Deep Work**. Developing ethical, generative, and discipline-specific AI pedagogy is not plug-and-play. It requires research, design, classroom testing, and critical reflection. Fellowships **legitimize this work as scholarly labor**, supporting it with stipends, course release, or summer funding.
- **Recognition of Faculty as Institutional Change Agents**. Fellows become **public ambassadors for pedagogical innovation**, catalyzing cultural change and modeling interdisciplinary AI engagement. This recognition can support **promotion, tenure, and teaching award portfolios**, reinforcing that AI innovation is both impactful and professionally meaningful.
- **Creation of Shareable, Peer-Tested Resources**. Fellows generate **reusable, field-tested materials** that form the basis of broader faculty development initiatives - extending their impact across programs, departments, and general education pathways.
- **Seeding of Long-Term Learning Communities**. By organizing fellows into **cohorts**, institutions foster interdisciplinary dialogue and trust. These cohorts often evolve into **ongoing communities of practice**, sustaining innovation well beyond the fellowship term.

Scaling and Sustainability Tips:

- **Start Small**. Begin with 4–6 fellows per year, representing a range of disciplines and teaching formats.
- **Provide Optional Tracks**. Allow for different levels of engagement - design-focused fellows, showcase-focused fellows, or research-and-publication fellows.
- **Embed Reflection**. Require structured reflection (written, recorded, or presented) to capture the **process of faculty growth**, not just the final product.
- **Elevate Visibility**. Feature fellows at teaching symposiums, on the university website, and in strategic communications to **signal institutional priority**.

Strategy 3. Peer Mentoring and Learning Communities: Building Trust, Reducing Isolation, and Amplifying AI Pedagogical Innovation

In a time of technological disruption, ethical uncertainty, and fast-evolving student behaviors, faculty benefit not only from institutional training - but from each other. **Peer mentoring and faculty learning communities (FLCs)** provide relational infrastructure where educators can share struggles, test ideas, and co-develop practices in a space of trust, rather than surveillance or performance. Unlike top-down models, these structures are **horizontal and dialogic**, enabling faculty to engage with AI literacy through **mutual inquiry, shared vulnerability, and iterative reflection** (Brookfield, 2017; Byars-Winston & Dahlberg, 2019). Peer-based development models are especially well-suited for AI-related pedagogy, where faculty must navigate:

- **Rapidly changing tools** without clear best practices.
- **Disciplinary differences** in how AI is perceived and applied.
- **Emotional and ethical tensions** around authorship, student trust, and assessment integrity.

By facilitating structured, ongoing, and relationship-centered learning, peer mentoring and FLCs transform AI pedagogy from a source of anxiety into a community of shared meaning-making and adaptive experimentation. Instead of approaching AI as an isolated or intimidating challenge, faculty build confidence by learning together, sharing both successes and missteps in a supportive environment. **This collaborative framework not only normalizes uncertainty but also fosters a culture of trust, reflection, and co-creation**, helping educators adapt AI pedagogy with resilience and collective wisdom.

Strategy 4. "Unlearning" as a Faculty Goal: Rethinking Originality, Authorship, and Academic Labor in the Age of AI

In the rapidly evolving landscape of generative AI, faculty are being asked not only to adopt new tools but rather to **reconsider long-held assumptions about what teaching, learning, and academic integrity truly entail**. This process requires more than upskilling - it calls for **unlearning**: the intentional, reflective dismantling of inherited norms that no longer align with present-day technologies, epistemologies, or student realities. Faculty may find themselves confronting deeply embedded beliefs such as:

- *"Original work is produced in isolation."*
- *"Using automated tools diminishes student effort or thought."*
- *"Authorship is a marker of individual mastery."*

While these assumptions have historically underpinned academic rigor and assessment, they are increasingly out of sync with how knowledge is created and shared in an AI-mediated world. Generative models such as ChatGPT, Claude, and Gemini challenge educators to **redefine creativity, rethink collaboration, and reconsider how originality is evaluated** - not to lower standards, but to align them with evolving realities (Bender et al., 2021; Selwyn, 2019).

Bridge Topic

Building AI Fluency One Click at a Time

In the face of fast-moving technological change, institutions must shift from episodic training to **sustained, responsive support ecosystems**. Just-in-time learning platforms provide faculty with the tools to act, reflect, and adapt on their own timeline - **bridging the gap between pedagogical curiosity and instructional confidence**. As a first-tier intervention, these hubs lay the groundwork for deeper faculty engagement with AI, while promoting **resilience, experimentation, and ethical integration** across the curriculum.

Bridge Topic

Investing in Faculty to Transform the Curriculum

Incentivized innovation models such as AI pedagogy fellowships shift the institutional narrative - from treating AI as an external disruption to embracing it as a catalyst for pedagogical renewal. By formalizing programs that reward experimentation, these **fellowships create space for faculty to test new teaching strategies without fear of penalization for failure**. They also encourage ethical leadership, positioning innovation not just as technological novelty but as a deliberate process of aligning AI with institutional missions and student-centered outcomes.

These programs reward faculty for risk-taking, critical experimentation, and ethical leadership, while helping institutions build a scalable, shareable knowledge base for AI integration. **Faculty participants contribute resources, case studies, and reflective practices that extend far beyond their own classrooms, creating ripple effects across departments and disciplines**. Over time, this growing repository of insights forms a durable infrastructure for AI pedagogy that supports both early adopters and those new to integrating intelligent systems.

By compensating labor, celebrating insight, and cultivating cross-disciplinary collaboration, fellowships position faculty not as late adopters - but as curators, critics, and co-creators of an educational future shaped by intelligent systems. **Faculty gain recognition for their contributions to institutional innovation, while students benefit from richer, more intentional engagements with AI in their coursework**. Ultimately, these strategic initiatives transform AI from a source of anxiety into a shared opportunity, reframing faculty as leaders actively shaping the trajectory of higher education in the age of automation.

Structures That Promote Collaborative Growth

Structure 1. Interdisciplinary Faculty Learning Communities (FLCs)

Faculty from diverse departments (e.g., literature, nursing, computer science, philosophy) meet regularly to:

- Explore common questions (e.g., *"How are our students using AI?"*).
- Read and reflect on shared texts (e.g., Benjamin, 2023; Crawford, 2021).
- Design cross-disciplinary activities or co-taught modules.

Example Format: A monthly 90-minute meeting anchored by a rotating facilitator and a thematic focus such as "AI and Creativity," "Algorithmic Fairness," or "Student Voice in Machine-Mediated Feedback."

Outcome: Breaks down disciplinary silos, builds shared vocabulary, and empowers faculty to see themselves as collaborators in a campus-wide curricular transformation. When educators from different fields engage in dialogue about AI, they begin to recognize common concerns and complementary strengths, creating a language of collaboration that transcends technical or disciplinary boundaries. **This shared foundation not only reduces isolation but also positions faculty as co-architects of institutional change**, capable of designing AI pedagogy that reflects the complexity and diversity of the academic community.

Structure 2. "Teach-and-Try" Workshops with Built-In Experimentation Time

Rather than passive presentations, **these workshops include interactive components designed to spark engagement and critical reflection**. Faculty might participate in live demonstrations of AI tools, small-group discussions that apply case studies to their disciplines, or design sprints where they co-create assignments and assessment strategies. This active format ensures that workshops are not just informational, but transformative - helping participants leave with concrete practices, shared insights, and renewed confidence in navigating AI pedagogy. These workshops include:

- A short introduction to a concept (e.g., "Ethical Prompt Engineering").
- A hands-on design sprint where participants create or revise an activity.
- Structured time to implement the idea in class within two weeks.
- A follow-up session to debrief, revise, and share student feedback.

Outcome: This approach shifts professional development from abstract discussion to hands-on practice, where faculty can test new ideas in manageable, low-stakes contexts. **By normalizing experimentation - even when outcomes are imperfect - it reduces fear of failure and reframes risk-taking as part of the learning process**. In doing so, it reinforces Brookfield's (2017) insight that genuine pedagogical leadership comes not from certainty, but from curiosity, reflection, and the courage to innovate in real time.

Structure 3. Reflective Practice Groups Using Brookfield's Critical Incident Method

Faculty meet in small cohorts to share one "critical incident" from their AI-related teaching - moments that surprised, challenged, or unsettled them. Using Brookfield's (2017) method, the group reflects on:

- *"What happened?"*
- *"Why did it matter?"*
- *"What did it reveal about teaching, technology, or power?"*
- *"How might this shape future practice?"*

Example Themes:

- A student openly admitted to using ChatGPT to revise their thesis - *"What now?"*
- An AI image generation exercise reproduced harmful stereotypes - *"How to respond?"*
- Peer review felt robotic after students relied on GrammarlyGo - *"What was lost?"*

Outcome: Normalizes discomfort, repositions reflection as expertise, and supports emotionally grounded faculty growth in a time of deep pedagogical ambiguity (Reiss, 2021). **Instead of viewing uncertainty as a weakness, this approach frames it as an essential part of learning how to navigate rapid technological change**. By making space for vulnerability, reflection, and dialogue, institutions help faculty transform ambiguity into resilience and cultivate confidence in their ability to adapt with integrity.

Why Peer Learning Matters for AI Pedagogy: Trust, Relevance, and Distributed Information

In a pedagogical landscape transformed by generative AI, faculty are not only adapting to new tools - but they are also confronting new questions about **ethics, authorship, equity, and expertise**. These are not merely technical challenges; they are **relational and reflective** ones. To navigate them well, faculty need more than guidance - they need **community**. Peer learning models offer the structure, support, and trust necessary to ensure that AI integration is not fragmented or fear-driven, but collaborative, intentional, and sustainable.

Peer-based faculty development creates space for educators to share ideas and challenges without the pressure of mastery or formal evaluation. It recognizes that **learning to teach in an AI-enhanced world is best approached collectively, among colleagues who share institutional realities and disciplinary contexts**. This collaborative spirit is realized through structures such as relational trust, contextual relevance, and collective capacity teaching clinics - three peer-learning approaches that normalize experimentation, dialogue, and reflective growth.

Peer Learning 1: Relational Trust

Faculty are more willing to explore new tools, confront their discomfort, and interrogate their assumptions when they do so within nonjudgmental, peer-led environments. **These spaces allow experimentation without fear of being judged** for not knowing enough or for making mistakes. In contrast to top-down workshops, peer learning communities cultivate psychological safety - giving faculty permission to admit uncertainty, share failures, and reflect openly with colleagues.

In the context of AI - where the stakes feel high and the pace feels overwhelming - this trust is essential. Faculty are often grappling with urgent questions about how to respond to AI-authored student work or how to design assessments that resist over-automation. To do this responsibly, they **need spaces where vulnerability is understood as strength**, where honesty is valued over perfection, and where reflection is recognized as a core part of professional growth (Brookfield, 2017).

For example, in one peer-learning circle, faculty from English, computer science, and education agreed to bring one "AI experiment gone wrong" to each session. An English professor shared an instance where ChatGPT flattened student writing into formulaic prose, while a computer scientist admitted struggling to explain hallucinations in large language models to undergraduates. **Together, the group unpacked these failures, reframing them not as shortcomings but as shared case studies that deepened everyone's understanding of AI's pedagogical limits**.

Peer Learning 2: Contextual Relevance

Peer learning thrives on local expertise. Faculty who teach similar students in the same institutional setting share a common understanding of classroom dynamics, curriculum pressures, and cultural norms that shape teaching and learning. **This shared context allows**

them to generate solutions that are both credible and adaptable, offering more practical value than one-size-fits-all professional development frameworks that overlook local realities.

For example, faculty at a commuter campus may work together to design AI-integrated assignments that account for device accessibility, limited campus presence, and asynchronous learning needs. **These faculty-generated solutions reflect an intimate knowledge of their students' lived realities and the barriers they face, which makes the assignments far more relevant and effective**. Similarly, in a fully online program, faculty may collaborate to build AI-driven discussion prompts that foster peer interaction across time zones, while also creating guidelines to ensure equitable participation for students balancing work, family, and study responsibilities.

Peer learning ensures that AI pedagogy is not detached from the environments in which it is practiced. It honors the unique constraints, resources, and opportunities that characterize specific institutions and disciplines. **By building on shared realities, it also fosters a culture of trust and mutual accountability**, where faculty feel empowered to innovate in ways that reflect their professional values and their students' needs (Byars-Winston & Dahlberg, 2019).

Peer Learning 3: Distributed Innovation

When faculty share tools, cases, prompts, and reflections across departments, innovation spreads organically - without the need for centralized control or top-down enforcement. This approach creates a living network of ideas, where lessons from one field are reinterpreted and adapted by others. **Such "networked pedagogy" ensures that AI integration reflects the diversity of institutional knowledge rather than a single prescriptive model**.

A philosophy professor, for instance, might design a reflection prompt about moral agency in machine learning, asking students to debate whether algorithms can ever make ethical choices. A biology professor could then reframe this prompt into a case study on algorithmic bias in clinical decision tools, encouraging students to analyze how machine predictions might overlook patient complexity. **By moving ideas horizontally across disciplines, creativity expands, and scalability becomes possible**, embedding AI literacy throughout the curriculum rather than limiting it to isolated early adopters (Floridi et al., 2018; Reiss, 2021).

Distributed innovation also mitigates burnout by making AI curriculum development a shared responsibility rather than an individual burden. **When resources, case studies, and activities are pooled across faculty, no one is left to carry the full weight of experimentation alone**. This collaborative approach fosters resilience, reduces duplication of effort, and creates a culture where AI literacy is continuously renewed through shared ownership and collective engagement.

Bridge Topic

Community as Infrastructure for Ethical AI Teaching

In an era of technological acceleration and epistemic instability, **peer learning becomes more than just a professional development strategy - it emerges as a form of collective**

resilience and solidarity. It allows faculty to engage in shared reflection and experimentation, creating space to navigate uncertainty with the support of colleagues who face similar challenges. By fostering trust and a sense of shared purpose, **peer learning ensures that educators lead with connection rather than fear or isolation**.

When institutions intentionally invest in peer-based structures - such as faculty learning communities, mentoring circles, and reflective cohorts - they lay the groundwork for a culture where AI pedagogy is not experienced as a disruption to endure, but as a collaborative project to shape. **These structures create continuity across disciplines, enabling diverse perspectives to inform how AI is integrated into teaching and research**. Ultimately, such investments transform the faculty community into co-creators of ethically grounded, socially responsive, and future-oriented approaches to AI in education.

Bridge Topic

Building Faculty Courage Through Community

Faculty development in the AI era must be as much about cultivating relationships as it is about mastering new content. In this context, peer mentoring and structured learning communities provide faculty with the space to navigate uncertainty together, share experiences that may otherwise remain hidden, and engage in collaborative experimentation that foregrounds ethical responsibility. **These structures allow educators to lean on one another as they explore how AI reshapes teaching, ensuring that innovation is scaffolded by trust and mutual support rather than isolated trial-and-error**.

In such communities, faculty are not pressured to present themselves as experts who have mastered every tool. Instead, they are invited to embody and model qualities of curiosity, humility, and transparency - demonstrating to both colleagues and students that learning in the AI era is iterative and collective. **It is within these nonjudgmental, trust-centered environments that the seeds of sustainable, mission-aligned AI pedagogy take root**, providing fertile ground for practices that are not only innovative but deeply connected to institutional values and human-centered education.

Faculty Reflection Activity: "Rethinking Originality"

This structured activity invites faculty to surface and interrogate their own assumptions about originality and authorship - an essential step toward building AI-integrated pedagogies that are ethically grounded and intellectually coherent. **By naming and reflecting on these assumptions, faculty gain clarity about how their disciplinary traditions define authorship and where those definitions may be challenged by machine collaboration**. This process not only strengthens academic integrity in the classroom but also equips educators to guide students in navigating AI's impact on creativity, accountability, and ownership of intellectual work.

Step 1: List Your Assumptions

Prompt: *"What are three assumptions I currently hold about originality in student work?"*

Examples Might Include:

- Originality means the work is entirely from the student's mind.
- Original ideas are more valuable than remixed or derivative ones.
- Authorship should be traceable to a single individual.

Encourage honesty without self-censorship, making clear that the exercise is about exploration rather than evaluation. **The goal is not to judge individual beliefs or practices, but to create space where unspoken assumptions can be named and reflected upon**. In doing so, faculty begin to uncover the invisible pedagogical scripts that guide their choices, opening the door to more intentional, ethically responsive approaches to AI-integrated teaching.

Step 2: Test Assumptions Using ChatGPT

Prompt: *"Choose a topic from your discipline and ask ChatGPT to generate a short essay or analysis. Then ask it to rewrite the same piece with different tones or citation styles."*

Reflection Questions:

- *"How predictable or surprising was the AI's output?"*
- *"Did it reproduce familiar academic tropes? Or generate something novel?"*
- *"How does the generative process compare to how students build ideas?"*
- *"What does this suggest about the **mechanics vs. meaning** of originality?"*

This exercise demonstrates that AI can generate responses that appear fluent and logically consistent, yet these outputs often mask a lack of intentional meaning-making. **Unlike human creators, AI does not exercise judgment, take interpretive risks, or embed knowledge within cultural, historical, or emotional contexts**. By contrasting machine coherence with human creativity, students learn to value the qualities of originality, critical discernment, and epistemic courage that define authentic intellectual and artistic work.

Step 3: Group Dialogue - "What Should Originality Mean Now?"

In small groups or facilitated sessions, invite faculty to explore the following:

- *"Should originality be redefined in terms of **process**, rather than product?"*
- *"Is ethical sourcing, synthesis, or personal voice a better measure of originality than novelty?"*
- *"What do we want students to learn about authorship and meaning-making in a co-creative environment?"*

These dialogues help **shift the faculty mindset from viewing AI primarily as a threat to recognizing it as a catalyst for pedagogical renewal**. Through reflective conversations, educators begin to see originality not as a fixed trait that can be "protected" from automation, but as a dynamic practice that evolves alongside new tools and contexts. In this reframing, originality becomes grounded in transparency, critical reflection, and ethical decision-making - qualities that both affirm academic integrity and expand the possibilities of creative scholarship (Brookfield, 2017; Slimi & Carballido, 2023).

Bridge Topic

Why Unlearning Matters

- **Ethical Consistency**. Many institutional policies on academic integrity still reflect pre-AI paradigms. Unlearning allows faculty to **align assessment practices with emerging norms**, reducing confusion and contradiction for students.
- **Pedagogical Freedom**. By loosening outdated constraints, faculty can **explore new models of creativity, collaboration, and assessment**, without fear of undermining academic rigor.
- **Professional Growth**. Unlearning invites faculty to engage in **metacognition about their teaching identity**, making space for personal and professional transformation in an era of profound change (Reiss, 2021).

Bridge Topic

From Resistance to Reinterpretation

Unlearning is not about abandoning academic values - it is about reimagining them in light of new realities. It asks faculty to revisit deeply held assumptions about originality, authorship, and academic labor, and to consider how these concepts might be reshaped in an AI-mediated environment. By engaging in this process, **educators can construct a more responsive, inclusive, and ethically grounded framework for AI-integrated teaching that aligns with both tradition and transformation**.

When educators embrace unlearning as a scholarly practice - not just a personal challenge - they model intellectual humility and adaptability for their students. This reframing positions faculty as leaders in navigating technological change, rather than as passive responders to disruption. In doing so, they affirm their role as thoughtful stewards of education in a machine-augmented world, committed to preserving human judgment while integrating new tools with care and integrity.

Shifting Roles: From Knowledge Gatekeepers to Learning Architects

The rise of generative AI and algorithmic assistance is not only changing what students produce - it is transforming how faculty are positioned in the educational process. In today's classrooms, information is instantly retrievable and endlessly reproducible, making the role of the educator less about guarding knowledge and more about shaping how it is engaged with. **Faculty must now design environments where students learn to question, critique, and apply AI outputs with ethical awareness, ensuring that learning becomes an active process rather than passive consumption**.

Faculty are no longer simply disseminators of content; they are becoming learning architects - professionals who intentionally craft experiences that guide students through complex interactions with information and technology. This involves **helping learners confront AI's assumptions, negotiate its limitations, and integrate human values into their academic and professional work**. To support this, faculty development must evolve to address not only technical adaptation but also the reimagining of teaching identities in an AI-saturated landscape.

Importantly, this shift does not diminish faculty authority. Instead, it re-centers faculty as the ethical compass and interpretive guide in AI-mediated learning, amplifying their importance in shaping how knowledge is created and validated. **By modeling transparency, critical reflection, and care, educators demonstrate that their role extends far beyond content delivery** - they are the relational and moral anchors of higher education in the AI era (Brookfield, 2017; Reiss, 2021).

Three Identity Shifts for AI-Era Faculty

Identity Shift 1. From "Sage on the Stage" to Guide for Responsible Tool Use

In classrooms where students can generate answers with a few keystrokes, the role of faculty shifts from being a transmitter of knowledge to being a guide in the intellectual process. Their primary responsibility is **to frame inquiry in ways that require critical thinking, context, and originality beyond what a machine can provide**. By modeling discernment and coaching students to use AI ethically, creatively, and reflectively, **faculty transform learning from a passive exercise into an active practice of judgment, accountability, and imagination**.

New Questions Faculty Pose:

- *"What assumptions shaped the AI's output?"*
- *"How do you know whether the answer is accurate - or biased?"*
- *"Where is your voice in this process?"*

Faculty guide students to move beyond simple tool use by shaping assignments that encourage active, thoughtful interaction with AI systems. **Rather than presenting technology as a shortcut, faculty frame it as a partner in inquiry - one that requires critical evaluation, creative adaptation, and ethical reflection**. In doing so, students develop digital citizenship skills alongside deeper habits of critical thinking, learning to treat AI not as an answer machine but as a catalyst for discernment and responsible engagement.

Identity Shift 2. From Content Expert to Curator of Trustworthy Sources

With AI now capable of generating summaries, mimicking voices, and producing content across nearly every discipline, the educator's task has expanded well beyond information delivery. **Faculty must act as curators - selecting and situating sources in ways that**

foreground rigor, context, and credibility - while also teaching students to critically appraise the outputs they encounter. In this role, educators help learners navigate overwhelming information landscapes, guiding them to see not only what content says, but also how and why it was produced, and whose perspectives or priorities are embedded within it.

Faculty Help Students:

- Distinguish between **credible and synthetic sources**.
- Recognize **biases in training data and algorithms**.
- Evaluate the **epistemic authority of different forms of knowledge** (Benjamin, 2023; Floridi et al., 2018).

This curatorial work is especially critical in an era where generative AI tools often obscure their sources, blur attribution, and reduce complex ideas into simplified summaries. **By carefully selecting, contextualizing, and interpreting materials, faculty provide the nuance and layered meaning that machines cannot replicate**. In doing so, educators model for students how to engage critically with knowledge systems - revealing the assumptions, gaps, and interpretive richness that sustain deep learning and ethical inquiry.

Identity Shift 3. From Grader of Answers to Mentor of Inquiry

AI has the potential to generate plausible answers, but it cannot mentor a student through confusion, curiosity, or moral ambiguity. This limitation highlights that the role of educators is not simply to verify correctness, but to accompany students in the deeper intellectual and ethical struggles that define genuine learning. In this way, faculty are repositioned as mentors of process rather than mere evaluators of product - guiding reflection, modeling discernment, and fostering resilience in moments where uncertainty becomes the gateway to growth.

This Mentoring Includes:

- Coaching students through **critical reflection and ethical tension**.
- Providing feedback that deepens thinking rather than corrects output.
- Helping students construct **intellectual identity in the midst of automation** (Brookfield, 2017; Reamer, 2023).

By shifting from answer-verification to question-generation, faculty reclaim the heart of education as dialogic, transformative, and human-centered. **This reframing emphasizes that the value of teaching is not in supplying facts that machines can reproduce, but in cultivating curiosity, critical dialogue, and the courage to wrestle with uncertainty**. In practice, this means positioning inquiry as the central act of learning - where students are challenged not only to respond, but to imagine, critique, and co-create knowledge alongside their peers and mentors.

Bridge Topic

Implications for Faculty Development

To Support These Role Transformations, Professional Learning Must:

- Emphasize **facilitation skills** and **critical tool analysis** over tool tutorials alone.
- Provide **reflection spaces** for educators to grapple with their changing identity.
- Equip faculty to design AI-integrated assignments that prioritize **transparency, creativity, and conceptual depth**.

Workshops, Fellowships, and Learning Communities Should Explicitly Address:

- *"What does it mean to teach when machines can write?"*
- *"How do I remain the ethical center of my course?"*
- *"What parts of my discipline are human - and must remain so?"*

These are not technical questions - they are **existential** ones, and faculty development must rise to meet them. **They challenge educators to reconsider what it means to teach, mentor, and uphold integrity in a world where intelligent systems are embedded into everyday practice**. Meeting these questions requires more than training in tools; it demands a shift in values, frameworks, and professional identity, so that faculty can guide students through uncertainty with confidence and care.

Bridge Topic

Reclaiming the Educator's Role in AI-Augmented Learning

In a world where generative AI can imitate expertise but not embody it, **faculty remain essential - not as dispensers of knowledge, but as designers of learning experiences, mentors of ethical engagement, and guardians of interpretive depth**. Their value lies in guiding students through the uncertainty of machine-generated content, helping them ask better questions and recognize the boundaries of automated fluency. Faculty bring lived experience, relational insight, and disciplinary nuance - elements no algorithm can reproduce.

This shift is not about loss - it is about reinvention. **It reframes the educator's role as one of transformation, where teaching becomes less about controlling access to information and more about cultivating wisdom, discernment, and ethical reasoning**. In doing so, faculty can reassert their relevance by designing learning environments where human creativity and moral agency are amplified rather than diminished by technology.

As institutions support this transition, they affirm that the future of teaching is not less human because of AI - it is more human, precisely because it must be. **The need for empathy, mentorship, and interpretive care grows stronger when students are navigating powerful, opaque systems**. By positioning faculty as anchors of integrity and relational depth, institutions make clear that education in the AI era is not a retreat from humanity, but its intentional reaffirmation.

Bridge Topic

Institutional Vision: Embedding AI Literacy into Faculty Life

To Institutionalize This Shift:

- Update teaching evaluation frameworks to reward **AI pedagogy innovation.**
- Create **AI education centers or strategic working groups.**
- Embed AI development into **new faculty onboarding, annual reviews, and strategic plans.**

Example:

- *A university includes AI fluency as a core competency in its faculty development roadmap, parallel to inclusive teaching and digital scholarship.*

Section Reflection: Reimagining Faculty Development as Ethical Adaptation and Collective Agency

This opening section reframes faculty development not as a static training regimen, but as a dynamic, reflective, and relational process - one urgently needed in an era defined by rapid AI acceleration. It challenges outdated assumptions that faculty need only occasional tool training or that pedagogical mastery is a fixed destination. Instead, the section positions AI not as a technical add-on, but as a paradigm shift that demands new epistemologies, evolving roles, and interdisciplinary collaboration. Faculty are invited to move from uncertainty and isolation into a culture of shared experimentation, guided inquiry, and critical solidarity.

By proposing a four-part framework - agile, continuous, collaborative, and reflective - the section outlines a faculty development model that is responsive to technological disruption while remaining deeply human-centered. Educators are not asked to become technologists; they are encouraged to become learning architects, curators of ethical inquiry, and mentors of critical engagement. This vision recognizes the emotional toll of pedagogical dislocation and counters it with structures of trust, adaptability, and community. Ultimately, the section calls on institutions to shift from transactional training to transformational support, ensuring that faculty are not left to navigate AI alone but rather are empowered to lead its integration with integrity, courage, and care.

Section 2: Core AI Competencies Every Faculty Member Should Build

---

As generative AI tools reshape how information is generated, evaluated, and communicated, all faculty - regardless of discipline - must develop a foundational **set of AI competencies** to engage ethically, critically, and practically. This does not mean turning every professor into a programmer or data scientist. It does mean cultivating **literacy, fluency, and**

confidence to guide students, model responsible practice, and participate in institutional decision-making.

The goal of this section is to **define essential AI competencies**, clarify levels of faculty engagement (**literacy - fluency - mastery**), and illustrate how these competencies map onto the core responsibilities of educators. By distinguishing these tiers of engagement, the framework helps institutions and faculty set realistic expectations while charting pathways for deeper growth and specialization. Ultimately, the section emphasizes that **AI skill-building is not an abstract exercise, but a practical foundation that strengthens teaching innovation, research excellence, mentorship practices, and institutional leadership in the AI era**.

AI Competency Levels: Literacy, Fluency, Mastery

Levels of Faculty Engagement with AI: A Developmental Framework for Literacy, Fluency, and Mastery

As institutions seek to build AI literacy across the curriculum, it is essential to recognize that faculty engagement with AI will occur along a **developmental continuum**, not a single threshold of "readiness." Faculty arrive with varying levels of experience, confidence, disciplinary alignment, and curiosity. To support inclusive, sustainable growth, colleges and universities must offer **tiered models of engagement** that honor different starting points, encourage reflective progression, and provide opportunities for leadership.

This three-tiered framework - **Literacy, Fluency, Mastery** - offers a flexible structure for designing faculty development programs, self-assessment tools, and recognition pathways. Importantly, it **does not presume that all faculty will become AI specialists**. Instead, it affirms that **ethical, context-sensitive engagement with AI is possible at every level**, and that faculty can make meaningful contributions to AI pedagogy regardless of technical background.

Literacy Level (Across Disciplines)

Goal: Build foundational understanding of AI terms, concepts, and social implications.

Description: Faculty at the literacy stage are beginning to explore what AI is, how it functions, and what its implications are for teaching, learning, and disciplinary practice. This level emphasizes **comprehension, curiosity, and ethical awareness**, not tool use.

Example Activities:

- Explain the function of large language models (LLMs) such as GPT-5 or Claude, including their reliance on training data and probabilistic generation.
- Identify common AI use cases in higher education (e.g., feedback summarization, lesson planning, image generation).
- Reflect on how generative AI might affect originality, assessment, or critical thinking in their field.

- Read and discuss foundational texts on algorithmic bias, surveillance, and data ethics (e.g., Benjamin, 2023; Noble, 2018).

Outcome: Faculty begin to build shared vocabulary, ask better questions, and position AI as a topic worthy of disciplinary and pedagogical inquiry (Selwyn, 2019). This shared language enables cross-departmental collaboration, allowing educators from different fields to discuss AI in ways that feel accessible and professionally relevant. Over time, these **conversations shift AI from being seen as a technical add-on to being recognized as a core subject of scholarly debate, teaching innovation, and ethical reflection**.

Fluency Level (Across Disciplines)

Goal: Responsibly integrate AI tools into teaching while evaluating outputs critically.

Description: Faculty at the fluency level can apply AI in instructional contexts while maintaining **critical distance and ethical reflection**. They can interpret AI-generated outputs, assess their limitations, and guide students in **transparent, equitable use**.

Example Activities:

- Use AI tools such as ChatGPT to draft rubrics, scaffold assignments, or create formative feedback templates.
- Identify and analyze bias in AI-generated summaries or representations (e.g., stereotypical images, Eurocentric examples).
- Teach students how to cite or document AI use in academic work.
- Facilitate classroom discussions on authorship, automation, and the cognitive risks and benefits of AI assistance.

Outcome: Faculty shift from avoidance or novelty use toward **pedagogically meaningful integration, with an emphasis on student agency, transparency, and critical thinking** (Brookfield, 2017; Reiss, 2021). Instead of treating AI tools as gimmicks or threats, they begin embedding them into assignments and discussions in ways that empower students to reflect on their choices and articulate their reasoning. This shift not only strengthens academic integrity but also positions AI as a resource for cultivating deeper inquiry, ethical judgment, and independent thought.

Mastery Level (Across Disciplines)

Goal: Lead institutional and disciplinary conversations about ethical, inclusive AI use.

Description: Faculty at the mastery level not only integrate AI into their own teaching - but they also **co-create structures, policies, and cultures** that support ethical AI adoption. Faculty mentor colleagues, contribute to AI governance, and develop a curriculum that anticipates future challenges.

Example Activities:

- Co-author institutional policies on generative AI, including academic integrity guidelines, documentation norms, and student equity considerations.
- Lead interdisciplinary workshops on AI-enhanced pedagogy, critical tool use, or reflective assessment design.
- Create assignments or modules that embed AI ethics, positionality, and epistemic critique across disciplines.
- Serve on university task forces or faculty learning communities focused on curricular innovation, student readiness, or workforce preparation in the AI era.

Outcome: Faculty become thought leaders and pedagogical architects, shaping how their institutions and disciplines respond to the epistemological and civic stakes of AI in education (Byars-Winston & Dahlberg, 2019; Floridi et al., 2018). In this role, they move beyond classroom-level adaptation to influence policies, frameworks, and public conversations about what constitutes knowledge, fairness, and accountability in an AI-mediated world. **By modeling reflective leadership, faculty demonstrate that AI literacy is not simply a technical matter but a civic and ethical responsibility that shapes the future of both education and society**.

Summary of AI Competency Levels (Across Disciplines): A Scaffolded Pathway to Thoughtful AI Engagement

This literacy - fluency - mastery framework allows institutions to move away from binary metrics of readiness ("tech-savvy" vs. "not ready") and toward a more inclusive, developmental approach. By **framing AI engagement as a spectrum of growth, rather than a fixed skill set, institutions can meet faculty where they are - whether they are experimenting with their first AI prompt or designing policy for campus-wide adoption**. It also reframes AI pedagogy as a matter of curiosity, reflection, and ethical responsibility, rather than simply technical proficiency or coding expertise.

By designing professional development opportunities that support faculty at every level - and by affirming that growth is ongoing - institutions can foster a culture of shared learning and continuous improvement. Such an approach encourages faculty to see AI not as a disruptive threat but as a catalyst for collective inquiry and pedagogical renewal. **Over time, this creates an environment where empowered, ethically grounded, and collaborative AI teaching becomes embedded across the curriculum, sustaining innovation and integrity in equal measure**.

Introduction to Core AI Competencies

The following pages of this section outline the **five core AI competencies** that every faculty member should develop to guide teaching and learning in the AI era. Because this material is both broad and detailed, the information provided here is deliberately structured to help readers navigate without losing sight of the larger picture. Each competency is introduced in the same way:

- **Core Competency Overview** – A narrative introduction explaining why the competency matters across disciplines and how it connects to faculty roles in teaching, mentoring, and scholarship.
- **Sub-Concepts or Component Competencies** – Breakdowns of specific knowledge, skills, or ethical considerations that define the competency. These may appear as "concepts" (e.g., ***What a Large Language Model Is***) or "competencies" (e.g., ***Detecting Inaccuracies or Unverifiable Claims***).
- **Applications in Practice** – Examples of how the competency translates into real classroom or faculty workflows. These applications highlight teaching activities, policy examples, or instructional practices that make the abstract tangible.
- **Pedagogical or Professional Outcomes** – A synthesis of why the competency is essential, what habits of mind fosters in students, and how it enhances faculty leadership in the AI age.

To support consistency and readability, each competency follows this pattern of **concept - application - outcome**. For some areas - such as faculty workflows or student guidance - the applications are grouped into sets (e.g., ***Responsible Applications of AI in Faculty Workflows* or *Core Instructional Practices for Ethical AI Mentorship***). These are not separate competencies but applied extensions of the larger competency. This layered design ensures that readers can:

- **Zoom in** on specific sub-skills (like prompt engineering or hallucination detection).
- **See how they fit** into the broader competency framework.
- **Connect theory with practice** through concrete examples and policy models.

Finally, each competency concludes with a short rationale - "**Why This Competency Matters**" - to tie the details back to the overarching goal: building reflective, ethical, and discipline-grounded AI capacity across higher education.

Core AI Competency 1: Understanding How Generative AI Works

As generative artificial intelligence becomes increasingly embedded in academic life - from writing tools such as ChatGPT to image generation platforms such as Midjourney - faculty across all disciplines must possess a **foundational understanding of how these tools operate**, what their capabilities and limitations are, and how they influence both cognitive processes and student work products. This knowledge is essential not only for integrating AI tools effectively but also for **teaching students to engage with them critically, ethically, and transparently**.

Faculty do not need to become machine learning experts or data scientists. However, they should be able to **explain in plain language** what generative AI is doing beneath the surface. This allows them to demystify the technology, surface its risks, and frame it as **a rhetorical, epistemological, and civic object**, not just a tool.

AI Competency Concept 1: What a Large Language Model (LLM) Is

LLMs such as GPT-5, Claude, or Gemini are trained on vast datasets of human language - books, articles, websites, and other digital text. They do not "understand" meaning in the human sense. Instead, they **generate text by predicting the next most likely word**, based on patterns observed in their training data.

This predictive process enables LLMs to produce fluent, coherent responses - but also means they can replicate bias, amplify misinformation, or generate plausible-sounding but factually incorrect content, known as "hallucinations" (Bender et al., 2021). Because the model relies on patterns in training data rather than genuine comprehension, it may reinforce stereotypes, normalize inaccuracies, or overlook nuance in complex contexts. For this reason, faculty and students must approach AI outputs with a stance of critical evaluation, recognizing that fluency is not synonymous with truth or reliability.

AI Competency Concept 2: How LLMs Are Trained

Faculty should be able to describe the general structure of how LLMs are developed:

- **Training Data**. Massive corpora scraped from the internet and licensed repositories.
- **Learning Mechanism**. Predictive modeling using neural networks to assign probabilities to sequences of words (tokens).
- **Fine-Tuning**. Post-training adjustments using human feedback or curated datasets to make outputs more aligned with user expectations.

Understanding this process highlights why these models are **influenced by the biases, omissions, and ideologies present in their training data** (Benjamin, 2023; Noble, 2018). Because AI systems learn by absorbing massive amounts of text and media from existing digital archives, they inevitably reproduce the worldviews and priorities embedded in those sources. This means **students and faculty must be trained to interrogate AI outputs critically, asking not only what the model says, but whose perspectives are amplified, whose are silenced, and what institutional logics are being reinforced**.

AI Competency Concept 3: Why Hallucinations Occur

Hallucinations arise because LLMs are not retrieving facts - they are **generating language that sounds statistically appropriate**. They lack access to verified knowledge bases (unless integrated into retrieval-augmented systems) and have no mechanism for validating claims unless explicitly directed to do so.

Faculty should prepare students to:

- Spot red flags in AI-generated content (e.g., incorrect citations, vague generalizations).
- Cross-check claims using credible, discipline-specific sources.
- Recognize that coherence does not equal credibility.

Additional reflection activities can **ask students to track where hallucinations emerge most often, noticing patterns across subject areas or assignment types**. This metacognitive awareness shifts the focus from blaming the tool to understanding the design limits of predictive language modeling. Ultimately, students who develop this discernment learn to **treat AI not as a truth engine, but as a conversational partner requiring oversight, verification, and critical judgment**.

AI Competency Concept 4: Prompt Engineering Basics

Effective use of generative AI requires an understanding of **how prompts shape responses**. Faculty should be familiar with:

- How specificity improves output quality.
- The importance of including context and constraints in a prompt.
- Techniques such as role-playing ("Act as a historian...") or chain-of-thought prompting to structure reasoning.

These basics are crucial for both guiding students in tool use and designing assignments that foster transparency and cognitive accountability (Reiss, 2021). **When faculty make explicit the difference between fluency and factuality, they empower students to see AI outputs as provisional drafts rather than final answers**. This clarity helps learners internalize habits of verification, situating **AI as a prompt for further inquiry rather than a replacement for disciplinary research**. Ultimately, grounding coursework in these principles ensures that students leave not only with technical competence but instead with judgment to navigate AI systems responsibly and critically in academic and professional contexts.

Teaching Example: Integrating AI Literacy in a Writing-Intensive Course

An instructor in a first-year writing seminar begins the semester with a workshop titled **"What ChatGPT Can and Cannot Do."** Students are shown how the tool generates responses by modeling statistical patterns in language. The instructor prompts ChatGPT with a generic essay question (e.g., *"What caused the fall of the Roman Empire?"*), then walks students through the response:

- *"Where is the information vague or unsubstantiated?"*
- *"What assumptions are embedded?"*
- *"Are sources cited - and if so, are they real?"*

The class then discusses **how AI-generated responses differ from scholarly writing** in terms of evidence, citation, critical stance, and authorial voice. Students are taught to treat AI output as a **starting point for critical engagement**, not a substitute for intellectual work.

Outcome: Students gain a clearer understanding of AI's mechanics and epistemic limitations, setting the foundation for more responsible use of the tool in drafting, brainstorming, or revising. **By seeing how outputs are shaped by training data and probabilistic prediction rather than verified knowledge, they learn to treat AI responses as provisional starting points** instead of authoritative sources. This awareness fosters habits of critique and verification, enabling students to integrate AI in ways that support - not undermine - their own reasoning and originality.

Why Core AI Competency 1 Matters Across Disciplines

Regardless of the field, faculty need this foundational understanding to:

- Design assignments that **anticipate and integrate AI use** rather than ignoring or policing it.
- Teach students to evaluate AI output in context, whether it is generating a business memo, visualizing a biology concept, or simulating a historical scenario.
- Promote **digital literacy and epistemological awareness**, preparing students for professional, civic, and scholarly environments shaped by algorithmic language production.

This competency is not just a matter of tool fluency - it is a prerequisite for ethical teaching, transparent expectations, and interdisciplinary AI literacy. **Without it, faculty risk sending mixed signals to students about what constitutes acceptable use, undermining trust and integrity in the classroom**. By treating AI competency as a shared foundation, institutions can foster coherence across disciplines, ensuring that students encounter consistent guidance while still engaging with diverse perspectives and applications.

Core AI Competency 2: Evaluating AI Outputs for Accuracy, Bias, and Appropriateness

---

One of the most critical competencies for faculty in the AI era is **the ability to critically evaluate the outputs of generative models, not only for surface-level coherence, but also for deeper issues of accuracy, bias, and epistemological appropriateness**. This requires recognizing that a fluent sentence or a polished paragraph may still misrepresent evidence, perpetuate stereotypes, or flatten nuance. As AI tools become more integrated into classroom assignments, student workflows, and institutional systems such as advising bots or grading platforms, **educators must be able to distinguish linguistic fluency from truth and synthetic confidence from scholarly rigor**.

This evaluation skill is not simply technical - it is disciplinary, ethical, and pedagogical in nature. The ability to critique AI-generated content determines whether faculty can responsibly model use for students, provide meaningful mentorship in how to engage critically with tools, and uphold the integrity of academic inquiry. It also **equips educators to make informed decisions about when AI enhances learning, when it should be constrained, and when human judgment must remain central**, thus reinforcing the values of care, rigor, and accountability in the AI-augmented classroom (Benjamin, 2023; Noble, 2018).

Evaluation Competency 1: Recognize Common Biases in AI Outputs

Generative models often reflect the **structural biases embedded in their training data**, reproducing assumptions about race, gender, nationality, ability, or ideology. Faculty should be equipped to:

- Identify when AI-generated text centers dominant perspectives or erases marginalized ones.
- Flag overuse of Western-centric examples or stereotypical characterizations.
- Interrogate visual outputs (e.g., DALL·E, Midjourney) for distortions related to identity, representation, or inclusivity.

These biases are not peripheral - they shape what students see as valid knowledge and whose experiences are considered credible (Benjamin, 2023; Crawford & Paglen, 2021). **When AI systems repeatedly elevate certain perspectives while omitting others, they normalize narrow epistemologies and obscure the diversity of human experience**. For students, learning to identify and question these embedded biases becomes essential to developing both disciplinary rigor and ethical responsibility in an AI-mediated world.

Evaluation Competency 2: Detect Inaccuracies or Unverifiable Claims

AI-generated text often includes **hallucinations** - fabricated facts, incorrect citations, or misrepresentations of disciplinary consensus. Faculty must learn to:

- Use domain knowledge to check factual accuracy.
- Guide students in verifying claims through trusted sources.
- Teach students to treat AI content as **generative, not authoritative**.

This also includes **recognizing when AI oversimplifies complex concepts or misuses technical vocabulary**. For example, a model might reduce nuanced theories in psychology to simplistic definitions, or apply biological terms in ways that distort their scientific meaning. By training students to identify these missteps, educators help them see that linguistic fluency is not equivalent to conceptual accuracy - and that careful verification is always required.

Evaluation Competency 3: Explain Why Generative Models Omit or Overgeneralize

Faculty should understand and communicate that:

- LLMs generate probabilistic text based on **training data**, not logical inference or evidence evaluation.
- These models often flatten nuance, omit counterexamples, and present **broad generalizations** that obscure discipline-specific debates.
- Their tone can mirror academic style, but **lack disciplinary depth or voice**.

This practice reinforces **the principle that AI should serve as a tool for inquiry rather than a final authority**. By learning to identify where outputs fall short, students develop the confidence to weigh AI suggestions against their own disciplinary knowledge. In turn, they gain the habit of treating AI as one perspective among many, encouraging active interpretation and critical engagement instead of passive acceptance.

Evaluation Competency 4: Compare AI Outputs to Academic Standards

Faculty should help students evaluate AI content through established academic criteria:

- **Logic**. *"Does the argument follow a clear, reasoned structure?"*
- **Evidence**. *"Are claims supported with credible sources or just asserted?"*
- **Voice**. *"Is there a discernible critical stance or positionality?"*
- **Purpose**. *"Does the text serve a scholarly aim, or simply imitate one?"*

By framing AI as a rhetorical actor, faculty help students recognize that machine-generated responses always carry assumptions, framing choices, and implied authority. This positioning makes clear that AI outputs are not neutral facts, but arguments shaped by training data, algorithms, and design priorities. In this way, students learn to weigh AI's contributions alongside, rather than above, human insight - developing the judgment to integrate, challenge, or reject them with intentionality (Reiss, 2021).

Pedagogical Application Example: Education or Social Science

Assignment: Students are given two literature reviews: one generated by ChatGPT and one excerpted from a peer-reviewed journal article. Working in pairs, they use an evaluation framework to compare:

- **What the AI version misses** (e.g., recent studies, methodological details, theoretical framing).
- **How linguistic bias or abstraction appears** (e.g., passive constructions, erasure of cultural context).
- Whether the AI synthesis **supports or dilutes** the ability to formulate a critical perspective.

Debrief Questions:

- *"What surprised you about the AI output?"*
- *"Did the model make assumptions about the field or the population studied?"*
- *"How would you revise the AI output to meet scholarly standards?"*

This exercise **builds metacognition by prompting students to think about how they think, rather than simply accepting outputs at face value**. It also strengthens media literacy, giving them the tools to analyze how AI systems frame, filter, and present information. Most importantly, it develops epistemic discernment, helping students distinguish between surface-level fluency and deeper reliability - an essential capacity for navigating both the promise and the limitations of machine-generated synthesis (Bender et al., 2021; Noble, 2018.

Why Evaluating AI Outputs for Accuracy, Bias, and Appropriateness Is Foundational

Evaluating AI-generated outputs is not simply a defensive posture against plagiarism or misuse. **It represents a cognitive skill set that lies at the very heart of critical inquiry, academic integrity, and ethical learning**. When students see faculty modeling this evaluation - naming hallucinations, interrogating bias, and questioning voice - they recognize that AI should not be treated as an infallible oracle but as a provisional tool to be challenged, adapted, and sometimes rejected in favor of human judgment.

As generative AI tools become more accessible and deeply embedded in educational workflows, **the challenge for faculty is not only to keep pace with new technologies but to equip students with the discernment to interrogate what these systems produce**. This involves teaching students to move beyond surface evaluation of whether the output "sounds right" and toward structured critique grounded in disciplinary standards and ethical reasoning. In doing so, educators reinforce that the purpose of evaluation is not to discredit AI entirely, but to ensure that its outputs are weighed carefully against context, evidence, and values.

Faculty who master this competency create classrooms where AI serves learning - not the other way around. By integrating critical evaluation into assignments, feedback, and class discussions, they ensure that students are active interpreters of AI-generated material rather than passive consumers. Ultimately, this positions faculty as stewards of thoughtful, ethically grounded engagement with technology, modeling for students how to navigate machine-produced knowledge with confidence, skepticism, and responsibility.

Core AI Competency 3: Ethical Use of AI in Academic and Creative Work

---

In a generative AI environment where students can access powerful tools capable of drafting essays, generating code, synthesizing summaries, or mimicking artistic styles, faculty must move beyond simple prohibition or vague warnings. Instead, they must be equipped to **explicitly define, teach, and model what constitutes ethical AI use** in their courses and disciplines. This requires both conceptual clarity and practical implementation strategies, grounded in academic integrity, disciplinary norms, and evolving professional standards.

The goal is not just to detect misconduct but to **foster transparent, reflective, and responsible engagement** with AI. When students are invited into conversations about fairness, authorship, and tool boundaries, they are more likely to internalize expectations and **develop their own ethical reasoning** - rather than relying on fear of punishment or institutional ambiguity (Brookfield, 2017; Reiss, 2021).

Ethical Use Competency 1: Define Appropriate vs. Inappropriate AI Use for Assignments

Faculty must articulate clear boundaries tailored to the assignment, learning objective, and disciplinary values. For example:

- In a computer science course, AI may be used to brainstorm pseudocode or troubleshoot errors, but not to submit auto-generated solutions.
- In a writing course, AI may assist with outlining or language refinement, but not with thesis development or argumentation.

Implementation Tip:

- Use assignment-specific language, not blanket statements. For example:

- ○ *"You may use ChatGPT to generate brainstorming ideas or vocabulary alternatives. All AI use must be disclosed and reflected upon in your process memo."*

Clear guidelines demystify AI's role and reduce confusion about what counts as authorship, collaboration, or misconduct. When expectations are spelled out, students understand the boundaries of acceptable use and can engage with AI tools transparently rather than secretly. This clarity not only s**upports academic integrity but also builds trust in the classroom** by reinforcing fairness, consistency, and shared responsibility between faculty and students.

Ethical Use Competency 2: Understand and Teach AI Citation and Disclosure Standards

As style guides evolve, faculty must stay informed about how to properly cite AI use across MLA, APA, Chicago, and other formats. Beyond technical citation, students should be taught how to **disclose AI involvement in a way that reflects transparency, process ownership, and academic honesty**.

Instructional Practices:

- Include examples of annotated citations for AI-generated content.
- Require reflection statements describing how AI was used, what was kept or revised, and why.
- Model responsible citation in instructor-created materials or slide decks.

Reference Standard:

The **Modern Language Association** recommends disclosing AI tool use in the works cited section (e.g., *"OpenAI. ChatGPT, 4.0 model, Mar. 2023 version."*). In addition to citation, they advise providing clarification in the body of the text or in footnotes whenever the AI's role in shaping an argument, summary, or draft is significant. This two-part approach ensures both formal acknowledgment and contextual transparency, helping readers understand how AI was used while preserving scholarly accountability and integrity.

Ethical Use Competency 3: Discuss Intellectual Ownership and Authorship in Collaborative Work

Generative AI raises complex questions about:

- *"What counts as original work?"*
- *"Can AI be considered a 'co-author'?"*
- *"Who is accountable for truth, clarity, and voice?"*

Faculty must guide students in understanding that **authorship implies intentionality, responsibility, and epistemic contribution** - none of which AI possesses. At the same time, co-creative practices in design, art, or media fields may warrant more nuanced models of attribution.

Pedagogical Opportunity: Facilitate discussions about AI authorship using case studies from publishing, journalism, or creative writing. Questions to explore include:

- *"Should AI be credited in academic or public-facing work?"*
- *"How does AI-assisted authorship differ from collaborative human authorship?"*
- *"What are the implications for copyright and moral ownership?"*

Ultimately, **conversations about AI and authorship open a space for students to grapple with the boundaries of creativity, accountability, and intellectual ownership in a digital age**. By moving beyond a binary of "allowed" versus "forbidden," faculty can help students explore the layered responsibilities that come with integrating AI into scholarly and creative work. These **dialogues ensure that students leave not only with technical skills, but with the ethical and epistemic grounding necessary to navigate authorship in an AI-saturated world**.

Ethical Use Competency 4: Navigate Student Questions Around Ghostwriting, Fairness, and Consent

Students may feel conflicted about AI use - especially if peers are using it differently, institutional policies are vague, or faculty are inconsistent. Faculty should be prepared to address questions such as:

- *"If I used Grammarly to revise, can I also use ChatGPT to reword?"*
- *"Is it cheating if I rewrite the AI's draft?"*
- *"Why is it okay for faculty to use AI to write recommendation letters, but not for students to use it on take-home exams?"*

These moments are not disciplinary flashpoints; they are ethical teaching opportunities that invite faculty to pause and model integrity in practice. Instead of framing AI-related dilemmas as rule violations, educators can use them to emphasize the shared values of clarity, fairness, and responsibility in academic work. By centering equity and informed consent, faculty turn potential conflicts into teachable moments that strengthen trust and reinforce the ethical foundations of learning communities.

Policy Example: Syllabus Language in a STEM Course

A faculty member teaching an introductory data science course includes the following syllabus statement:

- *"Generative AI tools (e.g., ChatGPT, GitHub Copilot) may be used for brainstorming code structure or troubleshooting error messages. However, all final submitted code must be written, annotated, and debugged by the student. For each major assignment, you are required to submit a one-paragraph AI-use reflection describing which tools were used, how they informed your thinking, and what changes you made."*

Rationale: This policy reinforces that AI is a learning aid, not a replacement for reasoning, by making clear that tools are meant to support - not supplant - student

thinking. It underscores that critical judgment, creativity, and intellectual effort remain the core criteria for assessment, even when AI is part of the process. In doing so, it protects student agency and ensures that academic evaluation remains centered on human insight and growth rather than automated fluency.

Why Ethical Use of AI in Academic and Creative Work as a Pedagogical Practice is Important

Ethical use of AI in academic and creative work is not merely a matter of compliance - **it is a teachable, assessable, and discipline-specific skill**. Faculty need to move beyond rigid, binary rules that treat AI only as a potential threat and instead establish transparent guidelines that clarify boundaries and expectations. **By embedding reflective assignments and fostering trust-building dialogue, educators can help students cultivate discernment and ethical judgment, skills that are essential for navigating AI responsibly across different contexts**.

When educators model clarity in their own use of AI, explain the rationale behind their expectations, and explicitly align policies with learning outcomes, they shift the focus from punishment to empowerment. This approach not only reduces ambiguity and misconduct but also builds a classroom culture where students see themselves as accountable participants in the ethical use of technology. Ultimately, such practices prepare students to become critical, reflective users of generative AI - capable of applying these skills in academic work, professional practice, and civic life where ethical decision-making is paramount.

Core AI Competency 4: Using AI to Enhance (Not Replace) Faculty Work

---

As generative AI tools such as ChatGPT, Claude, and Copilot become more sophisticated and widely available, faculty are increasingly exploring how to use these systems to support - rather than supplant - their professional responsibilities. When used thoughtfully, AI can help educators **save time, personalize learning, and expand accessibility**, particularly in high-volume, repetitive, or adaptive tasks. However, the integration of AI into faculty workflows must be guided by **critical discernment, ethical oversight, and professional judgment**.

The goal is not to automate away the relational, intellectual, and ethical core of teaching - but to ensure that those human dimensions remain at the center of education. By allowing AI to streamline repetitive or administrative tasks, faculty can redirect their energy toward mentoring students, facilitating meaningful dialogue, and guiding complex interpretive work. In this way, **technology becomes an assistant rather than a replacement**, freeing up cognitive bandwidth so that educators can invest more deeply in the forms of critical, empathetic, and context-rich pedagogy that machines cannot replicate (Crawford, 2021; Slimi & Carballido, 2023).

Application of AI in Faculty Workflows 1: Generating Quiz or Rubric Drafts

Faculty can use AI to generate **initial drafts of multiple-choice quizzes, discussion questions, or rubric criteria**, which can then be reviewed, revised, and tailored to course goals and disciplinary standards.

Example Practice:

- *A history professor asks ChatGPT to generate five quiz questions based on a given reading.*
- *After reviewing the output, the Faculty rephrases the questions for clarity, corrects a factual error, and adjusts the difficulty to align with Bloom's Taxonomy.*

Caution: Faculty must always **vet AI-generated content for accuracy, appropriateness, and cognitive rigor, since the technology often produces outputs that appear convincing but may oversimplify or distort complex concepts**. This vetting process includes checking factual claims against reliable sources, ensuring the framing aligns with disciplinary standards, and identifying when biased or reductive assumptions have shaped the response. By modeling this critical scrutiny, educators teach students that **effective AI use requires active interpretation and intellectual responsibility, not passive acceptance of machine-generated results**.

Application of AI in Faculty Workflows 2: Brainstorming Assignment Variations

Faculty can prompt AI to suggest **alternative formats for assignments** - such as switching from an essay to an infographic, simulation, or podcast - while still targeting the same learning outcomes. This can support **differentiated instruction and student choice**.

Example Practice:

- *A writing instructor exploring multimodal composition asks an AI tool for ways to scaffold an argument essay into a video script or visual story.*
- *The AI generates a rough outline, which the instructor then adapts into a flexible assignment guide with reflection checkpoints.*

Rationale: In this way, **vetting becomes a pedagogical act rather than just a safeguard, signaling to students that discernment is as important as content mastery**. It also underscores that intellectual rigor requires curiosity and skepticism, even in the face of seemingly authoritative responses. Ultimately, faculty who consistently demonstrate this practice help cultivate a culture of inquiry where AI is viewed as a starting point for deeper thinking, not a final authority

---

Application of AI in Faculty Workflows 3: Creating Learning Summaries or Review Sheets

Faculty can input their lecture notes or reading lists into AI systems to generate **unit summaries, study guides, or glossary lists**, particularly helpful for exam prep or review sessions.

Equity Benefit: These summaries can be further tailored for multilingual learners or students with reading challenges, providing scaffolds that enhance comprehension and participation. **When AI-generated summaries are adapted** to reflect plain language, translated phrases, or visual supports, **students who might otherwise struggle can engage more fully with course content**. This practice not only increases clarity but also reinforces equity by ensuring that diverse learners have meaningful access to the same intellectual opportunities as their peers.

Caution: At the same time, **summaries must be carefully cross-checked for omission, distortion, or overgeneralization since AI often condenses material without fully capturing nuance**. This is particularly critical when dealing with culturally sensitive content, complex theories, or context-dependent arguments, where subtlety matters as much as accuracy. Faculty who emphasize critical review teach students that accessibility should not come at the cost of precision or integrity, modeling responsible engagement with AI outputs.

Application of AI in Faculty Workflows 4: Supporting Neurodiverse Students with Accessible Explanations

AI tools can assist faculty in **rephrasing complex content into simpler language**, offering analogies, or providing multiple modalities of explanation (e.g., visual, step-by-step, audio-based) - beneficial for students with ADHD, autism, dyslexia, or processing differences.

Example Practice:

- *A math instructor uses AI to generate multiple explanations for solving quadratic equations - one narrative-based, one visual, and one step-by-step - which are reviewed and shared with students for use in learning accommodations.*

Ethical Reminder: Faculty must be aware of data privacy, particularly when inputting identifiable student information or feedback into third-party platforms. **Entering names, grades, or sensitive reflections into generative AI tools may violate institutional policies or legal protections such as FERPA, exposing students to unintended risks**. Responsible practice requires anonymizing inputs, using institution-approved systems, and teaching students to recognize that privacy is an ethical as well as a regulatory obligation in AI use.

Principles for Ethical AI-Augmented Teaching

To ensure AI enhances rather than undermines faculty work, three guiding principles should anchor its use:

- **Human Oversight**.
    - All AI-generated content should be **reviewed, contextualized, and edited** by the instructor. Tools can draft, but educators curate.
- **Pedagogical Alignment**.
    - AI output must be **aligned with course objectives, cognitive demands, and disciplinary values**. Use should not default to efficiency over substance.
- **Ethical Caution**.

- Faculty must consider:
  - **Data privacy**. *"Are student materials being submitted to public AI systems?"*
  - **Fairness**. *"Does use of AI reinforce inequity in expectations or support?"*
  - **Transparency**. *"Should students be informed when instructional content has been AI-assisted?"*

As Slimi and Carballido (2023) noted, **the ethical use of generative AI begins not with the tool's capabilities, but with the intentions and responsibilities of the human educator guiding its use**. This means that **faculty set the tone for how AI enters the classroom** - whether as a shortcut, a supplement, or a catalyst for deeper reflection. By foregrounding human judgment, educators demonstrate that ethical AI practice is less about what the machine can produce and more about how people choose to integrate, critique, and contextualize those outputs responsibly.

Why Using AI to Augment, Not Automate Faculty Work Is Important

When integrated thoughtfully, **AI can be a powerful amplifier of faculty creativity, efficiency, and inclusivity**. It **allows faculty to streamline routine tasks** such as quiz generation or content summarization, freeing up time for deeper engagement with students. At the same time, **AI can spark new ideas, offer alternative perspectives, and provide multilingual or accessibility support, ensuring broader student participation when guided by a human educator**.

It can streamline routine tasks, generate inspiration, and extend learning support - but only when faculty remain the ethical interpreters, relational anchors, and intellectual stewards of the classroom. **Faculty judgment ensures that AI outputs are accurate, appropriate, and aligned with learning goals, rather than accepted at face value**. This balance preserves the heart of teaching as a human-centered practice while using AI as a catalyst for innovation and inclusion.

In the age of automation, **the future of teaching depends not on what AI can do alone, but on how faculty choose to use it - with care, critique, and conviction**. Educators who approach AI with an intentionality model enables students to navigate technology responsibly and reflectively. In doing so, they show that teaching is not diminished by AI but strengthened, as the work of educators becomes increasingly about cultivating ethical discernment, creativity, and human connection.

Core AI Competency 5: Guiding Students in Ethical, Critical, and Reflective AI Use

---

As generative AI becomes embedded in academic, creative, and civic life, perhaps the most essential faculty competency is the ability to **mentor students in the ethical, critical, and reflective use of AI tools**. This involves more than setting usage boundaries or monitoring for misconduct. It requires **designing learning experiences that develop judgment, awareness, and epistemic responsibility** in a world where algorithmic outputs increasingly shape knowledge, labor, and decision-making.

In contrast to fear-based or rules-only approaches, ethical AI pedagogy invites students to engage AI tools as objects of critique, partners in process, and mirrors of human bias and design. Rather than focusing solely on prohibitions or compliance, this approach emphasizes curiosity, analysis, and reflection - **encouraging students to ask not just *"What can this tool do?"*** but ***"What does its design reveal about social values and institutional priorities?"*** By guiding students through these deeper questions, faculty foster a culture where AI becomes a site of inquiry into power, authorship, fairness, and human meaning-making, ensuring that technology serves as a catalyst for ethical and intellectual growth rather than a shortcut or threat (Benjamin, 2023; Noble, 2018; Reiss, 2021).

Instructional Practice 1: Encourage Reflection on How AI Influences Thinking

Students should be regularly prompted to reflect on how to use AI:

- Shapes their thought process and confidence.
- Influences their interpretation of problems.
- Affects their perception of authorship or originality.

Example Prompt:

- *"How did using ChatGPT shape the structure or tone of your draft?"*
- *"What did you keep, revise, or reject - and why?"*

These questions build metacognitive awareness, encouraging students to pause and reflect on their interactions with AI rather than accepting outputs at face value. By analyzing how they frame prompts, interpret responses, and decide when to accept or reject machine input, learners begin to recognize their own cognitive processes in action. This shift transforms students from passive users of AI into intentional inquirers, capable of applying critical thinking and reflective judgment to every stage of the learning process (Brookfield, 2017).

Instructional Practice 2: Assign Activities that Compare AI and Human Outputs

Design assignments where students must:

- Prompt an AI tool to complete a task.
- Complete the same task themselves.
- Compare, contrast, and critique the results using disciplinary criteria.

Skills Developed:

- Identifying stylistic, factual, or ethical differences.
- Recognizing when AI flattens complexity or lacks nuance.
- Evaluating where machine efficiency complements - or undermines - human insight.

This cultivates critical digital literacy by teaching students that effective AI use is not just about generating outputs, but about questioning the processes behind them. **Fluency in AI, therefore, involves both technical skill and the intellectual ability to identify errors,**

biases, or oversimplifications within machine-generated content. By practicing this form of critique, learners strengthen their capacity to engage responsibly with AI, recognizing its potential while remaining alert to its limitations and risks (Bender et al., 2021; Slimi & Carballido, 2023).

Instructional Practice 3: Provide Ethical Frameworks for Tool Use

Rather than relying solely on institutional policies, faculty should offer students **accessible frameworks** to guide their everyday AI decisions. These may draw from:

- **Fairness**. *"Does the AI reproduce bias or offer equitable representation?"*
- **Transparency**. *"Is the use of AI disclosed honestly in the final product?"*
- **Attribution**. *"Is the line between human and machine authorship clear?"*
- **Agency**. *"Is the tool being used to support thinking, or to bypass it?"*

Classroom Integration: Faculty can introduce ethical evaluation rubrics or reflection scaffolds tied to assignments, providing students with clear criteria for how to assess and report their use of generative tools. **These frameworks give learners a shared vocabulary to describe not only what the AI produced, but how they engaged with, modified, or critiqued it in the context of their discipline**. Over time, such practices normalize transparency, helping students recognize that ethical AI use is not a hidden practice but a reflective skill central to academic integrity and professional accountability.

Assignment Example: Philosophy and Machine Ethics

In a moral philosophy course, the instructor asks students to:

- Prompt ChatGPT to respond to a classic ethical dilemma (e.g., the trolley problem, euthanasia, corporate whistleblowing).
- Analyze the AI's reasoning using ethical theories studied in class (e.g., Kantian ethics, utilitarianism, virtue theory).
- Write a critique that addresses:
  - Whether the AI exhibited moral reasoning or merely mirrored training data.
  - What assumptions were embedded in its framing?
  - How human ethical reflection differs from statistical prediction.

Outcome: The **assignment concludes with a group dialogue on the limits of machine rationality and the necessity of human moral agency in algorithmic environments**. This conversation pushes students to reflect on where AI stops and human responsibility must begin, emphasizing that ethical decision-making cannot be outsourced to automated systems. In doing so, **students gain not only sharper critical perspectives on AI outputs but also a deeper appreciation of how their own values, interpretive frameworks, and voices remain essential** in shaping knowledge and practice in an era of automated content production.

Why Guiding Students in Ethical, Critical, and Reflective AI Use Matters Across Disciplines

Whether guiding a chemistry student interpreting AI-suggested lab methods, or a sociology student unpacking algorithmic bias in predictive policing data, faculty in all fields must help students:

- Approach AI use with **intellectual humility and discernment**.
- See themselves as **agents, not consumers**, in technological landscapes.
- Understand that ethical reflection is as important as technical skill.

As AI becomes increasingly embedded in public life - from hiring platforms to newsfeeds - **students must be equipped to ask better questions, not just generate faster answers** (Floridi et al., 2018; Gulya, 2023). This means cultivating the ability to interrogate how systems frame knowledge, whose priorities they serve, and what assumptions are hidden in their design. **By teaching inquiry over automation, educators prepare students to navigate AI as an active participant in society**, rather than passive consumers of machine-generated content.

Bridge Topic

Faculty as Ethical Mentors in the Algorithmic Age

The heart of AI pedagogy is not tool mastery - it is ethical discernment and critical inquiry. Faculty who embrace this mentoring role foster classrooms where students are encouraged to slow down, reflect on the implications of their choices, and actively question the authority of technological systems. In this way, **teaching AI becomes less about following instructions from a machine and more about cultivating principled frameworks for learning, collaboration, and authorship that center human agency**.

In doing so, educators reaffirm that while AI may offer information quickly and efficiently, it cannot substitute for wisdom, judgment, or purpose. **Only humans can situate knowledge within cultural, ethical, and relational contexts that give it meaning. By modeling this distinction, faculty demonstrate that teaching is not diminished in the AI era** - it becomes even more vital as a safeguard of empathy, care, and intellectual depth.

How Institutions Can Support AI Competency Building: Structures for Sustainable Faculty Growth

---

The transition to AI-enhanced teaching is not a single event - it is an evolving process that requires **long-term institutional investment in faculty capacity, confidence, and community**. While some faculty may already be experimenting with generative tools, most need clear pathways for exploring their use **ethically, reflectively, and pedagogically**. Institutions must recognize that building AI competency is not just about disseminating technical knowledge - it is about reshaping professional identity, assessment models, and disciplinary practice in a time of epistemic disruption (Brookfield, 2017; Reiss, 2021).

The following strategies provide a multi-tiered, inclusive approach to supporting AI engagement at scale. By layering initiatives such as peer learning circles, institutional training modules, and discipline-specific workshops, institutions create pathways for faculty at all levels of comfort and expertise to participate. **These efforts ensure that AI integration is not carried by a handful of early adopters but is embraced as a shared institutional priority, grounded in inquiry, collective support, and sustained critical reflection**.

Strategy for Institutional Support 1: Provide Scaffolded Faculty Training from Literacy to Mastery

Rather than offering one-off workshops, institutions should develop **tiered faculty development pathways** that move from foundational understanding (AI literacy) to applied usage (AI fluency) and finally to institutional leadership (AI mastery). This progression allows faculty to grow at their own pace and according to their disciplinary context.

Implementation Ideas:

- Faculty complete self-paced modules on topics such as AI bias, citation, prompt design, or assignment scaffolding.
- Those seeking deeper engagement participate in semester-long learning communities, project-based fellowships, or peer mentorship programs.
- Mastery-level faculty lead campus-wide initiatives, publish pedagogical resources, or support policy development (Byars-Winston & Dahlberg, 2019).

This tiered model not only builds individual competence but also cultivates a distributed leadership structure, ensuring that AI pedagogy does not rest on a small number of champions. As more faculty move along the pathway, institutions gain a sustainable pipeline of educators who can mentor peers, shape curricula, and influence policy. **Over time, this layered approach creates a culture where AI engagement is normalized, ethically grounded, and aligned with both disciplinary needs and institutional missions**.

Strategy for Institutional Support 2: Offer Modular AI Toolkits for Common Use Cases

To support just-in-time application, institutions can curate or co-create **modular toolkits** with examples of how AI tools can responsibly assist in common teaching scenarios. Each module should include ethical considerations, practical tips, and clear use limitations.

Toolkit Modules Might Include:

- Drafting quiz or rubric templates with AI.
- Designing AI-integrated reflection prompts.
- Using AI to generate content summaries or vocabulary glossaries.
- Creating accessible explanations for neurodiverse learners.

Each module should also include cautionary notes on data privacy, over-reliance, and student equity, helping faculty approach AI use with nuance and care (Crawford, 2021; Slimi & Carballido, 2023). **By surfacing these risks explicitly, faculty can frame AI as a technology that requires critical oversight rather than blind adoption**. This balance of opportunity and caution ensures that AI literacy training cultivates not only technical skill, but also ethical judgment and a strong commitment to inclusive educational practices.

Strategy for Institutional Support 3: Create Discipline-Specific Guidelines for AI Use and Interpretation

Different academic fields have different expectations around originality, authorship, collaboration, and source use. Institutions should support departments in **developing discipline-specific guidance** on AI integration that aligns with both pedagogical goals and professional standards.

Examples:

- *English or history departments create norms around how AI tools can be used in drafting or revising without erasing the authorial voice.*
- *STEM departments articulate when AI use in problem-solving or code writing enhances learning - and when it bypasses essential reasoning.*
- *Art and design faculty develop criteria for evaluating originality in generative outputs and attribution in co-creative practices.*

These guidelines foster ethical coherence and empower faculty to make consistent, transparent decisions. By providing a shared framework, they reduce ambiguity around AI use and ensure that faculty align their practices with institutional values and student needs. Over time, such clarity helps build trust across the academic community, reinforcing that AI integration is both principled and pedagogically intentional.

Strategy for Institutional Support 4: Host Faculty Showcase Events for AI-Enhanced Innovations

Publicly recognizing faculty experimentation sends an institutional message that **risk-taking, reflection, and co-creation are valued**. Showcase events create opportunities for peer-to-peer learning, collaborative critique, and curricular dissemination.

Event Formats Might Include:

- "AI Assignment Roundtables," where faculty present and critique each other's designs.
- Lightning talks on lessons learned from classroom AI use.
- Cross-disciplinary panels on challenges such as grading transparency, student trust, or authorship ethics.

These events model distributed innovation and collective ownership of pedagogical change (Floridi et al., 2018). **By engaging faculty from across disciplines in co-creation, they demonstrate that AI integration is not the responsibility of a single department, but a**

campus-wide endeavor. This collaborative approach not only generates richer ideas but also fosters long-term buy-in, ensuring that change is sustainable and reflective of diverse academic perspectives.

Peer Learning Structure: AI Pedagogical Cohorts

Peer-based cohorts provide sustained, faculty-driven spaces for collaborative exploration. Departments or colleges can form **AI pedagogy cohorts**, with rotating facilitation on thematic issues. These cohorts foster horizontal mentorship, normalize uncertainty, and create a protected space for testing new practices.

Facilitation Topics Might Include:

- **AI and Accessibility**. How generative tools can support multilingual or neurodiverse learners - and where they fall short.
- **Student Evaluation and Citation Practices**. How to assess AI-assisted writing, and what a transparent citation looks like across formats.
- **Discipline-Specific Challenges**. Addressing legal precedent synthesis in law schools, AI-assisted critique in studio courses, or data validity in social science research.

Each cohort session can include readings, tool demos, assignment walkthroughs, and critical incidents, reinforcing that AI pedagogy is as much about dialogue as design (Brookfield, 2017). These elements provide a balance of theory, practice, and reflection, allowing participants to see not only how tools function, but how they affect teaching values and student learning. By weaving structured content with open discussion, sessions cultivate a culture where experimentation is paired with critical inquiry, ensuring that faculty approach AI integration with both creativity and responsibility.

Why Institutions Supporting AI Competency Building Create a Collective Endeavor

Supporting AI competency is not a matter of producing more expert users - **it is about cultivating reflective, ethical, and interdisciplinary educators who can prepare students to live and learn alongside intelligent systems**. This means prioritizing judgment, transparency, and context-awareness over technical fluency alone. **When faculty understand that their role is to guide interpretation and ethical use, rather than to master every algorithm**, they become better positioned to mentor students in navigating the cultural and professional realities of AI.

When institutions scaffold faculty development, center peer learning, and align resources with values, they move beyond compliance toward a culture of confident, collaborative experimentation. **Such structures encourage faculty to approach AI not with fear or passivity, but with curiosity and collective accountability**. Over time, this creates a resilient academic community where innovation is normalized, ethical reflection is embedded, and experimentation becomes a shared responsibility rather than an individual burden.

In doing so, they ensure that AI becomes not a source of confusion or inequity - but a catalyst for pedagogical renewal and institutional integrity. **Faculty development programs that emphasize inclusivity, transparency, and shared learning transform AI from an isolated challenge into a unifying force for institutional mission**. Ultimately, AI becomes a tool for rethinking what education can be, helping institutions uphold their commitment to rigor, equity, and civic responsibility in a rapidly evolving technological era.

Section Reflection: Building Faculty AI Competence as a Foundation for Ethical and Disciplinary Leadership

This section establishes a comprehensive and pragmatic roadmap for developing the essential AI competencies that every faculty member - regardless of discipline - should build. Rather than framing AI engagement as a matter of technical expertise, the section reorients the conversation around ethical fluency, pedagogical application, and critical reflection. By introducing the Literacy–Fluency–Mastery model, it creates an inclusive developmental framework that validates diverse starting points while promoting upward growth through curiosity, integrity, and collaboration.

Each core competency - understanding how AI works, evaluating AI outputs, teaching ethical use, enhancing faculty workflows, and mentoring students in reflective engagement - reflects a shift in faculty identity from knowledge gatekeeper to guide, curator, and mentor in a machine-mediated world. Importantly, the section emphasizes that these competencies are not static checklists but evolving skill sets tied to faculty values, disciplinary norms, and broader institutional goals.

Finally, the section underscores that institutions play a crucial role in enabling this transformation by offering scaffolded training, modular resources, peer learning structures, and recognition for innovation. Together, these supports cultivate not only AI-capable educators, but also AI-conscious pedagogues - those who are prepared to model discernment, shape discourse, and lead responsibly within the algorithmic university.

Section 3: Creating Institutional Pathways for AI Training and Support

---

Higher education institutions cannot rely on one-time workshops or ad hoc tutorials to prepare faculty for the far-reaching implications of artificial intelligence. Brief interventions may raise awareness, but they rarely equip educators with the sustained skills and reflective practices needed to adapt in a rapidly shifting environment. **As AI continues to reshape student learning, faculty roles, and scholarly production, professional development must evolve into a strategic, embedded, and collaborative institutional priority** - woven into the culture of teaching, research, and service (Byars-Winston & Dahlberg, 2019; Slimi & Carballido, 2023).

To move from awareness to readiness, colleges and universities must invest in long-term pathways that build AI fluency across roles, disciplines, and teaching modalities. **These pathways should not only train faculty in the mechanics of AI tools but also guide them in framing ethical dilemmas, aligning technology with learning outcomes, and cultivating student agency**. By balancing technical skill development with ethical literacy, pedagogical relevance, and interdepartmental collaboration, institutions can position AI not merely as a set of tools but rather as a transformational force that redefines academic culture and the shared mission of higher education.

From Events to Ecosystems: Why Institutional Design Matters

While many colleges and universities have begun introducing generative AI to faculty through workshops, lunch-and-learns, and technology showcases, these efforts - though well-intentioned - often fall short of what is needed to foster long-term, mission-aligned transformation. Faculty development centered on AI remains largely **episodic, tool-driven, and structurally siloed**, limiting both its reach and impact. Without intentional design and institutional coherence, AI integration risks becoming **a scattered series of tech trainings**, rather than a coordinated strategy for preparing educators and students for the algorithmic age.

To move beyond episodic workshops, institutions must design faculty development that is iterative, scaffolded, and tied to broader academic priorities. This means creating long-term learning pathways that integrate AI into professional growth alongside ethics, pedagogy, and disciplinary expertise, rather than isolating it as a "tech skill." **When professional development is framed in this way, AI adoption becomes less about chasing the newest tools and more about building sustainable, values-driven practices** that align with institutional mission and student success.

Common Limitations in Current AI Faculty Initiatives

AI Faculty Initiative Limitation 1: Voluntary, One-Off Workshops

Most faculty development offerings around AI are optional and occasional, drawing primarily those who are already interested or confident. While this format may suit early adopters, it excludes faculty who are uncertain, overwhelmed, or time-constrained - those who may benefit most from guided exploration. One-time events also **lack the continuity** needed to develop ethical awareness, curricular integration, or reflective teaching practices (Brookfield, 2017).

To address this gap, **institutions must shift from optional workshops toward embedded, required, and tiered professional development**. This can take the form of AI-focused modules integrated into existing teaching academies, orientation programs for new faculty, or mandatory refreshers tied to curriculum renewal cycles. By making engagement systematic rather than voluntary, institutions ensure that all faculty - not just the curious few - develop the baseline competencies needed to guide students responsibly in the AI era.

In addition, ongoing development must be structured to provide continuity and growth, not one-off exposure. Semester-long learning communities, project-based fellowships, or cross-departmental mentorship networks allow faculty to build confidence, reflect on practice, and gradually scale their use of AI in teaching and research. **This continuous engagement transforms faculty development from an isolated event into a sustained culture of critical inquiry, innovation, and ethical stewardship, better aligning institutional support with the realities of technological change**.

AI Faculty Initiative Limitation 2: Centered Around Tools, Not Outcomes

Sessions often focus on tool demonstrations (e.g., "Using ChatGPT to Write Quiz Questions") without connecting to **learning goals, assessment frameworks, or epistemological implications**. This tool-first orientation reinforces a transactional mindset - AI as utility - rather than framing it as **a subject of inquiry and a force shaping knowledge and society** (Bender et al., 2021; Selwyn, 2019).

A more impactful model for AI faculty development links tool exploration directly to pedagogical outcomes. For example, **instead of simply showing how ChatGPT can generate quiz questions, sessions could invite faculty to critique those questions for cognitive depth, alignment with Bloom's taxonomy, or bias in framing**. This approach reinforces that AI is not just about efficiency but about shaping learning design, encouraging faculty to treat technology as part of a broader ecosystem of assessment and intellectual growth.

Equally important, faculty sessions must address the epistemological stakes of AI integration. Generative models are not neutral assistants; they embody assumptions about what counts as knowledge, how credibility is signaled, and which perspectives are prioritized or silenced (Bender et al., 2021; Noble, 2018). **By guiding faculty to interrogate these underlying logics, professional development can shift from surface-level tool adoption to deeper critical inquiry** - helping educators prepare students not only to use AI but to question its role in knowledge-making and civic life.

AI Faculty Initiative Limitation 3: Siloed in Instructional Technology or IT Departments

AI integration is frequently housed within tech units, separate from centers for teaching and learning, general education governance, or academic affairs. As a result, conversations about AI may remain narrowly focused on access, compliance, or functionality, rather than on **learning, ethics, and faculty identity**. This disconnection prevents **cross-functional integration** across pedagogy, policy, and curriculum (Reiss, 2021).

One way to overcome this disconnection is by embedding AI conversations directly within faculty governance structures and teaching centers. For example, **curriculum committees and general education boards can frame AI not just as a technical tool but as a subject of inquiry** - asking how it reshapes student agency, assessment design, or disciplinary epistemologies. This reframing ensures that discussions of AI move from the margins of compliance to the core of educational mission and identity.

Additionally, institutions should design cross-functional task forces where IT staff, teaching center directors, and faculty leaders collaborate on AI integration. **These groups can**

ensure that conversations about access and infrastructure are paired with equally robust dialogues about pedagogy, ethics, and faculty development. By bridging technical expertise with educational priorities, institutions can create a coherent strategy for AI adoption that supports not only system functionality but also meaningful and ethical learning outcomes (Brookfield, 2017; Selwyn, 2019).

AI Faculty Initiative Limitation 4: Misaligned with Faculty Reward Structures

Faculty who invest time in experimenting with AI pedagogy - designing new assignments, revising assessments, mentoring peers - often do so without institutional recognition. When teaching innovation is not rewarded in promotion, tenure, or merit reviews, educators may feel discouraged from investing effort in AI literacy, especially given the complexity and risk involved. This reinforces a culture where **AI engagement is seen as peripheral rather than central** to professional growth (Byars-Winston & Dahlberg, 2019).

A more sustainable approach is for institutions to explicitly incorporate AI pedagogy into evaluation criteria for teaching excellence. **Promotion and tenure dossiers, annual reviews, and faculty awards should include categories that recognize ethical innovation, interdisciplinary collaboration, and risk-taking in course design**. By institutionalizing these forms of recognition, universities affirm that exploring AI is not marginal work, but a central contribution to academic leadership and curricular renewal.

Equally important, recognition should extend beyond formal evaluation to public acknowledgment within the academic community. Highlighting faculty experiments in newsletters, teaching symposia, or campus-wide showcases signals to both peers and students that AI engagement is valued and celebrated. **This visibility not only reduces the stigma of experimentation but also creates a culture of inspiration and shared learning, positioning faculty as role models for how to navigate technology with creativity and integrity** (Brookfield, 2017; Slimi & Carballido, 2023).

The Consequence of These Limitations: Fragmentation and Fatigue

These structural limitations sustain a **fragmented campus culture around AI**, marked by:

- Uneven student experiences across courses.
- Faculty confusion about norms and expectations.
- A lack of shared language or institutional vision.
- Duplication of effort and missed opportunities for collaboration.

Faculty often express fatigue or disengagement, not because they lack interest, but because they lack pathways for meaningful, supported participation. **Without structured opportunities, recognition, or collaborative spaces, even motivated educators may feel isolated in their attempts to adapt to AI-driven change**. By creating clear avenues for engagement - such as mentoring networks, interdisciplinary workshops, or recognition programs - institutions can transform this fatigue into renewed energy and purpose, empowering faculty to see themselves as contributors to a collective transformation rather than as overwhelmed individuals.

Toward an Ecosystem Approach: What Faculty Need

To move from scattered events to sustainable ecosystems, institutions must design AI faculty development that is:

- **Accessible**. Clear entry points for all levels of AI fluency, from literacy to mastery.
- **Ongoing**. Recurring opportunities for exploration, implementation, and reflection.
- **Integrated**. Aligned with general education, equity initiatives, and academic leadership.
- **Recognized**. Tied to professional advancement, awards, and scholarly teaching pathways.
- **Collaborative**. Built on interdisciplinary dialogue and peer learning structures.

When these elements are in place, AI engagement becomes a shared, evolving, and supported institutional endeavor, not a solo experiment or compliance burden. **Faculty begin to see themselves as part of a larger learning community where responsibility, creativity, and ethical reflection are distributed across colleagues and departments**. This collective approach not only sustains energy and innovation but also signals to both educators and students that AI integration is a long-term cultural shift, grounded in institutional values rather than short-term technical fixes.

Summary: From Episodic to Embedded

AI is not a temporary trend - it is a paradigm shift in knowledge production, teaching practice, and academic integrity. Institutions that treat AI integration as a series of isolated events will fall behind. Those that invest in **ecosystem design - where faculty support, curricular alignment, and ethical inquiry are embedded across the campus - will cultivate a culture of curiosity, resilience, and pedagogical leadership**.

In short, AI fluency will not scale through workshops alone. It requires institutional structures that align capacity, values, and vision - turning sporadic engagement into collective transformation. **When professional development is woven into policy, curriculum design, and reward systems, faculty are positioned not just as tool users but as ethical leaders and collaborators in shaping the future of education with AI**. This broader infrastructure ensures that engagement is sustained, inclusive, and deeply connected to the mission of higher learning.

Key Structures for Scalable AI Support

AI in higher education cannot be sustained by one-off workshops or sporadic enthusiasm from early adopters. Institutions need **scalable, repeatable, and relational structures** that empower faculty to experiment, reflect, and share. **This section outlines five key models of**

support - Faculty Learning Communities, Faculty Fellowships, Cross-Role Collaboration Hubs, Seed Grants, and Scaffolded Pathways - each building toward a coordinated culture of ethical and innovative AI engagement.

Structure for Scalable AI Support 1: Faculty Learning Communities (FLCs) Focused on AI Pedagogy

---

Faculty Learning Communities (FLCs) offer one of the most powerful and sustainable structures for building AI literacy across campus. These small, cross-disciplinary cohorts provide the **relational continuity, protected space, and reflective scaffolding** needed for faculty to engage meaningfully with the pedagogical and ethical complexities of generative AI. Rather than framing AI integration as an individual technical challenge, FLCs treat it as **a shared inquiry into the future of teaching, learning, and knowledge production**.

FLCs also function as horizontal leadership incubators: they cultivate trust, normalize experimentation, and generate peer-reviewed practices that can scale beyond the group. Over time, these collaborative habits allow faculty to influence not just their own classrooms, but also departmental norms and institutional culture. As Cox (2004) and Brookfield (2017) emphasized, adult learning thrives when it is socially constructed, self-directed, and anchored in reflective dialogue - precisely the conditions that well-structured FLCs create.

Core Design Features of an AI Pedagogy FLC

A strong FLC focused on AI pedagogy typically includes:

- **8–12 faculty** from multiple disciplines and teaching roles.
- **Structured monthly meetings** facilitated by a rotating member or teaching center coordinator.
- **Shared artifacts** such as readings, assignment prototypes, or classroom reflections.
- **A culminating deliverable**, such as a campus showcase, resource guide, or departmental policy proposal.

Importantly, **FLCs are not passive learning environments**. They function as active laboratories of pedagogy, where faculty continuously design, test, and refine AI-integrated practices in direct response to classroom realities. **Members are both learners and contributors - engaging in cycles of experimentation and reflection that turn individual insights into collective knowledge, making innovation both sustainable and scalable across the institution**.

Sample Meeting Prompts and Activities

To move beyond tool tutorials and into reflective practice, each session can center on a thematic prompt or design challenge. For example, at a regional liberal arts college, a CTL-sponsored FLC launched a semester-long series with the following sequence:

- **"Redesign One Assignment Using Generative AI."** Faculty bring a current syllabus and workshop a revision that explicitly integrates AI tools (e.g., using AI for early-stage brainstorming, comparative text analysis, or prompt refinement). Reflections include how the revision alters learning outcomes, assessment criteria, and student agency.
- **"How Do You Explain AI-Generated Misinformation in Your Field?"** Members bring examples of hallucinated content from ChatGPT or Perplexity and discuss how these reflect disciplinary assumptions, gaps in training data, or representational bias. This opens broader conversations on **credibility, verification, and digital epistemology** (Bender et al., 2021; Noble, 2018).
- **"What Would an AI Ethics Statement Look Like in Your Department?"** In small groups, faculty draft discipline-specific ethics language that could appear on syllabi, departmental websites, or program learning outcomes. Statements address citation expectations, cognitive boundaries, and values-based guidance for AI use (Reiss, 2021; Slimi & Carballido, 2023).

Benefits of AI-Focused FLCs

Faculty Learning Communities (FLCs) dedicated to AI pedagogy are more than spaces for professional development; they are engines of cultural change within higher education. **By gathering faculty across disciplines into small, sustained cohorts, these communities foster the kind of trust, dialogue, and experimentation that one-off workshops cannot provide**. Their value lies not only in skill-building but in creating the conditions for peer accountability, cross-disciplinary insight, emotional support, and scalable institutional innovation - benefits that ripple outward to reshape both teaching practice and campus culture.

Benefit 1: Peer Accountability and Encouragement

Unlike one-time trainings, FLCs support iterative practice and encourage follow-through. **Faculty return to each session with reflections, student feedback, or revised materials, which fosters an ongoing cycle of learning and adaptation rather than a single event**. Over time, this iterative structure builds a culture of evidence-informed experimentation, where teaching practices are continuously tested, refined, and shared across the community.

Benefit 2: Cross-Disciplinary Fertilization

When an economics professor and a visual artist sit down to talk about AI authorship, or when a nursing instructor compares grading practices with a philosophy colleague, the resulting exchange deepens ethical awareness and reveals blind spots across disciplines. **These dialogues allow faculty to see how their assumptions, methods, and values differ from those in other fields, illuminating both shared challenges and discipline-specific tensions**. In turn, such cross-pollination enriches institutional conversations about AI, ensuring that policies and practices are informed by a diversity of perspectives rather than confined to siloed expertise.

Benefit 3: Emotional and Identity Support

Faculty grappling with AI-induced uncertainty, fear of being replaced, or frustration with shifting norms find empathy and perspective in a peer setting. **Within these groups, vulnerability is normalized, allowing faculty to share doubts and experiment with new approaches without fear of judgment or isolation**. Over time, these safe spaces foster resilience, mutual encouragement, and a collective sense of purpose, reinforcing that AI pedagogy is a shared journey rather than an individual burden.

Benefit 4: Institutional Scaling

Because FLCs generate **modular, peer-tested outputs**, their lessons can be adapted into broader initiatives such as:

- Teaching center resource guides.
- AI-integrated syllabi banks.
- Departmental policy templates.
- Faculty development workshops or retreats.

In this way, FLCs become the seedbeds for institution-wide capacity building. **What begins as small, peer-led experiments in pedagogy gradually produces scalable practices, policy templates, and shared resources that other departments can adopt**. Over time, the collective knowledge generated by these communities builds a durable foundation for campus-wide AI readiness, ensuring that innovation spreads through collaboration rather than isolated effort.

Summary: A Community Model for Cultural Transformation

FLCs are more than pedagogical support - they are change infrastructures, enabling institutions to move from fragmented AI responses to coherent, reflective ecosystems. **They help ensure that individual efforts do not remain isolated but instead contribute to a larger vision of institutional readiness and shared innovation**. By fostering collaboration and structured dialogue, they model what ethical AI engagement looks like: collaborative, iterative, and grounded in human connection.

As faculty learn to integrate AI into their classrooms, they also reimagine what it means to teach, learn, and lead in a world of algorithmic systems. **These communities offer space to test new ideas, share lessons learned, and align classroom experimentation with broader institutional values**. FLCs provide the relational and intellectual scaffolding to support this transformation - not just for individual faculty striving to adapt, but for the campus as a whole, creating a culture where ethical AI literacy becomes embedded in everyday academic practice.

Structure for Scalable AI Support 2: Faculty Fellowships for AI-Integrated Course Development

---

To foster widespread, sustainable innovation in AI-integrated pedagogy, institutions must move beyond informal experimentation and formally recognize the time, labor, and intellectual work involved in responsible course redesign. Without this structural support, AI teaching risks remaining fragmented, depending on the enthusiasm of individual faculty rather than institutional commitment. Faculty fellowships provide a proven structure for supporting educational innovation while elevating faculty agency, building institutional knowledge, and generating scalable curricular resources (Byars-Winston & Dahlberg, 2019).

An AI pedagogy fellowship is not merely a stipend - it is a coordinated developmental ecosystem, offering protected time, interdisciplinary support, and a public platform for reflection and dissemination. These programs create the conditions for faculty to take intellectual risks, experiment with pedagogy, and contribute to collective learning without fear of penalty. In doing so, fellowships validate faculty expertise while fostering a campus culture of collaborative innovation, ensuring that AI integration is not an isolated trend but instead a sustained transformation embedded in the academic mission.

Fellowship Structure and Supports

Semester-long fellowships should include both **individualized time for deep design work** and **communal learning opportunities** to situate course redesign within a broader pedagogical, ethical, and disciplinary conversation. Fellows might commit to 8–10 hours per month of structured engagement, with additional independent time for implementation and documentation.

Core Components:

- **Structured Workshops**. Topics might include:
  - Foundations of AI literacy and generative models.
  - Ethical frameworks for AI use in academic settings.
  - Designing assignments for transparent and accountable AI engagement.
  - Assessment models for AI-assisted work (e.g., citation, revision logs, reflective memos).
- **Dedicated Course Redesign Time**. Faculty are given course release, summer stipends, or protected research time to revise syllabi, create AI-integrated modules, and test new forms of student engagement.
- **Collaborative Consultations**. Fellows meet with librarians to source open educational resources, with instructional designers to integrate tools or assessments, and with accessibility specialists to ensure inclusive design for diverse learners.
- **Showcase and Dissemination**. At the end of the fellowship, each participant presents their revised course and key pedagogical insights through a public forum, roundtable, or recorded spotlight for the campus resource repository.

Summary: The fellowship model is built on four interconnected components that ensure both depth and scalability. **Faculty engage in structured workshops on AI literacy, ethics, and pedagogy, while also receiving dedicated time to redesign courses and test new learning approaches**. Collaborative consultations with librarians, instructional designers, and accessibility experts enrich the process, and the fellowship culminates in a public showcase, ensuring that insights and resources are shared across the institution.

Deliverables That Promote Institutional Scaling

Fellows commit to producing one or more artifacts that contribute to broader faculty development and curriculum transformation. These outputs provide **tangible returns on institutional investment** and support long-term scaling of AI pedagogy.

Sample Deliverables:

- **AI Literacy-Infused Syllabi**. Revised syllabi that clearly define AI expectations, integrate reflective assignments, and offer discipline-specific guidance for ethical tool use.
- **Open-Access Lesson Modules**. Modular, field-tested activities for teaching AI-related concepts - e.g., hallucination detection, authorship ethics, prompt critique, comparative analysis of machine and human writing.
- **Assessment Strategies for AI-Assisted Work**. Rubrics, policy templates, and assignment scaffolds that accommodate and assess AI-assisted processes without sacrificing learning integrity.
- **Departmental AI Pedagogy Guides**. Short, shareable primers that help other faculty navigate tool selection, student communication, and disciplinary implications of AI use.

Summary: The deliverables created through these fellowships are designed to extend well beyond the individual classroom. **By archiving syllabi, lesson modules, assessment strategies, and policy guides in a central repository, institutions create a living resource that can continually inform and inspire faculty across disciplines**. Optional Creative Commons licensing further amplifies the impact, enabling the dissemination of AI-integrated teaching practices to broader educational communities and supporting the growth of open, ethical, and scalable innovation.

Program Rationale and Long-Term Impact

These fellowships:

- **Legitimize faculty time investment**, recognizing course redesign as scholarly labor.
- **Elevate pedagogical leadership**, positioning faculty as innovators and peer mentors.
- **Ensure public dissemination**, building institutional capacity through reusable models and cross-disciplinary transparency.
- **Foster policy-relevant insight**, informing broader campus conversations around AI governance, digital literacy, and academic integrity.

Summary: Faculty fellowships provide a long-term mechanism for aligning AI integration with the deeper values of education rather than with trends or efficiency alone. **By resourcing faculty time, offering structured collaboration, and ensuring public dissemination, these programs embed AI pedagogy into the institutional fabric in ways that are sustainable**

and ethical. Over time, fellowships foster a culture where faculty innovation becomes a driver of institutional policy, curricular coherence, and responsible leadership in the evolving AI landscape.

Summary: Incentivizing Innovation with Integrity

Faculty fellowships create a stable and visible framework for advancing AI integration, ensuring that experimentation is resourced, structured, and institutionally supported rather than left to individual initiative. **By offering protected time, interdisciplinary dialogue, and opportunities for dissemination, these programs allow educators to move beyond ad hoc exploration toward systematic curricular innovation**. In doing so, fellowships elevate faculty as leaders of ethical and pedagogical change, transforming AI engagement into a shared institutional practice rather than a scattered response to technological disruption.

Structure for Scalable AI Support 3: Cross-Role Collaboration Hubs (Instruction + Innovation)

Successfully integrating AI into teaching and learning environments requires more than faculty training - it demands **institutional choreography**. Faculty cannot be expected to navigate the epistemological, technological, ethical, and curricular implications of generative AI alone. Instead, institutions must build **cross-role collaboration hubs** that leverage the diverse expertise of librarians, instructional designers, technologists, administrators, and scholars of ethics and pedagogy.

These hubs act as strategic incubators where innovation is guided by shared values and intentional design, rather than scattered individual efforts. By bringing together librarians, instructional designers, technologists, ethicists, and faculty, they ensure that **AI adoption is grounded in equity and pedagogical coherence instead of convenience or novelty**. In this way, institutions model that AI readiness is not the burden of a few but a collective, campus-wide commitment to ethical, scalable, and sustainable educational transformation (Crawford, 2021; Slimi & Carballido, 2023).

Key Roles in an AI-Integrated Instructional Ecosystem

Successfully embedding AI into teaching and learning requires more than individual faculty experimenting with new tools - it demands a coordinated network of expertise across the institution. AI integration touches pedagogy, ethics, technology, and governance, making it impossible for any single role to carry the responsibility alone. **Instead, effective ecosystems rely on librarians, instructional designers, ethicists, technologists, and academic leaders working in partnership to ensure that AI is deployed thoughtfully, equitably, and sustainably**.

This section highlights the unique contributions of each of these roles, illustrating how their collaboration builds coherence across classrooms, departments, and institutional policy. By recognizing the diverse expertise needed, institutions can move from fragmented adoption toward a holistic model of AI readiness that reflects both academic values and civic responsibilities.

Roles in an AI-Integrated Instructional Ecosystem 1: Librarians

Librarians bring essential expertise in **information literacy, source verification, citation practices, and digital authorship** - all of which are undergoing significant revision in the AI era. They can:

- Curate resources for teaching about algorithmic bias, hallucinated citations, and misinformation.
- Develop AI-related research instruction modules for students.
- Consult on citation and attribution frameworks for AI-assisted work.

Summary: Librarians play a pivotal role in ensuring that AI integration remains academically rigorous and ethically grounded. They help faculty and students **navigate emerging challenges in information literacy by curating resources on bias and misinformation, designing research modules that account for AI's limitations, and advising on evolving citation and authorship practices**. In doing so, librarians act as critical partners who safeguard accuracy, credibility, and intellectual integrity in the age of AI-driven scholarship.

Roles in an AI-Integrated Instructional Ecosystem 2: Instructional Designers

Designers help faculty move from curiosity to implementation by aligning tools with **learning outcomes, cognitive processes, and inclusive pedagogy**. Their support is essential for:

- Designing scaffolded, multimodal assignments that integrate AI reflectively.
- Reimagining assessment for transparency, reflection, and process documentation.
- Advising on UDL-aligned approaches to AI tool use for diverse learners.

Summary: Instructional designers are essential partners in moving faculty from curiosity about AI to effective classroom integration. **They help ensure that AI tools are not simply add-ons but are meaningfully aligned with learning outcomes through scaffolded assignments, transparent assessment models, and inclusive design**. By grounding AI use in principles of Universal Design for Learning (UDL), designers make it possible for diverse learners to engage critically, equitably, and reflectively with emerging technologies.

Roles in an AI-Integrated Instructional Ecosystem 3: Data Ethics Scholars

Faculty with backgrounds in digital ethics, philosophy of technology, law, or data justice can **anchor AI initiatives in ethical frameworks**. They provide:

- Faculty workshops on fairness, opacity, and algorithmic accountability.

- Case studies and curriculum modules for general education integration.
- Guidance on institutional AI use policies that center equity and autonomy.

Summary: Faculty with expertise in digital ethics, philosophy of technology, law, or data justice play a crucial role in grounding AI initiatives within strong ethical frameworks. **They contribute by leading workshops on fairness, accountability, and transparency, developing case studies and curriculum modules for integration into general education, and advising institutions on policies that prioritize equity and human autonomy**. Through this work, they ensure that AI integration remains not only technically sound but also ethically coherent and socially responsible.

Roles in an AI-Integrated Instructional Ecosystem 4: Academic Technologists

Technologists are responsible for **vetting platforms, maintaining security, and ensuring tool stability**. Their collaboration is essential for:

- Choosing AI tools that respect student privacy and comply with FERPA/GDPR.
- Advising on terms of use, bias risk, and system reliability.
- Supporting technical onboarding for new AI tools used in class contexts.

Summary: Technologists play a vital role in ensuring that AI tools adopted in educational settings are both secure and reliable. **They are responsible for vetting platforms to ensure compliance with privacy laws such as FERPA and GDPR, advising faculty on issues such as bias risk and system reliability, and supporting onboarding for classroom use**. By providing this expertise, technologists help safeguard both institutional integrity and student trust, while enabling smooth and ethical integration of AI into teaching and learning.

Roles in an AI-Integrated Instructional Ecosystem 5: Department Chairs and Academic Leaders

Chairs play a critical role in **aligning AI pedagogy with programmatic goals, evaluation criteria, and workload models**. They can:

- Ensure that AI-related innovations are reflected in teaching evaluations and peer review.
- Advocate for course release, professional development funding, or recognition in promotion processes.
- Support departmental conversations on ethical norms for AI use in teaching and scholarship.

Summary: Department chairs are pivotal in ensuring that AI pedagogy is aligned with broader academic goals and faculty responsibilities. **They can integrate AI-related innovations into evaluation and review processes, advocate for resources such as course releases or professional development funding, and support recognition of this work in promotion systems**. By facilitating departmental conversations on ethical AI use, chairs help establish shared norms and create an environment where responsible innovation is both supported and sustained.

Implementation Model: The Digital Futures Collaborative

To institutionalize these cross-functional partnerships, campuses can create a **Digital Futures Collaborative (DFC)** - a working group composed of representatives from each of the roles above, including student and community voices when appropriate.

Core Responsibilities:

- **Propose Policy for AI Use in Teaching and Learning**. Draft or review institutional language on appropriate AI use, academic integrity updates, documentation norms, and acceptable tool adoption processes.
- **Design Cross-Disciplinary Workshops**. Develop and lead sessions such as:
    - "Teaching with Generative AI: Pedagogy and Pitfalls."
    - "Redesigning Assessment in the Age of AI."
    - "Algorithmic Bias Across the Disciplines."
- **Support Research into AI and Pedagogy**. Coordinate internal grant programs, facilitate faculty learning communities, and co-author white papers or research briefs on AI teaching practices, impacts, and student outcomes.

Governance and Structure:

- Rotating leadership shared between faculty and teaching center staff.
- Meets monthly during the academic year.
- Reports to academic affairs and is integrated into strategic planning initiatives.

Why This Matters: From Ad Hoc to Coordinated Vision

In the absence of shared infrastructure, AI engagement remains uneven, reactive, and duplicative. Faculty may struggle to keep up with tool changes, policy updates, and classroom implementation - all while navigating student questions, assessment dilemmas, and disciplinary tensions. A cross-role collaboration hub brings **coherence, legitimacy, and sustainability** to AI integration efforts.

By aligning teaching, ethics, technology, and administration, institutions can reframe AI from being a narrow tool adoption issue into a broader transformational challenge that shapes both academic culture and civic life. **This alignment ensures that AI is not siloed in technical units, but embedded in curriculum, governance, and institutional mission, where its social and ethical implications are fully addressed**. In doing so, colleges and universities position themselves not only as adopters of innovation but instead as leaders in modeling responsible, democratic engagement with intelligent systems.

Summary: AI Readiness Requires Institutional Relationship-Building

No single office or individual holds all the expertise necessary to lead AI integration responsibly. It takes a **collective effort grounded in trust, humility, and interdisciplinary collaboration**. Cross-role hubs such as the Digital Futures Collaborative ensure that AI is not an isolated trend or a compliance burden - but a **campus-wide opportunity to reimagine what it means to teach, learn, and know** in the age of intelligent systems.

Structure for Scalable AI Support 4: Seed Grants and Micro-Innovation Funds

---

While major funding initiatives often garner attention, small, targeted investments can yield equally significant institutional impact when designed strategically. **When seed grants and micro-innovation funds are applied to localized experimentation, they allow faculty to pilot ideas at a scale that is manageable, adaptable, and immediately relevant to their teaching contexts**. These initiatives also promote interdisciplinary collaboration and produce scalable pedagogical models, multiplying the benefits of relatively modest financial commitments.

Seed grants and micro-innovation funds act as catalytic mechanisms that not only empower faculty to test new approaches but also encourage them to document, share, and refine their findings for institutional learning. **By lowering barriers to participation, they invite a wider range of educators - across disciplines, ranks, and comfort levels with AI - to contribute to the evolving culture of AI-integrated teaching**. These low-barrier, high-creativity structures signal that AI pedagogy is not simply a faculty-level task but a strategic institutional priority, one worthy of public investment, shared infrastructure, and scholarly recognition (Reiss, 2021).

Purpose of Micro-Innovation Funding

The core goal of seed grants is to create protected space and provide minimal yet meaningful financial scaffolding for faculty who wish to explore AI's potential in their teaching but might otherwise lack the time, incentive, or supportive infrastructure to pursue it. **By distributing smaller grants across a larger pool of participants, institutions ensure that experimentation is not limited to a select few but instead becomes a shared endeavor that represents the diversity of the faculty body**. This inclusive model fosters a culture of inquiry, lowers barriers to entry, and allows educators across disciplines, ranks, and technological comfort levels to contribute their unique perspectives to the collective exploration of AI in higher education.

Eligible Project Areas

Seed grants may range from $500 to $2,000 per award, offering flexible yet impactful funding to support early-stage pedagogical innovation. These modest awards are intentionally designed to encourage experimentation, making it possible for faculty to pilot ideas, test classroom strategies, or build small-scale collaborations without the pressure of large grant structures. By keeping the funding accessible and adaptable, institutions signal that creative engagement with AI is open to all faculty, regardless of discipline, rank, or prior experience with technology including:

Project Area 1: Piloting AI-Enhanced Assessment Strategies

Faculty design assignments and grading models that accommodate student use of AI tools while preserving critical reasoning, transparency, and authorship integrity.

Examples:

- *Annotated feedback memos that explain where and why AI tools were used.*
- *Dual-submission formats comparing human-generated and AI-supported drafts.*
- *Rubrics incorporating ethical reflection and revision commentary.*

Potential Deliverables:

- **Deliverable 1: AI Use Reflection Journal.** Students maintain a brief journal documenting their interactions with AI tools throughout the assignment. Each entry explains what tool was used, why it was chosen, and how the student critically evaluated its output. At the end of the term, the journal is submitted alongside their work, allowing faculty to assess transparency, intentionality, and growth in ethical reasoning.
- **Deliverable 2: Comparative Analysis Commentary.** In addition to submitting their human- and AI-supported drafts, students provide a 1–2 page commentary analyzing the differences between the two. This reflection highlights where AI supported their thinking, where it fell short, and what revisions they made to maintain originality and disciplinary voice. The commentary reinforces metacognition, showing that learning extends beyond the final product to the process itself.
- **Deliverable 3: Ethics-Infused Rubric Addendum.** Faculty integrate a new rubric category titled ***"Responsible AI Engagement"*** that explicitly evaluates transparency, reflection, and critical editing of AI outputs. Students are required to disclose prompt design, explain their editorial decisions, and demonstrate how their own reasoning shaped the final submission. This rubric add-on ensures that academic integrity and authorship integrity are central to the grading process.

Project Area 2: Building Interdisciplinary AI Modules

Faculty from different departments collaborate to develop cross-listed or co-taught instructional units - e.g., pairing a philosophy course on ethics with a computer science module on machine learning.

Examples:

- *"Can a Machine Make a Moral Decision?" (philosophy + engineering).*
- *"Bias in Data and Law" (criminal justice + statistics).*

Potential Deliverables:

- **Deliverable 1: Interdisciplinary Module Packet**. Faculty co-create a packet that includes a shared syllabus outline, key readings, and assignment prompts connecting both disciplines. For example, a philosophy–computer science collaboration might

include both ethical theory readings and hands-on coding exercises tied to machine learning scenarios. This packet can be archived and adapted by other faculty to scale interdisciplinary AI literacy across the institution.
- **Deliverable 2: Case-Based Teaching Resource**. Collaborating faculty develop a set of interdisciplinary case studies that situate AI questions within real-world contexts (e.g., predictive policing, algorithmic hiring, medical triage). Each case includes background readings, discussion questions, and an activity that draws on both disciplinary perspectives. The cases are designed to be modular, allowing faculty in other departments to integrate them into their own courses.
- **Deliverable 3: Public Showcase or Student Symposium**. At the end of the instructional unit, faculty organize a joint showcase where students present projects that integrate insights from both disciplines. For instance, computer science students might present a machine learning model, while philosophy students critique its ethical implications, culminating in a collaborative policy recommendation. This public forum becomes both a pedagogical outcome and an institutional artifact of interdisciplinary engagement.

Project Area 3: Developing AI Ethics Simulations

Faculty create classroom simulations that explore real-world scenarios involving AI in healthcare, law, media, or education.

Examples:

- *A nursing class debates the discharge recommendation of an AI triage system that ignores housing status.*
- *A journalism course critiques an AI-generated news feed for ideological skew and citation opacity.*

Potential Deliverables:

- **Deliverable 1: Simulation Scenario Repository**. Faculty document each simulation as a reusable teaching resource, including background context, student roles, prompts, and debrief questions. For instance, a nursing faculty member might prepare a written case about an AI triage system that overlooks housing insecurity, paired with structured reflection prompts. Over time, this repository becomes a shareable library that other faculty across disciplines can adapt for their own classrooms.
- **Deliverable 2: Student Reflection Compendium**. As part of the simulation, students produce short essays, policy memos, or multimedia reflections analyzing the ethical and institutional stakes of the scenario. Faculty then compile these reflections (with student consent) into a compendium that illustrates a range of disciplinary responses to AI decision-making. This resource highlights student voices and demonstrates how critical inquiry evolves across contexts such as law, health, and media.
- **Deliverable 3: Policy or Practice Briefs**. Each simulation concludes with students co-authoring a brief that recommends reforms or safeguards for AI use in the given scenario (e.g., transparency requirements for news algorithms, patient advocacy protocols in AI healthcare tools). Faculty can submit these briefs to an internal

repository or present them in public showcases, connecting classroom learning with civic and institutional engagement. These briefs serve as both student learning artifacts and potential resources for external stakeholders.

Project Area 4: Conducting Classroom Research on AI Impact

Faculty use the funding to study how AI-integrated assignments affect student learning outcomes, equity, or engagement.

Examples:

- *Pre- and post-course surveys on AI tool confidence and critical literacy.*
- *Comparative analysis of student work with and without AI assistance.*
- *Focus group discussions on cognitive and emotional responses to AI-generated feedback.*

Potential Deliverables:

- **Deliverable 1: Research Report on Student Outcomes.** Faculty prepare a structured research report that synthesizes findings from surveys, comparative work samples, and focus group data. This report highlights key trends in learning outcomes, equity of access, and engagement patterns across different demographics. It can be shared internally with teaching and learning centers or externally as a conference paper or journal article.
- **Deliverable 2: Evidence-Based Teaching Toolkit.** Based on their findings, faculty create a practical toolkit for colleagues that includes sample survey instruments, assignment templates, reflection prompts, and recommendations for equitable AI integration. This toolkit makes the research usable for other faculty who want to adopt similar strategies but may lack the time or expertise to design studies themselves.
- **Deliverable 3: Policy and Practice Recommendations Brief.** Faculty translate their findings into a concise policy brief that outlines implications for curriculum design, assessment practices, and institutional equity strategies. This brief may include recommendations such as safeguards for over-reliance on AI, guidelines for transparency in student work, or approaches to supporting students with lower confidence in digital tools. Such a deliverable ensures the project contributes not only to scholarly inquiry but also to institutional decision-making.

Case Example: Business School Innovation Microgrants

Consider, at a mid-sized university, the business school launched a microgrant program offering **$1,500 awards** to faculty interested in redesigning one major course assignment. Faculty were encouraged to integrate:

- **Prompt engineering** as a metacognitive skill.
- **AI-assisted drafts** paired with human revision and critique.
- **Reflective commentaries** on tool reliability, authorship, and ethical implications.

All grant recipients were required to document their process in detail, ensuring that their experimentation with AI pedagogy produced both evidence and transparency. Each participant uploaded assignment guides, reflection notes, and grading rubrics to an internal AI Teaching Repository, making their work accessible for review and reuse. **This practice not only preserved individual insights but also created a shared institutional resource**, allowing colleagues across departments to adapt, iterate, and scale these innovations in their own teaching contexts.

Strategic Benefits

While seed grants and micro-innovation funds may seem modest in scope, their strategic benefits extend far beyond the immediate projects they support. By empowering faculty to test new ideas, document outcomes, and share resources, these initiatives cultivate a culture of experimentation that is both sustainable and scalable. Importantly, the ripple effects of these investments include not only innovative classroom practices but also strengthened cross-disciplinary collaboration, institutional learning, and a shared sense of ownership over the evolving role of AI in higher education. These broader advantages translate into concrete institutional gains, which can be seen in several key areas where microgrants deliver immediate and lasting value

- **Low Risk, High Creativity.** Microgrants invite experimentation without requiring large-scale curricular overhaul. Faculty can **test ideas, learn from failure, and iterate quickly** - a necessary condition in a fast-changing AI landscape.
- **Cross-Pollination and Community Building.** By offering grants across disciplines, **institutions foster intellectual cross-pollination** by encouraging faculty to adapt ideas, methods, and practices from fields outside their own. These opportunities often spark interdisciplinary partnerships that extend well beyond the project term, laying the groundwork for long-term collaboration, joint publications, or future grant proposals.
- **Scalable Outputs for Institutional Learning.** Small grants, when documented and shared, become **building blocks of a scalable AI pedagogy ecosystem**. Institutions can compile outcomes into teaching guides, workshop curricula, or policy prototypes.
- **Early-Stage Pipeline for Larger Projects** Successful micrograntprojects often evolve into longer-term initiatives, grant proposals, or publications. The low-stakes environment helps faculty build momentum and confidence.

Summary: Empowering Innovation from the Ground Up

Seed grants and micro-innovation funds affirm that faculty insight, creativity, and professional judgment are the true engines of responsible AI integration. By resourcing small-scale projects, institutions acknowledge that meaningful innovation often begins with individual faculty experimenting at the classroom level. **These programs validate faculty as thought leaders while ensuring that AI adoption is guided by pedagogical care and intellectual responsibility rather than by top-down mandates**.

When institutions allocate even modest funding to this work, they create conditions where AI is not simply imposed as a tool, but instead explored, critiqued, and humanized as a pedagogical partner. **This allows faculty to investigate both the opportunities and risks of generative systems in ways that remain aligned with their disciplinary values**. In turn, institutions cultivate an environment where innovation thrives without compromising integrity, equity, or the human-centered mission of education.

By resourcing reflective experimentation at the classroom level, micrograants help ensure that the AI-enhanced university remains grounded in care, curiosity, and disciplinary integrity. They provide faculty with the freedom to take risks, test new methods, and generate shareable practices without the pressure of large-scale implementation. **Ultimately, this sustained, small-scale innovation creates a culture of iterative learning that strengthens both faculty agency and institutional resilience in an era of technological change**.

Structure for Scalable AI Support 5: Scaffolded Pathways from Literacy to Leadership

---

A successful institutional approach to AI integration cannot rely on isolated workshops, one-size-fits-all initiatives, or optional "tech add-ons." Instead, it requires a **strategically tiered model of professional learning** that recognizes where faculty are starting, honors the complexity of their disciplines, and provides structured opportunities for growth over time. The goal is to create clear, visible, and achievable entry points that help faculty progress from **initial awareness to sustained leadership**, while fostering a shared culture of curiosity, agency, and pedagogical integrity.

Scaffolded development models ensure that AI engagement is not restricted to a handful of enthusiastic early adopters but becomes a shared responsibility across the institution. By creating pathways that meet faculty at different levels of readiness, these models affirm that every educator - regardless of discipline or technical background - has a role to play in shaping AI's integration into teaching and learning. **They shift the narrative from faculty as passive recipients of technology to active contributors** who serve as critical thinkers, institutional stewards, and designers of ethical learning environments (Brookfield, 2017; Reiss, 2021).

Four-Stage Framework for Faculty Growth and Institutional Alignment

Integrating generative AI into higher education is not simply a matter of training faculty on new tools - it requires a strategic, institution-wide approach to professional learning, cultural change, and shared governance. **Faculty need opportunities not just to learn the mechanics of AI tools but also to question their implications for knowledge, authority, and equity in academic life**. As educators face shifting definitions of authorship, assessment, and academic integrity, they require scaffolded opportunities to explore, reflect, implement, and ultimately lead conversations about responsible AI integration.

The following four-stage framework offers a roadmap for building AI capacity across the faculty body, while aligning support structures with institutional goals. By progressing from **awareness** to **engagement**, from **implementation** to **leadership**, this **model recognizes that AI readiness is a developmental process rather than a one-time achievement**. It affirms that faculty are not passive recipients of technological change - they are the architects of pedagogical transformation, shaping how students encounter and interpret AI in their disciplines.

Each stage includes tailored support mechanisms that respect where faculty are starting, foster interdisciplinary collaboration, and promote a culture of ethical innovation. These supports ensure that faculty are guided step by step, moving from basic literacy to advanced fluency and eventually into leadership roles where they help shape institutional policy. **The framework thus provides a blueprint for campus-wide AI readiness**, grounded in reflective practice, equity-mindedness, and sustainable growth that benefits both educators and students.

---

1. Awareness

Objective: Build baseline knowledge of what generative AI is, how it works, and why it matters.

Support Mechanisms:

- Campus-wide **keynote events** with AI thought leaders to spark institutional conversation.
- Self-paced **AI literacy modules** that explain core concepts (e.g., hallucination, prompt engineering, bias in training data).
- **Introductory video series** that frame AI in discipline-specific contexts and model responsible engagement.

Outcome: This stage normalizes uncertainty and reduces the intimidation factor, helping faculty enter the conversation without fear of being left behind (Selwyn, 2019). **By lowering the barrier to entry, institutions create an environment where experimentation feels safe and curiosity is rewarded, rather than punished**. The outcome is a stronger foundation for long-term engagement, where faculty see themselves as participants in a collective learning process rather than as isolated novices struggling to keep pace.

---

2. Engagement

Objective: Facilitate structured faculty dialogue and early-stage classroom experimentation.

Support Mechanisms:

- **Faculty Learning Communities (FLCs)** focused on AI-integrated pedagogy, assessment, and equity.
- **Interactive workshops** on topics such as syllabus redesign, AI ethics, and assignment integrity.
- **Co-taught interdisciplinary courses** that explore AI from multiple disciplinary perspectives (e.g., AI and Creativity, Algorithmic Justice).

Outcome: This stage allows faculty to test ideas in the community, develop a shared vocabulary, and explore the pedagogical relevance of AI to their field. **By engaging in**

dialogue with colleagues, they begin to see how different disciplines frame similar challenges, which fosters cross-pollination of strategies and perspectives. The result is a richer sense of collective ownership over AI integration, where experimentation is reinforced by shared reflection and mutual accountability.

---

3. Implementation

Objective: Support faculty in translating ideas into practice through course redesign, scholarly experimentation, and institutional contribution.

Support Mechanisms:

- Paid **faculty fellowships** for AI-integrated course development.
- **Team-teaching opportunities** across departments to pilot AI-infused modules.
- **Assignment redesign microgrants** for integrating AI into learning outcomes, reflection, and assessment.

Outcome: At this stage, faculty become producers of AI pedagogy, not just consumers - sharing artifacts, documenting practices, and informing campus-wide learning (Byars-Winston & Dahlberg, 2019). **Their contributions begin to shape institutional culture, providing practical models and tested strategies that colleagues can adapt within their own contexts**. Over time, this collective authorship builds a sustainable repository of knowledge, positioning faculty as co-architects of the university's evolving approach to AI in teaching and learning.

---

4. Leadership

Objective: Elevate faculty as institutional co-designers of policy, curriculum, and professional learning infrastructure.

Support Mechanisms:

- Participation in **AI policy working groups** (e.g., academic integrity updates, citation protocols, authorship guidelines).
- Appointment to **campus AI task forces** to advise on ethical use, instructional integration, and vendor selection.
- Leadership in **cross-campus showcases**, symposia, or research groups on AI and pedagogy.

Outcome: This final stage allows institutions to recognize and amplify faculty innovation, positioning educators as central actors in shaping an ethical and inclusive future for AI in higher education. By elevating faculty contributions into policy discussions, curriculum frameworks, and public scholarship, institutions reinforce that innovation is not peripheral but mission-critical. Ultimately, **this outcome builds a culture where educators serve as both guardians of academic values and leaders in reimagining the role of AI across teaching, research, and civic life**.

Why This Four-Stage Framework Progression Matters

Without a clear developmental structure, AI pedagogy risks are framed as either:

- An **optional tool for tech-savvy faculty**, or;
- A **top-down requirement disconnected from faculty autonomy and values**.

By contrast, scaffolded pathways:

- **Honor Professional Identity**. Faculty see themselves not as replaceable by AI, but as curators of meaning in an AI-mediated world.
- **Build Cross-Functional Fluency**. Faculty learn to speak across disciplinary, technological, and ethical domains.
- **Cultivate Reflective Leadership**. Faculty are supported in asking not only "how" but also "why" and "when" AI should shape learning.

Outcome: This model aligns with adult learning theory, which emphasizes autonomy, application, and relevance as key conditions for engagement (Brookfield, 2017). As a result, **faculty are more likely to internalize AI pedagogy when they see it connected to their own disciplinary practices, immediate classroom challenges, and professional values**. The outcome is deeper ownership of the learning process, where educators actively shape AI integration rather than passively adopting tools.

Summary: From Entry to Influence

Scaffolded pathways ensure that faculty development is not a moment - but a movement. Rather than treating AI as a temporary trend, they frame it as an ongoing professional journey that grows alongside shifting tools, disciplines, and ethical challenges. **When designed with care, these pathways invite all faculty - regardless of role, rank, or discipline - to participate in a shared institutional journey from awareness to agency, from curiosity to contribution, from literacy to leadership**.

In doing so, institutions make clear that AI fluency is not merely a technical competency - it is a pedagogical and civic imperative. **By linking professional growth to mission, values, and equity, colleges and universities ensure that faculty see AI engagement as integral to both their teaching and their public responsibility**. This collective approach underscores that readiness for the algorithmic age must be built from the ground up, together, with transparency, inclusivity, and shared ownership at its core.

Institutional Readiness Indicators

As generative AI transforms the landscape of higher education, institutions face a choice: respond reactively with scattered, one-off initiatives - or build a coordinated, values-driven infrastructure that supports ethical, inclusive, and sustainable innovation. To determine whether AI development on campus is **systemic rather than sporadic**, leaders must assess not just adoption rates or workshop attendance, but the **coherence, alignment, and equity** of their institutional approach.

The following indicators serve as a diagnostic tool to evaluate whether an institution is **ready to support faculty, students, and staff** in navigating AI's academic and civic implications. These indicators are not exhaustive, but they reflect the **interdependent dimensions of leadership, culture, pedagogy, and accountability** needed for meaningful and mission-aligned AI integration.

Key Indicators of Institutional AI Readiness

Institutional AI Readiness Indicator 1: Is There a Campus-Wide Vision for Ethical AI Use in Teaching?

AI readiness begins with a **shared, articulated vision** - grounded in academic values, civic responsibility, and disciplinary diversity. Institutions that lead with intention have publicly accessible statements on:

- The pedagogical opportunities and ethical risks of AI.
- Core principles such as transparency, fairness, human agency, and academic integrity.
- The roles of faculty, students, and administrators in shaping AI use.

Such a vision is not merely a policy - it becomes a cultural anchor that guides decision-making, resource allocation, and faculty development priorities (Reiss, 2021; Selwyn, 2019). When institutions articulate AI principles as part of their mission, those commitments shape everything from how syllabi are designed to how funding is distributed. Over time, this shared vision provides coherence and accountability, ensuring that **AI adoption is pursued not just for efficiency but also for alignment with educational values and ethical standards**.

Institutional AI Readiness Indicator 2: Are AI Literacy Goals Integrated into General Education and Faculty Onboarding?

Systemic readiness requires that AI is not confined to specialized courses or tech-savvy departments. Institutions should embed AI literacy into:

- **General education learning outcomes**, especially around digital literacy, ethical reasoning, and critical thinking.
- **First-year faculty orientation and onboarding**, helping faculty across disciplines understand how AI intersects with assessment, authorship, and academic norms.
- Ongoing development for adjuncts, graduate faculty, and support staff to ensure **broad-based inclusion**.

This alignment affirms that **AI fluency is a core academic competency, not a niche specialization** (Brookfield, 2017; Byars-Winston & Dahlberg, 2019). By embedding AI literacy into general education and faculty development, institutions signal that all learners and educators - regardless of discipline - must engage critically with intelligent systems. In doing so, **campuses establish AI readiness as a shared academic expectation, positioning it**

alongside writing, critical thinking, and ethical reasoning as essential for success in higher education and beyond.

Institutional AI Readiness Indicator 3: Are Faculty Rewarded or Recognized for AI-Related Innovation?

Without structural incentives, AI pedagogical leadership remains dependent on personal interest and unpaid labor. Institutions can demonstrate readiness by ensuring that:

- AI-integrated teaching is eligible for **teaching awards, innovation grants, or merit recognition**.
- Curriculum redesign with AI is acknowledged in **promotion and tenure reviews**.
- Faculty who contribute to institutional AI policy, training, or research are recognized as **leaders in educational transformation**, not merely "early adopters."

This creates a culture of professional legitimacy around AI innovation and prevents burnout among those doing invisible digital labor (Reiss, 2021). When institutions formally recognize and reward faculty contributions to AI-integrated pedagogy, they transform what might otherwise be seen as extra, unacknowledged work into valued scholarly practice. This validation encourages broader participation, sustains momentum, and ensures that AI innovation becomes a collective responsibility rather than an isolated burden.

Institutional AI Readiness Indicator 4: Are Diverse Roles Included in Strategic Planning and Resource Allocation?

AI integration is a multi-role endeavor. Institutional readiness depends on including:

- **Librarians** who bring expertise in information literacy and citation practices.
- **Instructional designers** who support pedagogy and accessibility.
- **Academic technologists** who advise on platform security and privacy.
- **Adjuncts and contingent faculty** who often face different constraints but play essential roles in teaching and innovation.

When these voices are included in planning and resourcing, institutions avoid siloed implementation and cultivate campus-wide ownership of AI readiness (Crawford, 2021; Slimi & Carballido, 2023). This inclusive approach ensures that multiple perspectives - from librarians and instructional designers to technologists and adjunct faculty - are represented in decision-making, leading to solutions that reflect the realities of teaching and learning across contexts. By **distributing responsibility in this way, campuses foster a sense of shared stewardship, making AI integration more equitable, sustainable, and aligned with institutional values**.

Institutional AI Readiness Indicator 5: Is there an Evaluation Strategy to Measure the Impact of AI Development?

Readiness is not static - it must be **measured, reflected upon, and iterated**. Institutions committed to systemic AI development invest in:

- **Regular feedback mechanisms** (e.g., surveys, focus groups, course evaluations) to understand how faculty and students experience AI tools and policies.
- **Assessment frameworks** that track learning outcomes, engagement, and ethical understanding related to AI.
- **Annual reviews** of AI programming and resource use, with a transparent process for adjusting strategy.

Evaluation ensures that innovation is not only exciting - it is effective, equitable, and aligned with institutional mission. By embedding mechanisms such as surveys, focus groups, and outcome assessments, institutions can verify that new AI initiatives genuinely enhance learning and faculty practice rather than creating unintended inequities. This process also provides **a feedback loop that allows campuses to refine strategies over time**, ensuring that AI adoption remains mission-driven, sustainable, and responsive to the needs of students and educators alike.

Summary: Readiness as Culture, Not Compliance

AI readiness is not a checklist - it is a reflection of **institutional culture, leadership, and design**. The indicators above offer a framework for intentional growth, enabling campuses to move from reactive adaptation to proactive transformation. When institutions embed AI literacy into their policies, pedagogy, and practices - and when they do so collaboratively - they cultivate a **shared foundation for ethical and empowered engagement in the algorithmic age**.

Section Reflection: Designing Institutional Pathways that Transform AI Engagement into Collective Capability

This section reframes AI faculty development as an institutional responsibility rather than an individual initiative, emphasizing that systemic integration of AI into higher education demands more than sporadic workshops or tool-focused training. Instead, it requires the creation of coherent, scaffolded ecosystems that support faculty growth from literacy to leadership. Through its critique of common limitations - episodic offerings, tool-centric approaches, and siloed delivery - it calls for a coordinated infrastructure rooted in interdisciplinary collaboration, shared governance, and strategic alignment with institutional values.

By outlining concrete structures such as Faculty Learning Communities, course redesign fellowships, cross-role collaboration hubs, seed grants, and four-stage development pathways, the section offers a blueprint for sustainable, inclusive, and ethical faculty engagement with AI. It asserts that faculty innovation must be recognized, resourced, and connected to broader teaching and learning missions if institutions are to remain relevant and resilient in the AI era. Ultimately, this section makes clear that institutional AI readiness is not about adopting new tools - it is about cultivating a culture where curiosity, collaboration, and critical reflection are the engines of transformation.

Section 4: Faculty Learning Communities and Peer Mentorship Models

---

As higher education navigates the complexities of AI, one-size-fits-all workshops and hierarchical training structures often fall short. In contrast, **Faculty Learning Communities (FLCs)** and **peer mentorship models** offer **sustained, collegial, and interdisciplinary support**, enabling faculty to explore AI in a way that is **context-sensitive, curiosity-driven, and collaboratively scaffolded** (Brookfield, 2017; Cox, 2004).

These peer-based approaches foster:

- **Mutual accountability without surveillance.**
- **Cultural transformation over compliance.**
- **Grassroots innovation from faculty at all levels.**
- **Safe spaces for inquiry, failure, and iterative growth.**

Faculty learning communities (FLCs) and mentorship structures serve as powerful catalysts for institutional growth in the AI era. By creating intentional spaces for experimentation and reflection, these structures allow faculty to test innovative teaching strategies without fear of failure, refining their approaches through ongoing dialogue and peer feedback. **This process not only strengthens individual teaching practices but also builds institutional capacity** for ethical, sustainable, and innovative AI integration.

When institutions invest in FLCs and mentorship, they signal to faculty that curiosity, collaboration, and risk-taking are valued as part of professional development. This recognition empowers educators to engage deeply with AI while modeling the kind of reflective, adaptive learning that students themselves are being asked to cultivate. In this way, **professional development becomes both a practical and symbolic commitment** to building a resilient, future-ready academic culture.

Ultimately, these investments transform AI from an external disruption into an internal driver of pedagogical renewal. Faculty become co-creators of institutional knowledge, rather than passive adopters of external technologies. **By linking faculty development directly to mentorship and community-building, universities align innovation with their broader mission** of cultivating lifelong learners and ethical leaders.

Why FLCs Work for AI Capacity Building

As generative AI reshapes the landscape of higher education, faculty need more than tool training - they need sustained, reflective, and relational spaces to make sense of AI's instructional, ethical, and disciplinary implications. **Faculty Learning Communities (FLCs)** offer one of the most effective and scalable models for building institutional capacity in this area. Unlike one-time workshops or top-down mandates, FLCs foster **peer-driven, interdisciplinary inquiry** that aligns with how adults learn and how innovation actually spreads in complex academic environments.

AI is not a static subject - it is **fast-evolving, context-dependent, and ethically charged**. As such, it demands learning structures that accommodate ambiguity, invite experimentation, and foster collective meaning-making. FLCs meet this need by creating **trust-based, sustained cohorts** where faculty can explore, question, prototype, and reflect - together.

Core Strengths of FLCs for AI Pedagogy

Faculty Learning Communities (FLCs) bring unique advantages to the complex task of integrating AI into higher education. **Unlike one-off trainings or isolated workshops, FLCs foster continuity, collaboration, and reflection - qualities that are essential when navigating a fast-moving, ethically charged, and pedagogically disruptive technology such as generative AI**. Their strength lies not only in helping faculty understand tools but also in cultivating shared inquiry, cross-disciplinary dialogue, and cultural transformation, ensuring that AI pedagogy is grounded in values, equity, and human connection.

To illustrate these benefits more concretely, the following sections highlight four core strengths of FLCs for AI pedagogy, showing how they enable interdisciplinary dialogue, normalize uncertainty, center practical application, and create shared ethical language.

Strength of FLCs 1: Facilitate Interdisciplinary Dialogue

AI is not the domain of a single discipline. It touches law, medicine, literature, philosophy, business, and the arts. FLCs bring together faculty from across the curriculum, enabling rich conversations that **surface disciplinary blind spots**, challenge assumptions, and reveal opportunities for co-teaching and collaboration.

Example:

- *A data scientist and an art historian might co-develop a module on "Authorship and Originality in the Age of AI," examining both statistical patterns and aesthetic judgment.*

This cross-pollination strengthens institutional AI fluency, ensuring that innovation is **not confined to technical fields but broadly relevant and culturally responsive** (Bender et al., 2021; Floridi et al., 2018). By bringing together diverse disciplinary perspectives, **FLCs allow faculty to uncover new applications of AI that resonate with varied cultural contexts, ethical commitments, and student experiences**. In doing so, they help institutions build a more inclusive and adaptable approach to AI integration - one that recognizes both the technical possibilities and the human dimensions of educational change.

Strength of FLCs 2: Normalize Exploration and Uncertainty

Unlike formal training environments, FLCs are designed to **embrace uncertainty** as a necessary part of learning. This is essential in the context of AI, where:

- Tools evolve rapidly.
- Policies are still emerging.
- Student use patterns are unpredictable.

Faculty may enter AI-related conversations with excitement, anxiety, resistance, or skepticism. **FLCs provide psychological safety - a space where it is acceptable to ask "naive" questions, share imperfect experiments, and reflect on ethical dilemmas without fear of judgment** (Brookfield, 2017). In this environment, uncertainty is reframed as a catalyst for growth rather than a weakness, allowing faculty to build confidence, experiment openly, and develop more thoughtful and ethically grounded approaches to AI integration.

Strength of FLCs 3: Decenter Technical Expertise and Center Practical Application

FLCs do not require members to be AI experts. Instead, they create a culture where **practical, student-centered experimentation is prioritized** over technical fluency. This empowers faculty from non-STEM fields - often underrepresented in AI pedagogy discussions - to engage meaningfully and contribute valuable insight.

Example:

- *An English professor, for example, may bring expertise in authorship and rhetorical framing to conversations about AI writing tools, while a counseling faculty member might raise critical concerns about student identity, trust, and over-reliance on automation.*

This epistemic diversity deepens institutional AI pedagogy, **ensuring that implementation reflects values as much as capabilities**. By drawing from multiple disciplines and perspectives, faculty create approaches that balance technical utility with ethical, cultural, and relational considerations. As a result, **AI pedagogy evolves into a more inclusive and context-sensitive practice**, better equipped to serve diverse student populations and institutional missions.

Strength of FLCs 4: Create Shared Language for Reflecting on Ethics and Pedagogy

AI raises new questions about:

- *"What counts as original work?"*
- *"When is tool use educational vs. evasive?"*
- *"How do we assess thinking when machines produce the text?"*

FLCs support the development of **communal frameworks for discussing AI use** in teaching, moving faculty beyond personal opinions to **shared norms and reflective language**.

Through collective dialogue, participants begin to articulate shared expectations, ethical considerations, and pedagogical boundaries that transcend individual classrooms. Over time, these collaboratively developed frameworks shape not only classroom practice, but also **departmental policies, student-facing guidelines, and academic integrity standards**, ensuring coherence and trust across the institution.

Research Insight: The Power of FLCs in Times of Change

Cox (2004) and Richlin and Cox (2004) found that FLCs consistently:

- Increase **instructional innovation**.
- Improve **faculty satisfaction and morale**.
- Support **retention and professional development**, especially during periods of institutional transition or uncertainty.

Given the cognitive, emotional, and ethical stressors associated with AI adoption, these findings are particularly relevant. Faculty Learning Communities **provide not only a buffer against the uncertainty of technological change but also a supportive environment** where challenges can be shared and reframed as opportunities for growth. By fostering a sense of community, purpose, and resilience, FLCs help faculty navigate disruption in ways that reinforce both professional identity and institutional trust.

Summary: FLCs as Engines of Cultural Transformation

AI will not reshape higher education through technology alone. The true transformation will occur through **faculty who feel equipped, supported, and confident enough to guide their students in this new landscape**. Faculty Learning Communities (FLCs) create the ideal environment for this work, blending interdisciplinary collaboration, reflective pedagogy, and grassroots innovation in a structure that is both scalable and human-centered.

When institutions invest in AI-focused FLCs, they are not simply adding technical training sessions - they are building capacity for ethical, creative, and collective learning. These communities nurture inquiry, empathy, and shared accountability, helping faculty move from fragmented responses to coherent and sustainable practices. In this way, FLCs cultivate **a culture of care, curiosity, and pedagogical integrity** that ensures education remains deeply human, even in an algorithmic age.

Effective Design Elements for AI-Focused Faculty Learning Communities (FLCs)

Design matters. While Faculty Learning Communities are inherently powerful spaces for inquiry and collaboration, **their success in addressing AI pedagogy depends heavily on how they are structured and supported**. The most impactful FLCs are not accidental - they are intentionally crafted to balance diversity of perspective with psychological safety, blending practical experimentation with ethical reflection.

To achieve this balance, **institutions must pay attention to core design elements that shape how faculty enter, participate in, and sustain the work of AI integration**. These elements - ranging from cohort size and composition, to meeting cadence, to shared deliverables and visibility - create the scaffolding that transforms FLCs from informal conversations into engines of institutional change.

What follows is a set of key design elements that highlight how AI-focused FLCs can be organized for maximum depth, trust, and cultural impact. Each element offers both practical guidance and a vision for how faculty learning can be transformed into a driver of ethical, collaborative innovation.

Design Element 1: Size and Composition

The success of an AI-focused Faculty Learning Community (FLC) hinges in large part on its structure. While content matters, **cohort design - who is in the room, how they engage, and why they are there - ultimately shapes the depth and quality of inquiry, reflection, and collaboration**. In the context of generative AI - where uncertainty, novelty, and ethical tension are especially high - **intentionality in size and composition becomes critical** to ensuring that participants feel both supported and challenged.

A well-designed FLC balances **diversity of perspective with intimacy of dialogue**, creating a psychologically safe and intellectually generative environment. Such communities encourage faculty not only to experiment with AI tools but also to interrogate their broader **disciplinary implications, institutional constraints, and pedagogical possibilities**. This combination of experimentation and reflection ensures that faculty development is not limited to technical adoption, but is grounded in values-driven, context-sensitive innovation (Brookfield, 2017; Reiss, 2021).

Ideal Size: 6–12 Faculty Members

An optimal group size for an AI-focused FLC is 8 to 12 participants. This range is large enough to:

- Represent multiple disciplines and instructional contexts.
- Facilitate cross-pollination of ideas.
- Sustain dialogue even when some members miss a session.

At the same time, it is small enough to:

- Build trust and allow for personal reflection.
- Enable **rich, focused dialogue** instead of surface-level discussion.
- Support iterative learning, where members build on each other's insights over time.

Larger groups risk diluting engagement or defaulting to presentation formats, while smaller groups may struggle with sustainability or diversity of thought. Scholarship on Faculty Learning Communities suggests that an optimal size is typically **8–12 participants**, which balances diversity of perspective with intimacy of dialogue and accountability (Cox, 2004). Staying within **this range helps ensure active participation, equitable airtime, and sustainable collaboration across the life of the cohort**.

Mixed Disciplines and Experience Levels

AI impacts all fields - but not equally. A vibrant AI pedagogy community thrives on **disciplinary contrast**, where a computer science faculty member can learn from a writing instructor, and a design professor can exchange methods with a nursing educator. These conversations allow participants to:

- Explore **how AI reconfigures disciplinary knowledge** (e.g., what counts as original, rigorous, or ethical).
- Share **pedagogical tensions and adaptations** from diverse teaching formats (e.g., studio critique vs. lab report).
- Identify opportunities for **team-teaching, co-authored modules, or interdisciplinary assignment design**.

In addition to disciplinary breadth, **FLCs benefit from including participants at various levels of AI fluency - from hesitant first-time users to confident early adopters**. This intentional mix creates opportunities for reciprocal learning, where those with less experience can gain confidence while more advanced users are challenged to articulate their practices and assumptions. **The result is a culture of mutual mentoring**, where vulnerability and innovation are equally valued, and knowledge is constructed through dialogue rather than hierarchy.

Voluntary Participation with Incentives

FLCs work best when participants **choose to be there**. Voluntary participation ensures that members are intrinsically motivated, open to learning, and ready to share and reflect. However, to support meaningful engagement and honor faculty labor, institutions should provide **tangible incentives**, such as:

- **Stipends** for participation and deliverables (e.g., AI-infused assignments or syllabi).
- **Course-release or overload credit** for FLC facilitation or curriculum development.
- **Travel funds** for presenting AI pedagogy work at conferences or symposia.

These incentives do more than motivate - **they signal that AI integration is institutionally valued, and that pedagogical labor around innovation, ethics, and technology is a form of scholarly contribution** (Byars-Winston & Dahlberg, 2019). By offering stipends, course releases, or recognition in tenure and promotion processes, institutions communicate that **experimenting with AI is not peripheral work, but central to the mission of teaching and learning**. In this way, incentives function as both practical support and symbolic validation, affirming that faculty efforts in AI pedagogy are contributions to scholarship, institutional growth, and the evolving culture of higher education.

Framing Through Thematic Cohort Titles

The title of the FLC should do more than describe its function - it should reflect its **ethos, scope, and guiding inquiry**. Compelling titles invite curiosity and set the tone for collaborative reflection. For example:

- **"Teaching in the Age of AI."** A broad and inclusive title that welcomes educators from all disciplines and experience levels, focused on foundational awareness, exploration, and adaptation.
- **"AI and Authorship Across Disciplines."** A cohort focused on questions of originality, co-creation, and citation in AI-enhanced writing, design, and analysis. Ideal for faculty teaching writing-intensive, studio-based, or reflective assignments.
- **"Designing Human-Centered AI Learning Experiences."** A community dedicated to aligning AI use with student equity, accessibility, creativity, and critical thinking. Ideal for those concerned with **ethical design, inclusive teaching, and AI tool transparency**.

These thematic framings help faculty self-select based on their interests and concerns while providing structure for readings, workshops, and collaborative outputs. **By organizing FLCs around themes such as authorship, creativity, or ethics, institutions create clear entry points that feel relevant and motivating to participants**. At the same time, these framings ensure that discussions remain focused and generative, helping cohorts move from open-ended curiosity to tangible deliverables and shared institutional contributions.

Summary: Designing for Depth, Diversity, and Trust

Effective **AI-focused FLCs are not accidental - they are designed for relational depth, cognitive diversity, and pedagogical trust**. They thrive when intentionally structured to balance openness with focus, ensuring that faculty feel both supported and challenged as they navigate unfamiliar terrain. When institutions assemble small, interdisciplinary cohorts of voluntary participants - supported by meaningful incentives and anchored by compelling thematic focus - they create an environment where critical innovation is more likely to emerge, sustain, and scale.

In such spaces, **faculty are not only learning about AI - they are redefining what it means to teach, assess, and mentor in a world increasingly shaped by intelligent systems**. These communities encourage educators to move beyond surface-level tool use toward deeper reflection on how AI reshapes epistemology, equity, and academic identity. By engaging in this collaborative inquiry, faculty help chart a vision of higher education that is both technologically responsive and firmly rooted in human values.

Design Element 2: Meeting Structure and Frequency

To foster meaningful engagement and sustained inquiry, AI-focused Faculty Learning Communities (FLCs) must be intentionally structured - not rigidly prescriptive, but thoughtfully scaffolded to allow for both depth and flexibility. This intentionality ensures that participants are not only experimenting with tools but also wrestling with the larger pedagogical and ethical questions that AI raises. In the context of a rapidly evolving technological and educational landscape, **consistency and rhythm become essential**: they help build trust, support iterative experimentation, and guarantee that issues of fairness, bias, and academic integrity are considered alongside technical exploration.

The ideal meeting structure for an AI-focused FLC balances **content knowledge, collaborative practice, and reflective discussion, creating an environment where faculty can grow both individually and collectively**. Such a design ensures that sessions do not collapse into either abstract theorizing or narrow tool tutorials, but instead blend exploration with application. This balance allows faculty to move from curiosity to meaningful classroom integration - and ultimately to positions of broader institutional leadership, where they can help shape policy, culture, and strategic vision around AI pedagogy.

Meeting Cadence: 6–8 Sessions per Semester

A biweekly meeting schedule - typically 6 to 8 sessions across a semester - offers enough continuity to build momentum without overwhelming participants. This cadence allows faculty to:

- Engage in real-time tool experimentation and classroom implementation.
- Reflect between sessions on student response, instructional shifts, and ethical tensions.
- Build progressively toward shared deliverables, such as revised syllabi, teaching artifacts, or policy recommendations.

This rhythm also reflects the cognitive and logistical realities of academic calendars, ensuring that **faculty development is embedded in - not layered on top of - existing teaching responsibilities** (Brookfield, 2017; Cox, 2004). By aligning with the natural pacing of the semester, such structures help faculty integrate professional learning into their teaching cycles rather than treating it as an additional burden. This integration not only increases participation but also enhances sustainability, as development becomes part of the ongoing rhythm of academic life rather than a disruptive or temporary add-on.

Integrated Learning Modalities in Each Session

Each meeting should blend multiple modalities to support different types of faculty engagement. An effective session structure typically considers the following four modalities:

Integrated Learning Modality 1: Curated Readings

Select short, provocative texts that spark dialogue about AI's ethical, epistemological, or disciplinary implications. Examples include:

- *On the Dangers of Stochastic Parrots* (Bender et al., 2021).
- *Race After Technology* (Benjamin, 2023).

- *Atlas of AI* (Crawford, 2021).
- MLA and APA citation guidelines for generative AI.

These readings anchor technical exploration in critical reflection and socio-historical context, helping faculty see AI not just as a tool, but as a force shaping knowledge systems. **By engaging with scholarship that examines bias, equity, and epistemic authority, faculty develop a more nuanced understanding of how technological design reflects broader cultural and political values**. This process equips them to guide students in recognizing that every AI-generated output is embedded within human choices, historical conditions, and contested frameworks of knowledge.

Integrated Learning Modality 2: Tool Exploration

Each session should provide space for hands-on experimentation with one or more AI tools (e.g., ChatGPT, Perplexity.ai, DALL·E, Scite, Adobe Firefly). The aim is not just technical fluency, but **critical literacy** - testing, challenging, and contextualizing tool output. Faculty might:

- Compare outputs across tools using the same prompt.
- Reverse-engineer an AI-generated outline to identify disciplinary gaps.
- Evaluate the rhetorical tone or ethical framing in generated content.

This type of applied experimentation helps demystify AI, moving conversations away from abstract fears or uncritical enthusiasm into evidence-based practice. Faculty gain firsthand insight into the strengths and limitations of different platforms, while also identifying how their disciplinary values shape interpretation of the results. Over time, this reflective cycle builds a deeper form of critical AI fluency, where technical curiosity is balanced with ethical discernment and pedagogical intentionality.

Integrated Learning Modality 3: Case Study Discussion

Discuss real or hypothetical classroom scenarios that raise questions around:

- Academic integrity.
- Student trust and overreliance.
- AI and accessibility.
- Bias in generative content.

Faculty can bring examples from their own courses or respond to case studies drawn from teaching literature and current events. **This makes the discussion grounded in authentic practice, showing how AI challenges and opportunities manifest in real classrooms and disciplines**. By connecting broader debates to local teaching contexts, faculty are able to bridge theory and practice, fostering reflection that feels both relevant and actionable.

Integrated Learning Modality 4: Experimentation Planning and Reflection

Encourage each participant to **pilot a small AI-integrated change** in their course - an assignment revision, a policy clarification, a reflective prompt - and return to the next session with observations. These micro-experiments make innovation **safe, iterative, and grounded in context**. Reflection prompts might include:

- *"What surprised you about how students used AI in this assignment?"*
- *"What values did your policy language attempt to communicate?"*
- *"How did AI influence the depth or originality of student responses?"*

These reflections create a feedback loop that transforms classroom experimentation into collective learning for the entire community. **By surfacing patterns across multiple courses and disciplines, they allow FLC members to identify both common challenges and innovative strategies for integrating AI**. Over time, this process builds a shared knowledge base that strengthens institutional capacity while cultivating a culture of inquiry, transparency, and pedagogical care.

Sample Agenda (Week 3): Exploring Disciplinary Assumptions in AI Output

Pre-Meeting Reading:

- *Race After Technology*, Chapter 1 (Benjamin, 2023).
- Focus: How automated systems encode assumptions about behavior, knowledge, and value.

In-Session Activity:

- Prompt GPT-5 to *"generate a syllabus for an introductory course"* in a variety of disciplines (e.g., literature, nursing, economics, philosophy). Compare outputs for:
  - Voice and tone.
  - Assumed knowledge and values.
  - Types of assessment and reading assigned.

Discussion Questions:

- *"What implicit biases about disciplinary knowledge and academic labor appear in the outputs?"*
- *"How does the model reflect or distort your field's intellectual commitments?"*
- *"What might this suggest about using AI to scaffold student understanding - or misinform it?"*

Follow-Up Assignment: Revise one section of your own syllabus using an AI tool, and bring both the original and revised versions to the next meeting for peer feedback.

Learning Outcome: By completing this exercise, faculty will be able to identify how generative AI reproduces or distorts disciplinary norms, strengthening their critical AI literacy. They will develop the capacity to compare human- and AI-generated syllabus designs, drawing insight into the alignment - or misalignment - between pedagogical intent and machine output. Ultimately, participants will produce tangible artifacts that demonstrate reflective practice, which can be shared across the FLC to build a collective foundation for ethical and intentional AI integration.

Summary: Design for Depth, Dialogue, and Experimentation

Effective FLC sessions are not lectures; they are laboratories for thought, practice, and transformation. By designing meetings that balance theory and application, personal reflection and peer learning, AI-focused FLCs cultivate the **cognitive flexibility and ethical grounding** necessary for faculty to lead through uncertainty.

This design ensures that faculty are not just catching up with technology - they are shaping its place in higher education with **intentionality, care, and intellectual rigor**.

Design Element 3: Shared Deliverables and Visibility

Effective FLC sessions are not lectures; **they are laboratories for thought, practice, and transformation**. By intentionally designing meetings that balance theory with application, and personal reflection with peer learning, these **sessions become spaces where ideas are tested, refined, and contextualized**. In doing so, AI-focused FLCs help participants develop the cognitive flexibility and ethical grounding required to lead with confidence during times of technological disruption.

This design ensures that faculty are not just catching up with the latest technological shifts; they are actively shaping how these tools are integrated into higher education. By foregrounding intentionality, care, and intellectual rigor, **FLCs encourage faculty to critically question both the opportunities and risks of AI**. In this way, participants move from passive adaptation to proactive leadership, positioning themselves as co-creators of an ethical and pedagogically sound AI future (Byars-Winston & Dahlberg, 2019).

To maximize institutional impact, however, FLC learning cannot remain contained within the cohort. **The insights, practices, and experiments developed in these communities must be translated into tangible outputs that can inform broader teaching, policy, and professional development**. This is where *Deliverable and Dissemination Strategies* become essential, ensuring that the work of FLCs scales outward and shapes a collective culture of AI pedagogy.

Deliverable and Dissemination Strategy 1: AI-Infused Assignment or Syllabus Artifact

At the end of the semester, each participant should submit one redesigned assignment, syllabus section, or teaching activity that:

- Integrates AI use transparently (e.g., via a prompt, reflection task, or comparative analysis).
- Aligns with course learning objectives.

- Includes ethical scaffolding (e.g., a citation requirement or tool-use disclosure statement).
- Reflects disciplinary nuance in how AI is framed and evaluated.

These artifacts can be **compiled into a departmental or campus-wide teaching repository**, giving faculty across the institution a shared library of tested practices and pedagogical innovations. They may also be **integrated into a learning management system** (LMS), where faculty can easily access and adapt them for their own courses. In some cases, institutions may choose to make these resources public through digital collections of AI-enhanced pedagogies, extending their reach beyond the campus community.

Such deliverables function as peer-sourced models that showcase real examples of ethical and effective AI integration, **lowering the barrier for hesitant faculty to begin experimenting**. They not only provide concrete inspiration but also normalize responsible risk-taking, showing that innovation can be iterative and collaborative. Over time, **these shared outputs contribute to a growing culture of institutional knowledge**, where best practices in AI pedagogy evolve through collective effort rather than isolated trial and error.

Deliverable and Dissemination Strategy 2: Reflective Teaching Statement

Each FLC member should also write a **brief reflection (1–2 pages)** addressing questions such as:

- *"How has your understanding of AI's role in your discipline evolved?"*
- *"What surprised you about your students' use or response to AI?"*
- *"What risks did you take - and what did you learn from them?"*
- *"What ethical tensions emerged in your AI-integrated teaching?"*

These reflections serve several purposes:

- They create a record of pedagogical growth.
- They offer **personal narrative frameworks** for future workshops or publication.
- They model a **reflective stance** toward educational technology, rather than a compliance-based one (Brookfield, 2017; Reiss, 2021).

Compiled together, these statements can also inform program evaluation, offering evidence of how faculty are grappling with AI integration in authentic classroom settings. **They provide instructional designers and Center for Teaching and Learning (CTL) leaders with grounded insights into what is working, what challenges persist, and where additional support is most needed**. Over time, this feedback loop helps refine professional development offerings, ensuring they remain responsive to faculty experience, disciplinary diversity, and evolving institutional priorities.

Deliverable and Dissemination Strategy 3: Campus Symposium, Showcase, or Brown-Bag Talk

To promote **peer learning, institutional visibility, and cross-pollination**, FLCs should culminate in a public event where participants share insights, prototypes, or provocations from their semester of inquiry. Formats might include:

- A **faculty lightning round**, where each member shares a 5-minute "lesson learned."
- A **poster or resource fair**, displaying revised assignments or rubrics.
- A **panel discussion** on AI and pedagogy, moderated by a teaching center leader or librarian.

These events serve three important functions:

- **Model ethical and transparent AI use** in real classroom contexts.
- **Spark interest among non-FLC faculty** through relatable, grounded practice.
- **Normalize AI dialogue as pedagogical, not just technical**, making room for values-based engagement across disciplines (Benjamin, 2023; Selwyn, 2019).

These public showcases not only highlight the tangibles of an FLC but also create momentum for broader institutional engagement. By making experiments, challenges, and reflections visible, they encourage transparency and reduce the stigma around trial-and-error in AI pedagogy. Over time, these events can shift campus culture, **positioning AI integration as a collective academic endeavor rather than an isolated or optional pursuit**.

Why Visibility Matters

Without visibility, FLC outcomes risk remaining siloed - even when the cohort experience is transformational. Public deliverables and events:

- Extend the impact of FLCs by **creating institutional memory**.
- Establish AI pedagogy as a **collective, scholarly, and adaptive practice**.
- Support a culture of **collegial experimentation** rather than isolated implementation.
- Encourage wider campus buy-in and support **scaling through inspiration, not mandate**.

In short, **making the learning public invites others to join - not because they are required to, but because they see what is possible**. Publicly shared work sparks curiosity and demonstrates that experimentation with AI pedagogy is accessible and rewarding, lowering barriers for hesitant colleagues. Over time, this transparency creates a ripple effect, where individual efforts inspire collective innovation and help embed AI engagement into the culture of teaching and learning.

Summary: From Reflection to Institutional Diffusion

Shared deliverables and campus visibility transform the FLC from a closed community into an **engine of institutional learning and leadership**. They extend the influence of faculty work by creating tangible resources that colleagues across departments can adapt, ensuring that lessons learned are not lost but continuously built upon. In doing so, they **cultivate a**

culture where AI pedagogy is seen not as an isolated experiment but as a collective, evolving practice that strengthens institutional integrity and innovation.

Peer Mentorship Models for Scaling AI Fluency

While Faculty Learning Communities (FLCs) create structured, interdisciplinary cohorts for collective inquiry, **peer mentorship offers a complementary model for individualized support, trust-based experimentation, and scalable capacity building**. This form of mentorship allows faculty to learn in closer, more flexible relationships that respond to their immediate teaching challenges and questions. Especially in a landscape as fast-moving and uncertain as generative AI, peer mentorship provides an adaptive structure for **responsive, relational learning** grounded in collegial trust rather than hierarchical expertise.

Peer mentorship reduces isolation, flattens access to innovation, and promotes a culture of **collaborative knowledge exchange**, where all faculty - regardless of discipline, rank, or AI fluency - can contribute to institutional growth. By situating learning in reciprocal partnerships rather than formal training, it empowers faculty to co-create practical solutions that feel relevant to their classrooms and disciplines. Importantly, this approach redefines leadership not as authority over others, but as a commitment to shared reflection, ethical reasoning, and pedagogical stewardship (Brookfield, 2017; Byars-Winston & Dahlberg, 2019).

Together, FLCs and peer mentorship form a dual infrastructure for faculty development: one emphasizing community-scale innovation, and the other centering on personalized, trust-based growth. With this balance, **institutions can sustain both breadth and depth in their AI pedagogy efforts, ensuring transformation is both inclusive and scalable**. The following peer mentorship models illustrate how this complementary structure can be designed to support ethical, practical, and adaptive AI integration.

Peer Mentorship Model 1: Early Adopter Mentorship

In this model, faculty with more experience using AI in teaching partner with newer adopters to co-explore tool use, share assignments, and reflect on emerging challenges. Crucially, this is not a one-way transmission of knowledge - it is a **mutual learning partnership**, anchored in humility, trust, and shared purpose.

Key Design Elements:

- **Voluntary pairing**, based on expressed interest in mutual growth, not departmental assignment.
- **Focus on teaching goals** rather than disciplinary alignment - e.g., feedback loops, assessment, engagement.
- **Co-reflection over instruction** - mentors share what has worked (and not worked), while mentees bring fresh perspectives and contextual challenges.

Mentorship Activities May Include:

- Co-reviewing an AI-generated student product and identifying strengths/risks.
- Collaboratively designing a prompt-to-revision activity or reflective AI-use assignment.
- Holding informal debriefs after trying out a tool or policy in class.
- Co-authoring a department-wide FAQ or guidance document on appropriate AI use.

Example: Cross-Disciplinary Exchange

- *A* ***digital humanities professor*** *well-versed in using ChatGPT for natural language generation partners with a* ***sociology colleague*** *who is just beginning to explore AI's classroom potential. The digital humanist helps brainstorm ways to use ChatGPT for* ***drafting weekly discussion prompts****. In return, the sociologist introduces media literacy strategies for teaching students to identify* ***algorithmic bias in AI-generated summaries****.*
- *Together, they co-create a comparative activity that pairs* ***machine-generated discussion questions with student-written versions****, followed by reflection on source credibility, framing, and inclusivity.*

This **bidirectional mentorship approach democratizes expertise** by ensuring that both early adopters and newer faculty contribute to the learning process, making innovation a shared responsibility. In doing so, it cultivates humility and reciprocity, as experienced mentors share strategies while also learning new perspectives from colleagues less entrenched in AI practices. Ultimately, **this dynamic exchange strengthens critical AI fluency across fields**, embedding reflection, equity, and adaptability into the very fabric of faculty development (Benjamin, 2023; Noble, 2018).

Why Peer Mentorship Matters in AI Pedagogy

- **Trust Over Expertise**. Faculty are more likely to explore unfamiliar tools when the learning context is nonjudgmental. Peer mentorship lowers affective barriers by positioning exploration as a **shared endeavor**, not a performance of competence.
- **Contextual Responsiveness**. Unlike external workshops or generic modules, mentorship allows for **hyper-relevant problem-solving** based on teaching level, course structure, and disciplinary culture.
- **Distributed Innovation**. Mentorship relationships scale organically. As mentees gain confidence, they often become mentors to others - **scaling capacity through relationships**, not administrative mandates.
- **Integration with Departmental Culture**. Mentorship pairs can be nested within departments or across departments, depending on size and culture. In both cases, they **model professional learning as part of disciplinary engagement**, not just technical adaptation.

Summary: Reframing Mentorship as Mutual Inquiry

Peer mentorship is not about who knows more - **it is about who is willing to explore more thoughtfully, reflect more honestly, and share more generously**. In the context of AI integration, this model helps institutions **build relational infrastructure** that lasts beyond individual tools or training cycles. It promotes **ethical experimentation, interdependence, and pedagogical care** - qualities essential for navigating the uncertain terrain of AI-enhanced education.

Peer Mentorship Model 2: Cross-Disciplinary Pairing

Among the most powerful peer mentorship configurations for advancing AI fluency is **cross-disciplinary pairing** - intentionally matching faculty from different academic domains to co-explore the pedagogical, ethical, and epistemological implications of generative AI. This approach reframes AI integration not as a technical hurdle for specialists but instead as a shared intellectual space where diverse fields bring their values and methods into conversation. In doing so, the model transcends traditional mentorship hierarchies, **positioning all participants as co-learners in exploring the cultural, civic, and disciplinary stakes of AI**.

Cross-disciplinary pairing fosters **cognitive flexibility, pedagogical innovation, and ethical depth** by requiring faculty to encounter perspectives outside their own disciplinary comfort zones. These collaborations generate richer teaching strategies and surface insights that discipline-specific conversations might overlook, broadening the scope of inquiry. **In particular, they highlight overlooked questions** - such as who benefits from automation, whose knowledge is amplified or marginalized by data-driven models, and how relational care and human judgment should be preserved alongside efficiency and scale (Benjamin, 2023; Floridi et al., 2018).

Core Purposes of Cross-Disciplinary Mentorship

- **Cross-Pollination of Pedagogical Methods**. AI impacts writing, coding, analysis, and design - but each discipline brings different methods for **teaching those skills, scaffolding complexity, and assessing process**. By pairing faculty from different traditions, cross-disciplinary mentorship allows for creative integration and reimagination of assignment structures, tool use, and student dialogue formats.
- **Framing AI Beyond Function**. While many disciplines focus on what AI can do, cross-disciplinary conversations foreground **why, how, and for whom it should be used**. Humanities and social science faculty can introduce frameworks for power, bias, and positionality. STEM faculty can clarify what technical assumptions and affordances underlie model performance. Together, they build **shared language around AI's civic, epistemic, and cultural dimensions** (Crawford, 2021; Noble, 2018).
- **Re-centering Equity and Human Judgment.** Disciplines such as education, public health, counseling, and social work emphasize **relational intelligence, systemic critique, and the ethics of care** - essential counterbalances to the logic of automation. When paired with colleagues in fields such as computer science, economics, or

engineering, these perspectives help design AI-enhanced learning environments that are not only efficient - but humane.

Sample Pairing in Practice

Participants: A **nursing instructor** and a **philosophy professor**

Project: Together, they co-design a **role-play simulation** in which students respond to a hypothetical scenario: an AI-powered triage system recommends early discharge for a patient flagged as low-risk. Students play the roles of clinical staff, family members, ethicists, and health administrators. The task is to:

- Evaluate the AI's decision based on patient context, risk modeling, and ethical codes.
- Debate competing priorities (resource optimization vs. relational care).
- Reflect on **empathy, fairness, and systemic bias** in algorithmic decisions.

Mentor Exchange:

- The nursing instructor guides the design to reflect **clinical realities, patient safety protocols, and documentation practices**.
- The philosophy professor supports student preparation with **ethics readings** (e.g., deontology vs. consequentialism) and debriefs with questions on algorithmic accountability and justice.

Outcome: Students develop both **technical fluency and ethical discernment**, gaining the ability to critically assess AI outputs while understanding their broader implications. They learn not only to question how AI systems function, but also to evaluate the values, assumptions, and trade-offs embedded within their design and deployment. Ultimately, this prepares them to make informed decisions about **how AI should - and should not - be used in contexts where human lives, equity, and moral responsibility are at stake**.

Strategic Benefits of Cross-Disciplinary Pairing

- **Prevents Narrow Technocentric Implementation**. Encourages nuanced thinking about AI's role in meaning-making, not just efficiency or performance.
- **Models Scholarly Dialogue Across Knowledge Cultures**. Helps students see that knowledge is contested, interdisciplinary, and relational.
- **Builds Institutional Bridges**. Fosters collaboration across departments, units, and epistemologies - strengthening AI integration as a shared academic endeavor, not a niche concern.
- **Promotes Student Transfer of Learning**. When students encounter AI pedagogy across disciplines - paired with varied ethical and contextual frames - they learn to adapt critically, not blindly adopt.

Summary: Designing AI Pedagogy Through Intellectual Dialogue

Cross-disciplinary pairing turns AI fluency into an **intellectual and cultural dialogue**, not just a technical skill set. It demonstrates that the future of teaching with AI depends not only on prompt engineering - but on **ethical co-design, reflective conversation, and mutual learning across fields**. When faculty mentor one another across disciplines, they co-create a campus culture where AI is integrated not through uniformity - but through diversity of thought, care, and conviction.

Peer Mentorship Model 3: Peer Coaching with Classroom Observation

---

While faculty often share ideas about generative AI informally - over coffee, in hallway conversations, or via shared resources - **peer coaching with structured classroom observation** offers a deeper, more transformative form of professional learning. When implemented with intentionality, observation-based coaching turns AI pedagogy from theory into **lived practice**, providing a powerful context for **reflective teaching, ethical discernment, and co-learning**.

In this model, faculty volunteers observe one another's AI-enhanced lessons and then engage in structured debrief conversations. The goal is not to evaluate performance, but to surface critical insights about **student engagement, instructional clarity, ethical tensions, and pedagogical adaptation** in real time. This process strengthens both teaching practice and institutional capacity by creating a culture of **peer accountability, iterative experimentation, and mutual trust** (Brookfield, 2017; Byars-Winston & Dahlberg, 2019).

Structure and Principles of Peer Coaching

Peer coaching with classroom observation is most effective when it is guided by intentional design rather than left to informal habits. While the core of this model is trust and reciprocity, its impact depends on clear structures that support psychological safety, meaningful observation, and reflective dialogue. **Establishing these principles ensures that coaching is not mistaken for evaluation**, but embraced as a collaborative practice that deepens pedagogical reflection and strengthens institutional capacity.

To achieve these goals, peer coaching must be built on three interconnected principles that shape participation, observation, and reflection. Together, they provide a roadmap for structuring observation-based mentorship in ways that are practical, ethical, and transformative. The following sections outline these principles in detail, showing how they can be enacted across diverse teaching contexts to maximize both individual growth and collective learning.

Structure and Principle 1: Voluntary, Trust-Based Participation

Peer coaching must be opt-in and framed as a **reciprocal growth opportunity**, not a form of surveillance or performance management. Faculty pair or group themselves based on mutual curiosity or complementary goals - for instance, exploring how students respond to:

- AI-assisted drafting exercises.
- Syllabus policies on tool use.
- Generative feedback integration.

This ensures psychological safety and frames observation as a **collaborative inquiry** into teaching, not a critique of individual style. Faculty can approach the process with openness, knowing that the goal is mutual growth rather than evaluation or judgment. In this way, peer observation becomes a supportive exercise in curiosity, reflection, and shared exploration of AI pedagogy.

Structure and Principle 2: Observation of AI-Enhanced Lessons

Faculty observe a peer teaching a lesson that includes some element of AI integration - whether visible (e.g., tool demonstrations, student prompts) or embedded (e.g., AI-enhanced feedback, AI-curated materials). They may focus their attention on:

- How the instructor frames AI tool use for students.
- What kinds of questions do students ask about AI reliability or bias?
- Whether students use AI as a shortcut or a scaffolding aid.
- How ethical or disciplinary considerations are made visible in class dialogue.

Observers take **low-inference notes** and remain non-intrusive, focusing on **student responses, decision points, and moments of engagement or tension**. This method ensures that feedback is grounded in observable behaviors rather than subjective judgments, making it more actionable and less personal. **By concentrating on student learning dynamics, observers help faculty gain insight into how AI integration shapes classroom interaction** without undermining trust or confidence.

Structure and Principle of 3: Post-Class Debrief Using Brookfield's Critical Incident Protocol

Following the observation, the pair meets for a debrief using **Brookfield's Critical Incident Protocol** (Brookfield, 2017), which includes four reflective questions:

- **When were Students Most Engaged?** This identifies moments where AI-enhanced teaching sparked inquiry, clarity, or collaboration.
- **When were Students Most Distanced or Confused?** Highlights where tool use may have introduced cognitive overload, ethical ambiguity, or disengagement.
- **What Did You, as the Instructor, Find Most Affirming?** Surfaces confidence-building practices for teaching with AI.
- **What Felt Most Challenging or Unresolved?** Brings to light areas of ethical tension, instructional uncertainty, or gaps in student understanding.

These questions guide **nonjudgmental, evidence-informed conversation**, helping faculty move beyond "what worked" into **why and how teaching with AI affects student learning, trust, and disciplinary values**. By framing dialogue around evidence rather than opinion, faculty can identify deeper patterns and implications that might otherwise remain hidden. This process not only **strengthens individual practice but also contributes to a culture of collective reflection and ethical inquiry** around AI integration in education.

Benefits of Observation-Based Peer Coaching for AI Integration

- **Moves from Abstraction to Application**. Seeing AI pedagogy in action provides **concrete examples and unexpected insights** that cannot be gleaned from discussion alone.
- **Builds Reflective Teaching Habits**. The post-observation reflection cultivates **intentional, inquiry-based practice**, allowing faculty to refine not only their tools but also their framing, modeling, and ethical stance.
- **Reinforces Transparency and Collegiality**. By making classroom practice visible, peer coaching models **professional vulnerability and collaborative growth**, especially important in a time of technological flux and pedagogical uncertainty.
- **Surfaces Institutional Insights**. Patterns across observations can inform faculty development planning, policy revisions, or AI resource guides - grounded in what faculty and students are actually doing and experiencing.

Summary: Turning Dialogue into Guided Practice

In a moment when educators are being asked to adapt quickly to complex technological shifts, **peer coaching with classroom observation offers a grounded, relational, and reflective approach to change**. It transforms isolated experimentation into shared inquiry, supports pedagogical growth through dialogue, and centers AI not as a gimmick - but as **a catalyst for deeper reflection on what it means to teach well**. By situating faculty learning within real classroom practice, this model ensures that professional development remains authentic, context-specific, and immediately applicable.

When grounded in trust and structured reflection, peer observation becomes a **cornerstone of ethical AI integration** - not just for early adopters, but for the entire teaching community. It provides a scalable method for spreading innovation while maintaining equity, inclusivity, and accountability in pedagogical practice. Over time, this approach fosters a collective culture where **AI is engaged critically, integrated thoughtfully, and leveraged to strengthen - not diminish - the human dimensions of education**.

Sample Topics for FLCs and Mentorship Pairings

The complexity of AI integration in higher education cannot be addressed through technical skill-building alone - it requires **structured inquiry into pedagogical, ethical, cultural, and**

cognitive dimensions. Faculty must grapple not only with how AI tools function, but also with the deeper implications they carry for knowledge, equity, and academic integrity. Faculty Learning Communities (FLCs) and mentorship pairings benefit from clear thematic focus areas that invite participants to move beyond surface-level usage into **critical, values-driven exploration**.

The sample topics below serve as **anchor points for deep discussion, reflective teaching, and co-designed experimentation**. Each topic is designed to open space for faculty to interrogate AI in ways that are relevant to their disciplines, teaching contexts, and students' lived realities. Together, they provide layered questions that can guide semester-long inquiry, workshop sessions, or mentorship dialogues - helping faculty interrogate not only what AI does, but **what it asks of us as educators and learners**.

Topic 1: Bias in Generative AI

Core Inquiry: *"How do large language models encode and amplify societal bias - and how can educators respond responsibly?"*

Discussion Questions:

- *"What types of bias (e.g., gendered, cultural, ideological, or disciplinary) appear in AI-generated outputs in your field?"*
- *"How can faculty frame AI tools as objects of analysis rather than neutral assistants?"*
- *"What role do prompt design, tool selection, and student training play in reducing harm?"*
- *"How might we teach students to critique AI outputs through lenses of equity and representation?"*

Classroom Application: Design an activity where students compare multiple AI outputs on the same prompt and analyze differences using media literacy or sociological frameworks (Benjamin, 2023; Noble, 2018).

Outcome: The outcome of this inquiry is that students begin to see AI outputs not as neutral artifacts, but as reflections of underlying assumptions embedded in data and design choices. **By comparing multiple outputs and analyzing them through equity and representation frameworks, they practice identifying patterns of bias and considering their implications.** Ultimately, this cultivates critical digital literacy, equipping learners to engage responsibly with AI while recognizing both its potential and its risks (Benjamin, 2023; Noble, 2018).

Topic 2: Academic Integrity and AI

Core Inquiry: *"What does honesty look like when human and machine contributions are entangled?"*

Discussion Questions:

- *"Where should the line be drawn between allowable assistance and academic dishonesty?"*

- *"How do institutional policies and classroom norms need to evolve?"*
- *"What does meaningful attribution look like in collaborative human–AI work?"*
- *"How can we shift the conversation from surveillance to ethical reflection?"*

Classroom Application: Require students to submit an "AI Use Disclosure Statement" alongside assignments, describing which tools they used, how they used them, and what changes they made during revision (Reiss, 2021; Slimi & Carballido, 2023).

Outcome: The outcome of this inquiry is that **students learn to distinguish between legitimate collaboration with AI and actions that cross into dishonesty**, developing a clearer sense of academic integrity in the AI era. Through disclosure practices, **they build habits of transparency and accountability, reinforcing the principle that authorship requires intentional human judgment and responsibility**. Ultimately, this approach transforms AI from a surveillance issue into an ethical dialogue, empowering students to navigate human–machine collaboration with honesty and reflection (Reiss, 2021; Slimi & Carballido, 2023).

Topic 3: Teaching Prompt Engineering

Core Inquiry: *"How do we teach students to collaborate with AI tools without outsourcing their thinking?"*

Discussion Questions:

- *"What constitutes an effective prompt in your discipline - and how is that skill similar to or different from traditional research design or problem framing?"*
- *"What cognitive risks exist when students use AI to generate outlines, thesis statements, or literature summaries?"*
- *"How can prompt writing become a metacognitive practice rather than a shortcut?"*

Classroom Application: Design a side-by-side assignment: students write a human-generated essay plan and compare it to an AI-generated one. Then, reflect on clarity, originality, and epistemic ownership.

Outcome: The outcome of this exercise is that **students learn to see AI collaboration as a process that complements rather than replaces their own intellectual effort**. By comparing human-generated and AI-generated plans, they **gain metacognitive awareness of where critical thinking, originality, and disciplinary framing matter most**. This strengthens their ability to use AI as a reflective partner in inquiry, while maintaining ownership of reasoning and epistemic responsibility.

Topic 4: AI for Feedback and Assessment

Core Inquiry: *"Can AI tools meaningfully support formative feedback, or do they risk undermining learning?"*

Discussion Questions:

- *"How reliable is AI-generated feedback for guiding student revision?"*
- *"What does 'constructive' look like when machine-generated - especially for early drafts or multilingual learners?"*
- *"How do we prevent over-reliance on machine feedback, especially in courses emphasizing voice, nuance, or context?"*
- *"What ethical considerations arise when faculty use AI to generate comments on student work?"*

Classroom Application: Pilot a "co-feedback" model: students receive both AI-generated and instructor feedback, then write a reflection on what each offered, missed, or misunderstood (Nicol & Macfarlane-Dick, 2006).

Outcome: Through this exercise, **students learn to critically compare the strengths and weaknesses of human versus AI-generated feedback, recognizing where each contributes to revision**. They develop a more nuanced understanding of what constitutes constructive, context-sensitive guidance - particularly in assignments requiring nuance, originality, or voice. Ultimately, the process cultivates reflective judgment, **teaching students that effective feedback is not just about efficiency but about depth, accuracy, and ethical responsibility in learning**.

Topic 5: Human Creativity in the AI Era

Core Inquiry: *"What does originality mean when machines can mimic human expression?"*

Discussion Questions:

- *"How do we define creativity in writing, design, or performance when generative AI can simulate genre, tone, and visual style?"*
- *"What frameworks help students preserve or reclaim creative agency?"*
- *"How might we use AI as a* ***provocative constraint*** *rather than a producer?"*
- *"What tensions arise between speed, polish, and authenticity?"*

Classroom Application: Ask students to prompt an AI to generate a poem, logo, or short story, and then remix or critique it. Debrief with questions on authorship, intention, and emotional resonance (Bender et al., 2021; Crawford, 2021).

Outcome: By experimenting with remixing or critiquing AI-generated creative outputs, **students learn to distinguish surface-level imitation from authentic expression**. They begin to recognize that originality is not defined solely by novelty of form, but by intentionality, perspective, and human meaning-making. **This process deepens their creative agency**, helping them see AI as a tool for provocation and reflection rather than a substitute for genuine artistry.

Summary: Framing AI Topics as Questions of Meaning and Practice

These topics are not discrete - they intersect, evolve, and deepen over time, often surfacing in ways that challenge both faculty and students to reconsider assumptions about teaching and learning. As AI continues to expand its influence across disciplines, the overlap between issues such as bias, authorship, integrity, and creativity becomes increasingly visible and unavoidable. When FLCs and mentorship pairings adopt a **shared focus with layered questions**, they create a reflective culture in which AI integration becomes a **disciplinary, ethical, and pedagogical inquiry**, not just a technological adjustment.

By structuring dialogue around real tensions - bias, authorship, integrity, creativity - institutions equip faculty not only to adapt, but to **lead with discernment, humility, and vision**. This intentional framing allows faculty to practice ethical reasoning while navigating uncertainty, strengthening their ability to model critical engagement for students. Ultimately, the process fosters a culture of inquiry in which educators see themselves not merely as technology adopters, but as co-creators of meaning and stewards of higher education's evolving role in the AI era.

Strategies for Sustaining Momentum

While initial excitement often drives early AI integration efforts, lasting impact requires **infrastructure, shared ownership, and intentional renewal cycles**. Without these, even the most promising faculty development models - such as Faculty Learning Communities (FLCs), mentorship programs, or curriculum redesign fellowships - risk stalling out due to burnout, over-reliance on individual champions, or lack of institutional follow-through.

To ensure that generative AI capacity building evolves from episodic initiatives into a **sustainable pedagogical culture**, institutions must embed structures that **circulate leadership, reward experimentation, and create enduring connections across departments and roles**. These strategies emphasize **distributed stewardship**, visibility, and alignment with broader educational priorities - turning short-term innovation into **long-term transformation** (Brookfield, 2017; Slimi & Carballido, 2023).

While initial excitement often drives early AI integration efforts, lasting impact requires **infrastructure, shared ownership, and intentional renewal cycles**. Without these forms of support, even the most promising faculty development models - such as Faculty Learning Communities (FLCs), mentorship programs, or curriculum redesign fellowships - risk losing momentum over time. This stall can occur because of burnout, an over-reliance on individual champions, or the absence of institutional systems that sustain and scale innovation.

To ensure that generative AI capacity building evolves from episodic initiatives into a **sustainable pedagogical culture**, institutions must embed structures that **circulate leadership, reward experimentation, and create enduring connections across departments and roles**. By doing so, they foster resilience, continuity, and shared responsibility across the academic community. These strategies emphasize distributed stewardship, visibility, and alignment with broader educational priorities - turning short-term innovation into long-term transformation (Brookfield, 2017; Slimi & Carballido, 2023).

With these challenges and opportunities in mind, the following strategies illustrate concrete ways institutions can embed AI pedagogy into their culture. They provide models for distributing leadership, building momentum, and **ensuring that innovation remains meaningful, ethical, and sustainable across time**. Together, these approaches help translate enthusiasm into infrastructure and experimentation into lasting institutional change.

Strategy 1: Rotate Leadership Each Term to Avoid Burnout

AI-focused faculty programs should adopt a **shared governance model**, with rotating facilitators or co-leads to distribute labor and diversify perspectives. Leadership rotation:

- Prevents overburdening early adopters.
- Encourages emerging voices and perspectives.
- Builds leadership capacity across ranks and departments.

Facilitator handoffs can include **playbooks, facilitation guides, or reflection logs**, ensuring continuity while honoring local adaptation. These resources **provide incoming leaders with concrete tools and insights, allowing them to build upon the work of their predecessors rather than starting from scratch**. At the same time, they leave room for flexibility so that each new facilitator can adapt strategies to the specific needs, dynamics, and culture of their cohort.

Strategy 2: Host Campus-Wide "AI in Practice" Weeks to Highlight Outcomes

Celebrate and showcase innovation through dedicated campus-wide events such as **AI in Practice Week** or **AI-Pedagogy Spotlights**. These events may include:

- Lightning talks or poster sessions from faculty implementing AI in teaching.
- Student panels discussing ethical tool use and learning experiences.
- Tool demonstrations and workshops.
- Policy discussions with librarians, instructional designers, and academic integrity leaders.

By making pedagogical work public, these events **inspire wider adoption by showing colleagues what is possible and lowering the barrier to experimentation**. They also affirm the value of innovation, signaling that trying new approaches in teaching is recognized and celebrated within the institution. Finally, **the public nature of these events creates real-time feedback loops**, giving faculty practical insights that can inform ongoing refinement and future planning of AI-integrated pedagogy.

Strategy 3: Publish Internal Newsletters or Teaching Blogs Documenting Experiments

A low-cost, high-impact method for maintaining momentum is the creation of an **AI teaching newsletter, microsite, or collaborative blog**. Faculty and staff contributors can:

- Share reflective write-ups of classroom pilots.

- Offer annotated syllabi or sample assignments.
- Raise open questions about integrity, student feedback, or disciplinary tensions.

These communications sustain cross-pollination **by ensuring that insights, assignments, and experiments circulate across disciplines rather than remaining siloed**. They also normalize AI pedagogy as a collective and evolving practice, helping faculty see that participation does not require technical expertise but a willingness to engage critically. Over time, **this shared dialogue shifts the institutional culture**, positioning AI teaching and learning as an accessible, collaborative, and continually developing endeavor.

Strategy 4: Connect FLCs Across Departments Through an AI Teaching Consortium

Rather than allowing FLCs or working groups to function in isolation, institutions can create an **AI Teaching Consortium** - a network of AI-focused communities of practice across units. Consortium meetings might:

- Convene once per semester to share themes and challenges.
- Develop joint deliverables such as interdisciplinary modules or shared ethics rubrics.
- Advise campus AI policy working groups or general education committees.

This cross-FLC infrastructure **weaves a horizontal knowledge network** by linking faculty learning communities into a broader system of shared inquiry and exchange. In doing so, it strengthens institutional alignment, ensuring that innovations developed in one cohort can be adapted and scaled across other departments or disciplines. It also **minimizes duplication of effort, enabling faculty to build on each other's experiments and insights** rather than reinventing strategies in isolation.

Strategy 5: Build a Repository of Shared Syllabi, Policies, and Assignments

A centralized, searchable repository of faculty-created materials allows AI pedagogy to scale efficiently while respecting local nuance. The repository might include:

- AI-integrated syllabi with tool-use expectations and reflection policies.
- Sample assignments with annotated prompts and revision protocols.
- Rubrics for AI-informed assessment.
- Course policies on citation, disclosure, and tool limitations.

The repository becomes both **a living archive and a launchpad**, capturing a wide range of faculty innovations, reflections, and resources that continue to evolve over time. For new adopters, **it serves as a quick orientation tool, providing immediate access to peer-tested strategies and practical models that can be adapted into their own teaching**. For experienced faculty, it functions as a space to refine, iterate, and expand their approaches, ensuring that AI pedagogy remains dynamic, collaborative, and forward-looking.

Institutional Insight: Strategic Support Signals Legitimacy

Sustaining momentum also depends on **visible support from academic leadership and teaching infrastructure**. Endorsement and resourcing from:

- **Deans and department chairs** (who can provide course release, promotion credit, or teaching awards).
- **Centers for Teaching and Learning (CTLs)** (who can provide facilitation, documentation, and cross-role integration).
- **General Education committees and provost offices** (who can align AI literacy with institutional learning outcomes and strategic plans).

These signals help embed AI integration into **the institution's formal structures of recognition, reward, and academic excellence** - moving it beyond temporary projects into enduring culture (Byars-Winston & Dahlberg, 2019; Slimi & Carballido, 2023). When faculty innovation is formally acknowledged in tenure reviews, merit awards, and institutional showcases, it signals that experimentation with AI is not marginal but central to scholarly and pedagogical leadership. **Over time, this recognition shifts AI engagement from a series of isolated initiatives into a sustainable cultural norm**, woven into the core values and long-term vision of the university.

Summary: From Pilot to Practice to Pedagogical Culture

Sustaining momentum in AI pedagogy requires more than enthusiasm - it requires **design.** By rotating leadership, celebrating progress, connecting peer learning structures, and institutionalizing knowledge, campuses move from innovation to infrastructure. These strategies ensure that generative AI becomes not a one-time response to disruption, but an **ongoing opportunity for reflection, relevance, and educational renewal**.

Section Reflection: Cultivating a Faculty Culture of Trust, Inquiry, and Transformation through Peer-Based AI Pedagogy

This section positions Faculty Learning Communities (FLCs) and peer mentorship as essential infrastructures for navigating the ethical, pedagogical, and cultural challenges of AI in higher education. Rather than emphasizing technical training, it foregrounds relational learning, interdisciplinary dialogue, and reflective practice as the foundations for scalable, inclusive, and sustained AI integration. FLCs are shown to normalize uncertainty, decenter expertise, and foster collective agency - turning AI not into a compliance issue, but into a shared site of professional and pedagogical growth.

Peer mentorship further complements this approach by offering trust-based, context-sensitive support through early adopter partnerships, cross-disciplinary pairings, and observation-based coaching. These models decentralize authority, affirm vulnerability, and create reciprocal learning loops that demystify AI and democratize innovation. Together, FLCs and mentorship cultivate grassroots capacity for ethical experimentation, disciplinary dialogue, and curricular adaptation - helping institutions move from episodic adoption to a distributed, resilient faculty culture. This reflection affirms that building AI fluency is not just about tools - it is about connection, conversation, and co-creating the future of education.

Section 5: Incentivizing Faculty Innovation and Risk-Taking

Artificial intelligence represents both a disruptive force and a generative opportunity in higher education. To explore its implications for pedagogy, assessment, and research, faculty need **freedom to experiment, space to fail, and structures that recognize courageous innovation**. Yet too often, innovation is **expected but not supported** - or worse, **punished through evaluation metrics that privilege safety and conformity** (Brookfield, 2017; Reiss, 2021).

This section outlines how institutions can **align their incentives, evaluations, and recognition systems** with the kind of risk-taking required to thoughtfully integrate AI. It includes examples of how to embed innovation into promotion and tenure (P&T) structures, develop low-risk experimentation spaces, and celebrate AI leadership as a scholarly contribution.

The Innovation Paradox: Faculty Want to Innovate, But Fear the Risk

At the heart of many stalled educational technology efforts lies a persistent tension: **faculty are deeply motivated to innovate - but hesitant to take risks without psychological safety, institutional support, or peer validation**. This is the innovation paradox. It is not a lack of imagination or will that slows progress, but a **mismatch between individual creativity and systemic reinforcement**.

Nowhere is this more visible than in the rapid emergence of generative AI. Faculty across disciplines are curious - often excited - about exploring how AI might transform feedback loops, assessment design, authorship conversations, or critical thinking. Yet this enthusiasm is frequently tempered by a constellation of **pragmatic and emotional risks**:

- **Reputational Risk**. *"Will my colleagues view me as less rigorous if I try something unconventional with AI?"*
- **Assessment Risk**. *"What if my students misunderstand the assignment or misuse the tool?"*
- **Workload Risk**. *"Do I have time to redesign this course with no guarantee of support?"*
- **Policy Risk**. *"Will I run afoul of unclear or outdated institutional guidelines?"*

As Brookfield (2017) noted, adult learners - including faculty - will not experiment meaningfully unless they perceive the **environment to be supportive, the outcomes to be valuable, and the process to be collegial**. Without those conditions, innovation feels like exposure.

Why the Innovation Paradox Matters in AI Integration

The paradox is especially potent with generative AI because of the **high stakes and high speed** of the technology's development. Faculty sense that AI will reshape the academic landscape - and want to be active participants in that change - but many remain on the sidelines, unsure how to begin or whether it is safe to proceed.

This hesitation is not resistance; it is often a form of **protective professionalism**. Faculty recognize that generative AI challenges long-held academic norms - around authorship, originality, assessment, and cognitive labor - and they want time, guidance, and conversation to respond thoughtfully. When institutions mistake this caution for disinterest, they risk **missing the moment of engagement** that could lead to sustained innovation.

Addressing the Paradox Through Design and Culture

To resolve this paradox, institutions must create environments that **legitimize pedagogical risk-taking** and value AI-informed exploration as a form of scholarly work. This means:

- **Creating protected spaces** for experimentation (e.g., low-stakes fellowships, micrograants, pilot semesters).
- **Publicly recognizing faculty contributions** to AI-integrated teaching (e.g., awards, showcases, publications).
- **Aligning innovation with existing incentives** (e.g., inclusion in tenure review, teaching portfolios, and annual evaluations).
- **Modeling vulnerability** through peer observation, co-teaching, or rotating leadership roles.
- **Providing nonjudgmental support infrastructure**, such as CTLs, librarians, and instructional designers trained in AI pedagogy.

As Byars-Winston and Dahlberg (2019) suggested, when institutions treat innovation as **collaborative inquiry rather than compliance or competition**, faculty become more willing to experiment - not just with tools, but with **questions of meaning, ethics, and transformation**. This framing empowers educators to see themselves as co-creators of institutional culture, where experimentation is valued as a pathway to deeper reflection and long-term educational renewal rather than a risk to be avoided.

Summary: Innovation Is a Cultural Capacity, Not a Personal Trait

The innovation paradox reminds us that faculty are not risk-averse by nature; they are risk-aware by necessity. To nurture a campus culture where generative AI is approached with courage, care, and creativity, institutions must **lower the cost of entry and raise the value of experimentation**.

When innovation is embedded in community - not isolation - and reinforced through structure - not serendipity, faculty do not just adopt new tools - they help **co-author the future of learnin**g. This collective approach ensures that experimentation translates into sustainable cultural change, where shared practices, reflective dialogue, and institutional support anchor AI pedagogy as a long-term transformation rather than a passing trend.

Common Barriers to AI-Related Experimentation

While generative AI presents exciting opportunities for pedagogical transformation, many faculty find themselves caught between **intellectual curiosity and professional hesitation**. Even as interest grows, actual experimentation with AI tools in the classroom remains uneven - and for good reason. Innovation does not occur in a vacuum. It is shaped by the **structures, norms, and reward systems** that surround faculty work. Without intentional institutional support, these contextual factors become **invisible constraints**, discouraging risk-taking and reinforcing the status quo. Below are some of the most commonly cited barriers to AI-related experimentation. Each represents not a lack of faculty will, but a **mismatch between innovation goals and institutional realities**.

Common Barrier 1: Fear of Negative Student Evaluations

Faculty frequently report concern that trying new tools - especially those that are still evolving, unfamiliar to students, or not fully reliable - might result in **lower course evaluations**. This is particularly acute in:

- High-enrollment gateway courses.
- Courses where clarity and consistency are critical to student success.
- Teaching contexts where evaluations are weighted heavily in performance reviews.

Faculty may worry that students will perceive AI integration as "experimental," "confusing," or "less rigorous," even when pedagogically sound. Without mechanisms to contextualize innovation in evaluations (e.g., reflection prompts, mid-semester feedback opportunities, peer observation), **even thoughtful risk-taking may feel professionally unsafe**.

Common Barrier 2: Lack of Clarity in Promotion and Tenure (P&T) Guidelines

When promotion and tenure documents fail to specify how **pedagogical innovation, technology integration, or interdisciplinary curriculum design** is evaluated, faculty may reasonably ask: "*Does this work count?*" This ambiguity disproportionately discourages:

- Pre-tenured faculty balancing research and teaching priorities.
- Contingent or adjunct faculty whose renewal depends on stability.
- Scholars in fields where traditional scholarship is more clearly defined.

Without clear signals from P&T committees that **AI-integrated teaching is valued as evidence of pedagogical leadership**, innovation can feel like an extracurricular gamble rather than a meaningful contribution to academic excellence (Byars-Winston & Dahlberg, 2019). When institutions explicitly reward and recognize this work, faculty are more likely to view AI pedagogy not as a side project, but as a central pathway to advancing both their careers and the mission of higher education.

Common Barrier 3: No Formal Time or Compensation for Redesigning Courses

Effective AI integration requires more than adding a tool - it involves:

- Rethinking assessment models.
- Revising policies on authorship and collaboration.
- Designing scaffolds for ethical reflection and critical tool use.

These changes demand time for planning, consultation, pilot testing, and reflection. Yet many institutions do not offer:

- Course release.
- Summer stipends.
- Micrograms for curriculum innovation.

In the absence of **protected time or material recognition**, the labor of innovation becomes unsustainable - particularly for faculty already managing high teaching loads, research obligations, or service commitments (Reiss, 2021). Without structural support, even the most committed educators may retreat from experimentation, leaving AI integration uneven, fragile, and overly dependent on a handful of overextended early adopters.

Common Barrier 4: Concerns About Appearing "Non-Rigorous"

Generative AI challenges traditional markers of academic rigor - such as solo authorship, polished prose, or linear writing processes. Faculty may worry that using AI:

- Undermines disciplinary standards of originality.
- Suggests pedagogical "laziness" or shortcutting.
- Sends the wrong signal to students about critical thinking and intellectual effort.

These concerns are especially salient in fields where:

- Writing is central to disciplinary identity.
- AI is associated with automation, not insight.
- Historical bias has shaped perceptions of what counts as "serious" or "scholarly" work.

Without institutional reframing of AI as a cognitive partner rather than a replacement, some faculty may feel torn between curiosity and credibility. On one hand, they may want to experiment with AI tools to enhance learning and explore new pedagogical possibilities, but on the other, they may fear that colleagues or students will perceive this as a threat to rigor or professional authority. **Clear institutional messaging that positions AI as a collaborator in thinking - not a substitute for human expertise** - helps resolve this tension and creates space for faculty to engage with confidence and integrity.

Research Insight: The Conditions That Make Innovation Possible

As Cox (2004) and Byars-Winston and Dahlberg (2019) emphasized, **faculty are more likely to innovate when they feel psychologically safe, socially supported, and structurally enabled**. This includes:

- Clear recognition of innovation in evaluation processes.
- Peer communities that normalize experimentation.
- Access to design partners (e.g., instructional designers, librarians, technologists).
- Leadership that frames innovation as inquiry, not risk.

These factors turn experimentation into collective professional growth rather than isolated risk-taking. **When faculty engage in AI innovation within supportive structures** - such as peer communities, fellowships, or collaborative workshops - **they share both the challenges and the insights that emerge from their practice**. This shared approach not only distributes risk but also transforms experimentation into a cultural norm, reinforcing that learning, reflection, and adaptation are valued forms of scholarly contribution.

Summary: Remove the Barriers, and the Innovation Follows

Faculty do not need to be persuaded to care about AI - they need to be **resourced and recognized** for engaging with it critically, ethically, and reflectively. Addressing these barriers is not simply a matter of operational support - it is a matter of equity, trust, and long-term institutional vision. When innovation is scaffolded, not penalized, **faculty respond not with resistance - but with imagination.**

Institutional Strategies to Incentivize AI Pedagogical Innovation

---

For AI to become meaningfully integrated into higher education, institutions must move beyond one-off workshops and optional experiments to create systems that reward sustained, ethical, and creative engagement. **Faculty cannot be expected to shoulder the risks of innovation without recognition, support, and structural reinforcement**. Incentivizing AI pedagogy requires intentional strategies that elevate this work as central to academic excellence, aligning it with tenure, promotion, funding, and cultural values.

By embedding AI teaching innovation into institutional priorities, colleges and universities signal that **experimentation is not extracurricular - it is essential scholarship that shapes the future of learning**. These strategies ensure that innovation is not isolated to a few enthusiastic faculty but becomes a shared, mission-aligned endeavor that builds capacity across disciplines. In this way, **institutions can transform AI from a disruptive force into a catalyst for pedagogical renewal, equity, and leadership**. The following institutional strategies outline concrete ways to recognize, support, and scale AI pedagogical innovation, ensuring that faculty are empowered to lead this transformation with confidence and integrity.

Institutional Strategy 1: Explicitly Integrate AI Pedagogy into Promotion and Tenure Criteria

Incentivizing innovation requires more than encouragement - it requires **structural alignment**. When faculty are asked to redesign assignments, pilot AI-integrated modules, or lead institutional conversations around generative tools, their labor must be formally recognized as a legitimate form of scholarly teaching. One of the most powerful ways to affirm this work is by **embedding AI pedagogical leadership into promotion and tenure (P&T) frameworks**.

For many faculty - especially pre-tenure, contingent, or teaching-intensive faculty - P&T criteria serve as **the primary guidepost for professional decision-making**. If generative AI experimentation is not clearly identified as eligible for recognition under the teaching, service, or scholarly activity categories, it becomes a **perceived risk rather than a professional opportunity**. Faculty are left to wonder: *"Will this count? Or am I sacrificing evaluative stability to try something new?"*

Action Step: Update P&T Guidelines to Reflect Pedagogical Innovation in the AI Era

Departments and academic units should collaboratively revise their P&T language to reflect evolving expectations around **technology-enhanced instruction and cross-disciplinary innovation**. Clear, values-based language signals that **responsible, reflective engagement with AI is not only permitted - it is encouraged**.

Recommended Inclusions:

- **Curriculum Redesign**. Acknowledge the redesign of courses to incorporate AI-informed instructional strategies, such as tool-guided writing processes, reflective AI-use protocols, or prompt engineering instruction.
- **Interdisciplinary Collaboration**. Recognize co-teaching, module development, or grant-funded initiatives that bridge disciplines to explore the ethical, cognitive, or civic dimensions of AI.
- **Faculty Learning Leadership**. Include participation or facilitation of AI pedagogy-focused FLCs, working groups, mentoring programs, or campus-wide training as evidence of leadership and instructional innovation.
- **Reflective Scholarship**. Credit practitioner scholarship - such as reflective essays, case studies, conference presentations, or action research on classroom experiences with AI - as contributions to the scholarship of teaching and learning (SoTL).

Example Language for Faculty Handbook or Departmental P&T Guidelines:

- *"Innovative integration of emerging technologies, including artificial intelligence, into course design, assessment strategies, or institutional learning communities will be considered evidence of teaching excellence. Contributions may include curriculum redesign, interdisciplinary module creation, engagement in faculty learning initiatives, or reflective scholarship on AI-mediated instruction."*

This Phrasing:

- **Aligns innovation with teaching quality**, not just tech novelty.
- Emphasizes **intentionality, ethics, and reflection** over tool adoption alone.
- Creates **space for multiple forms of contribution**, including those beyond the classroom (e.g., workshops, mentoring, institutional policy input).

Why This Matters: Incentives Shape Participation

Without explicit mention in evaluation criteria, AI integration remains **peripheral to professional advancement**, despite its central role in shaping contemporary education. Faculty may remain cautious - especially those from underrepresented backgrounds or disciplines where digital labor is often overlooked (Reiss, 2021; Slimi & Carballido, 2023). In contrast, inclusive and transparent P&T language:

- Encourages **diverse participation** in AI innovation.
- Signals **institutional vision and coherence**.
- Rewards the **intellectual labor of reflection, experimentation, and ethical leadership**.

Summary: Make Innovation Count Where It Matters

Incentivizing AI pedagogical innovation is not only about encouraging creativity - it is about **removing institutional ambiguity and honoring intellectual risk**. By integrating AI-related teaching contributions into formal recognition structures such as promotion and tenure, institutions move beyond slogans of "innovation" and into **actionable alignment**. Faculty then have the confidence - and the professional security - to lead the future of learning with clarity, ethics, and purpose.

Institutional Strategy 2: Provide Release Time, Microgrants, and Fellowships for AI Experimentation

For AI pedagogical innovation to flourish, institutions must recognize that **thoughtful experimentation requires time, resources, and support infrastructure**. Faculty cannot be expected to redesign curricula, rethink assessment strategies, or study the ethical implications of generative AI while maintaining full teaching, research, and service loads. Without a designated space for inquiry and development, innovation remains **aspirational rather than achievable**.

To make AI integration both sustainable and equitable, institutions should invest in **tiered support mechanisms** that meet faculty at different stages of exploration. This includes **micro-innovation grants** for entry-level experimentation and **course releases or fellowships** for deeper, systemic redesigns. These supports affirm that pedagogical innovation is not extra - it is **core academic work deserving of institutional priority and recognition** (Byars-Winston & Dahlberg, 2019; Slimi & Carballido, 2023).

Micro-Innovation Grants: Scalable, Low-Barrier Entry Points

Microgrants in the range of **$500–$2,000** offer faculty the flexibility to pursue focused, short-term projects that align with their teaching goals and disciplinary expertise. These grants lower the threshold for participation and reward creative risk-taking by recognizing **small-scale efforts that yield high pedagogical value**.

Sample Use Cases:

- **Redesigning a general education module** to include AI-generated content analysis, prompt revision exercises, or comparative machine-human authorship discussions.
- **Conducting qualitative or survey-based research** on student perceptions of fairness, feedback, and learning outcomes related to AI use in the classroom.
- **Co-developing a cross-listed course** (e.g., philosophy + computer science) focused on AI ethics, bias in algorithms, or the cultural impact of automation.

Benefits of Microgrants:

- Encourages experimentation without the high stakes of a full course overhaul.
- Builds momentum among faculty across ranks and disciplines.
- Produces **artifacts for institutional repositories**, such as revised assignments, student reflections, or AI tool comparison guides.
- Offers a **pipeline to deeper fellowships or publications**, especially for teaching-focused faculty or new AI adopters.

Fellowships and Release Time: Deep Support for Transformative Design

For faculty ready to engage in comprehensive course redesign, **semester-long fellowships or course releases** offer the time, structure, and support necessary for strategic innovation. These programs recognize that meaningful integration of AI - especially in high-enrollment, interdisciplinary, or professionally accredited programs - requires more than curiosity: it requires **intentional collaboration, policy alignment, and sustained reflection**.

Key Features:

- **Mentorship pairings** with experienced AI-integrating faculty or instructional designers.
- **Peer cohort model** for shared reflection, critique, and artifact development.
- **Dissemination requirement**, such as a campus showcase, open-access module, or publication in a teaching journal.
- **Formal recognition** in annual reviews or promotion dossiers.

Example (STEM Department):

- *A biology professor receives a **course release** to co-develop a suite of "**AI for Biologists**" materials. These include:*
    - *Lab simulations using machine learning tools for ecological pattern detection.*
    - *Reflection prompts on ethical use of AI in medical diagnostics.*

- *A teaching guide co-written with an instructional designer and shared through the institution's* ***Open Educational Resources (OER) portal****.*

The project **culminates in a campus workshop and a published reflection** in a disciplinary teaching journal, ensuring that both the process and outcomes are shared widely with colleagues. **This dual dissemination bridges innovation with professional development**, while reinforcing transparency and modeling scholarly engagement with AI pedagogy.

Strategic Impacts: Beyond Individual Projects

These investments do more than fund isolated experiments - they:

- Build **institutional capacity** through documented, replicable models.
- Surface diverse perspectives on AI across disciplines and ranks.
- Normalize **risk-informed pedagogical leadership** as a recognized contribution to teaching excellence.
- Feed into strategic planning processes for curriculum development, digital literacy, and academic integrity policy.

When micrograints and fellowships are integrated with peer learning structures such as Faculty Learning Communities (FLCs), public showcases, and repository development, they create more than isolated opportunities for experimentation - **they form the foundation of an interconnected system**. This coherence ensures that faculty innovations are not only supported in the moment but also shared, iterated upon, and scaled across the institution. Together, **these elements build a sustainable AI pedagogy ecosystem** that embeds ethical reflection, collaborative practice, and curricular transformation into the very fabric of academic life.

Summary: Fund the Work You Want to See Flourish

Faculty innovation cannot be willed into existence - it must be **resourced, supported, and recognized**. By offering microgrants for exploratory redesign and release time for transformative projects, institutions move from passive endorsement of AI experimentation to **active co-creation of a new teaching and learning landscape**. These supports ensure that the future of AI in education is not determined by commercial platforms alone - but **authored by educators grounded in ethics, pedagogy, and purpose**.

Institutional Strategy 3: Create "Safe-to-Fail" Teaching Laboratories and Beta-Testing Spaces

---

Integrating generative AI into teaching is not a linear process - it is iterative, experimental, and often uncertain. Faculty need environments where they can test new ideas without fear of damaging their reputation, compromising student outcomes, or violating ambiguous policy.

"Safe-to-fail" teaching laboratories and beta-testing spaces provide this essential foundation by **normalizing risk as a condition of innovation**, not a threat to it.

In these settings, failure is reframed not as inadequacy but as **evidence of inquiry**, and success is defined not by polish but by learning. These models empower faculty to engage with AI tools authentically and reflectively, modeling for students what it looks like to navigate uncertainty with curiosity, humility, and ethical rigor (Brookfield, 2017; Reiss, 2021).

Why "Safe-to-Fail" Spaces Are Essential

Many faculty members hesitate to experiment with AI-enhanced assignments or tools because:

- **They fear appearing unprepared or unprofessional** in front of students.
- **They lack institutional assurance** that mistakes will be understood as part of growth.
- **They receive mixed signals** from policies, student expectations, and peer norms.

By creating protected, clearly designated experimental spaces, institutions **lower both the affective and reputational costs of pedagogical exploration**, making it safer for faculty to try new approaches without fear of failure. In these settings, faculty are encouraged to ask open-ended questions, test prototypes transparently, and refine their ideas iteratively with the support of peers. This **intentional design fosters a culture of innovation where experimentation is normalized** as part of professional growth, rather than treated as risky or peripheral.

Models for Safe-to-Fail Implementation

In higher education, experimentation with AI pedagogy often carries both promise and risk. Faculty may hesitate to innovate when the stakes are high, fearing reputational consequences, student pushback, or misalignment with institutional norms. To encourage creativity without penalty, institutions must design **safe-to-fail** environments - structured opportunities where trial, error, and iteration are framed as integral to professional growth rather than as shortcomings.

These models create intentional spaces where innovation is supported, reflection is prioritized, and failures are treated as valuable learning data for both individuals and the institution. By embedding safeguards and supports into the process, institutions can foster a culture of pedagogical resilience that prepares faculty to navigate the rapid evolution of AI. The following **Safe-to-Fail Models** illustrate practical strategies for creating these environments and sustaining faculty confidence in responsible AI experimentation.

Safe-to-Fail Model 1: "Teaching Sandbox Semesters"

Faculty are invited to pilot AI tools or alternative instructional strategies in designated courses or modules, with explicit framing that the course is in experimental mode. These pilots:

- May include ungraded or low-stakes assignments for AI comparison or prompt engineering.
- Emphasize **student metacognition over mastery**, using reflection logs or learning journals.
- Include **peer observation or documentation**, contributing to campus-wide learning.

Institutional Support Includes:

- Flexible syllabus language acknowledging the pilot.
- CTL consultation for design and student communication.
- Optional post-semester reflection session or write-up for teaching portfolios.

These pilot initiatives normalize experimentation as part of the teaching process, **signaling to both students and faculty that inquiry and iteration are valued outcomes**. They also ensure that insights from these trials do not remain isolated, but instead contribute to a collective institutional knowledge base that can inform broader policy and curricular design. Over time, this cycle of **safe-to-fail experimentation builds a culture of transparency, reflective practice, and continuous improvement in AI pedagogy**.

Safe-to-Fail Model 2: "Pedagogy Incubator Weeks" (Summer or Intersession)

Offer faculty a designated one- to two-week period - during January term, summer session, or intersession - to **try a speculative assignment, AI-driven activity, or revised module** with a small student cohort or community partner. These incubators:

- Encourage bold experimentation in a **low-stakes, opt-in setting**.
- Pair faculty with instructional designers or librarians for real-time support.
- Provide stipends or certificates for participation and documentation.

Deliverables may include a prototype assignment, an AI-use rubric, or a reflection brief for inclusion in a cross-disciplinary repository. T**hese artifacts serve as practical, shareable resources that demonstrate how AI integration can be approached transparently and ethically across different fields**. Over time, the accumulation of such deliverables creates a living archive of innovation that supports faculty learning, encourages adaptation, and scales institutional capacity for AI pedagogy.

Safe-to-Fail Model 3: "AI Pilot Roundtables"

Instead of traditional teaching evaluations, create **reflective communities of practice** where faculty can debrief classroom pilots with peers - not for approval, but for shared insight. Each roundtable might feature:

- One instructor sharing a 10-minute story of a classroom experiment (e.g., using ChatGPT to co-generate exam questions).

- A group discussion of challenges, surprises, and possible iterations.
- A rotating scribe to document key takeaways for broader campus dissemination.

These sessions normalize imperfection by framing experimentation as a legitimate and valuable part of pedagogical growth. They also foster community trust, creating a supportive environment **where faculty can share missteps, insights, and lessons learned without fear of judgment**. In doing so, they surface field-tested ideas that can be adapted across disciplines, turning individual exploration into collective institutional learning.

Illustrative Example: Co-Learning Through Uncertainty

In a **visual rhetoric course**, a communications professor partners with students to explore **Midjourney**, a text-to-image AI tool. Rather than arriving as an expert, the instructor frames the course module as a **shared exploration**, inviting students to:

- Generate AI visuals based on rhetorical prompts.
- Analyze how Midjourney encodes aesthetic bias and genre assumptions.
- Reflect on what it feels like to learn alongside a professor who is **openly navigating technological ambiguity**.

Student response centers not only on the tool itself, but also on the vulnerability, authenticity, and intellectual humility modeled by their instructor. **When faculty openly share uncertainties and invite dialogue about their own learning process, they humanize the use of AI and reduce the pressure for perfection in student work**. These qualities become essential to AI-era teaching, showing students that professional formation is not about mastery alone, but about ongoing reflection, adaptability, and ethical engagement.

Broader Impact: Shifting Culture Through Iterative Design

Safe-to-fail environments do more than support individual faculty - they begin to **redefine what pedagogical innovation looks like institutionally**. They encourage:

- A campus culture where faculty can **ask bold questions without penalty**.
- A view of AI literacy as **shared inquiry, not solo mastery**.
- Pedagogical leadership grounded in **collaborative risk-taking** and **public reflection**.

Creating designated teaching labs and beta spaces communicates a powerful message: **innovation is welcomed, supported, and expected to be imperfect**. These environments shift faculty development from compliance to creativity, and student experience from passive consumption to active epistemological engagement. In a world where AI changes faster than policy, **safe-to-fail structures provide the human infrastructure needed for sustainable, ethical adaptation.**

Institutional Strategy 4: Recognize AI Leadership in Annual Reviews and Awards

Faculty are more likely to engage meaningfully with generative AI when they see that **innovation is not only supported - but publicly valued**. Too often, however, the emotional, intellectual, and instructional labor involved in designing, piloting, and refining AI-integrated pedagogy goes unnoticed in formal evaluation processes. This creates a **disincentive for risk-taking**, particularly for contingent or early-career faculty who may feel that experimentation could be viewed as unprofessional or "non-rigorous."

Recognition is not merely a morale booster - it is a **cultural signal**. When institutions explicitly include AI-related teaching leadership in **annual review rubrics, award criteria, and campus storytelling**, they normalize innovation, legitimize reflective risk, and align faculty development with institutional vision (Byars-Winston & Dahlberg, 2019; Slimi & Carballido, 2023).

Institutional Action Steps for Visibility and Validation

For AI pedagogy to become embedded as an enduring part of academic culture, institutions must do more than encourage experimentation - they must make it visible and validate it as meaningful scholarly work. **Faculty innovation thrives when it is publicly acknowledged, rewarded, and shared across the campus community, ensuring that pedagogical leadership is seen as central to institutional excellence rather than peripheral**. Visibility not only amplifies the impact of individual faculty contributions but also signals to students, colleagues, and external stakeholders that ethical and thoughtful AI integration is a valued priority.

The following institutional action steps outline concrete ways to create this culture of recognition, ensuring that AI engagement is not treated as invisible labor but as a celebrated and validated dimension of academic practice.

Institutional Action Step 1: Add "AI Integration and Digital Pedagogical Innovation" to Annual Review Forms

Revising annual review forms to include a line item or checkbox for "AI and emerging technology in teaching" allows faculty to:

- Document experimental assignments, policies, or tool use.
- Reflect on student response and ethical considerations.
- Share lessons learned - even when pilots were imperfect.

This invites reflection as a form of scholarship, emphasizing that inquiry into process can be just as valuable as producing polished outcomes. **It reinforces to faculty and students alike that intellectual growth emerges through iteration, self-awareness, and critical dialogue rather than simply arriving at the "right answer."** In rapidly evolving educational contexts shaped by AI, this perspective affirms that adaptability, reflexivity, and ethical awareness are essential scholarly contributions in their own right.

Institutional Action Step 2: Include AI Leadership as a Criterion for Teaching Awards

Update teaching excellence award criteria to account for:

- Development of AI-infused assignments or curricula.
- Leadership in AI-focused Faculty Learning Communities (FLCs) or mentorship initiatives.
- Contributions to campus-wide AI literacy or integrity policy development.
- Cross-disciplinary or public-facing work (e.g., podcasts, open-access modules, student co-authored projects).

Award programs that celebrate **adaptive, reflective teaching in response to AI** signal to faculty that thoughtful experimentation is valued as a professional strength. They promote an institutional narrative where creativity, care, and responsiveness to change are recognized as central to effective pedagogy, rather than perfection or polish. **By elevating these qualities, institutions affirm that navigating uncertainty with integrity is a hallmark of educational leadership in the AI era**.

Institutional Action Step 3: Highlight AI Pedagogy in Campus Communications

Marketing and communication teams can play a pivotal role in amplifying teaching innovation. Profile AI-integrated courses, share short faculty interviews, or feature student reflections in:

- Faculty newsletters.
- New faculty orientation sessions.
- President or provost blogs and annual reports.
- Campus social media, emphasizing **student-faculty co-learning**.

This positions AI experimentation not as a fringe activity or something confined to specialized disciplines, but as **a shared institutional priority**. By framing it as a collective project of academic renewal, faculty from every field can see their role in shaping the ethical and pedagogical future of AI. **Such positioning fosters a sense of common ownership, reinforcing that AI integration is part of the broader mission of education** rather than an isolated initiative.

Illustrative Example: Recognition in Practice

- *At a liberal arts college, a* ***literature professor*** *designs a podcast series featuring students reflecting on their collaborative authorship experiences with ChatGPT. Each episode includes:*
    - *Reflections on what parts of the writing process students felt supported or challenged by.*
    - *Ethical dilemmas they encountered while using AI for brainstorming or revision.*
    - *Conversations on what "authorship" means in a machine-assisted world.*

- *The professor is nominated for the **Provost's Teaching Innovation Award**, and the podcast is shared in **faculty orientation**, sparking broader discussion on AI literacy, transparency, and trust in academic work.*

This Recognition:

- **Validates the emotional labor** of teaching in uncharted territory.
- **Models public pedagogy** and co-created learning.
- Inspires others to explore similar methods, knowing their work will be **seen, valued, and shared**.

This kind of recognition transforms individual experimentation into institutional learning, signaling that **AI pedagogy belongs at the center of academic renewal**. It also creates a ripple effect, **where faculty who may have been hesitant to explore AI feel encouraged to take risks, knowing their contributions will be acknowledged and shared**. Over time, these stories of innovation accumulate into a cultural archive of practice, reinforcing that AI integration is not only possible but professionally meaningful across disciplines.

Why Recognition Matters

Faculty are unlikely to take pedagogical risks if the **institutional reward structures are silent or ambiguous**. Recognition:

- **Counters fear-based resistance** by affirming thoughtful experimentation.
- Creates a **visible pipeline of exemplars** others can learn from.
- Supports equity by ensuring that **teaching innovation is rewarded across rank, role, and discipline**.

It also shifts campus culture toward a more **generative, inquiry-based understanding of excellence** - where AI tools are not shortcuts, but catalysts for deeper reflection, creativity, and student engagement. When institutions recognize AI teaching leadership in formal and informal ways, they move from passive endorsement to **active cultivation of pedagogical imagination**. Recognition systems - however small - send a message: ***This work matters. Your curiosity, care, and courage are central to how our institution meets the future***.

Institutional Strategy 5: Connect Risk-Taking to Leadership Pathways

One of the most effective ways to sustain innovation and institutional learning is to **link pedagogical risk-taking to formal leadership opportunities**. Faculty who experiment with generative AI - whether through syllabus redesign, ethical reflection, or collaborative teaching - should not remain isolated actors. Instead, their insights should be **amplified, integrated, and empowered** to shape campus-wide conversations about curriculum, ethics, and academic futures.

When institutions recognize that innovation is not only instructional labor but also **visionary leadership**, they create a culture in which **reflective experimentation becomes a pipeline to influence and stewardship**. This reframes risk not as deviation from norms, but as a valued contribution to the institution's evolving mission (Brookfield, 2017; Byars-Winston & Dahlberg, 2019).

Strategic Opportunities to Elevate Faculty Innovators

Recognizing faculty innovators is not only about celebrating individual achievement - it is about shaping a culture where risk-taking, reflective practice, and ethical engagement with AI are institutionally valued. In the rapidly shifting landscape of higher education, faculty who experiment with AI-integrated pedagogy often pioneer practices that others later adopt, refine, and scale. **By elevating these early innovators, institutions send a clear message that curiosity, creativity, and leadership in AI are central to their academic mission, not peripheral to it**.

To build on this momentum, the following **strategic opportunities** outline concrete ways institutions can highlight, reward, and amplify faculty innovation - turning local experiments into collective progress.

Strategic Opportunity 1: Invite Innovators to Join Curriculum or Gen Ed Committees

Faculty who are rethinking how AI affects learning outcomes, disciplinary assumptions, and assessment models bring a vital perspective to general education reform. Involve these educators in:

- Curriculum mapping.
- Digital literacy outcomes development.
- AI integration across Gen Ed tiers.

This ensures that **institutional learning goals keep pace with technological and epistemological change**, acknowledging that AI is reshaping not just how knowledge is delivered but how it is defined. **By grounding goals in classroom realities, institutions affirm that policy and pedagogy must move in tandem**, reflecting what faculty and students actually encounter in practice. In doing so, they create a living curriculum that evolves with the times while staying rooted in the principles of equity, rigor, and intellectual integrity.

Strategic Opportunity 2: Seat Innovators on AI Policy Task Forces

Many institutions are in the process of developing or revising:

- Academic integrity policies.
- Syllabus guidance for AI tool use.
- Student guidelines for ethical AI collaboration.

Faculty who have piloted tools, navigated student confusion, and designed reflection-based assignments bring grounded, practice-based insight that theory alone cannot provide. Their inclusion in AI task forces or working groups ensures that **institutional policies**

are shaped by lived classroom realities rather than by abstract speculation or reactive fear. This bridge between practice and policy helps institutions create guidelines that are not only ethical and forward-looking but also usable, credible, and responsive to faculty and student needs.

Strategic Opportunity 3: Invite Faculty to Mentor Others or Lead Institutional Initiatives

When experienced faculty lead mentorship programs, FLCs, or "AI Teaching Institutes," they:

- Build institutional memory around AI pedagogy.
- Normalize faculty-led professional development.
- Help peers move from anxiety to agency.

These roles **deepen the leadership bench** by ensuring that responsibility for AI pedagogy and governance is distributed rather than concentrated in a small circle of early adopters. When paired with protected time, recognition in annual reviews, or grant-funded facilitation, **faculty leaders are given both the resources and legitimacy to sustain their contributions**. This combination strengthens institutional resilience, signaling that AI innovation is not just an individual effort but a recognized, supported, and strategically valued dimension of academic life.

Example: From Pilot to Policy Leadership

- *After piloting an **AI ethics seminar** that blended philosophy, law, and case study analysis, a philosophy professor is invited to:*
    - *Co-chair a university-wide **AI and Society Working Group**.*
    - *Co-develop learning outcomes on AI literacy for the general education program.*
    - *Mentor early-career faculty on reflective assignment design.*

Their course experimentation - initially local and provisional - becomes **a catalyst for broader institutional transformation**, illustrating how small-scale innovation can ripple outward into systemic change. **The professor's influence extends beyond the classroom into policy discussions, curriculum redesign, and strategic planning**, where faculty perspectives are often underrepresented in technology-driven initiatives. In doing so, they help ensure that institutional decisions about AI integration remain anchored in lived teaching practice, pedagogical integrity, and the realities of student learning.

The Virtuous Cycle of Innovation and Influence

When risk-taking is structurally connected to leadership, a **virtuous cycle** emerges:

- A faculty member experiments with a new approach to AI integration.
- That work is recognized and documented.
- The faculty member is invited into **campus governance, mentorship, or strategic planning**.

- Their insights shape broader institutional conversations.
- This visibility and impact, in turn, **encourage further engagement and experimentation** - by them and others.

Rather than asking the same few innovators to do more, this approach **grows the circle of influence** by institutionalizing pathways from teaching to leadership. In the age of AI, leadership is not just about positional authority - it is about **pedagogical foresight, ethical reflexivity, and interdisciplinary imagination**. By connecting classroom experimentation to formal leadership roles, institutions elevate the work of faculty as **co-architects of the academic future**, not passive recipients of external change. This approach ensures that the people most attuned to student learning - faculty - are at the table when **policies, priorities, and pedagogical visions are defined**.

Closing the Innovation Loop: Feedback and Reflection

True innovation does not end at implementation - it continues through structured reflection, peer learning, and community dialogue. Yet in many institutions, pedagogical experimentation with AI remains **isolated and undocumented**, preventing the insights gained - both successes and struggles - from informing broader teaching practice. To fully support AI-enhanced pedagogy, institutions must close the innovation loop by **creating intentional opportunities for reflection, feedback, and knowledge sharing**.

This process not only improves individual teaching - it builds institutional capacity by transforming **private risk into collective learning**. Faculty feel affirmed when their insights are seen, their questions are validated, and their challenges become opportunities for peer exploration - not causes for judgment or silence (Brookfield, 2017; Cox, 2004).

Why Feedback and Reflection Matter

Without built-in mechanisms to revisit and reimagine innovation, institutions risk:

- Treating experimentation as a one-off event rather than an evolving process.
- Reinforcing perfectionism, where only "success stories" are shared.
- Losing valuable pedagogical knowledge that could inform policy, training, or curriculum design.

Closing **the innovation loop affirms that every pilot is meaningful data**, whether it succeeds fully or encounters obstacles along the way. By framing partial or “failed” attempts as valuable contributions, **institutions normalize risk-taking and encourage faculty to share lessons learned rather than hide them**. When held in community, these insights fuel collective growth, building an environment where experimentation is seen as essential to institutional learning and resilience.

Strategies for Reflective Innovation Culture

Building an AI-ready institution is not only about adopting new tools - it is about cultivating a culture of reflection that treats innovation as a cycle of inquiry, experimentation, and shared learning. **Faculty and administrators alike must see pedagogical change as iterative, where risks and revisions are as valuable as polished outcomes**. In this way, reflection becomes the glue that binds individual creativity to collective growth, ensuring AI adoption remains aligned with values of care, equity, and intellectual integrity.

The following strategies outline how institutions can embed reflective practices into the very fabric of innovation, creating a culture where experimentation is safe, inquiry is expected, and lessons learned fuel continuous transformation.

Strategy for Reflective Innovation Culture 1: Host "AI Innovation Showcases" Each Semester

Invite faculty to share:

- AI-infused assignments or assessment models.
- Reflections on classroom challenges and student feedback.
- Ethical tensions and how they were navigated.
- Lessons learned from both polished and messy implementations.

Showcases can take the form of poster sessions, roundtable discussions, or digital galleries. Including student voices - via testimonials or co-presentations - adds depth and authenticity. These events turn experimentation into **public pedagogy**, where the institution learns from itself.

Strategy for Reflective Innovation Culture 2: Publish Short Case Studies or Interviews on a Teaching and Learning Blog

Create an ongoing series where faculty:

- Briefly describe their AI-related course innovation.
- Reflect on what surprised them - about student engagement, tool behavior, or learning outcomes.
- Share key documents (e.g., rubrics, prompts, policies) as open educational resources (OER).
- Offer advice to colleagues considering similar experiments.

These narratives humanize the innovation process by showing the lived experiences of faculty who experiment with AI in their classrooms. **They provide accessible and relatable entry points for colleagues who may feel less confident about engaging with new technologies**, reducing the fear of failure by emphasizing shared challenges and incremental progress. At the same time, they preserve institutional memory, ensuring that lessons learned - both successes and missteps - remain available as practices evolve over time.

Strategy for Reflective Innovation Culture 3: Offer Peer Feedback Loops for AI Course Design

Facilitate structured peer consultations where faculty can:

- Present an idea, draft assignment, or policy for feedback.
- Use protocols such as the **critical friends method** or **Brookfield's critical incident analysis**.
- Receive input focused on **ethics, clarity, student experience, and disciplinary alignment**.

These feedback loops are most effective when framed not as evaluation, but as **collaborative co-design** - a space to revise, refine, and reimagine in dialogue. Optional structures may include:

- Department-based review circles.
- Cross-disciplinary teaching clinics.
- "AI Office Hours" hosted by instructional designers or faculty fellows.

These structures create continuity, ensuring that AI pedagogy is not a solitary experiment but a shared, iterative process across the institution. Faculty benefit from seeing how colleagues in different disciplines approach similar challenges, sparking cross-pollination of ideas and strategies. Over time, **these peer consultations cultivate a culture where innovation is normalized, supported, and refined collaboratively**, reinforcing AI integration as a collective academic project rather than an isolated burden.

Institutional Benefits of Reflective Closure

Closing the innovation loop does more than improve practice - it builds:

- **Institutional legitimacy** for experimentation.
- **Shared language** for discussing pedagogical use of AI.
- **Policy feedback channels** informed by grounded classroom realities.
- **Momentum for continuous improvement**, where iteration is normalized and celebrated.

This approach ensures that innovation is not framed as one-off heroics but as part of a **recursive process of design, implementation, reflection, and iteration**. Encouraging AI experimentation is only the first step. To build lasting pedagogical culture, institutions must create the structures that allow faculty to **make meaning from their efforts - and share that meaning with others**. When innovation is framed not just as a product but as a process, **reflection becomes an act of leadership**, and every course becomes a site of institutional learning.

Section Reflection: Aligning Institutional Structures with Faculty Courage in the AI Era

This section reveals a central truth of AI integration in higher education: meaningful faculty innovation will not scale through enthusiasm alone - it must be cultivated through structural alignment, cultural validation, and reflective feedback loops. It reframes the challenge not as faculty resistance to AI, but as an institutional failure to reward risk-taking, safeguard experimentation, and recognize pedagogical courage. The so-called **"innovation paradox"** - where faculty are curious but cautious - is shown to be a rational response to opaque policies, evaluation fears, and absent incentives.

By outlining concrete strategies - from revising promotion and tenure guidelines, to providing microgrants and fellowships, to establishing safe-to-fail laboratories and showcasing faculty leadership - this section illustrates how institutions can lower the cost of experimentation while elevating its value. Innovation is recast as both process and contribution: not a polished outcome to be performed, but a recursive journey to be resourced, reflected upon, and shared. Most importantly, **the section underscores that faculty are already positioned to lead the transformation AI demands - if they are trusted, supported, and invited into co-authorship of that future**. It is a call for colleges and universities to evolve from passive observers of change to active cultivators of the environments in which pedagogical transformation becomes not only possible - but inevitable.

Section 6: Addressing Resistance, Fear, and Misinformation

While artificial intelligence holds extraordinary potential for transforming teaching, learning, and scholarship, many faculty remain hesitant - or even resistant - to engage with it. This reluctance is not always a matter of technical capacity. More often, it reflects **philosophical discomfort, emotional fatigue, institutional distrust, or persistent misinformation** about what AI is and what it means for academic work (Brookfield, 2017; Selwyn, 2019; Slimi & Carballido, 2023). In many cases, these concerns are **reasonable and deeply rooted**, shaped by past experiences with poorly implemented technologies, shifting evaluation standards, or a growing sense that educational change is happening ***to*** faculty, rather than ***with*** them.

Too often, conversations about AI in higher education begin with functionality and end with compliance. But genuine adoption - and responsible integration - requires far more than access to tools or policy guidance. It demands **psychological safety, intellectual trust, and moral clarity**. Faculty are not merely content deliverers to be retooled - they are stewards of disciplinary meaning, professional identity, and pedagogical purpose. Their hesitations must be read not as resistance to change, but as calls for **dialogue, agency, and institutional coherence**.

To build AI-ready institutions, leaders must **resist the impulse to mandate and instead model engagement through empathy, transparency, and inclusive conversation**. This includes:

- Acknowledging the emotional labor of teaching in an era of accelerated disruption.
- Addressing misconceptions about AI's capabilities and limits.
- Creating space for reflective dialogue about ethics, purpose, and professional identity.

- Sharing stories of innovation that highlight care, co-creation, and student voice - not just efficiency.

This section explores the **common roots of faculty resistance**, not as barriers to be removed, but as **diagnostic windows into the culture of higher education itself**. By understanding where these concerns come from - and how they can be addressed with compassion and collaboration - institutions can begin to build the kind of culture where **AI is not feared, but thoughtfully integrated in service of human-centered learning**.

Common Roots of Faculty Resistance

Faculty resistance to AI integration is often misinterpreted as mere reluctance to adopt new technology, when in reality it reflects deeper concerns about identity, authority, workload, and pedagogical integrity. Many faculty worry that experimenting with AI might compromise their credibility, overwhelm their already stretched responsibilities, or erode the values they see as central to teaching and mentorship. **By examining these underlying roots, institutions can move beyond simplistic narratives of "fear" or "inertia" and instead address the structural and emotional realities that shape faculty engagement**.

With this in mind, we now turn to the **Common Roots of Faculty Resistance**, exploring the most prevalent concerns and the conditions that sustain them.

Common Root of Faculty Resistance 1: Fear of Being Replaced

One of the most prevalent - and often unspoken - drivers of faculty resistance to generative AI is the **existential fear of professional obsolescence**. This fear is not rooted in technical misunderstanding, but in **deep concern over the erosion of intellectual identity, pedagogical value, and institutional trust**. It surfaces especially in disciplines where teaching is traditionally anchored in:

- Content delivery (e.g., lectures, slide presentations).
- Writing and communication (e.g., essay-based assessment, rhetorical instruction).
- Human feedback (e.g., formative comments, grading, mentoring).

In these contexts, the rapid emergence of AI tools capable of drafting essays, summarizing texts, generating rubrics, or simulating feedback has led some faculty to ask, implicitly or explicitly:

- *"If ChatGPT can write an essay and grade it, where does that leave me?"*

This sentiment, gathered from recent faculty surveys and reflection groups, reflects more than anxiety - it reflects **an urgent call for institutions to articulate the enduring role of faculty in the AI era. Faculty are asking not simply for reassurance, but for clear visions of how their expertise, judgment, and mentoring remain indispensable in an age of**

machine-generated content and automated systems. Without this institutional clarity, uncertainty about the future of teaching risks deepening into disengagement or resistance, rather than fueling constructive adaptation and leadership

---

Understanding the Root of the Fear

This fear is not irrational - it is **a rational response to ambiguous institutional signals**, rapid technological shifts, and uneven professional development structures. It stems from:

- **Cultural messaging** that positions AI as more efficient, cost-effective, or scalable than human labor.
- **Unclear institutional strategy** around AI's place in teaching, assessment, and academic integrity.
- **Previous waves of automation** that have displaced professionals in other sectors - raising legitimate concerns about what "streamlining education" might mean.

For many educators, the concern is not just ***"Will AI replace me?"*** but:

- *"Will students value my feedback?"*
- *"Will my assignments be meaningful?"*
- *"Will my discipline be understood and respected in a machine-mediated world?"*

Reframing AI as an Extension, Not a Replacement

Institutions must respond not with dismissal or acceleration, but with **empathetic reframing**. AI is not a replacement for educators - it is a **tool that still requires human judgment, ethics, context, and relational insight** (Reiss, 2021). While it may shift what we do, it does not diminish why we do it - or who we are.

What AI Can Do:

- Generate first-draft content.
- Identify surface-level patterns.
- Simulate structure and coherence.
- Offer mechanical feedback based on syntax and keywords.

What Faculty Do That AI Cannot:

- Interpret nuance, voice, and lived experience.
- Build trust and motivation.
- Respond to cultural, emotional, and disciplinary context.
- Coach metacognition, curiosity, and intellectual resilience.
- Mentor students across identity development, scholarly inquiry, and ethical reflection.

Institutional Strategies to Address Replacement Anxiety

One of the most persistent fears among faculty in the AI era is the notion of being replaced - by automated grading tools, AI tutoring platforms, or algorithmic decision systems. This anxiety is not simply about technology itself, but about professional identity, academic value, and the human dimensions of teaching that cannot be automated. **Institutions have a responsibility to directly acknowledge these concerns and provide structures that affirm faculty as indispensable** architects of learning, mentors of ethical judgment, and stewards of student development in AI-integrated environments. The following strategies outline how institutions can move beyond reassurance to concrete action - embedding faculty identity, expertise, and leadership at the heart of AI integration.

Institutional Strategy 1: Affirm Faculty Purpose in Strategic Messaging

Faculty communications must emphasize that adaptation to AI is not a response to obsolescence but an affirmation of their continuing importance. Official statements should frame faculty as central to guiding ethical, inclusive, and student-centered uses of AI, positioning them as leaders in shaping how technology is implemented. By clearly articulating this role, institutions replace narratives of replacement with narratives of empowerment, strengthening trust and professional identity in the AI era.

Institutional Strategy 2: Center Faculty in AI Policy and Planning

Including teaching faculty - not just technologists or administrators - on AI task forces, curricular review boards, and ethics councils ensures that those who work most closely with students shape institutional decision-making. This approach signals that **the future of teaching is not being outsourced to external expertise, but co-authored by the educators who understand classroom realities and pedagogical needs**. By elevating faculty voices in governance, institutions foster legitimacy, transparency, and shared ownership of AI integration.

Institutional Strategy 3: Provide Development Spaces that Reframe Identity

Create reflective professional learning sessions titled, for example:

- *"What Cannot Be Automated?"*
- *"Teaching Presence in the Age of AI."*
- *"From Authority to Architect: Redefining Pedagogical Identity."*

These spaces help faculty reimagine their roles as **learning architects, ethical guides, and epistemic translators**, not merely as content distributors. By framing teaching as the design of reflective processes rather than the delivery of static knowledge, educators reclaim their central role in shaping how students think, question, and engage with AI. This repositioning highlights that **faculty authority in the AI era rests not on controlling information, but on cultivating wisdom, ethical discernment, and intellectual resilience in their students**.

Summary: Fear as a Call for Recognition and Redefinition

Faculty fear of replacement is not resistance - it is often a sign of **deep care for the craft of teaching and the role of human judgment in learning**. Rather than dismiss this fear, institutions must honor it, address it, and channel it into conversations about purpose, pedagogy, and professional agency. In doing so, we remind faculty - and ourselves - that in a world of intelligent machines, **it is the uniquely human elements of education that matter most**.

Common Root of Faculty Resistance 2: Overwhelm and Burnout

For many faculty, the introduction of generative AI into higher education arrives not as an exciting opportunity but as yet another disruption layered atop an already saturated landscape. The aftermath of the COVID-19 pandemic left educators managing **pedagogical redesigns, student mental health crises, shifting enrollment patterns, and ongoing digital fatigue**. In this context, the arrival of AI tools - often accompanied by media hype and institutional pressure - can feel less like innovation and more like **intellectual exhaustion**.

Faculty who are committed to their students, their research, and their service obligations often report that they **lack the time, energy, or clarity** to engage with yet another tool, particularly one as complex and fast-moving as generative AI. For faculty already juggling high teaching loads, limited support, and evolving assessment demands, AI is not perceived as transformational - it is perceived as **"one more thing."**

This exhaustion is not a reflection of resistance - it is a reflection of **unsustainable labor conditions**. It is also a warning sign. If institutions introduce AI solely through training sessions, policy documents, or efficiency rhetoric, they risk **compounding burnout rather than relieving it**.

Response Strategy: Reframe AI as Relief, Not Requirement

To engage faculty meaningfully, AI must be introduced not as an additional burden, but as a **strategic tool for rebalancing effort, simplifying complexity, and restoring time for human-centered work**.

Concrete Applications Include:

- **Drafting rubrics and assignment templates** that faculty can revise rather than create from scratch.
- **Summarizing open-ended student feedback** for mid-semester check-ins or teaching evaluations.
- **Providing first-pass suggestions** on syllabus language, reflection prompts, or discussion questions.
- **Helping students structure their ideas**, allowing faculty to focus on content, critical thinking, and personalized feedback.

When framed this way, AI becomes less about "keeping up" and more about **creating space to do what matters most**: building relationships, modeling ethical inquiry, and mentoring students through complex learning. **Rather than overwhelming faculty with a sense of obsolescence, this perspective emphasizes how AI can relieve cognitive and administrative burdens, allowing more time for human connection and intellectual depth**. In practice, it reframes AI as a tool for amplifying faculty strengths, ensuring that the heart of education remains relational, dialogic, and purpose-driven

---

Design Principle: Start Small, Start Supportive

Rather than asking faculty to "rethink their pedagogy" overnight, institutions should:

- Encourage micro-practices (e.g., using AI to suggest quiz questions or restructure a lesson plan).
- Create **low-stakes, opt-in learning spaces** where experimentation is scaffolded.
- Offer **faculty peer testimonials** that highlight how AI has saved time or eased cognitive load in manageable ways.

In this model, AI is not the endpoint - it is a **means of reclaiming time, focus, and energy** in an increasingly fragmented academic environment (Slimi & Carballido, 2023). By automating routine or repetitive tasks, A**I enables faculty to redirect their attention toward higher-order priorities** such as mentoring, inquiry, and fostering deeper student engagement, reinforcing the idea that technology should serve human-centered education rather than overshadow it.

Summary: Burnout Is Not Inertia - It Is a Call for Care

Faculty overwhelm should not be interpreted as stubbornness or stagnation. It is a clear signal that **systemic conditions must be addressed alongside technological advancement**. By presenting AI as a support mechanism - one that reduces unnecessary friction and re-centers faculty voice - institutions can build trust, re-engage their educators, and **turn exhaustion into renewed pedagogical agency**.

Common Root of Faculty Resistance 3: Philosophical Objections

---

Not all faculty resistance to AI stems from fear, fatigue, or technical uncertainty. For some, the hesitation is **deeply philosophical** - rooted in long-standing concerns about **the nature of knowledge, authorship, ethics, and the role of education in human development**. These faculty may not only question how generative AI functions but also whether it **should** be invited into certain aspects of teaching and learning at all.

From this vantage point, AI tools are not neutral assistants; they are **epistemic actors** that reshape the very processes of reasoning, expression, and interpretation. Some faculty -

particularly in the humanities, critical theory, or professional ethics domains - raise fundamental questions:

- *"Can a predictive language model* ***think****?"*
- *"What does it mean to* ***understand*** *in a machine context?"*
- *"How do AI-generated outputs affect students' development of agency, originality, and empathy?"*
- *"Is reliance on AI compatible with educational goals such as self-authorship, civic formation, or moral judgment?"*

Such questions are not distractions from AI implementation - **they are central to any responsible integration** of generative tools into higher education (Benjamin, 2023; Crawford, 2021). By surfacing concerns about ethics, equity, and institutional purpose, they ensure that adoption is guided by reflective inquiry rather than mere efficiency or novelty.

When Resistance Is Ethical Leadership

Faculty who express philosophical objections are not obstructing progress - they are often **modeling the very kind of critical inquiry that higher education aspires to teach**. Their caution reflects:

- A commitment to **non-instrumental learning**.
- A belief in the ethical weight of human presence in education.
- A desire to **resist the commodification of knowledge and creativity**.

In professional fields such as counseling, theology, social work, or writing instruction, faculty may argue that **no machine can - or should - replace the relational, interpretive, or spiritual dimensions of their disciplines**. These are not anti-technology stances; they are principled boundaries around **what must remain human**.

Facilitated Dialogue Example: Cross-Disciplinary Reflection on Limits

Sample Campus Event: Faculty–Student Dialogue Panel

Panel Title:

- *"Where Should Machines Never Teach?"*
- *"What Is Irreplaceably Human in Education?"*

Description: This panel brings together faculty from counseling, theology, creative writing, and computer science alongside student representatives. Each panelist offers a 5–7 minute reflection on what aspects of teaching and learning they see as distinctly human, followed by a facilitated discussion where participants debate questions such as:

- *"Can empathy be automated?"*
- *"Should spiritual or ethical reasoning ever be delegated to machines?"*
- *"What forms of mentorship cannot be simulated?"*

The event closes with small breakout groups, allowing attendees to articulate their own boundaries and principles for AI use in education

Panel Composition:

- A computer science professor discussing AI logic and limitations.
- A literature scholar reflecting on authorship and metaphor.
- A philosophy faculty member addressing epistemology and intentionality.
- A nursing educator discussing empathy and care ethics.
- A student representative describing lived experience with AI tutors.

Discussion Prompts:

- *"In which dimensions of your teaching is human presence non-negotiable?"*
- *"What do students lose when AI is used for cognitive shortcuts?"*
- *"Where can AI enhance reflection - and where might it flatten it?"*
- *"What forms of judgment or care cannot be replicated by machines?"*

Institutional Value-of-Validating Dissent

Creating spaces for philosophical objection:

- **Demonstrates respect** for academic freedom and ethical pluralism.
- Encourages **slow thinking in a fast-moving tech environment**.
- Surfaces valuable insights for AI policy, pedagogy, and student guidance.
- Helps faculty feel **heard rather than managed**, particularly those committed to the relational and moral foundations of teaching.

Rather than assuming adoption is inevitable, institutions should foster **normative debates** about what should - and should not - be delegated to AI in educational practice. **These conversations allow faculty, students, and administrators to articulate shared boundaries, clarify values, and surface disciplinary differences in what they consider irreplaceably human**. By treating AI integration as a matter of deliberation rather than destiny, higher education affirms that ethical choice and professional judgment remain at the heart of teaching and learning.

Summary: Resistance as Moral Presence

Philosophical objections to AI are not liabilities; they are **assets to be engaged with rigor and respect**. Faculty who voice these concerns uphold the integrity of education as a humanistic enterprise. By inviting them into institutional dialogue as ethical leaders - not late adopters - universities demonstrate that AI integration is not about compliance, but about **constructing a shared vision for education in a machine-augmented world**.

Common Root of Faculty Resistance 4: Misinformation and Media Distortion

One of the most persistent obstacles to faculty engagement with generative AI is not technological complexity, but **informational distortion**. Faculty - like students and the broader public - are inundated with **oversimplified, sensationalized, or contradictory narratives** about what AI is, what it does, and what it threatens. In the media landscape, AI is framed as either a miraculous solution to all educational inefficiencies or an existential threat to critical thinking and human authorship. Headlines alternate between proclaiming AI's sentience and warning of its collapse. This noisy environment cultivates **confusion, skepticism, and learned helplessness**, especially among those seeking to teach with integrity and care. Misinformation can lead faculty to:

- Overestimate AI's capabilities (e.g., assuming it can "think," "understand," or "evaluate").
- Underestimate its usefulness (e.g., dismissing it as a passing fad or gimmick).
- Misidentifies its origins (e.g., equating all AI with ChatGPT or with corporate surveillance).
- Misapply its outputs (e.g., trusting summaries, citations, or grading without validation).

In this context, resistance is often a protective response to **epistemic instability**. Faculty are not unwilling to engage; they are **unsure what is real, what is hype, and what is pedagogically appropriate**.

Response Strategy: Build Nuanced Understanding Through Myth-Busting Pedagogy

Rather than dismissing misinformation as ignorance, institutions should treat it as a **pedagogical opportunity**. By framing false or oversimplified claims as openings for deeper analysis, **faculty can help students interrogate the sources, assumptions, and power structures behind misleading narratives**. Faculty development offerings that include **myth-busting modules** not only correct errors but also cultivate epistemic awareness - empowering educators to confront misconceptions, guide students through complexity, and model informed decision-making in the AI era.

Myth-Busting Workshop Module: Sample Topics and Talking Points

This module can be offered as a stand-alone session or integrated into broader AI literacy seminars, FLCs, or department meetings.

Topic 1: AI Does Not Understand Language - It Predicts It

- Clarify that tools such as ChatGPT are **large language models (LLMs)** trained on massive corpora to predict the next most likely word.
- Emphasize that these models do not "know," "comprehend," or "reason" in a human sense - they **simulate coherence** without semantic awareness (Bender et al., 2021).

Topic 2: AI Can Hallucinate False Facts

- Introduce the concept of **AI hallucination** - the confident generation of incorrect or fabricated information.
- Illustrate how this undermines reliability, particularly in citation-heavy or scientific contexts.
- Encourage verification practices, especially in student work and academic writing.

Topic 3: Not All AI Is "ChatGPT"

- Define different types of AI (e.g., generative AI, predictive analytics, computer vision, recommendation systems).
- Provide examples across disciplines: DALL·E in art, Grammarly in writing support, Scite in research validation, Perusall in collaborative reading.
- Invite faculty to explore tools most relevant to their field, rather than assuming AI is monolithic.

Topic 4: AI Is Biased - Not Because It Is Malicious, But Because It Is Trained on Biased Data

- Introduce the concept of **algorithmic bias** as a structural - not intentional - phenomenon.
- Explain how datasets reflect existing social inequalities, stereotypes, and exclusions.
- Link to classroom discussions on **data ethics, equity, and digital literacy**, particularly in social sciences and humanities (Benjamin, 2023; Noble, 2018).

Supplement With Reputable, Accessible Readings

Pair myth-busting modules with short readings, such as:

- *On the Dangers of Stochastic Parrots* (Bender et al., 2021).
- *Race After Technology* (Benjamin, 2023).
- *Atlas of AI* (Crawford, 2021).
- Selections from the **MLA or APA guidelines** on AI citation and use.

Encourage small-group discussion, annotation, and critique to help faculty **develop both conceptual clarity and disciplinary perspective**. These activities give participants the chance to test ideas against multiple viewpoints, surface hidden assumptions, and practice articulating their own stance. Over time, t**he iterative exchange of perspectives deepens understanding, strengthens disciplinary grounding, and builds confidence in navigating AI's educational implications collaboratively**.

Outcome: From Passive Confusion to Informed Engagement

By addressing misinformation directly, these modules:

- Reduce anxiety by **clarifying boundaries between myth and function**.
- Equip faculty with a **shared language for AI critique and instruction**.

- Reposition educators not as late adopters, but as **critical stewards of knowledge and meaning** in the AI era.

Most importantly, myth-busting invites **intellectual humility without epistemic helplessness** - affirming that nuance, not certainty, is the most important faculty competency in a fast-evolving technological landscape. **By acknowledging complexity, educators can model the critical stance that questions assumptions rather than clinging to oversimplified answers**. This approach cultivates resilience and adaptability, equipping faculty to guide students through uncertainty with integrity, curiosity, and a commitment to thoughtful inquiry.

Summary: Misinformation Is Not Just a Knowledge Gap - It Is a Pedagogical Call to Action

In an age of media saturation and AI hype cycles, institutions must prioritize **clarity over cheerleading, transparency over persuasion, and reflection over compliance**. Faculty do not need to be sold on AI - they need to be **equipped to engage with it critically, ethically, and in alignment with their pedagogical values**. The goal is not blind adoption, but cultivating a culture where educators can weigh possibilities against risks and make intentional, informed choices about how - and when - to integrate AI into their teaching.

Institutional Strategies for Constructive Engagement

As artificial intelligence becomes a defining force in higher education, institutions must move beyond reactive policies or fragmented experiments and instead foster intentional, constructive engagement. Faculty and students alike need opportunities to explore AI not as a mandate, but as a shared subject of inquiry - where its possibilities and pitfalls can be tested, debated, and contextualized. **Constructive engagement means creating spaces that value dialogue over compliance, curiosity over fear, and reflection over simple adoption**, ensuring that AI integration aligns with both institutional mission and pedagogical values.

To make this vision actionable, campuses can adopt a range of strategies that invite faculty and students to engage AI critically, collaboratively, and ethically. The following institutional strategies highlight concrete ways to embed constructive engagement across teaching, learning, and policy.

Strategy for Constructive Engagement 1: Host "Ethical Dialogue Circles"

As generative AI reshapes the contours of academic work, faculty are not just adapting to new tools - they are **wrestling with profound questions of purpose, authorship, equity, and educational identity**. In this moment of epistemic flux, institutions must provide more than training - they must offer **spaces for ethical reflection, shared uncertainty, and communal meaning-making**. Ethical Dialogue Circles offer one such structure.

Unlike policy briefings or instructional workshops, Dialogue Circles are **non-instrumental, interdisciplinary spaces** grounded in mutual respect, active listening, and inquiry. Their goal is not to resolve policy dilemmas or promote tool adoption, but to **reclaim time for human reflection** - allowing faculty to ask:

- *"What are we really doing when we teach?"*
- *"What is being automated - and what must remain human?"*
- *"How do we steward student development in the face of algorithmic mediation?"*

Such conversations elevate AI discourse from technical implementation to **values-based exploration**, helping educators navigate change not only as professionals, but as citizens, mentors, and moral agents (Brookfield, 2017; Selwyn, 2019). **They transform dialogue into a shared ethical practice**, reminding faculty that the future of AI in education is ultimately a question of collective responsibility and human purpose.

Core Features of Ethical Dialogue Circles

Ethical dialogue circles provide a structured, reflective space where faculty can grapple with the pedagogical, cultural, and moral dimensions of AI in education. Unlike traditional workshops that focus on technical training, **these circles emphasize listening, reciprocity, and values-driven inquiry**. They are designed not to produce quick consensus, but to cultivate trust, surface complexity, and anchor institutional change in collective ethical reasoning.

Core Feature 1: Interdisciplinary Participation

Circles should include faculty from across fields - STEM, humanities, arts, social sciences, professional programs - to ensure diverse entry points and epistemologies. Differences in disciplinary framing (e.g., code vs. story, optimization vs. meaning) enrich the conversation and highlight the **pluralism of educational ethics**.

Core Feature 2: Facilitated, Non-Hierarchical Structure

Skilled facilitators - preferably from the Center for Teaching and Learning or trained faculty peers - guide the process using prompts, pause points, and inclusive speaking protocols (e.g., rounds, equity of voice, optional silence). This promotes psychological safety and **disrupts traditional hierarchies** that can inhibit vulnerability.

Core Feature 3: Reflective and Generative Aims

Dialogue Circles are not designed to reach consensus. Instead, they surface layered tensions and generate **shared language, open questions, and ethical commitments**. Participants may:

- Articulate personal or departmental AI principles.
- Map tensions between access and authenticity.
- Draft "what I believe" statements on authorship, empathy, or AI in learning.

These outputs are not mandates - they are **ethical anchors** that guide reflection across diverse teaching contexts. They **provide faculty with a shared moral compass** while still allowing flexibility for disciplinary differences and individual teaching philosophies. By framing guidance as an invitation to reflect rather than a set of rules to follow, **institutions encourage authentic engagement, ownership, and adaptation** in ways that strengthen both integrity and innovation.

Sample Prompts to Catalyze Inquiry

- *"What does it mean to teach when machines can mimic writing?"*
- *"When does student use of AI enhance learning - and when does it replace it?"*
- *"What is lost when AI performs reflection on behalf of students?"*
- *"How do we design classrooms that preserve justice, equity, and compassion amid automation?"*
- *"What can machines never mentor - and how do we safeguard that space?"*

These questions invite layered, nonbinary exploration - moving beyond ***"Use it or do not"*** into ***"What do we owe our students, our disciplines, and each other?"***

Outcomes and Impact

While not always tangible, the outcomes of Ethical Dialogue Circles are **culturally and pedagogically transformative**:

- Faculty report increased confidence in naming ethical tensions and pedagogical boundaries.
- Participants often shift from resistance or silence to **purposeful experimentation**.
- Dialogues surface **common fears and shared aspirations**, which inform institutional strategy and messaging.
- Reflections gathered can seed **living documents**, teaching statements, or departmental value frameworks.

By centering the **moral imagination** of faculty - not just their technical adaptation - institutions affirm that AI integration is not a compliance exercise, but an **invitation to re-clarify the human heart of education**. This framing helps educators see AI not as a threat to their role, but as an opportunity to reaffirm the enduring values of mentorship, dialogue, and human connection that machines cannot replicate.

Summary: Ethical Dialogue as Institutional Compass

Hosting Ethical Dialogue Circles signals that the institution sees faculty not just as implementers of change - but as **co-philosophers of educational purpose**. These circles help reclaim trust, surface unspoken tensions, and empower educators to engage with AI not from fear or fatigue - but from **discernment, community, and professional integrity**. In doing so, they transform AI from a technical issue into a shared ethical inquiry, one where faculty voice actively shapes the values and vision of institutional practice.

Strategy for Constructive Engagement 2: Offer Values-Centered Workshops, Not Just Tool Demos

---

Too often, faculty development workshops on AI focus narrowly on **features, functions, and workflows** - introducing tools such as ChatGPT or DALL·E as if they are plug-and-play enhancements to existing practice. While technical familiarity is necessary, this **tool-first orientation misses the deeper pedagogical challenge**: helping faculty integrate AI in ways that align with their goals, philosophies, and ethical commitments.

- Values-centered workshops begin not with the question ***"What can this tool do?"*** but rather:
    - ***"What are we trying to do as educators - and where might AI support or complicate that work?"***

By reversing the sequence - **starting with purpose, not products** - institutions affirm that **pedagogy comes first** and that AI is **a means, not a mission**. This framing keeps educational values at the center, reminding faculty and students alike that **technology should serve human development, not dictate it**.

Workshop Framing: From Adoption to Alignment

Values-centered workshops invite faculty to begin with questions such as:

- *"What is my philosophy of teaching and learning?"*
- *"What do I want students to walk away with that no machine can provide?"*
- *"Where in my practice do I want to preserve friction, reflection, or failure?"*
- *"What learning goals matter most in my discipline, and how do I know when they are achieved?"*

Only after surfacing these aims do facilitators introduce AI tools - not as replacements, but as **potential complements to human-centered practice**. This sequencing makes clear that **technology is in service to pedagogical goals, not the other way around**. It also helps educators frame AI critically, using it to enhance dialogue, reflection, and creativity while safeguarding the integrity of the learning experience.

Workshop Design Example: Aligning AI With Teaching Philosophy

Session Title: *"Aligning AI With What You Value as an Educator"*

Structure:

- **Opening Reflection Prompt**. *"What is one belief you hold about learning that you would never want to automate?"*
- **Small-Group Dialogue**. Faculty share core values or enduring teaching principles (e.g., empathy, critical thinking, student voice).
- **Scenario Mapping**. Facilitators introduce common use cases of AI (e.g., feedback generation, rubric drafting, student brainstorming).
- **Alignment Activity**. Participants evaluate where these tools might **enhance, undermine, or reshape** their teaching values.
- **Boundary-Setting Conversation**. Faculty articulate conditions for ethical use - what tools are acceptable when, for what purposes, and with what disclosures.

Outcome: Faculty leave not with a checklist of tools, but with a **personalized map** of AI practices that are pedagogically, ethically, and disciplinarily coherent.

Faculty Practice Example: Mission-First Integration

- Consider, at one institution's teaching and learning center, a facilitator begins a faculty workshop by asking:
  - *"What is your teaching philosophy - and how do you want students to grow as thinkers?"*
- Participants write down responses such as:
  - *"I want students to become independent researchers."*
  - *"I care about deep reading and civil discourse."*
  - *"My course is about cultivating reflective practitioners."*
- Only after this is shared does the facilitator introduce generative AI tools that **might align** with these aims:
  - Using AI to co-generate discussion prompts, which students then critique for bias or assumptions.
  - Using AI to simulate alternate interpretations of a text, prompting comparison with a human perspective.
  - Using AI to support first-draft clarity, with revision emphasizing voice, synthesis, and authorial intent.

This approach helps faculty see AI not as a **threat to their pedagogy**, but as a set of tools they can **selectively and critically mobilize** in service of their mission. It reframes integration as an act of professional agency, **where educators determine when, how, and why AI belongs in their teaching**. By positioning faculty as decision-makers rather than passive adopters, institutions affirm that the integrity of pedagogy remains human-led and value-driven.

Benefits of the Values-First Approach

- **Empowers faculty agency** by connecting innovation to existing teaching identity.
- **Fosters institutional trust**, signaling that AI use is not mandated, but professionally owned.

- **Promotes ethical experimentation** grounded in clarity of purpose, not novelty.
- **Supports cross-disciplinary dialogue** by linking tools to values that transcend content (e.g., curiosity, justice, metacognition).

It also creates a **shared pedagogical language** across units - enabling more coherent, thoughtful discussions about AI across disciplines, departments, and ranks. This shared language reduces the fragmentation that often arises when technology is framed only within technical or disciplinary silos. Over time, it fosters a sense of institutional alignment, **where faculty can exchange strategies and critiques with greater clarity and mutual understanding**.

Summary: Begin With Why - Then Decide on How

If higher education is to integrate AI ethically and responsibly, it must **start with what faculty value**, not just what vendors offer. Values-centered workshops reposition generative AI as a **mirror of pedagogical purpose** - a context-aware companion to be evaluated, adapted, and constrained. In doing so, they transform faculty development from tool adoption into **mission-aligned professional renewal**.

Strategy for Constructive Engagement 3: Acknowledge Resistance as an Asset, Not a Barrier

Too often, institutional discourse around faculty resistance to AI frames it as a **problem to be managed or overcome** - a sign of inertia, unfamiliarity, or unwillingness to adapt. But this view fundamentally misreads the nature of resistance in professional learning. In reality, resistance is often a **signal of care** - care for students, for disciplinary integrity, for equity, and for the purpose of education itself.

Faculty who raise concerns about generative AI are frequently those who have thought deeply about:

- The ethical dimensions of authorship and originality.
- The emotional and intellectual development of learners.
- The values that define their fields - whether creativity, critique, rigor, or empathy.

Rather than viewing resistance as obstruction, institutions should recognize it as **a form of ethical stewardship** - an act of educational integrity rather than defiance. Resistance often signals that faculty are holding onto values such as equity, relational trust, or disciplinary rigor, which may be at risk of erosion in rapid adoption cycles. By treating resistance as a reflective checkpoint rather than a barrier, **institutions can surface vital questions that ultimately strengthen the legitimacy and sustainability of AI integration**.

Resistance as a Diagnostic Tool

When faculty express hesitation, what they are often articulating are **unanswered questions or unacknowledged tensions**:

- *"Will this tool undermine critical thinking in my classroom?"*
- *"Will students lose confidence in their voice if they outsource reflection?"*
- *"Will this technology pressure me to automate the parts of teaching that matter most?"*

Such questions are not obstacles; they are **invitations to lead with intentionality and conversation**. As Cox (2004) and Slimi and Carballido (2023) reminded us, institutions that create space for these inquiries build **cultures of trust, not compliance** - and position themselves for long-term, ethical transformation.

Leadership Tip: Respond to Discomfort with Respect, Not Rebuttal

When a faculty member voices concern about AI, leaders - whether deans, department chairs, CTL staff, or faculty mentors - should treat the moment as **a relational opportunity, not a friction point**. The goal is not to convince, but to **listen with curiosity** and demonstrate that caution is **both welcome and valuable**.

Recommended Practices:

- **Listen actively** without redirecting or minimizing: *"I appreciate you naming that tension."*
- **Ask open-ended questions** that validate thoughtfulness.
  - *"What is your biggest concern about introducing this into your classroom?"*
  - *"Are there places where you feel AI would be especially inappropriate - or especially promising?"*
- **Offer optional, values-aligned engagement pathways** rather than one-size-fits-all sessions.
- **Publicly recognize resistant faculty as ethical thinkers**, inviting them to shape norms, not simply adopt them.

This approach reframes the hesitant voice as a **co-designer of institutional change**, not a passive recipient. By elevating resistance into dialogue, **institutions can uncover blind spots in their policies, curricula, or practices** that might otherwise go unexamined. In doing so, hesitancy becomes a generative force - shaping innovation through caution, reflection, and the insistence that change remain anchored in educational values.

Case Example: Ethical Hesitation as Leadership

In a campus-wide AI rollout, a writing instructor shares during a department meeting that they are uncomfortable allowing students to use ChatGPT for brainstorming because it could:

- Flatten personal voice.
- Shortcut the discomfort essential to the writing process.
- Obscure where ideas originate.

Rather than push back, the department chair invites this instructor to **join a working group on authorship and originality in AI-enhanced writing**. The result: a set of ethical use guidelines and assignment templates that help **all faculty think more critically about where**

AI belongs - and where it does not. What began as hesitation becomes an institutional contribution.

Institutional Benefit: From Defensive Culture to Ethical Reflexivity

When resistance is acknowledged as pedagogical reflection rather than obstruction:

- Faculty are more likely to engage in **dialogue rather than silence**.
- Policy becomes grounded in **lived values**, not theoretical assumptions.
- Early adopters and cautious colleagues can **co-exist and co-lead**, rather than polarize.

This shift allows innovation to proceed with **ethical depth, cultural coherence, and relational trust** - essential components of a sustainable AI transition. **It ensures that new practices are not only technically effective but also socially legitimate**, earning buy-in from diverse stakeholders. By rooting transformation in shared values, institutions build resilience, reducing the risk that AI adoption will fracture communities or undermine long-term credibility.

Summary: Resistance Is Not a Wall - It Is a Compass

In times of rapid technological change, resistance should be seen not as a deviation from institutional goals, but as a **barometer of educational values**. Faculty who hesitate are often the very people most invested in maintaining **thoughtfulness, equity, and care** in academic life. When institutions listen to that hesitation - and **elevate it as part of the leadership fabric** - they build not just capacity, but conscience.

Strategy for Constructive Engagement 4: Be Transparent About Institutional AI Goals

In moments of rapid change, faculty uncertainty is often not about the technology itself - but about **the institution's intentions**. When AI-related decisions are made behind closed doors or without clear communication, they breed confusion, mistrust, and speculation. Faculty begin to ask:

- *"Is this tool optional or being quietly mandated?"*
- *"Will I be judged if I do not adopt it - or punished if I do?"*
- *"Who is making these decisions, and do they understand teaching?"*
- *"Is this about pedagogy, or budget efficiency?"*

Such questions are not signs of resistance; they are **calls for transparency, clarity, and inclusion**. When faculty understand the institution's goals, rationale, and decision-making processes, they are far more likely to **engage with curiosity instead of caution** (Brookfield, 2017; Slimi & Carballido, 2023).

Transparency Is a Trust Strategy

Transparency does not require having all the answers - it requires:

- Naming uncertainty when it exists.
- Explaining what is being explored and why.
- Clarifying the lines between experimentation, recommendation, and requirement.

When institutions communicate early and often about their AI trajectory, they transform policy into **shared governance**. Faculty move from passive observers to **active co-designers of the educational future**. This transparency builds institutional trust, signaling that AI adoption is not a hidden administrative mandate but a collective, mission-driven endeavor.

What Faculty Need to Know - and Deserve to Be Told

In the rapid evolution of AI in higher education, faculty are often caught between hype, fear, and uncertainty. Too often, they are left to interpret rumors, fragmented trainings, or contradictory policy updates without clear guidance. **What faculty need is not more speculation but structured, transparent communication about how AI will affect their teaching, assessment, professional identity, and institutional responsibilities**. Clarity is not a luxury - it is an ethical obligation. Institutions that communicate openly empower educators to lead with confidence, integrity, and purpose rather than react from confusion or mistrust.

With this in mind, the following section outlines the core information that faculty not only ***need to know*** to navigate the AI era effectively, but also ***deserve to be told*** as part of their professional rights and responsibilities.

What Faculty Need to Know 1: Whether AI Use Is Optional or Expected

Institutions must clearly state:

- What autonomy do faculty have in AI integration?
- Where policy is suggestive (e.g., sample syllabus language) versus prescriptive (e.g., exam proctoring standards).
- How academic freedom and instructional flexibility are protected.

This clarity empowers faculty to make **ethically and pedagogically aligned choices** without fear of reprisal or confusion. **It reassures educators that their professional judgment is respected, even as new tools reshape teaching and learning practices**. It also establishes a culture of mutual trust, where institutional policies are experienced as supports rather than constraints, enabling faculty to innovate with confidence while staying true to their values.

What Faculty Need to Know 2: Which Tools Are Supported and Why

List the AI tools the institution endorses or licenses, along with:

- Use cases across disciplines.
- Accessibility and data privacy information.
- Equity and bias considerations.
- Known limitations.

When paired with pedagogical rationale (not just product features), this helps faculty select tools based on **teaching goals**, not trends. **It encourages a mindset where technology is evaluated in terms of its contribution to student learning outcomes, equity, and critical engagement rather than its novelty or popularity.** Over time, this alignment builds institutional coherence, ensuring that AI adoption reflects shared educational values rather than fragmented, tool-driven experimentation.

What Faculty Need to Know 3: Who Is Involved in AI Governance

Faculty want to know:

- Who is shaping AI policy and infrastructure?
- Whether instructional staff, librarians, adjuncts, and students are at the table.
- How power is distributed between IT, academic affairs, and faculty governance bodies.

Transparency about governance reassures faculty that **decisions are not being made without educational expertise**.

What Faculty Need to Know 4: How Faculty Input Is Gathered and Used

Institutions should clearly communicate:

- How feedback is solicited (e.g., surveys, roundtables, pilot reflections).
- How that input shapes decisions.
- What changes have resulted from faculty voice?

This feedback loop transforms participation into **visible impact**, reinforcing that the institution listens - and evolves. It signals that **faculty voices, disciplinary knowledge, and teaching experience are integral to shaping how AI is introduced and governed on campus**. This transparency builds trust, ensuring that policies are understood as collaborative frameworks rather than imposed directives.

Case Example: An "AI in Education Dashboard"

Consider, one university that launched an internal **AI in Education Dashboard**, and updated it monthly. The university then made it accessible via the teaching and learning center's website. It includes:

- A curated list of **approved and vetted AI tools**, categorized by function (e.g., writing, grading support, visual design).
- Summaries of **pilot programs**, including student outcomes and faculty reflections.

- An invitation to join or observe **AI governance working groups**.
- An FAQ addressing syllabus policies, authorship concerns, and student equity.
- Contact forms for feedback, ideas, and use-case sharing.

This dashboard does not just inform - it **models transparency, responsiveness, and shared responsibility**. By making institutional decisions, policies, and AI-related updates visible in real time, it demonstrates that **governance is a living process rather than a closed-door event**. In doing so, it invites **faculty and students alike to see themselves as active participants in shaping the educational ecosystem**, reinforcing a culture of accountability and shared stewardship.

Summary: Transparency Builds the Culture That Technology Alone Cannot

AI integration in higher education will not succeed through software alone. It requires a **culture of openness, clarity, and collective authorship**. When institutions are transparent about their goals, rationale, and governance, they invite faculty into a partnership - not a rollout. In doing so, they shift the AI conversation from policy to trust - and from adoption to agency.

Sample Structures for Dialogue and Exploration

Institutions seeking to foster a reflective and ethically grounded culture of AI adoption must go beyond tool demonstrations and policy memos. They must create sustained, flexible spaces for **dialogue, exploration, and narrative-building** - spaces where faculty and students alike can surface their hopes, fears, uncertainties, and aspirations. These structures are not peripheral to AI readiness - they are foundational. They build a culture where **questions are welcomed**, not just answers, and where **ethics, identity, and pedagogical purpose** take precedence over speed and compliance.

One such structure is the ***AI Town Hall*** - a public, inclusive forum where faculty, staff, administrators, and students gather for demonstrations, Q&A, and updates on institutional strategy. These events demystify institutional intent, offer real-time transparency, and validate questions that may otherwise remain unspoken. When thoughtfully facilitated, town halls become **arenas of shared governance**, where updates are paired with invitations to co-design policy and practice.

Equally valuable are ***Cross-Disciplinary Panels*** that feature voices from multiple academic cultures. A philosophy professor, a computer scientist, a media studies scholar, and a nurse educator might come together to discuss, ***"What is authorship in the AI era?"*** or ***"What should machines never teach?"*** These conversations make visible the **epistemological differences that AI surfaces**, while also revealing common ethical commitments across disciplines. By modeling both divergence and mutual respect, panels humanize AI discourse and signal that there is no single "correct" way to approach AI in higher education.

Another vital structure is the ***Critical Reading Circle***, where faculty and/or students engage with books and essays that challenge the dominant narratives about AI. Readings might include *Race After Technology* by Ruha Benjamin, *Atlas of AI* by Kate Crawford, or the now foundational article "Stochastic Parrots" by Bender et al. (2021). These groups prioritize **slow thinking, ethical awareness, and the social dimensions of technological design**. They offer a counterbalance to tool-centric training by inviting critical interrogation of AI's political, historical, and cultural assumptions.

For more personal and longitudinal engagement, institutions can promote ***Pedagogical Journaling*** - a reflective practice where faculty document their experiences integrating or resisting AI in their courses. Weekly prompts might ask: ***"Where did I feel aligned or in tension with my values this week?"*** or ***"What part of my teaching practice should remain machine-free - and why?"*** This form of inquiry fosters **metacognitive growth** and helps educators articulate their evolving philosophies of AI use in ways that support teaching statements, peer mentoring, and leadership development.

Finally, ***Open Mic "Ask Me Anything" Sessions*** offer a more informal, community-driven approach to AI engagement. These are casual, inclusive spaces - online or in-person - where anyone can pose questions without judgment. Faculty might ask, ***"What is a token in GPT-5?"*** or ***"Is using AI to help brainstorm ideas a violation of academic integrity?"*** These sessions are particularly important for **destigmatizing naivete** and encouraging participation from those who may feel excluded from more formal discussions. Hosted by librarians, instructional designers, or interdisciplinary faculty teams, these sessions model **humility, humor, and co-learning**.

Why These Structures Matter

Each of these structures - whether a panel, reading circle, journal prompt, or town hall - offers a different doorway into AI dialogue. Some faculty will enter through the lens of critique, others through curiosity or uncertainty. What matters is that **multiple formats exist**, allowing for reflection, participation, and meaning-making at every level of comfort and experience.

Together, these models help shift institutional culture from reactive adoption to **purposeful engagement**. They demonstrate that integrating AI in education is not a technical transaction, but an **intellectual, ethical, and relational project** - one best navigated in community.

Rationale: Normalize Inquiry, Not Just Adoption

What unites these formats is not tool mastery, but **cultural change through inquiry**. Institutions often emphasize AI competency as a destination. These structures reframe it as a **process of exploration**, where asking better questions is more important than reaching premature certainty.

By offering multiple entry points - dialogue, text, reflection, and open conversation - campuses create conditions for **distributed leadership, ethical experimentation, and shared pedagogical imagination**. This multimodal approach acknowledges that faculty and students bring different learning styles, comfort levels, and disciplinary perspectives to AI engagement.

It also reinforces that **no single pathway defines participation, making innovation a collective endeavor where diverse voices and approaches are not only welcomed but necessary for lasting cultural change**.

Summary: Dialogue Is Infrastructure

In the AI era, infrastructure is not just technical - it is cultural. Dialogue and exploration are the scaffolding through which trust is built, values are clarified, and innovation becomes relational. These sample formats offer a foundation for **campus-wide AI literacy grounded in humanity, humility, and collective growth**.

Section Reflection: Listening First - Building AI Integration Through Trust, Dialogue, and Human-Centered Understanding

This section offers a vital reframing of faculty resistance - not as a threat to innovation, but as a rich site of insight, care, and ethical leadership. It reveals how faculty hesitation toward AI is often rooted in legitimate professional fears, philosophical objections, misinformation, and burnout. Rather than viewing these responses as obstacles, the section calls on institutions to recognize them as diagnostic signals - indicators of a deeper need for clarity, support, and cultural alignment.

By elevating empathy, transparency, and dialogue as core strategies, this section affirms that successful AI integration requires more than training or policy - it requires trust. Structures such as ethical dialogue circles, cross-disciplinary panels, myth-busting workshops, and pedagogical journaling are not supplementary - they are foundational to building reflective, value-aligned adoption. When institutions invite resistance into the center of the conversation, they shift from pushing change onto faculty to co-creating a shared vision with them.

The heart of this reflection is clear: the most responsible and sustainable AI cultures will not be those that enforce adoption - but instead those that foster inquiry. Faculty are not merely adopters of technology - they are moral agents, cultural stewards, and meaning-makers. When institutions listen deeply, provide space for critical reflection, and validate discomfort as care, they lay the groundwork for ethical, thoughtful, and enduring transformation.

Section 7: Integrating AI Into Teaching Portfolios and Professional Identity

---

As AI becomes more deeply embedded in teaching and learning, faculty must be equipped to **document, reflect on, and communicate their engagement with these tools**. This is not just about recording tasks - it is about shaping an academic narrative that positions AI exploration as part of one's **scholarly identity, pedagogical growth, and leadership trajectory** (Brookfield, 2017; Slimi & Carballido, 2023).

This section provides strategies for integrating AI into:

- Teaching portfolios and course narratives.
- Curriculum vitae (CVs) and job materials.
- Annual reviews, promotion, and tenure (P&T) dossiers.
- Conference presentations and professional development statements.

By doing so, faculty not only increase institutional recognition but also **build confidence and clarity** in how their AI work contributes to broader educational goals. This visibility strengthens **the connection between individual innovation and institutional mission**, ensuring that **experimentation is seen as purposeful rather than peripheral.** It also encourages other educators to take part, knowing that their contributions will be valued, documented, and aligned with the shared trajectory of academic transformation.

What to Include in AI-Integrated Teaching Portfolios

As generative AI becomes a more prominent component of higher education, faculty portfolios must evolve to reflect **how faculty are ethically, creatively, and reflectively integrating AI into their teaching practice**. AI pedagogy should not remain invisible labor - especially when it involves thoughtful design, critical dialogue, and boundary-setting in uncharted instructional territory. Teaching portfolios provide a valuable space for faculty to **document, contextualize, and narrate their experimentation and learning** with AI tools, helping them demonstrate impact, intentionality, and innovation. The following outlines key components that can help faculty represent AI-integrated teaching in ways that are **pedagogically rigorous, ethically transparent, and institutionally compelling**.

Teaching Portfolio Component 1: Assignment Showcases with AI Integration

Faculty should include **1–3 representative assignments** that highlight meaningful integration of AI tools - not for novelty, but to support specific learning goals. For each assignment, the portfolio should describe:

- **How AI was used** by students (e.g., drafting outlines, generating visuals, simulating counterarguments, summarizing feedback, or co-developing research questions).
- **Why AI was introduced** (e.g., to develop metacognitive skills, explore algorithmic bias, scaffold reflective writing, or simulate workplace contexts).
- **What students learned** as a result (e.g., improved prompt engineering, critical evaluation of machine outputs, articulation of authorship boundaries, or heightened media literacy).

These entries should **frame AI not as a shortcut**, but as a catalyst for **higher-order thinking, ethical reasoning, or creative experimentation**.

Example Narrative:

- *Consider ... "In my Environmental Policy course, students used Perplexity.ai to conduct AI-assisted literature reviews during their capstone projects. After generating a list of sources using AI, they were required to verify each reference, assess its credibility, and compare the results to a manual search in peer-reviewed databases. Students documented discrepancies, discussed the implications of automation bias, and reflected on when and how AI can responsibly support research. Their annotated bibliographies became artifacts of both research literacy and AI critique."*

Whenever possible, include:

- Sample student work (with anonymized consent).
- Student reflections on the learning process.
- Feedback quotes that speak to **engagement, surprise, confusion, or insight**.

This enriches the narrative and shows that the assignment was not just technologically integrated - but **pedagogically transformative**. It highlights how AI use deepened student learning, fostered critical reflection, and advanced equity in ways that traditional methods might not have achieved. It also underscores that **the true value of AI integration lies in its ability to amplify pedagogy, not replace it**, thereby reinforcing the central role of faculty in shaping meaningful learning experiences.

Why It Matters in Evaluation

Including AI-integrated assignments in a teaching portfolio:

- Demonstrates alignment between **learning outcomes and instructional innovation**.
- Highlights **ethics-in-action**, showing how faculty are guiding students in responsible tool use.
- Provides concrete evidence for **teaching awards, promotion review, or grant applications**.
- Models transparency and thoughtfulness, distinguishing critical integration from trendy adoption.

It also signals to reviewers - department chairs, teaching committees, or tenure panels - that AI in your classroom is not accidental. It is **intentional, iterative, and mission-aligned**. It demonstrates that your integration of AI is guided by pedagogical goals and ethical reflection, making it part of a coherent vision for teaching and learning rather than a passing trend.

Summary: From Experimentation to Evidence

The teaching portfolio is no longer just a place for syllabi and student evaluations - it is a place for **documenting inquiry, caring, and complexity** in the AI era. Including AI-integrated assignment showcases gives faculty a way to narrate their own learning, **reclaim authorship of their teaching narrative**, and demonstrate that innovation in higher education can be ethical, experimental, and grounded in purpose.

Teaching Portfolio Component 2: Personal AI Use Philosophy Statement

As generative AI becomes increasingly embedded in higher education, it is no longer sufficient for faculty to simply adopt - or reject - these tools on technical grounds. Ethical and pedagogical reflection must accompany every instructional decision involving automation. One way to formalize and communicate this intentionality is through a **Personal AI Use Philosophy Statement**, included in the teaching portfolio alongside statements on inclusive pedagogy, experiential learning, or open educational practices.

This 1–2 page reflective statement allows faculty to **articulate their evolving relationship with AI in the classroom** - not as a static endorsement or critique, but as a dynamic, values-based stance rooted in critical inquiry and lived experience. It provides a structured space to capture growth, uncertainty, and intentional decision-making, while highlighting how AI integration aligns with both personal pedagogy and institutional mission.

Purpose of the Statement

The AI Use Philosophy Statement demonstrates:

- **Ethical self-awareness** in an era where transparency, student trust, and academic integrity are being redefined.
- **Clarity of purpose** in how AI tools are selected, constrained, or scaffolded.
- **Leadership readiness**, as institutions increasingly rely on faculty thought partners to shape AI governance, instructional policy, and digital equity efforts.

Rather than focus on technical mastery, this statement foregrounds the ***why*** behind the ***how***, encouraging faculty to reflect on what AI means in their discipline, their classroom, and their pedagogy. It **asks educators to move beyond describing tool use to articulating the values, priorities, and goals that guide their integration of AI**. In doing so, the statement becomes less a record of skills acquired and more a declaration of pedagogical purpose, situating AI within the broader ethical and intellectual commitments of teaching.

Key Elements to Include

Faculty might structure their statement around the following themes:

- **Core Beliefs**. *"What is your philosophical stance on the role of automation in learning? What must remain human in the learning process - and why?"*
- **Pedagogical Boundaries**. *"Where do you permit AI use in your classroom (e.g., brainstorming, feedback summaries), and where do you prohibit it (e.g., reflective writing, positionality statements)?" "How do these boundaries reflect your teaching goals and ethical commitments?"*
- **Balance and Intention**. *"How do you balance efficiency or accessibility benefits of AI with the need to preserve critical thinking, human dialogue, or developmental struggle?"*
- **Student Response**. ***"What have you learned from your students about how they engage with AI?" "How do their uses, misuses, or questions inform your approach?"***

- **Growth and Uncertainty**. *"Where are you still learning?" "What tensions or contradictions are you navigating as you experiment with generative tools?"*

Sample Prompt for Reflection

To scaffold the writing process, faculty can respond to an open-ended prompt such as:

- *"What does it mean to teach in an age when machines can simulate thought?"*
- *"How do I remain human-centered in my design choices, my assessment practices, and my relationship with students in an AI-enhanced classroom?"*

Such a question invites not only conceptual depth, but also narrative and vulnerability - key components of meaningful reflection in times of technological change. It encourages faculty to share personal stories, doubts, or shifts in perspective, revealing how they grapple with the evolving role of AI in their teaching. **This blend of intellectual rigor and human honesty transforms the exercise from a technical report into a richer exploration of professional identity and educational purpose**.

Why This Matters: Modeling Ethical Pedagogical Practice

Including an AI philosophy statement in a teaching portfolio is not merely performative - it models the kind of **intentional, ethically grounded practice** that modern academic leadership demands. As Benjamin (2023) and Selwyn (2019) emphasized, the sociotechnical systems that shape student experience must be interrogated - not merely implemented. This statement helps faculty signal that they are not simply using tools, but **thinking critically about what those tools mean** for equity, power, authorship, and learning.

Moreover, the act of writing the statement itself can serve as a **catalyst for professional clarity** - helping faculty refine their own practices, identify points of alignment with institutional mission, and prepare to lead AI-related dialogue in their departments and disciplines. **In articulating their reflections, faculty often uncover hidden assumptions, strengths, and tensions in their teaching philosophy that might otherwise remain unexamined**. Over time, these statements can also serve as living documents - resources to revisit, revise, and expand as both AI tools and faculty perspectives continue to evolve.

Summary: Teaching With Tools - and With Purpose

In an age where machines can mimic learning behaviors, **faculty distinction lies not in output, but in orientation**. A personal AI Use Philosophy Statement allows educators to express that distinction with clarity, humility, and scholarly voice. It affirms that AI integration is not a technical add-on, but a **pedagogical choice - grounded in ethics, reflective of values, and shaped by care**.

Teaching Portfolio Component 3: Documentation of Classroom Experimentation

As generative AI continues to evolve, its integration into teaching must be framed not as instant mastery but as **pedagogical experimentation** - a cycle of design, testing, reflection, and revision. Faculty teaching portfolios should include documentation of these experiments to demonstrate not just innovation, but **evidence-based, values-aligned responsiveness to a rapidly changing educational landscape**.

Much like a scholar documents a research study or a scientist logs lab trials, a teaching professional should track their instructional experiments with AI. These records offer valuable insight into **pedagogical reasoning, adaptive strategy, and ethical discernment** - qualities increasingly sought in promotion, tenure, and award reviews (Byars-Winston & Dahlberg, 2019).

What to Include in AI Teaching Experimentation Logs

This section of the portfolio should briefly but thoughtfully describe classroom experiments involving AI tools or practices, organized around the following key elements:

- **What Tool or Approach was Tested**? Identify the generative AI tool (e.g., ChatGPT, DALL·E, Perplexity.ai, Grammarly) and what role it played in the assignment or lesson (e.g., content generation, idea scaffolding, peer feedback simulation, multimodal design).
- **What Worked - and What Did Not**? Reflect honestly on what succeeded, what surprised you, and what created challenges or unintended outcomes. Emphasize **pedagogical insight**, not perfection.
- **How did Student Engagement or Learning Change**? Describe observed shifts in student participation, curiosity, critical thinking, or ethics awareness. Use student reflections, feedback, or examples (with consent) to support your claims.
- **How did the Approach Evolved Over Time**? Explain how you adapted the activity in future semesters or modules, showing **iterative learning and responsiveness to student needs**.

Example Entry Format (Narrative or Table)

Faculty may choose to present this information as a short narrative reflection or in tabular format for clarity and comparison across semesters.

Sample Table Entry:

Semester	Course	AI Tool Used	Purpose	Observed Impact
Fall 2023	Intro to Composition	ChatGPT	Brainstorming essay topics	Students generated more diverse topic ideas, especially in underexplored themes, but needed guided discussion on narrowing focus and avoiding overreliance on generic phrasing. Led

Semester	Course	AI Tool Used	Purpose	Observed Impact
				to follow-up assignment on evaluating AI-generated suggestions.

Sample Narrative Reflection:

- *Consider ... "In Fall 2023, I piloted a two-stage assignment in my 'Intro to Composition' course using ChatGPT. Students were asked to generate a list of possible essay topics with AI assistance and then annotate which ones they found promising. While the tool did help students identify new directions, I noticed that many initially accepted the AI's suggestions uncritically. I adjusted the activity mid-semester to include a "critique the chatbot" prompt, where students evaluated the cultural relevance, clarity, and depth of the generated topics. This led to stronger final proposals and more intentional topic selection in subsequent units."*

Why This Matters: Innovation as Reflective Practice

Inclusion of these experimentation logs signals that the faculty member is:

- **Not simply using tools, but thinking through their implications**.
- Willing to **iterate based on student learning**, not just novelty.
- Practicing **evidence-informed pedagogy**, grounded in observation, adjustment, and reflection.

This kind of documentation not only aligns with promotion and tenure criteria for teaching excellence - it also positions the instructor as a **thoughtful contributor to the evolving discourse around ethical AI integration**. It **signals that faculty are not simply reacting to new technologies, but actively shaping how those technologies intersect** with pedagogy, equity, and institutional mission. Over time, such documentation can serve as both personal evidence of innovation and a collective archive that informs broader policy, curriculum, and professional development efforts.

Summary: Evidence Over Enthusiasm

In a moment where AI can easily be oversold or misunderstood, portfolios that include clear, transparent records of classroom experimentation provide a **grounded narrative of pedagogical integrity**. They remind reviewers and colleagues alike that meaningful innovation is not measured by trend adoption - but by the ability to design, test, learn, and evolve in service of student development. In doing so, they **frame faculty as intentional leaders of change, demonstrating that ethical, reflective practice is as valuable as technical proficiency in the AI era**.

Teaching Portfolio Component 4: Student Learning Artifacts and Reflections

One of the most powerful ways to demonstrate the effectiveness and ethical integrity of AI-integrated pedagogy is through **student learning artifacts and reflective commentary**. While syllabi and assignment descriptions reveal instructional intent, it is student work that provides **tangible evidence of engagement, discernment, and growth**. When included thoughtfully in a teaching portfolio, these artifacts illustrate not just what was taught - but how students responded, adapted, and learned.

In the context of AI-enhanced learning, such evidence becomes especially important. It offers insight into how students:

- Navigate automation without surrendering authorship.
- Interpret, revise, or resist machine-generated suggestions.
- Develop a critical understanding of **bias, accuracy, and ethical implications** in digital tools.

These artifacts also support faculty in assessing whether their AI-infused assignments are fostering **metacognition, judgment, and conceptual depth** - or merely producing polished output without learning (Reiss, 2021). They provide a feedback loop for continuous course improvement, ensuring that assignments are not only technically innovative but also pedagogically aligned with deeper cognitive and ethical goals.

What to Include

Faculty may curate a selection of student artifacts that reflect diverse learning experiences and stages of engagement with AI. Examples include:

- **Annotated Samples of AI-assisted Student Work**. For instance, a student-generated paragraph with margin comments explaining which parts were written by AI, which were edited, and why. This reveals the student's thought process and capacity for critical editing.
- **Student Reflections on AI Use**. Short written reflections or discussion board excerpts in which students respond to prompts like:
    - *"How did using AI help (or hinder) your learning process in this assignment?"*
    - *"What decisions did you make about when to trust or revise the AI's suggestions?"*
    - *"How did using this tool change the way you think about authorship or originality?"*
- **Survey Results or Qualitative Feedback Summaries**. Aggregated responses from end-of-term surveys or anonymous feedback forms that specifically ask about the impact of AI-enhanced assignments on student engagement, understanding, or ethical awareness.

These forms of evidence should be framed with brief faculty commentary, clarifying context, instructional goals, and how the data informed future iterations of the course. **By situating evidence within reflective narrative, faculty demonstrate intentionality** - showing that innovation is not random but tied to explicit learning outcomes. This framing also helps reviewers and colleagues **understand how lessons learned in one course may scale, adapt, or inform institutional practices moving forward**.

Example Integration into Portfolio:

- *Consider ... "In my 'Media and Society' course, students used ChatGPT to generate summaries of competing news sources on the same topic. They then annotated the output to identify bias, omission, and source credibility gaps. I asked students to submit a short reflection explaining how the AI influenced their understanding of media literacy. One student wrote, 'It was helpful to start the summary, but I noticed it skipped anything critical of U.S. policy. That made me want to dig deeper into who trained this model and why.'"*

Such moments underscore how AI can become a tool for epistemic awareness, not just content generation. **When students pause to ask where an AI's assumptions come from, what frameworks it reproduces, and what voices are missing, they begin to see technology as a site of inquiry rather than a shortcut.** This reframing turns AI into a mirror for disciplinary methods and cultural values, helping learners understand not only what they know, but how knowledge itself is constructed and contested.

Ethical Considerations and Student Voice

When including student work in a teaching portfolio, always:

- Obtain written permission or anonymize the work.
- Contextualize the artifact with assignment descriptions and reflective framing.
- Avoid using only "success stories" - include examples that show struggle or ambiguity, as these often yield the richest learning.

This transparency aligns with the principles of **authentic assessment and ethical learning environments**, demonstrating that the instructor prioritizes **process over product**, and **student agency over automation** (Reiss, 2021). It **signals to students that their intellectual growth, critical reflection, and ability to make informed choices are valued as much as - if not more than - the final polished output**.

Summary: Centering Student Voice in the AI Era

In an educational landscape increasingly influenced by machine assistance, **the most compelling evidence of teaching impact will come from how students respond, reflect, and grow in relation to these tools.** Including their artifacts and voices in a portfolio affirms that AI pedagogy is not a one-way transmission - but a shared, iterative, and deeply human exchange. By foregrounding student perspectives, **faculty demonstrate that learning with AI is not simply about tool adoption, but about cultivating critical judgment, ethical awareness, and intellectual agency** in a world where automation and human creativity increasingly intersect.

Where to Position AI Work in Academic Materials

Faculty who are experimenting with AI pedagogy often ask a practical question: ***Where should this work appear in my academic record?*** While innovative teaching with generative tools is gaining visibility, it is not always obvious how to document AI-related assignments, reflections, or course redesigns in ways that align with traditional structures of academic evaluation. Positioning this work carefully matters, because it ensures that AI integration is recognized not as a passing trend but instead as evidence of thoughtful, mission-aligned teaching and scholarly leadership.

The following section - ***Where to Position AI Work in Academic Materials*** - offers guidance on how faculty can embed AI-related innovations across teaching portfolios, tenure and promotion documents, annual review narratives, and professional statements. It **highlights strategies that both preserve disciplinary credibility and signal pedagogical leadership in an era where AI is reshaping higher education**.

Where to Position AI Work in Academic Materials 1: Curriculum Vitae (CV)

As generative AI reshapes both the content and the method of teaching, faculty contributions in this domain must be **formally documented in the academic record**. The curriculum vitae, traditionally used to reflect scholarly productivity and pedagogical development, should evolve to include **AI-integrated teaching innovations, leadership in faculty development, and participation in AI ethics or policy initiatives**. Including these elements not only affirms the relevance and rigor of AI-related work but also helps evaluators **recognize it as legitimate scholarly and pedagogical labor**.

Given the accelerating centrality of AI in higher education, adding a dedicated section - such as ***"AI-Infused Teaching and Innovation"*** or ***"Digital Pedagogy and Emerging Technology"*** - ensures that faculty are not invisibilizing experimental or interdisciplinary work, particularly when it falls outside traditional course or publication categories. **This makes AI-related efforts legible to review committees**, positioning them as intentional contributions to teaching excellence and institutional mission rather than as peripheral add-ons.

Suggested Inclusions in the CV Section

Faculty might include entries that reflect a range of instructional, leadership, and scholarly engagement, such as:

- **Course Development and Delivery**. Titles and brief descriptions of courses that incorporate AI tools, critique AI systems, or explore interdisciplinary AI ethics. Indicate any new course approvals, instructional redesigns, or documented outcomes.
- **Workshops and Faculty Development**. Sessions designed or facilitated for colleagues on AI tools, syllabus language, responsible student use, ethical dilemmas, or AI-supported grading and feedback systems.

- **Panels and Presentations**. Participation in campus, regional, or national panels that address AI in teaching, assessment, equity, or disciplinary impacts. Note the audience and format (e.g., faculty roundtable, cross-disciplinary symposium).
- **Grants and Fellowships**. Competitive funding or release time secured for AI-enhanced curriculum innovation, interdisciplinary course creation, or contribution to institutional strategy on AI literacy (Byars-Winston & Dahlberg, 2019).
- **Published or Public-Facing Work**. Blog posts, opinion pieces, or podcast episodes featuring classroom experimentation, critical reflection on authorship, or public pedagogy in the AI era. Indicate venues and accessibility.

Sample CV Entry

AI-Infused Teaching and Innovation:

- *Spring 2024 – Developed and taught "AI, Argument, and Audience," a writing-intensive general education course exploring rhetorical appeals, authorship, and accountability in both human- and machine-generated texts. Students completed co-authored assignments with AI tools and critiqued algorithmic logic through classical rhetorical frameworks.*
- *Fall 2023 – Facilitated campus-wide faculty workshop: "Teaching in the Machine-Mediated Classroom," focused on boundary-setting, syllabus design, and inclusive AI literacy.*
- *2023 – Co-recipient, Innovation Microgrant for "Reimagining Peer Review with AI-Assisted Feedback," funded by the Center for Teaching and Learning.*
- *2022–24 – Member, Institutional Task Force on Generative AI Ethics and Academic Integrity.*

Framing AI Work for Academic Review

When positioned clearly and contextually, these CV entries help promotion and tenure committees:

- See the **breadth of faculty engagement**, from classroom practice to policy formation.
- Evaluate the work as **sustained and intentional**, rather than ad hoc.
- Recognize AI-related innovation as **pedagogically and institutionally aligned**.
- Understand the faculty member's contribution as part of a broader shift toward **evidence-based, ethically aware digital pedagogy**.

In short, thoughtful documentation on the CV helps ensure that **risk-taking is visible, leadership is legible, and reflective practice is professionally valued**. It also signals to external reviewers, grant committees, or interdisciplinary collaborators that **AI pedagogy is a recognized and serious scholarly contribution, not an experimental side note**.

Summary: Make AI Pedagogy Visible in Professional Identity

Your CV is not just a record - it is a narrative of who you are becoming as a scholar, teacher, and institutional contributor. In the AI era, those who are piloting new forms of teaching, asking ethical questions, and scaffolding digital literacy are not merely adapting - they are **leading the redefinition of academic practice**. The CV should reflect that leadership with **clarity, context, and confidence**.

Where to Position AI Work in Academic Materials 2: Annual Review Narratives

Annual review narratives offer faculty a unique opportunity to **contextualize their work**, reflect on instructional growth, and demonstrate alignment with both **personal pedagogical commitments and institutional priorities**. As artificial intelligence becomes more embedded in higher education, faculty should use this narrative space to make their AI integration **visible, purposeful, and pedagogically grounded**.

Rather than treating AI use as a stand-alone innovation, it is most impactful when framed as part of a **larger teaching philosophy, research inquiry, or disciplinary evolution**. This approach demonstrates that AI is not being used for novelty or efficiency alone, but is actively supporting **student learning, ethical engagement, and curriculum advancement**.

What to Include in the Annual Review Narrative

Faculty can thoughtfully incorporate AI-related work into their narrative by attending to three key areas. First, they can highlight **teaching innovations**, such as redesigned assignments, reflective practices, or curriculum development that integrates generative tools in meaningful and ethical ways. Second, they can emphasize **scholarly contributions and service**, including publications, presentations, workshops, or committee work that demonstrates leadership in shaping institutional or disciplinary approaches to AI. Finally, they can frame their **professional identity** around the values that guide their AI integration, showing how their work contributes not just to efficiency, but to equity, critical inquiry, and long-term pedagogical transformation.

Included in the Annual Review Narrative 1: Position AI Within a Broader Pedagogical or Scholarly Goal

Explain how AI tools were not used in isolation, but as a means to support:

- Critical thinking and analysis.
- Student authorship and agency.
- Inclusive learning or accessibility.
- Research skill-building or media literacy.

This helps reviewers see AI as a pedagogical strategy, not a distraction from core instructional outcomes. **It underscores that the integration of AI is directly tied to enhancing learning, cultivating critical inquiry, and advancing disciplinary goals, rather than being a mere experiment in novelty**. By framing AI use in this way, faculty demonstrate that their work aligns with institutional missions of rigor, equity, and innovation, making clear that technology serves as a tool for deeper educational purposes rather than as a detour from academic priorities.

Included in the Annual Review Narrative 2: Connect AI Integration to Departmental or Institutional Outcomes

Reference how AI-related teaching supports:

- General education goals (e.g., digital literacy, ethical reasoning, information evaluation).
- Program-level competencies (e.g., communication, interdisciplinarity, civic engagement).
- Strategic initiatives around **21st-century skill development**, **innovation**, or **equity**.

This signals alignment with institutional mission and **contributes to shared educational vision** (Byars-Winston & Dahlberg, 2019). It also reinforces that **faculty innovation in AI is not an isolated experiment**, but a deliberate contribution to the collective goals of teaching excellence, equity, and institutional growth.

Included in the Annual Review Narrative 3: Frame AI Use as Reflective and Iterative

- **Reflect on Initial Experimentation:** Describe the specific strategies, assignments, or tools you first tried, including what you hoped they would accomplish.
- **Identify Lessons Learned:** Explain what you discovered through student feedback, classroom dynamics, or personal reflection - highlighting both successes and challenges.
- **Document Changes Made:** Detail how you revised your approach in response to those insights, noting concrete adjustments in design, assessment, or instructional practice.

This shows that AI work is **intentional, data-informed, and pedagogically responsive** - key values in instructional assessment and faculty development (Brookfield, 2017). It also demonstrates a commitment to continuous improvement, where experimentation is not incidental but part of a deliberate cycle of reflection, revision, and ethical practice.

Sample Language for an Annual Review Narrative

- *Consider ... "This year, I piloted the use of DALL·E in my Visual Culture seminar as part of my ongoing work on visual rhetoric and representation. Students were asked to generate images based on literary and cultural themes, then analyze how the AI interpreted symbolism, race, and identity. This activity helped surface algorithmic bias and sparked discussions around authorship, originality, and visual ethics. While some students initially focused on aesthetics, they quickly shifted to questioning how training data shaped what the model produced - and what it left out. I revised the assignment mid-semester to include a short critical reflection prompt, which improved depth of analysis. This project aligned with our department's emphasis on media critique and our college-wide digital fluency initiative."*

This Type of Language Shows:

- **A clear teaching goal**.
- **Authentic student engagement**.
- **Ethical reflection**.
- **Instructional adaptation**.

This type of language also **demonstrates how faculty can situate AI use within broader curricular frameworks, showing alignment with departmental and institutional priorities**. It frames the assignment not as novelty, but as scholarship of teaching - where student outcomes, ethical awareness, and pedagogical design are explicitly documented. Finally, it provides reviewers with a narrative that is both reflective and actionable, helping them see how experimentation translates into long-term teaching growth and institutional value.

Why This Matters for Annual Review

Faculty narratives that include AI not only document innovation - they model a **scholarly approach to teaching**. They provide evidence that the faculty member is:

- Responsive to technological shifts.
- Engaged in ethical pedagogical experimentation.
- Contributing to institutional learning culture.
- A reflective practitioner, not merely a technology adopter.

This is particularly important in an era where **institutional policy on AI is still emerging**. Faculty who narrate their own thoughtful decision-making help **shape those policies from the ground up**.

Summary: Narratives as Advocacy for Reflective Innovation

The annual review is not just an evaluation mechanism - it is a platform for making one's evolving pedagogy **legible, defensible, and impactful**. By articulating how AI use aligns with values, enhances learning, and evolves through reflection, faculty help establish that **ethical AI integration is a form of leadership**, not risk. When framed this way, the review process becomes a space not only to report outcomes, but to narrate innovation - making visible the pedagogical risks, ethical choices, and reflective practices that define AI-era teaching.

Where to Position AI Work in Academic Materials 3: Promotion and Tenure Packets

As generative AI reshapes the landscape of higher education, faculty who engage in thoughtful, ethical, and student-centered AI integration must ensure that this work is **clearly documented and strategically framed within promotion and tenure (P&T) materials**.

Rather than treating AI engagement as an auxiliary interest, candidates should position it as a **core dimension of their teaching innovation, cross-disciplinary leadership, and institutional contribution**.

To be legible and persuasive to review committees - especially in traditional or discipline-specific environments - AI-related work must be mapped explicitly onto the **recognized categories of evaluation**: teaching effectiveness, scholarly innovation, service, and collegial impact. In doing so, faculty both advocate for their own advancement and help **legitimize AI pedagogy as meaningful academic labor** within the institution's evolving mission (Byars-Winston & Dahlberg, 2019).

Strategic Framing Across P&T Categories

Promotion and tenure (P&T) processes often rely on evidence that maps faculty contributions to established categories of evaluation, such as teaching, research, and service. **In the AI era, framing innovation within these categories becomes essential: it ensures that experimentation is not misread as peripheral tinkering, but recognized as a form of scholarly leadership**. By situating AI work within familiar structures, faculty demonstrate that their efforts advance institutional missions while also responding to technological transformation with intentionality and rigor. The following sections outline how AI-related teaching, scholarship, and service can be strategically framed across P&T categories to maximize recognition and impact.

Strategic Framing of AI Work 1: Teaching Innovation

Describe how AI tools have been used to:

- Support metacognitive writing strategies.
- Facilitate differentiated instruction and accessibility.
- Scaffold critical analysis of algorithmic systems.
- Promote ethical reasoning and academic integrity conversations.

Cite reflective assignments, student learning artifacts, and course redesigns that align with **program outcomes, general education goals, or institutional strategic themes**.

Sample Portfolio Language:

- *Consider ... "In my course 'Politics and Automation,' students used AI-generated policy briefs as the basis for critique and revision. This allowed them to interrogate not only the content but also the epistemological assumptions embedded in AI-generated discourse. This approach supported our department's emphasis on evidence-based argumentation and digital civic literacy."*

This example illustrates how AI can be integrated not as a shortcut, but as a catalyst for deeper disciplinary critique and reflection. By aligning student engagement with departmental outcomes and broader general education themes, **faculty demonstrate that AI assignments**

contribute directly to institutional learning goals. Such framing also makes clear that the purpose of AI use is not novelty - it is to cultivate transferable skills such as ethical reasoning, metacognition, and critical engagement with systems of knowledge.

Strategic Framing of AI Work 2: Interdisciplinary Collaboration

Highlight any cross-departmental or cross-functional projects involving AI, including:

- Co-taught or cross-listed courses.
- Joint workshops or panels.
- AI curriculum planning with colleagues from computer science, education, ethics, or design.

Show how this work bridges **technical and humanistic inquiry** and contributes to the institution's interdisciplinary vision.

Example:

- *"Co-developed a digital ethics module in partnership with colleagues from data science and sociology to integrate AI literacy into the core curriculum."*

These collaborations demonstrate that AI literacy is not confined to one department but emerges at the intersections of disciplines. **By showcasing how faculty co-create content across fields, institutions highlight their commitment to interdisciplinary innovation and ethical integration of technology**. Documenting these projects also provides concrete evidence that AI pedagogy contributes to institutional vision, accreditation priorities, and the preparation of students for complex, cross-sector professional environments.

Strategic Framing of AI Work 3: Student-Centered Assessment

Explain how AI integration has been used to:

- Improve formative feedback practices.
- Support inclusive and multimodal expression.
- Foster transparency and reflection in student learning.

Document student feedback (qualitative or survey-based) that highlights how AI-informed practices enhanced their sense of agency, clarity, or understanding. Such reflections can include direct quotes from course evaluations, focus groups, or reflective journals where students describe how AI-supported assignments helped them take ownership of their learning process. **When aggregated with survey data showing trends in engagement or comprehension, this feedback provides powerful evidence that AI integration supports both cognitive development and student empowerment**.

Strategic Framing of AI Work 4: Institutional Service

Describe your contributions to:

- Drafting AI usage policies.
- Participating in ethics committees or innovation task forces.
- Advising on AI-integrated curriculum development.
- Leading faculty development around emerging technologies.

This situates AI engagement not as siloed course experimentation, but as a service to the broader educational mission. **By framing classroom innovation in relation to institutional goals - such as digital literacy, equity, or civic readiness - faculty demonstrate that their work contributes directly to shared priorities rather than remaining isolated efforts**. This connection elevates AI pedagogy from individual trial-and-error to a collective practice that advances mission alignment, academic integrity, and institutional transformation.

Supporting Documentation to Include

To strengthen your case, supplement your core packet with:

- **Letters of support** from department chairs, instructional designers, collaborators, or teaching center staff who have observed or benefited from your AI leadership.
- **Student testimonials** (solicited with consent) that speak to the impact of AI-infused assignments, ethical modeling, or reflective practice.
- **Workshop evaluations** or event summaries from campus-wide offerings you have led or contributed to.

These endorsements are particularly useful in affirming **collegial influence and institutional alignment** - two critical but sometimes implicit dimensions of P&T evaluation. They demonstrate that a faculty member's AI-related work has not only advanced individual teaching but also contributed to collective growth, shared dialogue, and institutional priorities. **Such recognition underscores that innovation is not occurring in isolation but is actively shaping departmental culture and reinforcing the broader mission of the institution**.

Summary: Making AI Pedagogy Visible and Valued

In a period of rapid change, faculty who engage critically and reflectively with AI are not simply responding to disruption - they are **co-constructing the future of higher education**. Promotion and tenure packets that frame this work within recognized categories, supported by documentation and testimony, ensure that such contributions are **acknowledged, rewarded, and institutionalized**.

Section Reflection: Documenting the Future - AI Integration as Pedagogical Identity and Scholarly Leadership

This section powerfully reframes AI experimentation not as a peripheral activity, but as central to how faculty define, refine, and communicate their professional identity in a rapidly evolving academic landscape. It highlights that ethical, creative, and intentional engagement with AI is not only instructional - it is scholarly work that must be documented, narrated, and elevated through teaching portfolios, CVs, and professional review materials. Rather than allowing AI innovation to remain invisible or informal, this section urges faculty to foreground their reflective practices, classroom experimentation, and student outcomes as evidence of pedagogical depth and institutional contribution.

Through practical strategies - like integrating assignment showcases, personal AI use statements, and student reflections into portfolios - faculty can position themselves as thoughtful, values-driven educators navigating technological change with purpose. Furthermore, by framing AI work within promotion, tenure, and annual review materials, faculty ensure that their leadership in digital pedagogy is both visible and professionally valued. This narrative of AI-enhanced teaching is not about tools; it is about aligning innovation with learning outcomes, academic mission, and human-centered ethics. In doing so, faculty reclaim authorship of their evolving role in higher education and contribute to institutional clarity in defining what meaningful teaching looks like in the AI era.

Section 8: Designing the Future Together - Faculty as Co-Architects of AI-Ready Institutions

---

Artificial intelligence is not simply a technological shift - it is a **governance, culture, and values shift**. It alters how decisions are made, what kinds of evidence are considered credible, and how authority is distributed across institutions. As universities grapple with AI's implications for pedagogy, assessment, research, and administration, **the role of faculty must evolve beyond adaptation to intentional design**, shaping both the tools and the ethical frameworks that govern their use.

Faculty are not passive users of AI - they are **vision-makers, equity advocates, and educational futurists**. Their expertise positions them to anticipate unintended consequences, advocate for inclusive practices, and ensure that AI integration reflects academic values rather than just market pressures. Institutions that center faculty in AI strategy - from policy development to curriculum redesign - are more likely to create systems that are ethical, inclusive, and resilient (Byars-Winston & Dahlberg, 2019; Selwyn, 2019; Slimi & Carballido, 2023).

This section outlines how institutions can formally engage faculty as **co-creators of AI-ready ecosystems**, with case examples, participatory structures, and principles for governance. It emphasizes that sustainable AI adoption requires shared ownership, where faculty voices shape both vision and implementation. By embedding faculty perspectives into institutional planning, universities can transform AI from a reactive challenge into a proactive opportunity for academic renewal.

The Mindset Shift: From Adoption to Architecture

The initial phase of generative AI's integration into higher education was marked by individual experimentation. Many faculty have already begun using AI tools - whether to brainstorm assignments, streamline feedback, co-write rubrics, or encourage students to interrogate bias and authorship. But institutional readiness for AI cannot rest solely on the innovation of a few early adopters. What is needed now is a broader **mindset shift - from individual adoption to collective architecture**.

This means moving from **"How can I use AI in my classroom?"** to **"What kind of AI culture are we building as a university?"** It requires institutions to engage in **systemic, values-driven design**, and it calls on faculty not just to participate - but to **lead**.

From Tool to Infrastructure: The Architectural Imperative

As AI tools become embedded in campus-wide systems - learning management platforms, advising dashboards, curricular design, assessment protocols - the stakes expand beyond pedagogy. AI is no longer just a classroom tool; it is increasingly part of the **invisible infrastructure of academic decision-making**.

This raises urgent questions that cannot be left to technologists or external vendors alone:

- ***"What values should guide AI use*** *in grading, advising, or curriculum personalization?"*
- ***"How do we ensure transparency, explainability, and equity*** *in systems that increasingly influence student progress and instructor workload?"*
- ***"Who decides how AI is used,*** *and who is most likely to be impacted - especially across lines of race, ability, gender, or access?"*
- ***"What mechanisms exist for dissent, revision, and review,*** *especially when tools evolve faster than policies?"*

These are **not technical questions** - they are **pedagogical, ethical, and political**. And faculty are best positioned to ask - and help answer - them.

Faculty as Institutional Architects

The shift from adoption to architecture invites faculty to reimagine their role not only as faculty, but as **co-designers of the institutional ecosystem** in which AI operates. This includes:

- Shaping campus policies on AI authorship, accountability, and data use.
- Serving on cross-functional governance bodies that evaluate emerging tools.
- Collaborating with IT, librarians, student affairs, and advising to ensure **alignment between pedagogy and system design**.
- Modeling deliberative, inclusive leadership that prioritizes human judgment, educational equity, and academic integrity.

Faculty leadership in this space ensures that AI is not implemented as an **external mandate** but integrated as a **mission-aligned practice** - one that reflects the core values of higher education: inquiry, care, justice, and student development (Benjamin, 2023; Selwyn, 2019).

Summary: From Early Users to Ethical Engineers

The future of AI in higher education will not be determined by which tools are adopted - but by **how they are governed, who they serve, and what values they reflect**. Faculty have already begun exploring AI in their teaching. The next step is to scale that curiosity into **collective action** - moving from scattered experiments to shared frameworks, from improvisation to infrastructure.

To do so is not just to integrate AI - it is to **shape its role in the future of learning**. The mindset shift from adoption to architecture is ultimately a call to **reclaim institutional authorship** in an AI era. Faculty must not simply use AI - they must help **design the systems, policies, and pedagogies that define its use**.

Pathways for Faculty Co-Leadership in AI Integration

Pathway for Faculty Co-Leadership 1: Faculty Representation on AI Governance and Ethics Committees

As artificial intelligence becomes increasingly embedded in the instructional, administrative, and operational life of higher education, institutions must move beyond ad hoc decisions and begin building **formal structures of AI governance**. Central to these structures is the **meaningful inclusion of faculty** in the design, evaluation, and ethical oversight of AI systems.

Faculty are not merely stakeholders - they are **pedagogical experts, disciplinary stewards, and institutional historians**. Their engagement ensures that decisions about AI are grounded in **educational values, disciplinary nuance, and lived teaching experience**. This is especially important in contexts where AI is influencing student advising, assessment, accessibility services, and curriculum personalization - all areas where faculty insight is essential to protecting student learning, academic integrity, and equity (Brookfield, 2017; Reiss, 2021).

The Case for Faculty-Led AI Oversight

To ensure responsible and inclusive implementation, institutions should establish **standing or ad hoc committees** on AI governance and ethics, with faculty playing a central role. These committees should:

- **Review current and proposed use cases** for AI in teaching, advising, student support, admissions, and research infrastructure.

- **Draft and update ethical principles** for the use of generative AI in academic environments, aligned with institutional mission and disciplinary standards.
- **Evaluate AI tools** based on criteria of transparency, accessibility, data privacy, intellectual ownership, and potential bias.
- **Advise on procurement decisions and third-party partnerships**, ensuring that educational values - not just vendor promises - guide technology acquisition and deployment.

These committees should be **interdisciplinary by design**, ensuring that perspectives from the humanities, social sciences, STEM, the arts, professional programs, and student affairs are represented.

Example: R1 University's "AI in Education Ethics Task Force"

Consider at a major research university, the provost convened a faculty-led **AI in Education Ethics Task Force** composed of twelve members from departments including Philosophy, Computer Science, Education, Nursing, Sociology, and the Library. Over the course of one academic year, the task force:

- Conducted an audit of current AI-related teaching practices across departments.
- Hosted a series of listening sessions with students and faculty about AI's impact on learning.
- Published a white paper outlining **acceptable and unacceptable uses of generative AI in the classroom**, with particular attention to:
    - Student data protection.
    - Transparent use of AI in grading and feedback.
    - Optional participation in AI-assisted advising platforms.
    - Consent protocols for AI-mediated support services.

The task force's recommendations were formally adopted by the Faculty Senate and incorporated into campus-wide policy. They also became the basis for a new faculty development series, "Teaching with AI: Ethics and Practice," co-led by task force members.

Why It Matters: Legitimacy, Trust, and Shared Responsibility

When faculty are empowered to help **govern institutional AI strategy**, the results are more than procedural - they are cultural. Faculty inclusion ensures that:

- **Technology implementation is educationally aligned**, not just operationally efficient.
- **Policy reflects instructional realities**, not abstract aspirations.
- **Faculty concerns are addressed in dialogue, not in opposition**.
- **Institutions model participatory governance**, which enhances credibility and trust across stakeholder groups (Slimi & Carballido, 2023).

Moreover, when AI governance is housed within existing shared governance frameworks - e.g., through Faculty Senate subcommittees or provost-appointed working groups -

institutions reinforce that AI integration is not just a technical issue, but an **academic and ethical one**.

Summary: Faculty Governance Is AI Governance

As colleges and universities move from experimentation to infrastructure, faculty must be recognized not only as classroom innovators but as **institutional architects**. Their inclusion in AI ethics and governance committees ensures that higher education does not become a passive consumer of algorithmic tools - but instead emerges as a **deliberate, values-led shaper of AI's role in democratic and educational life**.

Pathways for Faculty Co-Leadership 2: Cross-Disciplinary Curriculum Councils

As artificial intelligence becomes a defining force in contemporary life, its integration into higher education cannot be siloed within computer science departments or relegated to optional workshops. It must be embedded thoughtfully and equitably into the **core curriculum**, where all students - regardless of major - engage with AI not only as a tool but as a cultural, ethical, and epistemological phenomenon. To accomplish this, institutions should empower faculty to lead **cross-disciplinary curriculum councils** that guide the development of AI-integrated learning across general education and degree programs.

These councils function as **curricular innovation hubs**, bringing together educators from humanities, social sciences, STEM, the arts, and professional fields to collaboratively design courses, pathways, and competencies that prepare students to **analyze, use, and challenge AI systems** in context. The aim is not only to teach technical literacy, but to cultivate **critical fluency, civic imagination, and ethical discernment** - capacities essential for democratic participation in an algorithmic age (Benjamin, 2023; Selwyn, 2019).

Faculty Leadership in Curricular Design

Cross-disciplinary curriculum councils should be faculty-driven and empowered to:

- **Embed AI Literacy Across General Education**. For example, integrating algorithmic bias into sociology courses, AI and authorship into first-year writing, or ethical decision-making in introductory business courses.
- **Design Interdisciplinary Courses that Center on AI-Society Interaction**. New offerings may include seminars like:
  - *"AI and the Human Condition"* (philosophy + engineering).
  - *"Algorithmic Futures: Policy, Power, and Public Life"* (public policy + data science).
  - *"Human–AI Collaboration in Creative Work"* (visual arts + computer science).
- **Ensure Alignment Between Departmental Outcomes and Digital Futures**. Councils can audit existing programs to identify gaps in data ethics, automation awareness, or digital communication, and recommend revisions that promote **future-proof competencies**.

Example: Interdisciplinary Collaboration at a Liberal Arts College

Consider at a liberal arts institution, a **faculty-led Curriculum Innovation Council** was formed with equal representation from arts, sciences, and professional programs. Co-chaired by a history professor and a computer scientist, the group was tasked with developing a new sophomore-level seminar required across all majors.

The result was a course titled **"Thinking With Machines,"** which invites students to examine:

- The philosophical roots of artificial intelligence.
- The labor, environmental, and social impacts of automation.
- Case studies in human-AI collaboration across medicine, education, journalism, and art.
- Ethical dilemmas raised by large language models, surveillance systems, and algorithmic decision-making.

Students read *Race After Technology* (Benjamin, 2023), coded simple machine learning models in Python, debated real-world AI policies, and completed a reflective essay on the role of machines in their intended profession. The course became a **signature element of the college's general education program** and sparked the creation of a faculty microgrant program to develop similar courses at the departmental level.

Why Cross-Disciplinary Curriculum Matters

- It **democratizes AI literacy**, ensuring all students - not just tech majors - are prepared to critique and co-shape algorithmic systems.
- It promotes **pedagogical inclusivity**, honoring the distinct contributions of each discipline in making sense of digital transformation.
- It supports **interdisciplinary community-building among faculty**, creating collaborative structures that outlast any single course or tool.
- It aligns with institutional missions to foster ethical leadership, global awareness, and lifelong learning.

Curriculum councils also help **institutionalize innovation** by ensuring that AI pedagogy is not dependent on a few early adopters, but is scaffolded into **governance, review cycles, and learning assessment**.

Summary: From Course Add-Ons to Curricular Foundations

In the AI era, colleges and universities must think beyond tool training and elective courses. They must build **intentional, interdisciplinary learning pathways** that prepare students to live, lead, and learn alongside intelligent systems. Faculty-led curriculum councils are essential to this work. They ensure that AI pedagogy is **rooted in disciplinary wisdom, responsive to emerging futures, and accessible to all learners** - not just the tech-savvy few.

Pathways for Faculty Co-Leadership 3: Co-Design Studios and Institutional Hackathons

To move beyond top-down implementation and passive adoption of artificial intelligence in education, institutions must create participatory spaces where **faculty, students, technologists, and administrators collaboratively design the future of AI-enhanced learning**. Co-design studios and institutional hackathons offer one such structure - blending creative problem-solving with critical pedagogy, and prototyping innovation that is **rooted in educational values, not just technical functionality**.

These short-term, high-intensity engagements - whether structured as 24-hour design jams, weekend hackathons, or multi-day AI-in-Education studios - invite participants to **co-create tools, assignments, feedback systems, and frameworks** that reflect the collective expertise of the academic community. They model **distributed leadership, mutual respect, and agile experimentation**, while surfacing divergent perspectives on what AI should do, where it should be constrained, and how it might be leveraged to deepen human learning rather than displace it.

Key Focus Areas for Co-Design

Co-design initiatives can be guided by themes that reflect institutional priorities or curricular opportunities. Potential prototypes include:

- **AI-augmented advising systems** that combine predictive analytics with contextual human judgment, while centering equity, consent, and transparency.
- **Collaborative feedback platforms** where AI generates initial suggestions, but students and faculty jointly annotate, revise, or critique the machine output - building metacognitive awareness.
- **Alternative assessment models** that prioritize ***process over product***, rewarding prompt engineering, reflection logs, and ethical use of generative tools, rather than polished but uncritical machine outputs.
- **Learning dashboards** that track not just outcomes, but ***how*** students interact with AI - surfacing patterns in dependence, revision, or resistance.

These design targets should be framed by critical questions:

- *"Who benefits from this system?"*
- *"Whose labor is made more visible or invisible?"*
- *"How are student agency and consent protected?"*

By integrating **ethics, usability, and pedagogy** into the design process, these studios prevent AI adoption from becoming purely instrumental or extractive.

Example: AI Pedagogy Design Sprint

Consider at a mid-sized liberal arts university, the teaching and learning center hosted a **48-hour AI Pedagogy Design Sprint**. Faculty from philosophy, education, computer science, and linguistics worked alongside instructional designers and undergraduate students to prototype a **multimodal grading rubric** for writing-intensive courses in the AI era. The rubric rewarded:

- **Prompt Crafting**. Students received credit for developing specific, ethically framed prompts used with generative tools.
- **AI-Use Reflection**. Students submitted a log documenting what the AI produced, what they kept, what they changed, and why.
- **Critical Editing**. Students demonstrated how they layered context, nuance, and disciplinary voice onto the AI-generated draft.
- **Citation Clarity**. Students were asked to disclose AI use in footnotes or process memos, normalizing transparency without penalizing experimentation.

The resulting prototype was tested in two first-year seminars the following semester and became the basis for a campus-wide faculty workshop: *"Grading With Generative AI: Transparency, Process, and Voice."*

Why This Matters: Innovation With Guardrails

Hackathons and design studios:

- **Democratize AI development**, allowing students and faculty to shape the tools that will affect them.
- Provide a venue for **low-risk experimentation**, where failure is reframed as learning.
- Surface **disciplinary tensions** and support shared vocabulary across silos.
- Enable institutions to **move faster than policy** by prototyping ethical practices before codifying them.

As Reiss (2021) and Brookfield (2017) reminded us, sustainable pedagogical change is rarely top-down - it emerges through **reflective communities of practice**, driven by curiosity, trust, and iterative design.

Summary: Prototyping the Future, Together

Rather than waiting for AI tools to arrive pre-packaged from vendors - or for ethical crises to demand reactive responses - colleges and universities can proactively build their AI pedagogical future through **intentional, interdisciplinary, and human-centered co-design**. Hackathons and studios send a powerful message: we are not simply recipients of AI - we are **co-authors of its academic role**, and we will shape that role in dialogue, not silence.

Pathways for Faculty Co-Leadership 4: Policy and Strategy Feedback Loops

As colleges and universities grapple with the ethical, pedagogical, and logistical implications of generative AI, they must move beyond surface-level consultation and toward **systematic, iterative mechanisms that formally include faculty in policy formation, review, and revision**. AI integration is not a one-time implementation - it is an ongoing negotiation of values, norms, and practices. Faculty are not just end users of AI policies - they are **co-creators of academic integrity, pedagogical rigor, and student development**.

Creating effective feedback loops ensures that the AI-related strategy remains **responsive, context-sensitive, and grounded in lived teaching experience**. Without such loops, institutions risk policy brittleness, faculty disengagement, and a misalignment between administrative intent and instructional reality (Brookfield, 2017; Reiss, 2021).

Key Areas for Ongoing Faculty Feedback

Faculty should be actively involved in the development and review of:

- **Academic Integrity Policies Involving AI**. This includes defining acceptable and unacceptable uses of AI in coursework, creating systems for transparent student reporting, and articulating proportional responses to violations. Faculty input ensures that integrity frameworks are not only enforceable but also **pedagogically coherent and ethically balanced**.
- **Syllabus Language Standards for Disclosure and Attribution**. As expectations around AI transparency evolve, institutions must offer guidance - but not mandates - on how faculty can frame AI use in course documents. Faculty should help draft **discipline-specific models** for citing AI, communicating boundaries, and fostering student agency.
- **AI Readiness Evaluations and Student Outcome Metrics**. Institutions should involve faculty in selecting and interpreting metrics that assess how AI integration affects student engagement, equity, retention, or performance. Faculty participation ensures that **quantitative data is contextualized with qualitative insights** and that accountability structures serve learning, not surveillance.

Practice Tip: Create Transparent, Collaborative Feedback Mechanisms

To operationalize these feedback loops, institutions can adopt **low-barrier, high-visibility practices** such as:

- Creating a **shared Google Doc** where draft AI policies are posted with open comment periods. Comments should be organized by theme (e.g., instruction, assessment, advising) and reviewed by a cross-functional committee.
- Asking department chairs to facilitate **structured faculty conversations** on AI integration, using a short discussion guide. Responses can be collected, synthesized, and brought back to leadership.
- Hosting **AI policy forums** where faculty can hear the rationale behind proposed guidelines, ask questions, and propose edits in real time.
- Most importantly, **close the loop**. Publish a brief response document summarizing faculty input, listing specific changes made, and explaining why others were not adopted. This builds **institutional trust, accountability, and shared ownership**.

Why It Matters: Legitimacy Through Process, Not Just Policy

Faculty are more likely to engage with and implement AI-related policies when:

- They understand the rationale.
- They see their voice reflected in the outcome.
- They are treated not as compliance targets but as **thought partners**.

This approach builds a culture where **change is co-authored**, rather than imposed - and where institutional agility is supported by **faculty trust and collaborative infrastructure** (Cox, 2004; Slimi & Carballido, 2023).

Summary: Policy Is Not Neutral - It Is Pedagogical

Every AI policy - whether about citation, grading, or tool access - carries implicit messages about **what learning should look like, who holds authority, and how knowledge is produced**. Faculty must be at the table when those messages are crafted, and feedback loops must ensure they are **not invited once but continually involved**.

The future of ethical, student-centered, and academically rigorous AI use depends not on perfect policies, but on **transparent processes where those closest to the classroom help shape institutional direction**.

Pathways for Faculty Co-Leadership 5: Faculty-Led Public Scholarship on AI and Higher Ed

As artificial intelligence increasingly shapes public discourse, labor markets, knowledge production, and democratic institutions, faculty have an essential role to play not only within their classrooms but as **public intellectuals and civic educators**. Institutions should actively support and elevate faculty who engage in public scholarship on AI and its implications for education, ethics, and society. Such work reflects **the university's mission to serve the public good** and positions faculty as trusted guides in an era of rapid technological change.

Public-facing scholarship on AI in higher education goes beyond academic publishing. It includes **community engagement, interdisciplinary research, media translation, and advocacy for equitable policy**. Faculty who take on this work act as bridge-builders between academic insight and public understanding - bringing nuance, ethics, and evidence to a discourse often dominated by hype, misinformation, or technocratic determinism (Benjamin, 2023; Selwyn, 2019).

Modes of Public Scholarship to Encourage and Recognize

Faculty co-leaders in this space may contribute through diverse platforms and practices:

- **Publishing in public-facing venues** on AI's influence on knowledge systems, educational labor, academic authorship, surveillance in learning platforms, or the commodification of student data. This may include op-eds, blog series, podcasts, or multimedia essays that translate academic expertise into accessible formats.

- **Hosting webinars, panel discussions, or town halls** that demystify generative AI for students, parents, policymakers, or local communities. Topics might include:
    - *"How AI Is Changing the College Classroom"*
    - *"Algorithmic Bias and Educational Equity"*
    - *"Can Machines Teach? Ethics of Automation in Higher Ed"*
- **Facilitating student–faculty research collaborations** on algorithmic ethics, academic integrity, AI bias, or educational data justice. These projects support undergraduate and graduate student development while advancing critical inquiry into the ethical dimensions of machine learning systems.
- **Serving as institutional representatives in public forums** on AI policy, workforce readiness, or education strategy - bringing an educator's lens to conversations often dominated by industry and infrastructure actors.

Recognition Strategy: Make Public Scholarship Count

To support this form of leadership, institutions should embed public scholarship into **promotion, tenure, and annual review frameworks** as a recognized form of:

- **Service** (e.g., institutional outreach, civic engagement).
- **Pedagogical innovation** (e.g., integrating public dialogue into coursework).
- **Academic leadership** (e.g., shaping AI ethics discourse within and beyond campus).

This can be reinforced by updating review guidelines to explicitly include language such as:

- *"Faculty contributions to public understanding of emerging technologies - including generative AI - through media engagement, community education, and interdisciplinary collaboration will be considered evidence of professional impact and academic leadership."*

Additionally, institutions might:

- Offer **media training** or support for public-facing writing.
- Create **microgrants or course releases** for faculty pursuing public scholarship initiatives.
- Highlight faculty voices on institutional websites, newsletters, and external communications.

Why This Matters: Reclaiming the Public Role of the University

In an era of algorithmic decision-making, misinformation, and educational uncertainty, faculty who engage publicly on AI do more than interpret technology - they **defend and reimagine the social mission of higher education**. They help communities understand not only how machines work, but **how society should work when machines are involved**.

Public scholarship affirms that AI literacy is not a technical skill alone - it is a **civic competency, a cultural critique, and a moral imperative**. Faculty must be empowered to bring this message beyond the classroom.

Summary: Scholarship as Stewardship

Supporting faculty-led public scholarship on AI is not just a matter of individual recognition - it is an institutional strategy for **restoring trust, modeling responsible innovation, and extending educational impact**. In this moment, the university's legitimacy will not be measured by how fast it adopts AI, but by how deeply it engages the questions AI forces us to ask - and how openly it shares those conversations with the world.

Guiding Principles for Faculty-Centered AI Design

As institutions move from early AI experimentation to systemic integration, the design of tools, policies, and infrastructure must be guided by **principles that center faculty expertise, values, and professional integrity**. Without these principles, AI adoption risks becoming extractive - serving administrative or technological agendas while marginalizing the lived experience of those who teach, mentor, assess, and support students.

Faculty-centered AI design is not about resisting innovation - it is about ensuring that **innovation is aligned with the mission of higher education**, including its commitments to equity, academic freedom, and ethical learning environments. The following five principles offer a foundation for institutions seeking to integrate AI thoughtfully, collaboratively, and sustainably.

Guiding Principle 1: Transparency

Faculty must be fully informed about any AI tools or systems being used across the institution - especially those that impact **grading, advising, student engagement metrics, or curricular mapping**. Transparency means:

- Clear communication about what AI tools are in use and what data they rely on.
- Access to documentation about how decisions are being made and how models function.
- Disclosure of vendor partnerships, data-sharing agreements, and algorithmic limitations.

Without transparency, faculty cannot adequately evaluate, critique, or contextualize the tools they are expected to engage with - or those used on their students' behalf.

Best Practice: Institutions should maintain a living inventory of all approved AI tools, their functions, their institutional rationale, and a point of contact for concerns. This should be paired with regular briefings and open forums for faculty questions.

Guiding Principle 2: Inclusion

AI design and policy must actively seek input from **underrepresented disciplines, epistemologies, and faculty groups**. Too often, AI governance is centralized within STEM or administrative units, overlooking the insights of humanities scholars, community-engaged educators, adjunct faculty, or those teaching in culturally sustaining frameworks. Inclusion requires:

- Cross-disciplinary representation in AI governance bodies.
- Compensation for faculty service in these roles.
- Support for participation from contingent, part-time, and minoritized faculty.

When inclusion is prioritized, institutions are more likely to design systems that account for **disciplinary nuance, ethical complexity, and the diversity of student experience** (Benjamin, 2023; Slimi & Carballido, 2023).

Guiding Principle 3: Agency

Faculty must retain pedagogical agency in deciding how, when, and whether to integrate AI tools into their teaching. This includes the right to:

- **Opt in or out** of institutional tools that automate aspects of instruction or feedback.
- Establish **course-specific norms** for AI use and student disclosure.
- Adapt or resist platform defaults that conflict with disciplinary or pedagogical goals.

Agency does not imply inconsistency - it recognizes that **meaningful AI integration requires professional judgment, contextual sensitivity, and ethical discretion**.

Policy Implication: Institutions should formally codify faculty rights to define AI use within their courses and ensure that platform changes or mandates are accompanied by opt-out provisions and robust consultation.

Guiding Principle 4: Ethical Stewardship

AI decisions must be guided not only by efficiency or innovation, but by **ethical commitments to students, communities, and the broader public**. This includes:

- Ensuring that AI implementation does not exacerbate inequity or surveillance.
- Prioritizing explainability and fairness in automated decision systems.
- Considering the social, labor, and ecological consequences of AI procurement and deployment (Crawford, 2021; Eubanks, 2018).

Faculty are uniquely positioned to act as ethical stewards because of their proximity to students, disciplinary norms, and the values of academic inquiry.

Recommendation: Every AI-related policy, platform rollout, or curricular initiative should be accompanied by an ethical impact statement and reviewed by a faculty ethics advisory body.

Guiding Principle 5: Reflexivity

AI policies must not be static. They should be **revisited annually** and iteratively revised based on:

- Teaching reflections gathered from across departments.
- Aggregated student feedback on AI-related learning experiences.
- Emerging research and social developments in AI ethics, authorship, and cognition.

Reflexivity recognizes that the AI landscape is not only changing technologically - it is evolving socially, politically, and educationally.

Implementation Strategy: Create a standing "AI Policy Reflection Week" each academic year, during which faculty share insights, tensions, and revisions from their courses. Use this as input for a campus-wide policy review.

Summary: From Governance to Design Culture

Embedding these five principles into institutional strategy is not simply a matter of governance - it is a matter of **designing a culture of ethical, inclusive, and reflective AI use**. Faculty must be seen not only as adopters of technology, but as **co-architects of the environments in which AI will shape learning, labor, and knowledge itself**.

Section Reflection: Faculty as Co-Architects of an AI-Ready Academic Future

This section stands as a culminating vision statement - a call for faculty not merely to adapt to AI, but to actively **architect** its integration into the institutional fabric of higher education. The shift outlined here - from passive tool use to proactive infrastructure design - elevates the role of educators from users to co-authors of AI's educational presence. This section highlights the need for intentional, collaborative, and values-driven approaches to AI governance, pedagogy, and policy, with faculty positioned at the center of strategic decision-making.

Crucially, this section reframes AI not as a technological disruption to be weathered but instead as a profound institutional turning point that demands clarity of mission, inclusivity of voices, and ethical stewardship. Faculty leadership is presented not as optional, but essential to ensuring that AI serves educational goals rather than undermining them. By engaging in governance committees, curricular councils, policy design feedback loops, public scholarship, and co-design initiatives, faculty help shape an AI culture rooted in equity, transparency, human judgment, and academic freedom.

Moreover, the five guiding principles - **Transparency, Inclusion, Agency, Ethical Stewardship,** and **Reflexivity** - offer an actionable ethical framework for institutions committed to designing an AI-integrated future that is both forward-thinking and human-centered. These principles not only protect the pedagogical core of academia but also signal that innovation without deliberation is not sustainable.

Ultimately, this section issues a compelling reminder: AI in higher education will not succeed through efficiency alone. Its success will depend on whether faculty are empowered to shape the **why, how,** and **for whom** AI is used. By elevating faculty as co-architects of institutional transformation, this section reaffirms that the future of education must be built - not bought - and that faculty are the rightful stewards of that design.

Chapter 9 Conclusion: Designing with Integrity - Building the Scaffolding for AI-Era Education

Chapter 9 examined the critical structures and supports that make responsible AI integration possible - not through policy alone, but through intentional design of teaching frameworks, assessment practices, and institutional environments. As generative AI continues to blur the boundaries between originality, assistance, and automation, faculty are tasked not only with guiding student behavior but with **reimagining the architecture of learning itself**. This chapter synthesized eight key dimensions of that design challenge, each contributing to a vision of academic integrity that is transparent, adaptive, and aligned with human values.

Section 1 reframed the traditional concept of academic integrity by arguing that **transparency and attribution** must become the new pillars in an AI-enhanced educational culture. Rather than assume a binary between cheating and honesty, the section called for environments where students are expected to ***disclose*** their AI use, reflect on it, and be held accountable for how it influenced their thinking - just as they would cite any collaborator or source.

Section 2 moved this idea into creative disciplines, showing how AI can become a **co-creative partner** when students are taught to iterate, remix, and reflect. Artistic innovation in the AI age requires not just tool fluency, but algorithmic material literacy - understanding how machine-generated aesthetics are shaped by data, bias, and platform constraints.

In **Section 3**, the chapter turned toward ethical pedagogy, emphasizing that students must **develop moral reasoning** alongside technical skill. Through human–AI case studies, role-play, and reflection, faculty can help students wrestle with questions of responsibility, bias, and justice - essential preparation for real-world AI dilemmas.

Section 4 challenged the myth of AI as a shortcut to creativity, highlighting the need to **cultivate divergence**, experimentation, and authentic voice. Faculty can design assignments that reward disruption over polish, process over perfection - ensuring that students do not merely **echo** AI's probabilities, but **surpass them with purpose**.

Section 5 underscored the urgency of teaching students to **evaluate AI-generated outputs**, reinforcing that fluency does not equal accuracy. Through fact-checking, lateral reading, and bias analysis, students can become not just users of AI but **critical interpreters** of its claims and consequences.

Section 6 returned to faculty modeling, reminding us that **what educators do with AI** - and what they share about it - deeply shapes student expectations. When faculty are transparent about their own uses, limitations, and ethical boundaries, they create a culture where **responsibility is learned through example**, not enforcement.

In **Section 7**, the chapter addressed the challenge of **designing new learning goals** for human–AI collaboration. It proposed revised outcomes that center on reflection, process documentation, disciplinary integrity, and ethical awareness - guiding students to think **with** AI, but never **through** it alone.

Finally, **Section 8** called on educators to leave a **legacy of ethical leadership**. This legacy is built not in grand declarations, but in the daily work of mentoring, co-designing, questioning, and modeling values-centered decision-making. Faculty who embrace this role prepare students not just for compliance - but for conscience.

The overarching message of Chapter 9 is clear: **Responsible AI integration begins with responsible design.** Integrity is not preserved through prohibition, but through scaffolding - through the creation of assignments, expectations, systems, and relationships that make **transparency, authorship, and ethical reflection possible**.

Faculty are not just adapting to new tools; they are **redefining the social contract of education**. When that contract is built on mutual trust, clearly communicated values, and shared responsibility, AI becomes a context for deeper learning - not a shortcut around it.

Ultimately, the integrity of the AI-era university will not be measured by how well it detects misconduct - but by how well it **cultivates judgment, invites transparency, and fosters meaningful human–machine collaboration**. Chapter 9 offers the design principles - and the ethical resolve - to make that future possible.

Chapter 10: Designing Forward: From Adaptation to Institutional Transformation

The previous chapters have equipped faculty with theoretical grounding, practical strategies, and ethical frameworks for navigating generative AI in the classroom, the curriculum, and the culture of higher education. From reimagining mentorship (Chapter 4), to unpacking AI literacy across disciplines (Chapters 5–7), to understanding the structural shifts in academic integrity and assessment (Chapter 3), this book has made one argument clear: **the future of AI in education is not about tools - it is about values, systems, and leadership**.

This final chapter bridges individual transformation and institutional design. It reframes faculty not merely as responders to technological change, but as **co-architects of the post-AI university** - a university that must be humane, ethical, inclusive, and future-ready. Each section that follows re-engages the core ideas of Chapters 1–9 while extending them toward sustained structural empowerment. In doing so, Chapter 10 serves as both a summative reflection and a strategic guide for long-term change.

Section 1: Redefining Empowerment in the Age of Intelligent Tools

---

The AI era challenges educators to revisit what empowerment means - not only for students, but for themselves as professionals navigating evolving systems of knowledge, authorship, and authority. As discussed in Chapter 1, the integration of generative AI into higher education does not represent a simple shift in instructional tools, but a fundamental reconfiguration of **how learners construct meaning, how faculty shape learning environments, and how institutions define success**.

Empowerment, in this new context, must move beyond access to digital tools. It must be defined as the **ability to critically engage with intelligent systems**, to interrogate their assumptions, and to reassert human judgment where automation pressures efficiency. As Chapter 2 emphasized, this requires AI literacy not just in functional terms, but in **epistemological, ethical, and civic dimensions** - helping students and faculty alike discern what it means to think, write, and learn when machines can simulate those acts.

Chapter 3 further deepened this view by situating AI within **systems of power and bias**, showing how the invisible infrastructures of algorithmic decision-making can obscure inequities and distort learning outcomes. For faculty to feel empowered, they must not only understand these forces - but they must also be structurally supported to challenge, modify, or opt out of harmful applications of AI in learning management, advising, and assessment platforms.

Importantly, empowerment is also relational. As explored in Chapter 4 on mentorship, faculty are increasingly called to become **guides, co-learners, and ethical anchors** for students who are experimenting with AI in both visible and covert ways. Empowerment, then, involves cultivating trust - trust in human process, intellectual struggle, and iterative learning. This is particularly vital when students are tempted to bypass learning through automation.

Chapter 6 extended this argument by redefining faculty roles - from content experts to **architects of learning systems that scaffold reflection, discernment, and judgment**. Faculty empowerment in this sense involves not just technical fluency, but institutional legitimacy. Educators must be recognized, supported, and rewarded for engaging AI critically and creatively - not penalized for moving slowly or asking foundational questions about fairness, authorship, or care.

Thus, redefining empowerment in the age of intelligent tools requires institutions to:

- Equip faculty and students with conceptual, not just technical, fluency (Chapters 2, 5).
- Protect space for dissent, experimentation, and reflective pause (Chapter 7).
- Codify pedagogical agency into policy - ensuring faculty retain control over disclosure norms, AI-integration boundaries, and assessment design (Chapter 3, Chapter 9).
- Center mentorship, storytelling, and community-based meaning-making as essential counterweights to machine-generated knowledge (Chapter 4, Chapter 8).

Empowerment in the AI era is not about having more data or faster systems. It is about reclaiming **purpose, voice, and professional identity** in a time of profound technological acceleration. Institutions that center this definition of empowerment - one that is ethical, dialogic, and scaffolded - will not only survive the AI transition. They will lead it.

Rethinking Student Agency in a World of Machine Intelligence

The rise of generative AI requires a fundamental redefinition of student agency. Traditionally, empowerment in education meant developing the capacity to think independently, solve problems autonomously, and produce work without external assistance. But as intelligent systems become capable of performing many of these once-defining tasks - drafting essays, analyzing data, composing code, summarizing research - faculty must shift from defending autonomy as a rigid ideal to **cultivating a more adaptive, reflective, and ethically attuned sense of agency**. As outlined in Chapter 2, the goal is not to resist AI's presence, but to teach students how to engage with it intentionally, critically, and transparently.

---

1. From Autonomy to Augmentation

In earlier models of education, independence was closely tied to **ownership over content production** - being able to generate work from scratch without outside influence. But in the AI era, where tools such as ChatGPT, GitHub Copilot, and Scite can generate competent drafts, code, or summaries within seconds, autonomy is no longer a simple absence of assistance - it is defined by **how, why, and when students choose to engage or intervene with AI systems**.

As introduced in Chapter 5, this redefinition of agency invites students to see themselves not as solitary producers, but as discerning collaborators. Empowerment now includes:

- Knowing when to use AI to scaffold, but not substitute.

- Understanding a tool's limitations and embedded assumptions (Chapter 3).
- Recognizing where human empathy, context, and creativity must intervene (Chapter 4).
- Owning not just the output, but the **decision-making process** behind it (Chapter 7).

This shift from autonomy to augmentation does not weaken student agency - it **amplifies it** by demanding greater reflection, intentionality, and epistemic awareness.

---

2. Teaching Judgment, Not Just Knowledge

As generative AI reduces barriers to information access and summary generation, educators must recalibrate learning goals away from content recall and toward **judgment, discernment, and critical engagement**. This pivot was reinforced in Chapter 7, where the design of AI-integrated learning outcomes emphasized not only the *use* of AI tools but rather the *evaluation* of their reliability, relevance, and consequences.

Example (Writing Course):

A student is asked to use ChatGPT to generate an essay outline and then reflect on:

- *What assumptions the model made?*
- *Which voices or perspectives were omitted?*
- *How their own outline would differ and why?*

As discussed in Chapter 6, such assignments cultivate metacognitive awareness, helping students **develop the judgment to challenge automation**, rather than blindly accepting machine fluency as authority. This positions them as critical editors and ethical decision-makers - roles that are increasingly vital in a world of algorithmically generated content.

---

3. Modeling Co-Creation, Not Competition

Many students approach AI with ambivalence or anxiety - either viewing it as a shortcut to be hidden or a threat to their originality. Faculty can reframe this binary by modeling a mindset of **co-creation** - where students partner with AI systems while preserving voice, values, and authorship.

This pedagogical shift echoes the mentorship strategies discussed in Chapter 4, where students were encouraged to engage AI tools iteratively and reflectively under faculty guidance.

Example (Design Course):

Students use Midjourney to generate three variations of a visual concept. They then annotate:

- *What aligns with their creative intent.*
- *What they would revise or reject.*

- *How the tool expanded their thinking.*

As seen in Chapter 8, this strategy supports **creative divergence**, not convergence. It reminds students that empowerment lies not in resisting tools altogether, but in directing them - **shaping outputs, not being shaped by them**.

---

4. Empowering Ethical Imagination

True agency in the AI era requires more than technical fluency - it demands **ethical imagination**. Students must be guided to consider how their use of AI affects others, reinforces or challenges bias, and contributes to (or resists) larger systems of algorithmic influence.

Chapter 3 introduced this through ethical case studies, encouraging students to identify gaps in AI-generated logic and imagine more just alternatives. Similarly, Chapter 5 illustrated how critical AI literacy requires students to ask:

- *"Who or what is being left out?"*
- *"Whose voices are silenced in the dataset?"*
- *"What harms might result from automated judgment?"*

Discussion prompts such as:

- *"What assumptions are embedded in this AI-generated content?"*
- *"What are the implications of using this tool in healthcare, education, or journalism?"*

... help move students from technical competence to **civic consciousness**, as encouraged by Benjamin (2023), Noble (2018), and Crawford (2021).

---

5. Empowerment Through Reflective Transparency

Transparency in AI use should not be treated as self-incrimination - it should be cultivated as a form of **intellectual integrity and ownership**. Students must be encouraged to narrate their process of working with AI tools, documenting their decisions as part of academic authorship.

As discussed in Chapter 9, reflection logs are an effective strategy for fostering this kind of process-based empowerment. For instance:

- *"Describe how you used AI in this project." "What prompted you to consult it?" "What did you keep, change, or discard - and why?"*

This metacognitive practice reframes AI use from something to obscure into something to **interrogate, disclose, and integrate** with clarity. Slimi and Carballido (2023) argued that such reflective transparency deepens ethical reasoning and affirms student agency in navigating complex learning environments.

From Tool Literacy to Transformation Literacy

As Long and Magerko (2020) emphasized, AI literacy must go beyond knowing how to operate software. Faculty should help students develop **transformation literacy** - the ability to understand how AI technologies shape social systems, cultural values, and professional practices, and how to respond in ways that are proactive, critical, and justice-oriented.

This aligns with Chapter 2's call to reframe AI education not as technical training but as a **liberal education in the digital age** - a way of cultivating ethical, civic, and reflective leadership in future professionals.

Section Reflection: Redefining Empowerment in the Age of Intelligent Tools

The section reframes empowerment as a multidimensional practice that demands more than functional AI fluency - it calls for critical agency, ethical clarity, and institutional support for both students and faculty navigating a rapidly evolving educational landscape. Drawing from the foundational perspectives introduced in Chapters 1–4 and extended through Chapters 6–9, this section positions empowerment not as a static ideal, but as a dynamic response to the epistemic, relational, and systemic disruptions posed by generative AI.

For faculty, empowerment involves reclaiming professional identity amid automation, resisting pressures to conform to efficiency-driven paradigms, and leading with pedagogical purpose. As this section emphasizes, true empowerment means having the authority - and the support - to shape how AI is used, questioned, or constrained within learning environments. Faculty are not simply adapting to intelligent tools; they are redesigning what it means to mentor, assess, and foster intellectual growth in an AI-mediated world.

For students, empowerment must be redefined from traditional autonomy to augmented agency. The section's discussion of augmentation, judgment, co-creation, ethical imagination, and reflective transparency illustrates how student learning shifts from isolated production to critical partnership with AI. It is not enough for students to know how to use tools - they must learn to question outputs, expose assumptions, and assert human values where algorithmic logic falls short.

By synthesizing themes of equity, authorship, metacognition, and civic literacy, this section articulates a vision of empowerment rooted in discernment rather than automation, care rather than compliance. It challenges institutions to go beyond access and inclusion toward redesigning pedagogical structures and evaluation systems that center ethical reflection and professional judgment. In doing so, it underscores a central truth: Empowerment in the AI era is not about mastering the machine - it is about mastering the meaning we make with it.

Section 2: Teaching AI as a Reflective Mirror, Not a Replacement

---

The growing presence of generative AI in academic settings has sparked fears of replacement - of human creativity, faculty authority, and student originality. But as established throughout this book, the most powerful role for AI in education is not substitution - it is

reflection. As articulated in Chapter 2, AI's predictive text, image generation, and analytical capabilities expose the contours of human thinking by mimicking it. This allows educators to **leverage AI not as an endpoint, but as a mirror - one that reflects habits, gaps, assumptions, and potential** in both teaching and learning.

To teach AI as a mirror, faculty must first cultivate students' capacity to examine what AI outputs reveal about their own process. Chapter 5 emphasized that AI tools often reproduce dominant logics - offering plausible but uncritical summaries, flattening nuance, or encoding bias into language and framing. When students analyze these tendencies, they gain deeper insight into **how arguments are structured, which voices are privileged, and how language can obscure or reveal complexity**.

This reflective framing also appeared in Chapter 3's case-based ethical reasoning approach, where faculty guided students to compare human and AI responses to dilemmas. By holding up AI's outputs as starting points for dialogue - rather than as authoritative answers - students learned to test claims, identify omissions, and articulate alternative pathways rooted in empathy, justice, and critical interpretation.

Chapter 6 reinforced that faculty can model this reflection themselves by openly discussing **when, why, and how they use AI** - such as to brainstorm feedback comments or synthesize meeting notes - while acknowledging where the tool falls short. This transparency helps normalize uncertainty and iterative thinking. It also creates a learning culture in which **process is visible, reasoning is valued, and technological limitations become teachable moments**.

In Chapter 7, the design of learning goals was shown to benefit from reflective AI use. Faculty who ask students not only to use generative tools but to **document their decisions, evaluate output credibility, and trace revision logic** are helping students build meta-awareness of their thinking. This scaffolds intellectual agency, particularly when students compare AI-generated drafts to their own, or when they encounter disagreements between human feedback and machine suggestions.

AI's reflective potential is also apparent in creative disciplines. As discussed in Chapter 4, students who remix, critique, or respond to AI-generated poetry, essays, or visual works begin to see their own authorship more clearly - not because AI devalues human work, but because it exposes **the mechanics and consequences of meaning-making**. These exercises also help students explore philosophical questions around originality, intent, and the nature of human expression - connecting technical engagement with timeless inquiry.

Finally, Chapter 8 argued that faculty themselves benefit from engaging AI as a mirror - especially in interdisciplinary spaces where divergent assumptions about rigor, creativity, and ethics become visible. Faculty learning communities, journaling prompts, and AI teaching studios offer structured opportunities for educators to reflect on **their role, their discomforts, and their aspirations in an AI-mediated academy**. To sustain AI as a reflective tool in education, institutions should:

- Encourage assignments that include AI-human comparison, process logging, and iterative critique (Chapter 5, Chapter 7).
- Train faculty in reflective questioning techniques that decenter the tool and recentralize thinking (Chapter 2, Chapter 3).

- Recognize the use of AI not as a shortcut or threat, but as a site of inquiry, critique, and ethical development (Chapter 6).
- Normalize transparency by inviting both faculty and students to share how they engage AI - what they trust, where they hesitate, and what they reject (Chapter 9).

AI does not replace human judgment. But when taught well, it **reflects and refines it**. When used in this way, AI becomes a cognitive partner - not a performer, but a provoker of better questions, deeper engagement, and more intentional authorship. Faculty who teach AI as a reflective mirror will help students understand not just what AI can do - but what it fails to do, and why that difference matters.

Teaching AI as a Reflective Mirror, Not a Replacement

As AI tools increasingly populate the intellectual and creative landscapes of higher education, the imperative is not to reject them, but to **teach students to use AI reflectively - to hold a mirror up to their own cognition, values, and voice**. Faculty must guide students away from overreliance and toward metacognitive discernment. When students see AI not as a replacement for human thought, but as a foil for examining and refining it, they begin to develop one of the most vital 21st-century dispositions: **intellectual self-awareness**.

This approach was previewed in Chapter 2, where students learned to question the epistemic assumptions of AI-generated content, and was further explored in Chapter 5's emphasis on critical evaluation of fluency versus factuality. Across disciplines, educators can use AI to surface what students believe, how they structure knowledge, and what they might otherwise take for granted.

AI as a Tool for Metacognition and Intellectual Ownership

---

1. Compare-and-Contrast Exercises with AI Outputs

One of the simplest yet most profound strategies for teaching AI as a mirror involves **juxtaposing human-authored and machine-authored responses**. As seen in Chapter 6, this comparison invites students to identify not only structural or stylistic differences, but also differences in **intent, voice, and originality**.

Sample Assignment (First-Year Writing):

- *Prompt students to write a one-paragraph response to a philosophical question (e.g., "What defines a meaningful life?"). Then, ask them to generate a response to the same question using ChatGPT. Students annotate both versions, noting:*
    - *Thematic strengths and weaknesses.*
    - *Stylistic differences.*
    - *Use of metaphor, tone, or rhetorical choices.*
    - *Evidence of cliché or pattern-based thinking.*

This task, as emphasized in Chapter 7, supports **visible thinking** - making cognition observable and discussable. It cultivates student voice, ethical authorship, and metacognition, while encouraging critical reflection on the **illusion of AI fluency** (Bender et al., 2021; Brookfield, 2017).

---

2. Teaching "Productive Dissonance" Through Confident Errors

Generative AI tools are prone to hallucinations - statements that sound plausible but are factually incorrect or misleading. Chapter 5 warned against uncritical trust in such outputs, especially when their surface coherence can obscure deeper flaws. Rather than treating these mistakes as liabilities, educators can use them as **productive dissonance** - opportunities to test, correct, and contextualize.

Example (Psychology Course):

- *Students ask an AI tool to explain Piaget's stages of cognitive development. They then fact-check the results using a scholarly source or textbook. Together, the class discusses:*
    - *Where the tool oversimplified or conflated stages.*
    - *How language choices shaped understanding.*
    - *Whether human error differs in nature from machine error.*

This activity mirrors the strategy in Chapter 3, where ethical case studies exposed gaps in machine reasoning. It teaches students to interrogate knowledge systems and apply **cognitive resilience** - the ability to challenge automation respectfully but rigorously (Crawford, 2021; Noble, 2018).

---

3. AI-Enhanced Peer Feedback and Revision Loops

Students often struggle to give and receive peer feedback constructively. As described in Chapter 4, AI can act as a **first-pass reviewer**, offering low-stakes suggestions that students can accept, reject, or revise - thus practicing **judgment in revision** before engaging with peer or instructor critique.

Assignment (STEM Communication Course):

- *Students submit a draft technical abstract to an AI writing assistant and request suggestions for clarity or conciseness. They then:*
    - *Identify which suggestions they accepted or ignored - and why.*
    - *Reflect on the tool's strengths and limitations.*
    - *Articulate how the tool affected their revision process.*

As seen in Chapter 6, this supports the development of **feedback literacy** - the ability to evaluate external critique, integrate it purposefully, and preserve ownership over one's voice (Reiss, 2021). When faculty narrate their own critical uses of AI in grading or content design, they model the reflective posture they ask students to adopt.

---

4. Using AI to Surface Hidden Biases and Patterns

AI systems do not just generate content - they **reveal the cultural assumptions of their training data**. This offers a unique opportunity for students to examine both machine and human bias. Chapter 3 called attention to how AI tools often reproduce dominant ideologies, while Chapter 8 emphasized the importance of cultural literacy in algorithmic critique.

Example (Ethics or Media Studies):

- *Students prompt ChatGPT to describe a "typical leader" or "ideal employee." They then:*
  - *Analyze who is centered or omitted.*
  - *Identify stereotypes or normative assumptions.*
  - *Compare the AI's response to their own definitions or lived experiences.*
- *Follow-up questions might include:*
  - *"What did this output reveal about mainstream representations?"*
  - *"Where do your own assumptions show up in how you evaluated the response?"*

This turns AI from a tool into a **cultural text**, enabling students to critique not just the technology but their own relationship to systems of knowledge and power (Bender et al., 2021; Benjamin, 2023).

---

5. Prompt Crafting as Reflective Expression

Prompt engineering is not simply technical - it is deeply **epistemological**. How students frame a question reveals what they believe matters, what answers they expect, and how they navigate ambiguity. As discussed in Chapters 2 and 7, prompt design becomes a window into intellectual habits and disciplinary assumptions.

Assignment (Education or Philosophy):

- *Students are asked to create three distinct prompts on a complex concept such as "justice" or "truth." After running each through an AI tool, they:*
  - *Compare the responses.*
  - *Reflect on how the wording shaped the AI's tone and depth.*
  - *Discuss which prompt best elicited nuance - and why.*

This task teaches that inquiry is not neutral - it is constructed. Students begin to see themselves not only as questioners, but as **shapers of the dialogue**, whether with humans or machines (Long & Magerko, 2020; Selwyn, 2019).

From Dependence to Discernment: AI as a Thinking Partner

As outlined in Chapters 6 and 9, the classroom must become a space where students learn **how to think with AI - without outsourcing thinking itself**. Rather than frame AI as a shortcut or a threat, faculty can treat it as a **sparring partner** - one that students must learn to question, refine, and debate. Educators can:

- Debrief AI hallucinations together in class.
- Share examples of their own prompting missteps and revisions.
- Discuss where AI helped inspire ideas - and where it failed to meet disciplinary expectations.

These practices create a culture of **co-learning**, where students and faculty alike engage AI not with passive acceptance, but with **critical agency**.

Section Reflection: Teaching AI as a Reflective Mirror, Not a Replacement

This section reframes the role of generative AI in education, moving away from narratives of threat and substitution toward a vision of AI as a catalyst for critical reflection and metacognitive growth. Rather than treating AI tools as competitors to human intellect, this chapter highlights their potential as pedagogical mirrors - revealing not only how language and knowledge are constructed, but also where assumptions, gaps, and biases reside. Through this reframing, faculty are empowered to guide students in developing discernment, authorship, and intellectual self-awareness.

Drawing on insights from Chapters 2, 3, 5, and 6, the section presents AI as a tool for surfacing epistemological blind spots and as a stimulus for deeper learning. Assignments that ask students to compare their own work with AI outputs, analyze hallucinations, or craft prompts intentionally become mechanisms for cultivating judgment rather than merely evaluating correctness. These practices position AI not as a threat to original thinking but instead as a foil against which student reasoning and voice can be clarified and strengthened.

Faculty transparency - about their own AI use, limitations, and hesitations - further models reflective practice and reduces the stigma or confusion students may feel about engaging with such tools. As shown in Chapters 4 and 8, when AI-generated artifacts are treated as cultural texts or ethical provocations, they open space for interdisciplinary dialogue and justice-oriented critique. This mirrors the growing need to shift from tool fluency to transformation literacy, as discussed in Chapter 7 and supported by scholars such as Bender, Benjamin, and Crawford.

Ultimately, this section advances a pedagogical culture where AI is not resisted nor uncritically embraced, but engaged as a thinking partner. By using AI to make cognition visible and judgment explicit, faculty foster not only digital literacy but reflective capacity - ensuring students do not just learn with AI, but learn about themselves in the process.

Section 3: Building Ethical Reasoning Through Human-AI Case Studies

---

In a world increasingly shaped by artificial intelligence, ethical reasoning is no longer an abstract academic exercise - it is a **survival skill**. Faculty have a unique responsibility to help students develop the capacity to assess not only what AI can do, but what it **should do**, and under what conditions. As introduced in Chapter 3, the use of real-world case studies - centered on human-AI interaction - provides a compelling strategy for developing this capacity, encouraging students to engage with ambiguity, consequence, and justice across disciplinary contexts.

Building ethical reasoning begins by situating AI not as a neutral tool, but as a **sociotechnical system** - one that is trained on human data, shaped by human decisions, and deployed within human institutions. Chapter 5 illustrated this with examples of algorithmic bias in search engines and predictive analytics, helping students surface questions about representation, access, and authority. When students investigate how these systems operate - who builds them, who they serve, and who they exclude - they begin to develop the critical lens essential to ethical engagement.

Chapter 7 added that ethical reasoning is not just about judgment after the fact - it is also about **designing learning experiences that prompt anticipatory reflection**. Faculty can do this by embedding structured decision points into assignments: *"Should you use AI here?" "What are the trade-offs?" "What disclosure is needed?" "What voices are missing from this model's training data?"* These questions encourage students to move beyond task completion and toward **values clarification**.

Case-based pedagogy brings this reflection to life. As detailed in Chapter 3, presenting students with nuanced scenarios - such as a nursing student confronting a flawed discharge recommendation from an AI system, or a teacher interpreting AI-generated "underperformance" alerts - requires them to reconcile institutional authority, machine logic, and lived human complexity. These cases cultivate students' capacity to **see dilemmas, weigh competing principles, and act with both empathy and accountability**.

Chapter 6 reinforced that ethical reasoning is developmental. Faculty play a vital role in modeling how to interrogate AI systems with humility, courage, and curiosity. When faculty narrate their own dilemmas - about using AI in grading, in feedback generation, or even in writing lectures - they show students that **ethical reasoning is not a checklist, but a posture of ongoing deliberation**.

Moreover, mentorship, as explored in Chapter 4, becomes a crucible for ethical development when it includes dialogue around AI use. When mentors invite mentees to discuss the ethical limits of generative tools - particularly in research, authorship, and peer collaboration - they help students form **habits of self-inquiry and moral imagination** that extend far beyond any one assignment.

Chapter 8 reminded us that ethical reasoning is also collective. Institutions that prioritize peer mentorship, interdisciplinary dialogue, and inclusive curriculum design create an environment where **ethics is not confined to philosophy courses - it becomes the connective tissue of educational culture**. This is particularly important in contexts where AI technologies are implemented without clear institutional values or safeguards. To scale ethical reasoning through case-based engagement, institutions can:

- Support faculty in developing **discipline-specific AI case studies**, grounded in lived practice and reflective of diverse identities (Chapters 3, 5, 8).
- Offer professional development on **facilitating ethical dialogue**, especially when students encounter tension between convenience and conscience (Chapter 6).

- Embed reflection prompts and scenario analysis into high-impact assignments across general education and the major curriculum (Chapter 7).
- Treat ethical reasoning as a **core learning outcome**, not a supplemental add-on - especially in the design of AI literacy pathways (Chapter 2).

AI case studies are not just pedagogical tools - they are **invitation points** for students to become the kinds of thinkers the world urgently needs: discerning, compassionate, and unwilling to outsource judgment to invisible systems. Faculty who teach through these cases prepare students not only to use AI, but to **govern, critique, and reimagine it**.

Building Ethical Reasoning Through Human–AI Case Studies

In an educational landscape increasingly shaped by automation, ethical reasoning cannot be treated as an elective concern or a discrete learning module - it must be central to how students are taught to think, decide, and act. The rise of generative AI has exposed fault lines in academic policy, professional norms, and public trust. As described in Chapter 3, AI systems are not neutral - they reflect social values, institutional priorities, and embedded assumptions that demand deliberate interrogation. Teaching ethics through case studies provides the structured ambiguity, interdisciplinary relevance, and moral complexity that AI-integrated learning requires.

Ethical reasoning, especially in relation to AI, is not about mastering a universal code. It is about **navigating messy intersections of values, consequences, and power asymmetries**. Case-based learning situates students in this ambiguity, helping them see that ethics is contextual, relational, and iterative. This pedagogy cultivates **moral imagination** - the capacity to envision more just futures, as urged in Chapter 8 - and connects to the larger goal of preparing students not just to comply with AI systems, but to shape them responsibly.

Why Case Studies Work: Ethics as Situated Judgment

Case studies excel because they anchor ethical reflection in real-world scenarios - scenarios that rarely offer neat solutions. Instead, they expose trade-offs, competing priorities, and gaps in policy or design. As highlighted in Chapter 5, AI systems are often deployed without full consideration of their downstream impact on marginalized communities, user autonomy, or democratic norms. Case-based pedagogy helps students:

- Grapple with **ambiguity** rather than memorize rules.
- Weigh **conflicting stakeholder perspectives**.
- Apply ethical frameworks to **fluid, fast-changing technologies**.
- Recognize how **technical functionality intersects with societal harm** (Reiss, 2021; Selwyn, 2019).

These experiences foster both **analytic clarity** and **empathic insight**, key dispositions for navigating ethically complex systems.

1. Choosing Case Topics That Resonate

The most impactful cases are those that intersect with students' lived experiences and civic concerns. Chapter 1 emphasized the importance of relevance in AI education - connecting the macro scale of technological transformation to students' identities, disciplines, and futures. High-impact case topics include:

- **Algorithmic Hiring Bias**. *"How résumé screening tools disadvantage nontraditional applicants?"*
- **Predictive Profiling**. *"How historical data reinforces existing inequalities?"*
- **Deepfakes and Misinformation**. *"What happens when political truth is algorithmically undermined?"*
- **AI-based Medical Triage**. *"How do automated decisions affect access to care during crises?"*
- **Automated Essay Scoring**. *"Who defines quality, and how are voice and fairness represented?"*

Example (Public Health Course):

- *Students debate the ethics of using AI to predict disease outbreaks by scraping social media data. They analyze:*
  - *Whose data is collected, and whether informed consent is involved.*
  - *Who benefits from the intervention - and who is surveilled?*
  - *What privacy, cultural, or political trade-offs are justified?*

This resonates with themes from Chapter 4, which framed mentorship as a space for ethical inquiry and relational trust.

---

2. Structuring Ethical Analysis with Clear Frameworks

Case analysis should be scaffolded using ethical reasoning models to prevent shallow or binary judgments. Chapter 7 emphasized that learning outcomes should reflect **deliberation, justification, and value articulation**, not just decision-making speed. Useful frameworks include:

- **Stakeholder-Impact Matrix**. Students identify all affected parties, map potential benefits and harms, and surface unintended consequences.
- **ACM Code of Ethics**. Widely used in computing and adaptable for disciplines such as media, design, and education. Emphasizes public good, transparency, and equitable practice.
- **AI4People Principles** (Floridi et al., 2018). A cross-sector ethical model focusing on:
  - Beneficence (well-being).
  - Non-maleficence (harm reduction).
  - Autonomy.
  - Justice.
  - Explicability (transparency).

Example Assignment (Criminal Justice Course):

- **Case:** *A predictive policing tool disproportionately flags Black-majority neighborhoods.*
- **Framework:** *Stakeholder Matrix + AI4People Principles.*
- **Prompt:** *"Analyze the ethical implications for each group (residents, law enforcement, developers, policymakers) and propose policy recommendations that balance safety with justice."*

This echoes the approach in Chapter 2, where students were encouraged to analyze systems not just for utility, but for underlying **values and harms**.

---

3. Fostering Dialogue, Not Just Judgment

Ethics education must be dialogic. Chapter 6 advocated for classrooms that make thinking visible, positionality discussable, and authority transparent. Similarly, Chapter 9 called for co-learning environments where students and faculty reflect on their own embedded assumptions. Strategies include:

- Structured controversy exercises or **Socratic seminars**.
- Role-play simulations with rotating perspectives (e.g., data scientist, community member, journalist, user).
- Reflective journaling on **personal dilemmas or decision-making tensions**.

Example (Sociology Course):

- *Students analyze TikTok's recommendation algorithm by taking the roles of:*
  - *A creator seeking visibility.*
  - *A marginalized user experiencing bias.*
  - *A platform moderator.*
  - *A concerned parent.*

The class then collaborates to develop a **set of ethical design guidelines**. This activity helps students move from critique to **co-constructed norms**, aligning with Chapter 8's emphasis on legacy-building and social responsibility.

---

4. Integrating Reflection and Action Planning

Ethical reasoning should culminate in **personal and professional commitments**. As Chapter 4 noted in the context of mentorship, helping students articulate their values fosters a sense of ownership and moral confidence. After the case study, students can be asked to:

- Write a **values statement** that they would want adopted in their future workplace.
- Draft a **code of conduct** for AI designers in their field.
- Submit a **policy memo** proposing ethical guardrails for AI deployment.
- Reflect on what shaped their decision-making - and what still feels unresolved.

These tasks reinforce the message that students are not just subjects of AI systems - they are **future architects** of those systems (Benjamin, 2023; Noble, 2018).

Example: Full AI Ethics Case Study Assignment

- **Course:** *Digital Journalism and Society.*
- **Case Title:** *"The Deepfake Candidate."*
- **Scenario:** *A hyper-realistic deepfake of a political candidate is released online 48 hours before an election. The video is viral. The tool used to generate it is legal and publicly available.*
- **Questions:**
  - *"Should social media platforms remove the video?"*
  - *"Is the tool developer responsible for downstream misuse?"*
  - *"What should journalists do when the story becomes the video itself?"*
- **Frameworks Used:**
  - *AI4People Principles.*
  - *Newsroom Ethics Codes.*
  - *Stakeholder-Impact Matrix.*
- **Deliverables:**
  - *Group presentation offering competing ethical arguments.*
  - *Individual reflection essay: "What role would I play in ensuring responsible media coverage of AI-generated content?"*

This case aligns with the values in Chapter 1: helping students see themselves not only as knowledge consumers, but as **civic participants** in a datafied democracy.

From Compliance to Moral Imagination

Too often, AI education defaults to compliance: **"Do not cheat."** But ethical leadership demands more. Students must be taught to **challenge harm, rethink assumptions, and imagine better systems**.

This echoes the call in Chapter 8 for students to become designers of humane institutions - not just competent users of tools. Ethical reasoning becomes a form of **public imagination** - the ability to foresee harms before they occur, advocate for change, and center justice even when rules lag behind.

Section Reflection: Building Ethical Reasoning Through Human–AI Case Studies

This section reframes ethical reasoning as a central, not peripheral, component of AI-integrated education. As discussed in Chapter 3, students must learn not only to use AI tools effectively but also to question their consequences, assumptions, and societal impacts. Through the use of case-based pedagogy, educators can immerse students in complex, ambiguous scenarios that invite values clarification, interdisciplinary thinking, and civic imagination.

Rather than teaching ethics as a compliance checklist, this approach positions it as a dynamic, dialogic practice that prepares students to become discerning actors in AI-shaped systems.

Chapter 5 highlighted that AI systems are not neutral - they are embedded with historical bias, cultural blind spots, and political implications. Teaching students to interrogate these systems helps cultivate what Chapter 8 describes as **moral imagination**: the ability to envision and advocate for more just, inclusive futures. Case studies facilitate this by contextualizing ethical dilemmas in disciplines ranging from public health and journalism to criminal justice and education. Students are challenged to identify impacted stakeholders, weigh competing priorities, and develop actionable responses - shifting from passive analysis to active agency.

Faculty play a key role in modeling ethical inquiry. As described in Chapters 4 and 6, mentorship and transparency - especially when faculty reflect on their own AI-related dilemmas - create a learning environment rooted in humility, trust, and co-exploration. When faculty share how they navigate ethical tension in grading, feedback design, or tool selection, students learn that ethical reasoning is a process, not a destination.

Chapter 7 reinforced that effective ethics instruction must also be scaffolded. Case study analysis gains power when guided by clear frameworks - such as the AI4People principles or stakeholder-impact matrices - that help students move beyond binary judgments toward thoughtful deliberation. Embedding reflection and action planning into these cases, as modeled in several examples, ensures that ethical reasoning translates into real-world responsibility.

Ultimately, this section deepens the argument - introduced in Chapter 2 - that AI literacy must extend beyond technical skills into domains of justice, empathy, and social critique. Faculty who build ethical reasoning through case-based engagement prepare students not just to navigate AI systems, but to reimagine and improve them. This is the heart of ethical education in the AI era: not avoiding complexity, but embracing it as the foundation for human agency and institutional transformation.

Section 4: Encouraging Creativity and Divergence in AI-Enhanced Work

---

As generative AI becomes more embedded in student workflows - capable of producing polished essays, structured summaries, and visually appealing designs - faculty face a critical challenge: how to ensure that AI use **amplifies creativity** rather than standardizing it. The role of educators is not to compete with the generative capabilities of machines, but to **design environments where students are rewarded for original thought, aesthetic risk, divergent interpretation, and critical authorship**.

Chapter 4 explored this imperative through the lens of creative disciplines, highlighting how AI can serve as both muse and foil. When students are encouraged to interrogate and remix AI outputs, they begin to see the **boundaries of machine creativity** - its tendencies toward safe, surface-level responses, its lack of emotional depth or subversive nuance. This not only sharpens student critique; it **opens new pathways for imagination**.

Divergence must be intentionally cultivated. As discussed in Chapter 7, learning environments that encourage students to experiment with prompts, revise AI-generated drafts, or translate machine output into multimodal responses help them **move beyond replication and toward transformation**. In these contexts, AI becomes a starting point - not a destination. Students can write speculative fiction based on AI-generated plot summaries, compose visual art that critiques the aesthetics of diffusion models, or annotate ChatGPT essays with metacommentary on what was missed.

This spirit of iterative creativity is especially vital in disciplines that are often misunderstood as technical or procedural. In Chapter 5, science and engineering faculty used AI-generated lab summaries to help students spot oversimplifications and redesign methodologies. In doing so, students practiced **scientific creativity**, challenging deterministic outputs and proposing new ways of knowing. Similarly, in Chapter 6, educators used AI as a scaffold to support neurodiverse learners - encouraging them to diverge from AI-generated templates with their own voices and structures.

Creativity in the AI era also involves questioning **the assumptions baked into the tools themselves**. Chapter 2 demonstrated how models trained on dominant cultural data often reinforce existing tropes, styles, and logics. When students compare their own linguistic or cultural expression with machine outputs - particularly when those outputs flatten nuance - they begin to reclaim authorship as an **act of resistance and self-definition**.

Chapter 8 emphasized that this form of creative empowerment must be supported structurally. Institutions can cultivate cultures of divergence by:

- Recognizing and rewarding **process-based assignments** that value reflection, experimentation, and risk-taking over final polish.
- Supporting **interdisciplinary collaboration** where creative and technical fields cross-pollinate - such as pairing design students with AI researchers to co-create speculative futures.
- Creating **assessment frameworks** that differentiate between surface-level automation and deeper cognitive synthesis.
- Developing **ethical creativity prompts**, where students respond to questions like, *"What can AI never imagine, and why?"*

The role of mentorship is also critical. As described in Chapter 4, mentors who share their own creative friction with AI tools - moments of failure, surprise, or dissonance - demystify the creative process. They help students understand that originality is not about speed or polish - it is about **curiosity, complexity, and ownership**.

Creativity, in this sense, becomes not only a product but a **practice of interpretation and intervention**. As Chapter 1 argued, the educational mission in an AI-enhanced world is not to protect human uniqueness by rejecting AI, but to **reaffirm human complexity by inviting students to stretch beyond AI's limits**.

In the AI age, the most urgent pedagogical task is not efficiency - it is divergence. Faculty who encourage creative deviation, critical reimagining, and expressive ownership will equip students to do what AI cannot: generate meaning, not just output; provoke thought, not just consensus; and pursue beauty, justice, or insight - on their own, human terms.

Encouraging Creativity and Divergence in AI-Enhanced Work

At its core, education in the AI era must do more than prepare students to use tools fluently - it must equip them to **create what machines cannot imagine**. Generative AI systems are optimized for pattern recognition, trained to deliver the most probable next word, image, or solution based on massive data sets. As a result, their outputs are often coherent, efficient, and even eloquent - but rarely disruptive, novel, or subversive. Chapter 4 first introduced this tension between fluency and originality, urging educators to cultivate spaces where students can use AI without being shaped by its limitations.

Creativity in the age of AI, therefore, must be framed not as spontaneous inspiration, but as **a conscious act of resistance against predictive conformity**. Students must learn to recognize AI's stylistic tendencies and cultural blind spots, and then **deliberately diverge**, remix, or reimagine.

The Risk of Replication

Generative AI systems, such as ChatGPT, Midjourney, and DALL·E, rely on statistical probabilities to create outputs. This means that:

- **Unconventional ideas are flattened.**
- **Culturally dominant narratives are reinforced.**
- **Safe, Western-centric language and imagery prevail.**
- **Creative unpredictability is filtered out as statistical noise.**

As Crawford (2021) and Noble (2018) warned, this pattern replication does not emerge from malevolent intent - but from the underlying data and design choices. Chapter 5 further emphasized that these systems, though "neutral" in presentation, carry **invisible ideologies**, often privileging familiarity over disruption.

If unexamined, students may internalize these norms - believing that sounding like an AI is the same as sounding "correct." Chapter 2 cautioned against this default fluency, reinforcing the need to treat AI outputs as texts to critique, not templates to emulate.

The Role of the Educator

In this environment, faculty are called to be **curators of divergence**. Their role is to:

- Prompt students to **notice when AI is being too safe or generic**.
- Encourage creative risk that exceeds algorithmic comfort zones.
- Design assignments where students are rewarded for **originality, not conformity**.
- Create conditions where cultural remix, narrative experimentation, and emotional depth are not only allowed, but required.

As discussed in Chapter 6, this modeling of creative agency by the educator - through annotated prompts, AI critiques, or co-authored revisions - helps students reframe the tool as **a springboard, not a script**.

Strategies to Promote Divergence in AI-Enhanced Assignments

---

1. Prompt Students to "Outthink the Machine"

Students should be challenged to identify the **limitations and omissions** in AI-generated content, and then respond with human insight.

Assignment (History or Literature):

- *Ask ChatGPT to write a summary of the causes of the French Revolution. Then:*
  - *Annotate for oversimplifications or historical bias.*
  - *Compose a counter-narrative from a lesser-known figure (e.g., a Haitian revolutionary, Parisian laundress, or exiled journalist).*
  - *Reflect on what the AI "missed" and why.*

This strategy, building on Chapter 5, teaches students to see AI outputs as **default narratives** and empowers them to **rewrite history from below** (Bender et al., 2021; Benjamin, 2023).

---

2. Remix AI Outputs with Personal Voice and Risk

Creativity is not merely invention - it is **revision with intent**. Students must be prompted to modify AI drafts in ways that infuse them with emotional complexity, political stakes, or personal truth.

Assignment (Creative Writing or Visual Design):

- *Generate a short story or base image using AI.*
- *Revise it by introducing a plot twist, stylistic disruption, or unexpected aesthetic element.*
- *Annotate changes with a rationale: "What was added, what was rejected, and why?"*

As Chapter 4 discussed, this process helps students reassert **agency over automation**, proving that authorship is not lost in collaboration - it is clarified.

---

3. Design Creative Constraints

Constraints force students to think beyond the predictable. As Reiss (2021) noted, constraint-based assignments encourage students to **push against algorithmic logic** and surprise both themselves and the system.

Assignment (STEM or Business Course):

- **Task:** *Use ChatGPT to write a pitch for a sustainable toothbrush.*
- **Rewrite it With:**
    - *No environmental clichés.*
    - *At least one metaphor from Greek literature.*
    - *A built-in counterargument.*

This exercise, echoing the design thinking strategies from Chapter 7, turns the assignment into a **creative puzzle**, where originality is sparked by structural pressure.

---

4. Critique and Extend AI Limitations

AI tools simulate coherence - but struggle with the **ineffable dimensions of human experience**. Students should be asked not just to use AI, but to **find where it fails - and then write into the void**.

Assignment (Philosophy or Ethics):

- *Ask an AI to generate a meditation on love or death. Then:*
    - *Identify where its language lacks vulnerability or insight.*
    - *Compare to a human-authored piece.*
    - *Write a response that addresses the emotional, cultural, or philosophical gaps.*

As discussed in Chapter 3 and Chapter 6, this critique allows students to frame AI not as the end of meaning, but as **an invitation to deeper expression** (Brookfield, 2017; Long & Magerko, 2020).

---

5. Celebrate Failure and Play

Fear of being wrong drives some students to over-rely on AI. To counter this, educators must **normalize uncertainty, embrace experimentation, and reward playfulness**.

Assignment (Performing Arts):

- Use AI-generated stage directions.
- Rehearse a scene with absurd or subversive interpretations.
- **Debrief**: *"What emerged that surprised you?"*

This method, aligned with Chapter 8's call for ethical improvisation and Chapter 4's embrace of mentorship-as-experimentation, positions **failure as generative**, not punitive.

Assessment: Rewarding Divergence, Not Just Polish

Creative assessment must evolve to reflect these priorities. Rubrics should:

- Reward experimentation, revision, and voice.
- Evaluate how students **intentionally diverged from AI norms**.
- Require documentation of the process and ethical reflection.

Sample Rubric Criteria:

- *Degree of departure from AI-generated content.*
- *Evidence of original thought and risk.*
- *Clarity of rationale for creative decisions.*
- *Awareness of tool influence and authorship ethics.*

This echoes Chapter 9's emphasis on process-based evaluation and Chapter 7's call for transparency in AI-integrated work (Slimi & Carballido, 2023).

Section Reflection: Encouraging Creativity and Divergence in AI-Enhanced Work

This section powerfully reframes the role of faculty in the AI era - not as gatekeepers of originality or competitors with machines, but as **curators of divergence**. As generative AI tools become increasingly adept at producing fluent, coherent, and technically correct output, the pedagogical challenge has shifted: educators must now cultivate creative resistance, aesthetic risk-taking, and reflective authorship in ways that transcend the efficiency and predictability of algorithmic design.

Drawing on insights from Chapters 4, 5, and 7, the section makes clear that creativity in AI-enhanced learning must not be defined by polish, but by **purposeful deviation**. AI's training on dominant cultural norms and probabilistic modeling makes it well-suited to replicate - but poorly equipped to disrupt. Therefore, the educator's task is not to prohibit AI use, but to teach students how to **remix, subvert, and reimagine** its outputs with human nuance and ethical imagination. This distinction echoes the concerns in Chapter 2 about default fluency being mistaken for insight, and reinforces the call in Chapter 8 for institutions to structurally reward experimentation over conformity.

Importantly, this section highlights how creativity can be scaffolded across disciplines - not only in the arts and humanities, but in STEM, business, and the social sciences. Chapter 5's examples of scientific redesign and Chapter 6's focus on neurodivergent student expression show that creativity is not a luxury but a **core competency** in every field, especially when supported by inclusive mentorship models and multimodal assessment frameworks.

Concrete strategies - including remix assignments, constraint-based design, reflective annotations, and failure-friendly environments - offer a roadmap for embedding creativity as a pedagogical ethos. These methods position generative AI not as a threat to student originality, but as a **mirror and foil**, helping students locate their voice by identifying what AI cannot authentically reproduce: vulnerability, cultural specificity, emotional insight, and transformative vision.

Ultimately, this section aligns with the broader argument from Chapter 1: that the purpose of education in the AI era is not to preserve uniqueness through rejection, but to **reclaim human complexity** through intentional engagement. Faculty who prioritize divergence as a learning goal - who assess risk-taking, celebrate revision, and model creative uncertainty - equip students not just to navigate the AI age, but to shape it with authenticity, agency, and ethical depth.

Section 5: Teaching Students to Assess the Integrity of AI Outputs

In a world increasingly saturated by algorithmically generated content, the ability to evaluate **what is true, trustworthy, or worth engaging with** has become an essential intellectual survival skill. As generative AI tools produce essays, summaries, designs, and even research overviews at unprecedented speed, faculty are called to shift focus from **information retrieval to information discernment**. This section revisits and extends insights from across the book to underscore that teaching students to assess AI outputs is not a technical add-on - it is a **central pillar of modern education**.

Chapter 5 addressed this directly by framing AI evaluation as a form of **digital source literacy**. Students must be taught that AI systems do not "know" in the human sense - they **predict**, based on training data, statistical regularity, and probabilistic coherence. This means that their outputs can be biased, outdated, incomplete, or confidently wrong. By surfacing these limitations through hands-on exercises, such as comparing AI-generated summaries to peer-reviewed texts or identifying misattributions in chatbot responses, faculty help students learn **how to read with skepticism and curiosity**.

Chapter 2 emphasized that this skill requires an understanding of how generative models are trained - what data they learn from, whose perspectives are embedded or excluded, and what assumptions underlie the fluency of their outputs. When students are taught the architecture of tools such as GPT-5 or DALL·E, they become better equipped to recognize the **boundaries between fact, fiction, and fabrication**.

But evaluation is not just about technical critique. As highlighted in Chapter 3, assessing AI integrity must also include **ethical and civic dimensions**. Students should ask: *"What values does this output reflect?" "Who might be harmed by trusting it uncritically?" "What is missing that a human scholar would include?"* These questions help students understand that integrity is not just about correctness - it is about **justice, transparency, and accountability**.

Chapter 6 illustrated how faculty can model this work through their own engagement with AI. When faculty openly critique AI-generated syllabi, citation lists, or rubrics - pointing out inaccuracies, inconsistencies, or ethical blind spots - they demonstrate what **responsible skepticism and academic rigor** look like in action. This models not only intellectual integrity but also professional humility.

Assessment of AI output also intersects with metacognition. As described in Chapter 7, students gain deeper learning when they are asked to **document and reflect** on their interactions with AI: *"What did they keep?" "What did they discard?" "Why did they trust or question certain results?"* These reflection logs become not only tools for transparency but also rich artifacts of critical thinking.

The evaluation of AI outputs also requires awareness of **disciplinary standards**. As Chapter 8 discussed, what counts as credible, logical, or rigorous varies across fields. A sociology student must evaluate not only whether an AI's summary of Goffman's theory is factually accurate but also whether it captures the theoretical nuance and social context. In a visual design course, students might be asked to critique not just aesthetic quality, but **representational equity and cultural bias** in AI-generated images.

To institutionalize this work, Chapter 9 urged that AI assessment skills be scaffolded through curriculum design, not relegated to one-off assignments. Institutions can support faculty by:

- Providing sample rubrics for evaluating AI-influenced work.
- Embedding AI integrity checks into writing centers or peer-review processes.
- Creating general education outcomes that emphasize **algorithmic literacy, interpretive judgment, and evidence-based reasoning**.

Chapter 4 also noted that mentorship plays a key role. When mentors prompt students with questions like, *"What assumptions did the AI make in this draft?"* or *"Whose voice is missing from this summary?"*, they help build habits of **critical vigilance** - a kind of intellectual integrity that is resilient to automation.

Ultimately, assessing the integrity of AI outputs is not about discrediting technology - it is about **honoring learning**. It ensures that students do not confuse fluency with accuracy, automation with authority, or coherence with credibility. In an educational climate shaped by predictive systems, faculty must help students become not just users of AI, but **evaluators of its claims, interpreters of its logic, and stewards of their own knowledge processes**.

Teaching Students to Assess the Integrity of AI Outputs

In a world where AI-generated content is proliferating across professional, civic, and academic domains, students must be trained not only to use AI - but to **question it**. The ability to assess the credibility, transparency, and bias of AI outputs is now a core literacy, akin to evaluating peer-reviewed research, cross-checking journalistic sources, or interrogating social media claims. As emphasized in Chapter 5, the fluency of AI responses can mask fundamental inaccuracies, omissions, or biases - making **critical scrutiny more essential than ever**. AI tools are being integrated into high-stakes environments:

- In **law**, for summarizing case precedents and drafting briefs.
- In **science**, for abstract generation or interpreting data trends.
- In **journalism**, for automating headlines and story leads.
- In **education**, for feedback generation or tutoring.
- In **healthcare**, for assisting with diagnoses and patient triage.

As explored in Chapter 3, the ethical consequences of uncritical use in any of these domains can be severe - ranging from reputational harm and misinformation to systemic discrimination or even loss of life (Benjamin, 2023; Crawford, 2021). Faculty, therefore, must prepare students to approach AI not as an oracle, but as a **fallible system that must be verified, contextualized, and ethically interrogated**.

Practical Strategies for Teaching AI Evaluation

---

1. Teach Students to Ask: "Where Did This Come From?"

Chapter 2 introduced the concept of AI as a black-box system - generating content without disclosing its sources or reasoning. Most large language models, including ChatGPT, do not cite their training data, and students often mistake fluency for factuality. This creates a dangerous epistemic illusion: **The appearance of knowledge without a verifiable origin**.

Assignment (Journalism Course):

- *Students prompt Perplexity or ChatGPT to summarize a recent news story, then:*
  - *Use lateral reading to check claims.*
  - *Compare key facts with primary sources.*
  - *Evaluate whether tone implies authority despite lacking evidence.*

This builds on Chapter 7's emphasis on sourcing and traceability, reinforcing **digital skepticism and epistemic vigilance** (Caulfield, 2017; Noble, 2018).

---

2. Introduce Lateral Reading and Source Triangulation

Lateral reading, originally developed to counter online misinformation, is an effective tool for AI source evaluation. As discussed in Chapter 9, lateral reading invites students to **step outside the original text and consult external sources** to evaluate accuracy.

Assignment (Science Course):

- *Ask ChatGPT to summarize recent CRISPR research. Students then:*
  - *Locate the actual peer-reviewed studies.*
  - *Analyze how accurately the AI conveyed findings.*
  - *Reflect on what was lost in simplification and what biases shaped the summary.*

This exercise develops **disciplinary sourcing habits** and reinforces the authority of vetted research - especially important in fields such as medicine, engineering, or public health.

---

3. Teach Students to Identify and Decode Bias

As discussed in Chapter 3, bias in AI is rarely intentional - but it is nearly always present. AI systems learn from the data they are trained on, and when those data reflect dominant ideologies or exclusionary histories, the outputs replicate them.

Assignment (Ethics or Media Studies):

- **Prompt the AI to describe:**
  - *A leader.*
  - *A family.*
  - *A criminal.*
- **Then ask students to analyze:**

- *Which identities are centered or erased?*
    - *What stereotypes are reinforced?*
    - *How prompt design shapes these representations.*
- **Follow-up:**
    - *Students revise the prompts to generate* ***more inclusive and critically aware outputs****, connecting the task to ethical prompt engineering and value-driven design* (Bender et al., 2021; Benjamin, 2023).

---

4. Emphasize Disciplinary Norms for Credibility

Chapter 6 illustrated that AI literacy is not one-size-fits-all. Each discipline defines credibility differently - through evidence, voice, citation practice, and epistemological framing. Students must learn not only to critique AI generally, but to do so **from within their disciplinary lens**.

Assignment (Law Course):

- *Provide students with AI-generated legal summaries.*
- *Ask them to compare with actual court rulings.*
- *Identify missing precedents, misinterpretations, or hallucinated citations.*

Discussion follows on the **risks of AI-generated legal misinformation**, helping students internalize why **disciplinary standards matter** in a machine-augmented world.

---

5. Model the Evaluation Process Explicitly

As emphasized in Chapter 10 Section 6, **faculty modeling is critical**. Faculty who walk students through their own process of evaluating AI content - publicly and transparently - demonstrate that intellectual integrity is **an active habit**, not a static expectation.

Classroom Strategy (Any Discipline):

- *Display a ChatGPT-generated answer on screen. Together with students:*
    - *Identify what seems oversimplified or misleading.*
    - *Cross-check claims live.*
    - *Discuss the tool's likely limitations based on training data.*

This kind of **real-time epistemic reasoning** invites students into the evaluative process and builds shared norms of academic rigor (Brookfield, 2017).

Assessment Ideas

To reinforce these skills, consider incorporating AI evaluation into formative and summative assessments:

Assignment Type	Focus
AI Fact-Check Journal	Students log and verify AI claims weekly, noting corrections and insights
Sourcing Map	Students reconstruct the citation trail of AI-generated outputs
Bias Reflection Essay	Students analyze how AI reflects or erases identity and culture
Cross-Tool Comparison	Students contrast ChatGPT with Perplexity and Google Scholar

These assessments encourage students to treat AI as a **textual object**, not a truth source - an idea central to Chapter 4's emphasis on divergent thinking and Chapter 7's learning goals.

Section Reflection: Teaching Students to Assess the Integrity of AI Outputs

This section reaffirms that in the age of generative AI, intellectual integrity depends not on content production alone, but on critical discernment. As emphasized throughout the book - particularly in Chapters 2, 3, 5, and 7 - faculty must shift from merely teaching students how to **use** AI to helping them **interrogate** it. The fluency and speed of AI-generated content often mask deeper issues of accuracy, bias, and source opacity. Thus, the ability to assess what AI says - and how, why, and to what effect - is a foundational skill of modern scholarship, civic literacy, and professional ethics.

What distinguishes this section is its call to reframe evaluation as a cross-disciplinary practice, one that reflects the epistemological standards of specific fields while cultivating broader habits of interpretive skepticism. In law, healthcare, journalism, or the sciences, AI outputs carry weight - and consequence. As explored in Chapter 3, ethical reasoning must therefore be embedded into the very act of AI critique, with students learning not only to check for factual errors, but to question whose voices are privileged, what values are encoded, and what harms may arise from uncritical acceptance.

The section's strategies - including lateral reading, source triangulation, prompt analysis, and real-time classroom modeling - turn AI into a **site of inquiry**, rather than a shortcut to answers. When students annotate AI outputs, trace phantom citations, or uncover bias in machine portrayals of leadership or identity, they begin to see AI not as a truth engine, but as a probabilistic artifact of human systems - one requiring careful interpretation.

By positioning evaluation as a metacognitive, disciplinary, and ethical act, this section aligns closely with the broader pedagogical goal of the book: to help students develop not just digital fluency, but epistemic resilience. Faculty who teach AI integrity are not merely protecting academic standards - they are equipping students to navigate a future where credibility must be constructed, not assumed.

Section 6: Modeling Responsible AI Use as Faculty

In a rapidly shifting digital landscape, faculty are not only educators - they are role models for how to navigate new technologies with integrity, discernment, and care. As students increasingly turn to generative AI to supplement (and sometimes replace) aspects of their academic work, faculty responses become part of the **hidden curriculum** - teaching students, implicitly or explicitly, what is acceptable, what is thoughtful, and what it means to be a responsible user of intelligent tools. Modeling responsible AI use is thus not ancillary to teaching - it is a **form of leadership**, shaping campus culture and student values.

Throughout this book, the importance of faculty modeling has been emphasized as a throughline. Chapter 6 positioned faculty as **learning architects** in the AI age - not just subject matter experts, but designers of environments where responsible engagement with technology is visible, scaffolded, and discussed. Responsible modeling starts with transparency. Faculty who disclose how they have used AI tools - for example, to generate a draft rubric, brainstorm lecture outlines, or summarize student feedback - signal that **AI can be integrated ethically and reflectively**, without diminishing academic ownership.

Chapter 2 reinforced this by suggesting that faculty share their own limitations and learning journeys with AI. When faculty say, *"I tried using this tool, and here is what I found helpful - and what I found lacking,"* they cultivate a culture where **curiosity, critique, and boundary-setting coexist**. This reframes AI not as a threat to human expertise, but as a site of ongoing professional learning.

Responsible modeling also involves **boundary-setting**, particularly around tasks where human judgment, empathy, and relational nuance are essential. As argued in Chapter 3, faculty should be clear about when AI may be used as a support (e.g., for brainstorming or outlining) and when it must not replace the student's voice or ethical reflection (e.g., in positionality statements, data interpretation, or reflective writing). Chapter 9 expanded this conversation by introducing the idea of "AI red zones" - contexts where automation may erode trust, misrepresent experience, or flatten meaning - and recommended that faculty articulate these zones in their syllabi and assessment criteria.

Mentorship, as discussed in Chapter 4, offers one of the most powerful arenas for modeling responsible use. When faculty invite students into open dialogue about the risks, promises, and limitations of AI - in research design, dissertation or capstone development, or career preparation - they build not only technical awareness but **moral agency**. A mentor who says, *"Let us reflect on how you used AI in this chapter, and how it shaped your argument,"* is teaching far more than compliance - they are modeling **intellectual self-awareness** and ethical practice.

In Chapter 7, this modeling extended into assessment design. Faculty who require students to submit AI-use logs or process memos are not policing behavior - they are signaling that **authorship is an act of transparency**, and that responsible use includes both strategic deployment and critical review. These habits become more powerful when mirrored by the instructor: *"Here is how I used ChatGPT to draft our feedback form - now let us revise it together based on our shared values."*

Chapter 5 reminded us that responsible AI use must include evaluation. Faculty who critique AI outputs for bias, inaccuracy, or oversimplification - whether in front of a class or in assignment design - demonstrate what it means to **engage tools without outsourcing judgment**. They model the difference between using AI as a thought partner versus a thought replacement.

Chapter 8 underscored that modeling is also cultural. When institutions recognize and reward responsible AI leadership - in teaching awards, tenure evaluations, or mentorship fellowships - they elevate modeling from an individual choice to an **institutional expectation**. In turn, this fosters a climate where faculty feel supported in experimenting with AI tools ethically, and where students see responsible engagement as a shared academic norm.

To support responsible modeling at scale, institutions can:

- Provide sample syllabus language that defines acceptable AI use and faculty rationale.
- Encourage faculty to narrate their use of AI tools during class design, grading, or content development (Chapter 6).
- Offer workshops where faculty reflect on their own AI learning curves and share responsible practices with colleagues (Chapter 9).
- Normalize co-learning with students - inviting them to critique, improve, and rethink the ways AI is used in shared academic spaces (Chapter 2, Chapter 4).

In the end, students may not remember every AI policy - but they will remember what their professors did when the rules were unclear, the tools were new, and the terrain was shifting. Modeling responsible AI use means showing students how to lead, how to question, and how to adapt with integrity. It means demonstrating that technology is not neutral - and neither are we.

Modeling Responsible AI Use as Faculty

One of the most powerful influences on student behavior is faculty behavior. When students observe their faculty navigating AI use with integrity, humility, and clarity, they are more likely to do the same. However, **when faculty remain silent or inconsistent about their own AI engagement - using tools quietly while expecting transparency from students - confusion and mistrust emerge**. As discussed in Chapter 9, inconsistency in expectations, especially when linked to academic integrity and ethical standards, undermines student confidence and diminishes opportunities for collaborative learning cultures.

Modeling responsible AI use is not a minor act. It is an **explicit commitment to leadership by example**, grounded in the values of transparency, reflection, and shared accountability. As Brookfield (2017) emphasized, ethical modeling by those in leadership positions is far more influential than abstract policy statements. When students see faculty disclose their AI use, critique the results, and reflect publicly on ethical boundaries, they are invited into a culture of **open inquiry, not secret compliance**.

This approach was supported in Chapter 4's mentorship models, where faculty were encouraged to **"teach aloud"** - making their cognitive and ethical reasoning visible to students. Likewise, Chapter 6 urged faculty to model feedback loops and revision processes rather than simply evaluate final outputs. In this way, **modeling becomes both a pedagogical strategy and a cultural intervention** - challenging shame, demystifying AI tools, and anchoring usage in shared values.

Practical Ways Faculty Can Model Responsible AI Use

---

1. Use AI in Course Preparation - Then Disclose and Reflect

Generative AI tools have become valuable aids for faculty behind the scenes. Faculty use them to:

- Draft or revise syllabi.
- Brainstorm assignment prompts.
- Generate formative assessments.
- Simulate common student misunderstandings.

These uses are not inherently unethical. But **undisclosed use sends the wrong message**: That AI is only legitimate in private, not in shared academic processes. As explored in Chapter 7, process transparency supports student trust, clarifies boundaries, and encourages intentional reflection.

Modeling Strategy:

- Include brief disclosures in syllabi, LMS announcements, or course introductions.

Example Syllabus Note:

- *"Some portions of this syllabus (e.g., weekly topic summaries and scaffolding for quiz design) were initially generated using ChatGPT. All content was revised by me to ensure clarity and alignment with course goals. I welcome your feedback on this process."*

This simple act demonstrates ethical awareness, invites student dialogue, and affirms **human editorial judgment over machine fluency** (Reiss, 2021).

---

2. Discuss AI Use in Research, Writing, and Brainstorming

Faculty often rely on AI to:

- Structure article outlines.
- Draft abstracts or social media summaries.
- Suggest keywords or titles.
- Rephrase technical writing for general audiences.

Rather than hiding this use, faculty can treat it as a professional development conversation. In Chapter 8, academic legacy was framed as a product of **transparency, mentorship, and responsible innovation** - which are modeled in moments such as these.

Modeling Strategy:

- Mention AI use in public talks or blog posts.
- Reflect on outcomes in department meetings.
- Note tool usage in acknowledgments or prefaces.

Example (Faculty Reflection Post):

- *"For my latest policy brief, I asked Claude.ai to suggest title options. While a few were useful, most defaulted to generic language. I selected one and reworded it. The process helped me clarify my argument, but also reminded me that AI tends to avoid edge or originality."*

This kind of candid reflection normalizes **tool use as iterative, imperfect, and guided by human discernment** (Bender et al., 2021; Crawford, 2021).

---

3. Invite Dialogue and Student Participation

Transparency is most effective when it is mutual. As students continue to use AI tools - whether invited or not - faculty can demystify the process by:

- Sharing their own experimentation.
- Asking students to reflect on their own transparency.
- Co-designing classroom norms for AI disclosure.

This aligns with the participatory mentorship frameworks in Chapter 4, where students and faculty co-created agreements that reflected evolving tech landscapes and learning goals.

Example (First Week Dialogue Prompt):

- *Here is how I have used AI tools such as ChatGPT or Perplexity in designing this course. "What experiences do you have with these tools?" "What would a fair, transparent AI policy look like for us this term?"*

Such dialogue promotes **collective agency** and reinforces that academic integrity is not a policing function - it is a shared value (Benjamin, 2023; Brookfield, 2017).

---

4. Acknowledge Limitations and Model Critical Engagement

No one - including faculty - is an AI expert across all domains. Modeling responsible use also means admitting:

- When tools failed to deliver accurate results.
- Where outputs lacked depth or cultural nuance.
- What the faculty member is still learning.

This echoes the reflective practices encouraged in Chapter 6, where faculty were urged to **disclose their own learning curves, not just their judgments**.

Classroom Example:

- *"I used ChatGPT to summarize this week's reading - but it missed the core argument entirely. This is a helpful reminder that sounding fluent does not mean being accurate. This is why your analysis matters more than ever."*

These moments build **intellectual humility**, one of the most essential traits for ethical leadership in AI-enhanced work.

---

5. Reflect Publicly on the Ethics of AI Use

Faculty modeling is most effective when it is not just **procedural**, but **principled**. Students benefit from hearing:

- What ethical values guide a professor's AI choices?
- What lines they choose not to cross (e.g., delegating certain types of grading or reflection).
- What social and institutional risks do they consider?

Modeling Strategy:

- Include a brief AI use statement in syllabi, course policies, or faculty handbooks.

Example Statement:

- *"I use AI to support administrative tasks and brainstorming, but I avoid it in grading student work or interpreting original arguments. Empathy, tone, and context are irreplaceable in those domains. You are encouraged to develop your own boundaries, and I am happy to discuss mine."*

This invites **values-centered conversation**, reinforcing points raised in Chapter 3 about justice, fairness, and AI's potential social consequences (Noble, 2018; Selwyn, 2019).

Examples Across Contexts

Domain	**AI Use Case**	**Modeling Strategy**
Teaching	Drafting rubrics, summaries	Share side-by-side human edits on Canvas with class commentary
Research	Brainstorming titles or outlining arguments	Include footnotes in shared slides or preprints noting AI's contribution

Domain	AI Use Case	Modeling Strategy
Communication	AI-assisted email drafts	Add a note: "Composed with AI assistance, revised by author for clarity and tone"
Committee/Policy Work	Writing proposals or curriculum updates	Use tracked changes to distinguish AI suggestions from faculty-authored decisions

These examples affirm that AI use is **neither hidden nor unquestioned**, but transparently integrated into professional practice.

Section Reflection: Modeling Responsible AI Use as Faculty

This section underscores a core truth of the AI era: students learn as much from what faculty **do** with technology as from what they **say** about it. Modeling responsible AI use, as explored throughout the book - particularly in Chapters 2, 4, 6, 7, and 9 - is not a supplemental act of transparency, but a cornerstone of ethical pedagogy in a machine-mediated academic culture. Faculty behavior becomes the interpretive lens through which students navigate their own choices with generative AI - especially when institutional policies remain emergent or ambiguous.

By making AI usage visible - whether in syllabus development, assessment design, or research workflows - faculty demystify the technology and foster a climate of co-learning. When faculty reflect aloud on what AI tools helped them do, what they rejected, and where their own judgment intervened, they humanize the integration process and model epistemic humility. As Chapter 4 illustrated, such mentoring reinforces student agency, allowing learners to see AI not as a shortcut, but as a prompt for reflection, discernment, and shared responsibility.

Importantly, this section expands the idea of modeling from technical demonstration to ethical stance. Faculty who declare their AI "red zones" - tasks where human judgment must remain primary - help students see that authorship, feedback, and interpretation are not just academic rituals, but moral acts. When responsible AI engagement is framed as both reflective and principled, it becomes a living curriculum: a way to teach transparency, invite critique, and resist the silent normalization of automation.

Ultimately, modeling responsible AI use is not about achieving mastery. It is about showing students what it looks like to lead with integrity, question with courage, and adapt without abandoning values. In a time of accelerating change, such modeling becomes not only pedagogically effective - but also culturally essential.

Section 7: Designing Learning Goals for Human-AI Collaboration

As AI becomes a ubiquitous part of knowledge work, students must be prepared not only to understand its functionality but to **collaborate with intelligent systems critically, ethically, and creatively**. Designing learning goals for human–AI collaboration requires educators to move beyond binary thinking - where AI is either banned or blindly embraced - and instead, **integrate AI literacy, discernment, and reflection into the fabric of academic development**.

This effort builds on the foundational premise of Chapter 2, which framed AI not as a standalone subject but rather as a **cross-disciplinary literacy**. Students need to be taught how to prompt, interpret, evaluate, and revise AI-generated content in ways that honor both disciplinary rigor and human judgment. Learning goals must therefore reflect a shift from content mastery alone to **process awareness, tool transparency, and ethical inquiry**.

Chapter 7 made this shift concrete by proposing layered competencies for AI-enhanced education: from foundational literacy (e.g., understanding what generative AI does), to fluency (e.g., applying it thoughtfully), to mastery (e.g., teaching others or shaping AI-integrated systems). Faculty were encouraged to align assignments and assessments with these stages, ensuring that students not only use AI but **reflect on its impact, critique its assumptions, and articulate their decision-making** throughout.

Importantly, as discussed in Chapter 5, these goals must also include the capacity to assess the credibility, integrity, and implications of AI-generated content. For example, students learning to summarize scholarly literature with the help of an AI tool should also be taught to verify citations, identify omissions, and revise outputs to include marginalized perspectives or context-specific nuance. In this way, collaboration with AI becomes an exercise in **active reasoning and academic authorship**, not passive consumption.

Chapter 3 added another dimension by emphasizing the importance of **ethically grounded case-based learning**. Learning goals should not merely reward successful tool use, but prioritize students' ability to navigate dilemmas - when to trust automation, when to intervene, and how to disclose AI use transparently. By embedding these questions into rubrics, reflection prompts, and grading criteria, faculty can reinforce that **collaboration includes responsibility**.

Human–AI collaboration also requires **creative divergence**, as outlined in Chapter 4. Learning goals should emphasize not just fluency with prompts or efficiency in drafting, but the ability to challenge, remix, and improve AI-generated outputs. In creative disciplines, this might mean asking students to annotate machine-generated poems with their own interpretive voice, or to produce visual counter-narratives in response to text-to-image systems. In technical fields, it might involve evaluating algorithmic decisions and proposing modifications that reflect user empathy or community accountability.

Chapter 6 reminded us that responsible collaboration also means understanding where human insight is irreplaceable. Learning goals should include articulating when **AI should not be used** - such as in writing positionality statements, interpreting personal narratives, or providing formative feedback on emotional expression. By identifying these boundaries, students learn that collaboration is not a default - it is a decision that must be contextualized and justified.

In mentorship contexts, as discussed in Chapter 4, learning goals can include the ability to co-analyze AI output with a mentor, reflect on its influence on scholarly direction, and revise research designs to retain originality and ethical coherence. Similarly, Chapter 8 emphasized that **goal-setting is cultural**: students from different linguistic, disciplinary, or social backgrounds may experience AI use differently, and learning goals must accommodate divergent ways of thinking, expressing, and questioning. To support faculty in designing these goals, institutions can:

- Provide sample outcome statements (e.g., "Students will critically assess AI-generated content for accuracy, bias, and disciplinary fit").
- Offer cross-departmental workshops on aligning AI use with learning outcomes and accreditation standards (Chapter 9).
- Create communities of practice where faculty share and revise AI-integrated rubrics based on student feedback and evolving tools (Chapter 6).
- Recognize the time and intellectual labor involved in adapting goals to AI-mediated contexts within promotion and review structures (Chapter 8).

Ultimately, designing learning goals for human–AI collaboration is not about future-proofing education - it is about **reaffirming the role of education in shaping the future**. These goals prepare students to work with, question, and ultimately reshape the systems that will influence every aspect of their professional and civic lives. And they remind us that collaboration, at its best, is a two-way process - one that challenges both humans and machines to grow beyond their limitations.

Designing Learning Goals for Human–AI Collaboration

As artificial intelligence becomes embedded in academic, professional, and civic life, faculty can no longer treat its presence as peripheral. The task now is not simply to regulate or tolerate AI, but to **design for it** - to create learning goals, assessment strategies, and pedagogical frameworks that treat human–AI collaboration as a site of critical thinking, ethical engagement, and creative growth. As Chapter 7 emphasized, when learning outcomes evolve to reflect real-world complexity, students gain agency and integrity, not confusion.

This section reframes instructional design in light of AI's affordances and limitations, building on principles introduced in Chapter 2 (AI as a reflective mirror), Chapter 5 (critical evaluation of outputs), and Chapter 6 (faculty modeling). At its heart is a question: ***"How do we teach students to work with AI without diminishing their originality, voice, or ethical compass?"***

Step 1: Define AI-Responsive Learning Outcomes

Traditional learning objectives often ask: ***"Can students do X on their own?"*** But in an AI-augmented world, the more meaningful question is:

- ***"Can students use AI to do X responsibly, creatively, and reflectively?"***

This shift, highlighted in Chapter 3's ethical case studies and Chapter 4's creativity scaffolds, emphasizes higher-order skills over rote performance.

Examples of Human–AI Collaboration Outcomes:

- Critically evaluate the **affordances and limitations** of generative AI in academic research.
- Demonstrate **transparent and ethical** use of AI in the writing or design process.
- Use AI tools to **ideate, iterate, and refine** creative products while maintaining personal voice.
- Assess **bias, sourcing, and credibility** in AI-generated content relevant to the student's discipline.
- Integrate AI tools into **problem-solving workflows** with attention to human oversight and ethical judgment.

These outcomes signal to students that AI is not banned nor blindly embraced - it is a tool to be **navigated with care and intention**.

Step 2: Align with Bloom's Taxonomy and Digital Literacy Frameworks

Well-designed learning outcomes should reflect a **developmental progression** - from understanding how AI works to applying it critically and creating new knowledge through collaboration. Bloom's Taxonomy provides a useful scaffold for this shift, as do digital literacy models referenced in Chapter 5 and Chapter 9.

Bloom's Level	AI-Aligned Learning Goal
Remember	Identify common uses of generative AI in your discipline.
Understand	Explain how large language models (LLMs) generate content and why errors may occur.
Apply	Use an AI tool to draft an outline, generate code, or visualize a dataset.
Analyze	Compare your own ideas with an AI-generated version to identify differences in reasoning, tone, or evidence.
Evaluate	Assess the ethical implications of using AI to make a decision in a real-world case.
Create	Co-author an artifact that synthesizes human creativity and AI-supported insight, with full reflection on process.

These outcomes can also be mapped to the **ACRL Framework for Information Literacy** and **JISC's Digital Capabilities Model**, reinforcing:

- Evaluative reasoning.
- Ethical tech use.
- Contextual information practices.
- Critical interpretation of AI outputs (ACRL, 2016; JISC, 2022).

This coherence across pedagogical models supports Chapter 10's broader theme: **clear design is a prerequisite for ethical innovation**.

Step 3: Embed in Career and Civic Readiness

Chapter 1 emphasized that AI is not simply an academic disruptor - it is a **societal force** reshaping employment, policy, and civic interaction. Learning goals should prepare students not just for course completion, but for **leadership in machine-mediated environments**.

Employers increasingly seek graduates who can:

- Leverage AI to **streamline research or communication**.
- Exercise **judgment** about when and how AI should be used.
- Collaborate in **human–AI teams**.
- Identify **automation bias** and data blind spots.
- Communicate their **AI use ethically** to stakeholders.

Sample Cross-Disciplinary AI Learning Goals:

- **Nursing.** Use AI-based diagnostic support tools while prioritizing patient dignity and equity in care.
- **Marketing.** Design a brand campaign that uses AI for segmentation, while preserving a human-centered narrative.
- **Journalism.** Critically review AI-drafted headlines for bias and accuracy before publishing.
- **Education.** Develop an inclusive learning activity that integrates AI, aligned with Universal Design for Learning (UDL) principles.

This reframing transforms AI literacy from a technical skill into a **professional imperative**, echoing the urgency in Chapter 8 around creating a legacy of ethical leadership (Benjamin, 2023; Selwyn, 2019).

Step 4: Assessing Human–AI Collaboration

Traditional assessments often evaluate products - but in AI-enhanced work, the **process matters just as much**. As Chapter 4 demonstrated, a polished AI output does not guarantee student learning or ethical discernment. Faculty must assess:

- **Transparency**. *"Did the student disclose AI use clearly and appropriately?"*
- **Strategic Prompt Design**. *"Did the student show intentionality and iteration in shaping AI output?"*
- **Human Editing and Synthesis**. *"Did the student modify AI output in ways that reflect deeper understanding?"*
- **Critical Reflection**. *"Did the student articulate what worked, what failed, and what they learned?"*
- **Disciplinary Integrity**. *"Was the AI use aligned with norms of evidence, voice, and academic honesty?"*

Example Assessment Rubric Dimensions:

Dimension	Indicators
AI Use Transparency	Clear disclosure of tools used, with rationale and documentation
Prompt Strategy	Evidence of prompt refinement and purposeful iteration
Human Insight & Revision	Substantive editing, synthesis, or expansion beyond AI output
Critical Reflection	Thoughtful engagement with strengths, limitations, and ethical implications
Disciplinary Alignment	Conformance to field-specific standards for credibility and originality

This multidimensional approach, as emphasized in Chapter 9, promotes **process-based, metacognitive learning** - not performance-based compliance (Slimi & Carballido, 2023).

Assessment Example: AI Use Portfolio (Any Discipline)

Assignment Description:

- *Students build a semester-long portfolio that includes:*
  - *Screenshots of prompts and AI outputs from assigned tasks.*
  - *Annotated revisions showing human intervention.*
  - *A final artifact (e.g., report, design, code, or argument).*
  - *A reflective statement addressing:*
    - *How was AI used?*
    - *Why specific choices were made?*
    - *What did the student learn about authorship, accuracy, and ethics.*

Purpose:

- *To evaluate not only the quality of the final work, but the* ***student's intentionality, process, and evolving agency*** *as a human collaborator with AI* (Brookfield, 2017; Reiss, 2021).

Section Reflection: Designing Learning Goals for Human–AI Collaboration

This section reframes the future of education not around content delivery, but around collaboration - between humans and machines, and more importantly, between values and technologies. Drawing from earlier chapters, it argues that teaching in the AI era is no longer about preparing students **despite** AI, but **through** and **with** it. Faculty must move past binary policies of prohibition or passive use, and instead design intentional learning outcomes that prepare students to navigate human–AI interaction with judgment, creativity, and ethical awareness.

As emphasized throughout Chapters 2, 3, 4, and 7, AI integration into learning outcomes must start with rethinking what success looks like. Rather than measuring isolated mastery, faculty are encouraged to scaffold competencies such as prompt strategy, critical revision, and ethical disclosure - skills that transcend disciplines and prepare students to act with agency in real-world AI contexts. The proposed frameworks move learning from task execution to process literacy, empowering students to critique, refine, and even resist AI-generated outputs where necessary.

Moreover, this section expands the scope of learning goals beyond academic performance to include civic responsibility and professional readiness. Drawing on the urgency expressed in Chapters 1 and 8, it insists that higher education has a duty to prepare students not just to use AI competently, but to shape its implications in journalism, medicine, engineering, policy, and beyond. This vision positions students as future leaders in human–AI collaboration - capable of wielding automation with care and confronting its blind spots with integrity.

Ultimately, designing learning goals for human–AI collaboration is about more than managing new tools. It is about cultivating the judgment to know when to partner with machines, when to intervene, and when to draw the line. It affirms that collaboration is not just technical - it is pedagogical, moral, and cultural. In shaping such goals, faculty are not merely teaching skills; they are building the foundations of human-centered leadership in an AI-mediated world.

Section 8: Creating a Legacy of Ethical Leadership in the AI Era

---

In times of rapid technological transformation, what faculty choose to teach - and how they choose to lead - becomes part of the **moral architecture of the academy**. As artificial intelligence redefines authorship, learning, creativity, and institutional operations, faculty are not simply adjusting their syllabi; they are **shaping the ethical climate of higher education**.

To create a lasting legacy, educators must center not only on what AI enables, but what it demands of us as mentors, colleagues, and civic actors.

This book has illustrated that ethical leadership in the AI era is not an abstract concept - it is grounded in daily pedagogical choices, curriculum design, policy critique, and community modeling. As discussed in Chapter 1, responding to AI requires not only technical upskilling but instead a reaffirmation of core educational values: **equity, reflection, humility, and care**. Faculty who embody these values through their teaching and mentorship extend a legacy far beyond the classroom - they shape how institutions remember themselves during a period of immense uncertainty.

Chapter 4 demonstrated that ethical leadership emerges most powerfully in mentoring relationships. When faculty guide students in using AI with transparency and purpose - inviting honest reflection about what they trusted, revised, or rejected - they instill habits of integrity that outlast the tools themselves. This is leadership through **relational pedagogy**, where students learn not just what is acceptable, but what is just.

As noted in Chapter 3, ethical leadership also means resisting the pressure to automate learning in ways that prioritize efficiency over ethics. Faculty who raise hard questions about AI-assisted advising, grading algorithms, or surveillance tools help institutions think **critically about their digital direction**. They serve as ethical stewards - protecting the human dimensions of education in environments increasingly mediated by code.

Chapter 6 reminded us that modeling is a form of leadership. Faculty who narrate their own uncertainties, make visible their process of trial and error, or share examples of responsible AI use are not undermining their authority - they are reinforcing **leadership as humility in practice**. They give students permission to ask questions, express doubt, and take ownership of their learning path - even when (especially when) that path is complicated by technology.

Chapter 8 emphasized that legacy is not only individual - it is cultural. Faculty shape ethical norms through department discussions, policy committees, hiring practices, and curriculum design. When they advocate for inclusive AI literacy, co-lead cross-disciplinary workshops, or embed algorithmic equity into general education goals, they create **structural conditions for future faculty and students to flourish**. This kind of legacy transforms campuses from reactive environments into **resilient ecosystems**.

Moreover, as discussed in Chapter 2 and Chapter 5, ethical leadership requires epistemic awareness - an understanding that truth, knowledge, and expertise are now being shaped by systems that simulate coherence but often lack context. Faculty who help students understand these dynamics - by critiquing AI summaries, revising hallucinated citations, or highlighting excluded voices - teach more than digital skills. They teach students to **defend truth as a deliberative process, not a computational output**.

To institutionalize this legacy, Chapter 9 called for faculty to be included in AI governance, policy design, and strategic planning. Ethical leadership must be supported structurally - through recognition in promotion and tenure criteria, funding for pedagogical innovation, and pathways for faculty voices to shape campus infrastructure. A legacy cannot be sustained if it is invisible.

Finally, Chapter 7 reminded us that leadership in the AI era must include the ability to **design for others** - to create learning goals, platforms, and tools that guide future generations of learners through ambiguity with ethical clarity. Faculty are not just teaching students how to think alongside AI. They are teaching them how to think **through AI** - with integrity, with courage, and with attention to who benefits, who is burdened, and who is believed.

To create a legacy of ethical leadership in the AI era, faculty must:

- **Name their values aloud**, even when those values challenge dominant narratives of automation or innovation.
- **Mentor with intentionality**, offering students a model of discernment rather than dependence.
- **Collaborate across difference**, building coalitions that reflect shared responsibility and diverse expertise.
- **Hold institutions accountable**, shaping structures that support long-term justice, not just short-term novelty.

Leadership in this moment is not about having the final word on AI - it is about **asking the right questions, in the right spaces, with the right people**, again and again.

By embracing clarity over confusion, courage over complacency, and curiosity over cynicism, faculty can transform the AI era from a perceived threat into an opportunity for educational renewal. The tools have changed. The mission remains the same: to cultivate thoughtful, ethical, and empowered learners ready to shape the future - and in doing so, become a faculty worthy of the moment.

Creating a Legacy of Ethical Leadership in the AI Era

Educators are not only content experts or curriculum designers - they are mentors, role models, and cultural stewards. In the AI era, this role takes on new urgency. As students begin to interact with tools that simulate intelligence, creativity, and decision-making, they will look to their faculty not just for permission or prohibition, but for guidance on **how to think, reflect, and act with discernment**.

As discussed throughout Chapters 1–9, faculty influence is amplified not only through what they teach but through what they **normalize, model, and reward**. Chapter 3 explored how ethical reasoning is taught through applied case studies, not abstract moral codes. Chapter 4 illustrated how creativity must be framed as intentional divergence from machine outputs. Chapter 6 emphasized the importance of faculty transparency in AI use, and Chapter 7 highlighted how human–AI collaboration requires new forms of assessment that prioritize reflection over automation. Now, in Chapter 10, the question becomes one of **legacy**: **"What will students remember - not just about the material, but about how their mentors helped them navigate a world shaped by intelligent systems?"**

Framing Faculty as Ethical Architects, Not Just Educators

Educators are often the first mentors students encounter as they confront the moral tensions of AI use. What faculty **highlight, ignore, or reward** - whether intentionally or not - shapes how students approach future decisions as developers, designers, policymakers, and citizens. Key questions to guide faculty reflection include:

- *"What values are embedded in the way I assign, evaluate, and discuss AI in my classroom?"*
- *"Do I teach students to* ***pause and question*** *- or to automate and execute?"*
- *"Am I preparing students to ask* ***what should be done****, not just what can be done?"*

As Brookfield (2017) emphasized, the role of the critical educator is to **surface assumptions, challenge power structures, and expand moral imagination**. In the AI era, this means faculty must lead students into ethical ambiguity, not shield them from it.

Strategies for Fostering Ethical Leadership Mindsets

---

1. Capstone Reflections on AI and Responsibility

To cultivate leadership, students must see themselves as **ethical agents**, not passive users. Capstone assignments that encourage reflective synthesis provide a powerful closure to AI-integrated learning journeys.

Example (Any Senior-Level Course):

- *Write a letter to your future self in your profession.*
- *Reflect on the challenges you may face in using AI tools responsibly.*
    - *"What principles will guide your choices?"*
    - *"How will you ensure your work promotes justice, equity, and human dignity?"*

This exercise, aligned with Chapters 7 and 9, transforms reflection into foresight - prompting students to **see ethical leadership as a lived practice**, not a classroom topic (Byars-Winston & Dahlberg, 2019; Slimi & Carballido, 2023).

---

2. Leadership Projects with Real-World Impact

Ethical leadership must extend beyond hypothetical scenarios. Students can be invited to lead projects that **intervene in public discourse, institutional policy, or community education**.

Examples:

- *Host a campus dialogue on AI bias in surveillance tools (Chapter 3).*
- *Design a toolkit for ethical AI use in nursing, journalism, or education (Chapter 5).*
- *Partner with local nonprofits to assess how AI is shaping public services.*

- *Publish student op-eds or community guides on misinformation and media literacy (Chapter 8).*

These initiatives shift students from classroom consumers to **civic actors and cultural critics** (Benjamin, 2023; Noble, 2018).

---

3. Interdisciplinary Ethics Debates

Complex AI dilemmas rarely have clear answers. Bringing together students from different majors encourages them to **inhabit competing value systems**, surfacing tensions between technical feasibility, economic incentives, and social justice.

Debate Questions:

- *"Should AI be allowed to make hiring decisions?"*
- *"Can autonomous vehicles be programmed to make ethical choices?"*
- *"Who is responsible when AI harms a vulnerable population?"*

Using formats such as Oxford-style debates or stakeholder simulations, students practice **dialogue, deliberation, and dissent** - foundational traits of ethical leadership explored in Chapters 3 and 6 (Bender et al., 2021; Selwyn, 2019).

---

4. Model Institutional and Civic Engagement

Faculty themselves must step into **public-facing roles** to demonstrate how scholarly expertise can inform ethical innovation.

Leadership Actions:

- Serve on institutional AI task forces or curriculum committees.
- Publish in public venues, such as blogs, op-eds, or policy briefs.
- Partner with civic organizations to promote AI literacy.
- Lead public webinars or town halls about AI's impact on education and society.

Example:

- *A faculty member co-authors a regional newspaper article about AI in K–12 classrooms and invites students to respond with their own letters, critiques, or community conversations.*

As discussed in Chapter 10 Section 5, such public modeling helps students see AI not as a technical issue - but a **cultural and ethical terrain** requiring active engagement.

---

5. Embed Ethical Principles into Course Culture

Leadership must be **modeled through the learning environment itself**. Syllabi, classroom norms, and grading policies should reflect a commitment to values-based learning.

Sample Norms:

- *AI use is welcome - but must be disclosed, explained, and critiqued.*
- *Experimentation is encouraged - but reflection is required.*
- *Efficiency is appreciated - but never at the expense of equity or originality.*
- *Grades reflect not only output, but process, transparency, and integrity.*

Sample Syllabus Language:

- *"This course emphasizes critical and ethical engagement with AI tools. You will be expected not only to use them - but to evaluate their assumptions, impact, and implications. Our goal is to prepare you not just as a user of technology - but as a leader of values."*

Such principles echo the call in Chapter 2 and Chapter 7 to **center inquiry over automation and meaning over convenience**.

Section Reflection: Creating a Legacy of Ethical Leadership in the AI Era

This final section invites faculty to envision their role not merely as faculty responding to rapid technological change, but as ethical architects actively shaping the future of higher education. Across Chapters 1–9, the book has emphasized that the integration of AI into academia cannot be measured solely by tool adoption, productivity gains, or technical proficiency. Instead, it must be judged by how faculty preserve and evolve the moral fabric of their institutions - through mentorship, modeling, curriculum design, and public engagement.

Ethical leadership, as articulated here, is a relational and reflective practice. It is demonstrated when faculty guide students through ambiguity rather than around it, when they teach discernment instead of dependence, and when they elevate questions of justice, authorship, and care above metrics of efficiency. Chapters 3, 4, and 6 reinforced that leadership happens through case-based dialogue, mentorship transparency, and critical self-disclosure. In this sense, faculty legacy is forged in daily choices - what gets rewarded, what gets questioned, and what gets reimagined.

This section also makes clear that legacy is cultural and institutional. As discussed in Chapters 8 and 9, educators extend their influence through policy development, governance participation, and community collaboration. By shaping norms around AI transparency, designing value-based assessments, and promoting interdisciplinary civic projects, faculty lay foundations that will guide future cohorts. They become, in effect, stewards of the university's conscience during a moment of systemic transformation.

Ultimately, creating a legacy of ethical leadership means anchoring AI innovation in timeless educational commitments: to truth, equity, empathy, and reflective agency. As the section reminds us, students may forget individual lectures - but they will remember how their faculty mentors responded when confronted with new, uncertain, and powerful tools. And if those responses model integrity, curiosity, and moral imagination, then the faculty of today will not just adapt to the AI era - they will define it.

Chapter 10 Conclusion: From Integration to Transformation - Reimagining Faculty Leadership in the Age of AI

Chapter 10 brought this book to its culminating vision: that faculty are not merely responders to artificial intelligence, but **architects of the future** of higher education. Across the previous nine chapters, we explored how generative AI reshapes writing, teaching, authorship, creativity, mentorship, assessment, and institutional culture. In this final chapter, we wove those insights together to articulate eight core leadership responsibilities that define what it means to be a faculty member in the AI era - not as a passive adapter, but as a **strategic, ethical, and cultural guide**.

Section 1 reframed the notion of **empowerment**, arguing that in the AI age, to empower students and faculty is to give them the skills and structures to think critically, challenge automation, and act with discernment. This empowerment is not technological - it is epistemological and relational, grounded in voice, judgment, and institutional legitimacy.

Section 2 proposed a new mindset: that faculty must teach AI not as a replacement for human intelligence, but as a **reflective mirror**. By using AI outputs as starting points for metacognition, critique, and deeper inquiry, faculty can help students better understand their own thinking - and the assumptions encoded in machine outputs.

Section 3 placed ethical reasoning at the heart of faculty work, highlighting the use of **human–AI case studies** to teach ambiguity, consequence, and value-based decision-making. In this model, students learn not what to think, but **how to evaluate** what AI proposes, what it omits, and what it disrupts.

Section 4 returned to the theme of creativity, but through a critical lens: **divergence**. Faculty must design for originality - not polished mimicry - by prompting students to remix, annotate, and challenge AI outputs. In doing so, educators reassert the irreplaceable complexity of human expression.

Section 5 addressed the urgent need to **teach students how to assess the integrity of AI outputs**, reframing digital literacy as a survival skill in an information landscape where fluency can mask falsehood. Faculty must equip students to identify hallucinations, trace sources, and evaluate claims within disciplinary contexts.

Section 6 emphasized that **faculty modeling** is not optional - it is a silent curriculum. When educators are transparent about their own AI use, admit limitations, and share ethical boundaries, they invite students into a culture of responsible inquiry and reflective experimentation.

Section 7 argued that **designing new learning goals** is foundational to meaningful AI integration. Learning outcomes must now include tool literacy, decision transparency, and critical reflection - skills that empower students not just to **use** AI, but to **understand, evaluate, and shape it**.

Finally, **Section 8** called faculty to a higher purpose: to **create a legacy of ethical leadership**. This legacy is not built through compliance or novelty, but through sustained acts of mentorship, policy critique, interdisciplinary collaboration, and values-centered teaching.

The ethical climate of higher education in the AI era will be shaped by those who choose to lead - not with certainty, but with clarity, courage, and care.

Concluding Themes

At its core, Chapter 10 advances two intertwined themes:

- **Faculty are the ethical infrastructure of the AI-era university.** Institutions may adopt tools, revise policies, or license platforms - but it is faculty who define the **moral tone** of their institutions. Through their decisions, disclosures, and designs, they model how to think with AI, without surrendering human discernment.
- **Leadership in the AI era means designing for uncertainty, not just outcomes.** Faculty must cultivate learning environments where process, reflection, dialogue, and dissent are not only permitted - but they are also **central**. In doing so, they help students develop not just technical skill but rather **ethical readiness and civic imagination**.

As we close this book, the message of Chapter 10 is ultimately a message of hope. AI does not diminish the role of educators - it **elevates it**. Faculty are not being replaced. They are being invited to lead with new relevance, new responsibility, and renewed purpose. The future of education will not be shaped by algorithms alone - but by those who teach others how to question, navigate, and transform them.

This is the legacy. This is the opportunity. This is the moment.

Afterword

Our Challenge to all Faculty of the AI Era

The age of artificial intelligence is no longer a speculative future - it is the defining reality of our present. In every corner of society, AI systems are reshaping how we live, work, and think. Nowhere is this transformation more urgent, and more contested, than in education. At the heart of this evolution stands the university - an institution historically committed to inquiry, rigor, and adaptation. And within it, faculty bear the responsibility not only to respond to this moment but to lead it.

The time has passed for debating whether AI belongs in the classroom. It is already there - on student devices, in research workflows, embedded in course design tools, and even within the very questions students ask. Faculty can no longer afford to ignore this reality. The traditional methods of teaching, mentoring, and preserving academic integrity must be reevaluated in light of this technological paradigm shift (see Appendix A). This is not a moment for fear - it is a moment for leadership, clarity, and courage.

Recognizing the Paradigm Shift

Generative AI, including tools such as ChatGPT, Claude, and Gemini, has rapidly transitioned from experimental novelty to mainstream utility. These systems now support natural language processing, content generation, coding, translation, tutoring, and even research synthesis. What began as assistance has quickly evolved into augmentation. And for many students and professionals, AI is already a default collaborator.

This acceleration poses both a challenge and an opportunity for university faculty. On one hand, it disrupts long-held assumptions about authorship, originality, and intellectual labor. On the other hand, it offers powerful tools to enhance learning, personalize instruction, and scale access to academic resources. Faculty who fail to engage risk becoming obsolete in their own classrooms. Those who embrace the shift can redefine what it means to teach, mentor, and uphold integrity in an AI-enhanced world.

Teaching in the AI Era

Pedagogy must evolve. The "chalk and talk" model, while still useful in limited contexts, is increasingly out of sync with how students learn, collaborate, and create in digitally mediated environments. Generative AI challenges the relevance of lecture-heavy instruction and rote memorization. If students can instantly generate summaries, essays, or code, then the role of the educator must shift toward designing experiences that cultivate critical thinking, synthesis, and human judgment - skills that AI cannot replicate.

To be clear, this does not mean lowering standards. Rather, it requires raising the level of intention in our instructional design. Assignments must ask students to critique AI-generated responses, compare sources, justify decisions, and reflect on their own learning process. Faculty must teach students how to **use** AI ethically and intelligently - not to avoid it, ban it, or pretend it does not exist.

Mentoring in an AI-Augmented World

Mentorship, too, must be reimagined. In an era where students increasingly turn to AI tutors and writing assistants for feedback and support, faculty advisors must shift their role from gatekeepers of knowledge to guides in discernment. Students need help not just accessing information, but interpreting, applying, and questioning it. They need models of ethical AI usage, strategies for integrating human insight with machine intelligence, and opportunities to explore complex problems that resist easy automation.

Faculty should encourage students to experiment with AI tools in their research and creative work, while simultaneously teaching them how to scrutinize algorithmic bias, data provenance, and the limits of computational reasoning. This type of mentorship prepares students not only for academic success but instead for more meaningful engagement in an AI-driven world.

Redefining Academic Integrity

Perhaps the most contested domain of all is academic integrity. The traditional definitions of cheating, plagiarism, and original work were developed in a pre-AI context. Faculty can no longer rely solely on similarity detectors or punitive codes of conduct. The presence of generative AI complicates what it means to "do one's own work." When students use AI to brainstorm, outline, or even co-write assignments, *"where does assistance end and misrepresentation begin?"*

This is not a call to abandon academic integrity. It is a call to redefine it. Integrity in the AI era must focus on **transparency of process, disclosure of tools,** and **demonstration of human understanding**. A student who submits an AI-assisted paper without acknowledging the tool may be violating ethical norms. But a student who can explain, critique, and contextualize the role AI played in their work is engaged in a new form of academic authorship - one that faculty must be prepared to recognize and assess.

The university system must also take bold steps toward a revised definition of plagiarism that distinguishes between generative synthesis and dishonest appropriation. Institutions must move beyond simplistic rules to nuanced frameworks that reflect how real-world professionals are already co-authoring with AI. Without this recalibration, we risk turning integrity policies into relics - outdated and unenforceable.

The Role of Faculty Leadership

This transition cannot be left to administrators, technologists, or student affairs officers alone. Faculty must lead. They are the stewards of academic culture, and their engagement will determine whether AI becomes a threat to integrity or a catalyst for innovation.

Leadership in this context means more than awareness. It means action. Faculty must:

- **Learn** the capabilities and limitations of current AI systems.
- **Revise** syllabi, learning objectives, and assessment strategies to reflect AI realities.
- **Model** responsible AI use in their own teaching and research practices.
- **Collaborate** with colleagues across disciplines to develop shared guidelines.
- **Mentor** students not just in content mastery, but in intellectual and ethical agency.

The courage to lead in uncertain times is not new to higher education. The academy has endured printing presses, calculators, the internet, and pandemics. Each disruption was met with resistance and reinvention. The AI era is no different.

Moving Forward: Practical Recommendations

To support this shift, institutions must provide resources, support, and incentives. The following steps can accelerate responsible integration:

- **Faculty Development Programs**. Offer workshops and certifications on AI literacy, pedagogy, and ethics.
- **Revised Integrity Codes**. Develop new policies that distinguish types of AI use and clarify expectations for disclosure.
- **Cross-Disciplinary Committees**. Form working groups of faculty, technologists, and students to continuously update guidance.
- **AI in Curriculum**. Embed AI literacy into general education and disciplinary coursework.
- **Research Funding**. Support scholarly inquiry into the educational impact of AI, including risks and innovations.

These are not luxuries. They are necessities if higher education is to maintain its relevance and rigor in a rapidly changing world.

Conclusion

The age of AI is not coming - it is here. And while it may upend many familiar practices in teaching, mentoring, and academic conduct, it also offers unprecedented possibilities for innovation and inclusion. Faculty are uniquely positioned to ensure that the university evolves with wisdom, responsibility, and purpose. This is not a time for fear. It is a time for leadership.

By embracing clarity over confusion, courage over complacency, and curiosity over cynicism, faculty can transform the AI era from a perceived threat into an opportunity for educational renewal. The tools have changed. The mission remains the same: to cultivate thoughtful, ethical, and empowered learners ready to shape the future.

It is our hope that this book serves as a practical guide and a source of encouragement as you lead that transformation - with bold action, thoughtful reflection, and a renewed commitment to the future of learning - becoming, in every sense, a true faculty of the AI era.

Steve and Barbara

References

Abdullah, Z., & Zaid, N. M. (2023). Perception of generative artificial intelligence in higher education research. *Innovative Teaching and Learning Journal*, *7*(2), 84-95.

ACRL (Association of College & Research Libraries). (2016). *Framework for information literacy for higher education*. https://www.ala.org/acrl/standards/ilframework

Altbach, P. G. (2007). Doctoral education: Present realities and future trends. In *International handbook of higher education* (pp. 65-81). Springer.

Anderson, L. W., & Krathwohl, D. R. (2001). *A taxonomy for learning, teaching, and assessing: A revision of Bloom's taxonomy of educational objectives: Complete edition.* Addison Wesley Longman, Inc.

Anderson, T., & Shattuck, J. (2012). Design-based research: A decade of progress in education research? *Educational Researcher*, *41*(1), 16-25.

Angwin, J., Larson, J., Mattu, S., & Kirchner, L. (2022). Machine bias. In *Ethics of Data and Analytics* (pp. 254-264). Auerbach Publications.

Ash, M. G. (2006). Bachelor of what, master of whom? The Humboldt myth and historical transformations of higher education in German-speaking Europe and the US. *European Journal of Education, 41*(2), 245–267.

Ash, S. L., & Clayton, P. H. (2009). Generating, deepening, and documenting learning: The power of critical reflection in applied learning. *Journal of Applied Learning in Higher Education, 1*, 25-48.

Austin, A. E. (2002). Preparing the next generation of faculty: Graduate school as socialization to the academic career. *The Journal of Higher Education*, *73*(1), 94-122.

Austin, A. E., & McDaniels, M. (2006). Preparing the professoriate of the future: Graduate student socialization for faculty roles. In *Higher education: Handbook of theory and research* (pp. 397-456). Springer.

Bailey, D. R., Almusharraf, N., & Almusharraf, A. (2023). Artificial intelligence in academic writing: Opportunities, challenges, and ethical considerations. *Journal of Academic Ethics, 21*(3), 451–468.

Balalle, H., & Pannilage, S. (2025). Reassessing academic integrity in the age of AI: A systematic literature review on AI and academic integrity. *Social Sciences & Humanities Open, 11*, 101299.

Ball, C. E. (2004). Show, not tell: The value of new media scholarship. *Computers and Composition*, *21*(4), 403-425.

Baptista, A., Frick, L., Holley, K., Remmik, M., Tesch, J., & Akerlind, G. (2015). The doctorate as an original contribution to knowledge: Considering relationships between originality, creativity, and innovation. *Frontline Learning Research*, *3*(3), 55-67.

Barker, M. J. (2011). Racial context, currency and connections: Black doctoral student and white advisor perspectives on cross-race advising. *Innovations in Education and Teaching International*, *48*(4), 387-400.

Barocas, S., Hardt, M., & Narayanan, A. (2023). *Fairness and machine learning: Limitations and opportunities*. MIT press.

Barthes, R. (1985). Rhetoric of the image. *Semiotics: An Introductory Anthology*, 192-205.

Becker, B. A., Denny, P., Finnie-Ansley, J., Luxton-Reilly, A., Prather, J., & Santos, E. A. (2023). Programming is hard-or at least it used to be: Educational opportunities and challenges of AI code generation. In *Proceedings of the 54th ACM Technical Symposium on Computer Science Education V. 1* (pp. 500-506).

Bender, E. M., Gebru, T., McMillan-Major, A., & Shmitchell, S. (2021). On the dangers of stochastic parrots: Can language models be too big? *FAccT '21: Proceedings of the 2021 ACM Conference on Fairness, Accountability, and Transparency*, 610–623.

Bengtsen, S. S. (2023). Doctoral education in-the-world: (Dis)connections between research and society. *From splendid isolation to global engagement. eds. B. Wolf, T. Schmohl, L. Buhin-Krenek and M. Stricker (WBV Media)*, 43-55.

Benjamin, R. (2023). Race after technology. In *Social Theory Re-Wired* (pp. 405-415). Routledge.

Biagioli, M. (2002). From book censorship to academic peer review. *Emergences: Journal for the Study of Media & Composite Cultures*, *12*(1), 11-45.

Binns, R. (2018). Fairness in machine learning: Lessons from political philosophy. In *Conference on fairness, accountability and transparency* (pp. 149-159). PMLR.

Birhane, A., Kalluri, P., Card, D., Agnew, W., Dotan, R., & Bao, M. (2022). The values encoded in machine learning research. In *Proceedings of the 2022 ACM conference on fairness, accountability, and transparency* (pp. 173-184).

Blair, K. L., & Monske, E. A. (2009). Developing digital literacies and professional identities: The benefits of E-portfolios in graduate education. *Journal of Literacy & Technology*, *10*(1).

Bok, D. (2003). *Universities in the marketplace: The commercialization of higher education*. Princeton University Press.

Boud, D. (2001). Using journal writing to enhance reflective practice. *New Directions for Adult and Continuing Education*, *90*, 9–18.

Boud, D., Costley, C., Cranfield, S., Desai, J., Nikolou-Walker, E., Nottingham, P., & Wilson, D. (2023). The pivotal role of student assessment in work-integrated learning. *Higher Education Research & Development*, *42*(6), 1323-1337.

Boud, D., & Falchikov, N. (2006). Aligning assessment with long-term learning. *Assessment & Evaluation in Higher Education*, *31*(4), 399-413.

Boud, D., Keogh, R., & Walker, D. (2013). *Reflection: Turning experience into learning*. Routledge.

Boyd, D., & Crawford, K. (2012). Critical questions for big data: Provocations for a cultural, technological, and scholarly phenomenon. *Information, Communication & Society*, *15*(5), 662-679.

Bretag, T., Mahmud, S., Wallace, M., Walker, R., James, C., Green, M., East, J., McGowan, U., & Patridge, L. (2011). Core elements of exemplary academic integrity policy in Australian higher education. *International Journal for Educational Integrity*, *7*(2).

Brickhouse, T. C., & Smith, N. D. (2000). Socratic teaching and Socratic method. In *Harvey Siegel (Ed.), The Oxford Handbook of Philosophy of Education*. MIT Press.

Brodin, E. M., & Avery, H. (2020). Cross-disciplinary collaboration and scholarly independence in multidisciplinary learning environments at doctoral level and beyond. *Minerva*, *58*(3), 409-433.

Brookfield, S. D. (2017). *Becoming a critically reflective teacher*. John Wiley & Sons.

Brookhart, S. M. (2010). *How to assess higher-order thinking skills in your classroom*. ASCD.

Broussard, M. (2019). *Artificial unintelligence: How computers misunderstand the world*. MIT Press.

Browne, S. (2015). *Dark matters: On the surveillance of blackness*. Duke University Press.

Buckingham-Shum, S., Ferguson, R., & Martinez-Maldonado, R. (2019). Human-centered learning analytics. *Journal of Learning Analytics*, *6*(2), 1–9.

Byars-Winston, A., & Dahlberg, M. L. (2019). *The science of effective mentorship in STEMM. Consensus study report*. National Academies Press. 500 Fifth Street NW, Washington, DC 20001.

Caillaud, E., & Skec, S. (2024). Supervision of design PHD students in an era of generative artificial intelligence. In *26th International Conference On Engineering and Product Design Education* (pp. 420-425).

Candy, L., & Edmonds, E. (2018). Practice-based research in the creative arts: Foundations and futures from the front line. *Leonardo*, *51*(1), 63-69.

Carless, D., & Boud, D. (2018). The development of student feedback literacy: Enabling uptake of feedback. *Assessment & Evaluation in Higher Education*, *43*(8), 1315-1325.

CAST. (2018). *Universal design for learning guidelines version 2.2*. http://udlguidelines.cast.org

Caulfield, M. (2017). Web literacy for student fact-checkers. Textbooks. 5. https://digitalcommons.liberty.edu/textbooks/5

Chen, M., & Decary, M. (2020). Artificial intelligence in healthcare: An essential guide for health leaders. In *Healthcare Management Forum* (Vol. 33, No. 1, pp. 10-18). Sage Publications.

Chiu, T. K., Ahmad, Z., Ismailov, M., & Sanusi, I. T. (2024). What are artificial intelligence literacy and competency? A comprehensive framework to support them. *Computers and Education Open*, *6*, 100171.

Cinelli, M., De Francisci Morales, G., Galeazzi, A., Quattrociocchi, W., & Starnini, M. (2021). The echo chamber effect on social media. *Proceedings of the National Academy of Sciences*, *118*(9), e2023301118.

Clark, B. R. (2008). *On higher education.* Johns Hopkins University Press.

Cobban, A. B. (1975). *The medieval universities: Their development and organization*. Methuen.

Cotton, D. R., Cotton, P. A., & Shipway, J. R. (2024). Chatting and cheating: Ensuring academic integrity in the era of ChatGPT. *Innovations in Education and Teaching International*, *61*(2), 228-239.

Cox, M. D. (2004). Introduction to faculty learning communities. *New Directions for Teaching and Learning*, *97*, 5-23.

Crawford, K. (2021). *The atlas of AI: Power, politics, and the planetary costs of artificial intelligence*. Yale University Press.

Crawford, K., & Paglen, T. (2021). Excavating AI: The politics of images in machine learning training sets. *AI & Society*, *36*(4), 1105-1116.

Creswell, J. W., & Clark, V. L. P. (2017). *Designing and conducting mixed methods research*. Sage Publications.

Dabis, A., & Csaki, C. (2024). AI and ethics: Investigating the first policy responses of higher education institutions to the challenge of generative AI. *Humanities and Social Sciences Communications*, *11*(1), 1-13.

Damsa, C., Rajala, A., Ritella, G., & Brouwer, J. (Eds.). (2024). *Re-theorising learning and research methods in learning research*. Routledge.

Davis, S. F., Drinan, P. F., & Gallant, T. B. (2011). *Cheating in school: What we know and what we can do*. John Wiley & Sons.

Deneen, C., & Boud, D. (2014). Patterns of resistance in managing assessment change. *Assessment & Evaluation in Higher Education*, *39*(5), 577-591.

Doshi-Velez, F., & Kim, B. (2017). Towards a rigorous science of interpretable machine learning. *arXiv preprint arXiv:1702.08608*.

Dweck, C. S. (2006). *Mindset: The new psychology of success*. Random House.

Eden, C. A., Chisom, O. N., & Adeniyi, I. S. (2024). Integrating AI in education: Opportunities, challenges, and ethical considerations. *Magna Scientia Advanced Research and Reviews*, *10*(2), 6-13.

Estima, S. (2020). *Multimodal meaning making and the doctoral dissertation–An exploration of academic forms* (Doctoral dissertation, University of Illinois at Urbana-Champaign).

Eubanks, V. (2018). *Automating inequality: How high-tech tools profile, police, and punish the poor*. St. Martin's Press.

Fahad, S., & Donni, R. (2024). *Ethical AI in education: Redesigning critical thinking pedagogies in the age of algorithmic discrimination*. ResearchGate Publications.

Farooq, Y. (2025). Exploring teachers' psychological readiness for effective AI integration in the classroom. *The Critical Review of Social Sciences Studies*, *3*(3), 351-364.

Fenwick, M., & Jurcys, P. (2023). Originality and the future of copyright in an age of generative AI. *Computer Law & Security Review*, *51*, 105892.

Fishman, T. (2009). *"We know it when we see it" is not good enough: Toward a standard definition of plagiarism that transcends theft, fraud, and copyright*. Proceedings of the 4th Asia Pacific Conference on Educational Integrity (Unpublished).

Fiske, A., Henningsen, P., & Buyx, A. (2019). Your robot therapist will see you now: Ethical implications of embodied artificial intelligence in psychiatry, psychology, and psychotherapy. *Journal of Medical Internet Research*, *21*(5), e13216.

Flammer, A. (1981). Toward a theory of question asking. *Psychological Research*, *43*, 407–420. doi:10.1007/BF00309225

Flick, L. B., & Lederman, N. G. (2004). *Scientific inquiry and nature of science*. Kluwer Academic Publishers.

Floridi, L. (2019). *The logic of information: A theory of philosophy as conceptual design*. Oxford University Press.

Floridi, L., & Chiriatti, M. (2020). GPT-3: Its nature, scope, limits, and consequences. *Minds and Machines*, *30*(4), 681–694.

Floridi, L., Cowls, J., Beltrametti, M., Chatila, R., Chazerand, P., Dignum, V., Luetge, C., Madelin, R., Pagallo, U., Rossi, F., Schafer, B., Valcke, P., & Vayena, E. (2018). AI4People - An ethical framework for a good AI society: Opportunities, risks, principles, and recommendations. *Minds and Machines*, *28*(4), 689-707.

Foucault, M. (2003). What is an Author? In *Reading Architectural History* (pp. 71-81). Routledge.

Friedman, B., Kahn, P. H., Jr., Borning, A., & Huldtgren, A. (2013). Value sensitive design and information systems. In *Early Engagement and New Technologies: Opening Up the Laboratory* (pp. 55-95). Springer.

Galanter, P. (2003). What is generative art? Complexity theory as a context for art theory. In *GA2003–6th Generative Art Conference*.

Gallant, T. B. (2008). Academic integrity in the twenty-first century: A teaching and learning imperative. *ASHE Higher Education Report*, *33*(5), 1-143.

Gardner, S. K. (2008). "What's too much and what's too little?" The process of becoming an independent researcher in doctoral education. *The Journal of Higher Education*, *79*(3), 326-350.

Gardner, S. K. (2009). The Development of doctoral students--Phases of challenge and support. *ASHE Higher Education Report*, *34*(6), 1-127.

Gay, G. (2018). *Culturally responsive teaching: Theory, research, and practice*. Teachers College Press.

Geethanjali, K. S., & Umashankar, N. (2025). Enhancing educational outcomes with explainable AI: Bridging transparency and trust in learning systems. *In 2025 International Conference on Emerging Systems and Intelligent Computing (ESIC)* (pp. 325-328). IEEE.

Glaser, R., Chudowsky, N., & Pellegrino, J. W. (Eds.). (2001). *Knowing what students know: The science and design of educational assessment*. National Academies Press.

Golde, C. M. (2005). The role of the department and discipline in doctoral student attrition: Lessons from four departments. *The Journal of Higher Education*, *76*(6), 669-700.

Golde, C. M., & Walker, G. E. (Eds.). (2006). *Envisioning the future of doctoral education: Preparing stewards of the discipline-Carnegie essays on the doctorate*. John Wiley & Sons.

Goldschmidt, G. (2019). Design creativity research: Recent developments and future challenges. *International Journal of Design Creativity and Innovation*, *7*(4), 194-195.

Gravett, K. (2021). Disrupting the doctoral journey: Re-imagining doctoral pedagogies and temporal practices in higher education. *Teaching in Higher Education*, *26*(3), 293-305.

Gray, M. L., & Suri, S. (2019). *Ghost work: How to stop Silicon Valley from building a new global underclass*. Harper Business.

Gulya, J. (2023). Rebranding originality for the age of AI. *International Journal of Emerging and Disruptive Innovation in Education: Visionarium*, *1*(1), 5.

Gundu, T. (2024). Strategies for e-Assessments in the Era of Generative Artificial Intelligence. *Electronic Journal of e-Learning*, *22*(7), 40-50.

Hagerty, A., & Rubinov, I. (2019). Global AI ethics: A review of the social impacts and ethical implications of artificial intelligence. *arXiv preprint arXiv:1907.07892*.

Han, Y. (2025). Beyond the algorithm: Reconciling generative AI and human agency in academic writing education. *International Journal of Learning and Teaching, 11*(1), 39-42.

Head, A. J., & Eisenberg, M. B. (2010). *Truth be told: How college students evaluate and use information in the digital age. Project Information Literacy Progress Report.* Project Information Literacy.

Heston, T. F., & Khun, C. (2023). *The good, the bad, and the ugly of ChatGPT in medical education* (SSRN Scholarly Paper 4532671).

Hoggan, C., & Kloubert, T. (2020). Transformative learning in theory and practice. *Adult Education Quarterly*, *70*(3), 295-307. doi:10.2139/ssrn.4532671.

Holmes, W., Bialik, M., & Fadel, C. (2022). *Artificial intelligence in education: Promises and implications for teaching and learning*. Center for Curriculum Redesign.

Iloka, P. C. (2025). Teaching integrity: Strategies for fostering ethical behavior in students. *UNIZIK Journal of Educational Research and Policy Studies*, *19*(1).

Jacoby, B. (2014). *Service-learning essentials: Questions, answers, and lessons learned.* John Wiley & Sons.

Javed, H., Muqeet, H. A., Javed, T., Rehman, A. U., & Sadiq, R. (2023). Ethical frameworks for machine learning in sensitive healthcare applications. *IEEE Access*, *12*, 16233-16254.

JISC. (2022). *Building digital capabilities: The six elements defined.* https://digitalcapability.jisc.ac.uk

Johnson, D. W., & Johnson, R. T. (2009). An educational psychology success story: Social interdependence theory and cooperative learning. *Educational Researcher*, *38*(5), 365-379.

Johnson, W. B., & Griffin, K. A. (2024). *On being a mentor: A guide for higher education faculty*. Routledge.

Kacena, M. A., Plotkin, L. I., & Fehrenbacher, J. C. (2024). The use of artificial intelligence in writing scientific review articles. *Current Osteoporosis Reports*, *22*(1), 115-121.

Kallunki, V., Kinnunen, P., Pyörälä, E., Haarala-Muhonen, A., Katajavuori, N., & Myyry, L. (2024). Navigating the evolving landscape of teaching and learning: University faculty and staff perceptions of the artificial intelligence-altered terrain. *Education Sciences*, *14*(7), 727.

Kamler, B. (2008). Rethinking doctoral publication practices: Writing from and beyond the thesis. *Studies in Higher Education*, *33*(3), 283-294.

Kapucu, M. S., & Avci, Z. Y. (2020). The digital story of science: Experiences of pre-service science teachers. *Journal of Education in Science Environment and Health*, *6*(2), 148-168.

Kearns, M., & Roth, A. (2019). The ethical algorithm: The science of socially aware algorithm design. Oxford University Press.

Kelly, F. (2016). *The idea of the PhD: The doctorate in the twenty-first-century imagination.* Routledge.

Kemmis, S., & McTaggart, R. (2007). Communicative action and the public sphere. *Strategies of Qualitative Inquiry*, *3*, 271-330.

Khreisat, M. N., Khilani, D., Rusho, M. A., Karkkulainen, E. A., Tabuena, A. C., & Uberas, A. D. (2024). Ethical implications of AI integration in educational decision making: Systematic review. *Educational Administration: Theory and Practice*, *30*(5), 8521-8527.

Klein, J. T. (2010). *Creating interdisciplinary campus cultures: A model for strength and sustainability*. John Wiley & Sons.

Knight, P., & Yorke, M. (2003). *Assessment, learning and employability*. McGraw-Hill Education.

Kochan, F. K., & Trimble, S. B. (2000). From mentoring to co-mentoring: Establishing collaborative relationships. *Theory into practice*, *39*(1), 20-28.

Kolb, D. A. (2014). *Experiential learning: Experience as the source of learning and development*. FT press.

Kovach, M. (2021). *Indigenous methodologies: Characteristics, conversations, and contexts*. University of Toronto press.

Kram, K. E. (1988). *Mentoring at work: Developmental relationships in organizational life*. University Press of America.

Kuhlthau, C. C. (2025). *Seeking Meaning: A Process Approach to Library and Information Services*. Bloomsbury Publishing.

Lancaster, T., & Cotarlan, C. (2021). Contract cheating by STEM students through a file sharing website: A Covid-19 pandemic perspective. *International Journal for Educational Integrity*, *17*(1), 1–16. https://doi.org/10.1007/s40979-021-00070-0

Lang, J. M. (2013). *Cheating lessons*. Harvard University Press.

Lee, A. (2008). How are doctoral students supervised? Concepts of doctoral research supervision. *Studies in Higher Education*, *33*(3), 267–281.

Long, D., & Magerko, B. (2020). What is AI literacy? Competencies and design considerations. In *Proceedings of the 2020 CHI Conference on Human Factors in Computing Systems* (pp. 1-16).

Lovitts, B. E. (2001). *Leaving the ivory tower: The causes and consequences of departure from doctoral study*. Bloomsbury Publishing PLC.

Luckin, R. (2017). Towards artificial intelligence-based assessment systems. *Nature Human Behavior*, *1*(3), 28.

Luckin, R., Holmes, W., Griffiths, M., & Forcier, L. B. (2016). *Intelligence Unleashed. An argument for AI in Education*. Pearson.

Manovich, L. (2018). *AI aesthetics*. Strelka Press.

Mayer, R. E. (2014). Incorporating motivation into multimedia learning. *Learning and Instruction*, *29*, 171-173.

McCormack, J., Gifford, T., & Hutchings, P. (2019). Autonomy, authenticity, authorship and intention in computer generated art. In *International Conference on Computational*

Intelligence in Music, Sound, Art and Design (part of EvoStar) (pp. 35-50). Springer International Publishing.

McKenney, S., & Reeves, T. (2018). *Conducting educational design research*. Routledge.

Mercer, N., & Howe, C. (2012). Explaining the dialogic processes of teaching and learning: The value and potential of sociocultural theory. *Learning, Culture and Social Interaction, 1*(1), 12-21.

Mesko, B., Hetenyi, G., & Gyorffy, Z. (2018). Will artificial intelligence solve the human resource crisis in healthcare? *BMC Health Services Research, 18*(1), 545.

Mienye, I. D., & Swart, T. G. (2025). ChatGPT in education: A review of ethical challenges and approaches to enhancing transparency and privacy. *Procedia Computer Science, 254*, 181-190.

Miller, A. I. (2019). *The artist in the machine: The world of AI-powered creativity*. MIT Press.

Moon, J. A. (2006). *Learning journals: A handbook for reflective practice and professional development* (2nd ed.). Routledge.

Nature Editorial. (2023). Tools like ChatGPT threaten transparent science. *Nature,* 613, 612. https://www.nature.com/articles/d41586-023-00191-1

Nicol, D. J., & Macfarlane-Dick, D. (2006). Formative assessment and self-regulated learning: A model and seven principles of good feedback practice. *Studies in Higher Education, 31*(2), 199-218.

Nicolescu, B. (2002). *Manifesto of transdisciplinarity*. Suny Press.

Niemi, H., & Multisilta, J. (2016). Digital storytelling promoting twenty-first century skills and student engagement. *Technology, Pedagogy and Education*, *25*(4), 451-468.

Nikolopoulou, K. (2025). Assessment redefined: Educational assessment meets AI-ChatGPT challenges. *Current Perspectives in Educational Research*, S*8*(1), 17-30.

Noble, S. U. (2018). Algorithms of oppression: How search engines reinforce racism. In *Algorithms of Oppression*. New York University Press.

North American Executive. (2025). Why the talent shortage is a major threat to growth in 2025. https://www.northamericanexec.com/news/why-the-talent-shortage-is-a-major-threat-to-growth-in-2025/

Nussbaum, M. C. (1997). *Cultivating humanity: A classical defense of reform in liberal education*. Harvard University Press.

Oakley, B., Felder, R. M., Brent, R., & Elhajj, I. (2004). Turning student groups into effective teams. *Journal of Student Centered Learning*, *2*(1), 9-34.

O'neil, C. (2017). *Weapons of math destruction: How big data increases inequality and threatens democracy*. Crown.

Ouyang, L., Wu, J., Jiang, X., Almeida, D., Wainwright, C., Mishkin, P., Zhan, C., Agarwal, S., Slama, K., Ray, A., Schulman, J., Hilton, J., Kelton, F., Miller, L., Simens, M., Askell, A., Welinder, P., Christiano, P., Leike, J., & Lowe, R. (2022). Training language models to follow instructions with human feedback. *Advances in Neural Information Processing Systems*, *35*, 27730-27744.

Paglis, L. L., Green, S. G., & Bauer, T. N. (2006). Does adviser mentoring add value? A longitudinal study of mentoring and doctoral student outcomes. *Research in Higher Education, 47*(4), 451-476.

Palmeri, J. (2012). *Remixing composition: A history of multimodal writing pedagogy*. SIU Press.

Pasquale, F. (2015). *The black box society: The secret algorithms that control money and information*. Harvard University Press.

Paul, C. (2002). Renderings of digital art. *Leonardo*, *35*(5), 471-484.

Peters, M. A. (2008). The history and emergent paradigm of open education. In *Open Education and Education for Openness* (pp. 1-15). Brill.

Pfund, C., Byars-Winston, A., Branchaw, J., Hurtado, S., & Eagan, K. (2016). Defining attributes and metrics of effective research mentoring relationships. *AIDS and Behavior*, *20*(2), 238-248.

Rafiq, S., & Qurat-ul-Ain, D. A. (2025). The role of AI detection tools in upholding academic integrity: An evaluation of their effectiveness. *Contemporary Journal of Social Science Review*, *3*(1), 901-915.

Rahm, L. (2023). Education, automation and AI: A genealogy of alternative futures. *Learning, Media and Technology*, *48*(1), 6-24.

Ray, S., & Ray, D. P. (2024). Artificial intelligence in education: Navigating the nexus of innovation and ethics for future learning landscapes. *International Journal of Research-Granthaalayah*, *11*(12), 163-174.

Reamer, F. G. (2023). Artificial intelligence in social work: Emerging ethical issues. *International Journal of Social Work Values and Ethics*, *20*(2), 52-71.

Reiss, M. J. (2021). The use of Al in Education: Practicalities and ethical considerations. *London Review of Education*, *19*(1), 1.

Repko, A. F., & Szostak, R. (2020). *Interdisciplinary research: Process and theory* (4th ed.). Sage Publications.

Rest, J. R., Thoma, S. J., & Bebeau, M. J. (1999). *Postconventional moral thinking: A neo-Kohlbergian approach*. Psychology Press.

Robin, B. R. (2008). *Digital storytelling: A powerful technology tool for the 21st century classroom. Theory Into Practice*, *47*(3), 220–228.

Ruiz-Rojas, L. I., Acosta-Vargas, P., De-Moreta-Llovet, J., & Gonzalez-Rodriguez, M. (2023). Empowering education with generative artificial intelligence tools: Approach with an instructional design matrix. *Sustainability, 15*(15), 11524.

Ryan, M., & Ryan, M. (2013). Theorizing a model for teaching and assessing reflective learning in higher education. *Higher Education Research & Development, 32*(2), 244-257.

Sanczyk, A., Merriweather, L. R., Howell, C. D., & Douglas, N. C. (2021). STEM doctoral mentoring: A call for a conscious, culturally responsive journey. *International Journal of Mentoring and Coaching in Education, 10*(3), 284-297.

Schon, D. A. (2017). *The reflective practitioner: How professionals think in action.* Routledge.

Selwyn, N. (2019). *Should robots replace teachers? AI and the future of education.* John Wiley & Sons.

Selwyn, N. (2021). *Education and technology: Key issues and debates.* Bloomsbury Publishing.

Slimi, Z., & Carballido, B. V. (2023). Navigating the ethical challenges of artificial intelligence in higher education: An analysis of seven global AI ethics policies. *TEM Journal, 12*(2), 590-602.

Smutny, P., & Schreiberova, P. (2020). Chatbots for learning: A review of educational chatbots for the Facebook Messenger. *Computers & Education, 151*, 103862.

Solaiman, I., Brundage, M., Clark, J., Askell, A., Herbert-Voss, A., Wu, J., Radford, A., Krueger, G., Kim, J.-W., Kreps, S., McCain, M., Newhouse, A., Blazakis, J., McGuffie, K., & Wang, J. (2019). Release strategies and the social impacts of language models. *arXiv preprint arXiv:1908.09203.*

Southworth, J., Migliaccio, K., Glover, J., Glover, J. N., Reed, D., McCarty, C., Brendemuhl, J., & Thomas, A. (2023). Developing a model for AI Across the curriculum: Transforming the higher education landscape via innovation in AI literacy. *Computers and Education: Artificial Intelligence, 4,* 100127.

Stokel-Walker, C. (2023). ChatGPT listed as author on research papers: Many scientists disapprove. *Nature, 613*(7945), 620-621.

Strubell, E., Ganesh, A., & McCallum, A. (2020). Energy and policy considerations for modern deep learning research. In *Proceedings of the AAAI conference on Artificial Intelligence* (Vol. 34, No. 9, pp. 13693-13696).

Sutherland-Smith, W. (2016). Authorship, ownership, and plagiarism in the digital age. In *Handbook of Academic Integrity* (pp. 575-589). Springer.

Taczak, K., Robertson, L., & Yancey, K. B. (2016). Reiterative reflection in the twenty-first-century writing classroom. In *A Rhetoric of Reflection* (pp. 42-63). Utah State University Press.

Taebi, B., van den Hoven, J., & Bird, S. J. (2019). The importance of ethics in modern universities of technology. *Science and Engineering Ethics*, *25*(6), 1625-1632.

Tan, M. J. T., & Maravilla, N. M. A. T. (2024). Shaping integrity: Why generative artificial intelligence does not have to undermine education. *Frontiers in Artificial Intelligence*, *7*, 1471224.

Topol, E. (2019). *Deep medicine: How artificial intelligence can make healthcare human again*. Hachette UK.

Tuck, E., & Yang, K. W. (2014). Unbecoming claims: Pedagogies of refusal in qualitative research. *Qualitative Inquiry*, *20*(6), 811-818.

Tufekci, Z. (2017). *Twitter and tear gas: The power and fragility of networked protest*. Yale University Press.

Uanachain, D. M. N., & Aouad, L. I. (2025). Generative AI in education: Rethinking learning, assessment & student agency for the AI era. *Thresholds in Education*, *48*(1), 111-132.

Van Dis, E. A., Bollen, J., Zuidema, W., Van Rooij, R., & Bockting, C. L. (2023). ChatGPT: Five priorities for research. *Nature*, *614*(7947), 224-226.

Vaughan, K. (2017). The role of apprenticeship in the cultivation of soft skills and dispositions. *Journal of Vocational Education & Training*, *69*(4), 540-557.

Vincent-Lancrin, S., & Van der Vlies, R. (2020). Trustworthy artificial intelligence (AI) in education: Promises and challenges. *OECD Education Working Papers*, *218*, 1-17.

Walker, G. E., Golde, C. M., Jones, L., Bueschel, A. C., & Hutchings, P. (2009). *The formation of scholars: Rethinking doctoral education for the twenty-first century*. John Wiley & Sons.

Wang, F., & Hannafin, M. (2005). Design-based research and technology-enhanced learning environments. *Educational Technology Research and Development*, *53*(4), 5–23.

Wang, X., Huang, R. T., Sommer, M., Pei, B., Shidfar, P., Rehman, M. S., Ritzhaupt, A. D., & Martin, F. (2024). The efficacy of artificial intelligence-enabled adaptive learning systems from 2010 to 2022 on learner outcomes: A meta-analysis. *Journal of Educational Computing Research*, *62*(6), 1348-1383.

Weber-Wulff, D., Anohina-Naumeca, A., Bjelobaba, S., Foltýnek, T., Guerrero-Dib, J., Popoola, O., Sigul, P., & Waddington, L. (2023). Testing of detection tools for AI-generated text. *International Journal for Educational Integrity*, *19*(1), 1-39.

Weidinger, L., Uesato, J., Rauh, M., Griffin, C., Huang, P. S., Mellor, J., Glaese, A., Cheng, M., Balle, B., Kasirzadeh, A., Biles, C., Brown, S., Kenton, Z., Hawkins, W., Stepleton, T., Birhane, A., Hendricks, L. A., Rimell, L., Isaac, W. S., … & Legassick, S. (2022). Taxonomy of risks posed by language models. In *Proceedings of the 2022 ACM Conference on Fairness, Accountability, and Transparency* (pp. 214-229).

Wiggins, G. P., & McTighe, J. (2005). *Understanding by design*. ASCD.

Williamson, B., & Eynon, R. (2020). *Historical threads, missing links, and future directions in AI in education. Learning, Media and Technology*, *45*(3), 223–235.

Wineburg, S. (2018). *Why learn history (when it's already on your phone)*. University of Chicago Press.

Yadav, D. S. (2024). Navigating the landscape of AI integration in education: Opportunities, challenges, and ethical considerations for harnessing the potential of artificial intelligence (AI) for teaching and learning. *BSSS Journal of Computer*, *15*(1), 38-48.

Yu, J. H., Chauhan, D., Iqbal, R. A., & Yeoh, E. (2025). Mapping academic perspectives on AI in education: Trends, challenges, and sentiments in educational research (2018–2024). *Educational Technology Research and Development*, *73*(1), 199-227.

Zawacki-Richter, O., Marín, V. I., Bond, M., & Gouverneur, F. (2019). Systematic review of research on artificial intelligence applications in higher education–where are the educators? *International Journal of Educational Technology in Higher Education*, *16*(1), 1-27.

Zellers, D. F., Howard, V. M., & Barcic, M. A. (2008). Faculty mentoring programs: Reenvisioning rather than reinventing the wheel. *Review of Educational Research*, *78*(3), 552-588.

Zimmerman, B. J. (2002). Becoming a self-regulated learner: An overview. *Theory Into Practice*, *41*(2), 64-70.

Appendix A: Paradigm Shift for Institutions of Higher Learning

Beyond the individual effect of AI on our daily lives, ready access to AI has also profoundly affected nearly every aspect of our lives, from daily routines to healthcare, entertainment, communication, to transportation, to education at all levels. Beyond the personal transformations from AI, it has profoundly changed the business landscape, redefining work roles and employment as well as the looming educational landscape, which has been somewhat reluctant to engage it. Roles are being redefined along with the creation of new job categories.

The benefits of AI cannot be underestimated. It has enhanced efficiency, productivity, and decision-making abilities with ready access to information. While AI has its benefits, it also presents new challenges. Foremost among these challenges are data privacy and ethical considerations regarding bias and transparency, which now have a significant and profound effect on education. Similar to business, education from kindergarten through higher education will require a paradigm shift. For higher education, universities and college must shift from the long-held responsibility as a center for knowledge transmission to becoming a curator of the learning experience. As such, both pedagogy must be redefined along with approaches to education and curriculum redesign is imperative.

One of the major challenges for businesses today is the shortage of talent (North American Executive, 2025). Higher education must plan a major role in addressing this challenge by first teaching students/learners how to use AI and generative AI ethically and responsibly. This will require significant curriculum change towards more reflective and reflexive assignments that not only teach responsible use of AI but also leverage AI to enhance the development of uniquely human skills such as critical thinking, creativity, complex problem-solving, and ethical reasoning.

These changes present a paradigm shift for educators/faculty. Learning in this environment requires the faculty to provide a rich learning experience in every class. To do so, faculty must also become trained AI users and leverage AI to assist in engaging students in a more collaborative approach. Teaching, in the AI environment, will become a highly interactive and experiential approach that engages learners to develop their critical thinking skills through complex and engaging conversations that stimulate intellectual curiosity and metacognitive thinking. Classroom supervision must shift to process management that emphasizes learning that requires students to document their thought processes and the role of AI in their work. This active experiential learning approach requires faculty to ask the right questions and leverage AI to create personalized feedback that fosters academic excellence and performance while ensuring academic rigor.

It should now be evident that all of these changes require a cultural shift within all higher education institutions that promotes ethical and responsible use of AI. These changes affect all aspects of how higher education institutions operate, teach, research, and interact. The following are some of the major shifts required:

- Developing AI literacy for students and faculty.
- Adaptability that promotes continuous learning.

- Learning experiences that instill lifelong learning.
- Creating a safe space for faculty and staff to experiment with AI, learn from what does not work, and share successes.
- Emphasizing AI as a tool to enhance human capabilities, not to replace human roles.
- Using and leveraging AI to free up faculty time for deeper engagement with students, more complex research, and creative problem-solving.
- Incentivize interdisciplinary collaboration between AI experts and faculty from various fields.
- Prioritizing Ethical AI and Responsible Use by developing AI guidelines, transparent use of AI, and critical thinking beyond AI.
- Redefine academic integrity and assessment.
- Cultivating a Student-Centric and Personalized Learning Environment.
- Streamlining Operations and Decision-Making.

Given all of these cultural and operational changes needed in the AI environment, the big question becomes, *"How does this change the role of faculty in higher education institutions?"* These changes will be significant as the focus shifts from *what* to *how* by shifting from the provider of information to how to find, evaluate, and analyze information, to include AI-generated content. Faculty also need to develop techniques to promote critical thinking, such as asking the right questions to differentiate between AI generative content and genuine understanding. Faculty will also need to develop AI literacy and be able to guide students on appropriate AI tools and how to use them ethically and responsibly. Faculty will need to develop an evolved pedagogy where they leverage AI to provide highly personalized feedback.

One of the key skills of faculty in this new environment is again the ability to ask the right questions that are tailored to the individual learner and engage in complex discussions and interactions. Leveraging AI to help with feedback will free up significant time to mentor, inspire, and foster enhanced, uniquely human skills that AI cannot provide. These include critical thinking, creativity, and complex problem-solving. Faculty will become the role models for ethically and responsibly integrating AI to enhance original work by demonstrating best practices. For mentors of those learners in the dissertation or capstone phase, AI has great potential for expanded opportunities for conducting research. Leveraging AI responsibly and ethically can contribute to a broader range of participants, enabling more societal, economic, and cultural impacts of the research. A broader cross-disciplinary approach to research where faculty collaborate with colleagues from different disciplines to address complex AI-related questions.

It should become clear that AI can become an adjunct to both learners and faculty. Faculty must evolve from the knowledge-dispensing role to becoming the essential guide, mentor, and innovator. Adaptability and creativity are needed to role model the ethical and responsible use of AI, along with learning how to ask the right questions. This is more than just Socratic questioning that simply probes by asking questions that serve as a guide to encourage analysis of information generated from AI. Faculty can then work with students to develop questions that will generate effective responses that refine their queries and specific prompts to guide students in leveraging AI and transforming that information into creative ideas. Responsible and ethical use of AI requires analysis and synthesis of the information to generate original thought. Faculty will also need to guide students in questioning and evaluating AI-generated responses. Rather than assessing that something is right or wrong, interacting and engaging with students collaboratively so that the understanding of what students are providing is mutually understood by both faculty and students. These changes do not mean throwing out the baby with the bath water, but rather evolving skills and learning new skills such as AI literacy. Open and ongoing discussions about AI use will be essential.

The Evolving Role of the Faculty

The accelerating pace of AI development is not just theoretical but an immediate reality for higher education. Institutes of higher learning must quickly shift from knowledge transmission to being curators of the learning experience, and the curriculum will also undergo a redesign to include leveraging AI as a means of enhancing unique human competencies of critical thinking, creativity, and complex problem-solving. The role of the faculty in this environment will necessarily have to evolve as well. Teaching will focus more on *how* instead of *what*. AI delivers the information more effectively and efficiently than textbooks or lectures (see Figure "Higher Education Paradigm Shift").

Faculty must become the student's guide on *how* to find the information, analyze it, and apply the AI-generated content. This shift directly aligns with moving students up Bloom's Taxonomy, from simply remembering and understanding to analyzing, evaluating, and creating. Every source on critical thinking attests that critical thinking is a learned skill. This is where faculty become crucial in teaching students how to critically assess AI outputs for accuracy, bias, and context. Faculty must master AI literacy, as they are the primary guides for students on which AI tools are appropriate for specific work, how to use AI ethically and responsibly, and how to interpret the results within a given discipline. Teaching thus involves prompt engineering and learning to ask the right questions to nuance effective human-AI collaboration. Prompt engineering involves crafting precise cues to elicit specific responses from AI language models (Heston & Khun, 2023), while questioning involves creating inquiries that reduce random speculation and uncertainty in favor of promoting critical thinking and meaningful discussions (Flammer, 1981). In essence, it extends Socratic questioning into the AI environment that challenges students to synthesize information, draw connections, and articulate their nuanced arguments. Faculty should encourage and lead open discussions about the responsibility and ethical use of AI in the students' discipline to explore academic integrity, plagiarism, bias, and the social impact of AI in their academic work, particularly in the advanced doctoral space.

Conclusion

AI's impact on knowledge generation is profound, fundamentally altering how we create, discover, and disseminate information. While AI does not *think* or *experience* in the human sense, its ability to process, analyze, and synthesize vast amounts of data at unprecedented speeds leads to what can be considered *new forms of knowledge* and significantly accelerates traditional knowledge creation processes. As such, AI has profoundly and irrevocably changed the landscape of learning, necessitating a call to action. A profound transformation in higher education is a necessary and beneficial adaptation for the future of higher education, shifting from the transmission of knowledge as its mission to becoming curators of the learning experience. This requires a profound change in culture, a redesign of the curriculum, and a different approach to teaching.

The learning experience involves the ethical and responsible leveraging of AI in students' academic work. As such, the curriculum must change to reflect this shift. With AI as a new form of knowledge, assignments must involve the use of AI along with reflective and reflexive assignments that promote critical thinking, creativity, and complex problem-solving. Faculty must evolve their teaching approaches concordantly with the change in the learning culture by developing AI literacy and mastering prompt engineering to encourage reflective debates on AI-generated content to maintain academic integrity and reduce bias and plagiarism. AI is here to stay. Higher education institutions and faculty must rapidly learn to leverage AI to enhance critical thinking, creativity, and complex problem solving, which, when combined with the power of leveraging AI, to achieve the desired outcome of academic excellence and instill a desire for their students to engage in life-long learning.

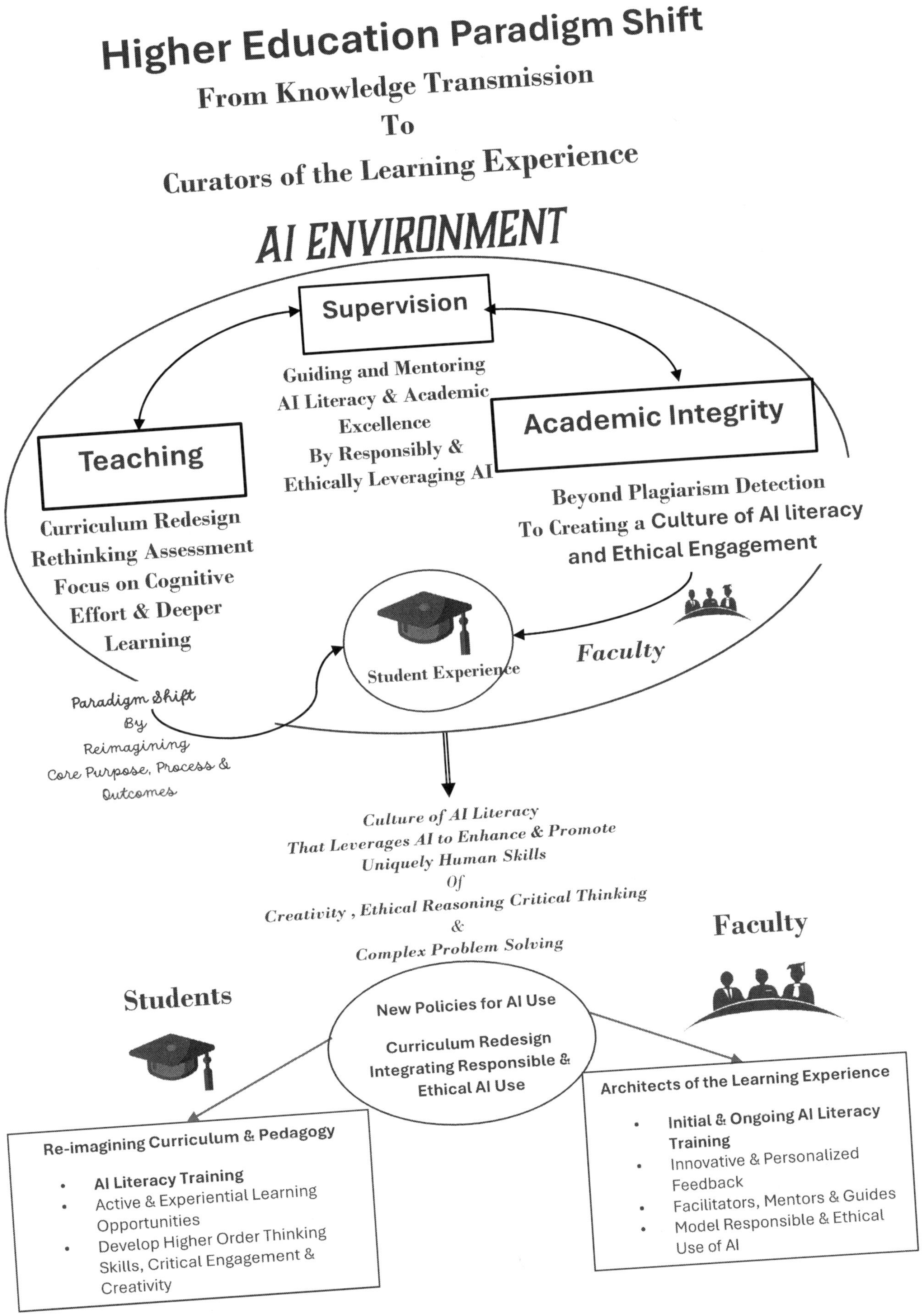
Higher Education Paradigm Shift
From Knowledge Transmission
To
Curators of the Learning Experience
AI ENVIRONMENT
Supervision
Guiding and Mentoring
AI Literacy & Academic
Excellence
By Responsibly &
Ethically Leveraging AI
Teaching
Curriculum Redesign
Rethinking Assessment
Focus on Cognitive
Effort & Deeper
Learning
Academic Integrity
Beyond Plagiarism Detection
To Creating a Culture of AI literacy
and Ethical Engagement
Student Experience
Faculty
Paradigm Shift
By
Reimagining
Core Purpose, Process &
Outcomes
Culture of AI Literacy
That Leverages AI to Enhance & Promote
Uniquely Human Skills
Of
Creativity , Ethical Reasoning Critical Thinking
&
Complex Problem Solving
Students
Faculty
New Policies for AI Use
Curriculum Redesign
Integrating Responsible &
Ethical AI Use
Re-imagining Curriculum & Pedagogy
AI Literacy Training
Active & Experiential Learning Opportunities
Develop Higher Order Thinking Skills, Critical Engagement & Creativity
Architects of the Learning Experience
Initial & Ongoing AI Literacy Training
Innovative & Personalized Feedback
Facilitators, Mentors & Guides
Model Responsible & Ethical Use of AI

Made in United States
Orlando, FL
04 November 2026

90200663R00391